Critical
Issues
in
History

Ancient Times to 1648

Critical
Issues
in History

UNDER THE EDITORIAL DIRECTION OF *RICHARD E. SULLIVAN*

SIX-VOLUME EDITION

TWO-VOLUME EDITION

Critical Issues in History

VOLUME I

Ancient Times to 1648

EDITED WITH INTRODUCTIONS BY

THOMAS W. AFRICA *University of Southern California*

RICHARD E. SULLIVAN *Michigan State University*

J. K. SOWARDS *Wichita State University*

D. C. HEATH *and Company, Boston*

ILLUSTRATION CREDITS

Page 1: Section, The Coliseum; Jacques-Francois Blondel,
Architecture Française, Paris, 1861.
Page 87: Restored exterior, Château de Coucy; Viollet le Duc,
Déscription du Château de Coucy, Paris, 1861.
Page 223: Section of chapel, Château D'Anet; C. T. Mathews,
The Renaissance Under the Valois, New York, 1893.

Printed August 1967

Boston
Englewood
Indianapolis
Dallas
San Francisco
Atlanta

PREFACE

The editors of this work are convinced that success in teaching introductory history courses ultimately depends upon the way in which each teacher exploits his own talents and taxes his own genius. However, their collective experience has convinced them that depth, sophistication, and thoughtfulness can be injected into introductory history courses by engaging students in *problem-resolving situations*. The editors are persuaded that this approach leads the student to the heart of the historical enterprise: the evaluation of evidence, the determination of the relationship among disparate bits of evidence, the arrangement of evidence into logical constructs, and the formulation of conclusions. The editors believe that encounters with historical problems develop historical-mindedness: a critical spirit, restraint in generalizing, caution in passing judgment, and suspicion of simplistic responses to human problems.

In arranging this book the editors have tried to face the realities surrounding the teaching of introductory history of civilization courses. They envisage the work as a supplement to other texts and to lectures, and therefore they have assumed a basic knowledge of history on the part of its users. The total time span embraced in the work has been divided into six large blocs, to each of which roughly equal space has been devoted: 4000 B.C.–A.D. 400; 400–1250; 1250–1648; 1648–1770; 1770–1870; and 1870 to the present. Thus half of the work (Volume I) is devoted to the period prior to 1648, and the other half (Volume II) to the period since 1648. This arrangement will fit the widely accepted practice of making the first semester in a year course break at 1648. Where a quarter system prevails two of the six sections can be utilized for each quarter of the academic year. To provide even greater flexibility, each section of the work is published as a separate volume. Five problems have been treated in each of the six sections, thus providing one problem for each of the thirty weeks of an academic year. An effort has been made to space the problems in each section on a chronological scale that will roughly match the pace at which the introductory course usually proceeds.

Each of the six sections opens with an interpretive essay seeking to establish a perspective toward the period in question which will give the problems relevance and significance. Each of the five problems within a section is preceded by a short statement which attempts to define the problem concisely and to draw the students' attention to the issues worthy of special note. The problem posed, the editor then provides four or five differing approaches, each representing the view of a competent historian whose case warrants attention. In selecting these treatments of an historical issue, the editors have tried to avoid generating conflict for conflict's sake. Rather they have sought to show how honest divergencies emerge among historians as a result of the complexities of the past, the different approaches to evidence, the varying assumptions made by historians, and all the other factors that enter into the interpretation of the past.

Although the editors share a belief in the efficacy of the problem-resolving technique in the teaching of history and although they have agreed upon a standard pattern of organization for preparing each section of the book, they have acted individually in the selection of the problems treated in their respective sections. The choices reflect each editor's own sense of what is important, a sense nourished by considerable teaching experience and a deep involvement in research. The decision to proceed in this fashion has produced a rich variety of approaches. In one problem a single man's role in history is debated, while only a few pages beyond the pressure of the silent, impersonal forces in history is measured. A single event is treated in depth in one problem; the next encompasses an entire culture. In one problem causes are sought, while in the next effects are weighed. One set of readings deals with the minute details of an episode in history, while the next justaposes vast ideological issues. The editors believe this varied fare is what is needed to stimulate interest, provoke questions, and sharpen the mental faculties of the many students who become involved in the complex and demanding task of trying to make sense out of the past.

CONTENTS

I. *The Ancient World to A. D. 400*

II.   *The Middle Ages, 400-1250*

III.   *The Eve of the Modern World, 1250-1648*

The Ancient World

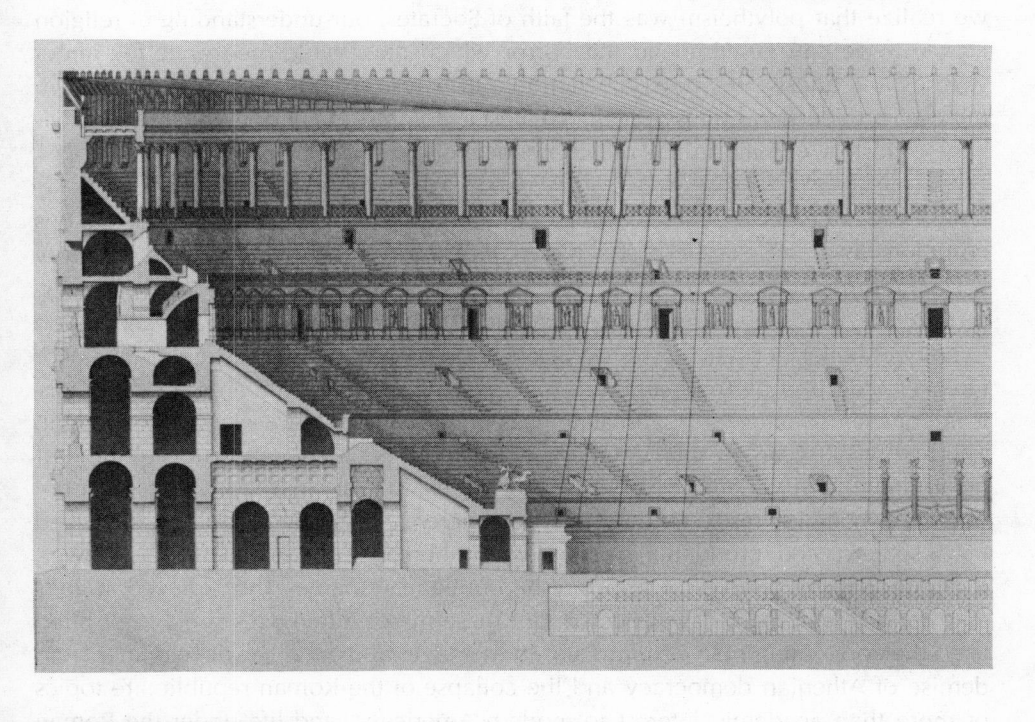

INTRODUCTION

There are many definitions of history, and all are highly personal. "History," said James Joyce, "is a nightmare from which I am trying to awake." Many modern students feel caught in the grip of events and agree with Joyce. History to Napoleon was "the only true philosophy," but he had imagined answers in history where there are usually only questions. The American folk hero, Henry Ford, announced, "History is bunk!" Some students may agree with him, but Henry was not well informed and thought that Benedict Arnold was a novelist. Had he known more about history, Ford might not have been a rabid anti-Semite. Ideally, knowledge of the past adds perspective to our view of the present and our hopes for the future. A sound grasp of history is an essential mark of the sophisticated man. The late John F. Kennedy was a member of the American Historical Association, and Winston Churchill won a Nobel prize for his historical works. Many people, particularly politicians, often claim that "history proves" whatever they are advocating, but it is a difficult matter to know what happened in the past and what it really proves. In the words of Marguerite Yourcenar, "here and there protrude the granite peaks of the inevitable, but all about is rubble from the landslides of chance." The complexity and multiplicity of human events is dazzling, and the historian (like anyone else) is presumptuous when he poses as a prophet. On the other hand, the study of history provides informed opinions on human behavior. Our own experiences are limited, and maturity is a slow and painful process—through history we may observe other men's trials without suffering their agonies. If we can see the world through their eyes, we gain new dimensions as human beings. When we realize that polytheism was the faith of Socrates, our understanding of religion grows. If we can comprehend the horror which reasonable men once felt about witches and ghosts, we may be better able to banish irrational fears from our own minds. To understand himself is the greatest accomplishment of man, and a knowledge of history can aid in this difficult endeavor.

Unlike the mute beasts, man is aware of the past experiences of his species, and this conscious awareness of the past is history. For 5,000 years he has kept a record of his achievements and follies—the record is not always edifying nor even necessarily clear, but it is always interesting and ever pertinent. Since each generation is unique, belief in cycles of history is an occult superstition. Yet, human behavior changes little if at all, and similar problems trouble men in different eras. History is full of useful analogies, but an analogy is not an answer but a stimulus to thought. The first 3,500 years of man's remembered existence is ancient history, a time of great vitality and variety in men and institutions. The ancient world differed from ours in two major respects: men had no inherent rights apart from those derived from society, and production depended on human and animal muscle power. It is true that the peoples of antiquity had outlandish names and believed in gods and notions which we have rejected, but these minor differences should not blind us to the common human denominator in their lives and ours. The development and demise of Athenian democracy and the collapse of the Roman republic are topics of more than academic interest to modern Americans, and life under the Roman Empire sheds considerable light on authoritarian society. The origins of Christianity and Judaism are vital subjects which deserve better treatment than they get in poor novels and worse films. In antiquity, man created civilization for better or worse, and it is imperative that we learn what he did with it and what it did to him.

About 3,000 B.C. history began in the city-states of Mesopotamia and the kingdom of Egypt. To an extent, both societies were managerial states with large educated bureaucracies. In Egypt the god-king preceded the bureaucracy but in Mesopotamia the bureaucrats preceded the kings. In the Near East the advanced societies kept tight controls over the masses and could mobilize great labor forces for irrigation work or the construction of temples, palaces, and pyramids. Trade flourished and with it a commercial mentality and an appreciation of mathematics; the Babylonians devised place-value notation, so dear to the heart of "new math" enthusiasts. In their heyday, the Egyptians had great concern for the afterlife and developed an elaborate funerary cult, but unlike modern Americans, they did not fear death and did not seek to hide it—rather they rejoiced at the prospect of serving the gods forever in paradise. The Mesopotamians took a gloomier view of death and felt that man returned to dust—the first novel of ideas, the Gilgamesh Epic, is based on this pessimistic theme of mortality and futility. In the first millennium B.C. great military empires arose. The grim Assyrians ruled with calculated cruelty and inflicted endless atrocities on their neighbors, but the policy of terror failed to break resistance and the Assyrians only reaped the hatred of their victims. When Assyria fell, the subject peoples "clapped their hands in glee." By the end of the sixth century B.C. the Persians ruled a great empire, stretching from the Balkans to the Indus valley. Cleverer than the Assyrians, the Persians won over their subjects by displaying great respect for local gods and customs. Wealthy, huge, and powerful, the Persian Empire was almost a universal state. The state religion of Persia was Zarathustrianism, which insisted on the immortality and moral accountability of man. To the Zarathustrian priests, the world was a battleground between the forces of darkness and the followers of God. In Palestine the Hebrews had evolved a highly ethical religion and a monotheistic view of God, who naturally was on the side of Israel. Because of the exclusiveness of Judaism, the religion of Israel had little appeal to the pagan world even after the Hebrew scriptures were translated into Greek.

Among moderns, the Greeks are the best known of ancient peoples, but they should not be judged solely by their poets and the Parthenon. Physically, the Hellenes lived in Greece and on the coasts of the Black Sea, Asia Minor, Libya, Sicily, Southern Italy, and Southern France. There was no Hellenic nation and only a vague cultural unity. Politically, the Greeks were fragmented into hundreds of tiny city-states, all fiercely independent and hostile to each other. Some Hellenic cities were ruled by dictators, more by wealthy oligarchies, but a few explored popular government and developed democracy. Athens, in particular, flourished under a highly workable democracy. However, Sparta was a unique totalitarian state devoted to military preparedness, yet reluctant to wage war, for the Spartans always feared that their oppressed serfs might rise against them. The exploitation of man was commonplace in Hellas, and Athens contained great numbers of slaves. The Greeks considered women inferior, stupid, and childlike. The gods cared little for ethics, and Greek religion was often orgiastic. In general, the Greeks were brutal, materialistic, and petty, but they also had a sense of humor and a love of beauty. Some were curious about the nature of man and the universe and laid the foundations of Western thought. Only a few Greeks knew or cared about science or philosophy, but Athens allowed considerable freedom of thought and expression, and no church imposed orthodoxy and hounded heretics. The Greeks were too emotional to be rationalists and too clever to be humble, and their literature abounds in silly ideas and brilliant insights. The variety of Greek thought was one of its most attractive features. The great sophist Protagoras said, "Man is the measure of all things," but Socrates insisted that the good man is the measure, and Plato believed that God is the measure. Despite their subtlety in many matters, the Greeks never realized the futility of war or the need for political unity. The Peloponnesian War between Athens and Sparta was the most famous and bloody of the many conflicts which drained the cities of men and treasure. By the late fourth century B.C., the exhausted cities of Hellas were absorbed into the military empire of Philip of Macedon.

Philip's son Alexander conquered the Persian Empire and founded the Hellenistic world. The Near East succumbed to Hellenic culture and the rule of Macedonian kings who built great nations from the debris of Alexander's empire. The new kings were military despots and living gods. City life and sophistication expanded, and Greek thought took on a cosmopolitan tone. The Ptolemaic kings of Egypt commanded a highly elaborate bureaucracy and subsidized science and learning. At Alexandria a great collection of books was assembled and a major institute of advanced research attracted scholars from many lands. The quality of Hellenistic science may be suggested by the work of two men: Eratosthenes estimated the size of the earth with amazing accuracy, and Aristarchus of Samos offered the hypothesis that the earth and the planets were satellites of the sun. As ideas expanded, cities, buildings, and machines grew larger. The Hellenistic peoples loved colossal statues and enormous equipment; war was fought with large armies and huge moving towers. At Syracuse, the great engineer Archimedes constructed elaborate weapons and defensive cranes which kept an entire Roman army at bay. Big and gaudy, the Hellenistic world was also divided and the kings exhausted each other in dynastic wars. For protection, the city-states of Greece experimented with federal unions but it was too late to provide real security. The Greek economy was unable to accommodate expanding populations, and reformers clamored for the abolition of debts and the redistribution of property. In the anxiety of the age, many men sought solace in the mystery cults of Isis and Serapis. For intellectuals, the Epicureans counseled a life of calm moderation in a cold atomic world, while the Stoics advised a stern acceptance of duty and destiny. The Cynics rejected society and convention and preached an anarchic return to nature. Astrology was the great pseudo-science of the Hellenistic age. When the Romans penetrated the East in the second century B.C., the divided and quarreling Hellenistic nations were easily subdued by the Western power.

Like Topsy, the Roman Empire grew without knowing it. While some wars were deliberate acts of aggression, others were unintended, and many were blunders. There was no consistent pattern of imperialism until the second century B.C. As a city-state, Rome had devised republican institutions which in theory maintained a balance between two executives, a popular legislature, and an aristocratic Senate. In practice, the nobles of the Senate ran the republic for their own benefit. The conquest of Carthage and the Hellenistic East made Rome an imperial power, but the stresses of constant war and running an empire ultimately eroded the republic. Many Roman citizens became landless paupers who resided in the capital and sold their votes for subsistence, but the upper classes enjoyed undreamed-of wealth and commanded hordes of slaves. Fierce political struggles by the nobles for glory and graft led to a series of civil wars in the first century B.C. One able politician, Gaius

Julius Caesar, emerged victorious and established a dictatorship, but he was murdered by his former peers in 44 B.C. Caesar's grandnephew and adopted son, Augustus, seized power in another civil war and founded a military despotism which governed efficiently and had the stability of dynastic succession. For the most part, the emperors of Rome were excellent rulers, and the empire was torn by only one brief civil war during the period 30 B.C. to 235 A.D. The Roman republic had exploited the provinces, but the emperors became increasingly generous toward provincials. The republic had been an Italian monopoly, but some of the most famous emperors came from Spain, Africa, and Syria. The much-publicized Roman Peace was a reality, and the peoples of the Mediterranean world enjoyed considerable prosperity and justice within the limits of an authoritarian regime. However, the Roman army turned against society in 235 A.D. and for a half-century set up and removed emperors at will, while the empire was assaulted by Persians in the East and Germanic barbarians in the North. In 285 A.D. the emperor Diocletian restored order and tried to guarantee stability with totalitarian controls. One of Diocletian's successors, Constantine, was a patron of Christianity, and the once-despised sect became the favored religion of the state. For a century the Roman Empire withstood foreign pressures until the Goths broke through in the late fourth century. In 410 A.D. Rome itself was sacked by barbarians and the Western provinces were soon lost to the invaders. The Eastern provinces became the Byzantine Empire, which had a lively history in the Middle Ages. With all of its faults, the Roman Empire in its heyday had shown that men of varied backgrounds could live together and share power with a minimum of injustice and exploitation.

Our knowledge of the ancient world is pieced together from inscriptions, monuments, coins, a few documents, and a sizable body of historical literature. The major historians of Greece and Rome are available in modern translations and are well worth reading. Any student will profit from contact with the curious and fair-minded Herodotus, the disciplined and gloomy Thucydides, Polybius and his attempts at scientific method, the dramatic and patriotic Livy, the grim and cynical Tacitus, Plutarch and his moralizing and hero worship, and the commonsensical Ammianus Marcellinus. The lesser writers—Xenophon, Sallust, Diodorus Siculus, Josephus, Dio Cassius, and even the *Historia Augusta*—also deserve attention, and the serious student will not neglect the New Testament, Eusebius, and the Hebrew books of Samuel, Kings, Chronicles, and Maccabees.

Not always careful with the facts, the ancient historians wrote with feeling and often with dramatic skill. In reading historians of any period, we must be alert for the biases and preconceptions which may have warped their judgment. We must also be on guard against romanticizing and rhetoric, which can make the most dubious "facts" convincing. When authorities conflict (and they always do), the problem can only be resolved with common sense, and the result will be at best a probability. Because the content of history is often emotional, the student of history should be a realist and a skeptic. When a historian's assertions happen to agree with our own prejudices, we can rarely spot the errors in his argument. A case in point would be the emperor Nero, who is portrayed in Christian tradition and cheap films as a monster of cruelty and vice. Maybe he was, but the saintly emperor Marcus Aurelius was also a persecutor of Christians and watched their torments with contempt. The Roman historians always exaggerated the virtues or villainies of famous men, and the anti-Nero sources are overdone and inconsistent. After he was overthrown, Nero received a "bad press" from writers who courted the favor of his successors. Yet, he had been popular in many parts of the empire, and his grave at Rome was strewn with flowers. Nero was not a model ruler and he did commit crimes, but his image in history is largely the result of fiction and libel. It is difficult to shed preconceived opinions, but the mature student of history must make every effort to do so. Even the devil is entitled to a fair trial, and too many men are condemned by historians on the basis of flimsy and biased evidence. While ancient writers were frankly partisan, modern historians try to be objective but they do not always succeed. It is too tempting to fight the battles of the present in the past and damn dead men who remind us of living ones. Though bias is always a defect, there can sometimes be an advantage in a partisan plea — if his bias is not ours, the writer may shock us into seeing things a little differently. The ultimate yardstick is reason tempered with humility.

1

AKHENATON AND MONOTHEISM

In George Orwell's novel *1984*, individuals who are condemned by the state are simply blotted out of history. Their names are deleted from all records, and all references to their existence are consigned to the flames. A similar fate befell the remarkable pharaoh, Amenhotep IV, who preferred to be called Akhenaton and who upset the religious life of Egypt in the fourteenth century B.C. His religious policies so offended the priests of Egypt that after his death the very name of Amenhotep IV was hacked out of all records and his memory was erased from history. Only the tombs at his holy city of Tell el-Amarna were spared, but they lay neglected until the nineteenth century A.D., when the existence of Akhenaton and his novel ideas were recovered for mankind. Unknown for over three thousand years, the episode of the heretic pharaoh threw unexpected light on the religious development of the Ancient Near East.

Amenhotep IV was one of the pharaohs of the Eighteenth Dynasty when Egypt was a great imperial power. Quite often, imperialism in secular affairs results in henotheism in religious matters: one deity becomes the national god and head of the pantheon. Of the myriad gods of Egypt, the Theban deity Amon-Re was the favored god of the pharaohs who attributed their victories to his intercession. The priests of Amon were rich and pampered, and Amon was considered the king of the gods. What is more, Amon had absorbed the attributes of the sun god Re and the creator god Ptah. As creator of the universe and sustainer of all life, Amon-Re was a universal god, omnipotent, omniscient, and concerned for mankind. However, Amon's supremacy did not endanger the cults of the other gods who also received the pious devotion of the Egyptian masses. In 1379 B.C. the young Amenhotep IV became pharaoh and soon drastically altered the state religion of Egypt. He deposed Amon and persecuted his priests, ignored the other gods, and insisted that the Aton was the supreme deity. Aton was an ancient term for the sun, which was venerated at the city of On (Heliopolis). The pharaoh claimed personal revelations from the Aton, changed his own name to Akhenaton,[1] and insisted that he was Aton's son. Since Thebes was a center of Amon worship, the pharaoh abandoned the capital and built a new city for Aton at Tell el-Amarna. A private world, the holy city was called Akhetaton (Horizon of Aton) and was dedicated to the Aton cult. In Egypt Akhenaton's officers ruthlessly hounded the priests of Amon, but the pharaoh was less concerned with foreign affairs and ignored reports of crises in Asia, where hostile neighbors seized the territories of Egypt's vassals in Syria and Palestine. Lost in his private devotions, Akhenaton allowed the Egyptian empire to crumble while Egypt itself was racked with religious strife. A court cult, the Aton religion had no appeal to the Egyptian masses, and the bigotry of the pharaoh infuriated the priests of the ancient gods. The holy city of Akhetaton became a remote isle of piety in a sea of hatred and discord. Oblivious to everything but the Aton, the pharaoh lost touch with reality.

About 1367 the situation changed. The pharaoh's strong-willed mother Tiy took drastic steps to restore order and save the dynasty. She visited Amarna and forced Akhenaton to accept one of his sons-in-law as co-ruler. Reigning at Thebes, the son-in-law halted the persecution and restored Amon-Re as the state god. Since Akhenaton's wife Nefertiti was devoted to the Aton cult, Tiy separated the pharaoh from his wife. The final years of Akhenaton are obscure, but he was dead by 1362. Though Nefertiti continued to worship the Aton in her palace, the priests of Amon ached for revenge on the hated cult. Another son-in-law of Akhenaton ruled from 1361 to 1352—a weak young man whose name Tutankhamon declared his dependence on Amon. His successor Eye was an adherent of the Aton cult but was overthrown in 1348 by a rough general, Horemheb, who was backed by the priests of Amon. The new regime took a thorough vengeance on the Aton cult and every vestige of the heretical faith was destroyed (except for the Amarna tombs). Contemporaries referred to Akhenaton as "the criminal of Akhetaton," and Amenhotep IV was dropped from the lists of Egyptian kings. The victory of Amon was complete, and the Aton cult and its founder vanished from history.

The bizarre reign of Akhenaton was not the only episode in world history in which a visionary ruler tried to impose his private religious views on a nation. The Babylonian king Nabonidus broke with the priests of the state god Marduk, who retaliated by aiding the Persians to take Babylon and overthrow the royal heretic. The Roman emperor Julian tried vainly to restore paganism as the state cult when the bulk of his subjects were Christians. Despite their sincerity and positions of

[1] In many older books, his name appears as Ikhnaton. [Editor's note.]

power, these rulers were failures, for a religion cannot be imposed from the top when it has no inherent appeal for the masses. The conversion of states has always been achieved by worldly princes who moved with the times and not against them. The personal tragedy of Akhenaton was probably heightened by a serious illness. The realistic art at Amarna depicts the pharaoh with a pear-shaped torso, tapering legs, and an unnaturally elongated face. Ironically, the grotesque appearance of Akhenaton became a standard of beauty for the Amarna circle, and his family and courtiers were portrayed with similar features. Though his wife Nefertiti was a strikingly beautiful woman, even she was sometimes shown with the eerie features of her husband. A recent study of the mummy of Akhenaton has suggested that the pharaoh probably suffered from a pituitary lesion which caused his progressive physical and psychological deterioration.[2] If so, the visionary pharaoh was a pathetic monster and in his final years a madman. In some respects, Akhenaton resembles the Florentine reformer Savonarola: Both were ugly, intolerant, god-intoxicated men with a deep sense of personal mission. Both reformers claimed divine inspiration, but the friar at least did not claim to be the son of god.

Whatever the weaknesses of the royal prophet, the Aton religion with its bigoted exclusion of other gods was a close approximation to monotheism. The American Egyptologist, James H. Breasted, deeply admired Akhenaton and insisted that the revolutionary pharaoh was "the first monotheist" and that the Aton doctrine had somehow influenced Hebrew thought. Breasted was a colorful and persuasive writer and his books convinced Freud and many others that Akhenaton was indeed a monotheist and that Mosaic monotheism was related to Atonism. Though still popular among general readers, Breasted's views were challenged by many scholars, and most Egyptologists reject his enthusiastic idealization of the Aton cult and its founder. The personality and beliefs of Moses present a historical problem of great complexity, because of the composite and contradictory nature of the Biblical texts which describe the man and his laws. Since the name Moses is Egyptian and he is associated with the Egyptian custom of circumcision, it is not unlikely that Moses was an Egyptian. The tradition that he was raised at the pharaoh's court reinforces this conclusion, and even if the tale of the babe in the bulrushes is true, Moses was a highly Egyptianized individual. However, any connection between Moses and Akhenaton is extremely doubtful, for the Exodus took place over a century after the death of the heretic pharaoh. The first and only reference in Egyptian annals to the existence of the Hebrews is an inscription by the pharaoh Merneptah, who boasted that he defeated Israel and other Asiatic tribes about 1232 B.C. If the Israelites were on the borders of Palestine by this date, Moses could not have been a contemporary of Akhenaton. Nor could the great lawgiver have had any knowledge of the Aton religion which had been destroyed root and branch years before. While it is possible that some memories of Atonism were preserved by the priests at On, there was an equally rich source of religious thought in the worship of Amon-Re, the all-powerful lord of the universe and father

[2] Cyril Aldred and A. T. Sandison, "The Pharaoh Akhenaten: A Problem in Egyptology and Pathology," *Bulletin of the History of Medicine* (1962), Vol. 36, 293–316.

of mankind. As one of the pharaoh's courtiers, Moses was surely familiar with the hymns to Amon-Re.

Moreover, the intolerant exclusiveness of the Aton cult with its hatred of other gods was not characteristic of early Hebrew religion, which accepted the existence of other national deities.[3] While Moses was on Sinai communing with Yahweh, his followers were dancing before a golden bull, and Solomon, "the Lord's anointed," later worshiped the gods of his many wives. The Israelites had great difficulty shaking free from an anthropomorphic concept of Yahweh. Only gradually did the religion of Israel evolve into a true monotheism. This momentous step in the history of religion took centuries to achieve and was the work of the great prophets who agonized over the nature of their national god and devised the premises of Judaism. Hebrew monotheism was a product of the tribulations of Israel and the intellects of the prophets—it was not a hollow echo of the bizarre cult of a fanatic pharaoh who had been swallowed by the mists of time.

[3] The author of II Kings 3:26–27 attributes the victory of the Moabites to the power of their god Chemosh. [Editor's note.]

TWO RIVAL HYMNS

1. A HYMN TO AMON-RE

The imperial god of Egypt, Amon-Re, was a blend of the Theban deity Amon and the sun god Re. To his worshipers, Amon-Re was "chief of all gods, the good god, the beloved, who gives life to all that is warm." The following hymn was composed before the reign of Akhenaton and celebrates Amon as the sun, as the creator, and as the protector of mankind.

The sweetness of thee is in the northern sky.
The beauty of thee carries away hearts;
The love of thee makes arms languid;
Thy beautiful form relaxes the hands;
And hearts are forgetful at the sight of thee.
Thou art the sole one, who made all that is,
The solitary sole one, who made what exists,
From whose eyes mankind came forth,
And upon whose mouth the gods came into being.
He who made herbage for the cattle,
And the fruit tree for mankind,
Who made that on which the fish in the river may live,
And the birds soaring in the sky.
He who gives breath to that which is in the egg,
Gives life to the son of the slug,
And makes that on which gnats may live,

From *Ancient Near Eastern Texts Relating to the Old Testament*, ed. James B. Pritchard, 2nd ed. (Princeton, 1955), pp. 366–67. Reprinted by permission of the Princeton University Press. Copyright © 1955 by the Princeton University Press. Translated by John A. Wilson.

And worms and flies in like manner;
Who supplies the needs of the mice in their holes,
And gives life to flying things in every tree.
Hail to thee, who did all this!
Solitary sole one, with many hands,
Who spends the night wakeful, while all men are asleep,
Seeking benefit for his creatures.
Amon, enduring in all things, . . .
Praises are thine, when they all say:
"Jubilation to thee, because thou weariest thyself with us!
Salaams to thee, because thou didst create us!"
Hail to thee for all beasts!
Jubilation to thee for every foreign country—
To the height of heaven, to the width of earth,
To the depth of the great green sea!
The gods are bowing down to thy majesty
And exalting the might of him who created them,
Rejoicing at the approach of him who begot them.
They say to thee: "Welcome in peace!
Father of the fathers of all the gods,
Who raised the heavens and laid down the ground,
Who made what is and created what exists;
Sovereign—life, prosperity, health!—and chief of the gods!
We praise thy might, according as thou didst make us.
Let us act for thee, because thou brought us forth.
We give thee thanksgiving because thou hast wearied thyself with us!"
Hail to thee, who made all that is!
Lord of truth and father of the gods,
Who made mortals and created beasts,
Lord of the grain,
Who made also the living of the beasts of the desert.
Amon, the bull beautiful of countenance,
The beloved in Karnak, ...
The horizon-dweller, Horus of the east,
From whom the desert creates silver and gold,
Genuine lapis lazuli for love of him.

A HYMN TO THE ATON

The most impressive of the Aton hymns was found in the tomb of Eye at Tell el-Amarna. Admirers of Akhenaton have seen a connection between this hymn and the 104th Psalm. The Aton hymn differs from the Amon-Re hymn, not in religious intensity or intellectual scope, but in slighting the other gods and celebrating the prophet Akhenaton.

From *Ancient Near Eastern Texts Relating to the Old Testament*, ed. James B. Pritchard, 2nd ed. (Princeton, 1955), pp. 370–71. Reprinted by permission of the Princeton University Press. Copyright © 1955 by the Princeton University Press. Translated by John A. Wilson.

Thou appearest beautifully on the horizon of heaven,
Thou living Aton, the beginning of life!
When thou art risen on the eastern horizon,
Thou hast filled every land with thy beauty.
Thou art gracious, great, glistening, and high over every land;
Thy rays encompass the lands to the limit of all that thou hast made:
As thou art Re, thou reachest to the end of them;
Thou subduest them for thy beloved son.
Though thou art far away, thy rays are on earth;
Though thou art in their faces, no one knows thy going.
When thou settest in the western horizon,
The land is in darkness, in the manner of death. . . .
At daybreak, when thou arisest on the horizon,
When thou shinest as the Aton by day,
Thou drivest away the darkness and givest thy rays.
The Two Lands are in festivity every day,
Awake and standing upon their feet,
For thou hast raised them up.
Washing their bodies, taking their clothing,
Their arms are raised in praise at thy appearance.
All the world, they do their work.
All beasts are content with their pasturage;
Trees and plants are flourishing.
The birds which fly from their nests,
Their wings are stretched out in praise to [thee.]
All beasts spring upon their feet.
Whatever flies and alights,
They live when thou hast risen for them.
The ships are sailing north and south as well,
For every way is open at thy appearance.
The fish in the river dart before thy face;
Thy rays are in the midst of the great green sea.
Creator of seed in women,
Thou who makest fluid into man,
Who maintainest the son in the womb of his mother,
Who soothest him with that which stills his weeping,
Thou nurse even in the womb,
Who givest breath to sustain all that he has made!
When he descends from the womb to breathe
On the day when he is born,
Thou openest his mouth completely,
Thou suppliest his necessities.
When the chick in the egg speaks within the shell,
Thou givest him breath within it to maintain him. . . .
How manifold it is, what thou hast made!
They are hidden from the face of man.
O sole god, like whom there is no other!
Thou didst create the world according to thy desire,
Whilst thou wert alone:
All men, cattle, and wild beasts,
Whatever is on earth, going upon its feet,
And what is on high, flying with its wings.
The countries of Syria and Nubia, the land of Egypt,

A Hymn to the Aton   11

Thou settest every man in his place,
Thou suppliest their necessities:
Everyone has his food, and his time of life is reckoned.
Their tongues are separate in speech,
And their natures as well;
Their skins are distinguished,
As thou distinguishest the foreign peoples.
Thou makest a Nile in the underworld,
Thou bringest it forth as thou desirest
To maintain the people of Egypt
According as thou madest them for thyself,
The lord of all of them, wearying himself with them,
The lord of every land, rising for them,
The Aton of the day, great of majesty.
All distant foreign countries, thou makest their life also,
For thou hast set a Nile in heaven,
That it may descend for them and make waves upon the mountains,
Like the great green sea,
To water their fields in their towns.
How effective they are, thy plans, O lord of eternity!
The Nile in heaven, it is for the foreign peoples
And for the beasts of every desert that go upon their feet;
While the true Nile comes from the underworld for Egypt.
Thy rays suckle every meadow.
When thou risest, they live, they grow for thee.
Thou makest the seasons in order to rear all that thou hast made,
The winter to cool them,
And the heat that they may taste thee.
Thou hast made the distant sky in order to rise therein,
In order to see all that thou dost make.
Whilst thou wert alone,
Rising in thy form as the living Aton,
Appearing, shining, withdrawing or approaching,
Thou madest millions of forms of thyself alone.
Cities, towns, fields, road, and river—
Every eye beholds thee over against them,
For thou art the Aton of the day over the earth. . . .
Thou art in my heart,
And there is no other that knows thee
Save thy son [Akhenaton,]
For thou hast made him well-versed in thy plans and in thy strength. . . .
All work is laid aside when thou settest in the west.
But when thou risest again,
Everything is made to flourish for the king, . . .
Since thou didst found the earth
And raise them up for thy son,
Who came forth from thy body:
The King of Upper and Lower Egypt, . . . Akhenaton, . . . and the Chief Wife of the
King . . . Nefertiti, living and youthful forever and ever.

JAMES H. BREASTED

AKHENATON: "THE FIRST INDIVIDUAL"

James H. Breasted (1865–1935) of the University of Chicago was a pioneer American Egyptologist. His doctoral dissertation (Berlin, 1894) dealt with Akhenaton. Learned, tireless, and enthusiastic, he was a popular speaker and a prolific writer. His lively books—*A History of Egypt* (1905), *Development of Religion and Thought in Ancient Egypt* (1912), *Ancient Times* (1916), *The Conquest of Civilization* (1926), and *The Dawn of Conscience* (1933)—were widely read, and his view of Akhenaton reached a large public. Originally, Breasted aspired to the ministry and his religious leanings are apparent in his interpretation of Akhenaton, the "first monotheist."

Amenhotep IV immersed himself heart and soul in the thought of the time, and the philosophizing theology of the priests was of more importance to him than all the provinces of Asia. In such contemplations he gradually developed ideals and purposes which make him the most remarkable of all the Pharaohs, and, we may even say, the first *individual* in human history. . . . It was universalism expressed in terms of imperial power which first caught the imagination of the thinking men of the empire, and disclosed to them the universal sweep of the Sun-god's dominion as a physical fact. In the Ancient East monotheism was but imperialism in religion. Already under Amenhotep III an old name for the material sun, "Aton," had come into prominent use, where the name of the Sun-god might have been expected. . . . A cult of the newly named Sun-god had . . . been inaugurated and . . . he had even been designated as "the sole god" by Amenhotep III's contemporaries. Amenhotep IV was soon closely associated with the new ideas. . . . Early in his reign we find him . . . engaged in the worship of Aton . . . but . . . it was not merely Sun-worship. . . . The king was evidently deifying the light or the vital heat which he found accompanying all life. . . .

Amenhotep IV possessed unlimited personal force of character, and he was moreover the son of a line of rulers too strong and too illustrious to be . . . set aside, even by the most powerful priesthood in the land. A bitter conflict ensued, in which the issue was sharply drawn between Aton and the old gods. It rendered Thebes intolerable to the young king. He decided to break with the priesthoods and to make Aton the sole god, not merely in his own thought, but in very fact. As far as their external and material manifestations and equipment were concerned, the annihilation of the old gods could be and was accomplished without delay. The priesthoods, including that of Amon, were dispossessed, the official temple-worship of the various gods throughout the land ceased, and their names were erased wherever they could be found upon the monuments. The persecution of Amon was especially severe. The cemetery of Thebes was visited and in the tombs of the ancestors the hated name of Amon was hammered out wherever it appeared upon the stone. . . . The royal statues of his ancestors, including even the king's father, were not respected, and . . . the young king was . . . obliged to cut out his own father's name in order to prevent the name of Amon from appearing. . . . The king's own name, likewise Amenhotep, . . . was of necessity also banished and the king assumed in its place the name "Ikhnaton," which means "Aton is satisfied." . . .

This terrible revolution, violating all that was dearest and most sacred in Egyptian life, must have been a

From James H. Breasted, "Ikhnaton, the Religious Revolutionary," *The Cambridge Ancient History* (Cambridge, Eng., 1926), Vol. II, pp. 109–17, 119–21, 125–28. Reprinted by permission of the Cambridge University Press.

devastating experience for the youthful king, perhaps not yet nineteen at this time. Thebes had become an impossible place of residence. . . . In the sixth year of his reign and shortly after he had changed his name, the king was living in his own Aton-city in Egypt. He chose as its site a fine and spacious bay in the cliffs . . . nearly three hundred miles below Thebes. He called it Akhetaton, "Horizon of Aton" — it is known in modern times as Tell el-Amarna. . . . All that was devised and done in the new city and in the propagation of the Aton faith bears the stamp of Ikhnaton's individuality. . . . The men about him, in spite of his youth, must have been irresistibly swayed by the young Pharaoh's unbending will. But Ikhnaton understood enough of the old policy of the Pharaohs to know that he must hold his party by practical rewards, and the leading partisans of his movement . . . enjoyed liberal bounty at his hands. . . . Although there must have been a nucleus of men who really appreciated the ideal aspects of the king's teaching, . . . many were not uninfluenced by "the loaves and the fishes." . . .

Of all the monuments left by this unparalleled revolution, the Aton hymns are by far the most remarkable; and . . . Psalm 104 shows a notable similarity to [one Aton] hymn both in the thought and the sequence. . . . In this great hymn the universalism of the empire finds full expression and the royal singer sweeps his eye from the far-off cataracts of the Nubian Nile to the remotest lands of Syria. It is clear that he is projecting a world religion. . . . He bases the universal sway of God upon his fatherly care of all men alike, irrespective of race or nationality. . . . Ikhnaton thus grasped the idea of a world-lord, as the creator of nature; but the king likewise saw revealed the creator's beneficent purpose for all his creatures, even the meanest. He discerned in some measure the goodness of the All-Father as did He who bade us consider the lilies. . . .

Our sources do not show us that the king had perceptibly risen from a discernment of the beneficence to a conception of the righteousness in the character of God, nor for His demand for this in the character of men. Nevertheless, there is in Ikhnaton's "teaching" . . . a constant emphasis upon "truth" such as is not found before or since. . . . He had himself depicted on the monuments while enjoying the most familiar and unaffected intercourse with

his family. . . . The art of the age was unavoidably affected by this extraordinary revolution, and . . . the king's person . . . was no exception to the law of the new art; the artists represented Ikhnaton as they *saw* him. . . .

Wholly absorbed in the exalted religion to which he had given his life, stemming the tide of tradition . . . , this young revolutionary of twenty-five was beset with too many enterprises and responsibilities of a totally different nature to give much attention to the affairs of the empire abroad. . . . Both in Syria and Palestine the provinces of the Pharaoh had gradually passed entirely out of Egyptian control, and . . . the Egyptian empire in Asia was for the time at an end. At Akhetaton, the new and beautiful capital, the splendid temple of Aton resounded with hymns to the new god of the empire, while the empire itself was no more. . . . The storm which had broken over his Asiatic empire was not more disastrous than that which threatened the fortunes of his house in Egypt. But he was steadfast as before in the propagation of his new faith. At his command temples of Aton had now arisen all over the land. He devoted himself to the elaboration of the temple ritual and the tendency to theologize somewhat dimmed the earlier freshness of the hymns to the god.

Meanwhile, the national convulsion which his revolution had precipitated was producing the most disastrous consequences throughout the land. The Aton faith disregarded some of the most cherished beliefs of the people, especially those regarding the hereafter. Osiris, their old time protector and friend in the world of darkness, was banished from the tomb, and the magical paraphernalia which was to protect them from a thousand foes was gone. . . . The Aton faith remained but the cherished theory of the idealist, Ikhnaton, and a little court-circle; it never really became the religion of the people. Added to the secret resentment and opposition of the people, we must consider also far more dangerous forces. During all of Ikhnaton's reign a powerful priestly party, openly or secretly, did all in its power to undermine him. Among the army and its leaders, the neglect and loss of the Asiatic empire must have turned against the king many a strong man. . . . Ikhnaton might appoint one of his favorites to the command of the army, but his ideal aims and his high motives for peace would be as unpopular as they were unintelligible to his commanders. . . . Thus, both the people and the priestly and military classes alike were fomenting plans to overthrow the hated dreamer in the palace of the Pharaohs, of whose thoughts they understood so little. To increase Ikhnaton's danger, fortune had decreed him no son, and he was obliged to depend for support, as the years passed, upon his son-in-law, a noble named Sakere. . . . Ikhnaton had probably never been physically strong; his spare face, with the lines of an ascetic, shows increasing traces of the cares which weighed so heavily upon him. He finally nominated Sakere as his successor and appointed him at the same time co-regent. He survived but a short time after this, and about 1358 B.C., having reached his seventeenth regnal year, he succumbed to the overwhelming forces that were against him. . . .

Thus disappeared the most remarkable figure in earlier oriental history. The sumptuous inscriptions on his beautiful coffin . . . call him "the living Aton's beautiful child who lives forever and is true (or just, or righteous) in sky and earth." To his own nation he was afterwards known as "the criminal of Akhetaton"; but however much we may censure him for the loss of the empire, which he allowed to slip from his fingers, however much we may condemn the fanaticism with which he pursued his aim, even to the violation of his own father's name and monuments, there died with him such a spirit as the world had never seen before—a brave soul, undauntedly facing the momentum of immemorial tradition, and thereby stepping out from the long line of conventional and colorless Pharaohs, that he might disseminate ideas far beyond and above the capacity of his age to understand. Among the Hebrews, seven or eight hundred years later, we look for such men; but the modern world has yet adequately to value or even acquaint itself with this man, who, in an age so remote and under conditions so adverse, became not only the world's first idealist and the world's first *individual,* but also the earliest monotheist, and the first prophet of internationalism—the most remarkable figure of the Ancient World before the Hebrews.

SIGMUND FREUD

MOSES AND THE ATON CULT

The founder of psychoanalysis, Sigmund Freud (1856–1939), was a man of wide interests with a particular fondness for Egyptology and antiquity. The figure of Moses attracted him, and Freud identified himself with the great liberator and lawgiver of Hebrew tradition. Despite his towering stature in psychology, Freud was not a historian and his version of Moses and the Aton cult was based on an uncritical acceptance of the theories of Breasted and a German scholar, Ernst Sellin. Aware that his interpretation of history was shaky at best, Freud admitted: "It is enough that I myself can believe in the solution to the problem. It has pursued me through my whole life." After publishing two articles on Moses in the psychoanalytical journal *Imago* in 1937, Freud returned to the topic in his final work, *Moses and Monotheism* (1939).

To deny a people the man whom it praises as the greatest of its sons is not a deed to be undertaken light-heartedly—especially by one belonging to that people. No consideration, however, will move me to set aside truth in favor of supposed national interests. . . .

The man Moses, the liberator of his people, who

Reprinted by permission of the publisher from *Moses and Monotheism* by Sigmund Freud (tr. Katherine Jones), pp. 3–71, excerpts. Copyright 1939 by Sigmund Freud. Reprinted also by special permission of the Hogarth Press and Mr. James Strachey.

gave them their religion and their laws, belonged to an age so remote that the preliminary question arises whether he was a historical person or a legendary figure. If he lived, his time was the thirteenth or fourteenth century B.C.; we have no word of him except from the Holy Books and the written traditions of the Jews. Although the decision lacks final historical certainty, the great majority of historians have expressed the opinion that Moses did live and that the exodus from Egypt, led by him, did in fact take place. It has been maintained with good reason that the later history of Israel could not be understood if this were not admitted. . . . The suggestion has long been made and by many different people that the name Moses derives from the Egyptian vocabulary. Instead of citing all the authors who have voiced this opinion, I shall quote a passage from a recent work by Breasted, an author whose *History of Egypt* is regarded as authoritative: "It is important to notice that his name, Moses, was Egyptian. It is simply the Egyptian word 'mose' meaning 'child,' and is an abridgement of a fuller form of such names as 'Amen-mose' . . . or 'Ptah-mose'. . . ." I have given this passage literally and am by no means prepared to share the responsibility for its details. I am a little surprised, however, that Breasted in citing related names should have passed over the analogous theophorous names in the list of Egyptian kings, such as Ah-mose, Thut-mose . . ., and Ra-mose. . . .

It might have been expected that one of the many authors who recognized Moses to be an Egyptian name would have drawn the conclusion, or at least considered the possibility, that the bearer of an Egyptian name was himself an Egyptian. . . . We are not at all surprised to find that the poet Chamisso was of French extraction, Napoleon Buonaparte, on the other hand, of Italian, and that Benjamin Disraeli was an Italian Jew, as his name would lead us to expect[1]. . . . Nevertheless, to the best of my knowledge no historian has drawn this conclusion in the case of Moses, not even one of those who, like Breasted, are ready to suppose that Moses "was cognizant of all the wisdom of the Egyptians." What hindered them from doing so can only be guessed at. Perhaps the awe of Biblical tradition was insuperable. Perhaps it seemed monstrous to imagine that the man Moses could have been anything other than a Hebrew. . . .

[*Freud discusses the legends of early heroes— Romulus and Remus, Sargon of Agade—who were cast adrift as babies in basket-boats. Such tales usually include the claim that the infant is of royal birth and thus justify his later rise to power from humble beginnings.*] . . . *It is very different in the* case of Moses. Here the first family—usually so distinguished—is modest enough. He is the child of Jewish Levites. But the second family—the humble one in which as a rule heroes are brought up—is replaced by the royal house of Egypt; the princess brings him up as her own son. . . . One of the families is the real one, the one into which the great man was really born and in which he was brought up. The other is fictitious, invented by the myth in pursuance of its own motives. As a rule the real family corresponds with the humble one, the noble family with the fictitious one. In the case of Moses something seemed to be different. And here the new point of view may perhaps bring some illumination. It is that the first family, the one from which the babe is exposed to danger, . . . is in all comparable cases the fictitious one; the second family, however, by which the hero is adopted and in which he grows up, is his real one. If we have the courage to accept this statement as a general truth to which the Moses legend also is subject, then we suddenly see our way clear. Moses is an Egyptian —probably of noble origin—whom the myth undertakes to transform into a Jew. . . . The divergence of the Moses legend from all others of its kind might be traced back to a special feature in the story of Moses' life. Whereas in all other cases the hero rises above his humble beginnings as his life progresses, the heroic life of the man Moses began by descending from his eminence to the level of the children of Israel. . . . But what could have induced a distinguished Egyptian—perhaps a prince, priest, or high official—to place himself at the head of a throng of culturally inferior immigrants and to leave the country with them, is not easy to conjecture. The well-known contempt of the Egyptians for foreigners makes such a proceeding especially unlikely. . . .

The Jewish people in Egypt were certainly not without some kind of religion, and if Moses, who gave them a new religion, was an Egyptian, then the surmise cannot be rejected that this other new religion was the Egyptian one. This possibility encounters an

[1] It should be noted, however, that Jews from Zerubbabel to Goldberg have often adopted the names of a host culture. [Editor's note.]

obstacle: the sharp contrast between the Jewish religion attributed to Moses and the Egyptian one. The former is a grandiosely rigid monotheism. . . . In the Egyptian religion, on the other hand, there is a bewildering mass of deities of differing importance and provenance. . . . A strange fact in the history of the Egyptian religion, which was recognized and appraised relatively late, opens up another point of view. It is still possible that the religion Moses gave to his Jewish people was yet his own, *an* Egyptian religion though not *the* Egyptian one. . . . If Moses was an Egyptian and if he transmitted to the Jews his own religion, then it was that of Ikhnaton, the Aton religion. . . . If Moses gave the Jews not only a new religion, but also the law of circumcision, he was no Jew but an Egyptian, and then the Mosaic religion was probably an Egyptian one: namely— because of its contrast to the popular religion—that of Aton, with which the Jewish one shows agreement in some remarkable points. . . . Let us assume that Moses was a noble and distinguished man, perhaps indeed a member of the royal house, as the myth has it. He must have been conscious of his great abilities, ambitious, and energetic; perhaps he saw himself in a dim future as the leader of his people, the governor of the Empire. In close contact with Pharaoh, he was a convinced adherent of the new religion, whose basic principles he fully understood and had made his own. With the king's death and the subsequent reaction, he saw all his hopes and prospects destroyed. If he was not to recant the convictions so dear to him, then Egypt had no more to give him; he had lost his native country. In this hour of need he found an unusual solution. The dreamer Ikhnaton had estranged himself from his people, had let his world empire crumble. Moses' active nature conceived the plan of founding a new empire, of finding a new people, to whom he could give the religion that Egypt disdained. . . . Perhaps he was at the time governor of that border province (Gosen) in which—perhaps already in the "Hyksos period"— certain Semitic tribes had settled. These he chose to be his new people. . . . He established relations with them, placed himself at their head, and directed the Exodus "by strength of hand." In full contradistinction to the Biblical tradition we may suppose this Exodus to have passed off peacefully and without pursuit. The authority of Moses made it possible, and there was then no central power that could have prevented it. . . .

The kernel of our thesis, the dependence of Jewish monotheism on the monotheistic episode in Egyptian history, has been guessed and hinted at by several workers. I need not cite them here, since none of them has been able to say by what means this influence was exerted. Even if, as I suggest, it is bound up with the individuality of Moses, we shall have to weigh other possibilities. . . . It is not to be supposed that the overthrow of the official Aton religion completely put an end to the monotheistic trend in Egypt. The School of Priests at On, from which it emanated, survived the catastrophe and might have drawn whole generations after Ikhnaton into the orbit of their religious thought. That Moses performed the deed is quite thinkable, therefore, even if he did not live in Ikhnaton's time and had not come under his personal influence, even if he were simply an adherent or merely a member of the school of On. This conjecture would postpone the date of the Exodus and bring it nearer to the time usually assumed, the thirteenth century B.C. . . .

In 1922 Ernst Sellin made a discovery of decisive importance. He found in the book of the Prophet Hosea (second half of the eighth century) unmistakable traces of a tradition to the effect that the founder of their religion, Moses, met a violent end in a rebellion of his stubborn and refractory people. The religion he had instituted was at the same time abandoned. . . . Naturally, I am not in a position to decide whether Sellin has correctly interpreted the relevant passages in the Prophets. If he is right, however, we may regard as historically credible the tradition he recognized; for such things are not readily invented—there is no tangible motive for doing so. And if they have really happened, the wish to forget them is easily understood. . . . Among all the events of Jewish prehistory that poets, priests, and historians of a later age undertook to portray, there was an outstanding one the suppression of which was called for by the most obvious and best of human motives. It was the murder of the great leader and liberator Moses, which Sellin divined from clues furnished by the Prophets. Sellin's presumption cannot be called fanciful; it is probable enough. Moses, trained in Ikhnaton's school, employed the same methods as the king; he gave commands and forced his religion on the people. Perhaps Moses' doctrine was still more uncompromising than that of his master; he had no need to retain any connection with the religion of the sun-god since the school of On would have no importance for his alien people. Moses met with the same fate as Ikhnaton, the fate that awaits all enlightened despots. The Jewish people of Moses were quite as unable to bear such a highly spiritualized religion . . . as were the Egyptians of the Eighteenth Dynasty. In both cases the same thing happened: those who felt themselves in tutelage, or who felt dispossessed, revolted and threw off the burden of a religion that had been forced on them. But while the tame Egyptians waited until fate had removed the sacred person of their Pharaoh, the savage Semites took their destiny into their own hands and did away with their tyrant. Nor can we maintain that the Biblical text preserved to us does not prepare us for such an end to Moses. The account of the "wandering in the wilderness" — which might stand for the time of Moses' rule — describes a series of grave revolts against his authority which, by Jahve's command, were suppressed with savage chastisement. It is easy to imagine that one of those revolts came to another end than the text admits.

HARRY R. HALL

AKHENATON: "THE FIRST DOCTRINAIRE"

Not all Egyptologists shared Breasted's enthusiasm for Akhenaton, but few were as caustic as Harry R. Hall (1873–1930), whose *The Ancient History of the Near East* (1913) enjoyed great popularity among British readers. As Keeper of the Department of Egyptian and Assyrian Antiquities, British Museum, Hall was a recognized authority on the ancient Near East. Though he did not admire Akhenaton, Hall accepted Breasted's notion that the heretical Pharaoh had been a monotheist. In the following passages, Hall falls into errors of his own, namely nineteenth-century racism.

The son of Amenhetep III and Tii was no Egyptian warrior like his ancestors. Of mixed race, with, probably, the alien blood of Aryan Mitanni inherited from his father and of the wild desert tribes . . . derived from his mother running in his veins as well as the ichor of the descendants of Ra, the son of a luxurious and art-loving father and of a clever and energetic mother, he was brought up under strong feminine influence. All the requisites for the creation of a striking and abnormal character were present. Amenhetep IV was a man of entirely original brain, untrammelled on account of his position by those salutary checks which the necessity of mixing with and agreeing with other men of lesser mental calibre imposes on those not born in the purple. His genius had full play. And the result was disaster. So insensate, so disastrous, was his obliviousness to everything else but his own "fads" in religion and art that we can well wonder if Amenhetep IV was not really half insane. Certainly his genius was closely akin to madness. Dithyrambs have been penned, especially in late years, in praise of this philosophic and artistic reformer, "the first individual in ancient history." We might point out that others have an equal right to this characterization, for instance [Hammurabi], Hatshepsut, or [Thutmose III]. . . . Certainly Akhenaten was the first doctrinaire in history, and, what is much the same thing, the first prig.

His religious heresy, the central fact of his reign, was not altogether his own idea. The veneration of the Aten, the disk of the sun, had been growing in court favor during his father's last years. Both Amenhetep III and Tii venerated the Aten as well as Amen-Ra and the other gods. Amenhetep III, as the son prob-

From Harry R. Hall, *The Ancient History of the Near East,* 11 ed. (London, 1950), pp. 298–99, 301–03, 304–08. Reprinted by permission of Methuen & Co., Ltd.

ably of a Mitannian mother, was half an Iranian and may well have felt drawn towards a cult which resembled not remotely Iranian religion. But at the same time he gives us (also an Iranian trait) the impression of a tolerant and easy-going prince, and even if he believed privately that the Aten was the one real god, he would be the last to make enemies of the priests and plunge his country into civil war by publicly announcing his belief. His son was of a different spirit. The feminine cast of his character showed itself at once in a reckless doctrinaire proclamation of a belief which could only be anathema to his less clever subjects, of an adhesion to a "principle" which admitted of no compromise even if it brought his kingdom about his ears and plunged the world in war, which it did. His reign lasted in all not more than eighteen years. . . . Much of the extravagance that followed would probably have been avoided had his father lived longer and been able to keep him in check. The influence of Tii, which must have been paramount during the first years of his reign, when she apparently acted as regent, can hardly have been wisely exercised.

At first the young Amenhetep IV was represented on the monuments in the conventional style of his forefathers. His real peculiarities of body (which was as strangely constituted as his brain) were ignored. Amen and the other gods are still officially worshipped by him five years after his father's death and his accession. In the thirteenth year of his age, probably, he was married to his sister Nefertiti, who evidently sympathized entirely with his ideas. Then came emancipation. In the sixth year of his reign, when he was presumably fifteen years old and therefore fully a man in Egypt, he openly proclaimed his heresy, and the religious revolution was begun. . . . The result was curious. The difficulty of governing Thebes must have been enormous, and it may well be that the king was not safe from assassination there. He therefore combined discretion with valor by ostentatiously shaking the dust of Thebes from off his shoes and proceeding to a new capital which should be free of Amen and his devotees. He would worship his god in his own way, and his court, as was fitting, should worship him too, in his way, in a spot uncontaminated by the previous presence of the absurd superstitions of his unenlightened ancestors. In a desert place, where the unregenerate did not exist, he would found a city called "Akhetaten," . . . where he could teach his "doctrine" to willing hearers only. . . .

We can imagine the effect of these proceedings upon his people: the fury of the priests of Amen; the bitterness of the soldiers and statesmen who saw the work of a dynasty abandoned and thrown aside at the caprice of a boy; the amazement of the Asiatics at the news that the young [Pharaoh] had gone suddenly mad and had vowed never to stir out of his city for the defence of his empire; the resentment of the mass of the Egyptians, soon to crystallize into active hatred of the "criminal of Akhetaten." Yet no overt resistance was possible. The whole machinery of the state was in the king's hands, and his behests were obeyed by the royal officers, probably many of them convinced adherents of the "doctrine." The king's religion was for the moment the religion of the empire, and Amen was deposed from his imperial throne to make way for the Aten. The whole of the property of Amen was simply transferred to the new god, and the Theban priests were driven out or proscribed. . . . Yet a king cannot abolish a national religion by decree, although he may obliterate the names of its gods from their temples, and this fact must soon have been learnt by Akhenaten. We do not know the details of the story, but for the last few years of his reign Thebes must have been in more or less open revolt, no doubt under the leadership of Amen's high-priest, whom the king did not recognize as existing. . . .

Foiled by the dispossessed priests of Amen in his attempt to abolish them and their god utterly, the king finally abandoned his empire to go its own way while he lived his own life with his family and court in the city which he had created. Many of his courtiers no doubt really believed in the new religion, but others, as we see from the readiness with which they abandoned it after his death, never really believed in it, but only conformed to it because it was the king's religion. . . . In the relief of Tell el-Amarna, . . . we see the king represented in what must be almost a caricature of his facial and bodily peculiarities. Probably he liked these peculiarities to be so exaggerated; his already long nose and chin to be made longer, his belly to be represented as pendulous, his legs as bowed. . . . Many of the courtiers . . . show in the reliefs a decided approximation to the same degenerate type. Probably fashion decreed that convinced adherents of the doctrine should be made to ape the countenance and figure, as well as the religion, of their royal teachers, whom the true courtier would vow to be the mirrors of all beauty as well as truth.

Akhenaton: "The First Doctrinaire"

It is on the walls of these tombs, too (for they were spared as inviolable houses of the dead when the temples of the Aten were destroyed), that we read the beautiful hymns to the sun-disk that were composed by the poet-king himself. Their phraseology is strangely reminiscent of that of Psalm 104. . . . Alas for the poet-king! His kingdom had already fallen into anarchy, and the foreign empire which his predecessors had built up had been thrown to the winds in his pursuit of his beautiful ideal. . . . Akhenaten died young and probably insane after a reign of some eighteen years. . . . The whole story is an example of the confusion and disorgani-zation which, *pace* Plato, always ensue when a philosopher rules. Not long after the heretic's early death, the old religion was fully restored, the cult of the disk was blotted out, and the Egyptians returned joyfully to the worship of their myriad deities. Akhenaten's ideals were too high for them. The debris of the foreign empire was, as usual in such cases, put together again, and customary, conventional law and order restored by the stupid, conservative reactionaries who succeeded him. Henceforward, Egyptian civilization ran an uninspired and undeveloping course till the days of the Saites and the Ptolemies.

JOHN A. WILSON

AKHENATON: MONOTHEIST OR HENOTHEIST?

A distinguished American scholar, John A. Wilson is a former Director of the Oriental Institute of the University of Chicago. His illuminating study, *The Burden of Egypt* (1951) (also available as *The Culture of Ancient Egypt*), is both stimulating and sound. A student of Breasted, Wilson recalls the great Egyptologist fondly: "He was persuasive: after forty years, I have some sense of apology if I cannot accept his high evaluation of the revolutionary Pharaoh Akhenaton or if I do not believe that conscience dawned for man pre-eminently in ancient Egypt. He offered his best for us to share."[1] However, Wilson's calm analysis of the Aton cult is more useful than Breasted's rhapsodic hero worship.

With certain exceptions . . . the Amarna texts omit mention of any gods except the Aton. . . . A violent change was the suppression of the former mortuary religion, with all its elaborate formulation centering on the god Osiris. Mortuary prayers and formulas were not now addressed to Osiris or Anubis, but directly to the pharaoh Akhenaton or through him to the Aton. . . . The most important observation about Amarna religion is that there were two gods central to the faith, and not one. Akhenaton and his family worshipped the Aton, and everybody else worshipped Akhenaton *as a god*. In addition to his formal names and titles, the pharaoh was referred to as "the good god," and he asserted that he was the physical son of the Aton. The abundant scenes in the Amarna tombs show him serving the living sun-disk, while all of his courtiers bow in adoration to him. Their prayers were not addressed to the Aton but directly to Akhenaton. The courtier Eye, who was later to become pharaoh, asked Akhenaton for mortuary benefits: "Mayest thou grant to me a good old age as thy favorite; mayest thou grant to me a goodly burial by the command of thy [spirit] in my house. . . . May I hear thy sweet voice in the sanctuary when thou performest that which pleases thy

[1] John A. Wilson, *Signs and Wonders Upon Pharaoh: A History of American Egyptology,* (Chicago: University of Chicago Press, 1964), p. 142.

father, the living Aton." Another noble did pray to the Aton, but prayed only on behalf of Akhenaton, with his petition for himself addressed to the pharaoh: "Mayest thou make thy beloved son Akhenaton to live with thee forever, to do what thy heart wishes, and to behold what thou dost every day, for he rejoices in the sight of thy beauty. . . . Let him remain here, until the swan turns black, until the raven turns white, until the mountains stand up to walk, and until the sea runs up the river. And may I continue in service of the good god Akhenaton until he assigns to me the burial that he gives." This is a stated acknowledgement of the centrality of the pharaoh in the worship of the Aton and of the dependence of the noble upon his god-king. . . . The Aton faith had no penetration below the level of the royal family as an effective religious expression; it was stated to be the exclusive faith of the god-king and his divine family, and the god-king welcomed and encouraged his subjects' worship of his divine being as the source of all the benefits which they might desire.

The self-centered nature of Akhenaton's faith, the fact that only the royal family had a trained and reasoned loyalty to the Aton, and the fact that all of pharaoh's adherents were forced to give their entire devotion to him as a god-king explain why the new religion collapsed after Akhenaton's death. Political and economic factors were also important, but . . . we cannot believe that [the courtiers] cherished within their bosoms the teaching about a benevolent and sustaining sole god, the Aton, when all of their religious exercise was exhausted in worship of Akhenaton. When that pharaoh died and the movement collapsed, they must have scrambled penitently back into the traditional faith, which they could understand and in which they were allowed wider devotion.

Two important questions face us. Was this monotheism? If so, was it the world's first ancestral monotheism, and did it come down to us through the Hebrews? Our own answer to each question is in the negative, even though such an answer may rest upon definitions of the terms, and such definitions must necessarily be those of modern distinctions.

Our modern Jewish, Christian, and Moslem faiths express the doctrine that there is one—and only one—God and that all ethical and religious values derive from that God. In . . . the Amarna religion,

we see that there were at least two gods, that the Aton was concerned strictly with creating and maintaining life, and that ethics and religion derived from the pharaoh Akhenaton. . . . The Amarna texts call the Aton the "sole god, like whom there is no other." This, however, was nothing new in Egyptian religious address. The form of expression was a fervid exaggeration or concentration, which went back to the earliest religious literature more than a thousand years before Akhenaton's time. In the period before the Amarna revolution, Amon, Re, Atum, Har-akhti, and Min were severally called "the sole god." Sometimes this term recalled the creation, when the one existent god was going to bring other gods into being. Sometimes it was a flattering exaggeration meaning the only important god, *like whom* there was no other. Often it was a focusing of the worshipper's attention upon one god, to the exclusion of others—what is called henotheism or monolatry. In no sense does it imply the absolute unity carried by the Moslem: "There is no god but God." In ancient times a man's name was a vital part of his being. . . . The same psychology applies to Akhenaton's attack upon Amon and topically upon other gods. If the philosophy of the new religion was that only the Aton was a god and that, therefore, Amon did not and could not exist, why was there so virulent an attack upon Amon, and why was his name systematically hacked out of the records? In those ancient terms he had still some kind of existence as long as his name was effectively a part of a single record. . . .

Atonism was at one and the same time native to Egyptian religion and unique within that religion. It was native because the Egyptian state was built upon the dogma that pharaoh was a god and stood between the people and the other gods; thus the double relationship at Amarna retained the past essentials. It was unique because the gods other than pharaoh were made one god, by a process of exclusion rather than syncretism. . . . Much more important was the elimination of Osiris from the mortuary faith, with the ascription of all mortuary benefits to the pharaoh. One could say that it was the closest approach to monotheism possible within the thought of the day. That would still fall short of making it a belief in and worship of only one god.

The question as to whether Atonism was ancestral to Hebrew monotheism and thus to modern expressions of religion is also difficult. However, it may be stated flatly that the mechanism of transmission from the faith of Akhenaton to the monotheism of Moses is not apparent. This was the personal religion of a pharaoh who later became a heretic within one generation. It was not accessible to Egyptians at large. Their subsequent reaction in a fervent return to the older forms, particularly the Osirian faith and the cherishing care of little personal gods, shows how little penetration Atonism had below the royal family. Even assuming that there were Israelite slave troops in Egypt in Amarna times, there was no way by which they could learn the teaching of Atonism, that there was a single, universal god, who made and continued life, toward whom the worshipper felt a warm sense of gratitude. Atonism taught that the pharaoh of Egypt was essential as the only intermediary between god and people. There is another discontinuity between Atonism and Hebrew monotheism as the latter developed, and that is the marked lack of ethical content in the hymns directed to the Aton. Akhenaton's faith was intellectual rather than ethical; its strong emotional content derived from the fervor of the discoverer and convert, who rejected past forms and preached new forms. The conviction of right and wrong was not ethical, but was a passionate reiteration that the new was right and the old was wrong. . . . The universalism of the Aton could have carried the implication that all men are equal under the god and should be so treated, but such a logical conclusion is strikingly absent from the texts. . . .

Much of the importance of the Hebrews to world history lies in the fact that they avoided some of the weakening and distracting phases of civilization. A concept which was imperfectly articulated and understood at pharaoh's court at Amarna would have been quite foreign to Asiatic tribes wandering in the desert. When the Children of Israel penetrated Canaan and settled down to work out a new way of life, their progressive religious steps were achieved

through their own national religious experience as their own God-given discoveries, without derivation from any foreign source. Such precious and inner expressions of religion can never be borrowed, but must be experienced. When they have been experienced, the *forms* in which they are uttered may be borrowed from others, but never the innermost spirit.

This brings us to a main argument for the contact between Atonism and Hebrew religion: the extraordinary parallelism in thought and structure between Akhenaton's hymn to the Aton and the 104th Psalm. . . . It has been claimed that such correspondences must show derivative connection and that the Hebrew psalmists must have known the Egyptian sun-hymn. Since the obliteration of Atonism was complete some six or seven centuries before the psalm was written, it is argued that the Aton hymn must have passed into Asia when Akhenaton was still in power and escaped destruction by translation into some Semitic dialect. So ingenious a mechanism of transmission is not necessary. We have already seen that the several ideas and modes of expression visible in Atonism were present in Egypt before Atonism and independent of Atonism. Since these were current forms in Egypt, not invented by the Amarna priests or scribes, it is not surprising to find them still in use after the fall of Atonism and without relation to the fact that the specific cult had been proclaimed a heresy. . . . [Wilson cites universalistic hymns to Amon from the Nineteenth and Twentieth Dynasties.] This is an adequate explanation of the similarity between the Aton hymn and the 104th Psalm. Hymns of this kind were current long after the fall of Akhenaton, so that when Hebrew religion had reached a point where it needed a certain mode of expression it could find in another literature phrases and thoughts which would meet the need.

2

DEMOCRACY IN ATHENS

It comes as a surprise to many moderns to learn that democracy has not always been looked upon with favor by Americans. Most of the founding fathers agreed with James Madison that "democracies have ever been spectacles of turbulence and contention, have ever been found incompatible with personal security or the rights of property, and have in general been as short in their lives as they have been violent in their deaths." Even today, some disenchanted people endorse H. L. Mencken's definition of democracy as "the art and science of running the circus from the monkey-cage," though it is doubtful that the wolf's lair or the snake pit would be any improvement. Madison and his contemporaries had never seen a democracy in action and had to rely on the classic historians of Greece who portrayed ancient democracy in dark colors. Later, the excesses of the French Revolution seemed to confirm the standing indictment of democracy as irresponsible and bloody, but the same reasoning ought also to have discredited Christianity since millions have been butchered in the name of the Prince of Peace. The crimes of states have less to do with forms of government than with the personalities of rulers and the imagined needs of the moment. In all fairness, democrats have spilled less blood than barons, bishops, and kings, and popular governments have generally reduced the misery which burdens most men throughout history.

Though there have been "democratic" elements in many societies of the past, true democracy existed only in a few Greek cities which utilized the full participation of all citizens in government. Such total democracy is impractical in large nations which must settle for representative government, but the Greek city-states were small and every citizen was important in politics. The apathy of many modern citizens was foreign to the Greeks who were fervent, even fanatical, in the exercise of their political rights. At times, political passions boiled over into outright factional warfare, and the cities were torn by civil strife. Yet Athens remained relatively free from the horrors of class war. At the city of Miletus, the democrats once trampled the children of oligarchs with oxen, and the oligarchs in turn coated the children of democrats with pitch and turned them into human torches. At no time did the Athenians descend to such atrocities, though Attic democracy was often endangered by oligarchic conspiracies and conservative secret societies whose members took solemn oaths to subvert democracy. We are singularly well informed on the political history of Athens, because of the histories, pamphlets, and philosophic studies which have survived from the era of democracy in Athens. However, the historians and political scientists who are the main sources for the history of Athens were usually unfriendly toward the theory and practice of democracy.

Popular government at Athens was a response to the failures of the Solonian constitution. In 594 B.C. Solon had established a political order in which decision making was in the hands of property owners and only the very wealthy were eligible to be magistrates. Under Solon's system, the masses elected their rulers and could punish them later for abuses of authority; the common people also had control of the courts, for they filled the large juries which decided all cases. By the middle of the sixth century, an able tyrant seized power and ruled Athens without disturbing the forms of Solon's constitution. The tyrant's henchmen filled important offices and executed his wishes. However, circumstances forced the next tyrant to raise taxes and impose a reign of terror against imagined enemies. His real foes soon overthrew him with military aid from Sparta. Though the Spartans preferred an oligarchic regime in Athens, the oligarchs overplayed their hand and were driven from the city about 508 B.C. The victor in the civil strife was a wealthy aristocrat, Cleisthenes, who established the democratic system in Athens with an emphasis on the equality and full participation of all citizens in government. Attic democracy gained great prestige by repulsing two Persian invasions—the naval victory in 480 B.C. was an additional boon to the democrats, for the common people manned the ships which defeated the fleets of Xerxes at Salamis. In the aftermath of the Persian wars, Athens became an imperial power in the Aegean area, extorting tribute from numerous cities which were nominally its allies.

Under the leadership of Pericles, Attic democracy was prosperous and powerful, and the citizens of Athens enjoyed a "Golden Age" of art and drama. In 431 B.C. Athens and Sparta blundered into a major conflict, the Peloponnesian War, which ended in 404 with the defeat of Athens and the loss of its empire. During the stresses of the long war, many Attic conservatives were pro-Spartan and hoped to bring peace by overthrowing the democracy. In 411 B.C. a group of extremists seized control of Athens, but more moderate conservatives gained the upper hand and democracy was restored within a year. In postwar Athens, the Spartans imposed a reactionary oligarchy on the defeated city. The oligarchic regime was called the Thirty and was led by a vicious extremist, Critias, whose purges led to a democratic counterrevolution. By 403 B.C. even the Spartans were disgusted with the Thirty and allowed the democrats to regain the city after a brief civil war. Disdaining reprisals, the restored democracy was remarkably restrained, and the conservative Plato praised it for not massacring its opponents. During the fourth century, Athens did not recover its former power, but democracy flourished despite the complaints of the rich who had to contribute more taxes in the absence of imperial tribute. The great orator Demosthenes warned that Athens and democracy were endangered by the aggressive plans of Philip of Macedon. In 338 B.C. Philip defeated the Athenians at the battle of Chaeronea and established a hegemony over the city-states of Greece. After Alexander, Macedonian warlords imposed oligarchy on Athens in 322 and 317 B.C., but the democrats finally regained control of the city. However, in the Hellenistic age the political life of Athens was irrelevant, for the city's policies were dictated by the kings of the powerful new nations which had been carved from Alexander's empire.

Most discussions of Attic democracy deal with the fifth century B.C., and a brief survey of the political system at the time of Pericles might be useful. All authority rested with the Assembly, which was a legislative body open to all adult male citizens. Anyone might address the Assembly, and its laws and decrees were literally the will of the people. However, the agenda for the Assembly was prepared by the Council of Five Hundred, whose members were chosen by lot. Through astute gerrymandering, the Council was a representative body reflecting the varied economic and geographic interests in the population of Attica. The urban masses of Athens packed the Assembly, but the Council protected rural voters and was largely controlled by machine politicians. The magistrates of Athens performed routine administrative duties and were chosen by lot, but decisions at the executive level were made by a board of ten elected generals, who were both military commanders and political bosses. For thirty years, Pericles dominated Athens as chairman of the board of generals. Because the empire provided prosperity, Periclean democracy had a middle-class tone, and wealthy men directed the destiny of the city. The poor manned the fleet, voted in the Assembly, could serve on the Council, and made up the juries whose activities had expanded since lawsuits involving residents of subject cities were heard at Athens. Imperial tribute paid the meager salaries of magistrates, military men, councilmen, and jurors; in the early fourth century, assemblymen also received a small pay for attendance. A distinctive characteristic of Attic life was the voluntary assumption by the rich of the cost of producing plays and supplying warships for the city. In the fifth century, wealthy men competed for the honor and prestige of such obligations, which became onerous in the fourth century.

Three aspects of Athenian democracy—the lot, ostracism, and demagogues—have often excited critics. In theory, the use of the lot in selecting magistrates and councilmen reflects a naïve faith in the equality of men, but in practice all Athenian officials, whether selected or elected, were first screened by the Council of Five Hundred as to their suitability. On a number of occasions, the voters of Athens ostracized prominent politicians, who were ordered to leave Attica but did not suffer the loss of their property. The pretext for ostracism was that the politician in question was a potential tyrant or a threat to the public weal. In theory, the device seems an absurd attack on talent, a weapon of the jealous masses against a man of ability. But, in practice the vote was instigated and rigged by rival leaders who would be eclipsed by the triumph of one man or who simply wished to break his political influence for a time. The Assembly was often swayed by glib orators who blocked the aims of the Council and the generals by eloquent speeches on the floor of the Assembly. Through oratory a politician could challenge the political machine by appealing to the sovereign people. Critics called the orators "demagogues" and claimed that they confused the electorate with rhetoric and emotion. Yet, politicians in any era employ emotional bombast to obscure issues and convince voters. Demagoguery is effective oratory, and an orator should be censured only if the policy he advocates is wrong or based on lies.

As an imperial power, Athens dealt high-handedly with its subjects and exploited them as do all empires. But the Attic fleet suppressed piracy in the Aegean and the subject cities prospered while they grumbled. In war the Assembly often made wrong decisions and at times acted cruelly, but what nation at war has not stained its hands with innocent blood? Compared to Sparta, the Athenian yoke was light and its crimes were few. A more cogent criticism of Attic democracy would take note of the lack of inherent human rights, for all rights were derived from society and could be abrogated by the state. No Athenian derived rights from his existence as a man. When faced with unjust laws, even Socrates could only say, "Change the laws or obey them." His own martyrdom was a private demonstration of philosophic faith and not an act of civil disobedience. His enemies and friends alike expected the aged philosopher to go into exile, but he wished to prove that a good man will die for the truth. Like Jesus, Socrates sought his own death, and his tragic fate was a glaring exception to the freedom of speech which was one of the glories of Athenian democracy. In the annals of muzzling men and censoring ideas, Athens stands indicted on a few occasions, but the record of Attic democracy is spotless compared to that of imperial Rome, medieval and modern Europe, and most nations today. Even if all were true that the critics of Athens have claimed, we can only concede with Winston Churchill that "democracy is the worst form of government except all those other forms that have been tried from time to time." Too often, moderns forget this simple truth.

"THE OLD OLIGARCH"

A SARCASTIC VIEW OF DEMOCRATIC ATHENS

Though this essay on the practice of democracy at Athens was preserved among the writings of the historian Xenophon, it is obviously the work of a conservative Athenian of the preceding generation who wrote before the Peloponnesian War. The anonymous author has aptly been nicknamed "the Old Oligarch," for he was no friend of democracy. Greek political polemics were generally abusive, but the Old Oligarch was a man of wit who employed sarcasm effectively. Instead of theorizing about the virtues of oligarchy, the author describes the fallible workings of democracy with graphic realism. Despite his hostile tone, he offers a rare glimpse of Athens in the fifth century B.C. In the following passages, the term "the People" stands interchangeably for the popular faction, the Athenian masses, and the Assembly which they controlled through their votes.

Now, as for the constitution of the Athenians and the type or manner of constitution which they have chosen, I praise it not, in so far as the very choice involves the welfare of the baser folk as opposed to that of the better class. I repeat, I withhold my praise so far; but, given the fact that this is the type agreed

From "The Old Oligarch," *The Constitution of the Athenians,* tr. Henry G. Dakyns, in *The Greek Historians,* edited by Francis R. B. Godolphin, Vol. II, pp. 633–37, 640–41. Copyright 1942 by Random House, Inc. Reprinted by permission.

upon, I propose to show that they set about its preservation in the right way; and that those other transactions in connection with it, which are looked upon as blunders by the rest of the Hellenic world, are the reverse.

In the first place, I maintain, it is only just that the poorer classes and the common people of Athens should be better off than the men of birth and wealth, seeing that it is the people who man the fleet and have brought the city her power. . . . This being the case, it seems only just that offices of state should be thrown open to every one both in the ballot and the show of hands, and that the right of speech should belong to any one who likes, without restriction. For, observe, there are many of these offices which, according as they are in good or in bad hands, are a source of safety or of danger to the People, and in these the People prudently abstains from sharing; as, for instance, it does not think it incumbent on itself to share in the functions of the general or of the commander of cavalry. The commons recognizes the fact that in forgoing the personal exercise of these offices and leaving them to the control of the more powerful citizens, it secures the balance of advantage to itself. It is only those departments of government which bring pay and assist the private estate that the People cares to keep in its own hands.

In the next place . . . , the fact that everywhere greater consideration is shown to the base, to poor people and to common folk, than to persons of good quality—so far from being a matter of surprise, this, as can be shown, is the keystone of the preservation of the democracy. It is these poor people, this common folk, this worse element, whose prosperity, combined with the growth of their numbers, enhances the democracy. . . . In fact, all the world over, the cream of society is in opposition to the democracy. Naturally, since the smallest amount of intemperance and injustice, together with the highest scrupulousness in the pursuit of excellence, is to be found in the ranks of the better class, while within the ranks of the People will be found the greatest amount of ignorance, disorderliness, rascality—poverty acting as a stronger incentive to base conduct, not to speak of lack of education and ignorance, traceable to the lack of means which afflicts the average of mankind.

The objection may be raised that it was a mistake to allow the universal right of speech and a seat in council. These should have been reserved for the cleverest, the flower of the community. But here, again, it will be found that they are acting with wise deliberation in granting to even the baser sort the right of speech, for supposing only the better people might speak or sit in council, blessings would fall to the lot of those like themselves, but to the commons the reverse of blessings. Whereas now, any one who likes, any base fellow, may get up and discover something to the advantage of himself and his equals. It may be retorted, "And what sort of advantage either for himself or for the People can such a fellow be expected to hit upon?" The answer to which is, that in their judgment the ignorance and the baseness of this fellow, together with his goodwill, are worth a great deal more to them than your superior person's virtue and wisdom, coupled with animosity. What it comes to, therefore, is that a state founded upon such institutions will not be the best state; but, given a democracy, these are the right means to secure its preservation. The People, it must be borne in mind, does not demand that the city should be well governed and itself a slave. It desires to be free and to be master. As to bad legislation, it does not concern itself about that. In fact, what you believe to be bad legislation is the very source of the People's strength and freedom. But if you seek for good legislation, in the first place you will see the cleverest members of the community laying down the laws for the rest. And in the next place, the better class will curb and chastise the lower orders; the better class will deliberate in behalf of the state and not suffer crack-brained fellows to sit in council or to speak or vote in the assemblies. No doubt; but under the weight of such blessings, the People will in a very short time be reduced to slavery.

Another point is the extraordinary amount of license granted to slaves and resident aliens at Athens, where a blow is illegal and a slave will not step aside to let you pass him in the street. . . . Supposing it were legal for a slave to be beaten by a free citizen or for a resident alien or freedman to be beaten by a citizen, it would frequently happen that an Athenian might be mistaken for a slave or an alien and receive a beating; since the Athenian People is not better clothed than the slave or alien, nor in personal appearance is there any superiority. . . . Slaves in Athens are allowed to indulge in luxury and . . . we must perforce be slaves to our slaves, in order that we may get in our slave-rents. . . . Where you have wealthy slaves it ceases to be advantageous that my slave should stand in awe of you. In [Sparta] my slave stands in awe of you. But if your slave is in awe of me, there will be a risk of his giving away his own moneys to avoid running a risk in his own person. It is for this reason then that we have established an equality between our slaves and free men, and again between our resident aliens and full citizens, because the city stands in need of her resident aliens to meet the requirements of such a multiplicity of arts and for the purposes of her navy. . . .

The common people put a stop to citizens devoting their time to athletics and to the cultivation of music, disbelieving in the beauty of such training, and recognizing the fact that these are things the cultivation of which is beyond its power. On the same principle, in the case of the [chorus producer], the management of athletics, and the command of ships, the fact is recognized that it is the rich man who trains the chorus and the People for whom the chorus is trained; it is the rich man who is naval commander or superintendent of athletics, and the People that profits by their labors. In fact, what the People looks upon as its right is to pocket the money. To sing and run and dance and man the vessels is well enough, but only in order that the People may be the gainer, while the rich are made poorer. And so in the courts of justice, justice is not more an object of concern to the jurymen than what touches personal advantage. . . .

Again, it is looked upon as a mistaken policy on the part of the Athenian democracy to compel her allies to voyage to Athens in order to have their cases tried. On the other hand, it is easy to reckon up what a number of advantages the Athenian People derives from the practice impugned. In the first place, there is the steady receipt of salaries throughout the year derived from the court fees. Next, it enables them to manage the affairs of the allied states while seated at home without the expense of naval expeditions. Thirdly, they thus preserve the partisans of the democracy, and ruin her opponents in the law courts. Whereas, supposing the several allied states tried their cases at home, being inspired by hostility to Athens, they would destroy those of their own citizens whose friendship to the Athenian People was most marked. But besides all this, the democracy derives the following advantages from hearing the cases of her allies in Athens. In the first place, the one per cent [tax] levied in Piraeus is increased to the profit of the state; again, the owner

of a lodging-house does better, and so, too, the owner of a pair of beasts or of slaves to be let out on hire; again, heralds and criers are a class of people who fare better owing to the sojourn of foreigners at Athens. . . . Every single individual among the allies is forced to pay flattery to the People of Athens because he knows that he must betake himself to Athens and win or lose his case at the bar, not of any stray set of judges, but of the sovereign People itself, such being the law and custom at Athens. He is compelled to behave as a suppliant in the courts of justice and, when some juryman comes into court, to grasp his hand. . . .

In the case of engagements entered into by a democracy, it is open to the People to throw the blame on the single individual who spoke in favor of some measure, or put it to the vote, and to maintain to the rest of the world, "I was not present, nor do I approve of the terms of the agreement." Inquiries are made in a full meeting of the People, and should any of these things be disapproved of, they can at once discover countless excuses to avoid doing whatever they do not wish. And if any mischief should spring out of any resolutions which the People has passed in council, the People can readily shift the blame from its own shoulders: "A handful of oligarchs acting against the interests of the People have ruined us." But if any good result ensue, they, the People, at once take the credit of that to themselves.

In the same spirit, it is not allowed to caricature on the comic stage or otherwise libel the People, because they do not care to hear themselves ill spoken of. But if any one has a desire to satirize his neighbor he has full leave to do so. And this because they are well aware that, as a general rule, the person caricatured does not belong to the People. . . . He is more likely to be some wealthy or well-born person or man of means and influence. In fact, but few poor people and of the popular stamp incur the comic lash, or if they do they have brought it on themselves by excessive love of meddling or some covetous self-seeking at the expense of the People, so that no particular annoyance is felt at seeing such folk satirized.

What, then, I venture to assert is, that the People of Athens has no difficulty in recognizing which of its citizens are of the better sort and which the opposite. And so recognizing those who are serviceable and advantageous to itself, even though they be base, the People loves them; but the good folk they are disposed . . . to hate. This virtue of theirs, the People holds, is not engrained in their nature for any good to itself, but rather for its injury. . . . For my part, I pardon the People its own democracy, as, indeed it is pardonable in any one to do good to himself. But the man who, not being himself one of the People, prefers to live in a state democratically governed rather than in an oligarchical state may be said to smooth his own path towards iniquity. He knows that a bad man has a better chance of slipping through the fingers of justice in a democratic . . . state. . . .

It not seldom happens, they tell us, that a man is unable to transact a piece of business with the [Council of Five Hundred or the Assembly], even if he sits waiting a whole year. Now this does happen at Athens, and for no other reason save that, owing to the immense mass of affairs they are unable to work off all the business on hand and dismiss the applicants. And how in the world should they be able, considering in the first place that they, the Athenians, have more festivals to celebrate than any other

state . . . of Hellas? . . . In the next place, only consider the number of cases they have to decide, what with private suits and public causes and scrutinies of accounts, more than the whole of the rest of mankind put together; while the [Council] has multifarious points to advise upon concerning peace and war, concerning ways and means, concerning the framing and passing of laws, and concerning the matters affecting the state perpetually occurring, and endless questions touching the allies; besides the receipt of the tribute, the superintendence of dockyards and temples. Can, I ask again, any one find it at all surprising that, with all these affairs on their hands, they are unequal to doing business with all the world? But some people tell us that if the applicant will only address himself to the [Council or the Assembly] with a bribe in his hand, he will do a good stroke of business. And for my part I am free to confess . . . that a good many things may be done at Athens by dint of money. . . . However, . . . as to transacting with every one of these applicants all he wants, the state could not do it, not even if all the gold and silver in the world were the inducement offered.

THUCYDIDES

FACTIONAL WARFARE ON CORCYRA

During the Peloponnesian War between Athens and Sparta, both sides tried to justify their war aims with ideological slogans—the Spartans posed as the liberators of Hellas while the Athenians claimed to be fighting for democracy. In 427 B.C. the democrats on the island of Corcyra took advantage of Athenian protection to massacre their oligarchic "pro-Spartan" opponents. The savage episode gave the great historian Thucydides an opportunity to digress on the grim nature of factional strife everywhere in Hellas. Born of a wealthy conservative Athenian family, Thucydides was critical of democratic errors but he admired Pericles and approved of a limited democracy in which the franchise would be restricted to property holders. When he composed this passage, postwar Athens was in the hands of a group of reactionary oligarchs, the Thirty, who ruthlessly purged the supporters of democracy. Thucydides intended his digression on Corcyra as a rebuke to all such bloodletting by either political faction.

When the Corcyraeans perceived that the Athenian fleet was approaching, while that of the enemy had disappeared, they . . . killed any of their enemies whom they caught in the city. . . . They also went to the temple of Hera and persuading about fifty of the suppliants to stand their trial, condemned them all to death. The majority would not come out, and, when they saw what was going on, destroyed one another in the enclosure of the temple where they were, except a few who hung themselves on trees or put an end to their own lives in any other way which they could. And during the seven days [while the Athenian squadron remained in the harbor], the Corcyraeans continued slaughtering those of their fellow-citizens whom they deemed their enemies; they professed to punish them for their designs against the democracy, but in fact some were killed from motives of personal enmity, and some because money was owing to them, by the hands of their debtors. Every form of death was to be seen, and everything, and more than everything that commonly happens in revolutions, happened then. The father slew the son, and the suppliants were torn from the temples and slain near them; some of them were even walled up in the temple of Dionysus and there perished. To such extremes of cruelty did revolution go, and this seemed to be the worst of revolutions because it was the first.

For not long afterwards the whole Hellenic world was in commotion; in every city the chiefs of the democracy and of the oligarchy were struggling, the one to bring in the Athenians, the other the [Spartans]. . . . In time of peace, men would have had no excuse for introducing either, and no desire to do so, but when they were at war and both sides could easily obtain allies to the hurt of their enemies and the advantage of themselves, the dissatisfied party were only too ready to invoke foreign aid. And revolution brought upon the cities of Hellas many terrible calamities, such as have been and always will be while human nature remains the same, but which are more or less aggravated and differ in character with every new combination of circumstances. In peace and prosperity, both states and individuals are actuated by higher motives, because they do not fall under the dominion of imperious necessities; but war which takes away the comfortable provision of daily life is a hard master and tends to assimilate men's characters to their conditions.

When troubles had once begun in the cities, those who followed carried the revolutionary spirit further and further, and determined to outdo the report of all who had preceded them by the ingenuity of their enterprises and the atrocity of their revenges. The meaning of words had no longer the same relation to things, but was changed by them as they thought proper. Reckless daring was held to be loyal courage; prudent delay was the excuse of a coward; moderation was the disguise of unmanly weakness; to know everything was to do nothing. Frantic energy was the true quality of a man. A conspirator who wanted to be safe was a recreant in disguise. The lover of violence was always trusted, and his opponent suspected. He who succeeded in a plot was deemed knowing, but a still greater master in craft was he who detected one. On the other hand, he who plotted from the first to have nothing to do with plots was a breaker up of parties and a poltroon who was afraid of the enemy. In a word, he who could outstrip another in a bad action was applauded, and so was he who encouraged to evil one who had no idea of it. The tie of party was stronger than the tie of blood, because a partisan was more ready to dare without asking why. (For party associations are not based upon any established law, nor do they seek the public good; they are formed in defiance of the laws and from self-interest.) The seal of good faith was not divine law but fellowship in crime. If any enemy when he was in the ascendant offered fair words, the opposite party received them not in a generous spirit but by a jealous watchfulness of his actions. Revenge was dearer than self-preservation. Any agreements sworn to by either party, when they could do nothing else, were binding as long as both were powerless. But he who on a favorable opportunity first took courage and struck at his enemy when he saw him off his guard, had greater pleasure in a perfidious than he would have had in an open act of revenge; he congratulated himself that he had taken the safer course, and also that he had overreached his enemy and gained the prize of superior ability. In general the dishonest more easily gain credit for cleverness than the simple for goodness; men take a pride in the one but are ashamed of the other.

The cause of all these evils was the love of power, originating in avarice and ambition, and the party-spirit which is engendered by them when men are fairly embarked in a contest. For the leaders on either side used specious names, the one party professing to uphold the constitutional equality of the many, the other the wisdom of an aristocracy, while they made the public interests, to which in name they were devoted, in reality their prize. Striving in every way to overcome each other, they committed the most monstrous crimes; yet even these were surpassed by the magnitude of their revenges which they pursued to the very utmost, neither party observing any definite limits either of justice or public expediency, but both alike making the caprice of the moment their law. Either by the help of an unrighteous sentence or grasping power with the strong hand, they were eager to satiate the impatience of party-spirit. Neither faction cared for religion, but any fair pretence which succeeded in effecting some odious purpose was greatly lauded. And the citizens who were of neither party fell a prey to both; either they were disliked because they held aloof, or men were jealous of their surviving.

Thus revolution gave birth to every form of wickedness in Hellas. The simplicity which is so large an element in a noble nature was laughed to scorn and disappeared. An attitude of perfidious antagonism everywhere prevailed, for there was no word binding enough, nor oath terrible enough to reconcile enemies. Each man was strong only in the conviction that nothing was secure; he must look to his own safety and could not afford to trust others. Inferior intellects generally succeeded best. For, aware of their own deficiencies and fearing the capacity of their opponents, for whom they were no match in powers of speech and whose subtle wits were likely to anticipate them in contriving evil, they struck boldly and at once. But the cleverer sort, presuming in their arrogance that they would be aware in time and disdaining to act when they could think, were taken off their guard and easily destroyed.

Now in Corcyra most of these deeds were perpetrated and for the first time. There was every crime which men might be supposed to perpetrate in revenge who had been governed not wisely but tyrannically, and now had the oppressor at their mercy. There were the dishonest designs of others who were longing to be relieved from their habitual poverty and were naturally animated by a passionate desire for their neighbor's goods; and there were crimes of another class which men commit not from covetousness but from the enmity which equals foster towards one another until they are carried away by their blind rage into the extremes of pitiless cruelty. At such a time the life of the city was all in disorder, and human nature, which is always ready to transgress the laws, having now trampled them under foot, delighted to show that her passions were ungovernable, that she was stronger than justice, and the enemy of everything above her. If malignity had not exercised a fatal power, how could any one have preferred revenge to piety, and gain to innocence? But, when men are retaliating upon others, they are reckless of the future and do not hesitate to annul those common laws of humanity to which every individual trusts for his own hope of deliverance should he ever be overtaken by calamity; they forget that in their own hour of need they will look to them in vain.[1]

[1] This last paragraph (III 84) may have been inserted by an ancient editor of the text. [Editor's note.]

GEORGE GROTE

A NINETEENTH-CENTURY LIBERAL DEFENDS
DEMOCRATIC ATHENS

The classic English history of Greece was composed by George Grote (1794–1871). Appearing in twelve volumes from 1846 to 1856, his *History of Greece* was a masterful work backed by sound scholarship and common sense and full of valuable insights. Though his treatment of some topics naturally is dated, the book has survived the passage of time remarkably well and is still useful for modern students. A successful banker and member of Parliament, Grote had an abiding interest in politics, ancient and modern. More liberal than his fellow members of the Liberal Party, he was a fervent believer in popular government and wrote at a time when "democracy happens to be unpalatable to most modern readers." Though he was also an authority on Greek philosophy, Grote felt that the development of democracy at Athens was an even greater achievement than the familiar Greek triumphs in art, thought, and literature.

The fruit of the fresh-planted democracy as well as the seed for its sustentation and aggrandizement continued progressive during the whole period. . . . But the first unexpected burst of it under the Cleisthenean constitution . . . is described by Herodotus in terms too emphatic to be omitted: . . . "Thus did the Athenians grow in strength. And we may find proof, not merely in this instance but everywhere else, how valuable a thing freedom is: since even the Athenians, while under a despot, were not superior in war to any of their surrounding neighbors, but, so soon as they got rid of their despots, became by far the first of all. These things show that while kept down by one man, they were slack and timid like men working for a master; but when they were liberated, every single man became eager in exertions for his own benefit." The same comparison reappears a short time afterwards where he tells us that "the Athenians when free felt themselves a match for Sparta, but while kept down by any man under a despotism, were feeble and apt for submission."

Stronger expressions cannot be found to depict the rapid improvement wrought in the Athenian people by their new democracy. Of course this did not arise merely from suspension of previous cruelties, or better laws, or better administration. These, indeed, were essential conditions, but the active transforming cause here was the principle and system of which such amendments formed the detail: the grand and new idea of the sovereign People, composed of free and equal citizens — or liberty and equality, to use words which so profoundly moved the French nation half a century ago. It was this comprehensive political idea which acted with electric effect upon the Athenians, creating within them a host of sentiments, motives, sympathies, and capacities, to which they had before been strangers. Democracy in Grecian antiquity possessed the privilege, not only of kindling an earnest and unanimous attachment to the constitution in the bosoms of the citizens, but also of creating an energy of public and private action, such as could never be obtained under an oligarchy, where the utmost that could be hoped for was a passive acquiescence and obedience. Mr. [Edmund] Burke has remarked that the mass of the people are generally very indifferent about theories of government; but such indifference — although improvements in the practical working of all governments tend to foster it — is hardly to be expected among any people who exhibit decided mental activity and spirit on other matters; and the reverse was unquestionably true in the year 500 B.C. among the communities of ancient Greece. Theories of government were there anything but a dead letter: they were connected with emotions of the strongest . . . character. The theory of a permanent ruling One, for example, was universally odious: that of a ruling Few, though acquiesced in, was never positively attractive, unless either where it was associated with the maintenance of peculiar education and habits, as at Sparta, or where it presented itself as the only antithesis to democracy, the latter having by peculiar circumstances become an object of terror. But the theory of democracy was preeminently seductive, creating in the mass of the citizens an intense positive attachment and disposing them to voluntary action and suffering on its behalf, such as no coercion on the part of other governments could extort. Herodotus, in his comparison of the three sorts of government, puts in the front rank of the advantages of democracy, "its most splendid name and promise" — its power of enlisting the hearts of the citizens in support of their constitution and of providing for all a common bond of union and fraternity. This is what even democracy did not always do, but it was what no other government in Greece *could* do: a reason alone sufficient to stamp it as the best government and presenting the greatest chance of beneficent results for a Grecian community. Among the Athenian citizens, certainly, it produced a strength and unanimity of positive political sentiment, such as has rarely been seen in the history of mankind, which excites our surprise and admiration the more when we compare it with the apathy which had preceded. . . . Because democracy happens to be unpalatable to most modern readers, they have been accustomed to look upon the sentiment here described only in its least honorable manifestations — in the caricatures of Aristophanes or in the empty

From George Grote, *History of Greece* (London: John Murray, 1847), Vol. IV, pp. 235–242.

The Ancient World

commonplaces of rhetorical declaimers. But it is not in this way that the force, the earnestness, or the binding value of democratical sentiment at Athens is to be measured. We must listen to it as it comes from the lips of Pericles, while he is strenuously enforcing upon the people those active duties for which it both implanted the stimulus and supplied the courage; or from the oligarchical Nicias in the harbor of Syracuse, when he is endeavoring to revive the courage of his despairing troops for one last death-struggle, and when he appeals to their democratical patriotism as to the only flame yet alive and burning even in that moment of agony. From the time of Cleisthenes downward, the creation of this new mighty impulse makes an entire revolution in the Athenian character. And if the change still stood out in so prominent a manner before the eyes of Herodotus, much more must it have been felt by the contemporaries among whom it occurred.

The attachment of an Athenian citizen to his democratical constitution comprised two distinct veins of sentiment: first, his rights, protection, and advantages derived from it—next, his obligations of exertion and sacrifice towards it and with reference to it. Neither of these two veins of sentiment was ever wholly absent; but according as the one or the other was present at different times in varying proportions, the patriotism of the citizen was a very different feeling. That which Herodotus remarks is, the extraordinary efforts of heart and hand which the Athenians suddenly displayed—the efficacy of the active sentiment throughout the bulk of the citizens; and we shall observe even more memorable evidences of the same phenomenon in tracing down the history from Cleisthenes to the end of the Peloponnesian War: we shall trace a series of events and motives eminently calculated to stimulate that self-imposed labor and discipline which the early democracy had first called forth. But when we advance farther down from the restoration of the democracy after the Thirty Tyrants to the time of Demosthenes—I venture upon this brief anticipation in the conviction that one period of Grecian history can only be thoroughly understood by contrasting it with another—we shall find a sensible change in Athenian patriotism. The active sentiment of obligation is comparatively inoperative—the citizen, it is true, has a keen sense of the value of the democracy as protecting him and ensuring to him valuable rights, and he is moreover willing to perform his ordinary sphere of legal duties towards it; but he looks upon it as a thing established and capable of maintaining itself in a due measure of foreign ascendency without any such personal efforts as those which his forefathers cheerfully imposed upon themselves. The orations of Demosthenes contain melancholy proofs of such altered tone of patriotism—of that languor, paralysis, and waiting for others to act, which preceded the catastrophe of Chaeronea, notwithstanding an unabated attachment to the democracy as a source of protection and good government. That same preternatural activity which the allies of Sparta at the beginning of the Peloponnesian War both denounced and admired in the Athenians, is noted by the orator as now belonging to their enemy Philip.

Such variations in the scale of national energy pervade history, modern as well as ancient, but in regard to Grecian history especially, they can never be overlooked. For a certain measure, not only of positive political attachment, but also of active self-devotion, military readiness, and personal effort, was the indispensable condition of maintaining Hellenic autonomy either in Athens or elsewhere, and became so more than ever when the Macedonians were once organized under an enterprising and semi-Hellenized prince. The democracy was the first creative cause of that astonishing personal and many-sided energy which marked the Athenian character for a century downward from Cleisthenes. That the same ultra-Hellenic activity did not longer continue, is referable to other causes. . . . No system of government, even supposing it to be very much better and more faultless than the Athenian democracy, can ever pretend to accomplish its legitimate end apart from the personal character of the people or to supersede the necessity of individual virtue and vigor. During the half-century immediately preceding the battle of Chaeronea, the Athenians had lost that remarkable energy which distinguished them during the first century of their democracy and had fallen much more nearly to a level with the other Greeks, in common with whom they were obliged to yield to the pressure of a foreign enemy. I here briefly notice their last period of languor in contrast with the first burst of democratical fervor under Cleisthenes . . .—a feeling which will be found . . . to continue for a longer period than could have been reasonably anticipated, but which was too high-strung to become a perpetual and inherent attribute of any community.

LORD ACTON

ATHENS: THE TYRANNY OF THE MAJORITY

John Emerich Dalberg-Acton, Lord Acton (1834–1902), was Regius Professor of Modern History at Cambridge. He was the author of many articles and essays and the driving force behind the famous reference work *The Cambridge Modern History*. His thoughts on history and liberty have had considerable influence on many moderns. Acton was a fervent libertarian and unalterably opposed any form of authoritarianism, secular or ecclesiastical. As a Catholic in Protestant England, he had felt the weight of official bigotry and was sensitive to the plight of minorities. Acton was equally opposed to papal absolutism and criticized Pius IX and the Vatican Council of 1870. Obsessed with abuses of authority, Acton planned to write a definitive *History of Liberty,* but he never got around to writing it—which is probably just as well since he felt that Thucydides' ''judgment in politics is never at fault.'' The learned baron was blinded by the class prejudices of his time. Though he worshiped liberty with all the fanaticism of a French revolutionary, Acton did not believe in equality and he was not temperamentally inclined toward fraternity.

Liberty, next to religion, has been the motive of good deeds and the common pretext of crime, from the sowing of the seed at Athens, two thousand four hundred and sixty years ago, until the ripened harvest was gathered by men of our race. . . . At all times sincere friends of freedom have been rare, and its triumphs have been due to minorities, that have prevailed by associating themselves with auxiliaries whose objects often differed from their own; and this association, which is always dangerous, has been sometimes disastrous. . . . The most certain test by which we judge whether a country is really free is the amount of security enjoyed by minorities. . . .

Pericles . . . resolutely struck away all the props that still sustained the artificial preponderance of wealth. For the ancient doctrine that power goes with land, he introduced the idea that power ought to be so equitably diffused as to afford equal security to all. That one part of the community should govern the whole, or that one class should make laws for another, he declared to be tyrannical. The abolition of privilege would have served only to transfer the supremacy from the rich to the poor, if Pericles

had not redressed the balance by restricting the right of citizenship to Athenians of pure descent. By this measure, the class which formed what we should call the third estate was brought down to 14,000 citizens and became about equal in numbers with the higher ranks. Pericles held that every Athenian who neglected to take his part in the public business inflicted an injury on the commonwealth. That none might be excluded by poverty, he caused the poor to be paid for their attendance out of the funds of the State, for his administration of the federal tribute had brought together a treasure of more than two million sterling. The instrument of his sway was the art of speaking. He governed by persuasion. Everything was decided by argument in open deliberation, and every influence bowed before the ascendancy of mind. The idea that the object of constitutions is not to confirm the predominance of any interest, but to prevent it; to preserve with equal care the independence of labor and the security of property; to make the rich safe against envy and the poor against oppression, marks the highest level attained by the statesmanship of Greece. It hardly survived the great patriot who conceived it; and all history has been occupied with the endeavor to

From John Emerich Edward Dalberg-Acton, First Baron Acton, *The History of Freedom and Other Essays,* eds. John Neville Figgis and Reginald Vere Laurence (London: Macmillan & Co. Ltd., 1907) pp. 1, 9–13, 16–17, 29.

upset the balance of power by giving the advantage to money, land, or numbers. A generation followed that has never been equalled in talent—a generation of men whose works in poetry and eloquence are still the envy of the world, and in history, philosophy, and politics remain unsurpassed. But it produced no successor to Pericles, and no man was able to wield the sceptre that fell from his hand.

It was a momentous step in the progress of nations when the principle that every interest should have the right and the means of asserting itself was adopted by the Athenian Constitution. But for those who were beaten in the vote there was no redress. The law did not check the triumph of majorities or rescue the minority from the dire penalty of having been outnumbered. When the overwhelming influence of Pericles was removed, the conflict between classes raged without restraint, and the slaughter that befell the higher ranks in the Peloponnesian War gave an irresistible preponderance to the lower. The restless and inquiring spirit of the Athenians was prompt to unfold the reason of every institution and the consequences of every principle, and their Constitution ran its course from infancy to decrepitude with unexampled speed. . . .

Their history furnishes the classic example of the peril of Democracy under conditions singularly favorable. For the Athenians were not only brave and patriotic and capable of generous sacrifice, but they were the most religious of the Greeks. They venerated the Constitution which had given them prosperity and equality and freedom, and never questioned the fundamental laws which regulated the enormous power of the Assembly. They tolerated considerable variety of opinion and great license of speech; and their humanity towards their slaves roused the indignation even of the most intelligent partisan of aristocracy. Thus they became the only people of antiquity that grew great by democratic institutions. But the possession of unlimited power, which corrodes the conscience, hardens the heart, and confounds the understanding of monarchs, exercised its demoralizing influence on the illustrious democracy of Athens. It is bad to be oppressed by a minority, but it is worse to be oppressed by a majority. For there is a reserve of latent power in the masses which, if it is called into play, the minority can seldom resist. But from the absolute will of an entire people there is no appeal, no redemption, no refuge but treason. The humblest and most numerous class of the Athenians united the legislative, the judicial, and, in part, the executive power. The philosophy that was then in the ascendant taught them that there is no law superior to that of the State—the lawgiver is above the law.

It followed that the sovereign people had a right to do whatever was within its power, and was bound by no rule of right or wrong but its own judgment of expediency. On a memorable occasion the assembled Athenians declared it monstrous that they should be prevented from doing whatever they chose. No force that existed could restrain them; and they resolved that no duty should restrain them, and that they would be bound by no laws that were not of their own making. In this way the emancipated people of Athens became a tyrant, and their Government, the pioneer of European freedom, stands condemned with a terrible unanimity by all the wisest of the ancients. They ruined their city by attempting to conduct war by debate in the marketplace. Like the French Republic, they put their unsuccessful commanders to death. They treated their dependencies with such injustice that they lost their maritime empire. They plundered the rich until the rich conspired with the public enemy, and they crowned their guilt by the martyrdom of Socrates.

When the absolute sway of numbers had endured for nearly a quarter of a century, nothing but bare existence was left for the State to lose, and the Athenians, wearied and despondent, confessed the true cause of their ruin. They understood that for liberty, justice, and equal laws, it is as necessary that Democracy should restrain itself as it had been that it should restrain the oligarchy. . . . The repentance of the Athenians came too late to save the Republic. But the lesson of their experience endures for all times, for it teaches that government by the whole people, being the government of the most numerous and most powerful class, is an evil of the same nature as unmixed monarchy and requires, for nearly the same reasons, institutions that shall protect it against itself and shall uphold the permanent reign of law against arbitrary revolutions of opinion. . . .

The ancients understood the regulation of power better than the regulation of liberty. They concentrated so many prerogatives in the State as to leave no footing from which a man could deny its jurisdiction or assign bounds to its activity. If I may employ an expressive anachronism, the vice of the classic state was that it was both Church and

State in one. Morality was undistinguished from religion and politics from morals; and in religion, morality, and politics there was only one legislator and one authority. The State, while it did deplorably little for education, for practical science, for the indigent and helpless, or for the spiritual needs of man, nevertheless claimed the use of all his faculties and the determination of all his duties. Individuals and families, associations and dependencies were so much material that the sovereign power consumed for its own purposes. What the slave was in the hands of his master, the citizen was in the hands of the community. The most sacred obligations vanished before the public advantage. The passengers existed for the sake of the ship. By their disregard for private interests and for the moral welfare and improvement of the people, both Greece and Rome destroyed the vital elements on which the prosperity of nations rests, and perished by the decay of families and the depopulation of the country. They survive not in their institutions but in their ideas, and by their

ideas, especially on the art of government, they are—

The dead, but sceptred sovereigns who still rule
Our spirits from their urns.

To them, indeed, may be tracked nearly all the errors that are undermining political society—Communism, Utilitarianism, the confusion between tyranny and political authority, and between lawlessness and freedom. . . . All that Socrates could effect by way of protest against the tyranny of the reformed democracy was to die for his convictions. . . . But when Christ said: "Render unto Caesar the things that are Caesar's, and unto God the things that are God's," those words . . . gave to the civil power, under the protection of conscience, a sacredness it had never enjoyed and bounds it had never acknowledged; and they were the repudiation of absolutism and the inauguration of freedom.

A.H.M. JONES

ATHENIAN DEMOCRACY: CRITICS AND REALITIES

Too often historians have, like Lord Acton, inferred a theory about ancient democracy and then damned the Athenians for adhering to such an absurd idea. However, a historian should be an investigator and not a judge—the nature of the past is complex and not always clear, and nothing is gained by rhetorical attacks on imagined evils. For those who wish to understand democracy at Athens, a safer guide than Acton or Grote is A. H. M. Jones of the University of Cambridge, who is a recognized authority on Greece and Rome. Widely respected for his books and articles, Professor Jones has recently written a monumental study of the later Roman Empire. Though sympathetic to Athenian democracy, he is not a partisan apologist, as Grote sometimes was. With learning and common sense, Jones contrasts the bitter attacks of ancient critics on Athens and the actual operation of democracy in the city.

All the Athenian political philosophers and publicists whose works we possess were in various degrees oligarchic in sympathy. The author of the pamphlet on the "Constitution of the Athenians" preserved among Xenophon's works is bitterly

hostile to democracy. Socrates, so far as we can trace his views from the works of Xenophon and Plato, was at least highly critical of democracy. Plato's views on the subject are too well known to need stating. Isocrates in his earlier years wrote pane-

From A. H. M. Jones, *Athenian Democracy* (Oxford, 1957), pp. 41–42, 44–46, 48, 50, 55, 61–62. Reprinted by permission of Basil Blackwell Ltd.

gyrics of Athens, but in his old age, when he wrote his more philosophical works, became increasingly embittered against the political regime of his native city. Aristotle is the most judicial in his attitude and states the pros and cons, but his ideal was a widely based oligarchy. With the historians of Athens, the same bias is evident. Only Herodotus is a democrat, but his views have not carried much weight, partly because of his reputation for naïveté, and partly because his explicit evidence refers to a period before the full democracy had evolved. Thucydides is hostile: in one of the very few passages in which he reveals his personal views, he expresses approval of a regime which disfranchised about two-thirds of the citizens, those who manned the fleet on which the survival of Athens depended. Xenophon was an ardent admirer of the Spartan regime. Aristotle, in the historical part of his monograph on the Constitution of Athens, followed —rather uncritically—a source with a marked oligarchic bias. Only the fourth-century orators were democrats; and their speeches, being concerned with practical political issues—mostly of foreign policy —or with private litigation, have little to say on the basic principles of democracy, which they take for granted.

The surviving literature is certainly not representative of Athenian public opinion. The majority of Athenians were proud of their constitution and deeply attached to it. The few counter-revolutions —in 411, 404, 322, and 317—were carried out by small extremist cliques, in 411 after a carefully planned campaign of deception and terror, in the other three cases with the aid of a foreign conqueror, and all were short-lived, being rapidly overwhelmed by the mass of the citizens. Nor was it only the poor majority, who most obviously benefited from the system, that were its supporters. Most of the great statesmen and generals of Athens came from wealthy families, and a substantial number from the nobility of birth; the leaders of the popular risings which unseated the oligarchic governments of 411 and 403 were men of substance. . . .

Freedom of action and of speech were the proudest slogans of Athens, and not only political but personal freedom; as Pericles says in the Funeral Speech, "we live as free citizens both in our public life and in our attitude to one another in the affairs of daily life; we are not angry with our neighbor if he behaves as he pleases, we do not cast sour looks at him which, if they can do no harm, cause pain."

Freedom of speech was particularly prized. As Demosthenes says, "in Sparta you are not allowed to praise the laws of Athens or of this state or that, far from it, you have to praise what agrees with their constitution," whereas in Athens criticism of the democracy was freely permitted. One only has to read the works of Isocrates, Plato, and Aristotle to see that this is true. The condemnation of Socrates is an apparent exception to the rule, but as Xenophon's account of the matter shows, the real [heart] of the charge against Socrates was that, of his pupils, Alcibiades had done more than any other one man to ruin Athens in the recent war, and Critias had been the ruthless ringleader of the Thirty who had massacred thousands of Athenians a few years before. . . .

Democrats in general approved of the egalitarian principle. Demosthenes in one passage argues that what makes all citizens public spirited and generous is "that in a democracy each man considers that he himself has a share in equality and justice," and in another praises a law forbidding legislation directed against individuals as being good democratic doctrine, "for as everyone has an equal share in the rest of the constitution, so everyone is entitled to an equal share in the laws." The Athenians were not, however, either in theory or in practice, absolute egalitarians, but drew a distinction between different political functions. On one point they admitted no compromise —equality before the law; as Pericles says, "in their private disputes all share equality according to the laws." This to us elementary principle needed emphasis, for Plato's friends in the Thirty, when they drew up a new constitution, ordained that only the 3,000 full citizens were entitled to a legal trial and that all others might be summarily executed by order of the government. It was secured in the Athenian constitution not only by the right of every citizen to seek redress in the courts, but by the character of the courts which consisted of large juries drawn by lot from the whole body of the citizens.

The Athenians also attached great importance to the equality of all citizens in formulating and deciding public policy. This was secured by the right of every citizen to speak and vote in the Assembly, and by the composition of the Council of Five Hundred which prepared the agenda of the Assembly; this body was annually chosen by lot from all the [wards] of Attica. Here democratic principle came into conflict with the oligarchic view, developed at length by Plato, that government was an art, demanding the highest skill, and should therefore be entrusted to a select few. . . . [However], it was not "the rulers of the city" who were chosen by lot, but officials charged with limited routine duties for which little more than "a sense of decency and fair play" was required. Furthermore, it must be remembered that a magistrate had to pass a preliminary examination which was, it is true, usually formal but gave his enemies an opportunity for raking up his past; was liable to be deposed by a vote of the Assembly taken ten times a year; and after his year was subject to a scrutiny in which his accounts were audited and any citizen could charge him with inefficiency or abuse of authority. It is unlikely that many rogues or nincompoops would expose themselves to these risks. . . .

Plato also objects to state pay: "I am told," he says, "that Pericles made the Athenians idle and lazy and garrulous and avaricious by first putting them on state pay." This is an oft-repeated accusation but has very little substance. In a population which never sank below 20,000 adult males and probably reached twice that figure at its peak, the Council and the magistracies did not provide employment except on rare occasions; a man might not hold any magistracy more than once or sit on the Council more than twice in his life. Assemblies were held only on forty days in the year. It was only as a juror that a citizen could obtain more or less continuous employment, and here the rate of remuneration was so low—half a laborer's wage in the fifth century and a third in the late fourth, in fact little more than bare subsistence—that in the fifth century, if the picture drawn in Aristophanes' *Wasps* is true, it attracted only the elderly, past hard work, and in the early fourth century, when economic conditions were worse, according to Isocrates, the unemployed. . . .

It is more difficult to answer the question whether the Athenian democracy did or did not in fact exploit the rich for the benefit of the poor. In the distribution of political power and influence, the rich seem to have fared well. In the minor offices and on the Council and in the juries the poor no doubt predominated, though even here it would seem that by the fourth century the well-to-do were by no means crowded out. To the important mili-

tary, diplomatic, and financial offices men of birth and wealth were generally elected. The orators who, normally holding no office, guided policy by their speeches in the Assembly were also mostly well-to-do, and many of them of good family. It was comparatively rarely that a self-made man . . . achieved political influence. A rich man or an aristocrat certainly did not find that his political career was prejudiced by his wealth or birth, while poor and humbly born politicians had to face a good deal of abuse from comedians and orators. . . .

The philosophers held that the state ought to mould and train the citizens in virtue, and assumed that the average man was naturally evil or at least foolish. Political power must therefore be given to a select group of wise good men, who would impose a good way of life on the rest by a rigid system of education and control. The Athenian democrats, on the other hand, took an optimistic view of human nature and believed that every citizen should be allowed to live his own life in his own way within the broad limits laid down by the law, and that all citizens could be trusted to take their part in the government of the city, whether by voting and speaking in the Assembly, judging in the juries, carrying on the routine administration as magistrates, or selecting the men to hold high political office. On one point the Athenians were distrustful of human nature, on its ability to resist the temptations of irresponsible power; hence their insistence on brief terms of office, regular review of the conduct of magistrates in office, and above all a searching scrutiny of the record of magistrates on completing their term. The philosophers are strangely blind to this danger and are content to rely on the virtue of their usually hereditary or co-optative oligarchies of wise men.

The ideals of the Athenian democracy are perhaps best summed up in a rather florid passage of the Funeral Oration attributed to Lysias. Our ancestors, he says, "were the first and only men of that time who cast out arbitrary power and established democracy, holding that the freedom of all was the greatest concord, and sharing with one another their hopes and perils they governed themselves with free hearts, honoring the good and chastising the bad by law. They held it bestial to constrain one another by force, and the part of men to define justice by law and to persuade by reason and serve both by action, having law as their king and reason as their teacher."

3

ALEXANDER THE GREAT
AND THE UNITY OF MANKIND

Whatever their virtues, the Greek city-states were hopelessly parochial in outlook. A fanatic obsession with autonomy at the municipal level isolated the cities from their neighbors and aborted attempts at federalism. Inherently divided, the Greeks were easily subdued by Philip II of Macedon. Like it or not, the cities were dragooned into his Hellenic League which subordinated local rivalries to a common aim (i.e. the supremacy of Macedon). In the name of the Hellenic League, Philip's son Alexander III conquered the Persian Empire, and the Greek cities suddenly became part of a vast international society. "Who could imagine fifty years ago the amazing world of today?" asked one awed philosopher. Politically, the Greek cities were either subjects or satellites of the national states which were established by Alexander's successors: the Ptolemies in Egypt, the Antigonids in Macedon, the Seleucids in Syria and Iraq, and later the Attalids in Asia Minor. The number of Greek cities expanded as settlements were founded throughout the Near East, and Alexandria in Egypt was the largest, most prosperous, and impressive city in the Hellenistic world. Culturally, Hellas extended from Marseilles to the Punjab, and a merchant or tourist from Sicily could feel somewhat at home visiting the Greek rajahs of the Indus valley. Hellenistic culture tended to overwhelm local art and literature, for intellectuals and social-climbers eagerly embraced Greek ways much as modern Asians and Africans adopt Western culture. A notable exception was the Maccabean movement in Palestine, but the Jews of the Diaspora (and indeed many Palestinian Jews) were highly Hellenized. The famous Septuagint translation of the Old Testament into Greek was a symptom of the overriding Hellenism of the age. Though the cities were no longer independent states, the mental horizons of their inhabitants were broadened—the Greek view of the world gained perspective, and many Greeks became cosmopolitan. However, the new attitude was not altruistic and humanitarian, for an awareness of others does not necessarily lead to love. Many of the Macedonian kings saw their non-Greek subjects, much as Kipling viewed the Indians, as useful taxpayers and servants but certainly not the equals of the Pukka Sahibs. Nevertheless, many Greek soldiers and businessmen married native women and produced a new breed of "Greeks," who were joined by the Hellenized intelligentsia and the citizens of Antioch and other new cities. Hellenistic art reflected the greater realism of the new age, and Hellenistic thought expressed a cosmopolitanism foreign to Pericles and Plato.

This broad new world with its sophistication and problems was created by Alexander, who had conquered it in a triumphal sweep through the Persian Empire. Born in 356 B.C., Alexander was the able son of an ambitious father, and he inherited Philip's plan to seize the Near East from the Persians. With Philip's hardy veterans and expert staff officers, Alexander carried out his father's aims and defeated the

Persian monarch Darius III by 331 B.C. Instead of merely holding the Near East, the young conqueror resolved to outdo his father and assumed the Persian throne. As King of Kings, Alexander openly sought the cooperation of the nobles of Persia. A compulsive adventurer, he also needed to outdo his Persian predecessors and embarked on the conquest of India. However, his exhausted troops refused to advance beyond the Punjab, and Alexander was forced to return to Mesopotamia. Frustrated by his failure in India and quarreling with his generals, Alexander succumbed to drink or poison and died in 323 B.C. Relations between the king and the Macedonians had been strained by his high-handed manner and his pro-Persian policies. The veterans did not appreciate it when Alexander adopted Persian dress and wanted courtiers to prostrate themselves before him. His claim to be the son of a god, Zeus-Ammon, probably offended the Zarathustrian Persians more than the polytheistic Macedonians and Greeks, but most men took it as the whim of an arrogant prince. However, Alexander's successors followed his precedent and utilized the concept of a god-king to bolster their military monarchies.

How great was Alexander? Unquestionably, he was a first-rate soldier, though much of his success was due to the superb military machine which Philip had forged, and the headstrong Alexander took unnecessary risks in battle. As King of Kings, he had sense enough to realize that he could not run his empire without the cooperation of the Persian aristocracy, and he astutely won their support by adopting Persian clothes and court protocol. The areas he conquered were immense, but so were the lands subdued by Genghis Khan, and the Mongols cleverly supported the religions of subject peoples. There have been few stupid successful conquerors in world history, but greatness is, or should be, a hallowed word. Caesar was a greater man than Alexander, and Socrates was greater than both of them. Not really a Greek, the Macedonian king imposed unity on the Near East in the name of Hellenism. Two other outsiders, the Corsican Bonaparte and the Austrian Hitler, imposed unity on Europe in the name of a supposedly superior culture, respectively that of France and Germany. The unity effected by all three conquerors was a fragile creation based on war and despotism, and the three empires shattered within a few years of their inceptions. Dante was not impressed by similar despots: "What mean their trumpets and their bells, their horns and their flutes, but 'Come, hangman—come, vultures!'?" In this sense, Alexander must be ranked among the spoilers of the earth. True, he was a man of ability and not a wholly destructive barbarian, but Alexander was not worthy of the title Great.

The personality of Alexander is well documented. The Macedonians were notorious as heavy drinkers. Even Philip was often drunk, and Alexander was a chip off the old block. The tradition favorable to Alexander concedes that he was overly fond of wine, and the hostile tradition depicts him as an alcoholic despot. In his cups, the king murdered a veteran officer, Cleitus, who had once saved his life in battle. Alexander's other crimes rarely were outbursts of drunken fury but were usually calculated political acts. In one purge, he killed the cavalry commander Philotas on a charge of treason and ordered the execution of Philotas's father Parmenion on general principles. Some of Alexander's victims were guilty of conspiring against the king, but others were struck down in far-reaching purges. Aristotle's tactless nephew Callisthenes was slain for criticizing the monarch. On occasion, the erratic Alexander released his anger by massacring luckless natives. One tradition attributes his death to poison administered by agents of the viceroy of Macedon, Philip's old friend Antipater, who was a bitter foe of Alexander's mother Olympias. A strong-willed emotional woman, she had poisoned her son with a more subtle venom years before. Jealous of Philip's infidelities, she engulfed Alexander in excessive maternal love and encouraged his boyish resentment of Philip's many accomplishments. Alexander's obsession to outdo Philip was the result of his mother's constant prompting. She also told her devoted son that the hated Philip was not really his father, but rather that he had been sired by a deity—thus, in later life Alexander insisted on being worshiped as the son of Zeus-Ammon. Antipater and the older officers were hardly pleased when Alexander claimed that Philip had been cuckolded by a god. Fearing that Philip might hand the throne to another son, Olympias had engineered the assassination of her husband, or so Antipater believed. As King of Kings, Alexander did not let his mother meddle in matters of high policy, but he also rebuffed Antipater's complaints of her constant intrigues. Even Alexander's admirer Tarn admits that "it is doubtful if he ever cared for any woman except his terrible mother." In essence, Alexander was a spoiled mamma's boy with a violent temper, paranoid traits, and a dependence on alcohol. On the other hand, he was, like Philip, politically astute and an able manipulator of men.

The meteoric career of Alexander had qualities of epic romance, and the Macedonian conqueror has been the subject of many legends. Alexander's image dazzled even Caesar in his sillier moments, and Napoleon struck an Alexandrine pose, strutting before the pyramids and boasting of a march on India. In the Middle Ages, both Christians and Muslims idolized the invincible Alexander as a hero of chivalry. Chaucer summarized the eternal image of Alexander:

The pryde of man and beste he layde adoun,
Wher-so he cam, unto the worldes ende.

In his own lifetime, Alexander aided the legendmongers by hiring Callisthenes as a public relations man. Callisthenes supplied Greek audiences with exaggerated tales of Alexander's prowess and divinity, but the publicist perished when the royal egomaniac began to believe the lies. In the twentieth century, Alexander has become the hero of a new myth. Sir William Tarn hailed him as an inspired prophet of world unity and the brotherhood of man:

There is certainly a line of descent from his prayer at Opis, through the Stoics and one portion of the Christian ideal, to that brotherhood of all men which was proclaimed, though only proclaimed, in the French Revolution. The torch Alexander lit for long only smouldered; perhaps it still only smoulders today, but it never has been, and never can be, quite put out.[1]

[1] Sir W. W. Tarn in *The Cambridge Ancient History* (Cambridge: Cambridge University Press, 1927), Vol. VI, p. 437.

Tarn's messianic Alexander has been widely accepted by modern readers who respond to the attractiveness of unity and brotherhood without inquiring into the validity of the notion that Alexander too believed in these commendable ideals. Once established, a myth is hard to shake (however easy it may be to refute), for a successful myth answers a deep need in its believers. Amid endless wars and mounting anxieties, we fear that life is a running sore and history a chamber of horrors. How comforting it would be if there had once been a brave young king who wanted to save mankind from its baser instincts and promote a reign of peace and justice; and if he had not been cut down in his prime, dead at the age of thirty-two, the messiah would have established the kingdom of God on earth. If only it were true. . . .

JUSTIN

ALEXANDER THE DESPOT

Like many American students, Roman readers were fond of oversimplified digests of complex subjects, such as science or history. A prime specimen of this instant education was the work of Justin, who composed a handy outline of history in the third or fourth century A.D. No scholar himself, Justin simply boiled down an earlier digest by Trogus Pompeius who had made a sketch of Greek history for hurried readers in the time of Augustus. At least Trogus consulted the major Greek historians, but filtered through Trogus and Justin we see them "through a glass darkly." One of the main traditions hostile to Alexander stemmed from the writings of the Peripatetic school, which took a dim view of the king who had executed Aristotle's nephew Callisthenes. Whatever his ultimate source (via Trogus), Justin depicts Alexander as a cruel, cunning despot.

Alexander assumed the attire of the Persian monarchs as well as the diadem, which was unknown to the kings of Macedonia, as if he gave himself up to the customs of those whom he had conquered. And lest such innovations should be viewed with dislike if adopted by himself alone, he desired his friends also to wear the long robe of gold and purple. That he might imitate the luxury too as well as the dress of the Persians, he spent his nights among troops of the king's concubines of eminent beauty and birth. To these extravagances he added vast magnificence in feasting; and lest his entertainments should seem jejune and parsimonious, he accompanied his banquets, according to the osten-

tation of the eastern monarchs, with games, being utterly unmindful that power is accustomed to be lost, not gained, by such practices.

During the course of these proceedings, there arose throughout the camp a general indignation that he had so degenerated from his father Philip as to abjure the very name of his country and to adopt the manners of the Persians whom . . . he had overcome. But that he might not appear to be the only person who yielded to the vices of those whom he had conquered in the field, he permitted his soldiers also, if they had formed a connection with any of the female captives, to marry them, thinking that

From Justin, XII, 3–7, 10–12, tr. John S. Watson, in *Justin, Cornelius Nepos, and Eutropius*, a volume in Bohn's Libraries (London, (1910), pp. 108–12, 115–17. Reprinted by permission of the publisher, G. Bell & Sons, Ltd.

they would feel less desire to return to their country when they had some appearance of a house and home in the camp and that the fatigues of war would be relieved by the agreeable society of their wives. He saw too that Macedonia would be less drained to supply the army if the sons as recruits should succeed their veteran fathers and serve within the ramparts within which they were born, and would be likely to show more courage if they passed not only their earliest days of service but also their infancy in the camp. This custom was also continued under Alexander's successors. Maintenance was provided for the boys, and arms and horses were given them when they grew up; and rewards were assigned to the fathers in proportion to the number of their children. If the fathers of any of them were killed, the orphans notwithstanding received their father's pay, and their childhood was a sort of military service in various expeditions. Inured from their earliest years to toils and dangers, they formed an invincible army; they looked upon their camp as their country and upon a battle as a prelude to victory.

Alexander, meanwhile, began to show a passionate temper towards those about him, not with a princely severity but with the vindictiveness of an enemy. What most incensed him was, that reflections were cast upon him in the common talk of the soldiers for having cast off the customs of his father Philip and of his country. For this offence, Parmenion, an old man next to the king in rank, and his son Philotas were put to death, an examination by torture having been previously held on both of them. At this instance of cruelty, all the soldiers throughout the camp began to express their displeasure, being concerned for the fate of the innocent old general and his son and saying at times that "they must expect nothing better for themselves." These murmurs coming to the knowledge of Alexander, he, fearing that such reports would be carried to Macedonia and that the glory of his victories would be sullied by the stain of cruelty, pretended that he was going to send home some of his friends to give an account of his successes. He exhorted his soldiers to write to their relatives as they would now have fewer opportunities on account of the scene of warfare being further from home. The packets of letters, as they were given in, he commanded to be privately brought to him, and having learned from them what everyone thought of him, he put all those, who had given unfavorable opinions of his conduct, into one regiment with an intention either to destroy them or to distribute them in colonies in the most distant parts of the earth. . . .

He invited his friends on some particular day to a banquet where mention being made, when they were intoxicated, of the great things achieved by Philip, he began to prefer himself to his father and to extol the vastness of his own exploits to the skies, the greater part of the company agreeing with him; and when Clitus, one of the older guests, trusting to his hold on the king's friendship in which he held the principal place, defended the memory of Philip and praised his acts, he so provoked Alexander that he snatched a weapon from one of the guards and slew him with it in the midst of the guests. Exulting at the murder, too, he scoffed at the dead man for his defence of Philip and his commendation of his mode of warfare. But when his mind, satiated with the bloodshed, grew calm and reflection took the place of passion, he began . . . to feel the deepest sorrow for the deed, grieving that he had listened to his father's praises with more anger than he ought to have listened to insults on his memory, and that an old and blameless friend had been slain by him at a feast and carousal. Driven therefore to repentance with the same vehemence with which he had before been impelled to resentment, he determined to die. Bursting into tears, he embraced the dead man, laid his hand on his wounds, and confessed his madness to him as if he could hear; then, snatching up a weapon, he pointed it against his breast and would have committed suicide, had not his friends interposed. His resolution to die continued even for several days after. . . . He reflected . . . what remarks and odium he must have occasioned as well in his own army as among the conquered nations; what fear and dislike of himself among his other friends; and how dismal and sad he had rendered his entertainment, appearing not less to be dreaded at a feast than when armed in the field of battle. Parmenion and Philotas, his cousin Amyntas, his murdered stepmother and brothers, with Attalus, Eurylochus, Pausanias, and other slaughtered nobles of Macedonia presented themselves to his imagination. He in consequence persisted in abstaining from food for four days until he was drawn from his purpose by the prayers of the whole army, who conjured him 'not to lament the death of one so far as to ruin them all, since, after bringing them into the remotest part of the barbarians' country, he would leave them amidst hostile nations exasperated by war." The entreaties of Callisthenes the philosopher had great effect upon him, a man who was intimate with him from having been his fellow-student under Arístotle and who had been subsequently sent for, by the king himself, to record his acts for the perusal of posterity.

Soon after, he gave orders that he should not be approached with mere salutation but with adoration, a point of Persian pride to which he had hesitated to advance at first, lest the assumption of everything at once should excite too strong a feeling against him. Among those who refused to obey, the most resolute was Callisthenes, but his opposition proved fatal both to himself and to several other eminent Macedonians, who were all put to death on the pretence that they were engaged in a conspiracy. The custom of saluting their king was however retained by the Macedonians, adoration being set aside. . . .

He married Statira, the daugher of King Darius [at Susa], but at the same time he gave the noblest virgins, chosen from all the conquered natives, as wives to the chiefs of the Macedonians, in order that the impropriety of the king's conduct might be rendered less glaring by the practice becoming general. He next assembled the army [at Opis] and promised that "he would pay all their debts at his own expense," so that they might carry home their spoil and prizes undiminished. . . . Discharging some of the veterans, he recruited the army with younger soldiers. But those that were retained, murmuring at the discharge of the older men, demanded that they themselves should be released likewise, desiring that "their years, not of life, but of service should be counted." . . . Nor did they address the king only with entreaties but also with reproaches, bidding him "carry on his wars alone with the aid of

his father Ammon, since he looked with disdain on his soldiers." Alexander, on the other hand, sometimes upbraided his men and sometimes charged them in gentle terms "not to tarnish their glorious services by mutiny." At last, when he could produce no effect by words, he leaped unarmed from his tribunal among the armed multitude to lay hands on the authors of the mutiny, and not a man daring to oppose him, he led thirteen of them . . . to punishment. Such submission to death did the fear of their king produce in the men. . . . He then addressed himself in a public speech to the auxiliary troops of the Persians apart from the Macedonians. He extolled their constant fidelity, as well as to himself as to their former kings; he mentioned the kindnesses which he had shown them, saying that "he had never treated them as a conquered people, but always as sharers in his successes; that he had gone over to the usages of their nation, not they to those of his; and that he had mingled the conquerors with the conquered by matrimonial connections. And now," he added, "he would entrust the guardianship of his person, not to the Macedonians only, but also to them." Accordingly, he enrolled a thousand of their young men among his bodyguard and at the same time incorporated into his army a portion of the auxiliaries trained after the discipline of the Macedonians. At this proceeding the Macedonians were much dissatisfied, exclaiming that "their enemies were put into their places by their king," and at length they all went to Alexander in a body, beseeching him with tears "to content himself rather with punishing than ill-treating them." By this modest forbearance they produced such an effect upon him that he released eleven thousand veterans more.

ARRIAN, ERATOSTHENES, PLUTARCH

ALEXANDER THE UNIFIER

The three following passages—a straightforward historical account, an inference of principle, and an exaggerated burst of rhetoric—have been used to justify the image of Alexander the unifier. The best extant life of Alexander was written in the second century A.D. by Arrian, who used the memoirs of the engineer Aristobulus and King Ptolemy I of Egypt. Eratosthenes was a famous polymath, literary critic, and scientist of the third century B.C. He served as Director of the great Alexandrian Library and is best known for his remarkably accurate estimate of the size of the earth. Plutarch was a Greek moralist and essayist of the late first and early second century A.D. His essay on the "Fortune of Alexander" was a youthful exercise in rhetoric and not a balanced historical estimate of the effect of Alexander on the East. In later life, Plutarch wrote a biography of Alexander which shows the king in a less favorable light.

1. ARRIAN

[Arrian has just described the suppression of the mutiny at Opis and Alexander's demonstration of favor toward the Persian soldiery. The Macedonians were shocked by the new policy.] When the news was reported to them about the Persians and Medes, . . . they were no longer able to restrain themselves, but running in a body to the palace, they cast their weapons there in front of the gates as signs of supplication to the king. . . . At length one of them, Callines by name, a man conspicuous both for his age and because he was a captain of the Companion cavalry, spoke as follows: "O king, what grieves the Macedonians is that you have already made some of the Persians kinsmen to yourself, and that Persians are called Alexander's kinsmen and have the honor of saluting you with a kiss, whereas none of the Macedonians has as yet enjoyed this honor." Then Alexander interrupting him, said: "But all of you without exception I consider my kinsmen, and so from this time I shall call you." When he had said this, Callines advanced and saluted him with a kiss, and so did all those who wished to salute him. Then they took up their weapons and returned to the camp, shouting and singing a song of thanksgiving. After this Alexander offered sacrifice to the gods to whom it was his custom to sacrifice, and gave a public banquet over which he himself presided, with the Macedonians sitting around him and next to them the Persians, after whom came the men of the other nations, preferred in honor for their personal rank or for some meritorious action. The king and his guests drew wine from the same bowl and poured out the same libations, both the Grecian prophets and the Magians commencing the ceremony. He prayed for other blessings and especially that harmony and community of rule might exist between the Macedonians and Persians. The common account is, that those who took part in this banquet were 9,000 in number, that all of them poured out one libation, and after it sang a song of thanksgiving. Then those of the Macedonians who were unfit for service on account of age or any other misfortune went back [to Macedon] of their own accord, to the number of about 10,000.

2. ERATOSTHENES

[The geographer Strabo makes a parenthetical remark on Eratosthenes' view of Alexander]: Towards the end of his treatise—after withholding praise from those who divide the whole multitude of mankind into two groups, namely Greeks and barbarians, and also from those who advised Alexander to treat the Greeks as friends but the barbarians as enemies—Eratosthenes goes on to say that it would be better to make such divisions according to good qualities and bad qualities, for not only are many of the Greeks bad, but many of the barbarians are refined—Indians and [Iranians] for example, and further, Romans and Carthaginians who carry on their governments so admirably. And this, he says, is the reason why Alexander, disregarding his advisers, welcomed as many as he could of the men of fair repute and did them favors.

3. PLUTARCH

[Plutarch is arguing that Alexander was really a philosopher in action]: Compare Alexander's pupils

From Arrian, "Anabasis of Alexander," VII, 11–12, tr. Edward J. Chinnock, in *The Greek Historians*, edited by Francis R. B. Godolphin, Vol. II, pp. 601–2. Copyright 1942 by Random House, Inc. Reprinted by permission.

From Strabo, I 4.9. Reprinted by permission of the publishers and the Loeb Classical Library from Horace L. Jones, *The Geography of Strabo* (Cambridge, Mass.: Harvard University Press, 1960; London: William Heinemann Ltd.), pp. 247–49.

From Plutarch, "The Fortune of Alexander," 328B–329D, 330A, C–E. Reprinted by permission of the publishers and the Loeb Classical Library from *Plutarch's Moralia*, tr. Frank C. Babbitt (Cambridge, Mass.: Harvard University Press, 1936; London: William Heinemann Ltd.), Vol. IV, pp. 393–99, 403, 405.

with those of Plato and Socrates. Plato and Socrates taught pupils of splendid natural endowment who spoke the same language, so that, even if the pupils understood nothing else, at least they understood the Greek tongue. And even so, Plato and Socrates did not win over many. But their pupils, such as Critias and Alcibiades . . . , were prone to spew the good word forth, as a horse the curbing bit, and turned them to other ways. But if you examine the results of Alexander's instruction, you will see that he educated the Hyrcanians to respect the marriage bond and taught the Arachosians to till the soil and persuaded the Sogdians to support their parents, not to kill them, and the Persians to revere their mothers and not to take them in wedlock. O wondrous power of Philosophic Instruction that brought the Indians to worship Greek gods and the Scythians to bury their dead, not to devour them! We admire Carneades' power which made Cleitomachus, formerly called Hasdrubal and a Carthaginian by birth, adopt Greek ways. We admire the character of Zeno which persuaded Diogenes the Babylonian to be a philosopher. But when Alexander was civilizing Asia, Homer was commonly read, and the children of the Persians [etc.] learned to chant the tragedies of Sophocles and Euripides. And although Socrates, when tried on the charge of introducing foreign deities, lost his cause to the informers who infested Athens, yet through Alexander, Bactria and the Caucasus learned to revere the gods of the Greeks. Plato wrote a book on the one ideal constitution, but because of its forbidding character he could not persuade anyone to adopt it, but Alexander established more than seventy cities among savage tribes and sowed all Asia with Grecian magistracies and thus overcame its uncivilized and brutish manner of living. Although few of us read Plato's Laws, yet hundreds of thousands have made use of Alexander's laws and continue to use them. Those who were vanquished by Alexander are happier than those who escaped his hand. . . . Alexander's new subjects would not have been civilized had they not been vanquished: Egypt would not have its Alexandria, nor Mesopotamia its Seleuceia, nor Sogdiana its Prophthasia, nor India its Bucephalia, nor the Caucasus a Greek city hard by; for by the founding of cities in these places, savagery was extinguished and the worse element, gaining familiarity with the better, changed under its influence. If then philosophers take the greatest pride in civilizing and rendering adaptable the intractable and untutored elements in human character, and if Alexander has been shown to have changed the savage natures of countless tribes, it is with good reason that he should be regarded as a very great philosopher.

Moreover, the much-admired Republic of Zeno, the founder of the Stoic sect, may be summed up in this one main principle: that all the inhabitants of this world of ours should not live differentiated by their respective rules of justice into separate cities and communities, but that we should consider all men to be of one community and one polity, and that we should have a common life and an order common to us all, even as a herd that feeds together and shares the pasturage of a common field. This Zeno wrote, giving shape to a dream or, as it were, shadowy picture of a well-ordered and philosophic commonwealth, but it was Alexander who gave effect to the idea. For Alexander did not follow Aristotle's advice to treat the Greeks as if he were their leader, and other peoples as if he were their master; to have regard for the Greeks as for friends and kindred, but to conduct himself toward other peoples as though they were plants or animals; for to do so would have been to cumber his leadership with numerous battles and banishments and festering seditions. But, as he believed that he came as a heaven-sent governor to all and as a mediator for the whole world, those whom he could not persuade to unite with him, he conquered by force of arms, and he brought together into one body all men everywhere, uniting and mixing in one great loving-cup, as it were, men's lives, their characters, their marriages, their very habits of life. He bade them all consider as their fatherland the whole inhabited earth, as their stronghold and protection his camp, as akin to them all good men, and as foreigners only the wicked. They should not distinguish between Grecian and foreigner by Grecian cloak and [shield] or scimitar and jacket, but the distinguishing mark of the Grecian should be seen in virtue and that of the foreigner in iniquity; clothing and food, marriage and manner of life they should regard as common to all, being blended into one by ties of blood and children. . . .

As sovereign of both nations and benevolent king, he strove to acquire the goodwill of the conquered by showing respect for their apparel, so that they might continue constant in loving the Macedonians as rulers and might not feel hate toward them as enemies. . . . Although paying due respect to his own national dress, he did not disdain that of his conquered subjects in establishing the beginnings of a vast empire. For he did not overrun Asia like a robber nor was he minded to tear and rend it, as if it were booty and plunder bestowed by unexpected good fortune. . . . Alexander desired to render all upon earth subject to one law of reason and one form of government and to reveal all men as one people, and to this purpose he made himself conform. But if the deity that sent down Alexander's soul into this world of ours had not recalled him quickly, one law would govern all mankind and they all would look toward one rule of justice as though toward a common source of light. But, as it is, that part of the world which has not looked upon Alexander has remained without sunlight.

WILLIAM W. TARN

ALEXANDER THE DREAMER

The late Sir William W. Tarn (1869-1957) was a scholar with vast learning and a vivid imagination. He was renowned for his study of *Alexander the Great* (1948), an excellent textbook *Hellenistic Civilization* (1927), and the chapters which he contributed to the monumental *Cambridge Ancient History*. More than any single individual, Tarn made the English-speaking world aware of the vitality and importance of the Hellenistic Age. His scholarly attainments are unquestioned, but he felt strongly about individuals in the past and his enthusiasm often overcame his common sense. Tarn's vision of Alexander as an apostle of "one world" and brotherly love was a noble dream which has influenced many writers and is still popular in some quarters. In 1933 Tarn delivered the Raleigh Lecture on History before the British Academy; his topic was "Alexander the Great and the Unity of Mankind."

What I am going to talk about is one of the great revolutions in human thought. Greeks of the classical period, speaking very roughly, divided mankind into two classes, Greeks and non-Greeks; the latter they called barbarians and usually regarded as inferior people, though occasionally some one, like Herodotus or Xenophon, might suggest that certain barbarians possessed qualities which deserved consideration, like the wisdom of the Egyptians or the courage of the Persians. But in the third century B.C. and later we meet with a body of opinion which may be called universalist; all mankind was one and all men were brothers, or anyhow ought to be. Who was the pioneer who brought about this tremendous revolution in some men's way of thinking? Most writers have had no doubt on that point; the man to whom the credit was due was Zeno, the founder of the Stoic philosophy. But there are several passages in Greek writers which, *if* they are to be believed, show that the first man actually to think of it was not Zeno but Alexander. This matter has never really been examined; some writers just pass it over, which means, I suppose, that they do not consider the passages in question historical; others have definitely said that it is merely a case of our secondary authorities attributing to Alexander ideas taken from Stoicism. I want to consider today whether the passages in question are or are not historical and worthy of credence; that is, whether Alexander was or was not the first to believe in, and to contemplate, the unity of mankind. This will entail among other things some examination of the concept which Greeks called Homonoia, a word which meant more than its Latin translation, Concord, means to us; it is more like Unity and Concord, a being of one mind together, or if we like the phrase, a union of hearts; ultimately it was to become almost a symbol of the world's

From William W. Tarn, "Alexander the Great and the Unity of Mankind," *Proceedings of the British Academy*, XIX (1933), pp. 123–27, 145–48.

longing for something better than constant war. For convenience of discussion, I shall keep the Greek term Homonoia. . . .

The Greek world, whatever its practice, never doubted that in theory unity in a city was very desirable, but though the word Homonoia was already in common use among Greeks, it chiefly meant absence of faction-fights, and this rather negative meaning lasted in the cities throughout the Hellenistic period, as can be seen in the numerous decrees in honor of the judicial commissions sent from one city to another, which are praised because they tried to compose internal discord. There was hardly a trace as yet of the more positive sense which Homonoia was to acquire later—a mental attitude which should make war or faction impossible because the parties were at one; and Isocrates extended the application of the word without changing its meaning. He took up a suggestion of the sophist Gorgias and proposed to treat the whole Greek world as one and the futile wars between city and city as faction fights—to apply Homonoia to the Greek race. For this purpose he utilized Plato's idea that the barbarian was a natural enemy, and decided that the way to unite Greeks was to attack Persia; "I come," he said, "to advocate two things: war against the barbarian, Homonoia between ourselves." But somebody had to do the uniting; and Isocrates bethought him of the Cynic Heracles, benefactor of the Greek race, and urged King Philip of Macedonia, a descendant of Heracles, to play the part. But if Philip was to be Heracles and bring about the Homonoia of the Greek world, the way was being prepared for two important ideas of a later time; the essential quality of the king must be that love of man . . . which had led Heracles to perform his labors, and the essential business of the king was to promote Homonoia; so far this only applied to Greeks, but if its meaning were to deepen, it would still be the king's business. The actual result of all this, the League of Corinth under Philip's presidency, was not quite what Isocrates had dreamt of.

This then was the background against which Alexander appeared. The business of a Macedonian king was to be a benefactor of Greeks to the extent of preventing inter-city warfare; he was to promote Homonoia among Greeks and utilize their enmity to barbarians as a bond of union; but barbarians themselves were still enemies and slaves by nature, a view which Aristotle emphasized when he advised his pupil to treat Greeks as free men but barbarians as slaves.

I now come to the things Alexander is supposed to have said or thought, and the gulf between them and the background I have sketched is so deep that one cannot blame those who have refused to believe that he ever said or thought anything of the sort. There are five passages which need consideration: one in Arrian; one from Eratosthenes, preserved by Strabo; and three from Plutarch, one of which, from its resemblance to the Strabo passage, has been supposed by one of the acutest critics of our time to be taken in substance from Eratosthenes, and as such I shall treat it. The passage in Arrian says that, after the mutiny of the Macedonians at Opis and their reconciliation to Alexander, he gave a banquet to Macedonians and Persians, at which he prayed for Homonoia and partnership in rule between these two peoples. What Eratosthenes says amounts to this. Aristotle told Alexander to treat Greeks as friends but barbarians like animals; but Alexander knew better and preferred to divide men into good and bad without regard to their race. . . . For Alexander believed that he had a mission from the deity to harmonize men generally and be the reconciler of the world, mixing men's lives and customs as in a loving cup, and treating the good as his kin, the bad as strangers; for he thought that the good man was the real Greek and the bad man the real barbarian. Of the two Plutarch passages, the first says that his intention was to bring about, as between mankind generally, Homonoia and peace and fellowship and make them all one people; and the other, which for the moment I will quote without its context, makes him say that God is the common father of all men.[1]

It is obvious that, wherever all this comes from, we are dealing with a great revolution in thought. It amounts to this, that there is a natural brotherhood of all men, though bad men do not share in it; that Homonoia is no longer to be confined to the relations between Greek and Greek, but is to unite Greek and barbarian; and that Alexander's aim was to substitute peace for war and reconcile the enmities of mankind by bringing them all—all that is whom his arm could reach, the peoples of his empire—to be of one mind together: as men were one in blood, so

[1] Plutarch, *Alexander* 27: "He said that God was a common father of us all, but especially of the best of us." The context is the episode at Siwah when the oracle hailed Alexander as the son of the god Zeus-Ammon. [Editor's note.]

they should become one in heart and spirit. That such a revolution in thought did happen is unquestioned; the question is, was Alexander really its author, or are the thoughts attributed to him those of Zeno or somebody else? . . . Plutarch says that behind Zeno's dream lay Alexander's reality, and no one doubts that Alexander was Zeno's inspiration, but the question is, in what form? Most writers have taken Plutarch to mean Alexander's empire, but to me this explains nothing at all. . . . It does seem to me that what Plutarch really means is not Alexander's empire but Alexander's ideas; after all, the frequent references in antiquity to Alexander as a philosopher, one at least of which is contemporary, must mean *something.* Zeno's inspiration, then, was Alexander's idea of the unity of mankind, and what Zeno himself did was to carry this idea to one of its two logical conclusions. Judging by his prayer at Opis for the Homonoia of Macedonians and Persians, Alexander, had he lived, would have worked through national groups, as was inevitable in an empire like his, which comprised many different states and subject peoples. . . . But Zeno abolished all distinctions of race, all the apparatus of national groups and particular states, and made his world-state a theoretic whole. . . . Alexander's way, or what I think was his way, led to the Roman empire being called one people. . . .

Only one conclusion from all this seems possible: the things which, in the tradition, Alexander is supposed to have thought and said are, in substance, true. He did say that all men were sons of God, that is brothers, but that God made the best ones peculiarly his own; he did aspire to be the harmonizer and reconciler of the world—that part of the world which his arm reached; he did have the intention of uniting the peoples of his empire in fellowship and concord and making them of one mind together; and when, as a beginning, he prayed at Opis for partnership in rule and Homonoia between Macedonians and Persians, he meant what he said—not partnership in rule only, but true unity between them. I am only talking of theory, not of actions; but what this means is that he was the pioneer of one of the supreme revolutions in the world's outlook, the first man known to us who contemplated the brotherhood of man or the unity of mankind, whichever phrase we like to use. I do not claim to have given you exact proof of this; it is one of those difficult borderlands of history where one does not get proofs which could be put to a jury. But there is a very strong presumption indeed that it is true. Alexander, for the things he *did,* was called the Great; but if what I have said today be right, I do not think we shall doubt that this idea of his—call it a purpose, call it a dream, call it what you will—was the greatest thing about him.

ARNOLD J. TOYNBEE

THE ARCHANGEL ALEXANDER

Probably the most famous historian in the modern world is Arnold J. Toynbee of the Royal Institute of International Affairs. Though a classical scholar of considerable stature, he is most renowned for his twelve-volume *A Study of History* (1934–1962) which in one form or another, usually in digest, has reached a wide audience. Essentially, Toynbee claims to understand the mechanics of the rise and fall of civilizations and he insists that the real function of a major society is the production of a "higher religion." Personally he is a man of charm, sincerity, and inherent goodness. At heart a poet and at times a mystic, Toynbee writes in a florid style which reflects the phraseology of the King James Bible. His persuasive style and religious tone have endeared his books to readers who are repelled by the grim pessimism of Spengler. However, Toynbee, like Spengler, has been unanimously condemned by competent historians who resent his pose of scientific objectivity and his cavalier distortions of fact. Heavily indebted to the ideas of Carl Jung, Toynbee is a meta-historian like Hegel[1] and his views are most impressive to those who are ignorant of the multiplicity and complexity of history. The Toynbee fad is a symptom of a time, and *A Study of History* will probably not survive the anxiety-ridden generation which has sought truth in its crowded pages. Needless to say, Tarn's vision of Alexander the dreamer struck a responsive note for Toynbee, the poet of history.

We children of the Western Society in the present generation are aware from our own experience how poignant this longing may be in an age when the unity of Mankind is being striven for unavailingly. In our day the universal state for which we yearn — the ecumenical commonwealth that will establish its peace from end to end of a Westernized and, by the same token, tormented world — has not yet made its epiphany even on the horizon; yet, in anticipation of its coming, its style and title — "the Great Society" — has been coined by a twentieth-century English sociologist [Graham Wallas] as a Western equivalent for the Hellenic "Inhabited World" and for the Sinic "All that is under Heaven."

It is this great longing for Peace on Earth after the tribulation of a "Time of Troubles" that has moved the subjects of the founders or preservers of the universal states to venerate them as Saviors of Society or actually to worship them as gods incarnate. And even the historian's colder judgment will single out as the greatest of all men of action those ecumenical rulers — a Cyrus, an Alexander, an Augustus — who have been touched with pity for the sufferings of their fellow men and, having caught the vision of the unity of Mankind, have devoted their personal genius and their political power to the noble enterprise of translating this dearly bought ideal into a humane reality.

Alexander's vision of Homonoia or Concord never faded out of the Hellenic World so long as a vestige of Hellenism remained in existence; and the compelling spiritual power of his humanitarian gospel is impressive in view of the recalcitrance of his Macedonian companions towards his efforts to induce them to fraternize with their defeated Iranian antagonists, and the equally stubborn recalcitrance of the rest of the Greeks towards his ordinance that the ruling faction in every city-state should reopen the gates to their exiled opponents of the contrary party.

All but a few of the Macedonian officers whom their royal leader had cajoled or dragooned into embarking with him on the pacific adventure of taking in marriage an Iranian bride might brutally repudiate their unwanted Oriental wives as soon as Alexander had been laid in his premature grave. Yet, some three hundred years after Alexander's death, we find Caesar Augustus putting Alexander's head on his Roman signet-ring as an acknowledgement of the source from which he was seeking inspiration for his arduous work of bringing a tardy peace and unity to a Hellenic World which Alexander's successors had thrown back into disunion and discord; and some two hundred years after Augustus' time, again, this Alexandrine tradition of humanitarianism still had power to move so coarse-grained and brutal a soul as Caracalla's to complete the process — which Julius Caesar had lavishly begun and Augustus cautiously continued — of conferring the Roman citizenship upon the subject majority in the population of the Roman empire.[2] Nor did Alexander's example merely influence the action of these later ecumenical rulers who sat in Alexander's seat and caught from that eminence Alexander's bird's-eye view of all his fellow men; the leaven also worked its way down through the variegated strata of a Hellenic Society which had now annexed the children of four submerged alien worlds to the Hellenic internal proletariat. It was Alexander's spirit that moved one Roman centurion at Capernaum to make his humble appeal to Jesus to heal his servant by simply speaking the word without coming under his roof, and that emboldened another Roman centurion at Caesarea to invite Peter to his house. It was Alexander's spirit, likewise, that inspired the Greeks who had come up to Jerusalem in order to worship at the feast to ask the disciples of Jesus whether their Master would grant them an audience; and we may believe that the same Alexandrine

[1] See Thomas W. Africa, "The City of God Revisited," *Journal of the History of Ideas*, XXIII (1962), pp. 281–292.

[2] The emperor Caracalla extended citizenship in order to increase the revenue on certain taxes which only Roman citizens paid. A paranoid despot, he fancied that he was Alexander reborn and was murdered while marching against Persia. [Editor's note.]

From Arnold J. Toynbee, *A Study of History* (London, 1939), Vol. VI, pp. 6–11. Published by the Oxford University Press under the auspices of the Royal Institute of International Affairs and reprinted by permission.

vision of the unity of Mankind was the human inspiration in the mind of Jesus himself when he broke out into a paean of exultation upon learning of the Greeks' request, and again when, in his encounters with the dissident woman of Samaria and with the Hellenized woman of Phoenicia, he broke away from an inhuman Jewish tradition of non-intercourse with unbelievers.

If we are convinced that Alexander's gospel of the unity of Mankind did indeed possess this power of creating concord between souls so far removed in time and creed and class from the Macedonian warrior-visionary, then we shall find ourselves impelled to search for the source from which this extraordinary power was derived; and, if we address our inquiry in the first instance to a humanist of the modern Western school, he will probably reply that the Brotherhood of Man is one of those fundamental truths which, once seen, are recognized, in the same flash, as being self-evident; and he will be likely to add that the duty and desire to serve Humanity require no sanctions outside themselves in any human heart that has become sensitively aware of its kinship with all its fellows. . . . The validity of the principle of Altruism is taken for granted by modern Western humanists of every sect. The Communist, for instance, believes, as devoutly as the Positivist, that Man's ultimate duty is owed to his fellow men in a Universe in which Humanity is monarch of all it surveys, because Man has no God above him; and yet we have seen reasons for believing that the dynamic elements in Communism—the springs of the action that has made Communism a force in contemporary human affairs—are derived, albeit unconsciously, from a trinity of theistic religions, if we are right in tracing back some of these elements to Christianity and others to Christianity's two forerunners, Judaism and Zoroastrianism. If we now return to our inquiry into the basis of the Humanism of Alexander, shall we find the theistic vein that is latent in Marx's Humanism anticipated in Alexander's vision?

There was, we must allow, in Alexander's life one arresting experience on the ordinary human plane which might have been sufficient in and by itself to open Alexander's eyes to the intellectual falsity and the moral indefensibility of the current Hellenic dichotomy of Mankind into "Hellenes" and "Barbarians"; and that was his sensational discovery of the unexpected virtues of his defeated Iranian adversaries. In the hostile caricature which had been the convention in Hellas during the interval of 146

years by which Alexander's passage of the Hellespont was separated from Xerxes' unluckier crossing of the same straits in the opposite direction, the Persian grandees had been held up to odium as monsters of luxury, tyranny, cruelty, and cowardice; and now, when Xerxes' abortive aggression had been avenged at last up to the hilt by Alexander's victorious "retaliation," the Macedonian champion of Hellas learnt through the intimate and illuminating intercourse of warfare that these arch-barbarians were in reality men capable of showing a bravery in battle and a dignity in defeat which even a Spartan might envy. The deepness of the impression which this unlooked-for discovery made upon Alexander's mind is notorious; but if we go on to ask whether in Alexander's opinion this experience of his own or others like it would suffice in themselves to awaken in human souls a consciousness of the unity of Mankind and a will to act upon this great discovery, our evidence (scanty though it is) will inform us explicitly that the answer is in this case in the negative. It is recorded that at Opis in Babylonia, Alexander once offered up a prayer that his Macedonians and his Persians might be united in Homonoia; and Plutarch reports as one of Alexander's sayings: "God is the common father of all men, but he makes the best ones peculiarly his own." If this "saying" is authentic, it tells us that Alexander's anthropology differed from that of Marx in the fundamental point of resting on an avowed theological foundation instead of professedly hanging in the air. It tells us that Alexander discovered the truth that the brotherhood of Man presupposes the fatherhood of God—a truth which involves the converse proposition that, if the divine father of the human family is ever left out of the reckoning, there is no possibility of forging any alternative bond of purely human texture which will avail by itself to hold Mankind together. The only society that is capable of embracing the whole of Mankind is a superhuman "City of God." . . . "Except the Lord build the house, their labor is but lost that build it; except the Lord keep the city, the watchman watcheth but in vain." The common experience of the Hellenic "Time of Troubles" taught this truth to Alexander the Greek and to Paul the Jew, . . . but the Hellenic Society has not been singular either in passing through great tribulation or in learning this lesson by suffering this affliction. In the Egyptiac World, more than a thousand years before Alexander made his pilgrimage to the oasis-oracle of Amon, the unity of Mankind was numbered among the mighty works of the divinity, manifested in the Sun-Disk, who was worshipped by Ikhnaton.

ERNST BADIAN

A CRITICAL APPRAISAL OF THE TARN THESIS

Professor Ernst Badian of the University of Leeds is highly regarded for his penetrating studies of Greek and Roman history. He is the author of *Foreign Clientelae* (1958), and a number of his essays were published in a collection in 1964. A pupil of Sir Ronald Syme, Badian is representative of the approach of many British scholars to antiquity. Pariculary since the Second World War, students of the Greek and Roman past have been noticeably drawn to a realistic solution to the complex problems of history. Though he can write with wit, Badian is engaged in the following passages with a straightforward critical appraisal of the Tarn thesis. Most of the quotations from Tarn are from his 1948 book on Alexander.

Twenty-five years ago Sir William Tarn delivered a Raleigh Lecture on History to the British Academy, to which he gave this challenging title [Alexander the Great and the Unity of Mankind] and in which he created the figure we may call Alexander the Dreamer: an Alexander "dreaming" of "one of the supreme revolutions in the world's outlook," namely "the brotherhood of man or the unity of mankind." . . . Six years later Tarn could write: "It is now, as I see it, certain." Ten years ago, in his great work on Alexander, certainty was apparently a little abated. But if there was less pretension, there was no more ability to think himself mistaken, and no more civility in dealing with opposing views. . . . Ever since 1933, Tarn's figure of Alexander the Dreamer . . . has haunted the pages of scholarship, and even source-books and general histories of philosophy and of ideas—at least in this country —have begun to succumb to the spell. Perhaps a quarter of a century is long enough for the life-span of a phantom: it is clearly threatening to pass into our tradition as a thing of flesh and blood. . . .

According to Tarn, Alexander developed "an idea which had three facets or aspects: . . . The first is that God is the common Father of mankind, which may be called the brotherhood of man. The second is Alexander's dream of the various races of mankind, so far as known to him, becoming of one mind together and living in unity and concord, which may be called the unity of mankind. And the third . . . is that the various peoples of his empire might be partners in the realm rather than subjects." Let us examine these "facets" in turn.

The first is not logically relevant to the other two: it is only by playing with imagery that we arrive from the idea of God as "the common Father of mankind" at that of the "brotherhood of man" in any ethically important sense. In fact, for reasons that nowadays need hardly be set out at length, the idea of God as "the common Father of mankind" is ethically neutral. On it, or on similar foundations, equalitarian and universalist ethics have in fact been founded—but also systems of chosen peoples, of lawful slavery, and all the class and race distinctions with which we are so familiar. To keep within the bounds of the image: God may still have all manner of favorite children, usually including the exponent of the theory advanced. This seems so elementary as to be hardly worth stressing. Yet it seems to have escaped Tarn's notice, as is clear from his exposition. Citing from Plutarch the report that Alexander "said that God was the common father of all mankind, but that he made the best ones peculiarly his own," he comments: "This, on the face of it, is a plain statement that all men are brothers." (And he goes on to say that it is the first.) On the face of it, it is hard not to see in it something quite different. Nor does scrutiny belie the first impression. Plutarch has been talking about Alexander's visit to Ammon and telling some of the stories that collected round

From Ernst Badian, "Alexander the Great and the Unity of Mankind," *Historia*, VII (1958), pp. 425–30, 432–33, 435–36. Reprinted by permission of Franz Steiner Verlag, publishers of *Historia*.

the oracle's replies to him; in particular, he has stressed the revelation to Alexander that he was to regard Zeus-Ammon as his father. . . . The story as Plutarch tells it . . . is not intended to, and it does not in the least, portray Alexander as believing in the brotherhood of man in any sense in which Greeks, ever since Homer, had not. . . . It is indeed surprising that such an elaborate house of cards should be built on a distortion of a reported saying. . . .

The other two "facets"—far more important—are fashioned out of the Opis banquet. . . . The scene is reported only by Arrian. . . . It is clear that to Arrian (i.e. to his source) the whole affair is not of outstanding importance. It is a tailpiece of merely two sections to the Opis mutiny, which *is* an important event . . . and it is immediately followed by the dismissal of the Macedonian veterans. This had been planned and announced before the mutiny and had been immediately responsible for its outbreak; and after its settlement it could at last be executed. The banquet, as we can see, just like the sacrifice that precedes it, marks the formal settlement of the dispute that had led to the mutiny; and it follows upon the account of the details of that settlement. The mutiny, as we are repeatedly and unanimously told, was due to the Macedonians' jealousy of the favor Alexander was showing to the "Persians." The reconciliation, therefore, might be expected to be between (a) Alexander and the Macedonians, whose quarrel *was* the mutiny; (b) the Macedonians and the "Persians," whose differences had caused it. . . . That the banquet marked "a greater reconciliation" or even the official conclusion of peace is neither stated nor implied in the source.

Tarn's scene-setting is at once splendid and misleading: . . . "No witness of the scene could ever have forgotten the sight of that great krater on Alexander's table and people of every nationality drawing wine from it for their common libation." It is a fit setting for a ceremony of international brotherhood. What, in fact, does Arrian (and we must agree with Tarn that that means Ptolemy) say? There is nothing about tables—how many were used and who used them—and certainly nothing about Alexander's own table; there is merely the statement that everyone was seated: apart from other reasons that might plausibly be conjectured, there were presumably too many people for everyone to be able to recline. Even a large refectory table could hardly have accommodated the crowd that Tarn wishes to place at

it. The source merely tells us how the guests were grouped within the area given over to the banquet—there is no implication that each group had only one table, and indeed numbers make it impossible. If Alexander had a table to share, he presumably shared it, on this occasion as on others, with a handful of high-ranking officers and courtiers.

On the *grouping,* however, the source is precise: around Alexander were Macedonians, next to them in order "Persians," next to them the rest. Thus, when "those around" Alexander join him in the libation from his krater, the emphatic repetition of the same phrase within a few words makes it clear that only the Macedonians are meant. No doubt the "Persians" and the rest poured the "same" libation—in an extended sense—from their own bowls: Arrian goes on to tell us that it is said 9000 people did so. But the sharing of Alexander's own krater was limited to the Macedonians. The inspiring ceremonial of an international love-feast is purely imaginary and due to misinterpretation of an unusually precise source. In fact, . . . treatment is carefully graded according to nationality—so far is it from being equal and cosmopolitan. . . . This fits in with what we have seen to be the purpose of the banquet and with the account of the mutiny and its settlement. Eager to regain the loyalty of his Macedonians (who were still his best soldiers and would be needed for his further plans of conquest), Alexander had called them "kinsmen" and thus made them—every common soldier of them—equal to the noblest of the "Persians." For he could be sure of the latter and their submissiveness, while the Macedonians had to be courted. He now reinforced this timely act of flattery by seating them "around him" at the banquet and letting them, and them only, use his own krater for the libation. After the banquet, of course, he proceeded to carry out his plans precisely as he had made them before the mutiny, and there was now no further protest: tact meant no surrender of principle. But the flamboyant gesture—as always, carefully calculated for political effect—reveals the unmistakable Alexander of history, who did not gain his empire by well-meaning muddle-headedness. The setting, then, is not that of an international love-feast. . . .

There is another passage in which Tarn seeks corroboration for his theory and in particular for his views on the Opis banquet: he claims the explicit support of Eratosthenes. Now Eratosthenes, of course, was far from being a contemporary of Alexander—so far that he could not even know any of his contemporaries; and though we admire him as a great scientist and mathematician, we have no means of assessing him as a historian or judging his skill in weighing historical evidence. . . . We are told that . . . Eratosthenes disapproved . . . of those who advised Alexander to treat Greeks as friends and barbarians as enemies: it would be more reasonable, he says, to make a division according to virtue and vice; . . . this was why Alexander disregarded all such advice and . . . conferred benefits upon all men of good repute. . . . So far there is no hint of Opis. But Tarn next brings in a passage in Plutarch's . . . "Fortune of Alexander"; there . . . Alexander is indeed credited with a cosmopolitan philosophy—as indeed it is the purpose of the [essay] to show that Alexander was a true philosopher. Plutarch first says that Zeno is much admired for the cosmopolitanism of his *Republic*, but that his ideal was translated into fact by Alexander. . . . Now, if Tarn had ascribed merely the general train of thought in the Plutarch passage . . . to Eratosthenes, we might well concede it. But that is just what he does not do: having

"got the limits of the Eratosthenes fragment," he uses precisely the last part—the part where the differences between Strabo's citation and Plutarch are manifold and striking—with its divine mission and its loving-cup as being genuine Eratosthenes, saddling the philosopher with the ascription of these ideas to Alexander and even with the use of these actual words. It is then only a small step to the assertion that Eratosthenes' loving-cup did actually exist; it was the great krater on Alexander's table at Opis. It follows that Eratosthenes had before him an impressive eyewitness account of the banquet, which gave him the ideas he ascribes to Alexander—a much more impressive one than Ptolemy's account. . . . It should now be clear that none of this is solidly based. . . . We must firmly assign to the realm of fantasy any attempt to connect Eratosthenes with the enunciation of Alexander's divine mission [or] with the simile of the cup. . . . As for the Opis banquet, there is not a shred of evidence that Eratosthenes had ever heard of it. . . , and certainly none that he thought it more important than Ptolemy did.

4

CAESAR AND THE TIDE OF FORTUNE

In the two centuries preceding the beginning of the Christian era Rome conquered the Mediterranean world, dragging Hellenistic kings and sullen Western barbarians behind the chariots of the victors. Unfortunately, Rome was still a city-state and the ruling class viewed the empire primarily as a source of tribute and a field for military exploits. Roman citizenship had only been granted to the Italians after they rose in arms at the beginning of the first century B.C. The republic was indifferent to the rights of provincials, and justice was only obtained for them under the emperors. The powerful nobles who ran the republic had also let Rome become a vast slum, crowded with unemployed and wretched citizens who sold their votes for a pittance. In theory the republic was a democracy, in practice it was an oligarchy, but it was a failure as either. To vote, Romans had to come to the capital, which was impractical for most Italians and provincials. Power lay with the urban masses who filled the Tribal Assembly, which was the legislative body of Rome. The nobles in the Senate manipulated voters, handed out military commands and patronage, and ran the empire. As Mommsen has suggested, a representative voting system would have pumped new life from the provinces into the moribund republic, but the nobles and the masses at Rome were unwilling to surrender their monopoly on political power. In the first century B.C. the assembly was a constant scene of violence and bribery as bitter factions struggled to intimidate or win over voters.

The chief factions were the conservative Optimates and the more liberal Populares, but both groups were led by noble families whose rivalries wrecked the republic. Ideology meant little to the practical Romans who relished honors, power, and the opportunity to ruin an enemy. Two useful magistracies were the consulship and the tribunate—the two consuls were the executives of the Roman state, and each of the ten tribunes could veto any governmental action in the capital. In office, the consuls commanded armies and held military commands as proconsuls in the provinces after their term as consul had expired. Since most offices were annual, electioneering was constant and there was no relief from political pressures.

The armies, which were necessary for the safety and expansion of the Roman republic, became the instruments of its downfall. The generals were politicians who counted on the loyalty of their veterans as voters and in extreme cases used combat troops to overthrow a rival when political maneuvers failed. Early in the first century B.C. the conservative general Sulla stormed Rome, slaughtered his enemies, and established a brief dictatorship. While Pompey and Crassus were Sulla's henchmen, young Caesar belonged to the Populares. Sulla resigned after strengthening the oligarchic hold on the republic, but within a decade Pompey and Crassus joined forces with the Populares to win power; their trump cards were the armies. In 60 B.C. harassment by the Optimates drove Pompey, Crassus, and Caesar into a coalition, the First Triumvirate, which ran Rome and gave Caesar a chance to win glory in Gaul. By 50 B.C. Crassus had died in a war with Parthia, and Pompey and Caesar had fallen out. Since Gaul was subdued, Caesar's enemies tried to relieve him of his military command—they were confident of breaking Caesar because they had won the support of Pompey. The result was a terrible civil war which ended in the victory of Caesar, who assumed a lifetime dictatorship. The rule of one man made a mockery of the republic, but earlier three men and then two had made the major decisions at Rome. Thinking in terms of partnership, Caesar had been particularly distressed that his peer Pompey did not effect a compromise with him within the facade of constitutional forms. The dictatorship was not Caesar's aim—(he had wanted to run for consul in 49 B.C.)—but a poor expedient, forced upon him by circumstances.

So much of history is full of presumptuous dullards and homicidal maniacs that we are pleased to run across an intelligent and urbane man like Caesar. He was a prisoner of his time as all men are, but the dictator proved to be an exception to the rule of witless or vicious men who shape much of history. As a man, Caesar was most interesting. Highly intelligent, he wrote well and he had a realistic grasp of the needs of the provinces and the poor at Rome. Caesar was willing to grant citizenship to provincials and even placed some in the Senate; he also cut the relief rolls at Rome and resettled over a hundred thousand of the urban poor as property owners in the provinces. Too witty for his own good, Caesar was sarcastic and mocked his rivals—even worse, he was calculatingly merciful and spared their lives after defeating them. They never forgave the contempt which his clemency implied. Unlike Alexander, Caesar avoided alcohol and chased women. His celebrated affair with Cleopatra was a relaxation, not an infatuation with the ambitious young queen. Though he was merciful to Romans, Caesar was ruthless in Gaul, where on one occasion he had captured rebels mutilated; he also slaughtered the women and children of an invading German tribe. All in all, he was no self-styled messiah and certainly no humanitarian superman, but rather a very able Roman noble with many of the biases of his class. Sir Frank Adcock has said of Caesar: "His genius was the hard practical genius of Rome raised to the highest power: he was a keen edge on the old blade." To later generations, Caesar was a god and the ancestor of a dynasty; to some, he was the prototype of a power-mad tyrant. The latter image has no relevance to the Caesar of history.

The dictatorship of Caesar distressed some of his contemporaries, and it touches raw nerves today. Yet, words taken out of their historical context obscure realities, and the Roman republic was not a Platonic ideal but a very human institution. Sir Ronald Syme has some helpful comments on the use of words in politics and war:

The political cant of a country is naturally and always most strongly in evidence on the side of vested interests. In times of peace and prosperity it commands a wide measure of acquiescence, even of belief. Revolution rends the veil. But the revolution did not impede or annul the use of political fraud at Rome. On the contrary, the vocabulary was furbished up and adapted to a more modern and deadly technique. As commonly in civil strife and class-war, the relation between words and facts was inverted. Party-denominations prevailed entirely, and in the end success or failure became the only criterion of wisdom and of patriotism. In the service of faction, the fairest of pleas and the noblest of principles were assiduously enlisted. The art was as old as politics, its exponents required no mentors. The purpose of propaganda was threefold—to win an appearance of legality for measures of violence, to seduce the supporters of a rival party, and to stampede the neutral or non-political elements. First in value come freedom and orderly government, without the profession of which ideals no party can feel secure and sanguine, whatever be the acts of deception or violence in prospect. At Rome all men paid homage to liberty, holding it to be something roughly equivalent to the spirit and practice of republican government. Exactly what corresponded to the republican constitution was, however, a matter not of legal definition but of partisan interpretation. . . . The liberty of the Roman aristocrat meant the rule of a class and the perpetuation of privilege.[1]

Caesar must be judged as a Roman and a ruler, and not as the embodiment of dictatorship which may be distasteful to us. In Caesar we find none of the pompous egomania of Napoleon, the manic vulgarity of Hitler, or the icy cruelty of Stalin. Caesar had his Roman faults and neglected the political and social regeneration of Rome and the empire for an invasion of Parthia ostensibly to avenge Crassus. In the midst of his war plans, the dictator was murdered by his friends. Of the twenty-three wounds which pierced his body, only one in the chest was fatal—except for a chance blow, Caesar would have survived the attack on his life. How merciful would he then have been, or would Caesar have become another Sulla? His assassins claimed that he had wished to be a monarch, but Caesar had seen the shabby kings of the East and did not crave a crown—"I am no king," he grinned, "but Caesar!" Shakespeare, who relied on Plutarch's inept sermons, is a poor guide to history, but he caught the real reason for Caesar's murder in the speech which he put in Cassius' mouth:

[1]Sir Ronald Syme, *The Roman Revolution* (Oxford: Clarendon Press, 1939), pp. 154–155. Reprinted by permission.

Why, man, he doth bestride the narrow world
Like a Colossus, and we petty men
Walk under his huge legs and peep about
To find ourselves dishonorable graves.
Men at some time are masters of their fates.
The fault, dear Brutus, is not in our stars,
But in ourselves, that we are underlings.

Jealousy, not ideology, cut Caesar down.

The march of history is a chaotic thing, and we impose order on it at the risk of distorting the past. Men rarely know the ultimate results of their acts, and historians often impute motives which would surprise the actors, who like blind men stumble through a crisis to glory or defeat. To know the moment and direction for action is difficult, and luck is a decisive factor in history. Shakespeare realized this numbing imperative:

There is a tide in the affairs of men
Which, taken at the flood, leads on to fortune;
Omitted, all the voyage of their life
Is bound in shallows and in miseries.

In the mouth of Brutus, such words have particular irony and stunning truth. The future is dark, and behind any turn may lurk some horror undreamed of in our careful calculations. When he crossed the Rubicon, could Caesar have foreseen the Ides of March, Antony's war against the assassins, the long strife between Antony and Augustus, or the grim annals of the Julian dynasty? The future dictator was then caught in events not of his own making and he aptly used a gambler's phrase: "The die is cast."

VELLEIUS PATERCULUS

CAESAR: A ROMAN VIEW

Under Augustus and his successors, Caesar was treated with ambivalence by historians who reflected the government's view. Caesar the god had adopted the emperor Augustus, but Caesar the rebel set an embarrassing precedent for ambitious generals. Velleius Paterculus was an amateur historian and retired officer who had served loyally under Augustus and his successor Tiberius. His admiration of Tiberius was excessive but provides a useful antidote to the malice of Tacitus. Most Augustan writers maligned Mark Antony, and Paterculus was no exception. In the following passages, he damns Curio, who was Antony's friend. As Caesar's henchman, the tribune Curio proposed that both Caesar and Pompey disband their armies; by an overwhelming vote (370 to 22), the Senate approved Curio's proposal and thus demonstrated that the civil war was actually the result of a factious minority which was irreconcilably opposed to Caesar. The enemies of Caesar vetoed Curio's compromise. Despite the slur on Curio, Paterculus tried to be fair in describing the origins of the civil war and the behavior of Caesar in victory.

It was in Caesar's consulship [actually the year before in 60 B.C.] that there was formed between himself, Gnaeus Pompeius, and Marcus Crassus the partnership in political power which proved so baleful to the city, to the world, and subsequently at different periods to each of the triumvirs themselves. Pompey's motive in the adoption of this policy had been to secure through Caesar as consul the long delayed ratification of his acts in the provinces across the seas, to which . . . many still raised objections; Caesar agreed to it because he realized that in making this concession to the prestige of Pompey he would increase his own, and that by throwing on Pompey the odium for their joint control he would add to his own power; while Crassus hoped that by the influence of Pompey and the power of Caesar he might achieve a place of preeminence in the state which he had not been able to reach single-handed. Furthermore, a tie of marriage was cemented between Caesar and Pompey, in that Pompey now wedded Julia, Caesar's daughter. . . .

[Both Pompey and Crassus were jealous of Caesar's conquest of Gaul, and Crassus died in 53 B.C. in an abortive invasion of Parthia, where he had hoped to win similar glory.] About the fourth year of Caesar's stay in Gaul occurred the death of Julia [54 B.C.], the wife of Pompey, the one tie which bound together Pompey and Caesar in a coalition which, because of each one's jealousy of the other's power, held together with difficulty even during her lifetime; and as though fortune were bent upon breaking all the bonds between the two men destined for so great a conflict, Pompey's little son by Julia also died a short time afterwards. Then, inasmuch as agitation over the elections found vent in armed conflicts and civil bloodshed, which continued indefinitely and without check, Pompey was made consul for the third time [52 B.C.], now without a colleague, with the assent even of those who up to that time had opposed him for that office. The tribute paid him by this honor, which seemed to indicate his reconciliation with the Optimates, served

more than anything else to alienate him from Caesar. Pompey, however, employed his whole power during this consulship in curbing election abuses. . . .

It was not long after this that the first sparks of civil war were kindled. All fair-minded men desired that both Caesar and Pompey should disband their armies. Now Pompey in . . . [55 B.C.] had caused the provinces of Spain to be assigned to him, and though he was actually absent from them, administering the affairs of the city, he continued to govern them for three years through his lieutenants, . . . and while he agreed with those who insisted that Caesar should dismiss his army, he was opposed to those who urged that he should also dismiss his own. Had Pompey only died two years before the outbreak of hostilities, after the completion of his theater and the other public buildings with which he had surrounded it, at the time when he was attacked by a serious illness . . . and all Italy prayed for his safety as her foremost citizen, fortune would have lost the opportunity of overthrowing him and he would have borne to the grave unimpaired all the qualities of greatness that had been his in life. It was Gaius Curio, however, a tribune of the people, who, more than anyone else, applied the flaming torch which kindled the civil war and all the evils which followed for twenty consecutive years. Curio was a man of noble birth, eloquent, reckless, prodigal alike of his own fortune and chastity and of those of other people, a man of the utmost cleverness in perversity, who used his gifted tongue for the subversion of the state. No wealth and no pleasures sufficed to satiate his appetites. He was at first on the side of Pompey, that is to say, as it was then regarded, on the side of the republic. Then he pretended to be opposed both to Pompey and Caesar, but in his heart he was for Caesar. Whether his conversion was spontaneous or due to a bribe of ten million sesterces [$500,000.00?], as is reported, we shall leave undetermined. Finally, when a truce was on the point of being concluded on terms of the most salutary character, terms

From Velleius Paterculus, II 44, 47–49, 56–58. Reprinted by permission of the publishers and the Loeb Classical Library from Frederick W. Shipley, trans., *Velleius Paterculus* (Cambridge, Mass.: Harvard University Press, 1955; London: William Heinemann Ltd.), pp. 145–47, 153–61, 173–77.

which were demanded in a spirit of the utmost fairness by Caesar and accepted by Pompey without protest, it was in the end broken and shattered by Curio in spite of Cicero's extraordinary efforts to preserve harmony in the state. . . . [Paterculus apparently refers to a proposal for a new reassignment of provinces, which was vetoed by Curio because it would leave Caesar without an army until he could be elected consul again. Caesar was authorized to run for the office while absent from Rome.]

In the consulship of Lentulus and Marcellus . . . [49 B.C.] the civil war burst into flame. The one leader seemed to have the better cause, the other the stronger; on the one was the appearance, on the other the reality of power; Pompey was armed with the authority of the Senate, Caesar with the devotion of his soldiers. The consuls and the Senate conferred the supreme authority not on Pompey but on his cause. No effort was omitted by Caesar that could be tried in the interest of peace, but no offer of his was accepted by the Pompeians. Of the two consuls, one showed more bitterness than was fair, the other, Lentulus, could not save himself from ruin without bringing ruin upon the state, while Marcus Cato insisted that they should fight to the death rather than allow the republic to accept a single dictate from a mere citizen. The stern Roman of the old-fashioned type would praise the cause of Pompey, the politic would follow the lead of Caesar, recognizing that while there was on the one side greater prestige, the other was the more formidable.

When at last, rejecting all the demands of Caesar who was content to retain the title to the province [of Cisalpine Gaul and Illyricum] with but a single legion, the Senate decreed that he should enter the city as a private citizen and should as such submit himself to the votes of the Roman people in his candidacy for the consulship, Caesar concluded that war was inevitable and crossed the Rubicon with his army. Gnaeus Pompeius, the consuls, and the majority of the Senate abandoned first the city, then Italy, and crossed the sea to [Greece]. . . . [In 48 B.C. Caesar defeated Pompey at Pharsalus and later occupied Cleopatra's Egypt where the fugitive Pompey had been murdered. In 46 B.C. Caesar defeated his enemies in Africa at the battle of Thapsus. Rather than accept Caesar's clemency, Cato killed himself. In 45 B.C. Caesar defeated the last of the Pompeians at Munda in Spain, and the civil war was over.]

Caesar, victorious over all his enemies, returned to the city and pardoned all who had borne arms against him, an act of generosity almost passing belief. . . . But it was the lot of this great man, who behaved with such clemency in all his victories, that his peaceful enjoyment of supreme power should last but five months. For, returning to the city in October, he was slain on the Ides of March [44 B.C.]. Brutus and Cassius were the leaders of the conspiracy. He had failed to win the former by the promise of the consulship and had offended the latter by the postponement of his candidacy. There were also in the plot to compass his death some of the most intimate of all his friends, who owed their elevation to the success of his party, namely Decimus Brutus, Gaius Trebonius, and others of illustrious name. Marcus Antonius, his colleague in the consulship, ever ready for acts of daring, had brought great odium upon Caesar by placing a royal crown upon his head as he sat on the rostra at the Lupercalia. Caesar put the crown from him, but in such a way that he did not seem to be displeased.

In the light of experience, due credit should be given to the counsel of Pansa and Hirtius, who had always warned Caesar that he must hold by arms the position which he had won by arms. But Caesar kept reiterating that he would rather die than live in fear, and while he looked for a return for the clemency he had shown, he was taken off his guard by men devoid of gratitude, although the gods gave many signs and presages of the threatened danger. For the soothsayers had warned him beforehand carefully to beware the Ides of March; his wife Calpurnia, terrified by a dream, kept begging him to remain at home on that day; and notes warning him of the conspiracy were handed him, but he neglected to read them at the time. But verily the power of destiny is inevitable; it confounds the judgment of him whose fortune it has determined to reverse. . . . Cassius had been in favor of slaying Antony as well as Caesar and of destroying Caesar's will, but Brutus had opposed him, insisting that citizens ought not to seek the blood of any but the "tyrant"—for to call Caesar "tyrant" placed his deed in a better light.

JULIUS CAESAR

"THEY WOULD HAVE IT SO"

A man's testimony on his own controversial actions is never impartial, often dangerous, and always useful, for it reveals the mind of the man if not the truth of the matter. In 48 B.C. Caesar justified his position by writing an account of the outbreak of the civil war which was still raging. Concerning Book I of Caesar's *Civil War,* Sir Frank Adcock has written: "Caesar is an advocate for himself, not wholly scrupulous, but wholly sincere. It is plain that he believed that he had not received the treatment which his exploits and his dignity deserved, and that his army shared his belief. He did not seek to overthrow the Republican constitution, but only to have it work for his interests and not against them. He was prepared to meet his enemies at least part of the way provided he did not forfeit his career, to come to terms with Pompey in a new coalition in which, however, he would be at an advantage over his former ally. The civic dissension need not be a civil war; it was not by his choosing that his enemies made it one. As he said at Pharsalus, 'they would have it so.'"[1] Caesar, of course, was not present at the Senate meetings which he described, but he had reliable information from the Senate's stenographers and from his supporters who did attend the debates. Late in 50 B.C., Caesar sent a letter to the Senate offering to resign his military command if Pompey would also give up his troops.

My letter was delivered to the consuls, but it was a difficult matter to get permission for it to be read aloud in front of the Senate. Indeed permission was only granted after the most vigorous agitation on the part of the people's tribunes. As for having a regular debate on the contents of the letter, it was found impossible to secure this concession at all. Instead, the consuls proceeded to bring in a motion on the political situation in general. The consul Lucius Lentulus addressed the Senate in a provocative manner. He assured them that he would play his full part in the defense of the republic, if the senators themselves would only show daring and resolution in the expression of their opinions. "If, on the other hand," he said, "as has happened on previous occasions, you are going to let your thoughts turn toward Caesar and the prospects of making yourselves popular in that direction, then I, Lentulus, am going to make my own decisions without reference to you. I too can, if I like, make myself safe by accepting Caesar's favor and Caesar's friendship." Scipio then made a speech to the same effect. Pompey, he said, was prepared to play his part in the defense of the republic, so long as the Senate would follow his lead; if, however, the Senate showed weakness and hesitation now, though they might beg for his help in the future they would beg for it in vain.

As the meeting of the Senate was being held in Rome and as Pompey was near the city at the time, it was considered that this speech of Scipio's had been dictated to him by Pompey himself. There were a few senators who expressed more moderate views. . . . There was Marcus Calidius who proposed that, in order that there should be no reason for a recourse to arms, Pompey should leave Italy and go to his provinces. "Caesar," he said, "has had two legions taken away from him by Pompey and is

[1] Sir Frank E. Adcock, *Caesar as Man of Letters* (Cambridge: Cambridge University Press, 1956), pp. 46–47.

From *War Commentaries of Caesar,* translated by Rex Warner, pp. 211–14, 217–18, ©1960 by Rex Warner. Published by arrangement with The New American Library, Inc., New York.

now apprehensive because of the impression that Pompey is holding these legions in reserve and keeping them near Rome with the idea of using them against him." Marcus Rufus also made a speech very much in the same terms as that of Calidius. All these speakers were vigorously attacked by the consul Lucius Lentulus in the most violent language. Lentulus absolutely refused to allow any discussion of the proposal of Calidius. . . . So, as a result of the consul's angry words, of the terror caused by an army actually on the spot, and of the threats of Pompey's friends, the Senate adopted the proposal of Scipio, the majority of the senators voting under force and pressure and against their wills. Scipio's proposal was that Caesar should disband his army before a fixed date, and that, if he failed to do so, he should be considered a public enemy. At this point, the people's tribunes, Mark Antony and Quintus Cassius, interposed their veto. Immediately the Senate was required to discuss whether this veto should be regarded as valid or not—a weighty and serious discussion—and the more bitter and savage a speech was, the more it was cheered by my enemies. The meeting of the Senate ended in the evening and all senators were then invited to visit Pompey outside the city. Pompey offered his congratulations to those who had shown themselves ready for action and encouraged them to preserve the same spirit in the future; he spoke sharply to the more lukewarm members and urged them to change their attitude. . . . Pressure was brought to bear on all who were friends of the consuls and all who were supporters of Pompey or of my old enemies to attend meetings of the Senate, and so vocal a crowd had the effect of terrifying the weaker spirits and forcing their own views on those whose minds were not made up. . . .

Other proposals . . . were made for sending a deputation to me to explain what the feelings of the Senate were. Every one of these speakers and every one of the proposals were attacked and opposed in speeches made by the consul, by Scipio, and by Cato. Cato was activated by his long hatred of me and by his bitter feelings at having failed in the elections [for consul in 51 B.C.]. The behavior of Lentulus can be explained by the fact that he had enormous debts and was looking forward to the command of an army and of provinces and to the bribes he would acquire for bestowing regal titles on native rulers; he boasted among his friends that he was going to become another Sulla, with supreme power in his hands. Scipio too was motivated by the expectation of a province and of armies which, since he was Pompey's father-in-law, he thought he ought to share with him; other motives can be found in the fact that he was frightened of prosecution, that he had a violent, ostentatious character himself and was led on by the flattery of men of like character who at this time had great influence both in politics and in the law courts. As to Pompey, he had been pushed into action by my enemies and also by his own wish that no one should be placed on the same level as himself. He had entirely broken off his old friendship with me and had become friends again with those who had been enemies of us both, most of whom he personally had turned against me during the time that he was my son-in-law. He was also concerned about the discredit he had brought on himself by keeping back the two legions to serve his power and supremacy instead of allowing them to go to Asia and Syria. Therefore, Pompey was eager to have things settled by force of arms. . . .

[On January 7, 49 B.C., the Senate decreed a state of emergency.] Decrees of the most savage and of the most insulting kind were passed depriving me of my command and the tribunes of their rights and dignity. The tribunes immediately fled from Rome and joined me at Ravenna where I was waiting to receive a reply to my own very moderate demands and hoping that a certain sense of fairness might be shown so that everything could end peacefully. . . . [On January 11, Caesar led the Thirteenth Legion across the Rubicon river which was the border of his province; the civil war had begun. Still hoping for a compromise settlement with his rival, Caesar sent a personal message to Pompey:] "I have always . . . put the good name and honor of the state first and have regarded them as more valuable than life itself. What distressed me was to find that my enemies in the most insulting manner were taking from me a privilege that had been granted to me by the Roman people. I was being deprived of six months of my command and was being dragged back to Rome, although the people had ratified the proposal that I should be allowed to stand for the consulship at the next elections without being personally present. Nevertheless, for the sake of the state I accepted this infringement of my rights and attack upon my honor with a good grace. But when I sent a letter to the Senate proposing that both sides should disband their armies, I failed even to gain this point. Troops are being raised all over Italy; two legions, stolen from me on the pretext that they were to be used against Parthia, are still in the country;

the whole state is under arms. How can all this be explained except on the assumption that there is a plan to destroy me? Yet for the sake of the state I am still prepared to make any concession and to put up with anything. I propose that Pompey should go to his provinces, that both of us should disband our armies, that everyone in Italy should return to civilian life, that the state should be freed from fear, that the holding of free elections and the general control of affairs should be handed over to the Senate and the Roman people. In order that this should be done with as little trouble as possible and on fixed terms which should be ratified by oath, I propose that either Pompey should come nearer to me or else should allow me to come nearer to him. A conference between the two of us would have the effect of settling all difficulties." . . .

[The consuls and Pompey insisted that Caesar retire to Gaul and disband his troops before Pompey would go to Spain; until Caesar promised to do so, they would continue to prepare for war.] These terms were unfair. It was unfair of Pompey to demand that I should retire to Gaul while he kept both his provinces and the legions that did not belong to him; to want me to disband my troops while he himself continued to recruit new forces; to promise to go to his province, but give no definite date for when he would do so. Thus, even if he stayed in Italy until my consulship was over, he could not be considered guilty of having broken his word. Finally, what showed that there was very little real hope of peace was the fact that Pompey allowed no time for a conference and made no suggestion that he should come near me personally.

THEODOR MOMMSEN

"CAESAR: THE PERFECT MAN"

Theodor Mommsen (1817–1903) of the University of Berlin was one of the giants of modern scholarship. Through his numerous essays and a monumental collection of Latin inscriptions, he helped to convert the study of ancient history into a critical discipline. Mommsen was a literary artist as well as a scientific historian, and he was awarded the first Nobel prize for literature in 1902. He wrote his immensely popular and influential *History of Rome* (1854–1856) when he was a young professor anxious for fame and money. In politics, Mommsen was a liberal and served in the German Reichstag, where he battled Bismarck on a number of occasions. As a professor, he opposed outbursts of anti-Semitism and ultranationalism on German campuses and staunchly defended academic freedom against religious bigots. His hatred of Prussian Junkers was so great that it warped his understanding of the late Roman republic. Despite his great learning, Mommsen saw the conservative opponents of Caesar as muddle-headed reactionaries and decadent caricatures of his hated Junkers. The partisan historian labeled Cato as a "stupid Don Quixote" and dismissed Pompey as a glorified sergeant major. His extreme adulation of Caesar as the "perfect man" was unscholarly, but Mommsen felt deeply about politics and Caesar seemed to him to have been a superhuman scourge of Junkers. Because of Mommsen's great prestige, his romantic image of Caesar has impressed uncritical readers as the verdict of history.

When Caesar was informed by the tribunes who had fled to his camp of the reception which his proposals had met in the capital, he called together the soldiers of the thirteenth legion . . . and unfolded before them the state of things. It was not merely the man of genius versed in the knowledge of men's hearts, whose brilliant eloquence shone forth in this gripping crisis of his own and the world's destiny. It was not even the generous and victorious commander-in-chief addressing soldiers whom he himself had called to arms, and who for eight years had followed his banners with daily increasing enthusiasm. There spoke, above all, the energetic and consistent statesman, who had now for nine-and-twenty years defended the cause of freedom in good times and bad; who had braved for it the daggers of assassins and the executioners of the aristocracy, the swords of the Germans and the waves of the unknown ocean, without ever yielding or wavering; who had torn to pieces the Sullan constitution, overthrown the rule of the Senate, and furnished the defenseless and unarmed democracy with protection and arms by means of the struggle beyond the Alps. And he spoke not to the Roman public, whose republican enthusiasm had been long burnt down to ashes and dross, but to the young men from the towns and villages of Northern Italy, who still felt freshly and purely the mighty influence of the thought of civic freedom; who were still capable of fighting and dying for ideals; who had themselves received for their country in a revolutionary way from Caesar the citizenship which the Roman government had refused. . . . And when he, the leader and general of the popular party, summoned the soldiers of the people, now that conciliatory means had been exhausted and concession had reached its utmost limits, to follow him in the last, the inevitable, the decisive struggle against the equally hated and despised, equally perfidious and incapable, and in fact ludicrously incorrigible aristocracy, not an officer or a soldier could hold back. . . .

Few men have had their elasticity so thoroughly tested as Caesar, sole creative genius of Rome and the last produced by the ancient world, which accordingly followed the path he marked for it until its sun was set. . . . Caesar was thoroughly a realist and a man of sense; and whatever he undertook was pervaded and guided by the cool sobriety which is the most characteristic mark of his genius. . . . To this he owed the "marvelous serenity" which remained steadily with him through good and evil days; to this he owed his complete independence, uninfluenced by favorite, by mistress, or even by

friend. As a result of this clarity of judgment Caesar never formed illusions regarding the power of fate and the ability of man. . . . As occasionally the most sagacious men enter into a pure game of hazard, so Caesar's rationalism at some points made contact with mysticism. Such gifts could not fail to produce a statesman. From early youth, accordingly, Caesar was a statesman in the truest sense, with the highest aim which a man is allowed to set for himself—the political, military, intellectual, and moral regeneration of his own deeply decayed nation, and of the still more deeply decayed Hellenic nation joined to his own. The hard school of thirty years' experience changed his views as to how this aim might be reached, but his aim itself remained constant both in time of hopeless humiliation and of unlimited power, both when as demagogue and conspirator he stole toward it by paths of darkness, and when as joint ruler and then as sole monarch he worked at his task before the eyes of the world. . . . A born ruler, he governed the minds of men as the wind drives the clouds. . . .

Caesar was monarch, but he was never seized with the giddiness of the tyrant. He is perhaps the only one among the earth's great who in large matters and small never acted from impulse or caprice, but always according to his duty as ruler, and who might look back on his life and doubtless find erroneous calculations to deplore, but no false step of passion to regret. . . . Such was this unique man, so easy and yet so infinitely difficult to describe. His whole nature is transparent clarity. . . . The secret lies in its perfection. As a man no less than as a historical figure, Caesar occupies a position where the great contrasts of existence meet and balance. . . .

Caesar was the entire and perfect man . . . just because more than any other he placed himself amid the currents of his time, and because more than any other he epitomized the essential peculiarity of the Roman nation—practical aptitude as a citizen. . . . As the artist can paint everything save consummate beauty, so the historian, when once in a thousand years he encounters perfection, can only be silent. For normality is doubtless capable of being described, but only by the negative notion of the absence of defect. Nature's secret, whereby she combines normality and individuality in her most finished productions, is beyond expression. We can only deem fortunate those who beheld this perfection, and gain some faint conception of it from the reflected luster which rests imperishably on the creations of so great a nature. . . .

It is proper to . . . protest against the custom—common alike to simplicity and perfidy—of using historical praise and censure as phrases of general application with no regard for circumstances. The present case involves construing the judgment of Caesar into a judgment of what is called Caesarism. . . . In this sense the history of Caesar and of Roman Imperialism, with all the unsurpassed greatness of the master worker, with all the historical necessity of the work, is in truth a sharper censure of modern autocracy than could be written by the hand of man. According to the same natural law by which the smallest organism infinitely surpasses the most artistic machine, every constitution, however defective, which expresses the free will of the majority infinitely surpasses the most brilliant and humane absolutism; for the former is capable of growth and therefore living, while the latter is what it is and therefore dead.

This law of nature demonstrates itself all the more completely in the Roman military monarchy, in that under the impulse of its creator's genius and in the absence of all foreign pressures, that monarchy developed in purer form than in any similar state. From Caesar's time . . . the Roman system had only an external coherence, repeating itself only mechanically; while internally, even under Caesar it was utterly withered and dead. If in its early stages and above all in Caesar's own soul, the hopeful dream of combining free popular development and absolute rule was still cherished, the government of the highly gifted emperors of the Julian house soon taught men a terrible lesson in how far it was possible to hold fire and water in the same vessel.

Caesar's work was salutary and necessary not because it was or could be a blessing in itself. But given the social organization of antiquity based on slavery and utterly foreign to republican-constitutional representation, and under the organization of the urban constitution which during five hundred years had ripened into oligarchic absolutism, an absolute military monarchy was both a logical necessity and the least of evils. When the slave-holding aristocracy of Virginia and the Carolinas shall have carried matters as far as their predecessors in Sullan Rome, Caesarism will there too be legitimized at the bar of history; where it appears under other circumstances, it is at once a caricature and a usurpation. But history will not deny the true Caesar his due honor, because her verdict in the presence of bad Caesars may lead fools astray and give rogues occasion for lying and fraud. . . . [In the second edition, Mommsen added a note to this passage:] When this was written—in the year 1857—no one could foresee how soon the mightiest struggle and the most glorious victory as yet recorded in human annals would save the United States from this fearful trial and secure the future existence of an absolute self-governing freedom not to be permanently kept in check by any local Caesarism. . . .

Caesar, wherever he acted as a destroyer, only carried out the pronounced verdict of historical development. . . . With the same self-reliant genius that accomplished the regeneration of Rome, he undertook also the regeneration of the Hellenes and resumed the interrupted work of the great Alexander whose image, we may well believe, was never absent from Caesar's soul. . . . [He] created, out of a state without distinctive culture or cosmopolitan civilization, a new whole in which culture and state again met in the rich fullness of blessed maturity. These are the outlines which Caesar drew for this work, according to which he himself labored, and according to which posterity—for many centuries confined to the paths which this great man marked out—endeavored to work generally in accordance with the intentions of the illustrious master, if not with his intellect and energy. Little was finished, much was merely begun. Whether the plan was complete, those who venture to vie in thought with such a man may decide. We observe no material defect in what lies before us. Every single stone of the building is enough to make a man immortal, yet all combine to form one harmonious whole.

JOHN H. COLLINS

CAESAR AND THE CORRUPTION OF POWER

Not all scholars have seen Caesar in a favorable light. Men of the twentieth century have witnessed too many sawdust Caesars and ersatz emperors to be able to read Mommsen without skepticism. John H. Collins of Northern Illinois University is a distinguished classicist who recanted on Mommsen's Caesar. His essay on "Caesar and the Corruption of Power" is lively and personally revealing. Whether or not he is correct in his indictment of Caesar, Collins has overstated the role of Cleopatra who, after all, was not "the serpent of the Nile." Before she was born, Caesar had seen Eastern luxury and vice in Bithynia, and when he dallied with Cleopatra, the dictator was a middle-aged man of the world and not an impressionable youth. As for Caesar's high-handed behavior as master of Rome, the details come from questionable sources and ultimately stem from the propaganda of his assassins. Caesar as Lucifer is no more plausible than Caesar as Messiah.

The figure of Caesar offered us in Shakespeare's play does not easily harmonize with the Caesar of the Commentaries, that is to say, with the Caesar of "history." Shakespeare's Caesar is a vain, pompous, cantankerous, aging egoist. . . . Of the farseeing statesman, the military genius, the master leader of men, . . . Shakespeare gives scarcely a hint in the earlier acts of the play . . . It is only after the murder that Caesar assumes this shape of greatness.

Thou art the ruins of the noblest man
That ever lived in the tide of times.
The foremost man of all this world.

I well recall the vague questioning that filled my beginner's mind when, fresh from the strong impression of Shakespeare, "at the cost of many tears and some blood I purchased the knowledge of Latin syntax" through the medium of the *Gallic War.* It seemed there were two Caesars, a great and a small, a leader and a tyrant. Some years later I read for the first time the brilliant chapter of Mommsen and under his powerful influence, became an incurable Caesarian. . . .

Although the great Caesar, Mommsen's Caesar, is . . . victorious on all major fronts, the human, all-too-human Caesar of Shakespeare cannot quite be relegated to the unhistorical region of subjective imagination. Aside from the fact that Shakespeare commanded a knowledge of human nature deeper than that of any other man of whom we have record, the purely historical evidence in favor of his general vision is weighty and derived from many independent sources. The honorific titles and privileges, the arrogant utterances and acts, the contemptuous disregard of the great traditions of the Roman republic that one finds catalogued in every biography of Caesar go far toward justifying the final condemnation of Suetonius [a biographer and gossipmonger of the second century A.D.] — "it was felt that Caesar had misused despotic power and was justly cut down." . . .

Out of the last eighteen months of Caesar's life, and more particularly out of the last six months, we have reports of a series of sayings and incidents, mostly from the secondary writers, but the most important also from Cicero, demonstrating a contempt for the republic and a striving for kingly and even divine honors in crass contradiction of the ancestral ways. . . . Suetonius, whose judgment must not be undervalued, devotes five chapters to Caesar's arrogance and insults. . . . The overall impression is that of a grovelling adulation by the Senate in the heaping up of titles and extravagant honors, and of

From John H. Collins, "Caesar and the Corruption of Power," *Historia,* IV (1955), pp. 445–46, 452–53, 455–58, 461–62, 464–65. Reprinted by permission of Franz Steiner Verlag, publishers of *Historia.*

an excessive power-lust on the part of Caesar. His conduct passed beyond occasional tactlessness or petulance; it shows deliberate and habitual insolence. The assumption of the life-time dictatorship in January 44, in flat contradiction of all Roman constitutional tradition, and the slightly later scene on the Lupercalia were merely the climax of a long course of usurpation. . . .

As is well known, the assassination of Caesar was called by Goethe "the most senseless deed in all history," and the verdict has been generally accepted by modern students. But leaving aside the question of its sense or folly, I would point out that it was also the result of the most successful plot in all history. Some sixty men were members of the conspiracy; it was discussed weeks if not months in advance . . .—yet the secret was not betrayed. History records many an assassination and many a plot, but the assassination of Caesar is absolutely unique in its elaboration and success. For a comparable murder plot we must look to the twentieth century and the attempt on Hitler in July 1944. The analogy is suggestive. The attack on Hitler was made by men who had grown desperate and who saw no means other than political murder of serving their country or of saving what might yet be saved. Knowing their circumstances, we do not judge them as criminals. Is it quite certain that we know enough about the Roman situation of 44 B.C. to be able to reverse the unanimous sentence of those sixty senators?

In calling attention to the case of Hitler, I have no wish to set up a general comparison or to see in Caesar an ancient fascist. I mean only to emphasize the extraordinary intensity of the hatred he had brought upon himself, and the amazing solidarity of his enemies. Few men can have reached such a degree of human isolation. Caesar's loneliness has been remarked by many of his biographers; it is less often remarked how far he had moved in his last months from the human geniality of the years in Gaul. . . . The tragedy of Caesar lies not so much in the fact that he was murdered by his friends, as in the fact that in the end he had no friends left, and had become such a menace to all that the best thought of the day identified with liberty and patriotism that sixty men could be found ready to risk their lives to kill him.

Modern opinion of Caesar has naturally been strongly colored by modern condemnation of the old republican system. The liberty for which Cicero so longed and for which Cato laid down his life meant in practice the liberty of a few hundred men to parasitize the Mediterranean world, and the liberty of . . . gangsters . . . to terrorize the capital. . . . But such considerations cannot be called on to justify Caesar's ruthless trampling on established and venerable forms unless it can be shown that he himself had some genuine vision of a future Reichsstaat in which the general welfare would replace the old game played for money and prestige. Such a vision has indeed been attributed to him, but its documentation is regrettably inadequate. . . . It is difficult to avoid the feeling that Caesar was thinking about out-Alexandering Alexander [as he prepared to invade Parthia]. It is possible that the Ides of March forestalled a military shipwreck comparable with Napoleon's disaster in Russia. The sure realism of Caesar's Gallic period had given way to dreams of world conquest. . . .

It appears to the present writer that we may profitably accept the ancient tradition with less of modern subtlety and modern re-interpretation than has usually been applied. It is not so much the ancient sources as our modern ways of thought that must be critically scrutinized to reach the historical truth. Our four best witnesses—Romans, drenched in Roman mores—Caesar himself, Cicero, Sallust, and Suetonius . . . , all tell essentially the same story. It is the story of a noble, genial, incomparably gifted nature corrupted by absolute power, quite in the sense of Lord Acton's famous aphorism. And the corruption of power, in Caesar's case, was aggravated by circumstances of enormous temptation, adequate to account for the fall of an archangel. . . .

Once the [civil] war had begun, Caesar continued to seek a compromise peace and demanded no extra-constitutional powers as the price. All his overtures were rejected, and the war went on to the bitter end. It would be impossible to imagine circumstances more conducive to hardening him into a cynical contempt for human stupidity. A second important factor in effecting the visible change in Caesar's character was, I cannot but think, the influence of Cleopatra and of the atmosphere of oriental pomp and luxury that Caesar found in Egypt. . . . The evidence that Cleopatra was still an important factor in Caesar's plans at the time of his death is supported by Cicero, and Augustus, at least, took the matter seriously enough to order the execution, on no visible grounds, of the young Caesarion.[1] . . . It does neither Caesar nor Cleopatra justice to degrade this vast human drama to the level of a scandal. With good right did the Romans a few years later fear Cleopatra "as they had feared none other but Hannibal." [Tarn's phrase.] I have suggested above that the Ides of March may have saved Rome from a military disaster in the Parthian desert. Quite as possibly they may have saved Rome and Europe for the West. . . .

There is adequate evidence that Caesar underwent a major change in character and outlook in his last phase, a change of character marked by cynicism and arrogance. It was a change which grew out of his disillusionment with his fellow citizens and with his older political ideals. It is less true to say that he rejected the republic than to say that the republic rejected him. His enormous genius shattered itself upon the impossible task of making the republic fit to rule the empire, and he turned to despotism in contempt and perhaps in bitterness. . . . An important factor in the outlook of his last years was undoubtedly the influence of Cleopatra. It would be too much to say that Caesar had become "orientalized" or "un-Roman," but that the flesh-pots of Egypt had touched him not at all is improbable in itself and against the weight of the evidence. A progressive megalomania shows itself in his conduct after Thapsus, and particularly after Munda. The insight of Blake.

The strongest poison ever known
Came from Caesar's laurel crown,

is justified by the history of his astounding career. The judgment of his contemporaries was more accurate than that of most modern reconstructions, and though the good that he did lived after him, it lived by wills and forces other than his.

[1] Cleopatra claimed that Caesarion was Caesar's son, and Antony recognized the claim. As the adopted son of Caesar, Augustus could not tolerate a rival; he also killed Antony's oldest son. [Editor's note.]

SIR RONALD SYME

CAESAR: A MODERN VIEW

Sir Ronald Syme of the University of Oxford is the most respected living authority on the history of Rome. In influence, he must be ranked with Gibbon and Mommsen. Born in New Zealand, Syme brought a "colonial" irreverence for authority to the study of Roman history. Many British scholars had identified the Roman Empire with Britannia's world sway and transformed Augustus into a proper British gentleman. Mommsen believed that Augustus was sincerely concerned with republican ideals, and the great German had convinced most scholars that the factions of the late Roman republic were political parties in the nineteenth-century sense. However, Syme harkened to earlier masters and embraced the lapidary style and trenchant pessimism of Tacitus and Gibbon. His *Roman Revolution* (1939) was an epoch-making study of the collapse of the republic and the establishment of the new order of Augustus. Impatient with slogans and images, Syme views politics as a struggle of men for power and not a conflict of vague ideas: "Power and chance are the presiding divinities." In Britain and abroad, the influence of Syme has been great on the postwar generation of scholars and students.

In all ages, whatever the form and name of government, be it monarchy, republic, or democracy, an oligarchy lurks behind the facade; and Roman history, republican or imperial, is the history of the governing class. . . . During the civil wars every party and every leader professed to be defending the cause of liberty and of peace. Those ideals were incompatible. When peace came, it was the peace of despotism. . . . The political life of the Roman republic was stamped and swayed, not by parties and programmes of a modern and parliamentary character, not by the ostensible opposition between Senate and people, Optimates and Populares, nobles and new men, but by the strife for power, wealth, and glory. The contestants were the nobles among themselves, as individuals or in groups, open in the elections and in the courts of law, or masked by secret intrigue. . . . The Roman constitution was a screen and a sham. . . . The general had to be a politician, for his legionaries were a host of clients, looking to their leader for spoil in war and estates in Italy when their campaigns were over. But not veterans only were attached to his cause—from his provincial commands the dynast won to his allegiance and personal following . . . towns and whole regions, provinces and nations, kings and tetrarchs. Such were the resources which ambition required to win power in Rome and direct the policy of the imperial republic as consul or as one of the leaders. . . .

The leaders strove for prestige and power, but not to erect a despotic rule upon the ruins of the constitution or to carry out a real revolution. The constitution served the purposes of generals or of demagogues well enough. When Pompeius returned [in 62 B.C.] from the East, he lacked the desire as well as the pretext to march on Rome; and Caesar did not conquer Gaul in the design of invading Italy with a great army to establish a military autocracy. Their ambitions and their rivalries might have been tolerated in a small city-state or in a Rome that was merely the head of an Italian confederation. In the capital of the world they were anachronistic and ruinous. . . . The remedy was simple and drastic. For the health of the Roman people, the dynasts had to go. Augustus completed the purge and created the new state. . . .

In the autumn [of 50 B.C.] men began to speak of an inevitable war. Fortune was arranging the scene for a grand and terrible spectacle. Caesar would tolerate no superior, Pompeius no rival. Caesar had many enemies, provoked by his ruthless ambition, by his acts of arrogance towards other leaders—and by his support, when consul and proconsul, of the domination of Pompeius, who now, for supreme

power, seemed likely to throw over his ally. On December 1st Curio's proposal [to disband both armies] came up in the Senate again, revealing an overpowering majority against both dynasts. . . . Then followed debate in the Senate, public attempts at mediation and negotiation in private. On January 1st a proposal of Caesar was rejected and he was declared contumacious: six days later his province was taken from him. The Caesarian tribunes M. Antonius and Q. Cassius, their veto disregarded, fled from the city. A state of emergency was proclaimed. Even had Pompeius now wished to avert the appeal to arms, he was swept forward by uncontrollable forces, entangled in the embrace of perfidious allies: or, as he called it himself, patriotic submission to the needs of the commonwealth. The coalition may summarily be described as four ancient and eminent families, linked closely with one another and with the Catonian faction. . . . It was the oligarchy of Sulla, manifest and menacing in its last bid for power, serried but insecure. Pompeius was playing a double game. He hoped to employ the leading nobles to destroy Caesar, whether it came to war or not, in either way gaining the mastery. They were not duped—they knew Pompeius: but they fancied that Pompeius, weakened by the loss of his ally and of popular support, would be in their power at last, amenable to guidance or to be discarded if recalcitrant. The policy arose from the brain and will of Marcus Cato. His allies, eager to enlist a man of principle on their side, celebrated as integrity what was often conceit or stupidity and mistook craft for sagacity. They might have known better—Cato's stubborn refusal to agree to the land bill for Pompeius' veterans [in 61 B.C.] only led to worse evils and a subverting of the constitution. After long strife against the domination of Pompeius, Cato resolved to support a dictatorship, though anxiously shunning the name. Cato's confidence in his own rectitude and insight derived secret strength from the antipathy which he felt for . . . Caesar. . . .

The conquest of Gaul, the war against Pompeius and the establishment of the dictatorship of Caesar are events that move in a harmony so swift and sure as to appear pre-ordained; and history has sometimes been written as though Caesar set the tune from the beginning, in the knowledge that monarchy was the panacea for the world's ills and with the design to achieve it by armed force. Such a view is too simple to be historical. . . . As the artful motion

From Sir Ronald Syme, *The Roman Revolution* (Oxford, 1939), pp. 7, 9, 11, 15, 38, 41–43, 45–51, 53, 59. Reprinted by permission of The Clarendon Press.

of a Caesarian tribune had revealed, an overwhelming majority in the Senate, nearly four hundred against twenty-two, wished both dynasts to lay down their extraordinary commands. A rash and factious minority prevailed. . . . Upon Caesar they had thrust the choice between civil war and political extinction. But Caesar refused to join the long roll of Pompeius' victims. . . . If he gave way now, it was the end. Returning to Rome as a private citizen, Caesar would at once be prosecuted by his enemies for extortion or treason. They would secure lawyers reputed for eloquence, high principle and patriotism. Cato was waiting for him, rancorous and incorruptible. A jury carefully selected, with moral support from soldiers of Pompeius stationed around the court, would bring in the inevitable verdict. After that, nothing remained for Caesar but to join the exiled Milo at Massilia and enjoy the red mullet and Hellenic culture of that university city.

Caesar was constrained to appeal to his army for protection. At last the enemies of Caesar had succeeded in ensnaring Pompeius and in working the constitution against the craftiest politician of the day: he was declared a public enemy if he did not lay down his command before a certain day. By invoking constitutional sanctions against Caesar, a small faction misrepresented the true wishes of a vast majority in the Senate, in Rome, and in Italy. They pretended that the issue lay between a rebellious proconsul and legitimate authority. Such venturesome expedients are commonly the work of hot blood and muddled heads. The error was double and damning. Disillusion followed swiftly. Even Cato was dismayed. It had confidently been expected that the solid and respectable classes in the towns of Italy would rally in defence of the authority of the Senate and the liberties of the Roman people, that all the land would rise as one man against the invader. Nothing of the kind happened. Italy was apathetic to the war-cry of the republic in danger, skeptical about its champions. The very virtues for which the propertied classes were sedulously praised by politicians at Rome forbade intervention in a struggle which was not their own. . . . Caesar, it is true, had only a legion to hand; the bulk of his army was still far away. But he swept down the eastern coast of Italy, gathering troops, momentum and confidence as he went. Within two months of the crossing of the Rubicon he was master of Italy. . . .

Yet, even so, until the legions joined battle on the plain of Pharsalus, the odds lay heavily against Caesar. Fortune, the devotion of his veteran legionaries, and the divided counsels of his adversaries secured the crowning victory. But three years more of fighting were needed to stamp out the last and bitter resistance of the Pompeian cause in Africa and in Spain. "They would have it thus," said Caesar as he gazed upon the Roman dead at Pharsalus, half in patriot grief for the havoc of civil war, half in impatience and resentment. They had cheated Caesar of the true glory of a Roman aristocrat—to contend with his peers for primacy, not to destroy them. His enemies had the laugh on him in death. . . . That was the nemesis of ambition and glory, to be thwarted in the end. After such wreckage, the task of rebuilding confronted him, stern and thankless. Without the sincere and patriotic co-operation of the governing class, the attempt would be all in vain, the mere creation of arbitrary power, doomed to perish in violence. It was rational to suspend judgment about the guilt of the civil war. Pompeius had been little better, if at all, than his younger and more active rival, a spurious and disquieting champion of legitimate authority when men recalled the earlier career and inordinate ambition of the Sullan partisan who had first defied and then destroyed the Senate's rule. Each had sought armed domination. Had Pompeius conquered in battle, the republic could hardly have survived. A few years, and Pompeius the dictator would have been assassinated in the Senate by honorable men at the foot of his own statue. . . . [Caesar] expressed alarming opinions about the republic—"it was only a name: Sulla, by resigning supreme power, showed that he was an ignorant fellow." Caesar postponed decision about the permanent ordering of the state. It was too difficult. Instead, he would set out for the wars again, to Macedonia and to the eastern frontier of the empire. At Rome he was hampered: abroad he might enjoy his conscious mastery of men and events as before in Gaul. Easy victories—but not the urgent needs of the Roman people. About Caesar's ultimate designs there can be opinion, but no certainty. . . .

Brutus and his allies might invoke philosophy or an ancestor who had liberated Rome. . . . Dubious history and irrelevant. The liberators knew what they were about. Honorable men grasped the assassin's dagger to slay a Roman aristocrat, a friend and a benefactor, for better reasons than that. They stood, not merely for the traditions and the institutions of the free state, but very precisely for the dignity and the interests of their own order. Liberty and the laws are high-sounding words. They will often be rendered, on a cool estimate, as privilege and vested interests.

It is not necessary to believe that Caesar planned to establish at Rome a "Hellenistic monarchy," whatever meaning may attach to that phrase. The dictatorship was enough. The rule of the nobles, he could see, was an anachronism in a world-empire; and so was the power of the Roman plebs when all Italy enjoyed the franchise. Caesar in truth was more conservative and Roman than many have fancied; and no Roman conceived of government save through an oligarchy. But Caesar was being forced into an autocratic position. It meant the lasting domination of one man instead of the rule of the law, the constitution and the Senate; it announced the triumph soon or late of new forces and new ideas, the elevation of the army and the provinces, the depression of the traditional governing class. Caesar's autocracy appeared to be much more than a temporary expedient to liquidate the heritage of the civil war and reinvigorate the organs of the Roman state. It was going to last—and the Roman aristocracy was not to be permitted to govern and exploit the empire in its own fashion. The tragedies of history do not arise from the conflict of conventional right and wrong. They are more august and more complex. Caesar and Brutus each had right on his side.

5

THE CONVERSION OF CONSTANTINE

The conversion of the Roman emperor Constantine to Christianity marked a turning point in the history of the church. Arising from obscure beginnings in the first century, Christianity was often at odds with the Roman state over the public worship of the state gods, which to Romans was a token act of loyalty but to Christians was idolatry. Sporadically the church felt the scourge of persecution, and rulers as varied as Nero and Marcus Aurelius believed that Christians were subversive enemies of society. The first empire-wide persecution began in 250 under the emperor Decius. Many Christians died for their faith, but some bowed to the will of the state, and others purchased false certificates of submission. In 260 the emperor Gallienus halted all persecutions, restored confiscated property to the bishops, and gave the church legal protection as a religion recognized by the state. Though still a minority in the empire, the number of Christians was considerable, and the sect had acquired the respectability of a hereditary religion. Apostolic simplicity had vanished long before—many Christians were affluent and worldly-wise, and a few were members of the ruling class. Some Christians embraced the un-Christlike profession of soldiering, and the bishops formed a highly able organizational elite. The Christian leadership did not hesitate to ask a pagan emperor, Aurelian, to unseat the bishop of Antioch on charges of heresy and misconduct. Stronger than ever, the church was able to withstand its last great trial, a severe persecution under Diocletian. The emperor himself had little enthusiasm for the persecution, but his younger colleague Galerius was a rabid bigot and produced an oracle from Apollo to justify the attack on Christianity. The persecution lasted from 303 to 311 when Galerius changed his policy and restored toleration. In the Eastern provinces, bigotry had reigned supreme, but in the West Galerius' colleague Constantius had done little more than close churches. In 313 Constantius' son Constantine and his colleague Licinius agreed on complete freedom of religion for their subjects. This policy—the miscalled Edict of Milan—was aimed at their rival in the East, Maximinus Daia, who had succeeded Galerius but revived a brief persecution. Not only had the Christians emerged intact from a long and bitter ordeal, but they now had a formidable champion, for one of the emperors, Constantine, had become their patron. In 324 Constantine was sole emperor, and the Christians were the favored religious faction in the Roman Empire. From Constantine on, all Roman emperors (save Julian) were Christians, and Christianity was the state religion by the end of the fourth century. The triumphant church promptly persecuted pagans and heretics.

The man responsible for the crucial shift in imperial religious policy was Constantine, an ambitious and battle-hardened politician who fought his way to supreme power through bloody civil wars. At the end of the third century, the emperor Diocletian had established a governmental system in which power was shared among four men at the highest executive level in the state. Diocletian and his colleague Maximian were senior emperors with the title of Augustus; Constantius and Galerius were junior emperors, or Caesars. After twenty years in power, the Augusti resigned and Constantius and Galerius moved up, appointing in turn new Caesars. Without the strong leadership of Diocletian, the system of collective rule collapsed in a power struggle between the new generation of rival Augusti—Constantine and Licinius against Maximinus Daia and Maximian's son Maxentius. Even old Maximian returned to politics long enough to back his son and then quarrel with him, turn to Constantine and quarrel again, and die in an abortive revolt against Constantine, who had married his daughter Fausta. In 312 Constantine defeated Maxentius at the battle of the Milvian bridge, and Licinius destroyed Daia the following year. For a decade the victors ruled as co-emperors, but Constantine and Licinius eventually fell out and Constantine alone survived. Though he secured absolute power in 324, the emperor was distressed by the Arian controversy which split the Christians of the East. In 325 Constantine convened an ecumenical council at Nicaea and influenced its decision against the beliefs of Arius. Personally, the emperor felt that the theologians were splitting hairs when they argued over the equality of God the Father and the Son. However, his authoritarian mind could tolerate no dissent, and he insisted that all churchmen subscribe to the vague Nicene creed. Beyond conformity in the interest of unity, Constantine asked nothing more, and some of his closest clerical friends were Arians. As he aged, the emperor grew obsessed with religion and spent great sums on churches and religious establishments. His mother Helena had followed his lead and become a Christian; in Palestine, the elderly lady discovered what she believed to be the cross on which Jesus had died. Constantine's piety was partly the result of an uneasy conscience, for he had executed his son Crispus on a false charge of attempted seduction made by the empress Fausta, whom the emperor later had steamed to death in her bath. In 337, knowing that he was dying, Constantine risked baptism and died in the odor of sanctity.

The date of Constantine's conversion to Christianity and the extent of his sincerity have been the subject of much scholarly debate. The ancient sources Lactantius and

The Conversion of Constantine   71

Eusebius contradict each other, and Eusebius freely twisted history to glorify the church and its heroes. Even after he became a patron of Christianity in 312, the emperor did not cease using pagan devices, but this may be explained as political opportunism, since most of his subjects were pagans. The famous vision of a cross in the sky (if it happened) was not the only heavenly visitation in Constantine's life. In 310 Constantine had abandoned the cult of Hercules, the patron of his discredited father-in-law Maximian, and proclaimed his renewed devotion to Sol Invictus, the solar god of his father Constantius. Somewhere in Gaul, the ambitious Constantine glimpsed the sun god, according to a florid panegyrist:

. . . when you had turned aside to the most beautiful temple in the whole world, nay rather to a god present in actuality. For, O Constantine, you saw, I believe, your protector Apollo in company with Victory, offering you laurel crowns, each of which bears the presage of thirty years. . . . But why indeed do I say, "I believe"? You really saw the god and recognized yourself in the appearance of one to whom the prophecies of poets have declared that the rule of the whole world should belong.[1]

Did Constantine actually claim to have seen the solar deity together with the goddess Victoria? In the fourth century, such a hallucinatory episode is quite possible. As for Apollo, the sun god was the favorite deity of the armies and had been the official god of the empire, Sol Invictus, under Aurelian. Sol Invictus was also the patron deity of the family of Constantius, and Constantine's cross in the sky was close to the sun. In 312, in response to a dream, Constantine placed a symbol on his soldiers' shields and, later, on his own imperial standard—the letter X divided by a vertical line which looped to the right on top. To Christians, this was the Greek monogram of Christ (*Chi Rho*), but it could also be a solar symbol, for the overall impression is of a round and spoked figure. To the pagan soldier, the emblem was a sign of Sol Invictus, and the Senate at Rome attributed Constantine's victory at the Milvian bridge to "the god of heaven." However equivocal the emblem was, Constantine acknowledged the Christian god as the bestower of his victory, but in the beginning the emperor's notion of Christ was probably much like his view of Sol Invictus, another god of battle.

Few doubt that in 312 Constantine had a dream of the emblem, which later seemed so lucky in war, but an earlier daylight vision of a cross in the sky raises doubts. Eusebius insists that he received the story of the cross from the emperor himself under oath, but Constantine was an elderly priest-ridden man when he confided the miracle to the bishop. It is noteworthy that Constantine did not inform his son's Christian tutor, Lactantius, of the wonderful vision. Lactantius was not one to disparage miracles, but he was only told of the dream of the magic emblem. If he could see Apollo in Gaul, the emperor could surely imagine another vision in his pious old age. Since his father Constantius was tolerant toward Christianity, it is not unlikely that young Constantine had a vague interest in Christ though not to the exclusion of other gods before 312. In the third century, the emperor Severus Alexander had a statue of Jesus beside pagan saints in his private chapel, and the emperor

---

[1] Panegyrici Latini 6(7) 21.3–5, translated by J. Stevenson, *A New Eusebius* (London: Society for Promoting Christian Knowledge, 1960), p. 298.

Philip was so pro-Christian that some people claimed he was a member of the sect. After the victory of 312 Christ was Constantine's patron deity, and the emperor was consistently grateful for the rest of his life. However, Constantine was never a Roman equivalent of the saintly King Louis IX of France, and Julian the Apostate was a more truly religious man than his uncle Constantine ever was. Though he believed in the god who had given him victory and power, Constantine never embraced the moral regimen of Christianity and never considered the church superior to the authority of a Christian emperor. Surrounded by bishops and saturated with Christian propaganda, he took a great interest in ecclesiastical politics and policy making, but Constantine was no more Christlike than Henry VIII or the other despots whom history calls Christian.

The American historian Henry Adams made a useful, if sardonic, comment on the first Christian emperor:

Good taste forbids saying that Constantine the Great speculated as audaciously as a modern stockbroker on values of which he knew at the utmost only the volume; or that he merged all uncertain forces into a single trust which he enormously overcapitalized and forced on the market; but this is the substance of what Constantine himself said in his Edict of Milan in the year 313, which admitted Christianity into the Trust of State Religions. Regarded as an Act of Congress, it runs: "We have resolved to grant to Christians as well as all others the liberty to practice the religion they prefer, in order that whatever exists of divinity or celestial power may help and favor us and all who are under our government." The empire pursued power—not merely spiritual but physical—in the sense in which Constantine issued his army order the year before at the battle of the Milvian bridge: *In this sign conquer!* using the Cross as a train of artillery which, to his mind, it was. Society accepted it in the same character.[2]

In our present irreligious age, we often lose sight of what religion meant to men like Constantine: supernatural power, magic protection, and little ethical content. After his death, the Greek church canonized him as a saint, and the Roman Senate made him a god. However, Constantine did not really qualify for either distinction.

LACTANTIUS AND EUSEBIUS

CONSTANTINE: THE CHRISTIAN SOURCES

The contemporary Christian sources for the conversion of Constantine in 312 are Lactantius and Eusebius. A convert to Christianity, Lactantius was a professor of Latin rhetoric who had been employed by the emperor Diocletian and later became the tutor of Constantine's son, Crispus. A fervent and prolific apologist for the Christian faith, Lactantius wrote a bitter treatise, *How the Persecutors Died,* in which he described with great relish the unhappy deaths of emperors who had oppressed the church. Lactantius died about 320, and his account of the events of 312 is our earliest version. Eusebius of Caesarea was born a Christian and became a bishop.

[2] Henry Adams, *The Education of Henry Adams* (New York: The Modern Library, 1931), pp. 478–479.

Scholarly and enthusiastic, he was the first major historian of Christianity. He revised his *Ecclesiastical History* four times to conform to shifts in imperial policy; the final edition was published after Constantine had destroyed his colleague Licinius in 324 and before Constantine executed his own son Crispus in 326. Eusebius also wrote a florid *Life of Constantine* after the emperor's death in 337. A poor source, the biography of Constantine is exaggerated and inaccurate—it also contains the most sensational account of Constantine's conversion, which Eusebius admits would be unbelievable had he not heard it from the aged and pious emperor himself.

1. LACTANTIUS

A civil war broke out between Constantine and Maxentius. Although Maxentius kept himself within Rome because the soothsayers had foretold that if he went out of it he should perish, yet he conducted the military operations by able generals. In forces he exceeded his adversary, for he had not only his father's army . . . but also his own, which he had lately drawn together out of Mauretania and Italy. They fought and the troops of Maxentius prevailed. At length Constantine, with steady courage and a mind prepared for every event, led his whole forces to the neighborhood of Rome and encamped them opposite to the Milvian bridge. . . . Constantine was directed in a dream to cause the heavenly sign to be delineated on the shields of his soldiers, and so to proceed to battle. He did as he had been commanded, and he marked on their shields the letter X, with a perpendicular line drawn through it and turned round . . . at the top, being the cipher of Christ. Having this sign, his troops stood to arms. The enemies advanced, but without their emperor, and they crossed the bridge. The armies met and fought with the utmost exertions of valor and firmly maintained their ground. In the meantime a sedition arose at Rome, and Maxentius was reviled as one who had abandoned all concern for the safety of the commonweal, and suddenly, while he exhibited the Circensian games on the anniversary of his reign, the people cried with one voice, "Constantine cannot be overcome!" Dismayed at this, Maxentius burst from the assembly and, having called some senators together, ordered the Sibylline books to be searched. In them it was found that—"On the same day the enemy of the Romans should perish." Led

by this response to the hopes of victory, he went to the field. The bridge in his rear was broken down. At sight of that, the battle grew hotter. The hand of the Lord prevailed, and the forces of Maxentius were routed. He fled towards the broken bridge, but the multitude pressing on him, he was driven headlong into the Tiber. This destructive war being ended, Constantine was acknowledged as emperor, with great rejoicings, by the Senate and people of Rome.

2. EUSEBIUS IN 325

Thus when Constantine . . . an emperor, born of an emperor, a pious son of a most pious and prudent father, and Licinius, second to him—two God-beloved emperors, honored alike for their intelligence and their piety—being stirred up against the two most impious tyrants [Maxentius and Maximinus Daia] by God . . . , engaged in formal war against them, with God as their ally, Maxentius was defeated at Rome by Constantine in a remarkable manner, and the tyrant of the East [Daia] did not long survive him but met a most shameful death at the hand of Licinius, who had not yet become insane. Constantine, who was the superior both in dignity and imperial rank, first took compassion upon those who were oppressed at Rome and, having invoked in prayer the God of heaven . . . and Jesus Christ himself as his aid, advanced with his whole army, proposing to restore to the Romans their ancestral liberty. But Maxentius, putting confidence rather in the arts of sorcery than in the devotion of his subjects, did not dare to go forth beyond the gates of the city but fortified every place and district and town which was enslaved by him, in the neighborhood of

From Lactantius, *How the Persecutors Died*, 44, tr. William Fletcher, in *The Ante-Nicene Fathers*, ed. Alexander Roberts (Buffalo: The Christian Literature Co. (1886), Vol. VII, p. 318. [This passage was written not long after 314. Editor's note.]

From Eusebius, *Ecclesiastical History*, IX, 9.1–12, tr. Arthur C. McGiffert, in *A Select Library of the Nicene and Post-Nicene Fathers*, ed. Philip Schaff (Grand Rapids, Mich., 1952), Vol. I, pp. 363–64. Reprinted by permission of Wm. B. Eerdmans Publishing Company.

Rome and in all Italy, with an immense multitude of troops and with innumerable bands of soldiers. But the emperor, relying upon the assistance of God, attacked the first, second, and third army of the tyrant and conquered them all; and having advanced through the greater part of Italy, was already very near Rome. Then, that he might not be compelled to wage war with the Romans for the sake of the tyrant, God himself drew the latter, as if bound in chains, some distance without the gates, and confirmed those threats against the impious which had been anciently inscribed in sacred books — disbelieved, indeed, by most as a myth, but believed by the faithful — confirmed them, in a word, by the deed itself to all, both believers and unbelievers, that saw the wonder with their eyes. . . . Maxentius . . . with his soldiers and body-guards "went down into the depths like a stone," when he fled before the power of God which was with Constantine and passed through the river which lay in his way, over which he had formed a bridge with boats, and thus prepared the means of his own destruction. . . . Then, the bridge over the river being broken, the passageway settled down and immediately the boats with the men disappeared in the depths, and that most impious one himself first of all. . . . Constantine . . . entered Rome in triumph. Immediately all the members of the Senate and the other most celebrated men with the whole Roman people, together with children and women, received him as their deliverer, their savior, and their benefactor, with shining eyes and with their whole souls, with shouts of gladness and unbounded joy. But he, as one possessed of inborn piety toward God, did not exult in the shouts, nor was he elated by the praises, but perceiving that his aid was from God, he immediately commanded that a trophy of the Savior's passion be put in the hand of his own statue. And when he had placed it, with the saving sign of the cross in its right hand, in the most public place in Rome, he commanded that the following inscription should be engraved upon it in the Roman tongue: "By this salutary sign, the true proof of bravery, I have saved and freed your city from the yoke of the tyrant; and moreover, having set at liberty both the Senate and the people of Rome, I have restored them to their ancient distinction and splendor." And after this both Constantine himself and with him the emperor Licinius, who had not yet been seized by that madness into which he later fell, . . . with one will and mind drew up a full and most complete decree in behalf of the Christians.

3. EUSEBIUS AFTER 337

Being convinced . . . that he needed some more powerful aid than his military forces could afford him on account of the wicked and magical enchantments which were so diligently practiced by the tyrant, [Constantine] sought divine assistance, deeming the possession of arms and a numerous soldiery of secondary importance, but believing the cooperating power of Deity invincible and not to be shaken. He considered, therefore, on what god he might rely for protection and assistance. While engaged in this enquiry, the thought occurred to him, that, of the many emperors who had preceded him, those who had rested their hopes in a multitude of gods and served them with sacrifices and offerings, had in the first place been deceived by flattering predictions and oracles which promised them all prosperity, and at last had met with an unhappy end, while not one of their gods had stood by to warn them of the impending wrath of heaven; while one alone who had pursued an entirely opposite course, who had condemned their error, and honored the one supreme god during his whole life, had found him to be the savior and protector of his empire and the giver of every good thing. Reflecting on this and well weighing the fact that they who had trusted in many gods had also fallen by manifold forms of death without leaving behind them either family or offspring, stock, name, or memorial among men: while the god of his father had given to him, on the other hand, manifestations of his power and very many tokens: and considering further that those who had already taken arms against the tyrant and had marched to the battlefield under the protection of a multitude of gods, had met with a dishonorable end . . . , he judged it to be folly indeed to join in the idle worship of those who were no gods . . . and therefore felt it incumbent on him to honor his father's god alone. Accordingly he called on him with earnest prayer and supplications that he would reveal to him who he was and stretch forth his right hand to help him in his present difficulties. And while he was thus praying with fervent entreaty, a most marvelous sign appeared to him from heaven, the account of which

From Eusebius, *Life of Constantine*, I, 27–29, tr. Ernest C. Richardson, in *A Select Library of the Nicene and Post-Nicene Fathers*, ed. Philip Schaff (Grand Rapids, Mich., 1952), Vol. I, pp. 489–90. Reprinted by permission of Wm. B. Erdmans Publishing Company.

it might have been hard to believe had it been related by any other person. But since the victorious emperor himself long afterwards declared it to the writer of this history, when he was honored with his acquaintance and society, and confirmed his statement by an oath, who could hesitate to accredit the relation, especially since the testimony of after-time has established its truth? He said that about noon, when the day was already beginning to decline, he saw with his own eyes the trophy of a cross of light in the heavens above the sun and bearing the inscription, Conquer by This. At this sight he himself was struck with amazement, and his whole army also, which followed him on this expedition and witnessed the miracle. He said, moreover, that he doubted within himself what the import of this apparition could be. And while he continued to ponder and reason on its meaning, night suddenly came on; then in his sleep the Christ . . . appeared to him with the same sign which he had seen in the heavens and commanded him to make a likeness of that sign which he had seen in the heavens and to use it as a safeguard in all engagements with his enemies.

EDWARD GIBBON

CONSTANTINE: AN EIGHTEENTH-CENTURY VIEW

Edward Gibbon (1737–1794) was a pompous little man but a giant among historians, for it is generally agreed that his *History of the Decline and Fall of the Roman Empire* (6 volumes: 1776–1783) is the greatest historical work written in the English language. He saw history on a grand scale and composed a prose epic on the collapse of a world which he admired. Gibbon had vast learning, a sharp wit, and a rhythmic style. Out of a welter of chaotic sources he made a coherent whole, and his account of Rome down to the fall of the Western empire is still worth the attention of scholars. However, Gibbon's view of Imperial Rome was warped by his Tory political bias and his thorough dislike of Christianity. Born an Anglican, he became a Roman Catholic as a youth, but his father soon sent him to a Calvinist minister in Switzerland to cure the boy of "Papism." After a thorough exposure to theological disputes and church history, Gibbon acquired a horror of organizational Christianity and became a skeptical deist. Such an attitude was useful when Gibbon tackled the problem of Constantine, who was regarded by most people as a plaster saint. Though indebted to the work of ecclesiastical historians, Gibbon was a man of the Enlightenment and pounced with glee on the threadbare image of Constantine.

In the consideration of a subject which may be examined with impartiality but cannot be viewed with indifference, a difficulty immediately arises of a very unexpected nature—that of ascertaining the real and precise date of the conversion of Constantine. . . . The learned Eusebius has ascribed the faith of Constantine to the miraculous sign which was displayed in the heavens whilst he meditated and prepared the Italian expedition. The historian Zosimus maliciously asserts that the emperor had imbrued his hands in the blood of his eldest son before he publicly renounced the gods of Rome and of his ancestors. The perplexity produced by these discordant authorities is derived from the behavior of Constantine himself. According to the strictness of ecclesiastical language, the first of the Christian emperors was un-

From *The Decline and Fall of the Roman Empire* (Vol. I) by Edward Gibbon. Everyman's Edition, pp. 634–36, 646–51, 653–54. Reprinted by permission of E. P. Dutton & Co., Inc., and J. M. Dent & Sons Ltd.

worthy of that name till the moment of his death, since it was only during his last illness that he . . . was admitted by the initiatory rites of baptism into the number of the faithful. The Christianity of Constantine must be allowed in a much more vague and qualified sense; and the nicest accuracy is required in tracing the slow and almost imperceptible gradations by which the monarch declared himself the protector and at length the proselyte of the church. . . .

[Lactantius[1]] affirms with the most perfect confidence that in the night which preceded the last battle against Maxentius, Constantine was admonished in a dream to inscribe the shields of his soldiers with the *celestial sign of God*, the sacred monogram of the name of Christ; that he executed the commands of Heaven, and that his valor and obedience were rewarded by the decisive victory of the Milvian Bridge. Some considerations might perhaps incline a skeptical mind to suspect the judgment or the veracity of the rhetorician whose pen, either from zeal or interest, was devoted to the cause of the prevailing faction. He appears to have published his *Deaths of the Persecutors* at Nicomedia about three years after the Roman victory; but the interval of a thousand miles and a thousand days will allow an ample latitude for the invention of declaimers, the credulity of party, and the tacit approbation of the emperor himself, who might listen without indignation to a marvellous tale which exalted his fame and promoted his designs. In favor of Licinius, who still dissembled his animosity to the Christians, the same author has provided a similar vision of a form of prayer, which was communicated by an angel, and repeated by the whole army before they engaged the legions of the tyrant [Daia]. The frequent repetition of miracles serves to provoke, where it does not subdue, the reason of mankind; but if the dream of Constantine be separately considered, it may be naturally explained either by the policy or the enthusiasm of the emperor. Whilst his anxiety for the approaching day which must decide the fate of the empire was suspended by a short and interrupted slumber, the venerable form of Christ and the well-known symbol of his religion might forcibly offer themselves to the active fancy of a prince who reverenced the name, and had perhaps secretly implored the power, of the god of the Christians. . . .

The Christian fable of Eusebius, which in the space of twenty-six years might arise from the original dream, is cast in an . . . elegant mold. In one of the marches of Constantine he is reported to have seen with his own eyes the luminous trophy of the cross placed above the meridian sun and inscribed with the following words: By This Conquer. This amazing object in the sky astonished the whole army as well as the emperor himself who was yet undetermined in the choice of a religion: but his astonishment was converted into faith by the vision of the ensuing night. Christ appeared before his eyes and displaying the same celestial sign of the cross, he directed Constantine to frame a similar standard and to march with an assurance of victory against Maxentius and all his enemies. The learned bishop of Caesarea appears to be sensible that the recent discovery of this marvellous anecdote would excite some surprise and distrust among the most pious of his readers. Yet, instead of ascertaining the precise circumstances of time and place, which always serve to detect falsehood or establish truth; instead of collecting and recording the evidence of so many living witnesses who must have been spectators of this stupendous miracle, Eusebius contents himself with alleging a very singular testimony, that of the deceased Constantine, who many years after the event in the freedom of conversation had related to him this extraordinary incident of his own life and had attested the truth of it by a solemn oath. The prudence and gratitude of the learned prelate forbade him to suspect the veracity of his victorious master, but he plainly intimates that, in a fact of such a nature, he should have refused his assent to any meaner authority. This motive of credibility could not survive the power of the Flavian family, and the celestial sign . . . was disregarded by the Christians of the age which immediately followed the conversion of Constantine. . . .

The protestant and philosophic readers of the present age will incline to believe that, in the account of his own conversion, Constantine attested a wilful falsehood by a solemn and deliberate perjury. They may not hesitate to pronounce that in the choice of a religion his mind was determined only by a sense of interest, and that . . . he used the altars of the church as a convenient footstool to the throne of the empire. A conclusion so harsh and so absolute is not, however, warranted by our knowledge of human nature, of Constantine, or of Christianity. In an age of religious fervor the most artful statesmen are observed to feel some part of the enthusiasm which they inspire, and the most orthodox saints

---

[1] Gibbon did not believe that Lactantius wrote the tract on the deaths of the persecutors, but most modern scholars do. The point does not impair Gibbon's thesis. [Editor's note.]

assume the dangerous privilege of defending the cause of truth by the arms of deceit and falsehood. Personal interest is often the standard of our belief as well as of our practice, and the same motives of temporal advantage which might influence the public conduct and professions of Constantine would insensibly dispose his mind to embrace a religion so propitious to his fame and fortunes. His vanity was gratified by the flattering assurance that *he* had been chosen by Heaven to reign over the earth; success had justified his divine title to the throne, and that title was founded on the truth of the Christian revelation. As real virtue is sometimes excited by undeserved applause, the specious piety of Constantine, if at first it was only specious, might gradually by the influence of praise, of habit, and of example be matured into serious faith and fervent devotion. The bishops and teachers of the new sect, whose dress and manners had not qualified them for the residence of a court, were admitted to the imperial table. . . . Lactantius, who has adorned the precepts of the Gospel with the eloquence of Cicero, and Eusebius, who has consecrated the learning and philosophy of the Greeks to the service of religion, were both received into the friendship and familiarity of their sovereign; and those able masters of controversy could patiently watch the soft and yielding moments of persuasion and dexterously apply the arguments which were the best adapted to his character and understanding. Whatever advantages might be derived from the acquisition of an imperial proselyte, he was distinguished by the splendor of his purple, rather than by the superiority of wisdom or virtue, from the many thousands of his subjects who had embraced the doctrines of Christianity. Nor can it be deemed incredible that the mind of an unlettered soldier should have yielded to the weight of evidence which, in a more enlightened age, has satis-fied or subdued the reason of a Grotius, a Pascal, or a Locke. . . .

The sublime theory of the Gospel had made a much fainter impression on the heart than on the understanding of Constantine. . . . He pursued the great object of his ambition through the dark and bloody paths of war and policy; and after the victory he abandoned himself without moderation to the abuse of his fortune. Instead of asserting his just superiority above the imperfect heroism and profane philosophy of Trajan and the Antonines, the mature age of Constantine forfeited the reputation which he had acquired in his youth. As he gradually advanced in the knowledge of truth, he proportionably declined in the practice of virtue; and the same year of his reign in which he convened the council of Nicaea was polluted by the execution, or rather murder, of his eldest son. . . . At the time of the death of Crispus the emperor could no longer hesitate in the choice of a religion; he could no longer be ignorant that the church was possessed of an infallible remedy, though he chose to defer the application of it till the approach of death had removed the temptation and danger of a relapse. The bishops whom he summoned in his last illness to the palace of Nicomedia were edified by the fervor with which he requested and received the sacrament of baptism, by the solemn protestation that the remainder of his life should be worthy of a disciple of Christ, and by his humble refusal to wear the imperial purple after he had been clothed in the white garment of a neophyte. The example and reputation of Constantine seemed to countenance the delay of baptism. Future tyrants were encouraged to believe that the innocent blood which they might shed in a long reign would instantly be washed away in the waters of regeneration. . . .

JAKOB BURCKHARDT

CONSTANTINE: "THE EGOIST ROBED IN PURPLE"

The Swiss writer Jakob Burckhardt (1818–1897) was a renowned cultural historian and art critic. His stimulating study of *The Civilization of the Renaissance in Italy* (1860) was extremely influential and gave rise to the image of the "Renaissance Man." *The Age of Constantine the Great* (1852) is less well-known but is also characterized by Burckhardt's wide learning and an overactive historical imagination.

Like his friend Nietzsche, Burckhardt disliked the nineteenth century with its crass materialism, bourgeois hypocrisy, and love of power and success. His books are less histories than extended historical essays, crammed with insights and biases. A man of great sensitivity, Burckhardt believed that the past could be recaptured through informed intuition. His intuition told him that Gibbon had been too soft on Constantine.

Constantine's historical memory has suffered the greatest misfortune conceivable. . . . He has fallen into the hands of the most objectionable of all eulogists, who has utterly falsified his likeness. The man is Eusebius of Caesarea and the book his *Life of Constantine*. The man who with all his faults was always significant and always powerful is here presented in the guise of a sanctimonious devotee; in point of fact his numerous misdeeds are amply documented in a number of passages. Eusebius' equivocal praise is basically insincere. He speaks of the man but really means a cause, and that cause is the hierarchy, so strongly and richly established by Constantine. . . . Virtually throughout his life Constantine never assumed the guise of or gave himself out as a Christian but kept his free personal convictions quite unconcealed to his very last days. That Eusebius is fully capable of ignoring and concealing such a fact he himself reveals by his earlier characterization of Licinius, whom he claims straightway as a Christian emperor beloved of God as long as the war against Maximinus Daia is involved, though he must have known that Licinius was nothing else than a tolerant pagan. It is highly probable that his treatment of Constantine is of a similar character. [If this is true,] the odious hypocrisy which disfigures his character would disappear, and we should have instead a calculating politician who shrewdly employed all available physical resources and spiritual powers to the one end of maintaining himself and his rule without surrendering himself wholly to any party. It is true that the picture of such an egoist is not very edifying either, but history has had ample opportunity to grow accustomed to his like. . . .

Eusebius is no fanatic; he understands Constantine's secular spirit and his cold and terrible lust for power well enough and doubtless knows the true causes of the war [with Licinius] quite precisely. But he is the first thoroughly dishonest historian of antiquity. His tactic, which enjoyed a brilliant success in his own day and throughout the Middle Ages, consisted in making the first great protector of the church at all costs an ideal of humanity according to his lights and above all an ideal for future rulers. Hence we have lost the picture of a genius in stature who knew no moral scruple in politics and regarded the religious question exclusively from the point of view of political expediency. . . . He found it advisable to attach himself more closely to the Christians after this war, and . . . the elevation of Christianity to the position of state religion was thus consummated. But Constantine was a more honorable man than Eusebius; he rather allowed these events to transpire than intervened actively on their behalf, and as regards his own personal conviction, he enjoined definite beliefs upon his subjects as little as did Napoleon in his concordat. To pass for a Christian would, indeed, have been a great presumption on his part. Not long after the council of Nicaea he suddenly had Crispus, his excellent son by his first marriage and a pupil of Lactantius, put to death . . . and soon thereafter he had his wife Fausta . . . drowned in her bath. . . .

Attempts have often been made to penetrate into the religious consciousness of Constantine and to construct a hypothetical picture of changes in his religious convictions. Such efforts are futile. In a genius driven without surcease by ambition and lust for power, there can be no question of Christianity and paganism, of conscious religiosity or irreligiosity; such a man is essentially unreligious, even if he pictures himself standing in the midst of a churchly community. Holiness he understands only as a reminiscence or as a superstitious vagary. Moments of inward reflection, which for a religious man are in the nature of worship, he consumes in a different sort of fire. World-embracing plans and mighty dreams lead him by an easy road to the streams of blood of slaughtered armies. He thinks that he will be at peace when he has achieved this or the other goal, whatever it may be that is wanting to make his possessions complete. But in the

From *The Age of Constantine the Great* by Jakob Burckhardt, tr. Moses Hadas, pp. 260–262, 283, 292, 294–296, 301, 323. Copyright 1949 by Pantheon Books, Inc. Reprinted by permission of Random House, Inc., and Routledge & Kegan Paul Ltd.

Constantine: "The Egoist Robed in Purple"   **79**

meantime all of his energies, spiritual as well as physical, are devoted to the great goal of dominion, and if he ever pauses to think of his convictions, he finds they are pure fatalism. . . .

After the war with Maxentius . . . Constantine not only permitted the toleration of Christianity as a lawful religion, but spread abroad in the army an emblem which every man could interpret as he pleased but which the Christians would refer to themselves. The interlocked letters X and P, which form the beginning of the word Christ . . . , were introduced on the shields of the soldiers, we are told, even before the war. At the same time or later the same emblem, surrounded by gold and jewels, was attached to a large battle standard [labarum]. . . . The emblem even had its own tent into which the emperor mysteriously retired before any important affair. Should not all this signify an open profession? First of all it is to be noticed that Constantine employed this sign not among the populace but in the army. . . . Among the Gauls and Britons in the army there were certainly many Christians and indifferent pagans, and to the Germans the religion of their leader was a matter of no consequence. On his part it was an experiment that obliged him to nothing more than toleration, which was already in fact the rule in his previous domains and which he now extended to his conquests also. For him Christ may have rated as a god along with other gods, and the professors of Christ's religion along with the servants of the pagan deities. We shall not deny the possibility that Constantine developed a kind of superstition in favor of Christ, and that he may even have brought that name into some kind of confused relationship with the sun-god. But without doubt he was concerned exclusively with success; if he had met with a powerful resistance against XP in Italy, the symbol would quickly have disappeared from shields and standards. . . .

As soon as his lucid, empiric logic informed him that the Christians were good subjects, that they were numerous, and that the persecution could no longer have meaning in a reasonably governed state, his decision was taken. From the political point of view, the practical execution of his decision is wholly admirable. In his victorious hands the labarum was a physical representation at once of rule, of warlike power, and of the new religion.

The esprit de corps of his army, which had been victorious over one of the greatest armies of ancient history, hallowed the new symbol with the aura of the irresistible.

But the familiar miracle which Eusebius and those who copy him represent as taking place on the march against Maxentius must finally be eliminated from the pages of history. It has not even the value of a myth, indeed is not of popular origin, but was told to Eusebius by Constantine long afterwards and by Eusebius written up with intentionally vague bombast. The emperor indeed swore a great oath to the bishop that the thing was not imagined, but that he actually saw in heaven the cross with the inscription "In this sign thou shalt conquer," and that Christ actually appeared to him in a dream, and the rest; but history cannot take an oath of Constantine the Great too seriously, because among other things, he had his brother-in-law [Licinius] murdered despite assurances given under oath. Nor is Eusebius beyond having himself invented two-thirds of the story.

A great inconsistency in Constantine's outward bearing persists; he accepts the monogram of Christ as the emblem of his army and has the name of Jupiter on his triumphal arch erased, but at the same time he retains the old gods on his coins and especially the sun-god as his unconquerable companion, and on important occasions his outward conduct is entirely pagan. This cleavage rather increases than decreases in his latter years. But he wished to give direct guarantees to both religions, and he was powerful enough to maintain a twofold position. . . . A glimmer of edification still clings to Constantine because so many admirable Christians of all centuries have claimed him for their own. But this last glimmer must also vanish. The Christian church has nothing to lose in this terrible though politically grandiose figure, just as paganism would have had nothing to gain by him. . . .

Let us now turn from the egoist robed in purple who measures and calculates all that he does or suffers to be done by the aggrandisement of his own power. Contrasted with this essentially frivolous authority of the state is the great and selfless devotion of many who gave away all of their possessions during their lifetime in order to "dedicate themselves to God."

FERDINAND LOT

CONSTANTINE: "AN ACT OF SUPERSTITION"

Ferdinand Lot (1866–1952) of the Sorbonne was one of the great medieval scholars of recent years. He wrote extensively and his *End of the Ancient World and the Beginnings of the Middle Ages* (1926) is a classic study of a vitally important period of transition. With urbanity and vast learning, Lot made a lasting contribution to the study of history, and his view of Constantine is a useful antidote to Burckhardt's total condemnation.

The edict [of toleration in 313] is no proof at all that Constantine passed over to Christianity. Was he even ever a Christian? This has been denied. Apart from Christian apologists, historians agree in seeing the founder of the Christian empire as a shrewd statesman, at bottom a religious skeptic, or at most a deist. They bring together all the points which show that up to his final victory over Licinius, Constantine kept the balance between paganism and Christianity. The Christian symbols to which Christian apologetics appeal they match with others which are definitely pagan. If the coins from a certain date onwards bear the Christian monogram, we read on the reverse "soli invicto comiti," an invocation to the sun-god, the god of the emperors and of the army since Claudius II and Aurelian . . ., the god also of Constantine himself in his youth. If the emperor grants privileges to the Christian churches, he does the same for the temples. He does not give up his purely pagan title of Pontifex Maximus. He entrusts the public offices to pagans as well as to Christians. At court, he is surrounded by philosophers and rhetoricians who naturally were pagans. He closed down the temples, it will be objected, but two or three only . . . which had become houses of ill fame. He prohibited sacrifices even in the home, but that was because he wished to bring everything into the light and under his control. Even after 324, after he had become a Christian "as far as he could be," he was still careful in his attitude to paganism. At most he defended Christianity and became a Christian at the end of his life, because he felt in this religion a "force which he did not wish to leave outside the grasp of his government." He seized the already fully established power of the episcopate. He realized what unique functionaries he would gain for his service by attracting to himself the bishops. Constantine resembles Bonaparte signing the concordat to reconcile the revolution and the church and to turn the bishops into more submissive prefects. "Supreme pagan pontiff by right, he would easily be the real head of Christendom and would thus rule over men's souls as well as over their bodies."

These interpretations of Constantine's thought are ingenious and probable. But they may also be entirely erroneous. There is a mania for crediting great men of the past with deep laid political schemes the idea of which perhaps never occurred to them. We forget that they may have been visionaries, and in that case the motives which they obeyed are of so special a kind that every psychological reconstruction based on political sense is bound to come to grief. In the first place, to think of Constantine as a disillusioned skeptic is more than arbitrary. There were no freethinkers at this time. All men from the lowest to the highest social stratum were religious or at least superstitious, even Diocletian, even Marcus Aurelius. Constantine when pagan was necessarily religious, Constantine when Christian was most certainly so. We see him concerned as to the problems of Christ's essential nature and his relation to the Father. He endeavored to restore unity to the church. Had he been indifferent, he would calmly have suffered the followers of Athanasius and of Arius to excommunicate each other and to set church against church, confining himself to maintaining the public peace and preventing the disciples of Jesus from killing each other. Doubtless

From Ferdinand Lot, *The End of the Ancient World and the Beginnings of the Middle Ages,* tr. Philip and Mariette Leon (New York, 1953), pp. 29–35, 37, 39. Reprinted by permission of Barnes & Noble, Inc., and Routledge & Kegan Paul Ltd.

he would have done better to adopt this attitude. But he intervened, and if he did so, it was because he believed in Truth, in the Absolute. In his adherence to Christianity sincerity played a part, and that part must have been great.

If we hold that he adhered to Christianity from policy we must believe that he had some interest in doing so. But what was this interest? A sovereign like Henry IV [of France], absolutely unable to bring over to his own faith subjects the majority of whom profess a doctrine different from his, may think it necessary to abandon his individual sentiments in order to bring about that unity of belief he deems indispensable for the good functioning of society. In that case, Constantine, even if he had been Christian at heart, would have been obliged to turn pagan. In spite of its marvellous power of expansion during the first three centuries of its existence, Christianity was far from having conquered the majority of the inhabitants of the Roman world. . . . The country in which Constantine was born and which had been ruled by his father and until 312 by himself, counts amongst the least Christian in the empire. It is a paradox that the emperor Constantine, a Westerner, should have imposed a religion which was widespread only in the oriental provinces of the empire. If there was any emperor to whose interest it was to embrace Christianity, it was Galerius and Maximinus Daia, but these on the contrary were its worst enemies. To go over to Christianity was, for a sovereign who reigned in the West, an act of sheer folly politically. It was even dangerous, for the army, the only real force in the state, was wholly pagan, addicted above all to the worship of the sun, and was destined for a long time to remain so. It being proved that Constantine had everything to lose and apparently nothing to gain by embracing Christianity, there is only one possible conclusion, namely that he yielded to a sudden impulse, which we may call one of a pathological or supernatural order as we prefer. He staked his fortune on the god of the Christians. Men's minds were troubled by the tragic fate of all those who had persecuted the Christians. Galerius himself, their fiercest adversary, had just done public penance and was asking his victims to pray for his salvation.[1] At Rome, Maxentius, who had the more numerous army, had invoked by incanta-

tions all the powers of the pagan world, infernal and supernal, and his magic practices disturbed men's imaginations. For Constantine there was left the possibility of trying his luck by making an appeal to the new god, the god of the Christians. His conversion was an act of superstition.

But was he really converted? This brings us back to the question already raised. If by conversion is understood an inner moral reformation, the answer will no doubt be in the negative. But that is not the point at issue. The point is whether the emperor, after his victory over Maxentius, gave any external official signs of his adherence to the new faith. These signs are indisputable. At the moment of engaging in battle with his rival Maxentius, Constantine was not content with a mental prayer to the god of the Christians but had the symbol [XP] engraved on his soldiers' shields. But to make use of this talisman was to enter on an irrevocable compact with the deity who granted victory. After that it was impossible to draw back without risking the wrath of heaven. On the day after the victory . . . he allowed the wholly pagan Senate to offer him a statue as a symbol of his divinity, but he had a cross put in its hand. . . . He constantly intervenes in the affairs of the church; for example, in the quarrel between the Catholics and the Donatists in Africa on the very day after his triumph over Maxentius. He calls together the council of Nicaea . . . the holding of which coincides with his [twentieth year as emperor]. Only twenty years separate this ceremony from Diocletian's triumph at Rome, and yet an abyss yawns between these two dates. He undertakes propaganda. He invites his subjects to become converted to Christianity; he distributes presents of gold and silver pieces with Christian designs. He will write to his Persian rival Sapor to beg him to protect the Christians and to induce him to become a Christian himself. He becomes aggressive. He condemns the worship of Apollo whose oracle had let loose the persecution of Diocletian. . . . He upbraids his soldiers for sacrificing to Jupiter Capitolinus and brings upon himself the scorn of the Senate and the Roman people who had in large majority remained pagan. He forbids (after 330) functionaries to offer sacrifices to the gods in official ceremonies. . . . It is true also that he received baptism only on his deathbed. . . . But in the fourth century it was far from unusual not to ask for baptism until reaching adult age. Performed *in extremis*, it was considered a sure means to eternal salvation.

[1] Not really. In his final illness in 311, Galerius halted the persecution on the grounds that the Christians were too obstinate to be converted to "proper" piety. In return for this clemency, he asked them as loyal Romans to pray for his health and the welfare of the state. [Editor's note.]

But the most striking manifestation of the emperor's sentiments is the foundation of Constantinople. . . . Having triumphed in a battle in which his rival [Licinius] put himself into his hands, Constantine owed the god of victories a striking sign of his gratitude. He showed the latter by transporting his capital from that Rome which was infected with an incurable paganism to a new city which was wholly Christian. . . . Constantine's conversion is the most important fact in the history of the Mediterranean world between the establishment of the hegemony of Rome and the setting up of Islam. To it is due the triumph of Christianity, which by transforming human psychology has dug an abyss between us and antiquity. Since the adoption of Christianity we have been living on a different plane.

NORMAN H. BAYNES

CONSTANTINE: A RECENT VIEW

Norman H. Baynes (1877–1961) of the University of London was a recognized authority on Byzantine history. His view of the conversion of Constantine was presented in the Raleigh Lecture on History in 1930.[1] The following passage is from the final chapter in the *Cambridge Ancient History* (12 volumes, 1922–1939), a monumental work of collective scholarship which is dated in parts but still indispensable for all students of ancient history.

Pope Marcellus, elected in 307, who was a rigorist, was opposed by a party which championed a more liberal treatment of [Christians who had renounced their faith during the recent persecution], and the two sections of the church met in bloody conflicts in the streets of the capital. In defence of public order Marcellus was banished by Maxentius. On April 8, 308 Maxentius permitted the election of Pope Eusebius, but he, too, met with opposition and was banished to Sicily. On July 2, 311 Miltiades was consecrated as bishop, and now Maxentius went farther than Galerius had done in his edict of toleration issued in the spring of the same year and restored to the church the property which had been confiscated during the persecution. It is important to realize that Maxentius in banishing two bishops was but doing his duty in maintaining order within the city. When Constantine marched upon Rome it was not to free the Christians from religious persecution.

Constantine as Caesar naturally continued to acknowledge Hercules as his official patron, especially when . . . Constantine married Fausta, Maximian's daughter, and received from his father-in-law the title of Augustus. But with the treachery and death of Maximian in A.D. 310, a Herculian title to imperial power became impossible: some new basis must be found for Constantine's authority. Thus the panegyrist forthwith explains, what had not been realized previously, that Constantine was connected with the family of the heroic third-century emperor Claudius Gothicus. What the precise relationship may have been the orator discreetly does not seek to determine: the essential point to bring home to his hearers was that the derivation of Constantine's title from the grant of the discredited Maximian was nothing but an error. Already there had been two emperors in his family; Constantine was *born* an emperor. He alone of all his colleagues was one of a dynastic line. The fiction prevailed: the dynasty of the Second Flavians was securely founded. With the change in the title to the throne was associated a change in the emperor's religious allegiance. He now returns to the sun-worship of his Balkan ancestors, and henceforth Sol Invictus—Apollo—becomes his divine patron. Constantine's Herculian past is buried. This has been

[1] Norman H. Baynes, "Constantine and the Christian Church," *Proceedings of the British Academy*, Vol. XV (1929), pp. 341–42.

From Norman H. Baynes in *The Cambridge Ancient History* (Cambridge, Eng., 1939), Vol. XII. pp. 679–85; 698–99. Reprinted by permission of the Cambridge University Press.

called Constantine's first conversion. The new imperial faith is duly celebrated in the panegyric delivered at Trèves after the death of Maximian. The orator gives free rein to his fancy and imagines the appearance to the emperor of Apollo in his temple to which Constantine has made his pilgrimage. . . . No small importance has been attached to this vision by some scholars: it has been interpreted as the model on which the later Christian vision was fashioned. This is to do too much honor to the panegyrist's invention. . . .

As Licinius becomes the ally of Constantine, so Maxentius and [Daia] are drawn together. The revolt in Africa suppressed, his corn supplies secured, Maxentius can shelter behind the walls of [Rome]. . . . In 312 Constantine . . . decided to march against the "tyrant" who held the Western capital. There follows the lightning campaign which ended at the Milvian Bridge. From Gaul Constantine struck across the Alps: he left behind him troops to guard the frontier of the Rhine, and though we can form no precise numerical estimate of the strength of the army of invasion, it was less than 40,000 men. Maxentius, we are told, had in Italy some 100,000 soldiers, though many of these remained with the "tyrant" in Rome. . . . Constantine's great fear was that Maxentius would not quit Rome. It was the guardians of the Sibylline books who achieved for Constantine that which he himself would have been powerless to enforce. Maxentius determined to leave to his generals the command of his forces. . . . In the first encounter the soldiers of Maxentius were victorious. Then "Constantine moved all his forces nearer to the city and encamped in the neighborhood . . . of the Milvian Bridge." The real difficulty of the battle, if we accept this statement of Lactantius, is to understand how it was that, in face of the superior numbers of Maxentius, Constantine was allowed to execute this flanking movement unmolested. Are we to understand a previous retreat and a wide detour? Just before dawn on October 28 "Constantine was sleeping when he was bidden to mark . . . on the shields of his men the sublime sign of God and thus engage the enemy. He did as he was bidden and marked on the shields the letter X with a line drawn through it and turned round at the top, i.e. Christus." Maxentius on the same day, . . . ordered that the Sibylline books should be consulted: the answer was given that on that day the enemy of the Romans would perish. The battle was already begun when Maxentius, assured

of victory, joined his army. Constantine with like confidence threw his cavalry against the enemy, and his infantry followed. It was a bitterly contested struggle, but when the lines of Maxentius broke they could not retreat, for the Tiber ran close behind them. The bridge of boats by which they had crossed gave way under the press, and Maxentius perished with the fugitives.

Constantine as victor entered the Western capital. Against the advice of the augurs, in despite of his military counsellors, unsupported by the troops of Licinius, with incredible audacity Constantine had risked everything on a single hazard—and won. How shall that success be explained? Constantine himself knew well the reason for his victory: it had been won "by divine instigation," by a "courage" which was no mere human valor, but was a mysterious force which had its origin in God. And as the ground of that conviction tradition has repeated the story of the Vision of the Cross athwart the afternoon sun—a vision which came to Constantine, it seems, while he was still in Gaul before he began his march into Italy. For that Vision of the Cross we have no contemporary evidence: indeed our only evidence is the assertion of Eusebius, made after Constantine's death in the *Life of Constantine*, that the emperor had on his oath assured him of the fact. No mention of that vision occurs in any of the editions of the *Church History* of Eusebius: this of course proves nothing: Eusebius did not come into close contact with Constantine until A.D. 325, which is the probable date of the last edition of his *History*. It has been contended that the whole account is an interpolation of the Theodosian period, but that contention is at present unproven. In the year 351 Constantius [II] was granted a vision of the Cross in the heavens and it was then remarked that the son was more blessed than the father: Constantine had but found in the earth the true Cross: Constantius had seen it in the sky. Does this denote ignorance of the story of Eusebius or a politic denial of Eusebius' statement? Who shall say? The one thing which is critically illegitimate is to treat the account given by Lactantius of the dream of Constantine before the walls of Rome as though it described the same vision as that related by Eusebius. In recent discussions the two quite distinct divine interventions have at times been confused. But even though at present the historical student may be forced to conclude any discussion of the Eusebian report with a judgment of "not proven or disproven," to the present writer it appears that the account of the church historian is at least a true reflection of the emperor's own thought—or at least of his afterthought. Victory had been promised him by the god of the Christians: he had challenged the Christian god to an Ordeal by Battle and that god had kept his pledge. This belief of Constantine remains of fundamental significance for the understanding of the policy of the reign. . . .

The solar imagery of an earlier religious conviction is retained because Constantine is a member of a dynasty, and that solar imagery has become a part of a dynastic heraldry which proclaims an inherited title to imperial power. The student must therefore be prepared to recognize a conscious ambiguity in the acts of Constantine—an ambiguity necessarily arising from the ambiguous position of a Christian emperor ruling a pagan empire and bound to a pagan past. . . . In any attempt to recover and interpret the thought of Constantine, it must never be forgotten that he is a Roman emperor and a statesman. The emperor's ecclesiastical policy is a part of his imperial statesmanship, for that statesmanship was based upon the conviction of a mission in the service of the Christian god. Thus Christian theology may become a danger if it threatens to create disunion amongst the faithful. The dispute between Arius and his bishop is for Constantine an idle enquiry on points of the smallest consequence. Other Christian rulers have shared his outlook. We are reminded of the contempt of Elizabeth of England for the disputes of the German Protestants concerning the omnipresence of the body of Christ: to the Queen these were "unprofitable discussions." . . . Constantine's refusal to enquire curiously how bishops might interpret the creed of Nicaea provided only that they accepted it recalls Elizabeth's denial that she sought "to make a window into men's souls." . . . [In many respects Constantine followed in the footsteps of his pagan predecessors, but] there is none the less at this time a break and a turning-point in Roman history; the first Christian emperor was, indeed, as [the historian] Ammianus described him, . . . a revolutionary. Constantine sitting amongst the Christian bishops at the ecumenical council of Nicaea is in his own person the beginning of Europe's Middle Age.

The Middle Ages

400-1250

INTRODUCTION

Somewhere around A.D. 400, a complex series of changes began to unfold to mark the opening of a new epoch in human history. In the seventeenth century, the term "Middle Ages" was coined to designate this new era. As is their way, historians have seldom agreed in their interpretations of the nature and significance of the Middle Ages. However, the labors of several recent generations of historians of this age have demonstrated that the period is of greater significance than was formerly believed. No longer can one dismiss it as a "dark age," marked only by violence, ignorance, superstition, and misery; a modern student cannot accept Voltaire's advice that "it is necessary to know the history of that age only to scorn it." Rather, he must approach the era as one which produced a remarkable series of positive achievements vitally related to all historical development since the Middle Ages.

It is no simple task to state briefly the fundamental place of the Middle Ages in the total historical continuum. At considerable risk of oversimplification, let us assume a bold perspective that has special relevance to the purposes of this volume. The Middle Ages was a pivotal period in history because this era produced for the first time a Western European civilization which since the Middle Ages has exerted a profound influence on the entire world. Prior to the Middle Ages, Western Europeans had developed no distinctive pattern of culture. Across the greater part of history, they had existed on the fringe of the civilized world, occasionally being drawn into the sphere of more highly developed peoples to benefit from their achievements, but rarely contributing anything of a positive nature. Then, almost suddenly, about 1500 years ago, something new began to appear in history — a dynamic civilization distinctly a product of Western Europe's people and environment, a mode of life different from those existing among all other inhabitants of the earth. The continued development of this new civilization, its impact on other peoples, and their reaction to it have been major — even dominant — themes in history since the Middle Ages.

The historical "problems" that follow will reflect certain aspects of the genesis of the "first Europe." Before involving ourselves in these issues, it might serve a useful purpose to indicate in broad terms the central characteristics of the medieval period. These points may help to focus attention on the achievements of the epoch and to establish a sense of the processes which produced these results.

The Middle Ages began with a radical — some would call it catastrophic — dislocation of an established, highly developed pattern of civilization. For several centuries prior to A.D. 400, the historical scene had been highlighted by a complicated chain of events tending always toward the unification of the lands and peoples around the Mediterranean Sea, a process that culminated at the beginning of the Christian era in the creation of the Roman Empire. By the third century A.D., the Roman Empire began to suffer internal maladies that endangered the unity of the Mediterranean world. In spite of efforts to correct these ills, the fabric of classical Mediterranean civilization continued to weaken until finally it faced a crisis it could not resolve. This crisis took the form of a vast movement of peoples into the Mediterranean area, a disturbance which historians call the "barbarian invasions."

The barbarian assault on the weakened Mediterranean world produced a world-shaking consequence: it split a unified culture into three distinct cultural areas. During the fifth and sixth centuries, Germanic barbarians established themselves as masters of the western provinces of the Roman Empire; in the process, they destroyed the Roman imperial regime there and set the stage for a new mode of life. Hardly had the Germanic intrusion into the Mediterranean world abated when another major barbarian assault began. Early in the seventh century, the impoverished, disunited nomads of Arabia were suddenly welded into a potent force by the new religion of Islam, proclaimed by Mohammed (c. 570–632). During the century following Mohammed's death, the adherents of the new faith conquered a vast empire reaching eastward far into Asia and westward across North Africa to Spain. A large segment of the old Roman Empire — Syria, Palestine, Egypt, North Africa, and

Spain—passed into the hands of the Muslims. The assaults of the Germans and the Arabs had compressed the Roman Empire into a small bloc of territory, embracing the Balkans, Asia Minor, and a few outposts in Italy. Although the emperors who ruled this area from the "second Rome" at Constantinople still insisted that eternal Rome lived on, the shock of the barbarian invasions had altered the whole pattern of life within this remnant of the Roman Empire. It has become customary to call this new entity the Byzantine Empire, a designation that signifies the passing of the old Roman Empire which had been the outward embodiment of the unified civilization of the Mediterranean Basin.

By 750, the Mediterranean Sea had ceased to serve as a high road across which flowed a multitude of forces uniting the destinies of the peoples who dwelt on and near its shores. It had now become a boundary zone, across which three distinctive groupings of peoples—the Muslims, the Byzantines, and the Germanic Western Europeans—faced each other, often in a hostile posture. Each was now set on a unique historical course. Beyond question, a new epoch in history had begun. While recognizing the vast significance of the tripartition of the Mediterranean world at the beginning of the Middle Ages, we must note that the three new cultures shared certain common characteristics which were to have a major bearing on their future development. First, each retained in varying degrees a precious inheritance from the dying classical world, a patrimony that provided models of civilized life upon which they could pattern their own youthful efforts to shape the future. Second, religion—in the form of Christianity and Islam—emerged out of the chaos of disintegrating classical civilization as the dominant force in life, providing meaning for human existence and inspiring constructive action in the face of chaos. As heirs of classical civilization and children of God (or Allah, as the Muslims named God), the peoples moving to the center of history at the outset of the Middle Ages were provided with potent forces to inspire their advance into the future.

A proper study of the Middle Ages ought to observe with equal emphasis the development of all three of the successors to the classical world. But we have decided to focus our attention on the shaping of the "first Europe." This is a saga centering around what the Germanic barbarians did with their Christian-classical heritage within the geographical confines of Europe.

The first stages of Europe's emergence were hardly auspicious. For several centuries following the dismemberment of the Roman Empire, the West was plunged into a "dark age." Compared with the preceding classical age or with contemporary Islamic and Byzantine cultures, the Germanic West was appallingly backward. From the fifth until the tenth century, political chaos, economic decline, cultural barbarization, and spiritual impoverishment characterized the European scene. The only relief was provided by a brief but abortive flurry in the eighth and early ninth century, when a Frankish dynasty, the Carolingians, made a premature effort to revitalize European society. However, despite the general atmosphere of decline and confusion, this first painful period of the Middle Ages held its own significance.

The Middle Ages

Step by step, the Europeans fashioned out of Germanic practices, Christianity, and the classical heritage basic institutions and a value system suited to the needs and capabilities of Europe's peoples. By the tenth century, this new pattern of life, unique to Europe, had been fairly well articulated. The acceptance of these modes of existence, the conduct of life within their limits finally assured the stability that for so long had been lacking in the West, and provided the departure point for a surge of creative activity which brought the "first Europe" to maturity during the eleventh, twelfth, and thirteenth centuries.

Where had the Europeans found their moorings? At the political and economic level of life, the answer lies in feudalism and manorialism. Painfully shaped out of Germanic and Roman precedents, these two institutions tended to fragment society into tiny, self-contained units. In this lay their strength, for the talents of the Europeans were not yet well enough developed to manipulate large groupings of people or to construct a complex interdependent economy. Feudalism succeeded in establishing a basic political order in society, and manorialism supplied an adequate material base for society. Without these conditions, any progress was impossible. Fragmented at the political and economic level, Europeans found a common ground in religion and culture. The faith that had swept to victory in the late Roman Empire, now modified to fit the situation in Europe, provided all Europeans with a common moral code, a common mode of worshiping God, and above all, a common purpose in life. It had required great effort to force Christianity down through all levels of Europe's society and to draw all people into the Church in a meaningful way. By the tenth century, success had been great enough to assure a shared system of values and world view among peoples otherwise isolated from one another. Above all else, the religious impulse had sustained cultural life and had oriented creative men in a common direction. By the tenth century, Europe's scholars and artists shared a precious body of knowledge carefully gleaned from classical culture and the early Church fathers. They had developed an educational system capable of transmitting this heritage from generation to generation, and they possessed the linguistic and artistic skills to permit a modest amount of self-expression. Their cultural horizons were narrowed by concentration on religious ends, but that same religion supplied stimulation for creative effort in an environment lacking any other source of inspiration.

Thus, by the tenth century, the basic ingredients of European culture had been established. The main actors in society were feudal nobles, churchmen, and serfs. Life gravitated around the noble's castle, the manorial village, the local church, and the monastery. Its conduct was regulated by feudal contract, manorial custom, and church rules. Over all presided a Christian world view which made this life a testing period in the eyes of God, whose omnipotent hand was always present to extend or withhold saving grace; only in the next world would the real prize come to man.

It was from this modest base that the "first Europe" grew to maturity. The maturing process occurred at a rapid pace between the eleventh and the thirteenth centuries, which certainly must be counted among the great creative ages in all history. A thick volume would be needed to describe adequately the surge of activity that filled these centuries and produced an amazing range of achievements. Such a description would always center around one theme: how Europeans realized the potential present in the institutions and ideals that had been established with such great effort between the fourth and tenth centuries.

If one wishes to extract the essential lines of development from the rich and complex details of the history of the period extending from the tenth to the thirteenth centuries, he must concentrate on a few basic themes. One such theme was the successful attempt by kings to exploit their rights as feudal lords to consolidate territorial states within which there were perfected courts of law, legal systems, financial systems, royal armies, and specialized officials capable of rendering positive services to all subjects living within these states. A second major feature of the High Middle Ages was economic expansion. Land clearance, improved agricultural techniques, and population growth produced a notable increase in agricultural production. Simultaneously, commercial activity, involving exchange both with non-European areas and within Europe, expanded at a rapid rate. Commerce bred industrial production. As the High Middle Ages proceeded, an ever-increasing number of people concentrated in cities, many of them newly founded in this era. This new class of city dwellers, called the bourgeoisie, created a wide range of new institutions suited to the mode of life prevailing in the cities. A money economy developed to meet the demands created by the expanded exchange of a greater number of products. At all levels of society, an urge was generated to accumulate wealth and to convert it into greater wealth; this essentially capitalistic spirit threatened to obliterate the older economic ideal of subsistence production. A third significant aspect of the history of the High Middle Ages was an energetic religious revival. Its facets were many: the effective centralization of Church administration under papal control, the codification of Church law, the definition of doctrine, the standardization of religious worship, the purification of the moral life of the clergy and the laity, the deepening of spiritual life, and the elimination of many forms of lay control over religious life. All these lines of development pointed toward a single end: to make the Church into a universal community capable of commanding the prime allegiance of all Europeans and of directing their lives toward the service of God. That goal was nearly achieved by the thirteenth century. Few other institutions in all history have exerted greater authority or commanded greater respect than did the Church of the age of Pope Innocent III. A fourth notable facet of the history of the era extending from the tenth to the thirteenth century was cultural enrichment. Again, the scene was characterized by a variety of developments: the infusion of a vastly increased amount of classical learning into the European cultural scene, the attempt of the scholastics to integrate this "new learning" into the Christian value system, the increasing reliance on human reason as a source of knowledge, the emergence of the universities, the development of a secular culture suited to the ideals of the increasingly refined nobility and of the bourgeoisie, and the perfection of the vernacular languages as a mode of expression. These complex developments produced a rich harvest of

The Middle Ages

cultural monuments; one thinks immediately of the *Summae* of the scholastic philosophers, Gothic cathedrals, the lyric poetry of the troubadors, the romances, the religious drama, *fabliaux,* and the feudal epics, each of which deserves respect as a noble reflection of a civilized society.

The growing vigor of European society was evidenced by its changing relationship with the outside world, especially with Byzantium and Islam. During the long era of its infancy, European society had been on the defensive in the face of non-Europeans. Moreover, European culture was unmistakably inferior, a situation that often led to European borrowing from foreign cultures without giving anything in return. Between the tenth and the thirteenth century, this situation changed radically. Europeans began to expand outward and to make their mode of existence felt abroad. The offensive thrust was many-sided. Missionaries carried Christianity into the Slavic and Scandinavian areas. Noble warriors and peasant colonists pushed eastward to occupy new lands, carrying with them European ways of life. European merchants made their presence felt increasingly in the rich markets of the Levant. Italian fleets asserted an ever-increasing dominance over the Mediterranean Sea. The most impressive display of Europe's new offensive capability was a military-religious assault on Islam, a crusading movement which re-established European control over most of Spain and established a Christian state in the Holy Land that lasted from 1099 until 1291. A by-product of the crusading movement was the European capture of Constantinople in 1204 and the subsequent Western domination of the Byzantine Empire for a considerable part of the thirteenth century. These broadening contacts with foreign cultures greatly enriched European life, especially economically and culturally. Equally significant, however, was the impact of European culture abroad. In this expansion of medieval Europe, lay the beginnings of a major theme in the future history of the world.

By the thirteenth century, the "first Europe" had been established and had taken a notable place in the world scene. The discerning student of history ought to ask certain questions about this new cultural entity. What were its essential features? Wherein did it differ from all other cultures? What constituted its vitality? These questions can only be answered if one is willing to undertake a thorough study of medieval European history and to compare what he discovers with the essential features of other cultures—past, contemporary, and future. This essay will not attempt to answer them; its purpose has been to pose the crucial issues which alone can make the study of medieval history meaningful. By now, it is hoped that the point of departure is clear: the proper study of the Middle Ages must focus on the unique configuration of a new cultural entity that emerged upon the world scene. That new culture was Western European civilization.

As the student increases his comprehension of the "first Europe," he will surely wonder about its ultimate passing. It has long been customary to count the fourteenth and fifteenth centuries as part of the Middle Ages. Scholars today are not fully convinced that these centuries should be so treated. Many aspects of European history between 1300 and 1500 suggest that the "first Europe" was being rapidly transformed into a new kind of Europe. In this volume we have decided to treat later medieval history in the context of a second stage in Europe's evolution. But this mode of periodization is not intended to suggest any sharp break in the continuity of European history.

By way of previewing something of the history of the fourteenth and fifteenth centuries and of the entire future of Europe's evolution, let us note here that even as the "first Europe" assumed its mature form in the thirteenth century, its entire fabric was marked by a series of tensions, a maze of conflicts emerging from its very essence. The universalism of the Church stood opposed to the divisions implicit in the emergent territorial states. The claims of the clergy to direct society sat ill with the claims of secular princes to the same end. The burgeoning power of centralized governments clashed with the remnants of feudal privileges claimed by the nobility. The ethos of the feudal nobility contrasted sharply with that of the bourgeoisie. The engrained modes of subsistence economy clashed with the economic methods fitted to a money economy and to a capitalistic spirit. The religious, otherworldly orientation of life was ill at ease in the face of secular, worldly values emerging rapidly during the High Middle Ages. The formalistic religion prescribed by the triumphant Church was challenged by personal, mystical approaches to the worship of God. The revealed wisdom of the mystic was difficult to square with the "discovered" wisdom of the rationalistic scholastic. A Latin culture contrasted with a vernacular culture. Men were at odds over the most effective pose to take toward the non-European world—missionary, economic, military, diplomatic. As one becomes more completely informed about the structure of the civilization of the "first Europe," he will become aware that these tensions provided vitality within European society. Even more significantly, he will comprehend that a good part of European history since the thirteenth century has revolved around the resolution of these tensions. Herein lies a major element of continuity in European history from the fall of Rome to the present. The new cultural pattern that emerged during the Middle Ages out of the ruins of the classical world generated within its own bosom a wide range of contradictions. Since the High Middle Ages, when these tensions became apparent, a major part of Europe's talent has gone into their resolution. Each step taken to resolve these tensions has in some way enriched European civilization. From this perspective, the history of the Middle Ages takes on a new meaning, for in creating the "first Europe," our forefathers shaped a world of contrasts and tension. It has required what Oswald Spengler called a Faustian spirit—a bold, adventuresome, resolute, intelligent, aggressive, idealistic spirit—to survive in such an ambience. But the rewards for the effort spent in resolving Europe's conflicts have been rich, as is witnessed by the civilization that emerged out of the "first Europe."

In the historical "problems" that are to be presented in the following pages, the student will be asked to focus his attention on only a minor part of the rich panorama of medieval history. It is regrettable that the range cannot be greater, but perhaps even a few, properly selected issues pertaining to the Middle Ages can help to bring each student closer to the essence of that era. The issues that have been selected for closer examination have been chosen because each touches on a theme that was vital in shaping the "first Europe." Each represents a major challenge that Western Europeans had to resolve in order to sustain the vitality of the society that they were shaping. Thus, an understanding of these problems involves one in the very pulse beat of the Middle Ages. The manner in which these issues were resolved had a great deal to do with the shape that the new society took. Consequently, our involvement in these problems will help us gain a deeper sense of the nature and the spirit of medieval European civilization. Finally, the fashion in which medieval men dealt with the issues we are to treat made a permanent mark on the European scene. Our comprehension of the material that follows will therefore help each of us to gain a broader perspective from which to view the European scene in its entirety.

1
THE EARLY MIDDLE AGES: CONTINUITY OR BREAK?

If, as our introduction has suggested, the Middle Ages warrants consideration as a unique period in the total history of mankind during which the basic patterns of human life were recast in new forms, then the problem of its beginnings has a special significance. For one must suppose that the configuration of events at the outset of the period had a decisive effect on everything that followed. Our first problem dealing with the Middle Ages will attempt to provide insights into the essential features of the first stage of the history of the medieval period, namely, the era extending roughly from A.D. 400 to 800.

By the very nature of his craft, the historian's instinct is to seek the particulars when he is confronted with a problem about the past. Applied to the problem of the beginnings of the Middle Ages, this impulse has driven numerous historians to search for certain specifics: a precise date when the Middle Ages began; a particular event that marked the passage from an old order to a new; the human actors to whom can be attributed the decisive acts which gave birth to the new order. A vast amount of labor has been spent in these pursuits and in defense of particular choices. The effort has proved futile. Every date, event, and human action that has been proposed by any historian or school of historians as marking the beginning of the Middle Ages has been found unacceptable by others—whose counterchoices in turn have been found wanting. The sterility of such an approach to the beginnings of the Middle Ages has gradually forced the issue into a new framework. Recognizing that the beginning of the Middle Ages is not an "event" in the conventional sense, recent historians have sought to redefine the problem. The selections that follow reflect the new orientation and must be studied from this perspective.

The new approach to the early Middle Ages centers on process. The first centuries of the Middle Ages are seen as a transition period within which complex chains of events interacted and subtle forces operated to alter patterns of life and modes of thought. From this angle of vision certain matters have become critical to historians seeking to characterize the nature of the early Middle Ages; these issues should be the student's major concern as he studies the following selections. He should try to discover how long the transition process lasted. He ought to seek how wide a geographical area and how large a number of people were involved. He should try to understand which facets of men's lives were most deeply affected by change. He should attempt to identify the forces causing alterations in patterns of life and thought. He ought to attempt to assess the nature of the change so that he can state wherein and to what degree the historical situation had become different during the transition era. Finally, he must face the perplexing task of formulating his own interpretation — even if only tentative — of the meaning of the particular segment of history here under consideration.

As each student listens to historians speaking to these several points, he will become aware that their interpretations differ. Their disagreements admittedly breed confusion. But at the same time they illustrate a hard reality with which the student of history must contend. The conflict reflected in these selections point up the extent to which the historian's presence is felt in interpreting a complex situation. The scholars represented in these selections share a common body of facts. But how differently they use them! In studying the selections the student should try to identify each writer's unique slant on the problem under consideration. What is his basis of selecting material? What assumptions about human nature and the historical process underly his approach? Does he have blind spots? Is he committed to any generalized interpretation of history? By concerning himself with these matters, the student can cultivate one of the prime talents required of the good historian: the critical spirit.

Despite different approaches and emphases, all the following selections grapple with one central issue: Was the early Middle Ages a period characterized basically by continuity or by a sharp break? The student should try to formulate a position on this issue. For upon it depends one's interpretation of all medieval history and even much of modern history. If he decides that the age was characterized by continuity with the classical age, then he will treat history beyond this era in terms of the evolution of survivals of the classical age. If he concludes that the early Middle Ages was an age of sharp, radical change, then he will look at future periods in terms of the new elements that entered the scene to replace the classical order. As one grapples with the problem of continuity or interruption in the early Middle Ages, he cannot help immersing himself in an even more profound question to which the historian alone can give an answer. Is the essential feature of the human experience a continuous stream of development embracing all history in an ongoing process? Or is the vital dimension of mankind's story those changes which from time to time obliterate an established order and require the creation of a new mode of existence?

P. BOISSONNADE

A CATASTROPHIC VIEW

Since the very beginning of the early Middle Ages men have felt that the era was one over which hung a pall of catastrophe. For those who are of this persuasion the perpetrators of catastrophe are obvious: the barbarians who overran the Roman Empire in the late fourth, fifth, and early sixth centuries. Already in his *City of God*, written as a consequence of the Visigothic sack of Rome in 410, St. Augustine seems to have sensed that tragic consequences would flow from the presence of the barbarians in the Empire. And as recently as 1947 André Piganiol could write that "Roman civilization did not die a natural death; it was assassinated."

Pursuing this broad theme, many generations of historians have treated the period after 400 in terms of its barbarous attributes: destruction, pillage, violence, ignorance, injustice, illiteracy, immorality, etc., etc. Typical of that view is the following passage from P. Boissonnade's *Life and Work in Medieval Europe*. Boissonnade, a French medievalist, wrote this work during World War I, a fact that may well have colored his view of the Germans. In spite of this bias, his treatment of the nature of the period following the invasions is typical of the view that prevailed until recently.

The great migrations began from about the end of the fourth and continued until the end of the sixth century, sometimes even longer. . . . [*The author now traces the course of the invasions down to c. 590*].

Almost all the bands of invaders and allies at first thought only to live within the empire, under the tutelage and in the shadow of the honoured name of Rome. Almost all of them proclaimed themselves its allies (*foederati*), its soldiers, and its defenders. In order to secure the obedience of the Roman peoples, they presented themselves in the guise of high Roman functionaries, *magistri militum*, consuls, and patricians, whose insignia they wore above their own robes as barbarian chiefs. These kings and princes ruled with the aid of the framework of the old bureaucracy, and with the support of the old Roman aristocracy and Church. But after a century or more they recognized the futility of a fiction which they began to find irksome. Strong in the servility of the Romanized peoples, and sure of retaining power so long as they kept the monopoly

of that military supremacy which Rome had abandoned to the barbarians, they delayed no longer to reveal themselves in their true colours. The civilized world then experienced the fatal effect of a change of rule from which it had been unable to protect itself, and the destructive results of the barbarian conquests began to be felt.

The first of these results was the disruption of the idea of the state. The barbarian monarchies, strange mixtures of Roman despotism and of the Germanic principate, struggled for three centuries in the grip of the leaders of their war bands, who had become the heads of turbulent aristocracies, they allowed the solid armour of the Roman administration to fall to pieces, and showed themselves powerless to prevent a fearful anarchy, in which Western society almost disintegrated. If the world gained thus by the disappearance of Roman absolutism and the Roman fiscal system, it lost for long centuries the blessings of order and internal peace.

Happily for the future of civilization the numerical

From P. Boissonnade, *Life and Work in Medieval Europe, The Evolution of Medieval Economy from the Fifth to the Fifteenth Century*, tr. Eileen Power (New York and London, 1927), pp. 14–31. Reprinted by permission of Routledge & Kegan Paul Ltd.

and social superiority of the Romanized populations was still so great that in the larger part of Europe the barbarian colonization was little more than a thin layer over the deep furrows left by the domination of Rome. The ancient peoples, Latins, Celts, Iberians, Thracians, Illyrians, and Hellenes, whose culture had become unified under the empire, rapidly assimilated, absorbed, or modified the Slav and Germanic and even the Asiatic peoples who were now established among them. If in the contact they lost a great deal of the character of civilized societies, they at least remained, above all in the domain of religion, the repository of Roman institutions. . . .

But if the invasions had little effect upon the ethnic foundations of the ancient Roman Empire in East and West alike, they had nevertheless disastrous results upon society and upon economic conditions. Humanity has rarely experienced misery as great as that of this period. The masses lost heavily by the change of masters. The upper and middle classes of the old Roman society were swept away in the storm or despoiled by the barbarians, and the surviving members were fused with the conquerors. Property changed hands, wholly or partially. . . . There came about a great transference of property in the West. It worked in favour of the growth of a landed aristocracy formed of predominant Germanic elements, mingled with assimilated Roman elements, to the detriment of the class of small free proprietors, whose number and influence naturally diminished very quickly. The large aristocratic estate, which since the end of the empire had been tending to absorb the soil, received an impetus in vitality and expansion from the invasions. At the same time the primitive forms of landownership, the collective property of the village and of the family, reappeared in the civilized West, where the Roman genius had brought about the prevalence of individual private property.

Far from bearing with them into the empire democratic principles of liberty and equality, the Germans only spread therein the oppression of poor by rich and of weak by strong, and subjected the masses to an oligarchy of chiefs of warbands, who were the masters of men and lands alike. Rome had fused within herself all classes and all races, and had brought them into an equality beneath her laws. The Germanic customs established profound inequalities between the divers peoples of the barbarian states. In Gaul there were as many as seven different codes of

law, according to the origin of the inhabitants, Romans, Salian, Riparian, and Chamavian Franks, Burgundians, Visigoths, and Alamanni. High barriers separated the different social ranks, to each of which a different penal legislation was applied, shamefully indulgent towards the upper classes and barbarously harsh towards the lower, for whom were reserved the punishments of mutilation and torture. The aristocracy, alone in its pride, was at pains to prevent any rise in the social scale by forbidding marriages between its members and those of other classes, on pain of a loss of rank. The barbarians dared not openly attack the liberty of freemen of Germanic origin, who were established side by side with the chiefs upon the lands of the empire. In the profoundly Romanized districts of Southern Gaul, Spain, and Italy, they allowed the continuance of a number of small free proprietors of Roman origin. But everywhere by means of a steady underground process, made easier by the disappearance of all authority and by the reign of force, the new aristocracies set to work to rob freemen of their landed property and of their personal liberty. In all regions wherein German settlements predominated, the ancient class of Roman landowners disappeared, either decimated or enslaved. . . . Thus the barbarians solved the problem of agricultural labour and were able to live in idleness upon the work of the old Roman landowners and cultivators. A similar fate overtook a smaller proportion of the old free classes of Celtic Gaul, Spain, and Italy; it became general in proportion as the rule of the barbarians grew firmer. Thus in the Italian peninsula the Lombards reduced all the free population, even the priests, to the condition of the Roman or Germanic *coloni*.

The colonate itself, which under the laws of the Christian empire had marked a stage in social progress, in the barbarian period took on the aspect of a retrogressive institution, whereby men became more, rather than less, dependent. While Roman law had assured to the *colonus* his personal liberty and stability on the soil which he cultivated, the customs and laws of the barbarians assimilated the *colonus* to the serf—*i.e.*, to the unfree, and to the urban or domestic slave, who could be separated from his family and transplanted from one domain to another. On the other hand, the serfs ceased to be distinguished from slaves, and their position became equally precarious. At the close of the Roman Empire slavery was on the point of becoming extinct; but during the three centuries which followed the first barbarian invasions, it was reconstituted and spread with extreme rapidity. Constant wars and raids, veritable man-hunts, analogous to those which still continue in Central Africa, threw thousands of men and women upon the market at miserable prices. The penal legislation of the barbarians multiplied the number of these unhappy wretches, decreeing the punishment of loss of liberty for the most inconsiderable misdemeanours, and, on the other hand, so great was the prevalent misery that for numbers of despairing creatures slavery was a sort of refuge. The greater part of the Roman populations . . . were thus reduced to servitude. The domestic servants of the aristocracy were similarly recruited, and the cultivation of the land and the care of herds and flocks was confided in part to bands of slaves (servi rustici, mancipia). These men, once more reduced to the level of beasts and things, were tied to their terrible condition by the law, which made enfranchisements rarer and more difficult, and forbade marriages between free and servile persons. It once more put the power of life and death into the hands of the masters and delivered over the slaves, almost without defence, to the atrocious and bestial fury of their owners. The enumeration of the cruel punishments to which men of servile condition were subjected—the loss of ears, nose, eyes, tongue, hands, and genital organs—and the various tortures to which they were submitted fills whole columns of the barbarian codes, until the reader cannot restrain a shudder. Mankind had passed far away from that great humanitarian movement which from the second to the fourth century had left its trace on Roman legislation upon slavery.

All the guarantees with which the expiring civilization of the ancient world had surrounded the life and possessions of the individual disappeared in the anarchy let loose by the barbarians. Even among the Visigoths, Ostrogoths, and Franks, who were already half Romanized by a long sojourn within the empire, the sudden awakening of ancestral ferocity transformed these "guests" into unchained murderers. . . . "For us," says Salvian, a priest of Marseilles, himself the apologist of the barbarians, "there is neither peace nor security." Another contemporary, Prosper of Aquitaine, cries, towards 416: "It is ten years since we fell beneath the sword of the Vandals and Goths; the people has perished, even children and young maids they slew." . . . Fiercer still were those Germans who were untouched by Roman civilization. Angles, Jutes, and Saxons were wild beasts, who must have blood

at all costs, and before setting sail they usually put to the sword a tenth of their prisoners. . . . The cruelty of the Alamanni left upon the memory of Western Europe almost as profound an impression as that of the Huns. The war bands which took part in the great invasion of 406 in Italy and Gaul spread terror far and wide by their atrocious exploits; they transformed the town of Treier into a charnel-house, in which the naked bodies of men and women were devoured by dogs and birds of prey. In Aquitaine and in Spain the faithful and the clergy were beaten, thrown into chains, and burned alive. Everywhere, at the sack of cities and towns, women suffered the supreme outrage. After the capture of Rome Alaric's Visigoths, reclining in the shade, forced the sons and daughters of the senators, captives of their harems, to serve them with Falernian wine in golden cups. With each expedition the women's quarters of the conquerors grew. Throughout the second half of the fifth century a contemporary witnesses that "the forest of swords mowed down the Italian nobility like corn." Later, in the sixth century, the savagery of the Lombards passed all bounds. "Murder is nothing to them," writes the annalist Paul Deacon. "Even as a sword leaping from the scabbard so did this fierce horde ravage, and men fell even as the ears of wheat beneath the sickle." In the East the same terrible sights were everywhere to be seen; men were massacred, women and children carried away, by the invading bands of Turanians, Germans, and Slavs in Macedonia, Thessaly, Greece, Illyria, Epirus, and the Danubian provinces. Ostrogoths hacked off the arms of labourers in Pannonia, and impaled the *coloni* of Illyria; Slavs crucified the peasants and artisans, whom they made prisoners, head downwards, or shot them full of arrows. Throughout the peninsula heaps of whitening bones marked the place where once stood villages, whose inhabitants had been massacred or had died of hunger.

The barbarians took the same delight in destruction and pillage that they took in killing and violence. They carried everything away as they passed, leaving behind them only the glare of fire and dreary heaps of ruins. From 406 to 416, according to St. Jerome's testimony, the barbarians destroyed every sign of civilization from the Alps to the Pyrenees, and from the ocean to the Rhine. "All Gaul burned upon the same bonfire," writes a Bishop of Auch. Prosper of Aquitaine expresses himself in the same terms in his poem. "The temples of God were delivered to the flames and monasteries were sacked. If the waves of the ocean had overflowed the fields of Gaul they would have done less damage." He shows the Visigoths themselves engaged in pillaging Roman villas, carrying off silver, furniture, and cattle, dividing up the jewels and drinking the wine. They bore away the sacred vessels of the churches, and to crown their work set fire to the houses. . . . At the very period when the barbarians had succeeded in making stable settlements, the wars of kings and peoples, tribes and families, perpetuated these customs, which were so destructive of a regular and productive social and economic life. In expeditions such as that of the Austrasians into Auvergne and Aquitaine in the sixth century, all that was left of the prosperity of the country disappeared beneath the brutal hand of the barbarians, who set fire to the harvest, cut down the fruit-trees, tore up the vines, pillaged barns and cellars, drove away before them troops of captives and domestic animals, and sowed desolation and death all around them. Sometimes the very excess of despair drove the peasants to take arms against them. . . . But in general there was no resistance, because the masses knew that it was useless.

In such a society, delivered over without mercy to all the abuses of brutal force and of unchecked barbarism, economic life waned, and sometimes seemed about to cease altogether. Agricultural labour became scarce, owing to the great slaughter of men, the slave raids, the famines and epidemics, which had become almost chronic. The growing insecurity discouraged all production, and everywhere in West and East alike stretched vast wastes, unpopulated and uncultivated. . . . The land, ill cultivated, according to primitive methods by these new masters, who knew nothing of the agricultural science of the Romans, now gave but uncertain harvests. The Germanic system of common cultivation with periodical divisions of the soil, which was introduced into part of the ancient imperial territory, only aggravated the evil. Rich crops, such as orchards, vineyards, and industrial plants, were partially abandoned in those lands where the Romans had introduced them. Nevertheless, the miserable populations which survived took refuge in the fields and the great domains, which were protected by ditches and palisades, or by embankments of earth and stones, or else in the shadow of the old Roman townships (vici), which could serve as a refuge for the small cultivators. Natural economy once more predominated, and life became con-

centrated and localized in the country districts, where the barbarians preferred to dwell.

Industrial economy, indeed, received its death-blow with that of the towns, which had been the home of the Graeco-Roman civilization. The barbarians showed a peculiar savagery in destroying those cities, in which the most flourishing varieties of industry and corporations of artisans had developed and still survived. Everywhere the conquerors dispersed the townsfolk and destroyed everything which might preserve the memory of civilized life —temples, churches, basilicas, theatres, circuses. Buildings and monuments alike were delivered to the flames, and throughout both West and East numbers of still flourishing towns disappeared, never to rise again. . . .

In the midst of the universal disorganization trade was reduced to a simple traffic in foodstuffs or in manufactures of primary necessity, and its range of circulation was very narrow. The great home and foreign commerce, which had developed so brilliantly under the empire, was no longer possible. Everything which was necessary to promote and to facilitate business was lacking. Land was now once more the sole capital, and natural products served as a medium of exchange. Trade by barter, the primitive method in use among the Germans, reappeared in the ancient Roman Empire, where money became rare and credit disappeared. The fine Roman roads, no longer kept in repair, deteriorated, the bridges fell down, the imperial post ceased, there were no more relays. All rapid movement became impossible. Everywhere insecurity reigned; brigands fell upon travellers and merchants on the edge of the woods and at the fords across rivers and marshes. Armed bands prowled about the country, and journeys became perilous expeditions, undertaken only in caravans and with armed escorts. The ports declined, the seas were infested with pirates, maritime trade became as uncertain as land commerce. . . .

There was misery and want everywhere in town and country alike. Bands of beggars whined for alms at the doors of the churches, the castles on the great estates, and the royal palaces. It was among these miserable beings that the bands of criminals who swarmed everywhere were recruited. . . . Death indeed mowed down in great swathes those who survived the invasions. Many who escaped sword and fire died of privation and hunger, or were carried off by the natural disorders which were now let loose upon mankind. Famine accompanied the invasions in Noricum, Gaul, Spain, and Italy. Even in times of peace the West and the East alike went in fear of dearth. "Anything rather than starvation" . . . was the saying on all lips. But famine reappeared periodically after droughts, floods, and the ravages of warlike bands, and sometimes in a form so terrible that there were sporadic scenes of cannibalism. . . . Epidemics, dysentery, typhus, and the Asiatic plague completed the deadly work. They flourished in the fifth century, and still more in the second half of the sixth and in the seventh, notably in Britain and Italy. . . . The wretched physique of the people caused nervous maladies, leprosy, and St. Anthony's Fire to multiply. The general exhaustion diminished fertility and reduced the birth-rate. The result of all this was that the population of West and East fell in this period to one of the lowest levels reached during the whole of the Christian era. . . . Contemporaries are unanimous in describing the desolation of the world, in West and East alike, the impression of solitude and of desert which it left upon their minds; and some believed that they had reached that end of the world predicted by the Scriptures.

The material and moral disaster was, indeed, immense, and seemed irreparable. Civilized life, especially in the East, had been thrust back into barbarism. Neither labour nor intelligence was honoured. Force reigned supreme, and the warrior band exploited Western society without pity. A minority of chiefs and fighters lived upon war and pillage, oppressed the wretched population of *coloni* and slaves on its domains, heaped up the fruits of its rapine, filled its harems with girls, its stables with horses, and its kennels with hounds, divided its leisure between banqueting and the chase, dog fights, and violent exercise. The nobility and freemen, shunning the ruined towns, lived in their *villae*, their family dwelling-places, or their hamlets on the edge of the great common forests,

like the idle, rude, and brutal conquerors they were. The working classes, who laboured for them, were exposed to all the risks of an unregulated and anarchical society, whose only rule was violence. The idleness, stupidity, coarseness, ignorance, credulity, and cruelty of the barbarians took the place of the well-regulated activity, the polish, culture, and relative humanity of the Romans. There was no longer any respect for the weak, for peasants and women and children. There was no discipline, no moral code to restrain these invaders, who merely added the vices of civilization to the depravity of barbarism. Far from regenerating the world, they very nearly wiped out civilization for ever. They destroyed the ordered societies of the West, only to replace them by anarchy. Far from bringing freedom in their train, they reestablished slavery. Far from diminishing class distinctions, they reared new barriers between the classes. Far from ameliorating the condition of the lower classes, they made it harder. Far from assisting economic development, they ruined all activity by sowing everywhere pillage, disorder, and destruction. They created nothing, but they destroyed much, and they put a stop to all progress for several centuries. In society and in labour the barbarian settlements produced one of the greatest retrogressions which the world has ever known. Their one useful result was that they gave finer spirits an impetus to energy and to action, and thus, out of sheer reaction, brought about a series of attempts to return to the traditions of Roman government, and roused the Church from its mystic dream, in order that it might save the remnants of civilization from shipwreck. In the East the Roman edifice had weathered the storm, and could serve as a model and framework for the restoration of society and of labour. In the West the spirit and institutions of Rome, adapted to new conditions of environment, were destined to inspire those attempts at economic and social restoration which took place towards the end of the Dark Ages.

HENRI PIRENNE

CONTINUITY—AND THEN A BREAK

In the following passage we encounter a concept that marked a milestone in the study of the early Middle Ages. This is the famous thesis of the Belgian historian Henri Pirenne (1862–1935), first published in an article in 1922 and then developed during subsequent years in further articles and in two books, *Medieval Cities* and *Mohammed and Charlemagne*. By posing a whole new series of issues concerning the early Middle Ages, Pirenne revolutionized the approach to the period. It will be evident immediately why the Pirenne thesis was so provocative. In sharp contrast with the opinion prevailing when he pronounced his views—basically the position reflected in the previous selection—Pirenne argued that the essential features of classical civilization persisted far beyond the traditional date set for its fall. His basic emphasis is on continuity as the essential feature of the period under question. As the student reads this selection, he should pay special attention to those aspects of society where Pirenne finds continuity most significantly evident. But, lest Pirenne's argument supporting the persistence of classical civilization prove too persuasive, the student must be reminded that Pirenne ultimately had to recognize a sharp break in history in order to account for the beginnings of the Middle Ages. His concept of when and where the break came was what gave his thesis an especially provocative turn. Each student should be sure to comprehend how, when, where, and why the break came from Pirenne's perspective. And finally he might ask whether Pirenne's interpretation is really so startlingly new or whether he merely presented a catastrophic interpretation shifted into a new setting.

The Roman Empire, at the end of the third century, had one outstanding general characteristic: it was an essentially Mediterranean commonwealth. Virtually all of its territory lay within the watershed of that great land-locked sea; the distant frontiers of the Rhine, the Danube, the Euphrates and the Sahara, may be regarded merely as an advanced circle of outer defenses protecting the approaches.

The Mediterranean was, without question, the bulwark of both its political and economic unity. Its very existence depended on mastery of the sea. Without that great trade route, neither the government, nor the defense, nor the administration of the *orbis romanus* would have been possible.

As the Empire grew old this fundamentally maritime character was, interestingly enough, not only preserved but was still more sharply defined. When the former inland capital, Rome, was abandoned, its place was taken by a city which not only served as a capital but which was at the same time an admirable seaport—Constantinople.

The Empire's cultural development, to be sure, had clearly passed its peak. Population decreased, the spirit of enterprise waned, barbarian hordes commenced to threaten the frontiers, and the increasing expenses of the government, fighting for its very life, brought in their train a fiscal system which more and more enslaved men to the State. Nevertheless this general deterioration does not seem to have appreciably affected the maritime commerce of the Mediterranean. It continued to be active and well

From Henri Pirenne, *Medieval Cities: Their Origins and the Revival of Trade* (Princeton, 1925), pp. 3–16, 19–26, 28. Reprinted by permission of the Princeton University Press. Copyright 1925 by Princeton University Press.

sustained, in marked contrast with the growing apathy that characterized the inland provinces. Trade continued to keep the East and the West in close contact with each other. There was no interruption to the intimate commercial relations between those diverse climes bathed by one and the same sea. Both manufactured and natural products were still extensively dealt in: textiles from Constantinople, Edessa, Antioch, and Alexandria; wines, oils, and spices from Syria; papyrus from Egypt; wheat from Egypt, Africa, and Spain; and wines from Gaul and Italy. There was even a reform of the monetary system based on the gold *solidus*, which served materially to encourage commercial operations by giving them the benefit of an excellent currency, universally adopted as an instrument of exchange and as a means of quoting prices.

Of the two great regions of the Empire, the East and the West, the first far surpassed the second, both in superiority of civilization and in a much higher level of economic development. At the beginning of the fourth century there were no longer any really great cities save in the East. The center of the export trade was in Syria and in Asia Minor, and here also was concentrated, in particular, the textile industry for which the whole Roman world was the market and for which Syrian ships were the carriers.

The commercial prominence of the Syrians is one of the most interesting facts in the history of the Lower Empire. It undoubtedly contributed largely to that progressive orientalization of society which was due eventually to end in Byzantinism. And this orientalization, of which the sea was the vehicle, is clear proof of the increasing importance which the Mediterranean acquired as the aging Empire grew weak, gave way in the North beneath the pressure of the barbarians; and contracted more and more about the shores of this inland sea. . . .

The appearance of the Germanic tribes on the shore of the Mediterranean was by no means a critical point marking the advent of a new era in the history of Europe. Great as were the consequences which it entailed, it did not sweep the boards clean nor even break the tradition. The aim of the invaders was not to destroy the Roman Empire but to occupy and enjoy it. By and large, what they preserved far exceeded what they destroyed or what they brought that was new. It is true that the kingdoms they established on the soil

of the Empire made an end of the latter in so far as being a *State* in Western Europe. From a political point of view the *orbis romanus*, now strictly localized in the East, lost that ecumenical character which had made its frontiers coincide with the frontiers of Christianity. The Empire, however, was far from becoming a stranger to the lost provinces. Its civilization there outlived its authority. By the Church, by language, by the superiority of its institutions and law, it prevailed over the conquerors. In the midst of the troubles, the insecurity, the misery and the anarchy which accompanied the invasions there was naturally a certain decline, but even in that decline there was preserved a physiognomy still distinctly Roman. The Germanic tribes were unable, and in fact did not want, to do without it. They barbarized it, but they did not consciously germanize it.

Nothing is better proof of this assertion than the persistence in the last days of the Empire—from the fifth to the eighth century—of that maritime character pointed out above. The importance of the Mediterranean did not grow less after the period of the invasions. The sea remained for the Germanic tribes what it had been before their arrival—the very center of Europe, the *mare nostrum*. The sea had had such great importance in the political order that the deposing of the last Roman Emperor in the West (476) was not enough in itself to turn historical evolution from its time-honored direction. It continued, on the contrary, to develop in the same theater and under the same influences. No indication yet gave warning of the end of that commonwealth of civilization created by the Empire from the Pillars of Hercules to the Aegean Sea, from the coasts of Egypt and Africa to the shores of Gaul, Italy and Spain. In spite of the invasion of the barbarians the new world conserved, in all essential characteristics, the physiognomy of the old. To follow the course of events from Romulus Augustulus to Charlemagne it is necessary to keep the Mediterranean constantly in view.

All the great events in political history are unfolded on its shores. From 493 to 526 Italy, governed by Theodoric, maintained a hegemony over all the Germanic kingdoms, a hegemony through which the power of the Roman tradition was perpetuated and assured. After Theodoric, this power was still more clearly shown. Justinian failed by but little of restoring imperial unity (527–565). Africa, Spain, and Italy were reconquered. The Mediterranean became again a Roman lake. Byzantium, it is true, weakened by the immense effort she had just put forth, could neither finish nor even preserve intact the astonishing work which she had accomplished. The Lombards took Northern Italy away from her (568); the Visigoths freed themselves from her yoke. Nevertheless she did not abandon her ambitions. She retained, for a long time to come, Africa, Sicily, Southern Italy. Nor did she loose her grip on the West—thanks to the sea, the mastery of which her fleets so securely held that the fate of Europe rested at that moment, more than ever, on the waves of the Mediterranean.

What was true of the political situation held equally well for the cultural. It seems hardly necessary to recall that Boëthius (480–525) and Cassiodorus (477–c. 562) were Italians as were St. Benedict (480–534) and Gregory the Great (590–604), and that Isidorus of Seville (570–636) was a Spaniard. It was Italy that maintained the last schools at the same time that she was fostering the spread of monarchism north of the Alps. It was in Italy, also, that what was left of the ancient culture flourished side by side with what was brought forth anew in the bosom of the Church. All the strength and vigor that the Church possessed was concentrated in the region of the Mediterranean. There alone she gave evidence of an organization and spirit capable of initiating great enterprises. An interesting example of this is the fact that Christianity was brought to the Anglo-Saxons (596) from the distant shores of Italy, not from the neighboring shores of Gaul. . . .

A brief survey of the economic development of Europe will give the crowning touch to the substantiation of the theory which has here been put forward. That development is, obviously, a clear-cut, direct continuation of the economy of the Roman Empire. In it are rediscovered all the latter's principal traits and, above all, that Mediterranean character which here is unmistakable. To be sure, a general decline in social activity was apparent in this region as in all others. By the last days of the Empire there was a clearly marked decline which the catastrophe of the invasions naturally helped accentuate. But it would be a decided mistake to imagine that the arrival of the Germanic tribes had as a result the substitution of a purely agricultural economy and a general stagnation in trade for urban life and commercial activity.

The supposed dislike of the barbarians for towns is an admitted fable to which reality has given the lie. If, on the extreme frontiers of the Empire, certain towns were put to the torch, destroyed and pillaged, it is none the less true that the immense majority survived the invasions. A statistical survey of cities in existence at the present day in France, in Italy and even on the banks of the Rhine and the Danube, gives proof that, for the most part, these cities now stand on the sites where rose the Roman cities, and that their very names are often but a transformation of Roman names.

The Church had of course closely patterned the religious districts after the administrative districts of the Empire. As a general rule, each diocese corresponded to a *civitas*. Since the ecclesiastical organization suffered no change during the era of the Germanic invasions, the result was that in the new kingdoms founded by the conquerors it preserved intact this characteristic feature. In fact, from the beginning of the sixth century the word *civitas* took the special meaning of "episcopal city," the center of the diocese. In surviving the Empire on which it was based, the Church therefore contributed very largely to the safeguarding of the existence of the Roman cities.

But it must not be overlooked, on the other hand, that these cities in themselves long retained a considerable importance. Their municipal institutions did not suddenly disappear upon the arrival of the Germanic tribes. Not only in Italy, but also in Spain and even in Gaul, they kept their *decuriones*—a corps of magistrates provided with a judicial and administrative authority, the details of which are not clear but whose existence and Roman origin is a matter of record. . . .

It is also well established that these cities were the centers of an economic activity which itself was a survival of the preceding civilization. Each city was the market for the surrounding countryside, the winter home of the great landed proprietors of the neighborhood and, if favorably situated, the center of a commerce the more highly developed in proportion to its nearness to the shores of the Mediterranean. A perusal of Gregory of Tours gives ample proof that in the Gaul of his time there was still a professional merchant class residing in the towns. . . . Care should of course be taken not to exaggerate its value. An equally great fault would be to undervalue it. Certainly the economic order

Continuity—And then a Break

of Merovingian Gaul was founded on agriculture rather than on any other form of activity. More certainly still this had already been the case under the Roman Empire.

But this does not preclude the fact that inland traffic, the import and export of goods and merchandise, was carried on to a considerable extent. It was an important factor in the maintenance of society. An indirect proof of this is furnished by the institution of market-tolls. Thus were called the tolls set up by the Roman administration along the roads, in the ports, at bridges and fords, and elsewhere. The Frankish kings let them all stay in force and drew from them such copious revenues that the collectors of this class of taxes figured among their most useful functionaries.

The continued commercial activity after the disappearance of the Empire, and, likewise, the survival of the towns that were the centers thereof and the merchants who were its instruments, is explained by the continuation of Mediterranean trade. In all the chief characteristics it was the same, from the fifth to the eighth centuries, as it had been just after Constantine. If, as is probable, the decline was the more rapid after the Germanic invasions, it remains none the less true that there is presented a picture of uninterrupted intercourse between the Byzantine East and the West dominated by the barbarians. By means of the shipping which was carried on from the coasts of Spain and Gaul to those of Syria and Asia Minor, the basin of the Mediterranean did not cease, despite the political subdivisions which it had seen take place, to consolidate the economic unity which it had shaped for centuries under the imperial commonwealth. Because of this fact, the economic organization of the world lived on after the political transformation.

In lack of other proofs, the monetary system of the Frankish kings would alone establish this truth convincingly. This system, as is too well known to make necessary any lengthy consideration here, was purely Roman or, strictly speaking, Romano-Byzantine. This is shown by the coins that were minted: the *solidus*, the *triens*, and the *denarius*—that is to say, the *sou*, the *third-sou* and the *denier*. It is shown further by the metal which was employed: gold, used for the coinage of the *solidus* and the *triens*. It is also shown by the weight which was given to specie. It is shown, finally, by the effigies which were minted on the coins. In this connection it is worth noting that the mints continued for a long time, under the Merovingian kings, the custom of representing the bust of the Emperor on the coins and of showing on the reverse of the pieces the *Victoria Augusti* and that, carrying this imitation to the extreme, when the Byzantines substituted the cross for the symbol of that victory they did the same. Such extreme servility can be explained only by the continuing influence of the Empire. The obvious reason was the necessity of preserving, between the local currency and the imperial currency, a conformity which would be purposeless if the most intimate relations had not existed between Merovingian commerce and the general commerce of the Mediterranean. In other words, this commerce continued to be closely bound up with the commerce of the Byzantine Empire. . . .

Here, then, is quite enough to support the conclusion that Merovingian times knew, thanks to the continuance of Mediterranean shipping and the intermediary of Marseilles, what we may safely call a great commerce. It would certainly be an error to assume that the dealings of the oriental merchants of Gaul were restricted solely to articles of luxury. Probably the sale of jewelry, enamels and silk stuffs resulted in handsome profits, but this would not be enough to explain their number and their extraordinary diffusion throughout all the country. The traffic of Marseilles was, above all else, supported by goods for general consumption such as wine and oil, spices and papyrus. These commodities, as has already been pointed out, were regularly exported to the north.

The oriental merchants of the Frankish Empire were virtually engaged in wholesale trade. Their boats, after being discharged on the quays of Marseilles, certainly carried back, on leaving the shores of Provence, not only passengers but return freight. Our sources of information, to be sure, do not tell much about the nature of this freight. Among the possible conjectures, one of the most likely is that it probably consisted, at least in good part, in human chattels—that is to say, in slaves. Traffic in slaves did not cease to be carried on in the Frankish Empire until the end of the ninth century. The wars waged against the barbarians of Saxony, Thuringia and the Slavic regions provided a source of supply which seems to have been abundant enough. Gregory of Tours speaks of Saxon slaves belonging to a merchant of Orleans, and it is a good guess that this Samo, who departed in the first half of the seventh century with a band of companions for the country of Wends, whose king he eventually became, was very probably nothing more than an adventurer trafficking in slaves. And it is of course obvious that the slave trade, to which the Jews still assiduously applied themselves in the ninth century, must have had its origin in an earlier era.

If the bulk of the commerce in Merovingian Gaul was to be found in the hands of oriental merchants, their influence, however, should not be exaggerated. Side by side with them, and according to all indications in constant relations with them, are mentioned indigenous merchants. Gregory of Tours does not fail to supply information concerning them, which would undoubtedly have been more voluminous if his narrative had had more than a merely incidental interest in them. He shows the king consenting to a loan to the merchants of Verdun, whose business prospers so well that they soon find themselves in a position to reimburse him. He mentions the existence in Paris of a *domus negociantum*—that is to say, apparently, of a sort of market or bazaar. He speaks of a merchant profiteering during the great famine of 585 and getting rich. And in all these anecdotes he is dealing, without the least doubt, with professionals and not with merely casual buyers or sellers.

The picture which the commerce of Merovingian Gaul presents is repeated, naturally, in the other maritime Germanic kingdoms of the Mediterranean—among the Ostrogoths of Italy, among the Vandals of Africa, among the Visigoths of Spain. The Edict of Theodoric contained a quantity of stipulations relative to merchants. Carthage continued to be an important port in close relations with Spain, and her ships, apparently, went up the coast as far as Bordeaux. The laws of the Visigoths mentioned merchants from overseas.

In all of this is clearly manifest the vigorous continuity of the commercial development of the Roman Empire after the Germanic invasions. They did not put an end to the economic unity of antiquity. By means of the Mediterranean and the relations kept up thereby between the West and the East, this unity, on the contrary, was preserved with a remarkable distinctiveness. The great inland sea of Europe no longer belonged, as before, to a single State. But nothing yet gave reason to predict

that it would soon cease to have its time-honored importance. Despite the transformations which it had undergone, the new world had not lost the Mediterranean character of the old. On the shores of the sea was still concentrated the better part of its activities. No indication yet gave warning of the end of the commonwealth of civilization, created by the Roman Empire from the Pillars of Hercules to the Aegean Sea. At the beginning of the seventh century, anyone who sought to look into the future would have been unable to discern any reason for not believing in the continuance of the old tradition.

Yet what was then natural and reasonable to predict was not to be realized. The world-order which had survived the Germanic invasions was not able to survive the invasion of Islam.

It is thrown across the path of history with the elemental force of a cosmic cataclysm. Even in the lifetime of Mahomet (571–632) no one could have imagined the consequences or have prepared for them. Yet the movement took no more than fifty years to spread from the China Sea to the Atlantic Ocean. Nothing was able to withstand it. At the first blow, it overthrew the Persian Empire (637–644). It took from the Byzantine Empire, in quick succession, Syria (634–636), Egypt (640–642), Africa (698). It reached into Spain (711). The resistless advance was not to slow down until the start of the eighth century, when the walls of Constantinople on the one side (713) and the soldiers of Charles Martel on the other (732) broke that great enveloping offensive against the two flanks of Christianity.

But if its force of expansion was exhausted, it had none the less changed the face of the world. Its sudden thrust had destroyed ancient Europe. It had put an end to the Mediterranean commonwealth in which it had gathered its strength.

The familiar and almost "family" sea which once united all the parts of this commonwealth was to become a barrier between them. On all its shores, for centuries, social life, in its fundamental characteristics, had been the same; religion, the same; customs and ideas, the same or very nearly so. The invasion of the barbarians from the North had modified nothing essential in that situation.

But now, all of a sudden, the very lands where civilization had been born were torn away; the Cult

Continuity—And then a Break   **105**

of the Prophet was substituted for the Christian Faith, Moslem law for Roman law, the Arab tongue for the Greek and the Latin tongue.

The Mediterranean had been a Roman lake; it now became, for the most part, a Moslem lake. From this time on it separated, instead of uniting, the East and the West of Europe. The tie which was still binding the Byzantine Empire to the Germanic kingdoms of the West was broken.

The tremendous effect the invasion of Islam had upon Western Europe has not, perhaps, been fully appreciated.

Out of it arose a new and unparalleled situation, unlike anything that had gone before. Through the Phoenicians, the Greeks, and finally the Romans, Western Europe had always received the cultural stamp of the East. It had lived, as it were, by virtue of the Mediterranean; now for the first time it was forced to live by its own resources. The center of gravity, heretofore on the shore of the Mediterranean, was shifted to the north. As a result the Frankish Empire, which had so far been playing only a minor rôle in the history of Europe, was to become the arbiter of Europe's destinies.

There is obviously more than mere coincidence in the simultaneity of the closing of the Mediterranean by Islam and the entry of the Carolingians on the scene. There is the distinct relation of cause and effect between the two. The Frankish Empire was fated to lay the foundations of the Europe of the Middle Ages. But the mission which it fulfilled had as an essential prior condition the overthrow of the traditional world-order. The Carolingians would never have been called upon to play the part they did if historical evolution had not been turned aside from its course and, so to speak, "de-Saxoned" by the Moslem invasion. Without Islam, the Frankish Empire would probably never have existed and Charlemagne, without Mahomet, would be inconceivable.

This is made plain enough by the many contrasts between the Merovingian era, during which the Mediterranean retained its time-honored historical importance, and the Carolingian era, when that influence ceased to make itself felt. These contrasts were in evidence everywhere: in religious sentiment, in political and social institutions, in literature, in language and even in handwriting. From whatever standpoint it is studied, the civilization of the ninth century shows a distinct break with the civilization of antiquity. Nothing would be more fallacious than to see therein a simple continuation of the preceding centuries. . . .

In the field of economics the contrast, which the Carolingian period shows to Merovingian times, is especially striking. In the days of the Merovingians, Gaul was still a maritime country and trade and traffic flourished because of that fact. The Empire of Charlemagne, on the contrary, was essentially an inland one. No longer was there any communication with the exterior; it was a closed State, a State without foreign markets, living in a condition of almost complete isolation.

WILLIAM C. BARK

CREATIVITY AMIDST CONTINUITY

Among the many critics of Pirenne's interpretation of the early Middle Ages has been William C. Bark, professor of medieval history at Stanford University. His book, *Origins of the Medieval World*, from which the following selection is extracted, by no means disallows the element of continuity; he sees much of the history of the early Middle Ages in terms of persisting facets of Roman society. Yet his basic emphasis is on the beginnings of a new society, one which he believes Pirenne completely overlooked. To Bark the major feature of the early Middle Ages was a creative reshaping of society out of a variety of elements—some carrying over from Rome and others completely new. His position consequently emphasizes a definite break between the classical and the medieval worlds, but a break that came gradually amidst rebuilding.

The following passage, coming near the end of Bark's book, must be read in the light of his previous arguments. He begins his study by raising several objections to the Pirenne thesis, most of which center on Pirenne's failure to see new forces emerging in the early Middle Ages. He then subjects Roman imperial society of the fourth century to close scrutiny and concludes that by that time in the West a "great social and economic revolution, namely, the destruction of the middle class, the acquisition of many small landholdings by the great proprietors, and the resulting vast increase in the power of the landed aristocracy" had already occurred. As a consequence of this revolution, the old order had reached a "dead-end"; "the more advanced but no longer workable imperial régime" had to be replaced and life had to be adjusted to the demands of a new setting, where the "landed estate under the domination of a local lord" was the center of existence. In Bark's opinion this adjustment was made in a remarkably creative fashion, as the following passage indicates.

If Julius Caesar or Hadrian . . . could have visited the Empire of the fifth or sixth century, they would have found many puzzling alterations in the external appearance of the world they had known. . . .

Both visitors would no doubt have regarded the later Roman West as sadly down at heel. . . . The "deterioration" they would have found would at least have been the deterioration of a more or less familiar set of visible and tangible Roman creations and practices. Much more startling would have been the discovery, if they had been capable of making it, that great though they found the external changes to be, they were minor compared with certain more subtle alterations in outlook, in values, in modes of thought, and in aspirations. . . . The other changes represented a movement *toward* something new and quite outside the experience of a Caesar or a Hadrian, and they were soon to be expressed in outward behavior as well as in thought and feeling. . . .

It is the purpose of this chapter to examine four different aspects of the new world taking shape behind, and partly obscured by, the mantle of the old. The epoch-making change or series of changes going on between the fourth and fifth and the ninth and tenth centuries took place both inwardly and outwardly, (1) in the way men thought and in what they thought about, (2) in the way they lived and expressed themselves, (3) in what they thought worth doing, and (4) in how they did it. . . .

The primary thesis of this chapter . . . is that something new, distinct, and essentially original began in the Western European portion of the Roman Empire; that its elements are distinguishable by the fourth century, and some of them earlier. This "something" is perhaps best described as a new attitude toward life. In the centuries of its formation, this attitude is partly obscured by the more familiar and eye-catching externalities of Roman survival, by the turbulence of the time, and by the scarcity of our sources. . . .

Changing Moods of Thought and Expression. It has long been recognized that the Church, to its own profit and that of the whole West, borrowed much from the organization of the Roman State, with such modifications as were necessary to meet the needs of a new institution operating in different conditions, performing new as well as old functions, and serving ends unheard of in the great days of Roman power. Thanks to the influence of the

Reprinted from *Origins of the Medieval World* by William Carroll Bark, pp. 67–80, 82–87, 89–95, 98–100, with the permission of the publishers, Stanford University Press. © 1958 by the Board of Trustees of the Leland Stanford Junior University.

Creativity Amidst Continuity

Church in every branch of aesthetic and intellectual endeavor, much of the order and system of Roman thought penetrated to where it could best be used. And yet in the new art of the Late Roman era and in the still newer art brought in by the barbarians there was much that was vigorous and original, much that owed nothing to Rome, that derived its inspiration solely from the new needs and values of the emerging medieval world. Nothing better attests the creative genius, the capacity both to learn and to originate, of Western European civilization, even in the period of its youth, than the mighty products of its religious art, which combined spiritual aspiration, warm human feeling, and artistic excellence in a way unknown to pagan, classical antiquity.

As it was with art, so it was with social and intellectual standards, and indeed with the very modes of thought. The intellectual life of the new world of the Middle Ages was cast in a mold essentially different from that of classical—chiefly Hellenic—antiquity. . . .

In the Late Empire the Hellenic fires burned dimly. Science lost vitality and the old union with philosophy was dissolved. There were new needs to be met. . . . Philosophy contracted a new alliance, this time with theology; henceforth for some centuries intellectual life was to proceed under the guidance of the Church. The learning of the past was in part kept and transformed, in part virtually ignored. Christian leaders, above all St. Augustine, strove with energy and success to reorganize the patterns of thought and to adapt such classical knowledge and intellectual endeavors as were retained to the new goals of human life, a life in which salvation had become the main concern of educated men.

St. Augustine is rightly given the place of prominence. Of all the tasks imposed upon the human intellect perhaps the most difficult is first to perceive in times of vast fundamental change what is dead and spiritless and devoid of meaning, and then to conceive, perfect and propagate values more suitable to the new age. Most men in all ages, and very likely more in times of turmoil than in times of stability, cling staunchly and blindly to the familiar and accepted, avoiding the cold discomfort of mental and spiritual readjustment. In recognizing what was dead or dying, and in giving meaning to what was living and being born, St. Augustine has had few equals. The *Confessions* and the *City of God* alone

tell us how powerful for him was the appeal of the past. His mastery lay in the recognition that for his own and future generations, in the conditions of life as they had come to be, the voices of Plato and the rest were but echoes from a tomb. He did not repudiate what he had borrowed from Plato; he used it. But he selected only what he considered valuable, adapted it to new conditions, and made it part of an intellectual structure that would have been incomprehensible to the Academy. . . .

There is discernible before the fourth century not a universal but a widespread decline in the quality of the intellectual and literary works belonging to the classical tradition. That tradition had lost a great deal of its vitality, and its followers seemed no longer convinced that the subjects with which they dealt were meaningful. The thinkers and writers of the Patristic tradition, by contrast, had complete faith in the urgency of what concerned them and wrote about it with energy and assurance, in apologetics, in exegesis, in homiletics, in works on ecclesiastical organization and supervision, on asceticism and hagiography, on the doctrinal controversies. It is generally the assumption of our age that these productions, particularly the last, represent wasted time. This is not the opinion, however, of those who know them well and recognize the place they hold in the development of the thought processes of Western man. Many of the controversies were dreary and futile affairs; many of the controversialists were inspired by economic and political motives or by personal interest, and wrote more passionately than intelligently. It remains true that the theological disputes very often dealt with subjects of undying concern to mankind, that frequently they were waged with sincerity and brilliance, and that they gave a strong impetus to the development of a method of thought keen, probing, and logical. Their contribution to the formation in later centuries of scholastic philosophy, one of the high points in the development of Western thought, is sufficiently well known to require no description here.

Thus we must be extremely cautious in passing judgment upon the intellectual accomplishments of the Patristic Age in comparison with those of classical antiquity. Divergence from the earlier standard we must recognize, simplification and even abandonment in some areas of learning we must acknowledge, but to issue a general condemnation of the intellectual life of the age as decadent, retrogressive, and benighted is simply to open the way to hopeless distortion of the historical realities and to make it impossible to understand them. There can be no denying that such evils as poverty, instability, and violence became worse after the time of St. Jerome and St. Augustine before they became better, and that intellectual pursuits suffered along with everything else. The essential consideration is that by the fourth century a new intellectual attitude toward the world had been well launched; that this attitude was not necessarily either superior or inferior to that of classical antiquity, but simply different; and that the circumstances and nature of its development were of the greatest consequence. It is doubtful that any attitude of mind and spirit less toughly welded, less aggressive, and less convinced of its mission could have weathered the storms that were to envelop Western Europe in the centuries ahead.

Remarkably enough, some at least of the intellectual leaders among the Christian clergy were aware that something very crucial, something requiring explanation, was taking place. . . .

It remained for Augustine of Hippo, however, to accept the challenge of his time on the highest intellectual plane and state the case for the rising Christian culture in his powerful philosophy of history. He saw that it was necessary not only to reply to the gibes of the pagans, but also to scotch the popular identification of the welfare of Christianity with the welfare of Rome. Though he doubtless thought of the problem primarily and immediately as one of apology, he was unquestionably aware that the whole meaning of history for Christians was also involved. He broke with certain contemporary and earlier historical theories and set about disabusing Christian minds of the expectation of steady material progress. Ultimately he rejected the concept of the materialistic progress of the earthly city for all future ages, and for his own time he cut the tie binding together the fates of the Christian religion and the Roman State. . . .

Did Augustine fully understand that he was helping prepare the road which the new world of the future would follow as it departed from the crumbling ruins of the Roman Empire and the classical past? So much could be expected of no man. . . . He was not omniscient. His accomplishment was to prepare the minds of his more thoughtful contemporaries and successors for the possibility of a change

in the political state of affairs as they knew it, and to enable them to adapt themselves to this change. He was a pioneer on the frontiers of thought; like all pioneers, he pushed into vast unknown areas, made his way as best he could, and did not always fully take in all he saw from mountaintops. He blazed new trails; others followed them, widened them, pushed them further. . . .

The Pioneer Society: Missionary Monks and the Winning of the West for Christianity. The foregoing description of St. Augustine as a cultural pioneer reintroduces a theme already briefly mentioned but to be stressed in the concluding sections of this interpretation; it is that in many respects the beginning of the Middle Ages was a pioneering movement. . . . In Europe from sixteen to thirteen centuries ago, much as in America in the last century, there were wildernesses and savages to contend with and a new way of life to create.

Although the expansion was guided and supported by a Church which had its administrative and cultural capital in Italy, the oldest and strongest center of culture in the West, the molders and bearers of the rising civilization had to rely mainly upon their own resources. Consequently what emerged was not simply the result of the transmission of a culture but the product of this transmission in the peculiar conditions of life found in semi-barbarous and materially backward northern and western European communities. To make possible a society in which paramount importance attached to individualism, to adjustment and adaptation, to experimentation and invention, and to a new standard of human values, it seems safe to say that the clash and fusion of classical, Germanic, and Celtic tastes, traditions, and cultures in something resembling a frontier environment and under the spiritual guidance of the Christian Church was necessary. . . .

During the chaotic age in which the Western tradition was born, new knowledge was only partly acquired in schools. The schools maintained by the Church, chiefly in monasteries, were repositories of the old knowledge, much of it meaningless to early medieval men; by necessity they were to some extent experimental in what they taught. Most of what men of this period learned, however, they learned directly, like men on all frontiers and in all times of turmoil, from the experience of living.

As new needs arose they were met on the spot as well as could be, just as they still are today in industry. Doubtless also successful solutions suggested ideas for new needs and additional improvements. . . .

Our best single illustration of the new way of life is afforded by the monastic expansion. When most of Western Europe, the once civilized as well as the uncivilized portions, took on the character of an agrarian society, it obviously became impossible for the old modes of propagating culture through urban centers to continue to operate. The State—i.e., the barbarian government—could not perform the task. The Church, which was in some respects more powerful than the State and in all respects better organized, could. The relationship between the two had been foreshadowed by St. Augustine in the City of God; according to this view, the Church as the representative of the eternal city was the superior, the State the subordinate partner. The Church, or rather its hierarchy of bishops, was both able to take an active part in secular affairs and willing to run the risk of being made worldly itself. No secular work harmonized better with its desires and capacities than the work of promoting Christian culture.

In the conditions of the time there was only one way of extending knowledge and building a new culture, and that was by sending agents out to live and work in the agrarian communities under barbarian rule. These agents were mainly monks, and the monastic centers they established—first among the predominantly pagan rural peoples of such Romanized regions as Gaul and then among the even less civilized barbarians, many of them beyond the bounds of the former Empire—were like outposts or fortresses in a hostile land. . . .

Gibbon erroneously describes these early monasteries as refuges, chiefly inhabited by fainthearted men of aesthetic and intellectual inclinations, by idlers and wasters looking for an easy life, and by others who were unwilling or afraid to face the world. The monastic life did attract some men of this type, as St. Benedict frankly remarks at the beginning of his Rule, and there were others, even in the West, whose strongly ascetic bent made them unfit to participate in the cooperative and constructive work of cenobitic life. Most, however, were active and courageous; it was these who worked among the Franks and other early invaders, faced the hostile Lombards

in Italy, went to Ireland, Scotland, England, Iceland, Germany, and the Scandinavian countries. They were sane and hardheaded men; they faced facts. Turning their backs on the solitary life of prayer, often no doubt with reluctance, they did the work which they alone were able to do.

The elements of the problem were clear. A relatively small number of men had to reach a great many, widely scattered in rural communities, and from the monastic centers of worship and instruction give visible proof of the superiority of their way of life. Thus it was—and it must have been so from the first, though we have more detailed information beginning with the Merovingian era—that the pioneer monks lived with the peasants and shared their labors in plowing and planting, in reclaiming land, and in clearing away forests. . . . When a party of missionaries moved into a new region, in some cases with an excellent boat, and began to clear land, to erect buildings (sometimes of stone), to plant a vineyard or divert a stream to their use, to construct a mill, or to do intricate work in metal, the pagans must have been deeply impressed. The missionaries were seen to be much more than preachers of a new religion; they were teachers, builders, physicians, metalworkers—above all, perhaps, they were farmers, like the people among whom they lived. . . .

A Changing Society: The Seigniorial System.
Are there other signs that in this impoverished agrarian world a new civilization and a new way of life were being brought into existence? The shadows are so thick, the obscurity so forbidding, that one may venture to say so only with great caution. Happily, the shadows have been in part dispelled by contemporary scholars, . . . especially . . . in clarifying the rise of the seigniorial system. . . .

In certain areas of economic activity there took place a reversion to simpler, pre-Roman conditions, and future progress—for progress there certainly was—went on from that state of affairs. This advancement, when it came, did not follow slavishly along the old Roman lines but sometimes struck off in quite different directions. The view is still strongly supported, however, that, save for a few exceptions, the transition from Roman to medieval agriculture meant the loss of much and the gain of very little. Actually although early medieval agricultural methods were at first in many respects far behind the most advanced Roman methods, in the long run the change was worth all it cost. Roman agriculture, despite all its contributions and achievements, had been following a blind alley; before new advances could be made, much of the way had to be retraced and a new beginning undertaken in simpler conditions. . . .

Of outstanding importance in the passage from Roman to medieval practice was the decline of slavery. Fewer slaves were acquired by war, and the Church staunchly opposed the enslavement of orthodox Christians. Most important of all, with the breakdown of the large-scale exchange-profit economy of earlier Roman times, which had required abundant capital, relatively stable conditions, and very careful supervision, including the keeping of accurate accounts, slaves became a burden. "To adopt tenancy as a solution was the line of least resistance." Thereafter labor took care of itself; families had their own small pieces of land; and custom soon dictated the laborers' days of work on the lord's demesne, the *mansus indominicatus.*

It is highly significant that the combining of tenure with service, though not unknown in the Late Empire, became widely established only after the invasions. . . .

It is clear that the origins of the medieval *seigneurie* (manor) reach far back into history, into Roman times and even beyond to a dim era of rural chiefdoms. The passing centuries encrusted this core with successive layers of customs. In the Roman era there came the great demesnes, the *latifundia,* which employed large numbers of slaves and usually a scattering of dependent peasants. Beginning with the second century, changing economic, military, and religious conditions combined with the invasions to transform the slaves into tenants. In time the free *coloni* also became tenants, and they were soon indistinguishable (except by law) from servile tenants. . . .

Although the transition from large slave gangs on the *latifundia* to servile tenure on *seigneuries* is reasonably easy to follow, the relationship between the Late Roman colonate and seigniorial tenure presents a thornier problem. Superficially so similar, the two institutions were yet essentially different. . . .

Where there was no such *seigneurie,* . . . conditions remained close to what they had been on the

latifundia of antiquity. The peasants were not protected by the customs that grew up in seigniorial communities; they had few rights and many burdens; they were harshly exploited and lived in a condition very close to slavery. There was virtually no improvement, even in methods of farming. . . .

The original cell of the *mansus* appears to have been the patriarchal family and its holdings, to judge from what we know of the taxing unit officially called *iugum* or *caput.* This unit corresponded to the *mansus* or hide, originally the landholding of one family (taken in the patriarchal sense rather than in the modern). . . . It is very likely that this system of land division . . . was simply taken over by Roman tax experts for the excellent reason that it was already established.

The significance of this . . . is tremendous; among other things it means no less than that a device long hailed as one of the most important of Roman survivals into the Frankish period had actually been borrowed by the Romans in the first place and already had centuries of history behind it. Another striking evidence of the antiquity and hardiness of the embryo *seigneurie* is the persistence in customs of the relationship between chief and lesser men and the continuation of the customs of the village community as a social force. The peasant owed certain things, gifts, to the chief, but he also had certain obligations—in such vital matters as grazing and rotation of crops—to the social group, the village, in which he lived. These obligations were all sternly maintained by custom, and since the society was collective, these customary obligations affected the chief or lord as well as the peasants. The relationship of gifts and customs to seigniorial dues and services is clear. Still another impressive parallel is found in the remote division between chief and dependent peasants and the medieval cleavage between nobles and villagers. In effect, the new trend simply continued a development that for some centuries had been halted, or directed into different channels, by Roman domination. . . .

A Changing Society: Technology, Adaptation, and Invention. Until thirty years ago historians paid little attention to technology in the Middle Ages; the general assumption was that, here as elsewhere, stagnation, unrelieved blight, and superstition prevailed. The man responsible above all others for rendering this hoary assumption disreputable was Commandant Lefebvre des Noëttes (d. 1936), a onetime French cavalry officer, who upon his retirement from military life turned his professional training to account by making a historical study of animal power. This work eventually led him to acumulate an impressive body of evidence on technical developments and their social consequences, and to suggest some extremely significant and far-reaching revisions in historical interpretations. . . .

Perhaps the most notable of the early barbarian innovations were in apparel, e.g., trousers and furs; in domestic architecture; in such household appurtenances as felt, skis, butter, barrels, and tubs; and in the cultivation of several new varieties of grain. . . .

Meanwhile we may consider briefly some of the most important of the inventions, both native and imported, that began to exert their influence upon the newly forming civilization of the West. Naturally a great many of these are closely connected with agriculture. Those in which Lefebvre des Noëttes first interested himself have to do principally with the horse. He was convinced by his study of documents and of artistic and archaeological evidence that antiquity, in its attempts to use animal motive power, had barely scratched the surface, that its methods of using draft animals were extremely inefficient. One of the chief difficulties derived from the ancient method of harnessing. Horses were harnessed by means of a yoke resting on the withers; oxen by the same method, or by a yoke tied to the horns. The trouble, especially for the horse, was that a strap attached to the yoke above the withers passed around the beast's neck. When he leaned forward to pull, this strap cut into his windpipe and greatly hampered his breathing. This drawback . . . was removed at the beginning of the tenth century or earlier with the introduction of the rigid horse collar resting on the shoulders. Thereafter the horse could lean his full weight into his collar without having his wind cut off.

There were other improvements in harness attachments and apparatus, but after the horse collar Lefebvre des Noëttes considered the principal advances to be the horseshoe and tandem harnessing. . . .

Just how long before the tenth century [this system of traction began to be used] we cannot say. . . .

Unfortunately, more than the satisfaction of idle curiosity depends upon the point. If a technique of such tremendous value and of such revolutionary potentialities was in the hands of Westerners as early as, say, the fifth century, obviously the medieval technological movement was already far advanced. If it was either a barbarian invention or an import, the claim of Roman cultural domination until the eighth century would be still further weakened.

About this last point there can be very little question—the harness was introduced by the barbarians. All the evidence we possess points toward a date several centuries before the first manuscript drawings [in the tenth century]. . . .

Of the other early medieval inventions known to us, one of the more important is the wheeled plow. It seems likely that the Germans either invented this device or brought it to the West, to Gaul and Britain, in very early times. . . .

Of the diffusion and use of the heavy wheeled plow in the early Middle Ages, we know nothing. . . .

Lynn White,[1] putting aside the disputed question of the date and origin of the heavy plow, links its development and effectiveness with the invention and introduction, attested from the later eighth century, of the threefield system, which measurably increased agricultural production. This method had very great advantages. Not only did it cut down the amount of labor relative to the amount of produce, but it reduced the risks of loss from poor harvests. It was better suited to the more humid and temperate climate of the North, where its labor-saving advantages easily compensated for its disadvantages: more numerous plots and decreased grazing area. . . .

A tremendously important technical apparatus of another kind was the water mill. Although water mills are known to have existed shortly before the birth of Christ, the device was scarcely exploited at all in antiquity. . . .

As . . . has [been] said, however, an invention is spread abroad only if there is a strong feeling of social necessity, and before the end of the Empire there were such abundant supplies of labor, much of it

---

[1] An American historian of medieval technology. [Editor's note.]

slave labor, that no such feeling was expressed. Other considerations also enter into the diffusion of inventions, but necessity is essential. The need for the water mill came to be felt toward the end of the Empire, with the decline of slavery. Like other technical improvements of the time, the water mill spread slowly, and older and simpler methods of grinding flour remained in use for centuries. First the monastic authorities, and later secular lords, learned to see substantial advantages for themselves in building water mills to be used by the neighboring peasants, both tenants and others. Beginning with the tenth century, when the great move came to transform established customs into rights, many a lord set up a monopoly for his mill. Here, as in several other instances, the later period developed what the earlier period invented or recognized as opportunity. It is necessary to give credit for the pioneer vision, the ground work, to the early Middle Ages.

Other technical improvements invented or first exploited in the early medieval period might be discussed here, among them the crank, a discovery of fundamental importance in the technological history of Western European civilization and a vast step forward in the acquisition of power devices. Enough has been said, however, to demonstrate the points at issue: the sharp break with the past, the inseparable connection of the new technology with the nature and conditions of the new society in which it grew. . . .

It becomes clear, as one examines the problem, that in industrial as well as in other activities the ancient world had lost its capacity to originate. . . .

How did it happen that after the break-up of the Western Roman Empire, the Occident became so inventive in its own right, so receptive of foreign contributions, so alert to the possibilities of devices that had been available but not availed of for centuries, such as the water mill? That is the basic question.

There is no basic answer. . . . The established patterns of the old civilization had been shaken up and scrambled beyond repair. Later developments demonstrated that whereas many of the pieces would fit well in new patterns, for the most part new pieces were needed. . . .

In societies and cultures just as in structures of stone and steel the forms, the architecture, the relationships, are paramount. So when the old order collapsed it meant either starting anew or doing without. Whether a new start would be made was up to the successors of Rome in the West. I have contended that the atmosphere in which they reached their decision was fortunate; that the breakdown of age-old set patterns, the formation of a new society, and the recognition of new needs all coincided with a time of conflict, the movement of peoples, adjustment and readjustment, and rapid change. Peoples, customs, and values met and clashed for centuries in the frontier-like society of Western Europe. The exchange of ideas in such an atmosphere was easy. The old restraints upon the introduction, examination, and application of new methods were broken down. In a society in which the supply of manpower was small, a premium was put upon the invention of labor-saving devices. The climate was favorable to exploration and invention, and the soil, so to speak, proved to be rich and productive. There is good reason to believe that if these conditions had not come into existence, all of them together, the great technical advance, which is so fundamental a part of the Western European achievement, could not have been set in motion in the early Middle Ages.

Yet, what has just been said about the impressive early medieval beginning in techniques must also be said about the rest of the four "changes" discussed in this chapter. Not only in technology but in all of them conditions were such as to permit, and even to encourage, an active, positive attitude toward life. It follows at once that the changes made in these various milieux—and they were much more often than not changes for the better—themselves became part of an environment affecting and affected by each of the others, an environment constantly changing through their reciprocal influences upon each other.

The element of freedom stands out, or more accurately, the *preparation* for eventual freedom and individualism and dignity. The deeds and events of the period served a pathfinding function. This was a time when those aforementioned important changes of direction were made, when new goals were headed for. One of those goals, perhaps the most important of all, was freedom—for we can now see and recognize what our predecessors could not discern. Certain fundamental adjustments had to be made before truly significant advances could be made in technology; the West had first to be free from the domination of rigid social institutions obstructive of new methods, free to invent, experiment, borrow, and apply. We have seen how those alterations began to come about in the intellectual sphere, in the changed relation between State and individual, in the honorable position accorded labor through the powerful monastic institution and the missionary activity of the monks, in the status of women through the teachings of Christianity. There was in simple truth a renovation literally from the ground up in the rural, agrarian society of medieval Europe. . . .

H. ST. L. B. MOSS

CONTINUITY WITHOUT A BREAK

For a statement which stresses the element of continuity and gradual transformation across the entire early Middle Ages, let us turn to a passage by H. St. L. B. Moss, a distinguished British medievalist whose speciality has been primarily Byzantine history but who has also investigated with great care the problem of the passing of the Roman Empire. The following selection, drawn from the concluding chapter of Moss's *The Birth of the Middle Ages, 395–814,* presents a view of the Early Middle Ages which would find some of the ideas expressed in the previous selections too drastic. As he reads this passage, the student should not only look for elements of continuity marking the period but should also seek some basis for evaluating the previous authorities. This will permit him to answer the basic question posed by this problem: Was the essence of early medieval history a continuity with classical civilization or a break which brought a new order into existence?

An attempt may now be made to present some picture of the changes wrought by four centuries of darkness and confusion. Viewed from a height, as if from an imaginary aeroplane travelling swiftly over time and space, the Eurasiatic land-mass appears to be undergoing an intensified phase of those continuous movements of population which form the substructure of world history. Urged on by primal needs, its peoples surge to and fro in sudden waves of invasion or slower tides of penetration, controlled, like flood-waters, only by unconscious forces and geographical obstacles, or by the unequal capacity of different areas for supporting human life. A nearer view discloses man's handiwork in the creation of artificial barriers. At one extremity, the Great Wall of China stands as the symbol of a settled Empire, a notable victory in the eternal conflict between the Steppe and the Sown Land. At the other, the Roman *limes,* flanked by the frontiers of the Persian Sasanids, obstructs the western movement of the Germanic tribes. Between them lie the immense plains of Central Asia, breeding-grounds for the nomad hordes which sweep out of the desert on to the fertile countries which border it, bringing destruction though often, also, an infusion of fresh vigour. Storm over Asia is the danger-signal for old civilizations. Mongols and Manchus breach the Great Wall, and age-long Chinese dynasties are overthrown. Huns and Avars roll through the steppe corridor of southern Russia, and the successive shocks of their impact drive the Germanic hosts before them to end Rome's dominion in the West, and —two centuries later—to hurl the Slav masses with centrifugal force against the mid-continental peoples. Close upon this comes the tide of Arab invasion, submerging Syria and Egypt, flowing on over North Africa and Spain, and advancing at the same time north-eastwards beyond Persia, till it meets the vanguard of the Turkish hordes, awaiting their cue for Asia's final entry on the stage of Europe.

From H. St. L. B. Moss, *The Birth of the Middle Ages, 395–814* (Oxford, 1935), pp. 242–65. Reprinted by permission of The Clarendon Press.

Coming closer to earth, we notice the network of Roman roads still covering the face of the countryside, but no longer, in A.D. 800, dotted with the busy long-distance traffic of merchants or officials, or threaded with the stone-built inns and posting-stations which a Chinese observer, in the first century after Christ, marked as characteristic features of the Roman Empire. Trade is by no means extinct, and it is clear that much of the economic structure of Imperial times remains in large districts of France and Italy. Even the town, in many instances, retains its former importance as a local centre of commerce. Boats pass up the Po, Rhine, and Rhône, and the ferries and bridges of Roman Gaul and Italy still continue to pay their tribute to the Franks and Lombards, though this does not necessarily indicate more than local traffic. Numberless examples of such commercial activity could be given but a broad contrast nevertheless remains between classical and early medieval economic conditions in Europe. . . . During the first and second centuries A.D., under the aegis of the *Pax Romana,* the mass-productions of the provinces were freely and systematically exchanged by land- and sea-borne traffic from Britain to Syria, furnishing the inhabitants or the armies with the ordinary necessities of life, corn, wine and oil, metals, lumber, clothes, and pottery. . . .

Very different is the situation round about A.D. 800. Making all allowances for variety, one may justly term the prevailing system in Western Europe a "closed house-economy" . . . , in which the needs of life were supplied by the labour of self-sufficient communities, and "exchange of goods takes a subordinate place to production." Long-distance trade, broadly speaking, is confined to luxuries for Court and Church—spices, jewels, ivories, incense, works of art. . . . This system of "local horizons" was directly due to the breakdown of Roman government, communications, and trade, and the turning-point may perhaps be placed not in the fifth century but rather during the fifty years of anarchy and invasion, 235–85, which virtually destroyed the intricate economic fabric of the Empire. . . .

So far as Western trade and industry, then, are concerned, the Late Roman and the Early Medieval periods show no definite break. Mediterranean shipping, or what remained of it by the fifth century, was crippled by the Vandal pirates, and no Carolingian revival was possible after the rise of Islamic sea-power. The overland route to the east was equally blocked by the troops of westward-marching invaders, by the subsequent occupation of Hungary by Huns and Avars, and by the immigration of Slavs. Certain local products, it is true, maintain or create their markets—Toledo weapons, Cordova leather, Frisian cloths. Northern towns such as Etaples, Utrecht, London, Slesvig, and Birka in Sweden find mention as trading centres. Annual fairs, as at Troyes and St. Denis, attract pedlars from all countries, kings legislate concerning trade, and big towns have their regular merchant quarters. The great frontier marts of the Rhine district under Roman rule are paralleled by Charlemagne's row of licensed trading stations on the Slav boundary. Certain long-distance routes, like the Baltic-Black Sea waterway, show increased activity in the eighth century, while Arabs, Jews, and Syrians, purveyors of eastern curiosities, are not unknown in the Frankish cities. Yet the fact remains that the early medieval period shows no regular commercial activity in the West which can be called indispensable to the maintenance of society. Conditions in the Byzantine Empire were quite otherwise, for here the Roman economic structure had remained intact, with its currency and credit, its markets and commercial legislation, and maritime trade connexions with the Far East, severed since the second century, had even been restored.

Agriculture presents a somewhat different picture, though here, too, the barbarian invasions produced no real break; the early Middle Ages in Western Europe are a continuation of a steady progress, dating from the time of Caesar, in which skilled methods of tilling the soil spread outwards from the circle of the Roman Empire into the heart of the Continent. From the Rhineland and north-eastern France, Roman instruments and technique crossed the frontier into Germany, and with the settling-down of the barbarian tribes, a pastoral and hunting existence was replaced by stable agricultural occupations over an ever-increasing part of Europe. Behind this zone lay the dim world of marsh, forest, and steppe, of nomad peoples and food-gatherers. The boundaries of this world were continually receding, but large portions of it lingered behind—immense virgin forests in France and Germany, shepherd-peoples roaming the Balkan uplands. Further diversity was introduced into the agricultural map of Europe by peculiarities of soil and climate, and by tribal and local custom. . . .

But the main line of cleavage in the West is one still visible to-day, between the Mediterranean intensive culture, on the one hand, with its individually owned patches of corn, vines, and olives, its short furrows, and light plough, and, on the other, the extensive husbandry of more northern latitudes, where a rough climate, a sparse population, and large districts of forest or morass produced systems of cultivation in which grazing plays a large and often a predominant part, human labour is scarce and unskilful, and the heavy plough with its eight oxen traces long furrows down the open field-strips.

The real importance of these contrasted conditions is psychological. The clear-cut Mediterranean system, which prevailed in Italy, southern Gaul, Spain, and North Africa under Roman rule, with its strong individualism, its self-sufficient, absolute ownership of land, lent itself admirably to purposes of taxation and definition of status. . . . Natural conditions in the North, however, produced a co-operative mentality, a world of thought in which rights of private ownership were dim and vaguely formulated. Rotation of crops, intermingling of strips, common use of wood and water, shared pasturage—habits of life arising from customs such as these created a rural economy more flexible, more irregular than that of the Mediterranean area. . . . They have left their traces upon village life and the local, self-governing institutions of medieval days, and they form an essential component in the growth of the Manor, delaying, and in many cases permanently preventing, the complete symmetry which feudal influences would otherwise have imposed.

It is, however, a false simplification to extend this contrast to the social evolution of Western Europe during the early Middle Ages, and to represent the issue as the submergence of German personal freedom and democratic institutions beneath the weight of Roman juristic conceptions, founded on centuries of organized oppression of the lower classes, and a Mediterranean view of the cheapness of human life and labour. It is true that this period is marked by a widespread "debasement and breaking-up of the class of common free men." . . . Yet it is clear that converging tendencies on both sides, Roman and Germanic, prepared the way for this "aristocratic transformation of society." The break-down of Roman government placed power, actual though not wholly constitutional, in the hands of the local magnates, who became petty sovereigns over their *coloni,* judging and taxing their tenants. The economic depression of the Empire, however, while it converted small freeholders into dependants of the landowner, and restricted their freedom of move-

ment, rendered them indispensable to him owing to scarcity of labour, and thus gave them a bargaining advantage; and meanwhile the improved status of the slave, due to humanitarian, and, later, Christian ideas and legislation, brought him nearer to the *colonus* and thus contributed to the formation of a large "half-free" class, the *laborantes,* who, together with the *orantes* (the Church) and the *bellantes* (the nobility) formed the constituent elements of West-European society.

The Teutonic side of the picture, on the other hand, is by no means one of ideal primitive freedom and democracy, as enthusiastic historians of the nineteenth century sometimes proclaimed. . . . The warriors of a primitive community, as in early Greece or Rome, were valuable to the State, and had therefore to be conciliated; they might even be given a certain share in policy. Yet even in the days of Tacitus there were inequalities of rank among the Germans; when the migrating tribes settled permanently, these inequalities were perpetuated by land-grants. A hereditary nobility might be replaced by a nobility of service, as the kings gained power; but this new nobility soon became hereditary, and from the earliest days of settlement, side by side with the free villages, we find a steady growth in the estates of nobles and abbatial landlords. The anarchy of Merovingian days produces a similar effect to that of the Roman collapse; free men "commend" themselves to gain the protection of a powerful landowner, while the central power is constantly found bartering or giving away its control. . . .

Developed political theories, which arise always from contemporary conditions, are naturally not to be looked for in centuries of turmoil, when the *de facto* maintenance of any authority at all is vastly more important than the *de jure* claims of him who exercises it. Yet two main changes may be noticed in men's ideas of the State, produced by the break-down of the Roman Empire in Western Europe, which were fated to influence the whole medieval period. The first is the altered relation of the secular and ecclesiastical authorities, which becomes fully apparent only after the dissolution of the Carolingian Empire. The second is the prevalence of habits of thought derived from barbarian tribal conditions. The mixed populations, of varying degrees of culture, in the Romano-German kingdoms provided difficult problems of administration, which were solved by adopting the curious principle of the "personality of law." Each man lived by the law of his people, Roman, Burgundian, Visigoth, Bavarian, Salian or Ripuarian Frank. . . . The process of fusion between these systems is a mirror of the larger cultural development of Western Europe. Personality, as a principle, gives place eventually to territoriality, but not before it has served its purpose in ensuring the survival, during a critical transition period, of legal customary variants. "Custom," in fact, comes to be regarded as the ultimate sanction, and in this we may recognize the triumph of "the ancient Germanic idea of a tribal law, immemorial in character, and binding upon king and people alike." Closely connected with this notion of the supremacy of law is that of the kingship "based primarily on service to the nation." This principle of responsible sovereignty, which contests with its Asian rival—the principle of the monarch ruling by divine right, mystic, sacerdotal, *solutus legibus,* vice-gerent of God—for the future of European government is essentially Germanic. . . .

All the more necessary, perhaps, in view of the momentous change which Constantine introduced, when by his identification of the interests and unity of Christianity and Empire he took the Church, as it were, into partnership, and intensified the hieratic cast of governmental authority. By the grant of jurisdiction to the Church, it became henceforth an organ of administration, and the gaps left by the gradual ousting of Imperial control in Italy were steadily filled up by the developing Papal organization. The barbarian rulers, despite their independent and sometimes threatening attitude towards the papal claims, likewise made use of the Church to serve their national ends, for only in its ranks did they find sufficient knowledge of Roman methods to cope with the complex problems of a civilized community. The turning-point in this process is reached in the remarkable "change of heart" in regard to the "barbarians" which Gregory the Great introduced into papal policy. To the minds of Leo I, Augustine, and Jerome, the mission of the Church might be universal in theory, but in practice it was limited by the boundaries of the Roman Empire. . . . Gregory's great missionizing and diplomatic activities in Western Europe ended all this, and prepared the way for new and undreamed-of possibilities, and with the growth of papal influence in the new kingdoms eventual severance from Byzantium, the Imperial world-centre, gradually became a conceivable thing. . . .

The character of the cultural transformation produced during these centuries by the collapse of Roman government in the West may perhaps be described as a crumbling and disintegration of the topmost layer of civilization. Fragments of this layer survived, in some places almost intact, but no longer as constituent parts of the universal pattern. Older, regional traditions, obscured for centuries by the standardized design created and superimposed by the Roman Imperial machine, emerged once more on the surface. New and revolutionary ferments, long working underground, became apparent in their effects. . . .

Artistically, the official Empire style, seen at its worst in the mass-productions exported to outlying provinces ("Samian" ware and the like) declines in company with the causes of its creation and distribution, and local, non-Roman traditions resume their sway in certain districts—flexible Celtic patterns, massive Teutonic jewellery, and the fanciful designs of the Scandinavian craftsman in wood and metal. . . . But it is a mistake to regard this either as "decadence" or, on the other hand, as an inherent development on purely artistic lines of evolution, conditioned by technical problems to be solved. The true "decadence" of ancient art is to be found in those photographically realistic statues of rheumatic fishermen, emaciated crones and brutal pugilists which satisfied Roman aesthetic demands in the third century. A decline both in skill and in public taste . . . but the change lies deeper than this. It is a change of spirit, of outlook, pervading every aspect of life, which here seeks expression, hesitatingly at first, but evolving later into the triumphant certainties of Byzantine and Romanesque. The predominant character of this change is Oriental. In religion, it appears in the prevalence of mystery-cults, and in the final victory of the greatest of these, Christianity. In thought can be traced a concomitant development of Eastern symbolism. In art, the Christian and mystical outlook transforms from within the products of classical tradition and is reinforced from without by the material influence of Asiatic styles and techniques. With the Empire centered at Byzantium, this influence becomes steadier and more powerful, and the cultural and economic supremacy of the capital results in the dispersion of its artistic output over the whole of barbarized Europe, to serve as models or correctives in the development of medieval art.

Similar tendencies—the emergence of old popular forms, the action of new ferments—can be seen at work in the transformation of literature and language. The aristocracy of Greek metres, with their delicate music of quantitative syllables, had maintained a precarious hold over Latin verse, the natural roots of which were fixed deep in the stressed peasant rhythms of threshing-floor, spinning-wheel and country dance, the gnomic saws of the rustic oracle, and the heavy tramp of the marching legionary. Fragmentary snatches of this folk poetry can be caught underneath the swelling chorus of Imperial singers—a children's rhyme, a ribald catch of Caesar's veterans, an amatory line scrawled on the street-wall of Pompeii. During the second century this accentual verse was adopted by a group of literary innovators. . . . The weakening of cultural standards encouraged such developments, and the new spirit discovered a congenial vehicle of self-expression in the broad emotional effects of strongly stressed rhythms. . . . Rhyme and assonance, features already familiar to folk-poetry, become prominent at the same time, and the creation of medieval hymnodic forms is thus practically complete.

Prose followed the same course. . . .

The spoken language itself undergoes a parallel transformation. Here, once more, the basis of the change is psychological. Caution is necessary in dealing with a medium so fluid and evanescent, but certain persistent tendencies are observable. Vulgar Latin, fundamentally speaking, is to be distinguished from high literary Latin by the quality of the thought which it expresses. Though not uninfluenced by the Hellenic discipline, noticed above, which pervaded educated speech and writing, its spirit remained impervious to the external impress of Greek antiquity, and it thus continued to be the property of the common folk, which survived the political and economic débâcle of the West, and was subsequently differentiated into the various Romance languages. "Hellenized Latin," on the other hand, "thanks to its literary mummification, could neither live nor die after the downfall of the Roman state. As 'Middle Latin' it led a supernatural existence in the Church, the school, on paper, on the tongues and in the ears of scholars." . . . It remained poised in mid-air, above the currents of everyday talk which are the effective forces in the development of language.

Meanwhile popular speech, freed from the constant pressure of alien modes of thought, lay open to the twin influences of this time—a revival of local tra-dition, and the action of new stimuli. Changes in vocabulary and syntax reflect the corresponding change of mentality. With the disappearance of the aristocratic, personal, Stoic attitude to life, there goes also the variable word order and studied emphasis, together with the inflexions which made them possible. In their place come the impersonal style, aiming at communication rather than self-expression, the overstatement characteristic of uneducated speech, and the altered meaning of the future, which is no longer accepted with resignation or determined resolve, but becomes the object of passionate hopes and fears. . . .

Greek development in literature and language brings out even more clearly the tendencies already outlined. . . .

The spirit of Christian mysticism found an outlet in the creation of new rhythms, inspired by Syrian models, which pervade the hymns of this period, with their Oriental refrains and ecstatic fervour, reaching their highest development in the magnificent liturgical chants of Romanus, which echoed under the great dome of St. Sophia.

The rich heritage of Hebraic thought and worship which had been taken over by the Church during her earlier centuries of existence profoundly influenced the formation of the Christian liturgy. But this heritage is itself only one manifestation of a religious consciousness, an approach to the mystery of the Unseen shared by the dwellers in the Near East, whose origins must be sought far back in the immemorial traditions of Egypt and Babylonia. The passive, brooding contemplation of the Divine essence, the eager abandonment of individuality which distinguish Oriental religiosity from the active, concrete, humanistic conceptions of Hellenic thought demanded for their expression new emotional rhythms, a new vocabulary, and even a new structure of the sentence. In the poetry and prayer-ritual of the Christian Church can be traced features common to the Old Testament, the Koran, and the magical papyri, and just as in the artistic sphere the revolutionary content transfigured the Graeco-Roman form which conveyed it, so here the negative, non-rational attributes of Deity, the preoccupation of the worshipper, not with the activities, but with the nature and being of God, found utterance in participial and relative constructions, in strange invocations and free-moving rhapsodies which finally, in the case of the liturgy, resulted in the creation of a new form of Greek poetical prose.

Oriental influence upon the art, religion, and literature of the Mediterranean world exercised a constant pressure, varying only in intensity, which stretches back far into prehistoric times. Mystery cults . . . spread rapidly throughout the West, and captured the imagination of the populace. Yet though Roman belief succumbed so completely to Asiatic modes of worship, the religious psychology of the West retained its distinct character, and more than one aspect of the dogmatic controversies of the early Christian centuries can be explained by the contrast, not only between the legalistic, concrete attitude of Latin theology and speculative, metaphysical proclivities of Greek writers, but between the emphasis laid by the West on the personality and saving activities of Christ, and the passionate absorption of Eastern thought in the supratemporal essence of the Divine nature.

Similar differences are displayed by the West in its use of symbolism and allegory, which may, broadly speaking, be taken as the characteristic mental processes of this period. . . . To look behind language, behind the visible world apprehended by mind and senses, to another, secret language, a secret world known only to the initiate, is the privilege of the poet and mystic in all ages. . . . The subjective method, however, is a dangerous one; lacking objective controls, the individual lies open to all the hidden currents of his time. Primitive animism—the conviction of the *mana* residing in words, actions, and inanimate objects—now recrudescent in a revival of sorcery and divination entered into Neoplatonism when its poetic powers of organization weakened, and the distinction between the symbol and that which it represented was disastrously obscured. Magic, which is fundamentally materialistic, destroyed the spiritual basis of allegory, and the decay of intellectual and imaginative energy ruined the appositeness of the symbol. . . . With the break-down of general culture, the sense of the word, unchecked by reason, gradually retreated into fantasy, and on this the Middle Ages reared its structure of thought. . . .

During the ages of transition, the Western Church as a whole definitely feared and distrusted the pagan learning; there were notable exceptions to this attitude, but the uncompromising tradition of Tertullian proved stronger, and finally prevailed

with the influence of Gregory. In a natural reaction from earlier depreciation of the "Dark Ages," stress has recently been laid on the "humanism" of the medieval Church; but it is not difficult to overstate this view, for it is certain that the sole purpose of education at this time in the West was to train ecclesiastics for the performance of their duties. The knowledge required for an understanding of the Latin services, and—in the case of more advanced pupils—for the study of Christian controversial and expository literature, the computation of Easter and other festivals, the legal and administrative system of the Church, provided in many cases an admirable curriculum, and the organized life of the monastery, with its regular hours, its library, and its economic security, gave opportunities for the preservation of culture in dangerous times which no other institution could have afforded. But the extraordinary achievements of scholars . . . must not blind us to the fact that our gratitude for the preservation of classical literature would have incurred the censure of the most orthodox ecclesiastical authorities, nor cause us to minimize the great gulf which divides the learning of this age from that of Jerome, and still more that of Origen, when all the resources of ancient civilization were still available. For several centuries these resources had been declining; and the Church further reduced and diluted the supply. Creative thought had long ceased; the taste of the time had turned to epitomes, anthologies, grammars, and works of reference. Genuine mastery of the Greek language disappeared wholly from the West; after Boethius there was no real assimilation of Hellenic philosophy. . . . Passive encyclopaedists, like Isidore of Seville and Raban Maur, are the characteristic product of the early Middle Ages—an indication of the stern necessity for the preservation of extant knowledge in face of the barbarism which threatened to engulf it.

The close of the sixth century witnessed a definite breakdown of culture in France and, to a lesser extent, in Italy also. Gregory of Tours, the foremost writer in Gaul, was not employing a figure of rhetoric when he bewailed his lack of grammar and education, and the generations which followed him were plunged into yet deeper abysses of barbarism. Literary Latin, the medium of thought, degenerated into a strange jargon, as may be seen in the scanty documents of this period, and the most polished poets of the Carolingian revival composed their Latin verses in a tongue nearly as foreign to them as it is to a French schoolboy at the present day. At the same time many popular beliefs and superstitions found their way into the official teaching of the Western Church. . . . With the break-down of communications, uncertain conditions of life, and confusion of standards and cultures, a powerful impetus was given to rumour and credulity, belief in marvels and demons and in the efficacy of magical objects.

It is not to be supposed that any more rational attitude had previously prevailed among the unlettered. There had always been more gods than men in the ancient world. . . . Nor did such tendencies vanish at the close of the Middle Ages; sorcery reached perhaps its highest development in the sixteenth, and witch-hunting in the seventeenth, centuries. Christianity, however, did not succeed in altering the situation in this respect, and just as the Roman State had finally given much of her organization to the victorious Church, so dying paganism also bequeathed its heritage to the medieval mind. Europe, moreover, during these centuries was only imperfectly Christianized. . . .

Yet paganism lived on throughout the Middle Ages, a tortuous underworld of mingled beliefs originating from various periods and racial strata, of vegetation-spirits from Italy, Celtic watersprites, Teutonic ogres and fairies, Scandinavian monsters, and the diminished forms of gracious Greek divinities. Beneath all changes of name and ceremonial, the peasant observed his ancient seasonal festivals, and paid his homage to the fertile spirits of seed-time and harvest. Tristan, Beowulf, and the heroes of the *Nibelungenlied* remained on the lips of men, and even the exploits of Alexander and the old tale of Troy were not utterly forgotten. Far removed from reality, however, were these medieval versions of classical history, fantastic variations on themes already distorted in late Roman times. Virgil the won-

der-working magician, Alexander the hero of a cycle of Oriental stories, dream-like as those in the *Arabian Nights,* are but dim reflections of their actual selves. The men of these centuries, indeed, saw as through a glass, darkly, the distant figures and events of the ancient world, remote from their own conditions as medieval Europe is from the present day. Rome itself, to the awestruck pilgrim, held no longer the memory of a busy and prosperous capital. It was a holy city of shrines and martyrdom, but a city also of haunted ruins, of strange legends and happenings of a marvellous past, a city where Popes exorcized plague-dealing snakes, or bound dragons by solemn incantations in caves under the Capitol.

Yet, though a vivid picture of antiquity may have been even more unattainable for the medieval than for the modern mind, the civilization of the Roman Empire still moulded the laws, the institutions and the forms of thought which governed human life in the Middle Ages, and which were destined finally to prevail in Europe. The sculptors and architects of Italy and southern France gave inspiration to their medieval successors. All human wisdom was acknowledged to reside in the ancient authors, and the literature of the Augustan age held with a powerful fascination even the half-unwilling reader. The Church retained the fabric of Roman organization, and the ideal of Imperial unity, with its hopes for a common European culture, though shattered at the death of Charlemagne, held ultimate promise of revival, for it had reared a fortress in France and the surrounding countries against which the storm-waves of Viking, Magyar, and Saracen were to dash their forces in vain, a fortress which guarded within its monastery and castle walls the treasures, spiritual and material, snatched so precariously from the wreckage of the ancient world.

2

THE CAROLINGIAN EMPIRE: ITS INSPIRATION

About 1310 Dante wrote in his *De Monarchia* that " . . . it is necessary in order that the world be at its best that there be a monarch of the world; and, in consequence, monarchy is necessary for the well-being of the world." This plea for a single world-state reflected in part the poet's passionate wish for a political miracle to pacify the troubled world of the fourteenth century. More significantly, Dante was echoing—as he so often did—one of the fundamental concepts that shaped the "first" Europe. Across the eight centuries that separated Dante from the collapse of the Roman Empire in the West the need to unite men into a single community had always been uppermost in the minds of the princes, prelates, and philosophers who shaped Europe's destiny. And for a good part of the medieval period the ideal of a universal state was embodied in a living institution—the Holy Roman Empire. Although the medieval Empire was disintegrating in Dante's generation and was destined to remain only a political ghost until its formal dissolution in 1806, the institution and the ideals which inspired it were of the greatest importance in shaping Europe's destiny prior to the fourteenth century.

Perhaps it is true, as one modern commentator has noted, that the medieval idea of world empire "has had a pathetic charm for modern men . . . because we are haunted by a wish to believe that there was an age in which such dreams could be widely dreamed." But whoever hopes to understand the "first" Europe must be more than charmed by medieval man's ability to dream such a dream; he must comprehend the substance of the medieval idea of empire. It was one of the prime forces working to create a sense of community in Europe, especially during the turbulent era between the fifth and the eleventh centuries when powerful centrifugal forces were fragmenting society.

There are many paths that might lead to a better understanding of the medieval concept of empire: through an examination of numerous medieval discourses on the imperial idea; through a study of the history of the actual medieval empire; through a reading of the best part of the mountain of scholarly literature that modern historians have produced on the subject. Perhaps the simplest and most direct approach lies through a single historical episode around which clustered the issues and the ideas basic to the medieval theory and practice of empire. Most historians would agree that the coronation of Charlemagne by Pope Leo III on Christmas Day, 800, was such an event. It marked the first attempt of Europeans to realize the imperial ideal, and therefore became an archetype for all later attempts. It was an event enacted by men powerfully moved by the ideological concepts basic to all later medieval concepts of the empire. It occurred at a decisive moment in the search for identity among Europeans that had been going on since the collapse of the Roman Empire. It created an institution, the Carolingian Empire, which had to face all the practical problems that beset the efforts of later Europeans to erect a single political community, and thus it exposed the troublesome gap between the theory and the practice of unity that has haunted the European conscience to this day.

In order to understand the following discussions of the Carolingian Empire each student must recall the chain of events that led to Charlemagne's coronation and to the efforts by Charlemagne and his successors to sustain the empire. In the background lay the establishment of the Frankish kingdom by Clovis and his successors in the sixth century, the decline of the Merovingian dynasty in the seventh century, and the rise of the Carolingian family through the clever exploitation of the office of mayor of the palace in the early eighth century. Then came the crucial events of mid-eighth century: the assumption of the Frankish crown by Pepin the Short with papal approval and blessing; the establishment of a Frankish protectorate over the papacy through the Donation of Pepin; and the beginning of a major reform of the Frankish church through the co-operative efforts of the new dynasty and the papacy. All these momentous events signified a new alignment of power and a fresh urge to regenerate society. Charlemagne (768–814) broadened and intensified these trends by a vigorous and successful program of conquest, internal reordering of his kingdom, and religious and cultural reform. By the end of the eighth century he was hailed as the ruler "supreme in the world and the mightiest of Europe." His successes led to his coronation as "emperor and augustus" on Christmas Day, 800. During most of the ninth century Charlemagne, his successors—especially Louis the Pious (814–840)—and many of the chief lay and ecclesiastical magnates labored to give that new title a positive meaning in political reality. Their efforts ultimately failed, but not before certain political concepts of the deepest significance to the formation of Europe were articulated and riven into the minds of men to become a permanent part of the European tradition.

The following selections represent only a few of the diverse interpretations of the nature and meaning of the Carolingian Empire. They have been selected because they reflect the motives and ideas which moved men of the eighth and ninth centuries to try to create a single political community for Western Europe. Although the various authors do not agree, their disagreement is not our major concern. The issue is the several layers of meaning that were involved in the Carolingian concept of empire. As he reads these passages, the student should first attempt to comprehend the assumptions that the Carolingians made concerning the nature of society. Beyond this crucial matter, he should look for areas where the architects of the Carolingian Empire disagreed concerning their enterprise. Finally, he should try to comprehend the realistic factors in Carolingian society which made difficult the maintenance of the empire. So armed he will be much better prepared to comprehend the history of the empire established later by the rulers of Germany, the quarrels between emperors and popes that repeatedly disturbed the medieval scene, and the basic political concepts that guided medieval rulers.

CONTEMPORARY ACCOUNTS

THE CREATION OF THE CAROLINGIAN EMPIRE

James Bryce summarized the opinion of many modern historians when he wrote as follows: "The coronation of Charles is not only the central event of the Middle Ages, it is also one of the very few events of which, taking them singly, it may be said that if they had not happened, the history of the world would have been different." This provocative statement prompts one to ask whether those actually involved in the coronation saw it in quite the same light. The following brief passages from sources nearly contemporary to the event of 800 will supply the best answer to this query. They represent virtually all that survives as first-hand, primary sources reporting the coronation. Upon first reading them one is tempted to conclude that men of Charlemagne's generation had only a faint notion of the import of events occurring about them—not an uncommon situation throughout all history. Yet these bare accounts contain the fundamental concepts which later historians use to explain the nature and significance of the coronation. They therefore deserve a close reading as a starting point for an understanding of the medieval idea of empire.

The first description, probably written by an official at the papal court shortly after 816, is from a collection of papal biographies called the *Liber pontificalis*. It should be read as a reflection of the interpretation placed upon the coronation by the papal court. The next two accounts are from contemporary annals which were compiled by authors who usually reflect the opinion of Charlemagne's court. The selection from the court annals (the *Annales regni Francorum*) was apparently written prior to the selection from the *Annales Laureshamenses*. The student should take special note of the shift in interpretation between the first and second accounts. The fourth selection was written not long after Charlemagne's death (814) by Einhard, an important court scholar who was an adviser and ardent admirer of the great ruler. As will be obvious, his account raises certain enigmas. The selection by Theophanes reflects how observers in Constantinople, long viewed as the seat of the one true emperor, saw the event in Rome.

In reading these accounts the student should look especially for evidence concerning certain key issues involved in the birth of the Carolingian Empire. What did those involved think they were doing? Why did they act as they did? What did they hope to accomplish? Who bore the prime responsibility for the coronation? These are the problems that have concerned historians since 800. The answers constitute the essence of the medieval idea of empire.

FROM THE BIOGRAPHY OF POPE LEO III[1]

After these things, the day of the birth of our Lord Jesus Christ having come, all were again gathered in the aforesaid basilica of the blessed Peter the Apostle. And then the gracious and venerable pontiff with his own hands crowned him [Charles] with a very precious crown. Then all the faithful people of Rome, seeing the defense that he gave and the love that he bore for the holy Roman Church and her Vicar, by the will of God and of the blessed Peter, the keeper of the keys of the kingdom of heaven, cried with one accord in a loud voice: "To Charles, the most pious Augustus, crowned by God, the great and peace-giving Emperor, life and victory." While he was invoking diverse saints before the holy confession of the blessed Peter the Apostle, it was proclaimed three times and he was constituted by all to be Emperor of the Romans. Then the most holy pontiff anointed Charles with holy oil, and likewise anointed his most excellent son to be king, upon the very day of the birth of our Lord Jesus Christ; and

[1] From *Liber pontificalis*, ed. L. Duchesne (Paris, 1886–92), Vol. II, p. 7. Translated by the editor.

when the Mass was finished, then the most serene lord Emperor offered gifts.

FROM THE FRANKISH ROYAL ANNALS (ANNALES REGNI FRANCORUM)[2]

On the most holy day of the Lord's birth, when the king, at Mass before the confession of St. Peter, rose up from prayer, Pope Leo placed on his head a crown; and he was acclaimed by the whole populace of Rome: "To Charles, Augustus, crowned by God the great and peaceful emperor of the Romans, life and victory!" And after these praises he was adored by the pope in the manner of ancient princes; and, the title of *patricius* being dropped, he was called emperor and augustus.

FROM THE ANNALES LAURESHAMENSES[3]

And because the name of emperor had now ceased to exist in the land of the Greeks and because they had a woman as emperor, it was seen both by the apostolic Leo himself and all the holy fathers who were present in that council [i.e., the council held to decide the fate of Leo III and before which he took his purification oath] and the rest of the people, that they ought to name as emperor Charles himself, king of the Franks, who now held Rome itself, where the Caesars were always accustomed to have their residence, and the rest of the places which they held in Italy, Gaul, and Germany. For Almighty God conceded all these places into his hands, and therefore it seemed to them to be just, that he—with the aid of God and with all the Christian people asking—should not be lacking that title.

King Charles did not wish to deny their request, and with all humility, subjecting himself to God and to the petition of the priests and all the Christian people, he received the title of emperor through the coronation of the lord pope Leo on the day of the birth of the Lord. And the first thing he did was to recall the holy Roman Church from that discord which existed there to peace and order.

FROM EINHARD'S LIFE OF CHARLEMAGNE[4]

His last voyage [to Rome] was a result of another cause. The Romans having caused Pope Leo many injuries—torn out his eyes and cut off his tongue—were moved to ask the aid of the king. Therefore, coming to Rome in order to put to order that which was causing too much disturbance in the order of the Church, he passed the whole winter there. It was at this time that he accepted the title of emperor and augustus. But at first he was so much opposed that he affirmed that, even though it was an important feast day, he would not have entered the church that day if he had known in advance the plan of the pope. He bore with great patience the envy of the Roman emperors, who were indignant at the title he had taken; and by his magnanimity by which he was so much superior to them he conquered their anger by sending to them many legates and by calling them "brothers" in his letters.

FROM THEOPHANES' CHRONICLE[5]

In this year in the month of December Charles, the king of the Franks, was crowned by Pope Leo.

[2] From *Annales regni Francorum*, a. 801, in *Quellen zur karolingischen Reichsgeschichte*, ed. Reinhold Rau (Berlin: Rütten & Loening, n. d.), 1. Teil, p. 74. Translated by the editor.

[3] From *Annales Laureshamenses*, a. 801, ed. G. Pertz, *Monumenta Germaniae Historica, Scriptores* [Hanover, 1826], Vol. I, p. 38. Translated by the editor.

[4] Translated by the editor from *Éginhard, Vie de Charlemagne*, chapter 28, ed. and tr. Louis Halphen, 3 ed., revised and corrected (*Les classiques de France au Moyen Âge*) (Paris, Société d'Éditions "Les Belles Lettres," 1947), p. 80.

[5] Translated by the editor from Theophanes, *Chronographia*, A. M. 6293 (J. P. Migne, ed., *Patrologiae Cursus Completus*, Series Graeca, CVIII, col. 956).

JAMES BRYCE

THE CAROLINGIAN EMPIRE AS THE REVIVAL
OF THE ROMAN EMPIRE

Four of the above sources—the biographer of Leo III, Einhard, and the two Frankish annalists—agree in suggesting that the coronation resulted in the bestowal of the titles "emperor" and "augustus" on Charlemagne and that he assumed rulership over the "Romans." This terminology immediately suggests that the coronation of 800 was in some way related to the ancient Roman Empire. Within a few years after 800 arguments began to be developed insisting that the coronation of Charlemagne involved a renewal (*renovatio*) or a transference (*translatio*) of the ancient Roman Empire (which had never ended) to a new setting. Throughout the Middle Ages this idea continued to find wide acceptance. And it is still cultivated, as is shown by the following classic statement by James Bryce (1838–1922), an eminent English historian, member of Parliament, office-holder in several Liberal governments, and British ambassador to the United States from 1907 to 1913.

The coronation of Charles is not only the central event of the Middle Ages, it is also one of those very few events of which, taking them singly, it may be said that if they had not happened, the history of the world would have been different. In one sense indeed it has scarcely a parallel. The assassins of Julius Caesar thought that they had saved Rome from monarchy, but monarchy became inevitable in the next generation. The conversion of Constantine changed the face of the world, but Christianity was spreading fast, and its ultimate triumph was only a question of time. Had Columbus never spread his sails, the secret of the western sea would yet have been pierced by some later voyager: had Charles V broken his safe-conduct to Luther, the voice silenced at Wittenberg would have been taken up by echoes elsewhere. But if the Roman Empire had not been restored in the West in the person of Charles, it would never have been restored at all, and the inexhaustible train of consequences for good and for evil that followed could not have been. Why this was so may be seen by examining the history of the next two centuries. In that day, as through all the Dark and Middle Ages, two forces were striving for the mastery. The one was the instinct of separation, disorder, anarchy, caused by the ungoverned impulses and barbarous ignorance of the great bulk of mankind; the other was that passionate longing of the better minds for a formal unity of government, which had its historical basis in the memories of the old Roman Empire, and its most constant expression in the devotion to a visible and catholic Church. The former tendency, as everything shows, was, in politics at least, the stronger, but the latter, used and stimulated by an extraordinary genius like Charles, achieved in the year 800 a victory whose results were never to be lost. When the hero was gone, the returning wave of anarchy and barbarism swept up violent as ever, yet it could not wholly obliterate the past: the Empire, maimed and shattered though it was, had struck its roots too deep to be overthrown by force, and when it perished at last, perished from inner decay. It was just because men felt that no one less than Charles could have won such a triumph over the evils of the time, by framing and establishing a gigantic scheme of government, that the excitement and hope and joy which the coronation evoked were so intense. Their best evidence is perhaps to be found not in the records of that time itself, but in the cries of lamentation that broke forth when the Empire began to dissolve towards the close of the ninth

From James Bryce, *The Holy Roman Empire* (London and New York: The Macmillan Company, 1897), pp. 50–52, 56–64, 67–74.

century, in the marvellous legends which attached themselves to the name of Charles the Emperor, a hero of whom any exploit was credible, in the devout admiration wherewith his German successors looked back to, and strove in all things to imitate, their all but super-human prototype. . . .

The impression which the [major contemporary accounts of the coronation] leave is essentially the same. They all show how little the transaction can be made to wear a strictly legal character. The Frankish king does not of his own might seize the crown, but rather receives it as coming naturally to him, as the legitimate consequence of the authority he already enjoyed. The Pope bestows the crown, not in virtue of any right of his own as head of the Church: he is merely the instrument of God's providence, which has unmistakably pointed out Charles as the proper person to defend and lead the Christian commonwealth. The Roman people do not formally elect and appoint, but by their applause accept the chief who is presented to them. The act is conceived of as directly ordered by the Divine Providence which has brought about a state of things that admits of but one issue, an issue which king, priest, and people have only to recognize and obey; their personal ambitions, passions, intrigues, sinking and vanishing in reverential awe at what seems the immediate interposition of Heaven. And as the result is desired by all parties alike, they do not think of inquiring into one another's rights, but take their momentary harmony to be natural and necessary, never dreaming of the difficulties and conflicts which were to arise out of what seemed then so simple. And it was just because everything was thus left undetermined, resting not on express stipulation but rather on a sort of mutual understanding, a sympathy of beliefs and wishes which augured no evil, that the event admitted of being afterwards represented in so many different lights. . . . Charles did not conquer, nor the Pope give, nor the people elect. As the act was unprecedented, so was it illegal; it was a revolt of the ancient Western capital against a daughter who had become a mistress; an exercise of the sacred right of insurrection, justified by the weakness and wickedness of the Byzantine princes, hallowed to the eyes of the world by the sanction of Christ's representative, but founded upon no law, nor competent to create any for the future.

It is an interesting and somewhat perplexing question, how far the coronation scene, an act as imposing in its circumstances as it was momentous in its results, was prearranged among the parties. . . . It is . . . on the whole . . . reasonable, to suppose that Leo, having satisfied himself of the wishes of the Roman clergy and people as well as of the Frankish magnates, resolved to seize an occasion and place so eminently favourable to his long-cherished plan, while Charles, carried away by the enthusiasm of the moment and seeing in the pontiff the prophet and instrument of the divine will, accepted a dignity which he might have wished to receive at some later time or in some other way. If, therefore, any positive conclusion be adopted, it would seem to be that Charles, although he had probably given a more or less vague consent to the project, was surprised and disconcerted by a sudden fulfilment which interrupted his own carefully studied designs. And although a deed which changed the history of the world was in any case no accident, it may well have worn to the Frankish and Roman spectators the air of a surprise.

Whether, supposing Leo to have been less precipitate, a cession of the crown, or an acknowledgment of the right of the Romans to confer it, could ever have been obtained by Charles is perhaps more than doubtful. But it is clear that he judged rightly in rating its importance high, for the want of it was the great blemish in his own and his successors' dignity. To show how this was so, reference must be made to the events of A.D. 476. Both the extinction of the Western Empire in that year and its revival in A.D. 800 have been very generally misunderstood in modern times, and although the mistake is not, in a certain sense, of practical importance, yet it tends to confuse history and to blind us to the ideas of the people who acted on both occasions. When Odoacer compelled the abdication of Romulus Augustulus, he did not abolish the Western Empire as a separate power, but caused it to be reunited with or sink into the Eastern, so that from that time there was, as there had been before Diocletian, a single undivided Roman Empire. In A.D. 800 the very memory of the separate Western Empire, as it had stood from the death of Theodosius till Odoacer, had, so far as appears, been long since lost, and neither Leo nor Charles nor anyone among their advisers dreamt of reviving it. They too, like their predecessors, held the Roman Empire to be one and indivisible, and proposed by the coronation of the Frankish king not to proclaim a severance of the East and West, but to reverse the act of Constantine, and make Old Rome again the civil as well as the ecclesiastical capital of the

Empire that bore her name. Their deed was in its essence illegal, but they sought to give it every semblance of legality: they professed and partly believed that they were not revolting against a reigning sovereign, but legitimately filling up the place of the deposed Constantine the Sixth; the people of the imperial city exercising their ancient right of choice, their bishop his right of consecration.

Their purpose was but half accomplished. They could create, but they could not destroy: they set up an Emperor of their own, whose representatives thenceforward ruled the West, but Constantinople retained her sovereigns as of yore; and Christendom saw henceforth two imperial lines, not as in the time before A.D. 476, the conjoint heads of a single realm, but rivals and enemies, each denouncing the other as an imposter, each professing to be the only true and lawful head of the Christian Church and people. Although therefore we must in practice speak during the next seven centuries (down till A.D. 1453, when Constantinople fell before the Mohammedan) of an Eastern and a Western Empire, the phrase is in strictness incorrect, and was one which either court ought to have repudiated. The Byzantines always did repudiate it; the Latins usually; although, yielding to facts, they sometimes condescended to employ it themselves. But their theory was always the same. Charles was held to be the legitimate successor, not of Romulus Augustulus, but of Leo IV, Heraclius, Justinian, Arcadius, and the whole Eastern line; and hence it is that in all the annals of the time and of many succeeding centuries, the name of Constantine VI, the sixty-seventh in order from Augustus, is followed without a break by that of Charles, the sixty-eighth.

The maintenance of an imperial line among the Easterns was a continuing protest against the validity of Charles's title. But from their enmity he had little to fear, and in the eyes of the world he seemed to step into their place, adding the traditional dignity which had been theirs to the power that he already enjoyed. North Italy and Rome ceased for ever to own the supremacy of Byzantium; and while the Eastern princes paid a shameful tribute to the Mussulman, the Frankish Emperor — as the recognized head of Christendom — received from the patriarch of Jerusalem the keys of the Holy Sepulchre and the banner of Calvary; the gift of the Sepulchre itself, says Eginhard, from Aaron king of the Persians. Out of this peaceful intercourse with the great Khalif the romancers created a crusade. Within his own dominions his sway assumed a more sacred character. Already had his unwearied and comprehensive activity made him throughout his reign an ecclesiastical no less than a civil ruler, summoning and sitting in councils, examining and appointing bishops, settling by capitularies the smallest points of church discipline and polity. . . .

Acting . . . thus when merely king, it may be thought, that Charles needed no further title to justify his power. The inference, is in truth rather the converse of this. Upon what he had done already the imperial title must necessarily follow: the attitude of protection and control which he held toward the Church and the Holy See belonged, according to the ideas of the time, especially and only to an Emperor. Therefore his coronation was the fitting completion and legitimation of his authority, sanctifying rather than increasing it. We have, however, one remarkable witness to the importance that was attached to the imperial name, and the enhancement which he conceived his office to have received from it. In a great assembly held at Aachen, A.D. 802, the lately-crowned Emperor revised the laws of all the races that obeyed him, endeavouring to harmonize and correct them, and issued a capitulary singular in subject and tone. All persons within his dominions, as well ecclesiastical as civil, who have already sworn allegiance to him as king, are thereby commanded to swear to him afresh as Caesar; and all who have never yet sworn, down to the age of twelve, shall now take the same oath. "At the same time it shall be publicly explained to all what is the force and meaning of this oath, and how much more it includes than a mere promise of fidelity to the monarch's person. Firstly, it binds those who swear it to live, each and every one of them, according to his strength and knowledge, in the holy service of God; since the lord Emperor cannot extend over all his care and discipline. Secondly, it binds them neither by force nor fraud to seize or molest any of the goods or servants of his crown. Thirdly, to do no violence nor treason towards the holy Church, or to widows, or orphans, or strangers, seeing that the lord Emperor has been appointed, after the Lord and his saints, the protector and defender of all such." Then in similar fashion purity of life is prescribed to the monks; homicide, the neglect of hospitality, and other offences are denounced, the notions of sin and crime being intermingled and almost identified in a way to which no parallel can be found, unless it be in the Mosaic code. There God, the invisible object of worship, is also, though almost incidentally, the judge and political ruler of Israel; here the whole cycle of social and moral duty is deduced from the obligation of obedience to the visible autocratic head of the Christian state.

In most of Charles's words and deeds, nor less distinctly in the writings of his adviser Alcuin, may be discerned the working of the same theocratic ideas. Among his intimate friends he chose to be called by the name of David, exercising in reality all the powers of the Jewish king; presiding over this kingdom of God upon earth rather as a second Constantine or Theodosius than in the spirit and traditions of the Julii or the Flavii. . . .

In civil affairs also Charles acquired, with the imperial title, a new position. Later jurists labour to distinguish his power as Roman Emperor from that which he held already as king of the Franks and their subject allies: they insist that his coronation gave him the capital only, that it is absurd to talk of a Roman Empire in regions whither the eagles had never flown. In such expressions there seems to lurk either confusion or misconception. It was not the actual government of the city that Charles obtained in A.D. 800; that his father had already held as Patrician and he had constantly exercised in the same capacity: it was far more than the titular sovereignty of Rome which had hitherto been supposed to be vested in the Byzantine princes: it was nothing less than the headship of the world, believed to appertain of right to the lawful Roman Emperor, whether he reigned on the Bosphorus, the Tiber, or the Rhine. As that headship, although never denied, had been in abeyance in the West for several centuries, its bestowal on the king of so vast a realm was a change of the first moment, for it made the coronation not merely a transference of the seat of Empire, but a renewal of the Empire itself, a bringing back of it from faith to sight, from the world of belief and theory to the world of fact and reality. And since the powers it gave were autocratic and unlimited, it must swallow up all minor claims and dignities: the rights of Charles the Frankish king were merged in those of Charles the successor of Augustus, the lord of the world. That his imperial authority was theoretically irrespective of place is clear from his own words and acts, and from all the monuments of that time. He would not, indeed, have dreamed of treating the free Franks as Justinian had treated his

half-Oriental subjects, nor would the warriors who followed his standard have brooked such an attempt. Yet even to German eyes his position must have been altered by the halo of vague splendour which now surrounded him; for all, even the Saxon and the Slave, had heard of Rome's glories, and revered the name of Caesar. And in his effort to weld discordant elements into one body, to introduce regular gradations of authority, to control the Teutonic tendency to localization by his *missi* — officials commissioned to traverse each some part of his dominions, reporting on and redressing the evils they found — and by his own oft-repeated personal progresses, Charles was guided by the traditions of the old Empire. His sway is the revival of order and culture, fusing the West into a compact whole, whose parts are never thenceforward to lose the marks of their connection and their half-Roman character, gathering up all that is left in Europe of spirit and wealth and knowledge, and hurling it with the new force of Christianity on the infidel of the South and the masses of untamed barbarism to the North and East. Ruling the world by the gift of God, and the transmitted rights of the Romans and their Caesar whom God had chosen to conquer it, he renews the original aggressive movement of the Empire: the civilized world has subdued her invader, and now arms him against savagery and heathendom. Hence the wars, not more of the sword than of the cross, against Saxons, Avars, Slavs, Danes, Spanish Arabs, where monasteries are fortresses and baptism the badge of submission. The overthrow of the Irminsul[1] in the first Saxon campaigns, sums up the changes of seven centuries. The Romanized Teuton destroys the monument of his country's freedom, for it is also the emblem of paganism and barbarism. The work of Arminius is undone by his successor.

This, however, is not the only side from which Charles's policy and character may be regarded. If the unity of the Church and the shadow of imperial prerogative was one pillar of his power, the other was the Frankish nation. The empire was still military, though in a sense strangely different from that of Julius or Severus. The warlike Franks had permeated Western Europe; their primacy was admitted by the kindred tribes of Lombards, Bavarians, Thuringians, Alemannians, and Burgundians; the Slavic peoples on the borders trembled and paid tribute; Alfonso

[1] A pagan temple which served as a symbol of Saxon resistance against Charlemagne's conquest of the Saxons. [Editor's note.]

of Asturias[2] found in the Emperor a protector against the infidel foe. His influence, if not his exerted power, crossed the ocean: the kings of the Scots sent gifts and called him lord: the restoration of Eardulf to Northumbria, still more of Egbert to Wessex, might furnish a better ground for the claim of suzerainty than many to which his successors had afterwards recourse. As it was by Frankish arms that this predominance in Europe which the imperial tide adorned and legalized had been won, so was the government of Charles Roman in semblance rather than in fact. It was not by restoring the effete mechanism of the old Empire, but by his own vigorous personal action and that of his great officers, that he strove to administer and reform. With every effort for a strong central government, there is no despotism; each nation retains its laws, its hereditary chiefs, its free popular assemblies. . . .

He repeats the attempt of Theodoric to breathe a Teutonic spirit into Roman forms. The conception was magnificent; great results followed its partial execution. Two causes forbade success. The one was the ecclesiastical, especially the Papal power, apparently subject to the temporal, but with a strong and undefined prerogative which only waited the occasion to trample on what it had helped to raise. The Pope might take away the crown he had bestowed, and turn against the Emperor the Church which now obeyed him. The other was to be found in the discordance of the component parts of the Empire. The nations were not ripe for settled life or extensive schemes of polity; the differences of race, language, manners, over vast and thinly-peopled lands baffled every attempt to maintain their connection: and when once the spell of the great mind was withdrawn, the mutually repellent forces began to work, and the mass dissolved into that chaos out of which it had been formed. Nevertheless, the parts separated not as they met, but having all of them undergone influences which continued to act when political connection had ceased. For the work of Charles—a genius pre-eminently creative—was not lost in the anarchy that followed: rather are we to regard his reign as the beginning of a new era, or as laying the foundations whereon men continued for many generations to build. . . .

There were in his Empire, as in his own mind, two

elements; those two from the union and mutual action and reaction of which modern civilization has arisen. These vast domains, reaching from the Ebro to the Carpathian mountains, from the Eyder to the Liris, were all the conquests of the Frankish sword, and were still governed almost exclusively by viceroys and officers of Frankish blood. But the conception of the Empire, that which made it a State and not a mere mass of subject tribes like those great Eastern dominions which rise and perish in a lifetime, the realms of Sesostris, or Attila, or Timur,[3] was inherited from an older and a grander system, was not Teutonic but Roman—Roman in its ordered rule, in its uniformity and precision, in its endeavour to subject the individual to the system—Roman in its effort to realize a certain limited and human perfection, whose very completeness shall exclude the hope of further progress. And the bond, too, by which the Empire was held together was Roman in its origin, although Roman in a sense which would have surprised Trajan or Severus,[4] could it have been foretold them. The ecclesiastical body was already organized and centralized, and it was in his rule over the ecclesiastical body that the secret of Charles's power lay. Every Christian—Frank, Gaul, or Italian—owed loyalty to the head and defender of his religion: the unity of the Empire was a reflection of the unity of the Church.

Into a general view of the government and policy of Charles it is not possible here to enter. Yet his legislation, his assemblies, his administrative system, his magnificent works, recalling the projects of Alexander and Caesar, the zeal for education and literature which he showed in the collection of manuscripts, the founding of schools, the gathering of eminent men from all quarters around him, cannot be appreciated apart from his position as restorer of the Roman Empire. Like all the foremost men of our race, Charles was all great things in one, and was so great just because the workings of his genius were so harmonious. He was not a mere barbarian warrior any more than he was an astute diplomatist; there is none of all his qualities which would not be

[3] Bryce refers here to three of the world's great conquerors and empire builders. Sesostris was a great Egyptian pharaoh. Attila (about A.D. 406–453) was king of the Huns at the time when the Hunnic empire extended over much of central Europe. Timur, or Tamerlane (about 1336–1405) was a Mongol conqueror who put together a great empire in Asia. [Editor's note]

[4] Roman emperors; Trajan ruled A.D. 97–117, several emperors bore the name Severus; Bryce probably refers to Septimius Severus, who ruled A.D. 197–211. [Editor's note]

[2] A small Christian principality in extreme Northern Spain. [Editor's note]

forced out of its place were we to characterize him chiefly by it. Comparisons between famous men of different ages are generally as worthless as they are easy; the circumstances among which Charles lived do not permit us to institute a minute parallel between his greatness and that of those two to whom it is the modern fashion to compare him, nor to say whether he was or could have become as profound a politician as Caesar, as skilful a commander as Napoleon. But neither to the Roman nor to the Corsican was he inferior in that one quality by which both he and they chiefly impress our imagina-tions—that intense, vivid, unresting energy which swept him over Europe in campaign after campaign, which sought a field for its workings in theology, science, literature, no less than in politics and war. As it was this wondrous activity that made him the conqueror of Europe, so was it by the variety of his culture that he became her civilizer. From him, in whose wide deep mind the whole medieval theory of the world and human life mirrored itself, did medieval society take the form and impress which it retained for centuries, and the traces whereof are among us and upon us to this day.

CHRISTOPHER DAWSON

THE CAROLINGIAN EMPIRE AS AN EMBODIMENT OF CHRISTIAN IDEALISM

Perhaps Bryce was too much impressed by those outward aspects of the contemporary descriptions of the creation of the Carolingian Empire which evoked the memory of ancient Rome. Are there not elements in these same accounts (especially the Annales Laurshamenses) which suggest a religious inspiration behind the dramatic events of 800? This has been the conclusion of many—perhaps the majority—of those who have discussed the Carolingian Empire. Few have expressed this view more eloquently than the British historian Christopher Dawson. The following passage, taken from one of Dawson's many volumes devoted to a defense of the positive, creative role of the Christian religion in shaping European civilization, sees Christian idealism as the generative force behind Charlemagne's Empire. In reading Dawson's interpretation of the Carolingian Empire one should pay special attention to the basic assumptions which undergirded Carolingian political thought. For the ideas that inspired the princes, the popes, and the intellectuals of the Carolingian age remained at the center of political thought throughout the Middle Ages. These same concepts were evoked again and again to defend the imperial idea and to justify political action aimed toward the establishment of a universal state in medieval Europe.

The historical importance of the Carolingian age far transcends its material achievement. The unwieldy Empire of Charles the Great did not long survive the death of its founder, and it never really attained the economic and social organization of a civilized state. But, for all that, it marks the first emergence of the European culture from the twilight of pre-natal existence into the consciousness of active life. Hitherto the barbarians had lived passively on the capital which they had inherited from the civilization which they had plundered; now they began to co-operate with it in a creative social activity. The centre of

From *The Making of Europe* by Christopher Dawson, pp. 214–222, 256–258, published by Sheed & Ward, Inc., New York. Reprinted by permission of The Society of Authors and Christopher Dawson.

mediaeval civilization was not to be on the shores of the Mediterranean, but in the northern lands between the Loire and the Weser which were the heart of the Frankish dominions. This was the formative centre of the new culture, and it was there that the new conditions which were to govern the history of mediaeval culture find their origin. The ideal of the mediaeval Empire, the political position of the Papacy, the German hegemony in Italy and the expansion of Germany towards the East, the fundamental institutions of mediaeval society both in Church and State, and the incorporation of the classical tradition in mediaeval culture—all have their basis in the history of the Carolingian period.

The essential feature of the new culture was its religious character. While the Merovingian state had been predominantly secular, the Carolingian Empire was a theocratic power—the political expression of a religious unity. This change in the character of the monarchy is shown by the actual circumstances of the installation of the new dynasty; for Pepin obtained Papal authority for the setting aside of the old royal house and was anointed king in the year 752 by St. Boniface according to the religious coronation rite which had grown up under ecclesiastical influence in Anglo-Saxon England and Visigothic Spain, but which had hitherto been unknown among the Franks. Thus the legitimation of the rule of the Carolingian house sealed the alliance between the Frankish monarchy and the Papacy which St. Boniface had done so much to bring about, and henceforward the Frankish monarchy was the recognized champion and protector of the Holy See. The Papacy had already been alienated from the Byzantine Empire by the Iconoclastic policy of the Isaurian emperors, and the extinction of the last survival of the Byzantine power at Ravenna by the Lombards in 751 forced the Pope to look for support elsewhere. In 754 Stephen II visited Pepin in his own dominions, and obtained from him a treaty which secured to the Papacy the Exarchate of Ravenna and the former Byzantine possessions in Italy, together with the duchies of Spoleto and Benevento. In return the Pope reconsecrated Pepin as King of the Franks, and also conferred on him the dignity of Patrician of the Romans. This was an epoch-making event, for it marked not only the foundation of the Papal State which was to endure until 1870, but also the protectorate of the Carolingians in Italy, and the beginning of their imperial mission as the leaders and organizers of Western Christendom.

The Carolingians were naturally fitted to undertake this mission since they were themselves the representatives of both sides of the European tradition. They traced their descent from Gallo-Roman bishops and saints as well as from Frankish warriors, and they combined the warlike prowess of a Charles Martel with a vein of religious idealism, which shows itself in Carloman's renunciation of his kingdom in order to enter the cloister, and Pepin's sincere devotion to the cause of the Church. But it is in Pepin's successor, Charles the Great, that both these elements find simultaneous expression. He was above all a soldier with a talent for war and military enterprise which made him the greatest conqueror of his time. But in spite of his ruthlessness and unscrupulous ambition he was no mere barbaric warrior; his policy was inspired by ideals and universal aims. His conquests were not only the fulfilment of the traditional Frankish policy of military expansion; they were also crusades for the protection and unity of Christendom. By his destruction of the Lombard Kingdom he freed the Papacy from the menace which had threatened its independence for two hundred years and brought Italy into the Frankish Empire. The long drawn out struggle with the Saxons was due to his determination to put an end to the last remains of Germanic heathenism as well as of Saxon independence. His conquest of the Avars in 793–794 destroyed the Asiatic robber state which had terrorized the whole of Eastern Europe, and at the same time restored Christianity in the Danube provinces, while his war with the Saracens and his establishment of the Spanish March were the beginning of the Christian reaction to the victorious expansion of Islam. In the course of thirty years of incessant warfare he had extended the frontiers of the Frankish monarchy as far as the Elbe, the Mediterranean and the Lower Danube, and had united Western Christendom in a great imperial state.

The coronation of Charles as Roman Emperor and the restoration of the Western Empire in the year 800 marked the final stage in the reorganization of Western Christendom and completed the union between the Frankish monarchy and the Roman Church which had been begun by the work of Boniface and Pepin. It would, however, be a mistake to suppose that the theocratic element in Charles' rule was based upon his imperial title or that he derived the universal character of his authority from the tradition of Roman imperialism.

Under the influence of his Anglo-Saxon adviser

Alcuin, which was no less decisive than that of Boniface had been during the previous period, he had already acquired an exalted view of his authority as the divinely appointed leader of the Christian people. But this ideal was based on the teaching of the Bible and St. Augustine rather than on the classical tradition of imperial Rome. For to Alcuin and the authors of the *Libri Carolini* Rome, even in its Byzantine form, was still the last of the heathen empires of prophecy and the representative of the Earthly Kingdom, whereas the Frankish monarch possessed the higher dignity of ruler and guide of the people of God. Charles was the new David and the second Josias, and as the latter had restored the law of God, so too Charles was the lawgiver of the Church and held the two swords of spiritual and temporal authority.

This theocratic ideal dominates every aspect of Carolingian government. The new Frankish state was to an even greater extent than the Byzantine Empire a *church-state*, the secular and religious aspects of which were inextricably intermingled.

The King is the governor of the Church as well as of the State, and his legislation lays down the strictest and most minute rules for the conduct of the clergy and the regulation of doctrine and ritual. The observance of Sunday, the performance of the ecclesiastical chant and the conditions for the reception of novices into the monasteries are all dealt with in the Capitularies, no less than the defense of the frontiers and the economic administration of the royal estate. On one occasion Charles even required a written answer from every parish priest as to the mode in which he administered baptism, the replies being forwarded by the bishops to Charles' palace for his personal inspection.

The government of the whole Empire was largely ecclesiastical, for the bishop shared equally with the count in the local administration of the 300 counties into which the Empire was divided, while the central government was mainly in the hands of the ecclesiastics of the chancery and of the royal chapel; the archchaplain being the King's chief adviser and one of the highest dignitaries of the Empire. The control and supervision of the local administration was ensured by the characteristic Carolingian institution of the *Missi Dominici,* who went on circuit through the counties of the Empire, like English judges of assize, and here too the most important missions were entrusted to bishops and abbots.

The theocratic spirit which inspired the Carolingian government is well shown by the curious address of one of Charles' Missi which has been preserved. "We have been sent here," he begins, "by our Lord, the Emperor Charles, for your eternal salvation, and we charge you to live virtuously according to the law of God, and justly according to the law of the world. We would have you know first of all that you must believe in one God, the Father, the Son, and the Holy Ghost, . . ." "Love God with all your hearts. Love your neighbours as yourselves. Give alms to the poor according to your means," and after recounting the duties of every class and state of life from wives and sons to monks and counts and public officials he concludes: "Nothing is hidden from God. Life is short and the moment of death is unknown. Be ye therefore always ready."

This address is more in the style of a Moslem Kadi than of a Roman official: indeed the Augustinian ideal of the City of God has become transformed by a crude simplification into something dangerously similar to a Christian version of Islam with Charles as the Commander of the Faithful. There was the same identification of religion and polity, the same attempt to enforce morality by legal means and to spread the faith by war. As Alcuin complained, the faith of the Saxons had been destroyed by tithes, and Charles' missionaries were plunderers (*praedones*) rather than preachers (*praedicatores*). The religion of Charles was like that of Islam, a religion of the sword, and his private life, in spite of his sincere piety, resembled that of a Moslem ruler. Yet for all that he claimed direct authority over the Church and intervened even in matters of dogma. In the words of his first letter to Leo III, he was "the representative of God who has to protect and govern all the members of God," he is "Lord and Father, King and Priest, the Leader and Guide of all Christians."

It is obvious that these claims were hardly reconcilable with the traditional authority of the Papacy. For Charles regarded the Pope as his chaplain, and plainly tells Leo III that it is the King's business to govern and defend the Church and that it is the Pope's duty to pray for it. Thus the destruction of the Lombard Kingdom seemed only to have increased the difficulties of the Papacy. It left Rome isolated between the two imperial powers of the Frankish monarchy and the Byzantine Empire, neither of which respected its independence. The dangers inherent in the situation soon became evident in the disputes that followed the Second Council of

Nicaea in 787. The latter was a victory of the allied forces of Rome and Hellenism over the oriental heresy of the Iconoclasts. But Charles, whose religion had something in common with the militant simplicity of the Isaurian emperors, refused to accept the conciliar decisions. The Franks could hardly appreciate the importance of the question of image-worship for the peoples of Hellenic tradition. For . . . the art of the Northern peoples was essentially at one with that of the East in its abstract aniconic character. Moreover, the influence of the Old Testament which was so strong in the Caroline circle led to a Puritanical attitude in the question of image-worship no less than in that of the observance of Sunday. Consequently Charles in person entered the theological lists against Byzantium and Rome. He caused his theologians to compile a series of treatises against the council which were published in his name as the *Libri Carolini*. He sent a Missus to Rome with a capitulary of eighty-five *reprehensions* for the Pope's instruction, and finally, in 794, he called a great council of all the western bishops at Frankfurt in which the Council of Nicaea was condemned and the doctrines of the image-worshippers refuted.

The position of Pope Hadrian was one of intense difficulty, and he was forced to temporize. He found himself in agreement with the Byzantine Empire against the Frankish kingdom and the Western Church; and yet the Byzantines had robbed him of his patrimonies in the East and regarded him as no better than an alien. In the event of a schism between East and West he would have been left isolated and powerless. Politically he was entirely dependent on the Frankish power, and on the death of Hadrian in 795, his successor did homage to Charles as his overlord.

This anomalous state of things was ended by the Pope's recognition of Charles as Roman Emperor and his coronation at Rome on Christmas Day in the year 800. It is difficult to say how far the Pope acted on his own initiative or whether he was the instrument of Charles and his Frankish advisers. The testimony of Charles' biographer, Einhard, is in favour of the former alternative, but it has met with little favour from modern historians, at least in France and England. Certainly Charles was the gainer, for his universal authority in the West now received the sanction of Roman law and tradition. For the Papacy, however, the advantage was no less clear. The supremacy of the Frankish monarchy which had

threatened to over-shadow that of Rome was now associated with Rome, and consequently also with the Papacy. The political allegiance of the Pope was no longer divided between the *de jure* authority of the Emperor at Constantinople and the *de facto* power of the Frankish King. As King, Charles had stood outside the Roman tradition; as Emperor, he entered into a definite juridical relationship with the head of the Church. His power was still as formidable as ever, but it was no longer indefinite and incalculable. Moreover, the idea of the Roman Empire was still indispensable to the Church. It was synonymous with Christian civilization, while the rule of the barbarians was so identified with heathenism and war that the Liturgy couples together "the enemies of the Roman name and the foes of the Catholic Faith." Consequently it is by no means improbable that the Papacy as the representation of Roman universalism should have taken the initiation in the restoration of the Empire in 800. . . .

However this may be, it is certain that the restoration of the Roman Empire, or rather the foundation of the new mediaeval Empire, had a religious and symbolic value which far outweighed its immediate importance from a political point of view. Charles used it, no doubt, as a diplomatic counter in his negotiations with the Eastern Empire, but his coronation made no difference in his life or government. He never attempted to ape the ways of a Roman or Byzantine Caesar, as did Otto III[1] and other mediaeval emperors, but remained a thorough Frank, in dress and manners as well as in his political ideals. He even imperilled his whole work of imperial unification by dividing his dominions among his heirs in 806 according to the old Frankish customs, instead of following the Roman principle of indivisible political sovereignty; and the same tradition reasserted itself among his successors and proved fatal to the unity and continuity of the Carolingian Empire.

It was the churchmen and the men of letters rather than the princes and statesmen who cherished the ideal of the Holy Roman Empire. To them it meant the end of the centuries of barbarism and a return to civilized order. To Einhard Charles is a new Augustus, and he views his achievement in the light of the Augustan ideal; while Modoin, the Bishop of Auxerre, writes of his age as the Renaissance of classical antiquity. . . .

[1] A later Holy Roman Emperor of Germanic origin; he ruled from 983 to 1002. Otto III lived in Rome during most of his reign and tried to make it his capital. [Editor's note]

The storm of barbarian invasion that fell upon Europe in the ninth century seems sufficient of itself to explain the premature decline of the Carolingian Empire and the dissolution of the newly-acquired Western unity. Nevertheless, it is easy to exaggerate its importance. It was far from being the only influence at work; indeed, it is almost certain that the fortunes of the Carolingian Empire would have followed a similar course, even if it had not had to undergo the attacks of the Vikings and the Saracens.

The germs of decay were inherent in the Carolingian state from its origins. For in spite of its imposing appearance, it was a heterogeneous structure without an internal and organic principle of unity. It claimed to be the Roman Empire, but it was in fact the Frankish monarchy, and so it embodied two contradictory principles, the universalism of the Roman and Christian traditions on the one hand, and the tribal particularism of barbaric Europe on the other. Consequently, in spite of its name, it bore little resemblance to the Roman Empire or the civilized states of the old Mediterranean world, it had much more in common with those barbaric Empires of the Huns and the Avars and the West Turks which were the ephemeral products of military conquest and which succeeded one another so rapidly during these centuries on the outskirts of the civilized world.

The Roman Empire of the Carolingians was a Roman Empire without the Roman law and without the Roman legions, without the City and without the Senate. It was a shapeless and unorganized mass with no urban nerve centres and no circulation of economic life. Its officials were neither civic magistrates nor trained civil servants, but merely territorial magnates and semi-tribal war leaders. And yet it was also the embodiment and representative of an ideal, and this ideal, in spite of its apparent failure, proved more durable and persistent than any of the military or political achievements of the period. It outlived the state to which it had given birth and survived through the anarchy that followed, to become the principle of the new order which arose in the West in the eleventh century.

The champions of this ideal were the great Carolingian churchmen, who played so large a part in the administration of the Empire and the determination of the imperial policy from the time of Charles the Great to that of his grandson Charles the Bald.

While the counts and secular magnates for the most part represented local and territorial interests, the leaders of the ecclesiastical party stood for the ideal of a universal Empire as the embodiment of the unity of Christendom and the defender of the Christian faith. Agobard of Lyons[2] even ventures to attack the traditional Frankish principle of personal law and to demand the establishment of a universal Christian law for the universal Christian commonwealth. In Christ, he says, there is neither Jew nor Gentile, Barbarian nor Scythian, neither Aquintanians, nor Lombards, nor Burgundians, nor Allemanni. "If God has suffered in order that the wall of separation and enmity should be done away and that all should be reconciled in His Body, is not the incredible diversity of laws that reigns not only in every region or city, but in the same household and almost at the same table, in opposition to this divine work of unity?"

Thus the Emperor was no longer the hereditary chieftain and war leader of the Frankish people; he was an almost sacerdotal figure who had been anointed by the grace of God to rule over the Christian people and to guide and protect the Church. This involves, as we have seen, a strictly theocratic conception of kingship, so that the Carolingian Emperor was regarded, no less than the Byzantine Basileus, as the vicar of God and the head of the Church as well as of the state. Thus Sedulius Scotus (c. 850) speaks of the Emperor as being ordained by God as His vicar in the government of the Church and as having received power over both orders of rulers and subjects, while Cathulf goes so far as to say that the king stands in the place of God over all his people, for whom he has to account at the Last Day, while the bishop stands in the second place as the representative of Christ only.

But the Carolingian theocracy differed from the Byzantine in that it was a theocracy inspired and controlled by the Church. There was no lay bureaucracy such as existed in the Eastern Empire; its place was taken by the episcopate, from whose ranks the majority of the Emperor's advisors and ministers were drawn. Consequently, as soon as the strong hand of Charles the Great was removed, the theocratic ideal led to the exaltation of the spiritual power and the clericalization of the Empire rather than to the subordination of the Church to the secular power. . . .

[2] Agobard was bishop of Lyons and an important intellectual leader in the ninth century. [Editor's note]

C. DELISLE BURNS

THE CAROLINGIAN EMPIRE
AS AN EXERCISE IN POWER POLITICS

The interpretations given by Bryce and Dawson may raise some questions in the student's mind. Are these men not too idealistic? Do they not expect us — in the best traditions of nineteenth century liberalism (Bryce) and religious idealism (Dawson) — to believe that great political leaders are moved primarily by high ideals and by an enlightened consciousness of what human experience has demonstrated to be good? Have they not taken too seriously certain idealistic concepts written into the accounts of Charlemagne's coronation which in fact may be only rationalizations of naked political facts? These queries are normal for all of us nourished in an age where politics are viewed as a quest for power, prestige, and personal advantage. This typically twentieth century approach has led some historians to view the Carolingian Empire as just another episode in man's timeless search for some basis from which to exert his dominance over other men.

Such a view is reflected in the following selection by C. Delisle Burns (1879–1942), a British writer whose career involved government service, party work in the British Labor Party, and a teaching career at the University of London. In reading this selection special attention should be given to the motives which may have moved Charlemagne and to the political advantage that he might have gained from his accession to the imperial throne. These matters have been of utmost importance to many historians of the medieval empire. Some of them, especially those interested in the origins of a German state in Europe, have interpreted the medieval empire as the first articulation of Germanic nationhood and have viewed the medieval emperors from Charlemagne onwards as political leaders fundamentally concerned with establishing Germanic power on some kind of sound, practical basis. Others, no less concerned with German destiny, have viewed the dream of empire handed down by Charlemagne to such figures as Otto I, Henry IV, Frederick Barbarossa, and Frederick II as a tragic heritage which spurred rulers to an ambition incapable of realization and which doomed Germany and Italy to political chaos throughout much of modern history.

On Christmas Day, A.D. 800, Charles the Great, the king of the Franks, was crowned as Emperor and Augustus in the basilica of St. Peter in the Vatican by Pope Leo III.[1] Each of the chief actors in this episode was playing a part. And in view of the later history of the Holy Roman Empire, which was supposed by some historians to have then come into existence, the parts make the play almost a comedy. But that is from the point of view of a much later age. At the

[1] Charles the Great and not Charlemagne will be the name used here, because "Charlemagne" means the mythical figure of the romances.

From C. Delisle Burns, *The First Europe: A Study of the Establishment of Medieval Christendom, A.D. 400–800* (London, 1948), pp. 569–78, 580, 601–2, 605–11, 612–14. Reprinted by permission of George Allen & Unwin Ltd.

time and throughout the Middle Ages, the majority of men who thought at all on such subjects, no doubt, seriously believed that Charles was a successor of the Emperor Augustus, and that the successor of St. Peter had the power to make him so.

It may be difficult in modern times to recognize the power of make-believe in the ninth century and the Middle Ages. The historical imagination was entirely lacking. The habits and customs of the ninth century could easily be confused with what was then supposed to have occurred in the first century, just as the Hebrew records of kings and prophets could be confused with the actions and policies of Germanic warriors and their bishops. Eight hundred years divided the first Augustus from Charles the Great, and Peter the Apostle from Pope Leo III. . . . Charles the Great may have thought that he was a successor of that Augustus; but it is by no means certain that he himself took his new titles as seriously as did some of his followers. He may have known that the pageant in which the part of Emperor had been assigned to him, had very little connection with real life. . . .

Charles the Great was a play-Emperor. The "Holy Roman Empire" in the West, throughout the Middle Ages, was an historical pageant, without any relation to the realities of the time. No doubt it was believed by some to be a continuation of that Empire which had disappeared in western Europe four centuries before Charles the Great. But that same Empire continued to exist in the East with its capital at Constantinople, as in the days of the first Christian Emperor; and both Charles and the Pope knew that the Roman Empire was actually in existence, with its central government and its military forces, at the time when the episode in the basilica of St. Peter's in Rome was being performed. It is impossible to believe that either the barbarian king or the Pope who had been lately rehabilitated by him, thought that the coronation in St. Peter's, either in right or in fact, transferred the central government of the Roman Empire from Constantinople to Rome. And neither their words nor acts, as recorded, give any grounds for believing that they thought that they were establishing a new system of government. . . .

It may be assumed as obvious that there never had been two Roman Empires—one of the East and one of the West. In practice, as well as in theory, the whole Empire had, at certain times, been administered by two Emperors of equal authority, just as

under the Roman Republic two consuls of equal authority had administered different parts of the Roman Dominions. Thus when the rule of the Roman Emperor ceased to exist in western Europe in A.D. 479, the Roman Empire continued unchanged, except for its lost territory. It is therefore quite misleading to speak of a western Roman Empire; and thus, when Justinian restored Italy and Africa to the Empire again, no "western" Empire came into existence. Charles the Great and Pope Leo III knew quite well that there was only one Roman Empire; but they may have imagined that two Emperors of equal authority could exist in the ninth century as in the fifth. Even if, however, that was their belief, they cannot have supposed that the people of Rome or the bishops of that city had any right or power to give to Charles, as Emperor and Augustus, control of the imperial system centred in Constantinople. . . .

That no new institution was founded and no old one revived in A.D. 800 is proved by the action of those who bore the title of Emperor. Rome was never made the seat of imperial authority by Charles the Great or his successors. No "palace" (*palatium*) or central office was established in Rome. But the newly crowned "Emperor" returned immediately to his old seat of government at Aachen; and almost all the Frankish and other barbarian successors of the new Emperor resided and exerted what authority they had, north of the Alps. The conception of a Roman Empire, therefore, in western Europe during the Middle Ages, was entirely fantastic; and the ceremony which was supposed to found that Empire in A.D. 800 was as fantastic as any of the documents to which the ninth century gave birth—the false Decretals and the rest.

What then made it possible to impose upon western Europe a play-Emperor? The steps made in conscious policy by the kings of the Franks and the Popes of the eighth century were, no doubt, the chief causes of the coronation of Charles the Great as "Emperor." Conscious policy on the part of the Popes . . . had led to their centralization of control over the Latin Churches. And conscious policy, especially on the part of the usurper, Pippin the Frank, led to an extension of the Dominions of his descendants. But before discussing the character and purpose of any such conscious policy, it is useful to notice, as in the case of the Papacy, the more indefinite forces which tended to support the idea of a new kind of Emperor.

PRESTIGE OF IMPERIAL ROME

In the first place, the prestige of imperial Rome had never entirely faded from the minds of the kings of the Franks. . . . The prestige of imperial Rome was used for many generations by the Frankish kings as an instrument of their policy.

The interest in imperial Rome, however, as contrasted with ecclesiastical Rome, revived in northern Europe most vigorously under Charles the Great. Charles collected at his Court scholars from different countries, whose one common interest was the revival of Latin literature and learning. The king and his closest friends among these scholars shared a very simple form of humorous intercourse, in which each person was given a nickname. Thus Charles himself was referred to as "David" or "Solomon," and sometimes, in verses, as "Augustus"—meaning "revered majesty" or as "Caesar." . . . Again, in Angilbert's[2] poem, "Charles the Great and Pope Leo," written just before the coronation of A.D. 800, Charles is said to have established a "Second Rome," with a "forum and sacred senate" and marble halls and aqueducts all of which is taken word for word from the first book of Virgil's *Aeneid*. The verses of Alcuin and Angilbert and Theodulf of Orleans[3] are full of phrases taken from Virgil and Ovid. And the *Life of Charles the Great* by Einhard, also a member of his Court, is a patchwork of quotations from Suetonius's *Lives of the Caesars*. Evidently the Court of Charles the Great enjoyed "make-believe," as children do. They knew they were pretending; and yet, like children, they were not very certain where pretence ended and reality began. But in the minds of them all the life and literature of early imperial Rome had a profound significance.

CHRISTIAN ROME

Christian Rome—the Rome of the martyrs and successors of St. Peter—had also an influence upon the kings of the Franks. When Charles Martel was in conflict with the older Churches of Gaul or western France (*Francia occidentalis*) his support of the missionary bishops in Germany or eastern France (*Francia orientalis*) brought him into direct contact with the Roman See, because these bishops looked to Rome to direct their policy of reform and missionary work. Again when Pippin, the son of Charles Martel, decided to usurp the throne, he is said to have appealed to the bishop of Rome for a judgment upon his rights. But Christian Rome exerted an even greater influence in north-western Europe, as a source from which the relics of martyrs could be brought. Thus both Gregory of Tours and Bede[4] report travels of envoys from the North seeking relics in Rome. As early as the fifth century Prudentius[5] wrote: "It is hardly known how full Rome is of buried saints—how richly the city's soil blossoms with sacred tombs. . . ."

THE ROMAN CHURCH

The unconscious tendencies which drove the Roman Church towards the establishment of a new Emperor were probably these. First, an increasing need for an alternative to the Emperor at Constantinople as protector and defender. This need, as it will be shown later, was hardly conscious in the Roman See before the middle of the eighth century; and it cannot be said that, at any stage, the popes deliberately substituted any other civil authority for that of the Roman Emperor. Nevertheless the conquests of the Mohammedans and the weakness of the Government at Constantinople in defence of its Italian dependencies undermined the respect which the Popes continued to show for the Roman Emperor. Pope Stephen had appealed to the Emperor at Constantinople before he sent his first appeal to Pippin, king of the Franks. But the Emperor failed him. Secondly, the desire to promote unity among the Latin Churches, which led to the establishment of the medieval Papacy, also created a tendency in the Roman Church to support any movement which might lead to a unity of the civil and military authorities in western Europe. Obviously it would obstruct the unity of the Churches if the bishops in the different kingdoms or dukedoms found their kings or dukes at war one with another. It is a difficulty which the Christian Churches have not yet solved.

---

[2] An abbot (about 740–814) who was one of Charles's chief advisers and a leading poet in the circle of intellectuals and artists that gathered at Charles's court. [Editor's note.]

[3] Another close adviser of Charlemagne and an important figure in the court circle of intellectuals. [Editor's note.]

[4] An English monk and scholar (673–735) who wrote extensively on a wide range of subjects and whose works were widely used as textbooks by later generations. His chief work was the *Ecclesiastical History of the English People*. [Editor's note.]

[5] A Christian poet of the late fourth and early fifth century; his works included hymns, saints' lives, and theological treatises. [Editor's note.]

Although war between Christian nations may not theoretically affect the Christianity of either side, clearly the bishops of one area could not practically oppose the military policy of the king on whom they depended. And because bishops and abbots as landowners had to supply military forces, even when they did not lead them to battle—as some did in defiance of the canons—the Churches were so closely associated with the military lordships of the day that continuous war naturally tended to divide the Churches of one area from those of another. It was natural, therefore, for the Church in Rome, representing the unity of the Christian Churches, to desire to unite all Christian kings. But unity in the eighth century and throughout the Middle Ages was assumed to involve subordination to the authority of one person. This assumption was partly due to the tradition of imperial Rome and partly due to the primitive conception that the ideal unity of men was like that of a war-band under its leader. This primitive conception in the ninth century was naturally stronger among peoples east of the Rhine than it was in the older civilization further west. The conception that an Empire, including many kingdoms or superior to them, is desirable, is not explicitly stated before the coronation of Charles the Great. But there was clearly an unconscious tendency in this direction, which affected the Popes in the second half of the eighth century, because of their desire to use any means for preserving and increasing the unity of the Churches. This same tendency to seek unity for the Christian Churches by means of political unity under one ruler certainly affected Alcuin and his friends at the Court of Charles the Great. . . . All the bishops and abbots of the ninth century, in Rome and northwestern Europe, who desired the reform of the Church, were affected by the same tendencies, which eventually produced the medieval Empire.

THE NEW NORTH

A third unconscious tendency leading towards the medieval conception of an Empire was due to the influence of what may be called "the new North." As late as the middle of the sixth century, writers in most of western Europe still seemed to have thought of Roman civilization as dependent upon the connection between the East and the West or the Greeks and the Latins, embodied most clearly in the connection between old Rome and new Rome. Even when in the seventh century the bishop of Rome had come to be known, among bishops in the West,

as above all others, "Apostolicus" and "Pope," the connection between Pope and Emperor, between supreme power in the spiritual and supreme power in the temporal sphere, meant the relationship between the Latin Churches and the Roman Emperor then reigning at Constantinople. But while the conscious policy of the Churches in Italy and Spain was still affected by the traditional respect for the Emperor in the East, unconsciously the influence of writers, missionaries, bishops and abbots in northern Gaul (or Francia), in England and in Ireland had made a deep impression on all the Latin Churches and particularly the Church of Rome. Before the eighth century the chief influences affecting the thought and policy of the Roman Church had come either from Africa or from Syria and Alexandria. By the middle of the eighth century, however, the chief influences were coming from northern France and England. . . . But the result was that these countries, newly conquered for the Roman See and now producing their own literature, brought their influence to bear upon all the Latin Churches, including that of Rome. Therefore, by the middle of the eighth century, an unconscious tendency had begun to operate which made men look from Rome, not eastwards, but northwards, in their conceptions of Catholic Christianity. At the end of the eighth century, Paris, Tours, Reims, Canterbury, York, and afterwards Mainz and Cologne, had become centres of Christian life, replacing, at any rate for the Latin Churches, the African and Asiatic cities which had been reduced to subjection by Mohammedan invaders. In that atmosphere—the new currents of doctrine and practice flowing from the North—conscious policy was devised and carried out. . . .

THE POLICY OF THE CAROLINGIANS

The steps taken by those in control of social power, which led eventually to the crowning of Charles the Great, may be shortly described as follows. They are all connected with the three names—Charles Martel, Pippin his son, and Charles the Great his grandson. It is the story of the conquest of supreme power by a Frankish family, of its entanglement in Italian rivalries and of the final acceptance of a theocratic authority, as a method of preserving and extending military conquests. Conscious policy was that of barbarian warriors who could extend their power by armed force but found, as all barbarians are surprised to find, that they could not hold their conquests except by acquiring some moral authority. . . .

[Burns proceeds with a detailed analysis of the policies of Charles Martel, Pepin the Short, and Charlemagne between 714 and 800. He lays special emphasis, as suggested in the sentences immediately above, on Frankish military conquests and aggressive diplomacy leading to an ever expanding influence for the dynasty. Editor's note.]

THE CORONATION

The play at this point reaches the scene in St. Peter's when Charles was crowned by the Pope. . . . In the view here maintained the coronation was arranged beforehand between the Pope and Charles, and was probably the outcome of the policy, not of the Pope but of Charles himself. Secondly, the ceremony was intended by Charles to indicate the assumption of a *title*, and not the establishment of an *institution* —still less the claim to control an ancient institution already in existence, the Roman Empire. Thirdly, the title was intended to add prestige to the king of the Franks in all his territories indeed but primarily to express his new position in relation to the Pope. It implied the recognition of a higher status than that of Patrician; and from the Pope's point of view, it expressed the assumption that the king of the Franks was the official protector of the papal territories. . . .

THE TITLE AND ITS MEANING

But what actual title had Charles been given in the West? The earliest accounts say that "the *Roman* faithful" or "the whole *Roman* people" cried out— "Long live the Emperor." That is to say, the title referred only to his relation with the clergy and people of the city of Rome, and expressed only a change from the title of "patricius." It did not refer to the whole western world. Charles remained king of the Franks and Lombards; and in addition he was Emperor in the city of Rome. But in the later accounts "the whole *Christian* people" asked him to be their Emperor—a wholly fantastic idea.

The title of Emperor and Augustus, adopted by Charles, although it had little or no reference to the Roman Empire, undoubtedly added and was intended to add dignity or prestige to the barbarian king of the Franks. Like his predecessors, Alaric and Theodoric,[6] Charles was willing enough to dress himself in the Roman fashion, at any rate on the Roman

stage. But besides prestige, the new title, no doubt, expressed the king's new position in relation to the Pope. As *Patricius* he could not claim so definite a status as an Augustus. But the title of Emperor gave Charles at least the conventional right of being informed at each election of a Pope; and it gave the Pope a right to regard him as protector of the Church of the city of Rome. Again, the new title expressed no additional power, but a new relationship between the king of the Franks and all Christians in the West. From this time the ruler of the Franks, whether in western France or eastern France (*Francia orientalis*)—Germany, was regarded as protector of Christians in the Holy Land and other Mohammedan territories. The "whole Christian people," to which the documents of the early ninth century refer as the "faithful" (*fideles*) of Charles the Great, are now confined to the Latin Churches which from this date called themselves—using a Greek word—"Catholic." And this word, in the Middle Ages, continued to be used to distinguish the Churches of the West from the Christian Churches of the East—Latin from the Greek Christianity. Nobody after the ninth century would have dreamt of including among the "faithful" of Charles in the "Catholic" Church the subjects of the Roman Emperor who were members of the Greek Churches.

The attitude and policy of Charles the Great, after his assumption of the new title, are indicated by his actions during the thirteen years of his life, remaining after the year A.D. 800. He never returned to Rome; nor did he treat it as a capital in any sense, although he left his agents (*missi*) there. He governed his dominions chiefly from his residence at Aachen, holding his councils there, and issuing from the *palatium* there his general Capitulary and his orders to his officials. The Frankish kingdom, indeed, and its subordinate kingdoms of Lombardy and Aquitaine had no capitals in the civilized sense of the word. The king of the Franks remained the leader of warbands and their attendant clergy, whose central office (*palatium*) moved with him on his expeditions or in his changes from one royal residence to another. . . .

In A.D. 814 Charles the Great died; and Louis the Pious succeeded to his throne as king of the Franks.

---

[6] Alaric was the king of the Visigoths when this barbarian nation sacked Rome in A.D. 410. Theodoric, the king of the Ostrogoths, led his nation against Italy in A.D. 489 and from A.D. 493 until his death in A.D. 526 he was the actual ruler of Italy. [Editor's note.]

But in A.D. 816 Louis was again crowned, this time by Pope Stephen IV—and at Reims, not at Rome. Louis, however, continued the practice of his father; and in A.D. 817 after a general Congress, held at Aachen, he crowned his own eldest son, making him a "partner of his own title and Empire." He also named his two other sons "kings"—one of Aquitaine and the other of Bavaria. Coronation, therefore, had not yet become an act of papal authority and was still considered as the transference of a title. As late as A.D. 823, when Pope Paschal crowned Lothair[7] in Rome, the Chronicler says that "he received the crown of the kingdom and the title of Emperor and Augustus." Clearly neither Charles nor his immediate successors thought of an Empire in the modern sense of the word, nor even in the old Roman sense. Political authority implied the existence of a kingdom whose ruler might or might not be given the title of Emperor or Augustus, just as he might be called "Caesar," without any clear reference either to the original holders of that name or to its later meaning under Diocletian.

If anything more were needed to show that Charles the Great did not establish an Empire, and was not in anything but name an Emperor, a brief review of the actual situation in which he left Europe would be conclusive. There was no capital or permanent centre of administration and law. The old barbarian custom continued of moving the king's officials and retinue from villa to villa. It made no difference in practice that a villa or country residence of a king might be called a "palace" (palatium). Indeed, this use of the word is merely another sign of make-believe by which the central offices of ancient Rome on the Palatine Hill gave their name to any of the scattered houses of a barbarian chieftain. Again there was no central administration. The king's agents (missi dominici) were quite unable to control the counts or other local landowners who had established themselves in almost independent power over different districts. Worse still, there was no permanent armed force, either for internal order or for defence against foreign enemies. Charles the Great followed the old practice of summoning for an expedition as many armed men as he could collect in the early summer, and of allowing them to return to their scattered homes in the autumn. He did, indeed, attempt to establish small permanent outposts on his northeastern frontier, manned by counts and

their armed retainers; but that there was no single defensive system is proved by the number of expeditions the king had to make, to help these outposts. Finally, in the system established or rather continued under Charles the Great, there was none of that "providence" (providentia) with which the Emperor was credited under the old Roman system. He made no roads. His system of government did not require them. He conceived a plan of a canal between the Main and Danube; but when the work was begun, it was abandoned because the sides fell in, owing to the lack of competent workers. He repaired the old Roman harbour at Boulogne, but seems never to have grasped the need for new harbours, as a protection against the raids of the Northmen. He did, indeed, give money and land for the building and maintenance of churches and monasteries—which may be taken to correspond to the building of temples and public baths by the Roman Emperors; but the administration of what would now be called "social services" was in the hands of the clergy and not of the king or his counts.

In short, Charles the Great, stripped of the romances which adorned "Charlemagne," was simply a barbarian warrior of great energy, limited intelligence, no education and great simplicity of mind. Like Clovis, three hundred years before him, he believed that he could promote Christianity in the form familiar to him by killing some of those who had never heard of it and compelling the others to be baptized. He was intelligent enough to appreciate the services of scholars and to support their efforts for the promotion of learning and music among the clergy. His ambitions and ideals were those of a barbarian chieftain; and his leisure was spent in hunting and swimming. He was frugal in food and drink and clothing, but somewhat expansive in his affections. The number of his concubines and illegitimate children is not known; and he enjoyed having about him all his daughters. But in an age in which savage cruelty and reckless treachery were not uncommon, even at the Court of the Roman Emperor, which claimed to be the centre of civilized life, Charles the Great was exceptional in attracting faithful supporters and in exciting admiration for the power of his personality. . . .

GENERAL CONCLUSIONS

. . . The conclusions to be drawn are as follows. The Carolingian "Empire," or at least the adoption of the titles "Augustus" and "Emperor," was an

[7] The oldest son of Emperor Louis the Pious; after 840 he became ruler of a part of Louis' empire and bearer of imperial title. [Editor's note]

attempt to use the prestige of Rome for the support of a military system. The Frankish kings took advantage of the work of the Christian missionaries in Germany and of the Roman Church in Italy. The coronation of an "Emperor" was a kind of consecration, giving moral authority to military power by connecting it with Christian Rome—the Rome of the martyrs and apostles. Charles the Great, no doubt, was a sincere Christian, in his understanding of Christianity. He honestly believed, as many medieval warriors and kings did after him, that his wars were waged in the interests of Christianity, even when he attacked a Christian and Catholic king of the Lombards or duke of Benevento. The Christian Churches of Germany and France did indeed derive some advantage from the support given by Charles the Great to missionaries and reformers. And it is difficult to disentangle the motives of any man who has great power over his fellows. Charles may have thought of himself sometimes as the instrument of Christian Rome. But clearly he was never a passive instrument controlled by the policy of others. He expressed definite ideas of his own on ecclesiastical and even theological matters. It is, therefore, probable that he, like his father and grandfather, was not unaware of the use to which Christianity could be put in extending his conquests. The Christianity, for example, imposed by Charles the Great upon the Saxons was not "a way of life" supported by reasoning on evidence, but submission to a military leader and his ecclesiastical and lay officials.

But the titles "Augustus" and "Emperor" were not Christian in origin; and the second was definitely military. The prestige attached to them therefore came, not from Christian, but from pre-Christian imperial Rome. Indeed, difficulties arose in later times from the doubt whether the successor of St. Peter could have any power to confer a title which had existed before Christianity was accepted by the Emperors. In the ninth century Frankish poets described the transfer of power from the Romans to the Franks, as if the Franks had inherited a universal dominion which the Romans had transferred to them. Again Hincmar, in his life of St. Remy, says that the Franks came from Troy, as the Romans did, and that the Emperor Valentinian named them "Franks," "using the Greek word which means fierce." The Franks were, therefore, associated with the Romans as warriors and conquerors, not as makers of laws or of roads.

But the prestige of imperial Rome, in the ninth century and indeed in later times, perhaps even until modern times, had two very different meanings. The Roman Empire, to which medieval Europe looked back, was in fact both a military system of conquest and a civilian system of law and of administration. The Rome to which Charles the Great looked back was *military*, even if the sword was now in the service of St. Peter and not of the Caesars. But the Rome which remained the traditional source of the civilization of Gaul, surviving in Neustria or western France, was *civilian*—the Rome of law, administration and trade. The contrast between these two aspects of the Roman system in the minds of men in the ninth century must not be exaggerated. No doubt, Charles the Great was influenced by Roman Emperors as law-givers when he issued his Capitularies. But he was, above all, a soldier—a leader of expeditions against the Saracens and against the Saxons—a successor therefore of Alaric and Theodoric, as well as of Roman Emperors who had extended the Empire. . . .

WALTER ULLMANN

THE CAROLINGIAN EMPIRE
AS A CREATION OF THE PAPACY

So far our inquiries into the Carolingian Empire have emphasized the role of Charlemagne as the creative agent. However persuasive such arguments are, they never are absolutely convincing. Forever challenging any attempt to attribute to

Charlemagne sole responsibility for the event of 800 is the testimony of Einhard that the great ruler did not want the imperial crown and would have absented himself from the church of St. Peter on that fateful Christmas day had he known what was going to happen. If not from Charlemagne, from where, then, could the initiative have come? The contemporary sources provide an obvious clue—from the papacy. Several historians have approached the establishment of the Carolingian Empire from a papal point of view and have found persuasive reasons for arguing that the papacy was indeed the prime mover.

One of the most exhaustive studies of this theme has been made by Walter Ullmann, an English scholar who has specialized in the study of the growth of papal government throughout the Middle Ages. His acute analysis of papal problems and ideology at the end of the eighth century warrants close scrutiny. Not only does it contain a possible explanation of the origin of the Carolingian Empire, but it also provides a key to most later papal concepts of the medieval empire. The ideas and the interests that moved popes Hadrian I and Leo III to act as they did were little different than those which inspired later popes to support the empire and yet to engage in desperate battles against aggressive emperors in an attempt to make them conform to the papal idea of empire. Ullmann's argument thus provides an introduction to one of the great issues of medieval history: the struggle between papal and imperial universalism.

[Ullmann's interpretation of the establishment of the Carolingian Empire is based on a closely knit argument that takes us back to the beginning of papal history. A brief summary of that argument may be helpful in understanding the following selection.

Prior to about 500 the papacy had developed certain basic principles upon which was erected a theory of papal government. First, the popes argued that membership in the Christian community, gained through baptism, did not bestow any right to rule. The governance of the Church belonged to those who were qualified, such qualification being recognized by ordination. Thus the governance of the Church belonged to the ordained, i.e, the clergy. Second, successive popes developed the theory that church government was monarchic. Supreme authority was vested in the bishop of Rome, the successor of St. Peter to whom Christ had transmitted the power to rule over the Christian community. The bishop of Rome thus possessed a principatus, i.e., a real jurisdiction over the entire Christian body. Third, the papacy held that the secular head of society was divinely constituted to perform a specific duty in society, namely, to support and carry out the ends dictated by the Christian faith as defined by the priestly power. The secular ruler was subordinated to priestly authority and was obligated to accept the direction of the spiritual authorities for the good of society.

This theory of government encountered a rival theory of government subscribed to by the Christian emperors of the late Roman Empire. The imperial, caesaropapist theory exalted the emperor above the clergy and made of him a priest-king ordained by God to direct all aspects of society. This theory came into sharp conflict with the papal theory after Emperor Justinian (527–565) reconquered Italy and reestablished imperial control over Rome. Between the sixth and the eighth centuries the papacy had small opportunity to apply its concepts of government because of the presence of imperial forces in Italy. However, during this period the imperial power in Italy slowly deteriorated, creating ever greater opportunities for the popes to act as the possessors of a real principatus. Moreover, divergent developments in liturgy, doctrine, and disciplinary practices worked to create a growing chasm in religious life between the East and the West. Over

From Walter Ullmann, *The Growth of Papal Government in the Middle Ages* (London, 1955), pp. 87–102. Reprinted by permission of Barnes & Noble, Inc., and Methuen & Co., Ltd.

The Middle Ages

much of the West men grew increasingly accustomed to look to Rome for spiritual guidance. The popes were not timid about expanding their spiritual realm, especially through missionary work.

The conflict between the papal and the imperial ideology reached a climax in the first half of the eighth century. The papacy, long frustrated in its contention that it had a right to govern the Church, sought its freedom in a revolutionary way. It undertook to liberate itself constitutionally from the Roman Empire centered in Constantinople. This end was achieved by using the Frankish rulers. Ullmann traces in detail the skilled exploitation by the popes of the Lombard threat in Italy, of the Frankish religious respect for the see of St. Peter, and of the desire of the Carolingian family to acquire the Frankish crown to bring affairs to a climax in 751–754. As a consequence of the events of these years the papacy gained a new protector in the person of the Frankish ruler who now had the added title "patricius of the Romans" and a legally constituted state in Italy that was outside the jurisdiction of the Byzantine emperor. Thus liberation was achieved.

In the meantime, the popes continued to perfect papal ideology. The Donation of Constantine was manufactured to provide a legal basis for the papal state. This document stated that Constantine had granted the empire in the West to Pope Silvester I; thus the donation made by Pepin the Short in 754 involved nothing more than what legally belonged to the papacy by virtue of Constantine's grant. The popes also expanded the argument that the true Christian commonwealth consisted of all Christians faithful to Rome; this gave the popes spiritual authority over a community that no longer coincided with the Roman Empire ruled by the emperor in Constantinople. And finally the popes of the eighth century nourished the idea that the Frankish ruler had as his first obligation the protection and promotion of the spiritual community headed by the pope. While this idea was not excessively popular with Pepin the Short, who saw himself primarily as king of the Franks, it did sharpen the ancient papal principle that the secular head of society was obliged to protect the Church as directed by the priestly order.

By 755 or 760 the new order was clearly established. From thence we proceed to the age of Charlemagne. Editor's note.]

Although it had emancipated itself from the constitutional framework of the Eastern empire, the papacy had little cause to rejoice in its newly won "freedom." The position of the pope as the lord of the Duchy of Rome drew the Roman nobility conspicuously to the fore: it now demanded a share in the making of the pope and the "election" of Constantine (II), himself a soldier, and the subsequent tumultuous scenes brought forth a vigorous opposition party under the able leadership of Christophorus. The Council held at Rome in April 769 in which many Frankish bishops as well as of course still more Italian bishops participated, proceeded to the condemnation of Constantine (II) and, what is more important for us, to the promulgation of an election decree. This election decree was later to serve as the model on which a better known papal election decree was built. The synodists of 769 laid down that no layman must partake in the election of a pope — only clerics were allowed to vote, whilst all the laymen were permitted to do was to salute the thus elected pope as the "lord of all."

This election decree, however, lacked proper backing. And the subsequent history of papal elections and consecrations and the ever-increasing military influence of the Roman nobility made it imperative for the papacy to appoint an effective protector, a protector who was to guarantee the "freedom" of papal elections and thereby also to guarantee the authority of the newly elected pope. . . .

None was better qualified for this office than the Frankish "patricius Romanorum." Whilst the father [Pepin] had refused to bear the title, the son [Charlemagne] adopted it, certainly from 774 onwards. The intimate connection between the Roman Church and the Frankish Church no less than the strengthening of the bonds between it and the Frankish monarchy in the two decades since Ponthion,[1] were not without effects upon the mind of Charlemagne. The acceptance of the title and office of "patricius Romanorum" by Charlemagne is, we think, the effect, not of any political consideration on his part, but of his purely religious views. To him "Romanitas" and "Christianitas" were tautological expressions. Romanism for Charlemagne was not a historical-political term, but had an exclusively religious connotation: it signified the contrast to "Grecism," to that kind of faith which was not Roman-directed. Romanism simply meant Latin Christianity

[1] That is, since the meeting of Pepin and Stephen II in 752. [Editor's note.]

The Carolingian Empire as a Creation of the Papacy

—that Christian faith which was directed and orientated by the Roman Church. The Bonifacian work, its concomitant close association with Roman-papal organization, the spreading of the characteristically Roman liturgies and their prayers, the religious orientation of the Frankish domains towards Rome, led to a complete amalgamation of Christian and Roman elements. This Roman ferment in that eighth-century Christianity of the Franks was of decisive importance, because "Christianitas" and "Romanitas" became virtually indistinguishable. . . .

Set against this background it is perhaps understandable that Charlemagne should have had no hesitation in adopting the title and in playing the role of the "patricius Romanorum." When "Romanus" equalled "Christianus," there was indeed no obstacle to prevent his assuming that role which virtually meant no more than that of a military defender of the "Romans," that is the "Christians," a role which in fact he was accustomed to play in any case. What the title meant to him was that his protective function naturally embraced also those Romans who were the epitome of all the Romans in the world, that is, the geographical Romans: they were merely the Christians, as it were, in a condensed and crystallized form. And it was in his function as "patricius Romanorum," in his function as a protector of the Church of Rome, that he not only confirmed the "donation" of his father,[2] but also added a considerable part of Italy to the territories which his father had "restored" to their rightful owner, the Church of Rome. . . .

It seems clear that the Easter transaction of 774 had the same character as its precursor of twenty years earlier: in each case the transaction concerned "restoration" of property, stolen by the Lombards from its legitimate owner, the Roman Church. The test here as there lies in the transfer of property that was not in the hands of the Lombards—in our case, Venetia and Istria, to mention only the two most conspicuous examples. For both Venetia and Istria were still Byzantine and therefore belonged to the empire. The insistent demands of the pope put to Charlemagne for the implementation of the "donation" of 6 April 774, show us the rift between the

pope's intentions and the king's actions, a rift that seems to have become particularly clear after Charlemagne's assumption of the title "Rex Langobardorum" on 5 June 774. What is, moreover, very characteristic of these many letters sent by the pope, is the emphasis on the function of the Roman Church as the "spiritualis mater" of the king and the emphasis on his duty of protecting his spiritual mother—for this reason, if for no other, he ought to be a fighter "pro justitiis beati Petri exigendis" ["for seeing that justice is done for St. Peter"]. The prospect of appropriate reward is not omitted in these papal letters: if he fulfilled his promises the king would exalt the Roman Church and herewith the universal Church, and thereby the orthodox Christian faith would be preserved.

The exaltation by Charlemagne of the Roman Church is in fact the dominant theme in all these numerous papal appeals to the Frankish king. In one of his communications the pope goes even so far as to remind Charlemagne of the exaltation of the Roman Church by the Emperor Constantine: he is held up to the Frank as the model, for he had exalted the Church through his grant and had bestowed upon the pope these parts of the West, so that the "sancta Dei ecclesia" might flourish and blossom forth. "Et pro hoc petimus eximiam precellentiam vestram, ut in integro ipsa patrimonia beato Petro et nobis *restituere* jubeatis." ["And we beg your most distinguished excellence for this, that you order to be restored to blessed Peter and to us that patrimony in its entirety."] Divers emperors, Adrian I claims, patricians and other God-fearing men had conceded to St. Peter and the apostolic Roman Church territories, such as Tuscany, Spoleto, Corsica, and so forth, and "of these transactions we have the documents in our Lateran archives." Hence Charlemagne should imitate the great emperor Constantine who had exalted the Church under Silvester so enormously and who had given the Roman Church the "potestas" over these Western parts of the world.

Even though the pope's territorial ambitions remained largely unfulfilled, the papal creations of Pippin, Charles's son, as "King of Italy," and of Louis as "King of Aquitaine," when there was no precedent for these offices and for papal conferments of royal dignity and function, should be appraised adequately as regards their symbolic significance. Taken in conjunction with the creation of the Carolingian "patricius Romanorum" by Stephen II, these actions throw into clear relief the steady

[2] This confirmation of the Donation of Pepin occurred during Charles's trip to Rome in 774. The Easter transaction of 774, referred to below, was the meeting between Charlemagne and Pope Hadrian I at which Charlemagne renewed his father's grant to the papacy. [Editor's note.]

continuity of papal doctrine and plainly herald the much more significant act on Christmas day 800. Ponthion, Kierzy, Pavia, the creation of the "patricius Romanorum," Charlemagne's donation, the creation of the Italian and Aquitanian kings—these are powerful preparatory steps culminating in the creation of Charlemagne as "Imperator Romanorum." It is as if the papal theme gained momentum towards the closing years of the eighth century.

For we must bear in mind that during the pontificate of Leo III there were some very specific signs pointing to great changes. It will be recalled that . . . the newly elected pope was to announce his election to the emperor or, in order to save time, to the exarch at Ravenna, so as to obtain imperial confirmation of the election. But when Leo III became pope, there was no longer an exarch nor did the papacy consider itself as part of the Roman empire. Yet Leo III sent a "decretalis cartula" to Charlemagne immediately after his election. We hold that the reason why the deed of the election was despatched, was not indeed to adhere to an obnoxious system—the requirement of imperial confirmation was of course fundamentally inimical to the papal point of view—but in order to utilize this old rule for quite a different purpose: the papacy thereby implied clearly the role for which the Frankish king was destined—that of an emperor, for it was the emperor (or on his behalf the exarch) who had to give imperial confirmation to the papal election. But whilst the purpose of notification was previously to obtain imperial confirmation, the purpose now was, we consider, to implement the duty of the protector of the Roman Church and of the pope. The notification was to serve as the signal to the "patricius Romanorum" that a new pope had assumed his office, who is now to be protected by the patrician.

Furthermore, Adrian I had disregarded the rule laid down by Justinian that all documents, including therefore papal ones, must be dated according to imperial years. Leo III definitely abandoned this prescription of Justinian, but substituted in a document issued on 20 April 798, the regnal years of Charlemagne's rule in Italy for the imperial years (of the Eastern emperor). The idea behind this innovation was the same as in the case of notification: it was to indicate the role for which the Frankish king was destined.

The plan of Charlemagne to erect a Second Rome at Aix-la-Chapelle was an additional motive for Leo III to expedite matters in the direction in which they had already been moving. This plan of Charlemagne was revealed to him on the occasion of his visit to Paderborn in the summer of 799. Expelled by the Romans Leo sought to implore the help of the protector, the "patricius Romanorum." We shall have an opportunity to make some observations on what may be called Charlemagne's imitative rivalry with the Eastern emperor, but for the moment it must suffice to state that the residence of the Frank at Aix was largely modelled on the residence of the Eastern emperor, who lived in "New Rome" and, moreover, had at hand his chief priest, the patriarch. According to Charlemagne, the "Old Rome" was to be transplanted to Aix: next to the minster and the *"sacrum palatium"* which was the residence of the Frankish king, there was a third building, the "Lateran." Like Constantinople, Aix was to be the Second Rome: the Lateran is in fact the "house of the pontiff" in Einhard's description. And the court poet tells us of the "coming Rome"—"ventura Roma"—which Charlemagne is about to erect at Aix. It was the *secunda Roma*.

When Leo III implored the help of Charlemagne, the latter's intentions cannot have remained hidden from the pope. Did not in fact everything point to a most uncomfortable exchange of Byzantium for Aix? Was this exchange not a repetition of the set-up which the papacy had hoped to relegate to the past? Did not Charlemagne's exhortation of the pope have an ominous ring: he should lead an honest life, respect the canons, guide the Church religiously and diligently and fight simony—when this is compared with Justinian's view on the functions of the priesthood? What other role but that of an archpriest was the pope to play in the scheme of things devised by the Frank? For the king's task was the effective strengthening, consolidating, propagating, and preserving the faith—the pope's task was to support the king in this duty by praying for him like Moses did with elevated hands.

The Carolingian idea of a Second Rome at Aix, we hold, was one of the most severe challenges which the papal programme had to meet. For if this scheme of things had gone through, the foundations of the papal theme would have been sapped. European Christianity drawing its life blood from Romanism and nurtured by the Church of Rome, would have been deprived of its strongest and most attractive foundations. To have acquiesced in this plan of Charlemagne would have been a betrayal of all the Church of *Rome* stood for. And had not the instrument been carefully prepared, though primarily as a weapon against the East? The Donation of Constantine was precisely the handle by which the emancipation of the papacy from the clutches of the Eastern emperor could be effected: and the threatening clutches of the Frankish king were a sufficient justification for employing the same weapon against him. The "vacancy" in the empire provided the pretext; Leo's trial by Charlemagne two days before Christmas provided the additional stimulus for the momentous action on Christmas Day—for the transfer of the empire from the Bosphorus to the Tiber, by making the Frank the *Imperator Romanorum*. The historic significance of the act is only heightened when this twofold objective is appraised: the coronation was aimed against the empire as well as against the Frankish king. The seat of the empire was where the pope wished it to be—the seat of the *Roman* empire was *Rome,* not Constantinople, not Aix-la-Chapelle.

It was a magnificent political and symbolic device which Leo adopted. There can be no doubt that the initiative lay in papal hands: the act was well prepared—the Romans knew exactly what they had to shout, although no pope had ever crowned an emperor in Rome. The accounts in the official papal book[3] and in the Frankish annals[4] are substantially the same: because the pope had put the crown on Charlemagne's head, the Romans acclaimed him, in accordance with the previous arrangements, "imperator Romanorum." This acclamation by the Romans was to announce publicly the meaning of the papal act. Charlemagne became, by virtue of the pope's action, "imperator Romanorum"; but he also had to be designated and named as such in a public manner by the Romans present. That all this must have been carefully arranged, goes without saying: these previous arrangements, however, appear in the official papal accounts as the spontaneous inspiration of the Romans. Because the Romans—we follow the account—saw how much Charlemagne defended and loved the Roman Church and its vicar, they unanimously in a raised voice exclaimed, at the bidding of God and of St. Peter: "To Charles, the most pious Augustus crowned by God, the great and peace loving emperor, life and victory." It is plain that the "spontaneous inspiration" was well planned and need not detain us.

[3]See above, p. 123–24 where this account is reproduced.

[4]See above, p. 124 where this account is reproduced.

It is not, however, without significance that the Romans witnessing the act with their own eyes, acclaim Charlemagne as "a Deo coronatus." And it is as a result of divine and Petrine inspiration that they shout thus. The significance of this lies in that the whole ceremony is presented as the working of the divine will—it is not the pope who crowned the Frank, but God Himself: "a Deo coronatus."

If we wish to understand this, we must keep in mind that, according to the papal standpoint, there was no difference at all between the function of the newly created emperor and that of the patrician of the Romans: he was the protector and defender of the Roman Church. In both of our sources this vital point breaks through. The *Liber Pontificalis* declares that out of recognition for Charlemagne's *defence* of the Roman Church the Romans had acclaimed him emperor; according to the Frankish annals the patrician became absorbed in the emperor. And this is exactly what the papal book also says: "et ab omnibus constitutus est imperator Romanorum." This means that the patrician was now acclaimed or called—as the Frankish annals have it—or was "set up" as "emperor of the Romans" because the pope had crowned him: papal action preceded the acclamation—the Romans acclaimed the thus crowned Frank an "imperator" who had as a consequence of the papal coronation been raised from the office of patrician of the Romans to the dignity of the emperor of the Romans. The constitutive act was that of the pope: the acclamation derives its meaning from the papal act: the papal act is announced to the world. The patrician wears no crown; the emperor does, and he wears it because the pope has imposed it: the crowned emperor is acclaimed.

The "vacancy" on the imperial throne—and we take note that the increase of the indications pointing to fundamental changes coincides with Irene's rule as empress—provided the pretext for transforming an office into a dignity: the office of the patrician was transformed into the dignity of Roman emperorship. Functionally, however, nothing changed, as far as papal intentions went: whether patrician or emperor his function was defence and protection of the Roman Church. Constitutionally, however, there was a radical change for there was now an emperor of the Romans where previously there had been none—the consequence was the emergence of the "problem of the two (Roman) emperors." Charlemagne's coronation was, so to speak, the final and solemn and public act by which the papacy emancipated itself from the constitutional framework of the Eastern empire. There remains to be answered the question, By what authority did the pope proceed in the manner in which he did?

If we keep in mind that according to the accepted doctrine all power comes from God; if we recall that ideologically there was no difference between the famous Gelasian statement and the Donation of Constantine; if we consider the function which, in the papal view, the (secular) Ruler was to play—if we duly appraise all this, it will not be too difficult to realize that the pope acted not only as the mediator between God and man in imposing the crown—hence Charlemagne is "a Deo coronatus"—but also as the dispenser of the highest available dignity and power (*potestas*), of Roman emperorship. In fact, the dignity and power conferred by the pope could be no other but a conceptually universal one: the Roman Church, being the epitome of universal Christianity, can confer through the pope only a universal Christian power: and the only universal power that was available at the time was that designated by the title "emperor of the Romans." Moreover, although the imperial crown was in Constantinople, it was there on sufferance by the pope (Silvester): not only was there no emperor now, but those emperors who had been there before, were not worthy being called *Roman-Christian* emperors. For—we try to follow papal reasonings—these emperors had in fact constantly infringed the—for the papacy—most vital principle, that of the *principatus* of the Roman Church. With particular reference to this point Gelasius had declared that the emperor held his empire as a trust, as a *beneficium,* from God: but by demonstrably setting aside the divinely instituted papacy, the Eastern emperors had misused their trust—hence the pope considered himself entitled to withdraw his consent which by implication he had given to Constantine's taking his crown to Constantinople.

The emperors in the East, although ostentatiously styling themselves *Roman* emperors, had, by virtue of their opposition to the *Roman* Church, forfeited their claim to be *Christian* emperors. They were considered—as later terminology will have it—unsuitable emperors, and the papacy therefore was, always provided that the Donation was efficacious, entitled to transfer Roman emperorship from Constantinople to Rome: the Donation was the basis upon which Leo could proceed. This is nothing extraordinary, for, as we pointed out, the Donation was originally intended to be employed as a weapon against the East, so as to effect the emancipation of the papacy from the Eastern constitutional framework. And the possibility of a withdrawal of Roman emperorship from the East was as much inherent in the document as the papal consent to Constantine's taking the crown thither.

Gelasius had maintained that Christ was "Rex" and "Sacerdos" the "potestas regalis" [regal power] —signifying the "Rex"—and the "auctoritas sacrata pontificum" [Sacred authority of priests]—signifying the "Sacerdos"—were united in Him, but "by a marvellous dispensation" He had distinguished between the function of the priest and that of the king. It was Christ's own act: Christian imperial power therefore originated in Christ. There was no possibility of asserting that the pope conferred imperial power: until his position as the vicar of Christ was fully developed there was indeed no possibility for him to combine—like Christ—"potestas regalis" and "auctoritas sacrata"; therefore, there was also no possibility of conferring imperial power or of withdrawing it. This defect was made good by the Donation: as a consequence of Constantine's grant, the pope disposed of the crown, the external symbol of imperial power. And in this capacity Leo III acted on Christmas Day 800. Had not his predecessor, Adrian I, declared that the Roman Church was the "caput totius mundi," [head of the whole world], . . . and was it not the same Adrian who quoted the Donation? The "mundus" could be nothing else but Christendom, of which the Roman Church was the epitome and head: Charlemagne should conquer the barbaric nations; he in fact was already hailed as *the* Christian Ruler, Christian, because the spiritual son of the *Roman* Church. The empire in the East, though so ostentatiously calling itself Roman and Christian, could not justify these appellations—Leo took the step which was, from the point of view of papal doctrine, wholly understandable. The Roman Church being the "caput" of the (Christian) universe ("Mundus") creates through the pope a universal (Christian) protector who alone deserves the dignity of an "emperor of the Romans." This is his dignity—his function is that of a protector and defender, in the Roman-papal sense: the *principatus* of the Roman Church over the ideational universal entity, the *corpus Christi* (the universal Church), can be exercised through the agency of an ideational universal *potestas*, the emperor of the Romans.

3

MEDIEVAL ECONOMIC GROWTH: ITS SOURCES

The preceding two problems have suggested at least two forces that nourished some sense of community in Western Europe during the long period of gestation of a new civilization: the classical heritage and the ideal of empire. Their role must never be underestimated. Yet these forces, even when combined with the constructive efforts of the Church and the all-pervading influence of Christianity, were not sufficient to deliver a viable Western European way of life. During the early Middle Ages the survivals of classical civilization, the splendid ideals of a single political community, and the exalted spirit of Christianity influenced the actions of only a few men in any decisive way. At the foundations of society life proceeded in an atmosphere of disorder, poverty, ignorance, fear and insecurity. Nothing reveals the tenuous character of a society struggling to find solid foundations better than the fate of the Carolingian Empire during the last half of the ninth and the early tenth centuries. For in that brief time a combination of forces—outside invasions, dynastic quarrels among Charlemagne's heirs, usurpations of power by greedy nobles, and petty localism—wiped out the meager progress made by the Carolingians and their ecclesiastical supporters toward political order, spiritual regeneration, economic stability, and cultural revival. Many historians have viewed the post-Carolingian era, especially the tenth century, as the nadir of European history. The events of that troubled century give credence to this opinion. The havoc wreaked by Viking, Magyar, and Saracen invaders, the rowdy politics of undisciplined feudalism, the secularization and demoralization of the Church, the paucity of cultural achievements, and the uniform poverty of most men combine to present a gloomy picture. As one reads the laments of tenth-century observers, he is nearly persuaded that the future promised nothing. He is ready to agree with several contemporary writers who interpreted their miseries as signs of the fulfillment of the ancient prophesy that at the end of a thousand years after Christ's birth the world would end.

With the benefit of hindsight the historian knows that the tenth century gloom was unwarranted. A modern medievalist has put the point well when he said that "if it [the tenth century] was dark, the darkness was that of the womb." In fact, during the tortured centuries lying between the fall of Rome and 1000 a firm base had been created for Western European civilization. In the very institutions that seem to epitomize tenth-century "darkness"—feudalism, manorialism, the secularized Church—were the generative forces. At the base of society, so to speak, were stored up the vital energies and dynamic forces capable of delivering the "first" Europe from the womb. Already in the tenth century these energies and forces began to find release. And with amazing rapidity they interacted to transform the face of Europe during the eleventh, twelfth, and thirteenth centuries.

An eleventh century chronicler provides a clue to one of the most fundamental manifestations of Europe's emergence. After recounting at length the travails of the tenth century, he wrote:

So on the threshold of the aforementioned thousandth year, some two or three years after it, it came to pass throughout the world, but especially in Italy and Gaul, that the structures of the churches were rebuilt, although many were still seemly and needed no such repair. But every nation of Christendom became rivals with the others to see which would worship in the fairest buildings. So it was as though the very world had shaken itself and cast off its old age, and began clothing itself everywhere in a white garment of churches.

Indeed, as the chronicler implies, men only rebuild churches because they will to do so. But they can never build churches without the material means. The above passage is but one of a multitude of signs that Europeans began to dispose of a greater amount of material wealth by the opening of the eleventh century. A large scale economic revival had begun and would continue until the fourteenth century. This economic growth was a fundamental factor in shaping the "first" Europe. Without it the political, social, religious, and cultural resurgence marking the history of the eleventh, twelfth, and thirteenth centuries would have been impossible. Some consideration of economic growth is thus essential to an understanding of medieval European civilization at its peak.

The most intriguing problem involved in the economic expansion of Europe in the Middle Ages is the question of the origins of the revival. Where and how did a society so impoverished and so disorderly, so dispirited and hopeless as that of post-Carolingian Europe discover the talent, energy, and resources required to fashion an almost spectacular economic growth? The selections that follow grapple with this issue. They seek to explain how an "underdeveloped" society was suddenly able to put itself on its economic feet and create a greatly expanded material base capable of sustaining progress in all other aspects of civilization.

In selecting the following passages attention has been confined to rather recent scholarship. This choice has been conscious. When the economic history of the Middle Ages first commanded the serious attention of historians in the nineteenth century, there was a tendency to explain economic growth in terms of highly abstract, generalized theories of economic development. Since then the patient work of many scholars has produced a body of facts about the medieval economy that makes most of the older generalized explanations of growth extremely dubious. It now seems impossible to fit medieval economic development into any great overarching law of economic process. Rather the origins of economic revival were not only complex and varied but also unique to the European scene.

As he studies these selections the student ought first to try to identify the various forces that promoted economic growth. He will soon discover that various authors place their emphasis on different points. This calls for an effort at evaluation, for an attempt at assigning greater importance to some causes of economic growth than others. Although it may appear at first glance that there is substantial disagreement among the authors of the following selections, perhaps the student might try to probe a little more deeply into the issue at hand. For in economic history one is dealing with one of those baffling aspects of history where the complexity is so great that no single approach makes much sense. The student should perhaps seek to fit all the divergent views represented in these selections into his own synthesis which will accommodate a multiple explanation for Europe's economic resurgence. Genuinely sophisticated historianship indeed demands blending of many strands into complex explanations.

B. H. SLICHER VAN BATH
ROBERT S. LOPEZ

A POPULATION EXPLOSION?

The mere mention of population growth is apt to create a sense of panic to the intelligent observer of the modern world. And rightly so, for large sectors of the world are currently threatened with economic catastrophe as a consequence of population growth. However, historians view other ages in a different perspective. Some medieval economic historians argue that the *prime* factor stimulating economic growth was a medieval population explosion. Although others would not go quite so far, most of them attribute considerable importance to this phenomenon.

The two selections that follow will introduce the reader to the population problem in the Middle Ages. B. H. Slicher van Bath, a Dutch historian of agriculture, supplies some statistical data useful in estimating the magnitude of medieval population change within a long-range historical setting. Robert S. Lopez, professor of medieval history at Yale University and one of the foremost experts on medieval trade, offers some explanations of that growth. These selections do not quite do justice to the complex question of medieval demography, but they will at least suggest the broad dimensions of this dynamic factor in medieval society and help to clarify some of the discussions of economic growth below.

B. H. SLICHER VAN BATH

Accurate statistics, which show the size of the population and its growth or shrinkage since the preceding census, have appeared only in the last hundred and fifty years, and even then they apply only to individual nations. Most population figures before 1750 rest on estimates, which though sometimes based on numbers of homes or families known from tax-rolls, are more or less guess-work. Since the size of population of a single country in the past is so hard to ascertain, it is understandable that figures dealing with the population of the whole of Europe can be based only on conjecture. Because of the uncertainty of such data, one might be tempted to shelve the whole subject with the verdict, "Better no figures than false ones," but it is perhaps preferable, as will be done here, to take up the opposite

From B. H. Slicher van Bath, *The Agrarian History of Western Europe, A.D. 500–1850,* tr. Olive Ordish (New York: St. Martin's Press, 1963; published in Great Britain by Edward Arnold Ltd.; published in the original by Uitgeverij Het Spectrum, Holland), pp. 77–80. Reprinted by permission of Edward Arnold Ltd.

attitude, "Better a few figures—which, though not entirely reliable, give at least *some* guidance—than no figures at all." We shall not run much risk of being misled if we always bear in mind the doubtful character of the figures.

In his book *The World's Food*, M. K. Bennett, making use of the latest researches in the demographic field, gives the following statistics on the population of Europe.

YEAR	IN MILLIONS	YEAR	IN MILLIONS
400 B.C.	23	1400	45
A.D. 1	37	1450	60
200	67	1500	69
700	27	1550	78
1000	42	1600	89
1050	46	1650	100
1100	48	1700	115
1150	50	1750	140
1200	61	1800	188
1250	69	1850	266
1300	73	1900	401
1350	51	1949	548

These figures show that the high points were reached during the Roman Empire at about A.D. 200, just after the full flowering of the Middle Ages in 1300, and after 1750, when the great expansion of modern times began. A period of decline occurred at the time of the late Roman Empire and the barbarian invasions. The low point shown in the graph at the year 700 probably came, in fact, between 543 and 600, when serious epidemics were raging. The upswing which follows 700 (the Carolingian era) sinks again in about 900. After the spectacular rise from about 1150 to 1300 there follows the decline in the fourteenth century. This is partly due to the Black Death which took such toll between 1347 and 1350. But this epidemic was only one of a long series which had already begun in the second decade of the fourteenth century. From 1400 to 1450 a fairly quick recovery took place, followed by a steady rise till 1750. Perhaps the growth of population between 1550 and 1650 was somewhat greater than appears from the above figures, and that between 1650 and 1750 slightly less. The remarkable ascent after 1750 stems from many causes, the chief being that after that date the death-rate fell considerably in many European lands, while the birth-rate till 1880 remained at about the same level as before 1750; perhaps it may even have risen in the second half of the eighteenth century, in comparison with the preceding period. . . .

ROBERT S. LOPEZ

It can never be repeated often enough: the significant events of the tenth century are not to be found in the chronicles and scarcely involve the famous men. The dawn of Europe beginning to gleam at that time can only be observed by leaving the lofty spheres of political history and descending to the very springs of life.

There is every reason for believing that the general demographic decline of the early Middle Ages was halted soon after that "world plague" of 742–743. . . . It is even possible that a very modest revival may have shown itself from the ninth century: the Carolingian attempts at colonization, the beginnings of social organization amongst the Slavs, the progress of Byzantine and Arab trade, the advance of Indo-China and Japan, and even the revival of the T'ang empire after the disasters which had struck it in the eighth century could support such a hypothesis. But the indications are too slight, above all too little studied, to allow us to draw definite conclusions on the subject of a sudden demographic change, the effects of which could at first only affect populations reduced to a minimum.

In the tenth century, doubt is no longer possible: in Spain and China, in Sweden and in Egypt, humanity began to multiply. Men are the basic raw material of history: this continuous increase which went on without wavering to the last years of the thirteenth century and only ceased completely in the middle of the fourteenth, is the prime mover of all the events of the late Middle Ages. It may not have been the most important phenomenon, for the universities and cathedrals, parliaments and cities are more significant than the number of births and deaths, but the upsurge of population was definitely the initial phenomenon which made all else possible.

Causes of the Recovery   The demographic revival can be explained more easily than the decline which preceded it. The natural tendency of every species is to increase, if external causes do not impede it, to the very limits set by the resources of

From Robert S. Lopez, *The Birth of Europe*, © 1962 Librairie Armand Colin, © 1966 translation J. M. Dent & Sons Ltd. Published 1967 by M. Evans & Co., Inc. by arrangement with J. M. Dent & Sons Ltd. Reprinted by permission.

food it can obtain. Between the tenth and the thirteenth century none of the great scourges of humanity, except perhaps leprosy, seems to have raged at full force. In particular there is no further talk of grave outbreaks of plague, and malaria, it seems, assumed a less malignant form.

War, that other obstacle, played only a negligible part in the demographic history of the late Middle Ages. In spite of its reputation, the age of feudalism used only very small armies, and if it delighted in innumerable skirmishes, it fought very few battles. The prestige of the knights was based on the fact that they were not anonymous fighters lost in the crowd, but an elite of warriors who knew how to take hard blows without being killed.

Some thousands of combatants, some hundreds of dead: these are the terms for evaluating the most bloody contests, those described in the most dramatic tones by the chroniclers. There were often more victims amongst the non-combatants, for instance when Jerusalem was captured by Godefroy de Bouillon, 'they rode in blood up to the horsemen's knees'; not a single Jew escaped, we are told. But a letter recently discovered in the synagogue of Old Cairo asks for help for the survivors of the massacre of Jerusalem. It is true that, even where there was no question of hatred, feudal armies gladly burned harvests and cottages so as to starve the hostile lord. All the same, they were not sufficiently numerous, did not campaign long enough, and did not possess equipment efficient enough to produce the destruction which war creates in our time.

As for available resources, it is certain that at the beginning of the tenth century virgin territories exceeded considerably the total area of cultivated lands, and that even the lands easiest to cultivate and most densely populated were short of hands: was there not a marsh at the gates of Paris, another outside the Moorgate of London, and a wood in the middle of Milan? There was therefore no lack of space to feed a larger population.

In addition, the possibilities for agriculture were gradually enlarged by a slow improvement in the climate. We have proof of this, such as the retreat of polar ice in the sea and of glaciers in the mountains of the north, the extension of wine-growing to countries like England, where it is no longer practicable today, and the plentiful supply of water in the regions of the Sahara later reclaimed by the desert. Lastly, a series of technical improvements enabled farmers to extract, with less expenditure of effort than before, more frequent and more plentiful harvests from the soil, and to transport them more easily to distant markets.

EUROPE'S GOOD FORTUNE

It would be interesting to compare the immediate and the long-term effects of the demographic growth in all the countries which experienced it. It seems that in China it brought an economic, cultural and political revival under the Sung dynasty, without, however, very greatly modifying the agrarian, almost static, nature of its civilization. In Moslem Africa it seems to have brought about a rapid, exuberant flowering soon followed by a profound decline. But these spectacles are only marginal to our book: we will restrict ourselves to observing what happened in Catholic Europe.

Here the demographic upsurge of the tenth century was the beginning of a chain reaction which has not yet ended after a thousand years. Well before the fourteenth century, as soon as the demographic revolution becomes an agricultural revolution which in turn becomes a commercial revolution, Catholic Europe will pass from the rear to the lead in world economic development. Then, at the end of the middle ages and the beginning of the modern age, a crisis will hinder her progress but the solid foundations laid by the commercial revolution of the Middle Ages will prove firm enough to endure and support the huge impetus of the industrial revolution from the eighteenth to the twentieth century.

HENRI PIRENNE

COMMERCE AND ECONOMIC REVIVAL

When historians first began to give serious attention to medieval economic conditions, they were especially struck by the role of commerce as a dynamic aspect of economic life. Perhaps overly impressed by the part that trade plays in the modern world economy, they tended to view the "first" Europe's commercial growth as the starting point for all other economic developments. Special attention was given to the revival of trade in the tenth and eleventh centuries as the prime mover in an economic chain-reaction that transformed medieval society. And there are still a great many economic historians who see this "commercial revolution" as the basic cause of growth.

This view of medieval economic change was given classic expression by Henri Pirenne, the Belgian historian whose ideas we have encountered before (see above, pp. 101 – 6). The following passage from his *Economic and Social History of Medieval Europe* provides a concise summary of commercial revival set against the background of an agricultural economy. The student might note with special care how Pirenne explains the beginnings of commercial revival and how the fruits of commerce penetrated European economic life in its entirety.

INTRODUCTION

It is quite plain, from such evidence as we possess, that from the end of the eighth century Western Europe had sunk back into a purely agricultural state. Land was the sole source of subsistence and the sole condition of wealth. All classes of the population, from the Emperor, who had no other revenues than those derived from his landed property, down to the humblest serf, lived directly or indirectly on the products of the soil, whether they raised them by their labour, or confined themselves to collecting and consuming them. Movable wealth no longer played any part in economic life. All social existence was founded on property or on the possession of land. Hence it was impossible for the State to keep up a military system and an administration which were not based on it. The army was now recruited only from among the holders of fiefs and the officials from among the great landowners.

In these circumstances, it became impossible to safeguard the sovereignty of the head of the State. If it existed in principle, it disappeared in practice. The feudal system simply represents the disintegration of public authority in the hands of its agents, who, by reason of the very fact that each one of them held a portion of the soil, had become independent and considered the authority with which they were invested as a part of their patrimony. In fact, the appearance of feudalism in Western Europe in the course of the ninth century was nothing but the repercussion in the political sphere of the return of society to a purely rural civilisation.

From the economic point of view the most striking and characteristic institution of this civilisation is the great estate. Its origin is, of course, much more ancient and it is easy to establish its affiliation with a very remote past. . . .

From *Economic and Social History of Medieval Europe* by Henri Pirenne, pp. 7 – 10, 12, 13 – 23, 25 – 29, 33 – 39. Reprinted by permission of Harcourt, Brace & World, Inc., and Routledge & Kegan Paul Ltd.

Thus the organisation of the great estate was not, in any respect, a new fact. But what was new was the way in which it functioned from the moment of the disappearance of commerce and the towns. So long as the former had been capable of transporting its products and the latter of furnishing it with a market, the great estate had commanded and consequently profited by a regular sale outside. It participated in the general economic activity as a producer of foodstuffs and a consumer of manufactured articles. In other words, it carried on a reciprocal exchange with the outside world. But now it ceased to do this, because there were no more merchants and townsmen. To whom could it sell, when there were no longer any buyers, and where was it to dispose of a produce for which there was no demand, because it was no longer needed? Now that everyone lived off his own land, no one bothered to buy food from outside, and for sheer want of demand, the landowner was obliged to consume his own produce. Thus, each estate devoted itself to the kind of economy which has been described rather inexactly as the "closed estate economy," and which was really simply an economy without markets. It did so not from choice but from necessity, not because it did not want to sell, but because buyers no longer came within its range. The lord made arrangements not only to live on his demesne and the dues of his peasants, but also to produce at home, since he could not procure them elsewhere, the tools and garments which he needed for the cultivation of his lands and the clothing of his servants. Hence the establishment of those workshops or "gynaeceas," so characteristic of the estate organisation of the early Middle Ages, which were simply designed to make up for the absence of commerce and industry. . . .

Thus, from every point of view, Western Europe, from the ninth century onwards, appears in the light of an essentially rural society, in which exchange and the movement of goods had sunk to the lowest possible ebb. The merchant class had disappeared. A man's condition was now determined by his relation to the land, which was owned by a minority of lay and ecclesiastical proprietors, below whom a multitude of tenants were distributed within the framework of the great estates. To possess land was at the same time to possess freedom and power; thus the landowner was also a lord. To be deprived of it, was to be reduced to serfdom; thus the word *vilain* was used both for the peasant living on a domain (*villa*) and for the serf. It is of no importance

that here and there among the rural population a few individuals happened to preserve their land and consequently their personal liberty. As a general rule serfdom was the normal condition of the agricultural masses, that is to say, of all the masses. . . .

In this strictly hierarchical society, the first place, and the most important, belonged to the Church, which possessed at once economic and moral ascendancy. Its innumerable estates were as superior in extent to those of the nobility, as it was itself superior to them in learning. The Church alone, moreover, thanks to the gifts of the faithful and the alms of pilgrims, had at its disposal financial resources which allowed it, in times of scarcity, to lend to necessitous laymen. Furthermore, in a society which had relapsed into general ignorance, it alone still retained those two indispensable instruments of culture, reading and writing, and it was from churchmen that kings and princes had necessarily to recruit their chancellors, their secretaries, their "notaries," in short, the whole lettered personnel without which it was impossible for them to function. From the ninth to the eleventh century the whole business of government was, in fact, in the hands of the church, which was supreme here, as in the arts. The organisation of its estates was a model which the estates of the nobility sought in vain to equal, for only in the Church were there men capable of drawing up *polyptycha*, keeping registers of accounts, reckoning up receipts and expenditure, and, consequently, balancing them. Thus, the Church was not only the great moral authority of the age, but also the great financial power.

Moreover, the Church's conception of the world was admirably adapted to the economic conditions of an age in which land was the sole foundation of the social order. Land had been given by God to men in order to enable them to live here below with a view to their eternal salvation. The object of labour was not to grow wealthy but to maintain oneself in the position in which one was born, until mortal life should pass into life eternal. The monk's renunciation was the ideal on which the whole of society should fix its gaze. To seek riches was to fall into the sin of avarice. Poverty was of divine origin and ordained by Providence, but it behoved the rich to relieve it by charity, of which the monasteries gave them an example. Let the surplus of their harvests, then, be garnered and distributed freely, just as the abbeys themselves advanced freely sums borrowed from them in cases of need.

. . . Lending at interest, or "usury" (to employ the technical term used for it, which now took on the derogatory meaning which it has retained down to our own day), was an abomination. It had been forbidden from the very beginning to the clergy, and from the ninth century the Church succeeded in prohibiting it also to the laity and in reserving it for the jurisdiction of ecclesiastical courts. Moreover, commerce in general was hardly less disreputable than commerce in money, for it too was dangerous to the soul, which it turned away from the contemplation of its latter end. . . .

It is easy to see how well these principles harmonised with the facts and how easily the ecclesiastical ideal adapted itself to reality. It provided the justification for a state of things by which the Church itself was the first to benefit. What was more natural than the reprobation of usury, commerce, and profit for profit's sake, in those centuries when each estate was self-supporting and normally constituted a little world of its own? And what could have been more beneficent, when we remember that famine alone compelled men to borrow from their neighbours and hence would at once have opened the door to every abuse of speculation, usury and monopoly, to the irresistible temptation to exploit necessity, if these very abuses had not been condemned by religious morality? Of course, theory and practice are miles apart and the monasteries themselves very often transgressed the Church's order. But, for all that, so deeply did it impress its spirit upon the world, that it took men centuries to grow used to the new practices demanded by the economic revival of the future and to learn to accept as legitimate, without too great a mental reservation, commercial profits, the employment of capital, and loans at interest.

THE REVIVAL OF COMMERCE

I. The Mediterranean.   The irruption of Islam into the basin of the Mediterranean in the seventh century closed that sea to the Christians of the West, but not to all Christians. The Tyrrhenian Sea, it is true, became a Moslem lake, but this was not the fate of the waters which bathed Southern Italy, or of the Adriatic or the Aegean Sea. . . . The south Italian towns, Naples, Gaeta, Amalfi, and Salerno in the west, and Bari in the east, continued to recognise the Emperor at Constantinople, and so also did Venice, which, at the head of the Adriatic, never had

anything seriously to fear from the Saracen expansion.

The tie which continued to unite these ports to the Byzantine Empire was, it is true, not very strong, and it grew steadily weaker. The establishment of the Normans in Italy and Sicily (1029–91) definitely broke it as regards this region. Venice, over which the Carolingians had been unable to establish their control in the ninth century, had been all the more willing to continue under the authority of the Basileus, because he prudently refrained from exerting it, and allowed the town to be gradually transformed into an independent republic. For the rest, if the political relations of the Empire with its distant Italian annexations were not very active, it made amends by carrying on a very lively trade with them. In this respect, they moved in its orbit and, so to speak, turned their backs on the West and looked towards the East. The business of provisioning Constantinople, whose population numbered about a million inhabitants, kept up their exports, and in return the factories and bazaars of the capital furnished them with silks and spices which they could not do without.

For urban life, with all the luxury demands which it made, had not disappeared in the Byzantine Empire as it had done in that of the Carolingians. To pass from the latter to the former, was to pass into another world. Here, economic evolution had not been rudely interrupted by the advance of Islam, and an important maritime commerce continued to supply towns peopled with artisans and professional merchants. No more striking contrast could be imagined than that between Western Europe, where land was everything and commerce nothing, and Venice, a landless city, living only by trade.

Constantinople and the Christian ports of the East soon ceased to be the sole objective of the navigation of the Byzantine towns of Italy and Venice. The spirit of enterprise and the search for gain were too powerful and too necessary to allow religious scruples to prevent them for very long from renewing their former business relations with Africa and Syria, although these were now in the power of the infidels. From the end of the ninth century connections were formed which grew steadily more active. The religion of their customers mattered little to the Italians, provided that they paid. The love of gain, which the Church condemned and stigmatised by the name of avarice, was manifest here in its most brutal form. The Venetians exported to the harems of Egypt and Syria young Slavs, whom they carried off or bought on the Dalmatian coast, and this traffic in "slaves" unquestionably contributed quite as largely to their growing prosperity as did the slave trade of the eighteenth century to that of so many French and English shippers. To this was added the transport of timber and iron, with which the countries of Islam were unprovided, although there was no room for doubt that the timber would be used to build vessels and the iron to forge weapons which would be employed against Christians, perhaps even against the mariners of Venice. The merchant, here as always, could see nothing beyond his immediate profit, and bringing off a good business deal. It was in vain that the Pope threatened to excommunicate the sellers of Christian slaves, or that the Emperor prohibited the supply to infidels of articles capable of being employed in warfare. Venice, whither merchants in the ninth century had brought back from Alexandria the relics of St. Mark, went her own way, secure in their protection, and considered the steady progress of her wealth as the just reward of the veneration in which she held them.

That progress was, indeed, uninterrupted. By any and every means, the city of the lagoons devoted itself with astonishing energy and activity to advancing that maritime trade, which was the very condition of its existence. The entire population practised and depended on it, as on the Continent men depended on the land. So serfdom, the inevitable consequence of the rural civilisation of the peasants of this time, was unknown in this city of sailors, artisans and merchants. The hazards of fortune alone established between them social differences independent of legal status. From very early times, commercial profits had created a class of rich traders, whose operations already present an incontestably capitalistic character. . . .

II. *The North Sea and the Baltic Sea.*   The two inland seas, the North Sea and the Baltic, which bathe the coasts of Northern Europe, as the Mediterranean, to which they form a pendant, bathes its southern coasts, presented, from the middle of the ninth century to the end of the eleventh, a spectacle which, profoundly as it differs from that which we have been describing, resembles it nevertheless in one essential character. For here, too, on the coast and, so to speak, on the very edge of Europe, we find a maritime and commercial activity which is in

striking contrast with the agricultural economy of the Continent.

. . . Lacking a fleet, the Carolingian Empire was unable to defend itself against the Northern barbarians as the Byzantine Empire had defended itself against the Moslems. Its weakness had been only too well exploited by the energetic Scandinavians who, for more than half a century, subjected it to annual raids, not only by way of the estuaries of the northern rivers but also by those of the Atlantic. But the Northmen must not be represented as mere pillagers. Master of the sea, they could and did combine their aggressions. Their object was not and could not be conquest; though they won a few settlements on the Continent and in the British Isles, that was the most they could do. But the incursions which they pushed so deeply into the mainland were essentially great razzias. Their organisation was obviously carefully planned; they all set off from a fortified camp as centre, where booty collected from neighbouring regions was piled up while awaiting transport to Denmark or Norway. The Vikings, in fact, were pirates, and piracy is the first stage of commerce. So true is this that from the end of the ninth century, when their raids ceased, they simply became merchants.

To understand Scandinavian expansion, however, it must also be remembered that it was not directed exclusively towards the West. While the Danes and the Norwegians threw themselves on the Carolingian Empire, England, Scotland and Ireland, their neighbours, the Swedes, turned to Russia. From our point of view it is immaterial whether they had been asked for assistance by the Slav princes in the valley of the Dnieper in their struggle with the Patzinaks, or whether, in search of gain, they made a spontaneous thrust towards the Byzantine shores of the Black Sea, by the great natural route which from remotest times had been followed by Greek merchants from the Chersonese and the Sea of Azov seeking Baltic amber. It is enough to state that from the middle of the ninth century they established entrenched camps along the Dnieper and its tributaries, similar to those that their Danish and Norwegian brothers were establishing at the same date in the basins of the Scheldt, the Meuse and the Seine. Constructed at so great a distance from their mother country, these *enceintes* or, to use the Slavonic word, *gorods,* became permanent fortresses, from which the invaders dominated and exploited the not very warlike people who surrounded them. It was there that they amassed the tribute imposed on the vanquished and the slaves taken from among them, as well as the honey and furs which they obtained from the virgin forests. But before long, the position which they occupied inevitably led them to engage in trade.

Southern Russia, where they had installed themselves, lay, in fact, between two areas of superior civilisation. To the east, beyond the Caspian Sea, stretched the caliphate of Baghdad, to the south, the Black Sea bathed the shores of the Byzantine Empire and led to Constantinople. The Scandinavians in the basin of the Dnieper at once felt this double attraction. The Arab, Jewish and Byzantine merchants, who were already frequenting this region before their arrival, showed them a road which they were more than ready to follow. The country conquered by them put at their disposal products particularly suited for trade with rich empires leading a life of refinement: honey, furs and above all slaves, the demand for whom from Moslem harems, as well as from the great estates, promised the same high profits which tempted the Venetians. . . .

. . . It is impossible to doubt the part played by Scandinavia as a middleman, when we consider the astonishing progress of its navigation in the tenth and eleventh centuries, that is to say, during the period which succeeded the invasion of the Danes and Norwegians in the West. It is quite clear that they ceased to be pirates and became merchants after the example of their Swedish brothers; barbarian merchants, perhaps, who were always ready to become pirates again on the slightest occasion, but merchants all the same, and what is more, merchants navigating the high seas. . . . In short, the Nordic people gave proof at this time of an energy and a spirit of enterprise which reminds us of the Greeks in the Homeric era. Their art was characterised by a barbarous originality, which nevertheless betrays the influence of that East with which their commerce brought them into communication. But the energy which they displayed could have no future. Too few numerically to retain the mastery over the immense expanses where their ships had sailed, they had to yield place to more powerful rivals, when the extension of commerce to the Continent brought about a revival of navigation to compete with their own.

III. The Revival of Commerce. Continental Europe was bound soon to feel the force of the two great commercial movements which appeared on its borders, the one in the Western Mediterranean and the Adriatic, the other in the Baltic and the North Sea. Responding as it does to the craving for adventure and the love of gain which are inherent in human nature, commerce is essentially contagious. Moreover, it is by nature so all-pervasive that it necessarily imposes itself on the very people whom it exploits. Indeed it depends on them by reason of the relationship of exchange which it sets up and the needs which it creates, while it is impossible to conceive of commerce without agriculture, since it is sterile itself and needs agriculture to supply food for those whom it employs and enriches.

This ineluctable necessity was imposed on Venice from its very foundation on the sandy islets of a lagoon, on which nothing would grow. In order to procure a livelihood its first inhabitants had been forced to exchange salt and fish with their continental neighbours for the corn, wine and meat which they could not have obtained otherwise. But this primitive exchange inevitably developed, as commerce made the town richer and more populous, and at the same time increased its demands and sharpened its enterprise. At the end of the ninth century, it was already commandeering the territory of Verona and above all the valley of the Po, which provided an easy avenue for penetration into Italy. A century later its relations had extended to a number of points on the coast and mainland: Pavia, Treviso, Vicenza, Ravenna, Cesena, Ancona, and many others.

It is clear that the Venetians, taking the practice of trade with them, acclimatised it, so to speak, wherever they went. Their merchants gradually found imitators. It is impossible, in the absence of evidence, to trace the growth of the seeds sown by commerce in the midst of the agricultural population. That growth was no doubt opposed by the Church, which was hostile to commerce, and nowhere were bishoprics more numerous and more powerful than south of the Alps. . . .

[There is evidence which] illustrates the moral conflict which the revival of commerce was to provoke everywhere, and which indeed never ceased during the whole of the Middle Ages. From the beginning to the end the Church continued to regard commercial profits as a danger to salvation. Its ascetic ideal, which was perfectly suited to an agricultural civilisation, made it always suspicious of social changes, which it could not prevent and to which necessity even compelled it to submit, but to which it was never openly reconciled. Its prohibition of interest was to weigh heavily on the economic life of later centuries. It prevented the merchants from growing rich with a free conscience and from reconciling the practice of business with the prescripts of religion. For proof of this we need only read the many wills of bankers and speculators, directing that the poor whom they had defrauded should be repaid and bequeathing to the clergy a part of the property which at the bottom of their hearts they felt to be ill-gotten. If they could not refrain from sin, at least their faith remained unshaken and they counted on it to obtain absolution for them on the day of judgment.

It must, however, be recognised that this ardent faith contributed largely all the same to economic expansion in the West. . . .

[Pirenne summarizes the offensive action which the Christians took against the Muslims in the Mediterranean area, beginning with the efforts of Pisa and Genoa in the early eleventh century and culminating with the Crusades during the twelfth century. Editor's note.]

Thus the one lasting and essential result of the crusades was to give the Italian towns, and in a less degree, those of Provence and Catalonia, the mastery of the Mediterranean. Though they did not succeed in wresting the holy places from Islam, and though no more than a few places on the coast of Asia Minor and in the islands remained of their early conquests, at least they enabled Western Europe not only to monopolise the whole trade from the Bosphorus and Syria to the Straits of Gibraltar, but to develop there an economic and strictly capitalistic activity which was gradually to communicate itself to all the lands north of the Alps.

Islam did not react against this triumphant advance until the fifteenth century and the helpless Byzantine Empire was forced to submit to it. From the beginning of the twelfth century its supremacy in the eastern Mediterranean was at an end. It rapidly fell under the influence of the maritime towns, which now monopolised its import and export trade. Sometimes in an endeavour to shake off their yoke, the emperor tried to play off the Pisans and Genoese against the Venetians, or allowed the populace to massacre the detestable foreigners indiscriminately, as, for example, in 1182. But he could not do without them, and willy-nilly had to abandon Byzantine

commerce to them, even more completely than Spain in the seventeenth century was to abandon hers to the Dutch, the English and the French.

The revival of maritime commerce was accompanied by its rapid penetration inland. Not only was agriculture stimulated by the demand for its produce and transformed by the exchange economy of which it now became a part, but a new export industry was born. In both directions the lead was taken by the Lombard plain, admirably situated as it was between the powerful commercial centres of Venice, Pisa and Genoa. Country and towns shared equally in production, the former with its grain and wines, the latter with their linen and woollen stuffs. As early as the twelfth century Lucca was manufacturing silk fabrics, the raw material for which came to her by sea. In Tuscany, Sienna and Florence communicated with Pisa by the valley of the Arno and shared in her prosperity. Behind Genoa the movement spread to the coast of the Gulf of Lyons and reached the basin of the Rhône. The ports of Marseilles, Montpellier and Narbonne traded all over Provence as did Barcelona over Catalonia. So vigorous was the trade of the maritime countries that in the eleventh century it began to spread northwards through the Alpine passes, which the Saracens of Garde-Frainet had blocked so dangerously in the tenth century. From Venice it reached Germany by the Brenner, the Saône and Rhine valleys by the Septimer and St. Bernard, and the Rhône valley by Mont Cenis. The St. Gothard was long impassable, but eventually a suspension bridge was slung from rock to rock across the gorge and it too became a route of transit. In the second half of the eleventh century we hear of Italians in France. It is more than probable that they were already frequenting the fairs of Champagne at this period and met there the flow of commerce from the coast of Flanders.

Indeed, the economic revival which was in process of achievement in the Mediterranean, was matched on the shores of the North Sea by revival which, if it differed from it in extent and character, proceeded from the same causes and produced the same result. As we have seen above, the Northmen had established, in the estuary formed by the arms of the Rhine, the Meuse and the Scheldt, a mart which soon attracted trade from far and wide along these rivers. . . . At the same period, a trade developed in the Meuse valley, extending as far as Verdun by way of Maastricht, Liége, Huy and Dinant. The Scheldt enabled Cambrai, Valenciennes, Tournai,

Ghent and Antwerp to communicate with the sea and the large rivers which emptied their waters among the Zealand Islands. The harbour of Bruges at the end of the Gulf of Zwyn, now silted up, was so convenient that from the end of the eleventh century ships began to put in there in preference to other ports, and the future glory of the city was thus ensured.

It is certain that at the end of the tenth century Scandinavian trade kept Flanders in close relations with the North Sea and Baltic countries. . . . Her trade was naturally still more active with England. . . . The Channel was less frequented than the North Sea, but there was a regular trade between the Norman and English coasts, by way of Rouen and the estuary of the Seine, and thence along the river to Paris and to the confines of Champagne and Burgundy. The Loire and the Garonne, by reason of their distance, did not experience until later the effects of the commercial revival in the northern seas.

Flanders soon came to occupy a privileged position, which it was to keep until the end of the Middle Ages. Here we meet with a new factor, industry, which was nowhere else in operation at so early a date and with such remarkable results. . . . The fineness of the [Flemish] cloths soon caused a demand for them along all the coasts frequented by the Northern seamen and, to meet that demand, their manufacture increased to proportions hitherto unattained. It was already so considerable that at the end of the tenth century native wool was insufficient for its needs, and wool had to be imported from England. The superior quality of English wool naturally improved that of the cloth, the sale of which increased as its fame grew. In the course of the twelfth century the whole of Flanders became a country of weavers and fullers. Cloth-making, which up till then had been carried on in the country, was concentrated in the merchant towns, which were founded on all sides and supplied an ever-growing commerce. It was cloth which created the nascent wealth of Ghent, Bruges, Ypres, Lille, Douai and Arras. Already an essential article of maritime trade, it now brought into existence an extremely important trade by the land routes. From the beginning of the twelfth century Flemish cloth was being taken by sea to the fair of Novgorod, while the Italians were coming to Flanders to buy it in exchange for the spices, silks, and goldsmiths' work which they imported from south of the Alps. But the Flemings themselves frequented the famous fairs of Champagne, where, midway between the North Sea and the Alps, they met buyers from Lombardy and Tuscany. These carried Flemish cloth in enormous quantities to the port of Genoa, whence under the name of *panni francesi* they were taken by sea as far as the ports of the Levant.

Of course, Flanders was not the only place where cloth was manufactured. Weaving is by nature a domestic occupation, which is known to have existed from prehistoric times and is met with wherever there is wool, i.e., in all countries. It was only necessary to stimulate its production and perfect its technique for it to become a real industry. This was not neglected. In the thirteenth century, Genoese notarial instruments mention the names of a number of towns which were sending cloth to that port: Amiens, Beauvais, Cambrai, Liége, Montreuil, Provins, Tournai, Châlons, etc. Nevertheless, Flanders and soon afterwards its neighbour, Brabant, occupied an unrivalled place among their competitors. The proximity of England enabled them to obtain excellent wool on the best terms and in much larger quantities than the latter. In the thirteenth century the overwhelming superiority of the Flemish industry is reflected in the admiration which it inspired in foreigners. Throughout the history of medieval Europe no other region presented this character of an industrial country which distinguished the basin of the Scheldt. It offers, in this respect, a contrast to the rest of Europe which brings to mind England in the eighteenth and nineteenth centuries. . . .

In striking contrast to the Italian towns, Flanders and Brabant, as they became more industrialised, became also less interested in the maritime commerce for which their geographical situation seemed to have destined them. They abandoned it to the foreigners whom their industry attracted in ever-increasing numbers to the port of Bruges, Scandinavians in the eleventh century, and later Hansards. . . .

[Pirenne now proceeds in the remainder of his book to describe the consequences that stemmed from the revival of trade: the emergence of cities and city institutions, the development of a bourgeoisie class, the transformation of agriculture, the development of a money economy, banking, and credit, the appearance of capitalism, etc. Editor's Note.]

GEORGES DUBY

AGRICULTURE AND ECONOMIC REVIVAL

The large role which Pirenne assigned to commercial expansion as the driving force regenerating the medieval economy has in recent years received a serious challenge from a rather surprising quarter: the historians of medieval agriculture. By taking up once again the investigation of an aspect of medieval life that has long been considered the epitome of economic stagnation and conservatism and by bringing to this study new techniques and insights, the historians of farming have opened new and exciting vistas. The most significant of these historians have been Frenchmen, many of them inspired by the seminal works of Marc Bloch, the great French medievalist who met a tragic death at the hands of the Nazis during World War II as a consequence of his role as a resistance leader. Bloch's works on feudal society and rural life not only revitalized the study of agricultural history but also encouraged his followers to apply the new insights of the social sciences to medieval economic and social history.

One of the most eminent perpetrators of Bloch's tradition is Georges Duby, a professor at the University of Aix-Marseille. His recent two-volume study, entitled *L'Economie rurale et la vie des campagnes dans l'Occident médiéval* (1962), is a masterful reinterpretation of medieval agricultural history, representing a skilled synthesis of the most up-to-date scholarship. The following passage was written by Duby for a large-scale work on world history. Not as full as his more specialized *L'Economie rurale*, it still conveys the essential conclusions that have been formulated as a consequence of the most recent investigations of agricultural history. In reading this selection the student should note the main features of the agricultural "revolution" and the by-products for the rest of the economy. Perhaps he will then have some reason to challenge the argument presented by Pirenne in the preceding selection.

Restrained for more than a century by the invasions of the Norsemen, the Saracens, and the Hungarians, the renewal of economic activity . . . asserted itself decidedly in Europe around 950. It was at that moment . . . that there spread rapidly in the countryside of reconstructed Christendom many technical inventions of very great consequence, inventions which were certainly much older but whose application in the West had remained very limited up until then. . . . Everything leads one to think that the great revival of the medieval West was intimately bound to a fundamental renovation of agricultural practices, to a veritable revolution whose progress was in truth very slow but which by permitting the production of slightly more than subsistence altered completely the conditions of economic life.

Technical Improvements.   That renewal was complex and affected each of the elements of the cultural system; for greater clarity it is convenient to isolate the diverse improvements which, in reality, depended closely one upon another and which are

From Edouard Perroy, et al., *Le Moyen Age*, Vol. III of *Histoire Générale des Civilisations*, ed. Maurice Crouzet (Paris, 1955), pp. 251–59. Used by permission of Presses Universitaires de France. Translated by the editor.

inextricably mixed together. The first improvement consisted of a better utilization of the power of streams; after the beginning of the tenth century it seems that by the generalized application of procedures long known the streams were regulated . . . so as to run grain mills and oil presses. The water mills, causing hand grinding implements to be useless, released the domestic labor force from the extremely heavy burden of the preparation of the grain and permitted it to be devoted to other more productive tasks. At the same time that they captured the energy of water, men succeeded in making better use of animal power. In effect, there simultaneously was developed and diffused a considerable improvement in the methods of harnessing animals: for the horse the rigid shoulder-collar replaced the loose breast-collar which strangled the beast and considerably reduced its power; for the oxen, the yoke, best suited to the vital forces of the animal, was no longer applied to the withers but to the horns. To this initial progress there was united an improvement of implements: in the hoe and the pitchfork iron was substituted for wood, making the tool more efficient; the use of the harrow was also begun; and, especially, to the harnessing methods which produced greater power one could link plowing implements of greater efficiency. In effect at that moment in all of northern Europe, on the heavy, rich soil which was not threatened with depletion by too heavy cultivation, the use of the large, heavy wheeled plough equipped with a mold-board spread, and the old wooden plough, capable only of scratching the earth, was progressively relegated to soils that were thin and dry.

Turned over more completely and better aerated, the soil also benefitted from progress in manuring, from marling which spread through the west of France, and from the irrigation employed on a large scale in Lombardy after the beginning of the twelfth century. As a consequence the yields of agricultural labor were increased. Finally there was another revolution, this time in the cycle of cultivation: for the Roman system of rotation or biennial rotation, for the still more primitive and less productive nomadic or temporary cultivation or of burnt-over cultivation was substituted little by little the triennial rotation. The substitution was in reality very slow (it appears that these new usages were introduced in the Carolingian age on the very large royal and monastic establishments) and would always remain only partial, but it marked decisive progress. This technique, in effect, permitted the putting of the land under cultivation two years out of three instead of one year out of two, and therefore increased by at least one half the production of foodstuffs. At the same time that triennial rotation developed, there also spread the use of a new cereal, oats, in the face of which barley declined. Oats served most often as food for humans in the form of porridge; but it was also used for animals and contributed to increase the number and improve the quality of the beasts. The raising of horses in particular was expanded. This significant phenomenon, which marked the beginning of a complete transformation of the methods of warfare and which as a result oriented the entire evolution of the western aristocracy, was not without reverberations on the rural economy: from the end of the eleventh century in northern Gaul the horse—more expensive to maintain, but faster and capable of producing larger yields because of an increase in the working of the land—began to replace the oxen. Such are the principal technical innovations. Again we must note that they spread slowly and at first in the most important agricultural enterprises, that their center of diffusion was seemingly located in the great loamy plains . . . between the Loire and the Rhine, that during the Middle Ages they penetrated only the lands of southern England, France, and northern Germany. The South, essentially for climatic reasons, retained archaic customs, including the use of the old plow and of biennial rotation.

Production and Population. This technical revolution gave rise to a complete renovation of rural life. First of all, on all of the establishments the harvests were much increased with the same amount of labor. In order to put under cultivation the large pieces of arable land on that portion of the manor reserved to the lord, the master no longer had need of so large a force of compulsory labor: a few men were sufficient. He no longer called upon the others and made with them an arrangement by which they rendered to him as a substitution for that service [that is, for labor service or the *corvée*] money payments or agricultural produce. Thus there gradually disappeared most of the *corvées* demanded on the landed estates of the Carolingian period. . . . Little by little the dependent agricultural establishments ceased any longer to participate in the exploitation of the lord's reserve. . . . As a direct effect of the improvement of techniques the conversion of the ancient labor services into rents procured for the master of the soil supplementary resources: resources in produce which by assuring the maintenance of his household permitted him to reduce the size of his reserve, to rent part of it, and to increase the number of his tenants and thus his profits; resources in money which allowed him to purchase more. In that way the lord was less closely attached to his land; rents took an ever larger place in his revenues; and the exploitation of the manorial enterprise tended to be opened to the outside world.

On the peasant holdings the benefits accruing from the implements of labor and the reduction of the corvees . . . permitted more abundant harvests to be taken from the plots allotted to the peasants. Without doubt it was necessary to deliver over in kind or to sell part of that yield in order to discharge the payments which replaced the old labor services. . . . However, there remained sufficient surpluses to assure a better nourishment for peasant families. . . . That was the solution for the chronic undernourishment (the skeletons exhumed from the cemeteries of the early Middle Ages bear witness to this) which for many prior centuries had weighed on the rural world, had increased to a high level the rate of infant mortality, and had checked all possibility of population expansion. After the year 1000 famines became rarer and eventually disappeared, while the population of the West began to increase regularly. This is a phenomenon difficult to measure, . . . but one which can be recognized as having extraordinary amplitude; . . . [on the basis of some evidence] one can admit that during the three hundred years which followed the year 1000 the population in Western Europe became three or four times more numerous.

It seems that at its beginnings this increase in population was marked by an increase of the density of the population on the old lands under tillage; the same amount of labor might, in effect, feed many more people without difficulty. A half or a quarter of a holding formerly sufficient for one family now provided a living for an agricultural household. Thus the family holdings of the old type were divided into half- and quarter-holdings, and at the same stroke the households and the inhabitants of the village multiplied. But soon the demographic pressure was accompanied by an extension of the land under cultivation at the expense of areas which heretofore had been left idle because, given the state of techniques, they were either too little productive or too difficult to work. Three interrelated facts—the utilization of methods of traction and of agricultural implements much more efficient and capable of rooting out deep stumps and of turning over the

heavy soils which no plow up to now had been able to touch; the surplus of hand labor freed by the use of more efficient agricultural practices; and finally the natural abundance of births which is no longer offset by infant mortality—were the point of origin for a large movement of land clearance which, depending on the part of Christendom, began between 950 and 1100.

Land Clearance.   Peasants and lords collaborated in these undertakings, destined to transform progressively the forest and the marsh into productive lands. The peasant often took the initiative because the exploitation of the old arable lands required less labor than ever. When his labors ended, there remained time for the head of the family to attack the waste land which bounded his fields, to push forward with the plow and to extend little by little his holding. During the winter he burned the brush, cut down the large trees, and dug up the stumps. In the spring the clearing had become a meadow which the year after one could work and sow, and still later plant to vines. If the reclaimed land belonged to a vigilant lord, he might require that a rent be paid; if not, the peasant would lay claim to the new plot as his private property. And by this slow progress, carried on around the entire edge of the holding, the cultivated clearing was enlarged. Soon the new fields were a long distance from the village. Those who had conquered these new lands from the waste installed their dwellings there, and thus there was created on the periphery of the estate a dispersed habitation. Often the clearers of the land ended by meeting at the limits of their clearings those who had come from other villages, and the belt of uncultivated lands which had formerly isolated the parishes entirely tended to be reduced to a few sparse remnants on the most sterile soil. Besides, when in the peasant households children grew to adulthood, all could not be employed on the paternal holding; some of them had to search their fortune elsewhere. Those who did not go to the cities or did not go to enlarge the crowds of converts to the new monasteries were welcomed by the lords of the great forested hilly regions, were established there with some companions, and after practising for a few years an itinerant cultivation on burned over ground, created in the middle of the forest a new estate.

As to the landed lords, they too began to extend their direct exploitation. In order to employ to the full their domestic labor force which now had greater leisure and to utilize the part of the *corvées* of their tenants which had not been converted to rents, they undertook the cultivation of certain parts of their reserved land that had been abandoned to woods or to pasture. But most of the lords tried especially to increase their rents, and thus to multiply their tenancies. They therefore offered to young men in search of land pieces of virgin soil to put under cultivation. To attract these young men they often furnished them with implements, beasts of burden, and the capital needed to begin the installation. In a general way, they gave up the most burdensome dues. They promised not to levy the arbitrary head tax (*taille*) and to maintain the other exactions at a reasonable rate. Guaranteed against the hazards of the first years, the colonist was required simply —aside from a light money rent for the house which he occupied—to deliver a fraction of his harvests, varying according to the region between a fourth and a twelfth. These conditions were tempting; their advantages were sometimes publicized afar and caused the displacement of population over a long distance from the regions long populated and with the greatest density of people toward the pioneering zones. . . .

This intense agricultural colonization rapidly modified the landscape of the countryside of the West. In all the old cultivated areas the uncultivated stretches were reduced; to such a point that sometimes the equilibrium of the village economy was found to be broken, since there remained too few of the wooded plots which, by furnishing wood for heating, berries, the prime material of almost all of the peasant buildings, and nuts for the feeding of pigs, constituted one of the essential elements of the agrarian economy. And likewise there was a reduction of the pastures and the vacant lands which, as a result of the rarity of meadows and the absence of fodder raising, were indispensable to the maintenance of animals. The great forested solitudes were broken up, opened up by new clearings. . . . Finally, cultivation progressed equally along the alluvial banks of streams and in the low, marshy valleys of the great rivers. There it was not against the tree but against the water that the battle was waged, and the conquest, based on a network of dikes, presupposed a collective management of drainage, carried on by a strict community discipline in order to support a system of protection. Thus everywhere there increased lands capable of producing grain. It was in the middle of the twelfth century that the movement attained its greatest intensity. The land clearances, the effects of which added to those caused by technical progress, increased still more the volume of subsistence and permitted the demographic expansion to continue.

Circulation of Goods and of Men. The immediate consequence of that simultaneous increase of men and of goods for consumption was the revival of exchanges. In the year 1000 the class of "laborers" was made up almost exclusively of peasants who struggled to draw from the soil that from which to live and from which to satisfy the basic needs of the knights and the clergy; and with rare exceptions all transfers of wealth took place through the channel of dues within the manor which was an organism almost completely closed. But progressively, the better return from agricultural labor . . . provoked a visible expansion of manorial resources. The members of the upper classes were thus incited to raise their standard of living and were no longer content with incomes required for their subsistence. The same phenomenon permitted on the other hand an increasing number of workers to detach themselves from the land, to devote themselves to activities not exclusively agricultural, and in response to the demands of the rich to take up new functions as artisans or in commerce. These specialists were fed by the excess production of the rural exploitations; but they had to buy that food. And thus it was that exchanges increased outside the framework of the manor, . . . and that the rate of the circulation of wealth was accelerated. As a natural effect money took a more important place in current life. Coins were more necessary; little by little precious metals which had been immobilized in treasuries of the metal-smiths were put into circulation. That stock was insufficient and in the mints there were struck coins of less weight and of poorer alloy. At the same time that the coinage became more common, it was debased; in every way, its purchasing power was lowered. . . . A final consequence of economic expansion was a slow but continued rise of prices. . . . In a certain region of France cereals sold at the end of the thirteenth century for about twenty times more than in 1100.

A new quickening of travel [marked the period after 1000]. . . . Circulation was facilitated by the clearance of land which by thinning out the natural obstacles which were formed by the great forests and the humid valleys, helped to draw together human groups. The techniques [of travel] were still rudimentary. . . .

In spite of the slowness of travel and the difficulties and dangers of the routes, very numerous were those in the feudal centuries who left their family or their community in order to travel — men or women, clerks or monks, knights or men of inferior status. In effect, travel was the great distraction of the times. . . . Any pretext for movement was good enough; very often the pilgrimage was the occasion for setting out. In the first rank of practices of piety stood the visit to certain holy places. . . . After 1000 these spiritual journeys took on larger proportions; most of the pilgrims now chose as their destination either Rome or Jerusalem or the holy places of Palestine, or finally the tomb of St. James at Compostella [in Spain].

All these travellers, whose progress was slow, were unable to carry with them enough food supplies for the entire journey; they could not always benefit from the free hospitality of charitable establishments. They therefore carried money to pay along their way for their lodging, their food, food for their animals, and the service of ferrymen. They left their coins with the sellers of agricultural produce, with the innkeepers established along the side of the roads, with the butchers and with the bakers who . . . established themselves in ever larger numbers at the stopping places and who made a fortune. Thus, as a result of the increasing intensity of movement along the routes, new outlets were opened for agricultural workers; the peasants could sell to the outside the part of their harvests which the improvement of practices of cultivation rendered in excess, and by virtue of that money penetrated into the rural milieu.

It is true that the small cultivators hardly profited from that money; the return of their sales was in effect absorbed in large part by the manorial fiscal system which at that moment . . . was adapted to the acceleration of the circulation of money. The money spread about by the travelers was in the last analysis collected by the manorial lords [and other wielders of power] . . . who were evidently the first to reap the profit from that movement. For that reason, the members of the aristocracy, lay and ecclesiastical, could increase their expenditures considerably. The churchmen in particular utilized their new revenues in money for the embellishment of the sanctuaries. With their incomes they undertook new constructions, opened workshops for sculpture, and enriched their sacristies with new adornments; the artistic flowering at the end of the eleventh century, as well as the development of specialized crafts, especially that of stoneworkers, was intimately connected with the rebirth of the money economy.

As to the knights, it was especially for the pleasure of making a show, of being brilliant in the worldly assemblies — one of the essential joys of the noble — that they surrendered their money resources. They were no longer content with the products of their domain and of their household industry. They became accustomed to luxury. Luxury of the table: it was proper to serve to their guests rare articles of food, the wines of the lands of the North, and especially spices. Luxury in dress: they abandoned the common fabrics for furs, precious and exotic materials, and colored cloths that were uncommon. The taste for fine imported objects which had never been destroyed and which had maintained a flow of long-distance commerce during the periods of greatest economic contraction, suddenly expanded and gave rise to a new expansion of luxury trade. While the purchase of oriental products increased and was paid for by larger sales to the Muslim lands, the production and exchange of certain expensive products was intensified in the interior of the western world: traffic in wines from the region of the Seine and the Oise, . . . and from the banks of the Loire and the Atlantic coast towards England and the Low Countries; diffusion of high quality cloth woven and dyed in the cities of Artois and Flanders. Thus the circulation of merchandise increased along the routes at the same time as did the movement of pilgrims. . . . In the midst of the ranks of laborers an economic class was formed. Numerous enough at the beginning of the eleventh century to be made the object of special prescriptions in the oaths of the peace of God, that class grew without cease, joining together those who occupied themselves with furnishing to the members of the upper classes the luxury items which they desired. These were the merchants.

P. BOISSONNADE

EFFECTIVE ORDER AND ECONOMIC RECOVERY

In the modern world we have grown accustomed to think that factors other than purely economic ones can have a powerful influence on economic systems. Perhaps the same was true in the medieval world. At least that is the position taken by the French social and economic historian P. Boissonnade in the following selection from his book *Life and Work in Medieval Europe*. This work for a long time has constituted one of the most widely read of all treatments of medieval economic history. Intensive research since its publication in 1921 has produced new information which requires adjustments of many of Boissonnade's generalizations. But it is possible that his remarks on the relationship between economic growth and political forces contains an important element of truth.

The selection that follows is inserted in Boissonnade's book after he has described tenth- and eleventh-century feudalism and manorialism in particularly harsh terms. His characterization of these institutions highlights disorder, violence, arbitrary abuse of power by feudal bullies, cruel exploitation of the peasantry, and technical stupidity—all combining to constitute an economic regime that was little less than savage. If this was the character of the feudal-manorial system (many scholars, like Georges Duby, would question such a view), then the point Boissonnade seeks to make in the following passage may have validity. At least it has to be placed alongside the other explanations of economic growth that we have encountered.

The primary condition necessary to stimulate the activity and progress of labour was the formation of some tutelary authority able to assure the necessary protection and order to the masses. . . .

Feudal government, indeed, never succeeded in fulfilling at all efficaciously the tutelary functions of a regular power, the permanent and enlightened protector of labour. Born out of the fear of the invasions and the need for protection against anarchy, it was for its subjects little more than a prolonged military dictatorship, with all the inconveniences of a despotism established upon brutal force. Instead of order it had only an ill-determined hierarchy, which merely gave rise to confusion, and the freedom of the feudal contract perpetuated this lack of discipline. Several hundreds of thousands of little local sovereigns, as turbulent as they were brutal, served by rapacious agents, who were both unscrupulous and ignorant, crushed the subject classes beneath an irritating tyranny, which was often no better than a kind of regular brigandage. A rough and incoherent fiscal system erected arbitrariness and extortion into a system. "The lords," declares a cleric of this period, "seek to fleece and to devour their subjects." Justice itself fell into their hands, and became, not an institution guaranteeing social peace and equity, but an instrument of extortion, the essential object of which was to *exploit* the person under jurisdiction—that is to say, to overwhelm him with fines and confiscations. The worst of it was that the villeins had no recourse against the abuses of this government, which were aggravated by the total absence of an organized police and by the multiplicity of feudal wars.

From P. Boissonnade, *Life and Work in Medieval Europe, The Evolution of Medieval Economy from the Fifth to the Fifteenth Century*, tr. Eileen Power (New York and London, 1927), pp. 150–58. Reprinted by permission of Routledge & Kegan Paul Ltd.

In the absence of a real system of regular government, to take up arms was the sole resource left to feudatories, in order to secure respect for their power or their rights. Thus war was perpetual; it died down in one place, only to break out again in another. It was the usual accompaniment of spring and summer, and let loose upon thousands of little states all the horrors of devastation, fire, and murder. Cottages went up in flames, harvests were burned, cattle killed or driven away, vines and fruit-trees cut down or uprooted, mills destroyed, and even churches profaned. When the peasants were unable to take refuge in the heart of the woods they were seized, fleeced, tortured, mutilated, hanged. Sometimes their hands and feet were cut off, or they were flung upon the fire; captives had their eyes put out, women were violated and their breasts were hacked off. After exploits such as these whole provinces became deserts. Not infrequently famine followed in the train of prolonged feudal warfare to complete the work of destruction and death. It was essentially this chronic state of insecurity and robbery which for 200 years caused the stagnation of all cultivation and the poverty of the mass of the people. The feudal warrior, indeed, easily became a brigand, and war degenerated into an enterprise of pillage. "Honour," says a troubadour at the beginning of the twelfth century, "is (for a gentleman) to steal and to plunder."

Thus as long as the feudal régime was all powerful, order, the elementary necessity of every society, was lacking to stimulate the progress of labour. Strangers to any idea of a real economic administration, the feudatories deprived labour of any possibility of improvement or of a lasting emancipation. It was only when great centralized feudal states were formed, side by side with reviving monarchies, that the Middle Ages began to move towards a happier future. From the eleventh century, in Normandy, Aquitaine, Anjou, and Flanders, then in the county of Barcelona and the marches of Brandenburg and Austria, there sprang from the feudal world itself governments, which took up once again, in concert with the monarchies of France, Germany, England, Navarre, Castile, Aragon, and the two Sicilies, the tradition of the supreme state, the dispenser of justice, the defender of order and public interest. Great politicians and administrators, such as William the Conqueror, Henry II Plantagenet, Philip Augustus, St. Louis, Henry II and Henry III of Germany, Frederick Barbarossa, Frederick II of Swabia, Roger II of Sicily, Alphonso

VII and Jaime I of Spain once more established the framework of a strong civil and military administration and set to work to reduce the abusive power of the feudatories, and to substitute the interest of national groups for those of individuals or of local groups. Everywhere they sought first to re-establish order by decreeing what was called in some parts the Duke's Peace, as in Normandy, in others the Count's Peace, as in Flanders and Catalonia, and in others still the King's Peace, as in France, Germany, Castile, or the two Sicilies. They made repeated efforts to limit and then to forbid feudal and private wars, and to prohibit the bearing of arms, trying to transform the anarchical and warlike society of their time into a peaceful and ordered one. Thus they laid the first foundations of a national economy, and, in the teeth of many obstacles, began to inaugurate a more far-reaching régime than that of the feudal economy, which never looked beyond local considerations.

The princely or monarchical state had henceforth a more or less clear-cut economic policy, the object of which was to protect and favour labour in its various forms, and to encourage production and exchange. Great feudatories and kings were among the most ardent promoters of agricultural colonization. They often protected the rural masses against the abuses of seigniorial government, and even favoured the mitigation or suppression of serfdom, sometimes on their own domains, but, above all, outside them. Everywhere laws began to be put forth to protect agriculture, to prevent the seizure of cattle and farm implements, to encourage reclamations, or to prevent their abuse by forbidding the destruction of forests. Some rulers, such as the counts of Flanders, the dukes of Normandy, and the kings of the two Sicilies, set up model farms and studs, introduced new crops, or legislated, like the kings of Castile, for the development of stock-breeding and the prevention of murrains. They were the enlightened protectors of all manifestations of the industrial renaissance, of urban activity, and of the corporations of artisans, and they promoted the exploitation of mines. Sometimes, as in the two Sicilies, they even anticipated the economic system of modern monarchies by creating veritable state manufactures. Their policy was wider in scope than that of the feudal governments, and they devoted all their efforts to promoting the development of circulation and exchange; merchants were granted not only security, but a whole host of exemptions and privileges, the interests of external trade were protected, and within their realms they created fairs and markets with special franchises, improved the means of communication both by sea and by land, and restricted the multiplicity of weights and measures, which they sometimes, as in England and France, even attempted to unify. They tried at the same time to develop credit, and to repress its abuse. They granted foreign bankers permission to set up banking-houses, and regulated the rate of interest and the exchanges. They restricted the circulation of feudal coinages, and promoted the movement in the direction of monetary unity by bringing about the prevalence of the royal coinage, and sometimes reserving the right to mint it for themselves. For the first time in centuries England, the two Sicilies, Flanders, Hainault, France (in the time of St. Louis) knew a fixed and pure coinage. But more often yet they proved to be still unable to shake off the practices of the feudal governments, and destroyed the effect of their more enlightened economic policy by a fiscal policy which bristled with abuses and was a mass of hampering restrictions and incoherent customs regulations. The national economy of which they were the representatives was painfully seeking its way in the chaos of feudalism, from which it had not yet completely emerged.

In the foreground at this period we must place the action of the Church, which was superior in continuity, power, and scope to that of the secular governments. With the whole of Western Christendom under its eyes, the Church inaugurated therein the first international economy, and sought to give to labour a system of protective regulations designed to increase its efficacy. The Papacy and the French monastic orders took the lead in this work of reconstruction. Under the inspiration of the religious idealism professed by the monks, the great medieval popes from Gregory VII to Innocent III succeeded in partially freeing the Church from the feudal bonds which threatened to stifle it, and set its feet boldly in the path of progress. In concert with the Cluniacs and Cistercians they restored the idea of authority, the conception of the solidarity of interests of Western Christendom, and tried to establish order and public peace in feudal Europe. The Church assisted monarchical government to re-establish itself, playing a tutelary rôle towards it which was useful at the time. Its doctors revived the Christian and Roman tradition of the state as protector of the community of labour and defender of collective interests. It propagated the common basis of Christian civilization throughout the West, proclaimed the

necessity and dignity of labour, and was the sole society open to the lower classes, wherein the son of the villein or artisan could rise to the bishop's mitre, nay, even to the papal tiara, as did the erstwhile swineherd Nicholas Breakspear (Adrian IV). Strong in its spiritual and temporal power, recruited by dint of its elective system from the élite, furnished with a centralizing government served by the ever-increasing monastic militia, the Church in this period of the Middle Ages can justly claim the honour of having taken the lead in social and economic progress and in material civilization, as it led in intellectual and moral civilization.

Popes and councils, monks and clerks, sought to regulate feudalism, to soften its manners, and to raise its ideal by the institution of chivalry. They tried to reform the abuses of feudal government and to prevent the exploitation of its subjects. In 1179 the Lateran Council was bold enough to condemn arbitrary tallages, and in the thirteenth century the Franciscans are found encouraging the movement against the payment of seigniorial dues, and supporting the emancipation of peasants and burgesses. Themselves victims of feudal brutality, clerks and monks often made common cause with the people against the feudatories. The ideal of the Church was a well-ordered society, in which work should be able to go on in security, and of this society it constituted itself the guardian. Likewise from the eleventh century onwards it began a missionary campaign, in part fruitless, and yet a true source for pride, to limit, regulate, and even to suppress war. With the support of popes and princes, the French Church, promoter of so many generous ideas, spread the Peace and the Truce of God throughout the West. By virtue of these two institutions, feudal expeditions were entirely forbidden for part of the year —Advent, Lent, religious festivals, and were prohibited every week from Wednesday to Monday morning. Non-combatants, clerks, merchants, peasants, and their goods were placed under the safeguard of religion so as to protect them from the brutality and devastation of the soldiery. Armed associations (*paixades*, "fraternities of peace" or "fraternities of the cowl") were founded under oath to maintain these salutary regulations. Ecclesiastical censure, the withholding of the sacrament, and excommunication fell upon those who disturbed public order or work. The Church lacked the power to bring an effective force to bear in support of its generous conceptions, but it had at least the merit of showing the way to the monarchical state, which was later to carry out the great social work thus planned by churchmen.

At the same time the Church gave to the masses the powerful, moral, and idealistic armour of its Faith. It multiplied schools and universities for the people as well as for the chosen few, and spread abroad the teaching of which it had the monopoly. It was the Church which founded higher education, and in the professorial chairs of its doctors political economy was born and problems were discussed relating to the organization of labour, the origin and limits of property, individual or communal ownership, wages and the just price, the rôle of commerce and of money. All these high questions were there studied with the utmost boldness, and the audacity of speculative thought on this point knew no bounds among theologians and canonists, though practical reason tempered the boldness of theoretical reason, as the mendicant orders found at the end of the thirteenth century, when they were minded to take up communism and an anarchical equalitarianism.

In the social order the Church had been at pains to organize the relief of the labouring classes, the poor, the sick, and the captive, multiplying, with the help of the laity, alms-houses, hospitals, *maisons Dieu*, lazar-houses, and organizations for the ransoming of prisoners. Charity, a Christian form of social solidarity, was made a formal obligation, and a corrective of the right of property. In the economic sphere the Church then played a part of the first importance, for it united organizing ability with the breadth of mind and idealism of the most talented body of men to be found anywhere in that age. Its domains became centres of attraction, by reason of the superiority of the agricultural methods employed there and the favourable condition of the peasantry. It was "good to live beneath the cross," provided that one gave up all spirit of independence. It was in the Church that there appeared the first signs of pity for the working classes; theologians and preachers, Yves de Chartres, Geoffrey de Troyes, Raoul Ardent, Maurice de Sully and their like, proclaimed the social value of the work of the poor and humble and the original equality of serf and free-man before God and His sacraments, even while they preached obedience to the villeins. They castigated the oppressors of the poor, and some even raised a voice against the institution of serfdom.

The clergy, a tradition-loving class and conservers of the feudal order, showed scant favour to the political and social emancipation of the peasants, but they set an example in the amelioration of their lot in the economic sphere. They showed immense activity in pushing on the agricultural colonization of the West, in which the great French monasteries were the leaders, and deserve the eternal homage of history. The ecclesiastical domains were centres in which agricultural science was developed, forestry and scientific breeding improved, model farms created, new crops tried, and agricultural production regenerated and stimulated. It was on the lands of the Church, and in towns in which episcopal authority ruled, that there appeared the professional division of labour, the first perfected industrial technique, the first schools of arts and crafts; and there, too, the working classes first organized themselves. Above all, the monasteries, during this period of three centuries, taught to one generation after another the various higher forms of industry, the production of luxury fabrics, tapestry, embroidery, enamel work, goldsmith's work, porcelain, glasswork, architecture, sculpture, painting. From the schools of Moissac, Saint-Savin, Saint-Denis, Fossanova, Chiaravalle, Saint-Gall, and many another abbey there went forth craftsmen who taught the men of their day the skilled practice of industrial arts. Finally, the Church began early to assist the development of a new form of wealth based upon movables. It favoured the formation of groups of merchants round the centres of its dominion, both urban and rural; it sought to secure the safety and to provide the means of transport, organizing under its aegis the first associations for the repair of roads and bridges and creating the first long distance transport services by road or river; it stimulated the creation of markets and fairs; and it tried to repress or abolish barbarous customs, such as piracy and wreckage, which hindered maritime commerce. Although the Church tended to consider mercantile activity as sterile and the trade in money as usurious, it was nevertheless the first to create reserves of capital, to inaugurate the system of deposits, credit, and banking, to proclaim the wise doctrine of a stable coinage, and to take part in large commercial enterprises. In short, by establishing between the states of Western Christendom the bonds of a true international solidarity, the Church prepared the way for the renaissance and development of a money economy which was destined to give to labour an expansion and a freedom hitherto unknown to it.

ROBERT S. LOPEZ

PRIVATE INITIATIVE AND ECONOMIC RECOVERY

In direct challenge to Boissonnade's argument that the increasing effectiveness of centralized authority spurred economic growth is the position taken by Robert S. Lopez in the following passage. This brief selection from a general history of the Middle Ages forms a part of a discussion in which Professor Lopez identifies four basic forces acting to promote economic growth in the tenth and eleventh centuries. The first three factors promoting economic expansion were population growth and movement, a more favorable attitude toward the merchant as a respectable member of society, and technical development. The fourth factor is described as follows: "The extreme political fragmentation and the feebleness of governments which favored local initiative and private associations." In the passage that follows Lopez suggests the intriguing possibility that the magic ingredient that is supposed to be unique to modern economy—private enterprise—was already at work in the medieval world.

[*Professor Lopez has just finished a discussion of new technological advances emerging in the tenth century*]. Machines do not deserve the scorn poured upon them, even in our own time, by certain intellectuals: for are they not creations of human intelligence equally with works of art? However, nor must one exaggerate their importance. No machine on its own can be the beginning of an economic revolution: rather, we believe it is the revolution which produces the machine or endows it with its usefulness. The instrument has value only through the hand which uses it and the brain which directs it.

Still, if one turns to intellectual equipment and initiative, one feels once again that the tenth century and the years immediately following mark a new dawn. There is then a collective reaction against that inertia of spirit and will which for five or six centuries had condemned the whole of Europe to ignorance and poverty, isolation and slavery. . . .

ORIGINAL ASPECTS OF EUROPEAN INITIATIVE

From the tenth century onwards private, local initiative takes a new leap forward in all spheres—economic, political, religious, intellectual. Particularism reacts in this way against the weakness of the central authorities who had promoted the modest cultural renaissance and the weak material revival of the ninth century. Some, being strong enough to do without all assistance, make their own laws. The others—the great majority of individuals—form groups as they are able, by contract or oath, according to the bonds of parentage or neighbourhood, and according to their community of aspirations and interests. This is how, between the tenth and the twelfth centuries, two apparently opposite tendencies are revealed at the same time: on the one hand, anarchic individualism; on the other, the fraternities and voluntary private associations.

Individualism, the spirit of association, absence of governmental restrictions; these are the indispensable characteristics of all rapidly expanding economies until the era of contemporary state planning. During the centuries of the great medieval growth of population we find one or other of these characteristics in the Moslem states as well as in the Byzantine and Chinese Empires. But in these Empires private initiative is hampered by governments wishing to stabilize the economy. In the Islamic world, on the other hand, it is weakened by a society ill adapted to organization and voluntary collaboration. It is only in Europe that the three conditions are united, once at the beginning of the Western commercial revolution of the Middle Ages; a second time at the beginning of the Industrial Revolution of the modern age. And in both cases this combination seems to have helped Europe to get ahead of the rest of the world.

COMMERCIAL CONTRACTS

In maritime commercial contracts individualism makes to the spirit of organization the indispensable minimum of concessions necessary for the temporary unification of capital and consequent spreading of the risks. The most typical agreement is certainly the *commenda,* unknown to classical antiquity, sparsely outlined in the Near East in the seventh century, mentioned for the first time in a Venetian document of the tenth century but widespread in all the Mediterranean ports, both Christian and Moslem, in the twelfth and thirteenth centuries. This contract binds, for one single commercial venture—an outward and return voyage—the money-lender and the traveller. The former takes three-quarters of the profit in case of success but takes responsibility for any loss involved. The traveller risks his trouble for the sake of a quarter of the possible profit. The sharing of risks and profits introduces a social element into an agreement which originates in the loan pure and simple, the lender running no risk beyond the capital he has advanced, and taking no direct part in the management of the affair.

Commercial 'adventure', we said: in fact, in the oldest contracts, the voyage is called *taxedion* (from the Greek: "military expedition"), the activity of the traveller *procertari* (from the Latin: "to engage in a struggle") and the action of lending money is *iactare* (to "throw" it at random). But this risk is, generally speaking, well calculated. We know a case in the twelfth century where a Genoese capitalist tripled his first investment in two years, thanks to three successive *commenda* contracts, while the traveller amassed a sum almost equal to that which the capitalist had entrusted to him at the start. In this particular case it seems that the traveller was a young man whose only luggage was his initiative and intelligence. But the roles were often

reversed: The humblest people entrusted their mite in *commenda* to a capitalist merchant in the hope of being thus linked with his fortune. Also two merchants often took turns in the roles of lender and traveller.

In a more rudimentary form, contracts similar to the Mediterranean *commenda* are found in the commerce of the North Sea and the Baltic from the thirteenth century onwards. Is this a derivation or a chance similarity? It is possible that their origin goes back to the even more informal contracts mentioned in the Scandinavian sagas, and thence to the Byzantine maritime customs of the tenth century. The influence of Jewish and Italian law can also be invoked. But all things considered, it seems more reasonable to believe that the parallel demands of maritime commerce spontaneously suggested to the men of the north solutions comparable to those which the sailors of the south had found.

In inland commerce the contract which played the largest part—the fraternal society or company (literally, "sharing of bread")—was founded on the principles which governed the communal administration of individual inheritances. Did it not often happen that the rightful claimants to the succession of a fief, a landed property or a fiscal due formed a consortium in order to keep the property intact? Similarly the members of a company are often brothers, cousins, sometimes brothers-in-law who came to an agreement to unite their capital and their labour for a certain number of years. They share risks and profits in proportion to their contribution to the general capital and assume a corporate unlimited responsibility for all the obligations contracted by one of them.

This union was as narrow and rigid as the *commenda* was adaptable and transitory. The company was better suited to long-term projects, to enduring and powerful construction. But it was more vulnerable: the mistake of a single partner could cancel out the gains of several years and sweep away the other partners in a common ruin.

PROFESSIONAL ASSOCIATIONS

Side by side with the contracts between individuals and families (the two examples we have given show but imperfectly their variety and elasticity), must be mentioned the professional associations. Even in the advanced towns, indeed, the great merchants and the capitalists were only the elite. The mass consisted of retailers, shopkeepers, pedlars, artisans and apprentices. However, the "great ones" did not at all like to be mixed with the "small," nor to submit to a group discipline. At the most they made common cause when they went abroad, in the reassuring promiscuity of caravans and convoys, or in the cartels, hansas or guilds which they normally formed for dealing with foreign powers. Moreover, they got rid of these collective organisms as soon as they were able to transform their towns into autonomous political powers and use them for the protection of their private interests. On the other hand, the guild or corporation remained in general the typical organization of the small merchants and it was *par excellence* the organization of the manual workers.

What is the origin of these trade associations which blossomed suddenly in the tenth century in several cities of Europe, and soon became an essential part of urban life? Some of them were probably descended from the professional corporations of the Romans and Byzantines, which were state-controlled, or from the gangs of serf workers of the early Middle Ages. Others were perhaps attached to the religious brotherhoods or the primitive Germanic guilds which had no professional character, their members meeting to pray, or rather to drink and help each other in case of need. Whether or not there was an existing tradition, trade associations were formed wherever there was a nucleus of workers wishing to protect their collective interests. This phenomenon was not restricted to Catholic Europe. From the tenth century onwards trade guilds, generally less free than the Western corporations, sprang up in China, in the Islamic world and at Byzantium.

The aims of trade associations have often been misunderstood by historians who are haunted by the problems of their own age. Some have taken too literally the moral precepts which embellish the corporate statutes. Whatever he may say, the main object of a manufacturer could not be to serve God and humanity, but to sell his goods at a profit. The measures taken to guarantee quality and limit price spring less from a regard for honesty than from the necessity of avoiding unpleasant surprises for difficult customers; for in the Middle Ages, even at the height of the commercial revolution, the customer (as we say nowadays) is always right. On the other hand, the modern critics of medieval guilds found their reasoning on the restrictions adopted after the fourteenth century, in an atmosphere of depression which engendered mistrust and ill-feeling on the part of the trade guilds towards every newcomer. In general, the medieval guilds of Catholic Europe, *in their early stages,* welcomed into their ranks as many new recruits as economic progress allowed them to absorb. They welcomed them on an equal footing; the apprentice being destined to become master in his turn.

In order to appreciate fully the role of the guilds, it must never be forgotten that while the merchant could increase indefinitely the volume of his business the artisan was limited by the moderate return of manual work. He could not increase his return either by exploiting cheap manual labour which since the disappearance of slavery no longer existed; or by the large scale utilization of machinery which was still at an embryonic stage. Even in a fully expanding economy, therefore, the artisan ran the risk of acquiring very little wealth and of being exploited by the capitalist merchant. The guild strove to protect him by unifying the profession without suppressing autonomy in the workshop. It only partly succeeded, at the price of restrictions, several of which hampered the development of industry. But in as far as it succeeded, it prevented the commercial revolution from inflicting on the workers the sufferings which accompanied the beginning of the Industrial Revolution.

Moreover, the guild had in addition a positive part to play. It often worked as a political party to influence on behalf of its members their own town or foreign governments. It also acted as a cartel in buying raw materials or making a kind of publicity. By standardizing the production of the workshops it facilitated international distribution. One had to be a native of Ypres to know the names of its weavers, but "Ypres cloth" guaranteed by the seal of the guild was known and sought after from Novgorod to Crete.

4

THE CRUSADES: THEIR CAUSES

History may never repeat itself in exact detail, but, as one looks over the whole course of the past, there are certainly broad types of phenomena that appear again and again. One such recurrent phenomenon centers around changes in the relationships between large groupings of peoples confronting each other in a hostile pose. There are repeated cases through history where a potent nation, empire, or civilization suddenly collapsed after a long career of exerting powerful influences on a neighboring people. And there likewise are many examples where long-suffering societies, buffeted about by more aggressive and resourceful outsiders, suddenly were able to pass from a defensive to an offensive stance — taking vengeance in some instances on those who had previously been exerting pressure on them. A strong argument can be made that these great fluxes in power relationships mark major turning points in history. Have we not, in fact, encountered shifts of this kind that had an immense impact on the shape of history? Did not Alexander the Great's career mark a dramatic outward thrust of the Greek world against the aggressive forces of Near Eastern civilization as those had been concentrated in the Persian Empire? And did not the fall of the Roman Empire involve a dramatic reversal in which peoples of the Mediterranean area lost their dominance over peoples to the north and became the victims of aggression at the hands of their former "inferiors"? This whole issue has a special relevance in the twentieth century. For we may be witnesses (and victims?) of another major shift in which Western European civilization finds itself on the defensive after several centuries of outward expansion against and dominance of a large part of the world.

One of these great shifts in the power relationships between adjacent communities occurred in the High Middle Ages. For several centuries after the collapse of the Roman Empire the peoples of Western Europe were on the defensive. Germans, Byzantines, Arabs, Norsemen, Slavs, and Magyars repeatedly overran large parts of the West, took possession of various areas, and were responsible for untold chaos and misery. During these long centuries the Western Europeans could do little but suffer; only briefly during the early Carolingian age was there anything resembling a counteroffensive. To a very considerable degree the slowness of Europe's recovery over the centuries between 500 and 1000 was a direct result of incessant attacks on Europe from the outside.

During the tenth and eleventh centuries the situation showed signs of changing. European resistance began to stiffen, and the invaders discovered that ingress was not as easy as it had once been. Western Europeans began to edge outward in a more positive fashion. Missionaries ventured into the Slavic and Scandinavian areas. Germanic knights and their peasant dependents pushed eastward across the Elbe and down the Danube rivers. The fleets of the Italian cities began to clear the waters of the Western Mediterranean of the Muslims. Italian and North European merchants appeared more frequently in the marketplaces of Constantinople. European armies became actively engaged in aggressive warfare against Islam and Byzantium in Spain, Southern Italy, and Sicily. These were all harbingers of the resurgence of the West—the beginning of a story that leads through the age of discovery in the sixteenth century, the establishment of European colonial empires in the seventeenth and eighteenth centuries, their enlargement in the nineteenth century—developments all accompanied by the inexorable spread of Western European ideas and techniques to all parts of the world.

Certainly the most dramatic manifestation of medieval Europe's increasing ability to take the offensive was the movement we know as the Crusades. Perhaps no single aspect of the history of the Middle Ages has been more widely discussed; many who know nothing else about medieval history have at least heard of the heroic deeds of those who took up the cross for the purpose of winning and holding the holy places in the East. To this very day we reflect a link with the Middle Ages by calling our sacrifices in behalf of great causes "crusades." We have constant crusades against crime, vice, corruption, and poverty. The fathers of today's students participated in a "crusade in Europe" between 1942 and 1945, and some argue that a "crusade against communism" is in order at the moment. Such expressions may sound silly and sentimental, but as one historian of the Crusades of the Middle Ages has said, they are vestiges of an episode in the European past "which left behind in the consciences of modern peoples a certain ideal of generosity and a taste for noble causes which the harshest lessons of reality will never erase completely."

The historical problems involved in the medieval Crusades are immense. The events and personalities connected with a movement that lasted for at least five centuries are so varied that one can never be completely informed on crusading history. The Crusades embrace so wide a range of human behavior—from the noblest to the most abject—that anyone with the least historical interest can find something which will intrigue him in the long story of the crusading effort. In the selections that follow we shall have to neglect most of this rich vein of history, hoping that every student will avail himself at some time of the opportunity to read some of the excellent histories of the Crusades that occupy the shelves of any library.

There is one fundamental question that must be treated before any aspect of the history of the Crusades makes sense. What was it that evoked the crusading movement? What were the forces that caused the rich and the poor, the famous and the unknown, saints and sinners to leave behind home, family, and possessions in order to undertake the hard journey into lands about which they knew virtually nothing except that great danger awaited them? Were they caught up in some sort of collective madness? Were they dupes to skilled operators who stood to profit by exploiting them? Were they men dedicated to ideals in a way that escapes our comprehension? Were they crude, self-seeking opportunists who saw a chance for personal and collective advantage? The selections that follow seek to answer these questions by attempting to define the causes of the crusading movement—especially the First Crusade. A mastery of these selections will certainly throw light on the nature of the crusading movement. And it will provide new insights into the dynamism of the society that produced the Crusades. It is of special importance that this last matter be grasped, since the particular form that Europe's first major thrust outward took impressed on many non-Europeans a view of the European mentality that has not yet been effaced.

POPE URBAN II'S SPEECH

THE CALL TO ACTION AT CLERMONT

Most historians of the Crusades agree that the decisive event which launched the attack on the East was the famous speech delivered by Pope Urban II at Clermont in France in November 1095. Unfortunately, no clear record of that speech has survived; rather there are several versions that do not agree in particulars. But all the versions emphasize certain essential themes. Two descriptions of the speech are given below. The first is by Fulcher of Chartres, a well-educated clergyman who accompanied the First Crusade and remained in the Holy Land for the rest of his life. He recorded his adventures in a work entitled *Gesta Francorum Hierusalem peregrinantium,* the first part of which includes Urban's speech and was written about 1101. The second version of the speech was recorded by a certain Robert the Monk in his *Historia Hierosolymitana,* an account of the First Crusade which was not written before 1122. Both Fulcher and Robert were present at Clermont and thus were in a position to provide an accurate summary of what was said.

It seems logical to suppose that Urban made a conscious effort to shape his remarks in terms of what he knew or thought would appeal to his audience. Therefore his speech may contain important clues as to what it was that made the crusading movement possible. In reading these versions of the speech the student should seek to discover the Pope's major themes on the assumption that they are clues to the spirit of the era.

1. VERSION GIVEN BY FULCHER OF CHARTRES

[*According to Fulcher, Urban devoted the first part of his speech to a plea for peace within the Christian community and asked all present to take an oath to* uphold the Truce of God. Then he continued in this fashion:]

Since, oh sons of God, you have promised the Lord more earnestly than heretofore to maintain peace in

From *Translations and Reprints from the Original Sources of European History* (Philadelphia; University of Pennsylvania Press), Vol. I, No. 2, pp. 4–8. Reprinted by permission of the publisher.

The Middle Ages

your midst and faithfully to sustain the laws of the church, there remains for you, newly fortified by the correction of the Lord, to show the strength of your integrity in a certain other duty, which is not less your concern than the Lord's. For you must carry succor to your brethren dwelling in the East, and needing your aid, which they have so often demanded. For the Turks, a Persian people, have attacked them, as many of you know, and have advanced into the territory of Romania as far as that part of the Mediterranean which is called the Arm of St. George;[1] and occupying more and more the lands of those Christians, have already seven times conquered them in battle, have killed and captured many, have destroyed the churches and devastated the kingdom of God. If you permit them to remain for a time unmolested, they will extend their sway more widely over many faithful servants of the Lord.

Wherefore, I pray and exhort, nay not I, but the Lord prays and exhorts you, as heralds of Christ, by frequent exhortation, to urge men of all ranks, knights and foot-soldiers, rich and poor, to hasten to exterminate this vile race from the lands of our brethren, and to bear timely aid to the worshippers of Christ. I speak to those who are present, I proclaim it to the absent, but Christ commands. Moreover, the sins of those who set out thither, if they lose their lives on the journey, by land or sea, or in fighting against the heathen, shall be remitted in that hour: this I grant to all who go, through the power of God vested in me.

Oh, what a disgrace if a race so despised, degenerate, and slave of the demons, should thus conquer a people fortified with faith in omnipotent God and resplendent with the name of Christ! Oh, how many reproaches will be heaped upon you by the Lord Himself if you do not aid those who like yourselves are counted of the Christian faith! Let those who have formerly been accustomed to contend wickedly in private warfare against the faithful, fight against the infidel and bring to a victorious end the war which ought long since to have been begun. Let those who have hitherto been robbers now become soldiers of Christ. Let those who have formerly contended against their brothers and relatives now fight as they ought against the barbarians. Let those who have formerly been mercenaries at low wages, now gain eternal rewards. Let those who have been striving to the detriment both of body and soul, now labor for a two-fold reward. What shall I add? On

this side will be the sorrowful and poor, on the other the joyful and the rich; here the enemies of the Lord, there His friends. Let not those who are going delay their journey, but having arranged their affairs and collected the money necessary for their expenses, when the winter ends and the spring comes, let them with alacrity start on their journey under the guidance of the Lord.

2. VERSION GIVEN BY ROBERT THE MONK

Oh, race of Franks, race from across the mountains, race chosen and beloved by God—as shines forth in very many of your works—set apart from all nations by the situation of your country, as well as by your catholic faith and the honor of the holy church! To you our discourse is addressed and for you our exhortation is intended. We wish you to know what a grievous cause has led us to your country, what peril threatening you and all the faithful has brought us.

From the confines of Jerusalem and the city of Constantinople a horrible tale has gone forth and very frequently has been brought to our ears, namely, that a race from the kingdom of the Persians,[2] an accursed race, a race utterly alienated from God, a generation forsooth which has not directed its heart and has not entrusted its spirit to God, has invaded the lands of those Christians and has depopulated them by the sword, pillage and fire; it has led away a part of the captives into its own country, and a part it has destroyed by cruel tortures; it has either entirely destroyed the churches of God or appropriated them for the rites of its own religion. They destroy the altars, after having defiled them with their uncleanness. They circumcise the Christians, and the blood of the circumcision they either spread upon the altars or pour into the vases of the baptismal font. When they wish to torture people by a base death, they perforate their navels, and dragging forth the extremity of the intestines, bind it to a stake; then with flogging they lead the victim around until the viscera having gushed forth the victim falls prostrate upon the ground. Others they bind to a post and pierce with arrows. Others they compel to extend their necks and then, attacking them with naked swords, attempt to cut through the neck with a single blow. What shall I say of the abominable rape of the women? To speak of it is worse than to be silent. The kingdom of the Greeks is now dis-

---

[1] The Hellespont.

[2] That is, the Seljuk Turks [Editor's note]

membered by them and deprived of territory so vast in extent that it can not be traversed in a march of two months. On whom therefore is the labor of avenging these wrongs and of recovering this territory incumbent, if not upon you? You, upon whom above other nations God has conferred remarkable glory in arms, great courage, bodily activity, and strength to humble the hairy scalp of those who resist you.

Let the deeds of your ancestors move you and incite your minds to manly achievements; the glory and greatness of king Charles the Great, and of his son Louis, and of your other kings, who have destroyed the kingdoms of the pagans, and have extended in these lands the territory of the holy church. Let the holy sepulchre of the Lord our Saviour, which is possessed by unclean nations, especially incite you, and the holy places which are now treated with ignominy and irreverently polluted with their filthiness. Oh, most valiant soldiers and descendants of invincible ancestors, be not degenerate, but recall the valor of your progenitors.

But if you are hindered by love of children, parents and wives, remember what the Lord says in the Gospel, "He that loveth father or mother more than me, is not worthy of me." "Every one that hath forsaken houses, or brethren, or sisters, or father, or mother, or wife, or children, or lands for my name's sake shall receive an hundred-fold and shall inherit everlasting life." Let none of your possessions detain you, no solicitude for your family affairs, since this land which you inhabit, shut in on all sides by the seas and surrounded by the mountain peaks, is too narrow for your large population; nor does it abound in wealth; and it furnishes scarcely food enough for its cultivators. Hence it is that you murder and devour one another, that you wage war, and that frequently you perish by mutual wounds. Let therefore hatred depart from among you, let your quarrels end, let wars cease, and let all dissensions and controversies slumber. Enter upon the road to the Holy Sepulchre; wrest that land from the wicked race, and subject it to yourselves. That land which as the Scripture says "floweth with milk and honey," was given by God into the possession of the children of Israel.

Jerusalem is the navel of the world; the land is fruitful above others, like another paradise of delights. This the Redeemer of the human race has made illustrious by His advent, has beautified by

residence, has consecrated by suffering, has redeemed by death, has glorified by burial. This royal city, therefore, situated at the centre of the world, is now held captive by His enemies, and is in subjection to those who do not know God, to the worship of the heathens. She seeks therefore and desires to be liberated, and does not cease to implore you to come to her aid. From you especially she asks succor, because, as we have already said, God has conferred upon you above all nations great glory in arms. Accordingly undertake this journey for the remission of your sins, with the assurance of the imperishable glory of the kingdom of heaven.

When Pope Urban had said these and very many similar things in his urbane discourse, he so influenced to one purpose the desires of all who were present, that they cried out, "It is the will of God! It is the will of God!" When the venerable Roman pontiff heard that, with eyes uplifted to heaven he gave thanks to God and, with his hand commanding silence, said:

Most beloved brethren, to-day is manifest in you what the Lord says in the Gospel, "Where two or three are gathered together in my name there am I in the midst of them." Unless the Lord God had been present in your spirits, all of you would not have uttered the same cry. For, although the cry issued from numerous mouths, yet the origin of the cry was one. Therefore I say to you that God, who implanted this in your breasts, has drawn it forth from you. Let this then be your war-cry in combats, because this word is given to you by God. When an armed attack is made upon the enemy, let this one cry be raised by all the soldiers of God: It is the will of God! It is the will of God!

And we do not command or advise that the old or feeble, or those unfit for bearing arms, undertake this journey; nor ought women to set out at all, without their husbands or brothers or legal guardians. For such are more of a hindrance than aid, more of a burden than advantage. Let the rich aid the needy; and according to their wealth, let them take with them experienced soldiers. The priests and clerks of any order are not to go without the consent of their bishop; for this journey would profit them nothing if they went without permission of these. Also, it is not fitting that laymen should enter upon the pilgrimage without the blessing of their priests.

Whoever, therefore, shall determine upon this holy

pilgrimage and shall make his vow to God to that effect and shall offer himself to Him as a living sacrifice, holy, acceptable unto God, shall wear the sign of the cross of the Lord on his forehead or on his breast. When, truly, having fulfilled his vow he wishes to return, let him place the cross on his back between his shoulders. Such, indeed, by the two-fold action will fulfill the precept of the Lord, as He commands in the Gospel, "He that taketh not his cross and followeth after me, is not worthy of me."

J. J. SAUNDERS

THE CRUSADES AS HOLY WAR

The themes struck by Urban II in his speech at Clermont indicate that religious aspirations provided a major force in unleashing Europe's military forces against the East. Not a few modern scholars are convinced that religion must be viewed as the major cause of the crusading movement. The following selection supplies a brief, concise summary of that approach to the Crusades. It was written by J. J. Saunders, a lecturer in history at the University of Canterbury in New Zealand. It is especially important to note where Saunders places the responsibility for molding the religious drives that found expression in holy war.

Of the three great world-religions, Islam is the only one which was born militant. When Muhammad was driven from his native Mecca to seek refuge in the rival city of Medina, it was not unnatural that he should use the enmity between the two towns to overcome his pagan foes by force. The victory of Islam in Arabia was largely accomplished by the sword, and circumstances induced the Prophet's heirs to employ the armies of tribesmen at their disposal in the propagation of the new faith in the world beyond. The aim of the *jihad*, or holy war, was to enlarge the domain of Islam until the entire globe had been subdued, but this did not imply forcible conversion: on the contrary, the Peoples of the Book (that is, nations with holy scriptures of their own) were to be assured of freedom of worship, and thus under the Caliphs, Christians and Jews all enjoyed toleration.

Buddhism and Christianity, unlike Islam, grew up within the framework of ordered and civilized societies and did not possess the means, even if they had had the will, to conquer the world in the name of their founders. In the days when Rome was still pagan, Christian theologians doubted if a faithful Christian could lawfully serve in an army whose emperor was worshipped as a god; and a strong anti-militarist sentiment pervaded the early Church and even after the conversion of Constantine, St Basil of Cappadocia recommends the soldier who has killed his enemy in war to abstain for three years from holy communion. Yet in face of the example of the Hebrews in the Old Testament, war could not be condemned as immoral *per se*, and St. Augustine, in *The City of God*, concedes that it may be waged 'by command of God.' The German scholar Erdmann, in his *Entstehung des Kreuzzügsgedankens* (1935),[1] holds that the early Christians were essentially pacifist, and that militarization came in with the Germans, to whom war was a natural and continual activity: one recalls the story of Clovis, who after listening to a recital of the passion and death of Christ, exclaimed: "Had I been present with my brave Franks, I would have avenged his injuries!" The primitive and barbarous society of the Germanic West was thoroughly war-minded: by contrast the civilized Byzantines treated war as a re-

[1] This work is the most thorough study of the religious aspects of the crusading movement. [Editor's note]

From J. J. Saunders, *Aspects of the Crusades* (Christchurch, N. Zeal., 1962), pp. 17–21. Reprinted by permission of the Publications Committee, University of Canterbury.

grettable necessity, to be avoided as far as possible by diplomacy and other means.

It has often been argued that the Crusading spirit was born in the West in the time of Charlemagne, who was indeed represented in later legend as fighting the Saracens in Palestine: his wars against the pagan Saxons and Avars enlarged the domain of Christendom as well as the Frankish Empire, and the forced baptisms in which he indulged are evidence of a new and startling aggressive type of Christianity. Yet there is a big difference between Charlemagne's campaigns and the later Crusades. The former were all fought in Europe and could be treated as defensive, as necessary for the protection of Latin Christendom: the latter were unmistakably offensive operations conducted far away across the sea, and (this is the essential point) sponsored and organized by the Church for a purely religious purpose, the recovery of the Holy Places in Palestine.

How did the Latin Church come to adopt war as an instrument of ecclesiastical policy? It has been suggested that, paradoxically, Crusading warfare grew out of the peace movement which the Church had vigorously promoted from the late tenth century onwards in order to check the frightful evils of private war waged, after the collapse of the Carolingian State, by irresponsible and unrestrained feudal lords. Partly out of genuine idealism, partly out of a desire to protect its property in an age of wild licence and political anarchy, the Church set out to mobilize public opinion against lawless brigands in high places: missions were preached, a Truce of God was proclaimed, and crowds were invited to subscribe to a peace oath, the lead being taken by such sovereigns as Robert the Pious in France and the Emperor Henry III in Germany. The results were but meagre: to curb the fighting propensities of feudalism was beyond the Church's power, and clearly the most effective means of putting down the evil would be to come to terms with these turbulent barons and enlist them in campaigns abroad against the enemies of Christendom.

Spain offered a promising field. After the collapse of the Omayyad Caliphate in 1031, Muslim Spain had lapsed into chaos, thus inviting Christian intervention for the recovery of what was after all a lost province of the Latin Church; and in 1063 Pope Alexander II offered an indulgence to all who fought for Christ against the Moors. This brought a crowd of French knights and adventurers streaming across the

Pyrenees, and with these powerful reinforcements, Alfonso VI of Castile was able to capture the old Visigothic capital of Toledo in 1085. The influence of Cluny is discernible here: the reform movement so intimately linked with the great Benedictine abbey in Burgundy had stimulated, among other things, pilgrimages to the shrine of St James at Compostella in Galicia, and the monks of Cluny, if they did not actually organize military expeditions, managed the pilgrim-roads across France into Spain. It was in the inns and hospices along these roads that there grew up the Chansons de Geste, which reflected the new spirit of a vigorous if brutal anti-Saracen religious patriotism. We have not yet reached the chivalrous age of Arthur and the Holy Grail: we are still in the barbarized world of the Song of Roland, which was in fact the world of the First Crusade.

Yet this Spanish fighting was no true Crusade: the Popes concerned themselves only indirectly with it, and a figure like the Cid, who fought indifferently for Christian or Moor, would have been unthinkable in the Palestine of the next generation. What was needed to bring into being the Holy War proper was that the Popes should proclaim universal peace among Christians and mobilize the faithful in a great offensive against the enemies of the faith, not in Spain or North Africa but in the very cradle of the Christian religion. This could only be done in the peculiar circumstances of the late eleventh century.

First, the great reform movement, which aimed at freeing the Church from the corrupting grip of the feudalized monarchies and lordships, had been driven to look to Rome for leadership and to build up a new conception of papal supremacy. The tremendous conflict over lay investiture between Gregory VII and Henry IV of Germany had underlined this new role of the Papacy and prepared the way for Urban II, in his famous speech at Clermont in 1095, to seize the moral mastery of Europe.

Secondly, the breach between the Greek and Latin Churches, which had been steadily widening, impelled the Hildebrandine Papacy to seek a restoration of Christian unity. We know now . . . that the schism of 1054 was not in fact final and definitive: it came about almost accidentally, and relations between Rome and Constantinople were not wholly broken off. The references in Urban's speech to 'the churches of the East' do hint that a grand reunion of the Christian body was envisaged as a consequence of the defeat of the infidel.

Thirdly, the irruption of the Seljik Turks into Western Asia, which endangered the Byzantine Empire and interrupted the pilgrim traffic to the Holy Land, supplied the final stimulus. The loss to the Turks of central Anatolia, long the chief recruiting-ground of the imperial armies, and the threat to Constantinople itself, drove the Byzantine emperors to seek urgently for reinforcements from the West. The appeal of Michael VII to Pope Gregory in 1073, and of Alexius I to Count Robert of Flanders in 1091 could not go unanswered, and by 1095 it may well have seemed to a shrewd statesman like Urban II an excellent opportunity to achieve at one blow several desirable ends: the relief of the Byzantine Empire from Turkish pressure, the reunion of the Churches, and the rescue of the Holy Places from the enemies of Christ. Given the strong current of religious revivalism then sweeping over the Latin world in the wake of the reform movement, this last would have the strongest appeal.

Thus the Holy War, the very concept of which was unintelligible to the Christian East, was the creation of the reformed Hildebrandine Papacy seeking to make good its bold claims to the overlordship of a united Christendom. It was no conscious imitation of the Muslim *jihad*, for this aimed at *expansion*, whereas the Crusades aimed at *recovery*, though the notion of fighting for God and the Faith appeared in both. Recent writers, reacting against the tendency of the last generation to ascribe every historic movement to politico-economic motives, have perhaps overstressed the moral and spiritual elements. Thus Paul Alphandery, in his *La Chrétienté et l'Idée de Croisade* (1954), sees the Crusade as a genuine expression of popular faith, animated by a kind of collective mysticism and rising up out of an atmosphere of visions, prophecies and miracles, typified by the affair of the Holy Lance at Antioch. Adolf Waas, also, in his *Geschichte der Kreuzzüge* (1956), appears to trace its origin to an ideal of dedicated knighthood, of feudal vassalage to God, which goes back to Charlemagne and perhaps even to the pre-Christian society of ancient Germany. This is far-fetched indeed: more prosaically we may say that the Crusades are the outcome of the Latin Church's attempt to tame feudal barbarism and harness it to the service of religion, an attempt which, as we might expect, was only half successful. Swashbuckling scoundrels like Bohemund of Taranto rubbed shoulders with sincere idealists like Godfrey of Bouillon: the saying attributed to the latter, when he was offered the throne of Jerusalem, that he would not wear a crown of gold in the city where his Saviour had worn a crown of thorns, whether authentic or not, remains one of the sublimest phrases of history and reflects the noblest side of the Crusading movement. Certainly the Crusades were the product of a feudal society and could have arisen out of no other: this is why they do not occur in any other age or any other part of Christendom, and this is why the fastidious and peace-loving Byzantines could never see the Frankish soldiers of the Cross as anything but coarse and bloodstained barbarians.

PAUL ROUSSET

THE RELIGIOUS ATMOSPHERE

Professor Saunders' analysis of the crusading movement as a holy war raises a related issue of great significance. What kind of religious convictions were present among Europeans that would make the idea of holy war appealing? Among several historians who have addressed themselves to an assessment of the religious temper of the society that responded enthusiastically to Urban II's appeal is the Swiss historian Paul Rousset. His major work, *Les origines et les caractères de la première Croisade* (1945), provides a searching quest for the religious psychology prevailing in eleventh-century Europe. In another study, presented as a paper before the Tenth

International Congress of Historical Sciences held at Rome in 1955, he tried to summarize the fundamental religious concepts associated with the crusading movement. That paper constitutes the next selection. The student should try to identify the popular religious aspirations that found expression through participation in the crusading venture. Then he may be in a better position to comprehend the real significance of "holy war" and to evaluate religion as a causative force in the Crusades.

The Crusade was not only a major political event of the Middle Ages . . . ; it was also a visible sign of the ephemeral unity of Europe and the expression of Europe's ambitions and fervors. It is therefore interesting to study the crusading idea (idée de Croisade) held by those who told about it or sang about it, and to see how the Crusade was justified and described by its direct and indirect witnesses.

For several reasons we shall limit this study to the period which extends from the end of the eleventh century to the middle of the twelfth century. . . . Only the First Crusade ought to be considered as a true and typical crusade. . . . The sources for our study will then be essentially those of the Crusade of 1095: charters, annals, chronicles, and poems compiled from the end of the eleventh century to about 1140. . . .

We intend to show first how the chroniclers explained and justified the Crusade, specified its aims and its forms. [We shall also show] how the crusader—that new man of the end of the eleventh century—was designated. . . . We shall describe the interior characteristics of the Crusade: belief in divine election, biblical mentality, evangelism. Finally we shall try to grasp what it was that truly made the Crusade a war apart from other wars, an event at one and the same time both old and new, an idea of great influence in the history of the West in the eleventh and twelfth centuries.

In the prologue to his Historia Hierosolymitana, Robert the Monk declared that the Crusade was not a human undertaking, but a divine one. Likewise for Ordericus Vitalis the expedition to Jerusalem owed its origin to a divine impulse. Many chroniclers recorded that prodigies preceded the departure of the crusaders: falling stars, earthquakes, and signs in the sky. One can think that these cosmic manifesta-

tions constituted arguments capable of persuading the knights. . . .

These extraordinary signs and the lessons which a simple people drew from them already justified a new war. This war appeared as one different from others, as an expedition which earned for its participants the approval of the clergy and not their condemnations. The Church, preoccupied for a long time by the problem of "fraternal wars," that is to say, wars among Christians, saw in the Crusade a means to put an end, at least for a time, to the wars which ravaged Christendom. At Clermont Urban II proposed to the knights to turn their arms against the Muslims and to substitute for sinful combat a worthy and meritorious combat. For the brutal and pious feudal lords the Crusade came to be the just war, the combat which saved, the enterprise of salvation. The privilege of indulgence—a new privilege in war— would give to the Crusade a supplementary justification and would make of that enterprise a pious work.

The avowed aim of the Crusade—the liberation of the Holy Sepulcher—likewise constituted a sufficient justification. The chroniclers developed an extensive literature concerning the Holy Land, Jerusalem, and the Holy Sepulcher. The Holy Places, because they and they alone were the setting elected by Christ, were the land of the Incarnation and the Redemption, demanded deliverance from Muslim subjugation and possession in full ownership. Guibert of Nogent sang of the glory of Jerusalem, the holy city which deserved to attract to itself all the Christian kingdoms. Jerusalem is the source of Redemption, the place of salvation, the head of the Church, the navel of the world, the most excellent land that was like a second paradise. The crusader fought for two kingdoms: he fought to secure possession of the terrestrial Jerusalem in order that he

From P. Rousset, "L'idée de Croisade chez les chroniqueurs d' Occident," Relazioni del X Congresso Internazionale di Scienze Storiche, Vol. III: Storia del Medioevo (Florence, 1955), pp. 547–63. Used by permission of G. C. Sansoni, Editore. Translated by the editor.

might ultimately possess the celestial Jerusalem where he would live eternally.

All these expressions . . . of the chroniclers reflect the thought of the clergy, but they should not be separated from the thought of most men. These expressions are not formulas empty of meaning; they faithfully reproduce the thought and the state of feeling of an epoch. Moreover, this language, which is the language of the pilgrim, shows forcefully that the Crusade is the war-like extension of the pilgrimage to Jerusalem, the brutal realization of that pilgrimage. It is without doubt that for many the Crusade preached by Urban II signified this first of all: to make free the route to the Holy Sepulcher, to recover the territory and the places which by right . . . belonged to the Christian world.

The crusading idea in the form in which it developed around the year 1100 can be grasped here in its original purity and in all its living force. As a gigantic pilgrimage the Crusade inherited the characteristics of traditional pilgrimages. It was a journey toward a precise point, a long and difficult trip which demanded daily efforts and which brought about purification. Formerly pacific, the pilgrimage to Jerusalem was transformed little by little . . . into a military pilgrimage. A psychology of fear was born and a hostility ever more violent fortified the pilgrims. To the spirit of pilgrimage was added in the crusader-pilgrim the spirit of war with all that that implies in terms of violence and hate. In epic poetry which was spreading at that moment — and especially in the *Chanson de Roland*—there is eloquent testimony of that spirit of implacable warfare.

The crusader already saw his undertaking justified by the reasons which we have discussed. Beyond that, he was persuaded that the new war would permit him to exalt the name of Christ and expand Christendom. There was confusion between the temporal order and the spiritual order. . . . For the crusading leaders the crusading idea was confused with the missionary idea. . . . The expansion of Christendom, by establishing rulership over Syria from this time forward, constituted for the crusaders a supplementary justification: it was not only a matter of defending Christian territories; it was necessary to enlarge the Christian world.

A divine work, a privileged war thanks to the summons of the pope and to the indulgence, the geo-graphical and spiritual aim of recovering the Holy Land, the exaltation of Christendom: all these characteristics explain and justify in the eyes of the crusading chroniclers the expedition to Jerusalem. And they give to the crusading idea, originating in a distant past and recently developed, a meaning that is at once intellectual and emotional. It is an explanation and a justification that is insufficient in the eyes of modern historians, but it was satisfactory to the chronicler who did not feel the need to go far back in time (the very notion of time escaped him) to discover the first origins of the Crusade.

In fact, it appears certain that the chroniclers felt no need to seek the origins of the expedition which they recounted. What struck them was the novel character of the expedition and the changes which it brought to life in the West. Guibert of Nogent sees in the Crusade a new mode of life, a new social order. When Bernard of Clairvaux composed a panegyric for the Order of the Temple, he made conspicuous the newness of the institution: "I speak of a new kind of soldier." The Templars, declared the abbot of Clairvaux, were occupied in a dual combat that was spiritual and temporal. The war which they fought—a war of defense against the Muslims of the Holy Land—did not condemn them but saved them; if victory was beneficial, death was an even greater benefit. The pages in which Bernard eulogized the Templar, the soldier of Christ, the warrior of the new age, constitute an important witness showing the transformation of war and of the warrior in the West. War, for so long carried on by the knights against the common people, was henceforth to be directed against the Muslims, and the knight, known as a criminal when he waged war in the lands of Christendom, benefited from ecclesiastical favors when he battled the Muslims in the Holy Land.

Many chroniclers took pleasure in making known the importance of the change brought to the West by the Crusade, that is to say, by the transformation of the knight, a warrior by profession and habits, into a crusader. For many the Crusade was bound to appear first of all as the liberation of the West. By quitting Europe to deliver the Holy Places the knights freed Christendom from its endemic wars. From that point of view the Crusade was a form of anti-war; it was peace, the peace of God finally realized; it was the final result of the evolution of the institutions of peace. . . .

The Crusade was a new war and the chronicler did not know how to designate its heroes. It is striking to note that the terms "crusade" and "crusader" have no equivalents in the Latin of the eleventh and twelfth centuries. The term crucesignati used to designate crusaders is rare. . . . The chroniclers call the Crusade "the Jerusalem journey," "the Jerusalem expedition," "the pilgrimage," "the way of the sepulcher of the Lord." This is the language of the pilgrimage which proves that, in the mind of those who lived it and spoke of it, the Crusade continued the tradition of pilgrimages to the Holy Land and that it also constituted a new enterprise which did not yet have a name. It was thus something both old and new. As for the crusaders, they were called "the pilgrims of Jerusalem," "the Hierosolimitani." They are "the warriors of the Lord," "the soldiers of Christ," "the fellow-workers of God," . . . "the people of God." They are marked by the sign of the Cross, cruce signati. . . .

That new war . . . allowed for certain characterizations which, if not always new, were at least apt in defining it and distinguishing it from other wars. Here again we see that for the man of the twelfth century the Crusade appeared as a war apart from others, as an enterprise with particular aspects.

The enumeration of the themes of the Crusade developed by the chroniclers is meaningful. Some of them are themes which holy war had rendered familiar and which usage had sanctioned; others are new or at least are presented in a form which is surprising. The crusading idea . . . is at once old and new, but the chroniclers took pleasure in showing first of all the new elements (in contrast to the modern historian, preoccupied primarily with binding the present to the past).

To grasp the crusading idea as contemporaries felt it, it is necessary to describe its principal characteristics, leaving aside the characteristics intended as means of justification and already treated above.

A pilgrimage and an enterprise of conquest, a holy war and a penitential expedition, the Crusade involved multiple and contradictory characteristics. These are the characteristics which define the Crusade in its inner nature, in its soul: a persuasion to defend a just cause; more generally, a conviction that the friends of God ought necessarily to triumph over His enemies; the prospect of the palm of the

martyr for fallen heroes; a biblical mentality . . .; and the spirit of poverty. . . .

God is immanent and His justice is exercised in the world immediately, here and now; He grants His aid to those who have a pure heart and He abandons those who abandon Him. Sinful conduct explains the failure of any undertaking. This is the explanation supplied by [the chroniclers] for the difficulties of the siege of Antioch: "God ordained that we suffer this poverty and misery on account of our sins." The expression "because of sins," which comes constantly from the pens of the chroniclers . . . , is the universal explanation (epic poetry expresses the same thought). For men of this time divine justice is imminent, and events show forth brilliantly to the eyes of the good and the wicked the sudden fury of that justice. As a consequence, history indicts or glorifies men, and at the same time it reflects divine omnipotence. The title which Guibert of Nogent gave to his history of the Crusade—Gesta Dei per Francos—is significant; the great expedition of 1099 is not like any other expedition; its origin and its aims recommend it to the eyes of God, make it His work par excellence, and the Franks have been elected for that sacred task. Without doubt there are involved here . . . language and formulas which are biblical and ecclesiastical and which recall the religious impregnation of the minds of the writers. But these formulas and that impregnation are those of the Crusade and of the times which saw it born and develop. All the historiography of the eleventh and twelfth centuries possesses an apologetic character. Even St. Bernard himself, when he was questioned on the subject of the failure of the Second Crusade, which he had preached and put in motion, would respond by examples drawn from the Old Testament which demonstrated the importance of a moral view in the events: the crusaders themselves were the cause of their own defeat, he says, because they had sinned. One sees then that in the opinion of contemporaries the Crusade admits of a meaning that surpasses the Crusade itself and which makes of it an act at once temporal and spiritual, a witness, a sign.

A military pilgrimage and a war for salvation, the Crusade offered to its participants important spiritual favors: indulgence and the death of the martyr. The reading of cartularies is significant in this respect: one sees that the knights who, upon their departure for Jerusalem, ceded their lands, did this because they thought that this renunciation would earn them spiritual merits. . . . The Crusade permitted a warrior who was today condemned and damned to assure his salvation and to save Christendom. . . . The crusaders venerated the dead crusaders . . . and marveled before the innumerable martyrs.

Combat against the Muslim offered to the knight the fulfillment of heroic prowess and the glory of the martyr. The Crusade with its spiritual favors extended his domain, enlarged it over a new land; the crusader was not only he who abandoned his goods and took the road to Jerusalem, but he was first of all one who fought the Muslim and defended Christendom. Here was an extension and a deformation of the crusading idea which bears witness to the force of that idea and to its exact adaption to the necessities of the age.

The crusading idea had need to develop a doctrinal support, a written authority. That support and that authority could only be scriptural. The Old and the New Testaments came to furnish to the chroniclers the texts and the necessary references for the explanation and the justification of their accounts. One must immediately note the considerable importance of the Old Testament in that scriptural documentation. . . .

The clerical origin of most of the chroniclers explains in large part these references and these citations; it will not however suffice to explain the willingness among the chroniclers to compare constantly their heroes to the Hebrews and to see in the Crusade a renewal of biblical history. The crusaders are the chosen people, the new Hebrews, the true children of Israel. To them pertain the promises made long ago to the Hebrews. . . . The history of the Crusade, like the history of the Hebrews, is filled with miracles. The actions of the crusaders . . . are even more grand than those of the Hebrews. Comparisons between the Hebrews and the crusaders flow in numbers from the pens of the chroniclers: Adhemar of Monteil [bishop of Puy] and Raymond of St. Gilles[1] are compared to Moses and Aaron; the march of the crusaders to the Holy Land is compared to the march of the Hebrews toward the Promised Land; the death of Adhemar one year before the capture of Jerusalem is likened to the death of Moses on the eve of his entrance into the land of Canaan. When described in this fashion, the Crusade appeared as an imitation of the Hebrews, as a

parallel history which the chronicler transmitted in a spirit of piety and of triumph. The poets were also inspired by the Old Testament; Charlemagne . . . is represented as a biblical king. . . .

These innumerable references to the Old Testament, this intimate knowledge of the history of the Hebrews, this constant need to rely on sacred examples, this parallelism established between biblical facts and the deeds of the crusaders pose for the historian of the Crusades a problem difficult to resolve. [One authority, P. Alphandery,] thinks that these citations are "the outcroppings of a subconscious work of assimilation of contemporary facts to biblical facts and traditions." This phenomenon of assimilation . . . is not unique with the chroniclers of the Crusade; it is an element of the mentality of the age which witnessed the beginning and the development of the Crusade. For the Christians of the eleventh and twelfth centuries the Old Testament is not old and outmoded, but real and living; and they relive its adventures and accomplish its prophecies. The concept of time was badly comprehended by the feudal man who felt no need to state dates precisely, to fix time intervals; having abolished time, he brought back the past in the present.

That explanation still does not suffice to account for the extreme importance of the Old Testament in the thought of the chronicles of the Crusade. It must be extended by a complementary explanation. The crusading men (and their historians) reveal a mentality which is often that of a childlike people. Their reactions are often primitive, naive, childish, reflecting a need to cover all, to explain and to realize all things. To that primitive people there is need of doctrinal support, of a justificative text: the Old Testament is that which answers to these reactions (and which sometimes determines them) and which is suited to the needs of a simple soul, of the heart of a child.

The important part played by the Old Testament in the spirituality of the Crusade should not cause one to neglect the role of the New Testament, of evangelism, of the Cross; nor can one overlook the role which devolved on the poor in the expedition.

The crusading idea drew a considerable part of its force from the Cross, the distinctive sign of the new warrior and the sign par excellence of the Christian. The Cross was the standard of the army while on the march toward Jerusalem and later of the knights

---

[1] These two figures played a prominent role as leaders of the First Crusade. [Editor's note]

who protected the Latin states against Muslim assaults. It grouped all the crusaders under the same sign, it sealed their unity, it was for each of them an assurance of divine friendship and an indication of the contract between them and God. . . . The banner of the Cross was a weapon; it was an element of the strategy of Holy War. . . . It is not difficult to recognize in this appeal of the Cross, which regarded it as a protective sign and an assurance of victory, an ancient Christian belief, the "resurgence" of an abolished practice. [One chronicler] went back to Constantine to explain the trust which the Crusaders had in the Cross. . . . The Crusade, in giving again to the sacred sign the sense which it had long ago had, in reuniting with a past which still had not been destroyed in memories and feelings, had discovered a moving and striking symbol. . . .

The words of Christ, "If anyone wishes to come after me, let him renounce everything and take up his cross and follow me," provided the occasion for [one chronicler] to transfer a sacred text to the use of the Crusade. There occurred then, he says, a great movement in all regions of Gaul, so that whoever desired to follow the Lord and faithfully bear the Cross with Him, hastened to take the road to Jerusalem. Perhaps an interpretation of a preacher, certainly a clerical commentary which shows how the crusading idea could graft itself on a gospel text and take on an accent that was both messianic and prophetic.

The Crusade, so lived and understood, was an acceptance of the appeal of Christ: to take His Cross and follow Him. This involved acceptance at the level of the warrior life and the transformation of a pacific message into a war-like enterprise. The Crusade appeared then as a gigantic way of the Cross, an unexpected application of a devotional exercise which Peter Damien, a resolute adversary of all war, had preached more than five years earlier. The counsel of Christ, "If anyone wishes to come after me . . ." related as a general rule to those who left

the world to enter a monastery; here it was applied to profane and war-like acts. The Crusade had caused a precept with a spiritual sense to be transformed into one with a material sense (in the same fashion, the expression "soldier of Christ," commonly employed in the Middle Ages to designate a monk, took on the sense of a warrior occupied in holy war, of the crusader).

The evangelical value of poverty was alluded to by certain chroniclers of the First Crusade. The presence of the poor . . . gave the expedition its spiritual value and furnished to the warriors many precious prayers. One must note . . . the decisive part of the presence of the poor, the common people in the heart of the feudal army. . . . At a decisive moment, when after the battle of Antioch the nobles were lost in feudal disputes and delayed the final march on Jerusalem, it was the threat of the common people that served to force a departure. . . . And the taking of Jerusalem (15 July 1099) signified—if not the triumph of poverty . . . —at least the role that virtue never ceased to enjoy in the final stage of the Crusade and its share, alongside the spirit of gain and ambition, in the ideology of the expedition.

The crusading idea was never fixed. It took its origins from the holy war practiced over the course of the centuries; it was born of the appeal of Urban II, and, too soon, it was subjected to transformations and deformations. . . . The Crusade—the First Crusade—is unthinkable outside the age which saw it come into being; it is a "child of the time"; but because it was a widely influential idea, the Crusade rapidly modified institutions and conditions, and, by virtue of these modifications, was itself modified, and soon lost that which constituted its essence and its efficacy. Already the Second Crusade—an expedition to aid—was not identical with the first. . . . The Fourth Crusade . . . is the tragic witness of the deformation of the idea of the Crusade.

RENÉ GROUSSET
CLAUDE CAHEN

THE EASTERN PROBLEM

The religious spirit of the late eleventh century was certainly a prime factor in making the crusading movement possible. But why were these religious forces loosed when they were? Several historians have found the answer to this question in that part of Urban II's speech which referred to the East. They argue that it was the threat to Christendom from the Muslim world, of an international crisis, which compelled Urban II to call upon Western Europeans to take military action. As one historian has put it, the Crusades were the Frankish answer to the eastern problem in European history, an issue that is almost as old as human history itself.

The following two selections examine this issue. The first is by René Grousset, a French scholar who has written extensively on the history of the Near and Far East. His three-volume *Histoire des Croisades* (1935) is one of the outstanding major works on the whole crusading movement. In it he works out in great detail the problem of East-West relations as a factor explaining the Crusades. His basic ideas have been summarized in briefer form in the following passage from a popular history of the Crusades entitled *L'Épopée des Croisades*.

Grousset's position is questioned in the second selection by Claude Cahen, a professor at the University of Strasbourg. Cahen is a specialist in Islamic history and views the crusading movement from a Muslim perspective. The selection below represents part of a paper which he read before the Tenth International Congress of Historical Sciences in Rome in 1955. In his remarks to the Congress, Cahen summarized the argument he had developed in an earlier article in English printed in the journal *Past and Present* in 1954.

RENÉ GROUSSET

When in the final days of June, 1095, Pope Urban II passed from Italy into France to preach the First Crusade, no one, it would seem, suspected as yet the object of his voyage. Before making public the project which would upset the world, this native of Champagne wished once again to establish contact with the province of his birth and to meditate under the vaults of the monastery of Cluny where he had pondered in his youth. Likewise the voices which rose from that land were eminently suited to confirm him in his resolution, if they had not inspired the original idea. Was it not from Cluny which had de-parted, along with the great movement of pilgrimages of the eleventh century, the first expeditions to deliver the Spanish Christians from the Muslim yoke? When Urban, who was still called Eudo de Châtillon, was not yet twenty years old, had he not seen in 1064 his compatriot, Eble de Roucy, along with French knighthood of eastern France, take the road to the Pyrenees to drive the Arabs from Aragon? Faithful to these memories as well as to the example of his predecessor, Gregory VII, Urban, once he had become pope, had in 1089 himself launched on the way to Spain another French expedition, composed largely of knights from the Midi. By that time the Spanish *reconquista* was already like the great maneuvers of the Crusade.

How did Urban II decide to extend to the East the war of deliverance which had begun in the extreme West? To answer that question it would be necessary to follow the great pope in his meditations when, from the Lateran palace or from his exile in Salerno or from the windows of Cluny, he turned his view outward over the world.

Islam, having arisen four hundred years earlier from the sands of Arabia, now covered from Syria to Spain nearly half of the ancient Roman territory, and the cradle of Christianity was already in its power. For one moment—it was now a century ago—a person had been able to think that the Holy Land was about to be delivered. That had occurred when the Byzantine Empire, by an unexpected revival and in a great counter-assault against the Arabs, had pursued them into Syria. In 969 the city of Antioch had been again restored to Christianity. In 975 Emperor John Tzimisces, one of the most glorious sovereigns in Byzantine history, had traversed all of Syria as a conqueror and had held his court under the walls of Damascus. From there he had penetrated into the holy land of Galilee. He had been seen at the head of his "Roman" legions coming to pray on the banks of Lake Tiberias, to save in the memory of the Virgin the inhabitants of Nazareth, to climb as a pilgrim the mountain of the Transfiguration, Tabor. There seemed little that could happen to prevent him from pushing on to Jerusalem, as he had shown to be his intention. But the obligation which he felt to go to combat the Arab garrisons who remained masters of the Lebanese ports halted his progress, and after being so near to his goal, he had returned to die in Constantinople without having delivered the Holy City. The persecution which the caliph of Cairo had carried on against the Holy Sepulcher shortly after, in 1005, had rendered more visible to the eyes of Christendom that insolvency of Byzantine armies and of the Byzantine church. Byzantium had decidedly let escape the glory of attaching its name to the crusade.

The situation grew worse following this with the appearance of the Turks. Arabs and Persians, the old masters of eastern Islam, had long since lost their initial combativeness under the influence of a refined civilization. On the contrary, the Turks were a military race par excellence, hardened by centuries

of nomadism and misery in the bleak solitude of Asia. They brought to the Muslim world a new force. All was changed on that day in 1055—a memorable date in the history of Asia—when the chief of one of the Turkish hordes emerging from the [Asian] steppe, Tughrul-Beg the Seljuk, entered Baghdad and imposed himself on the Arab caliph as temporal vicar and sultan, superimposing thereby on the Arab empire a Turkish empire, and when with him the Turks had become the dominant race in the Muslim world. The Muslim conquest, arrested for two centuries, now resumed its course. The future Urban II, still a monk at Cluny, would undoubtedly have heard the pilgrims tell how the Seljuk Turks, after horrible ravages, had been able to take away from the Byzantine Empire the ancient Christian land of Armenia. Soon even more terrible news would reach him, that of the disaster at Manzikert.

A last energetic soldier, Emperor Romanus Diogenes, had mounted the throne of Byzantium. In the spring of 1071 with a hundred thousand men, among whom were numerous Norman mercenaries, he resolved to deliver Armenia from the Turks. The leader of the Turks, Alp Arslan, . . . the second sultan of the Seljuk dynasty, went forth to meet him. The encounter took place near Manzikert, north of Lake Van, on 19 August 1071. On that decisive day Romanus was betrayed by his lieutenants. Left alone with a handful of faithful, he defended himself heroically until, wounded and his horse killed under him, he was made a prisoner and taken to Alp Arslan, who treated him with honor. It would be the Byzantines who, after he had gained his liberty, would tear out his eyes because of political hatred.

The defeat at Manzikert, too little mentioned in our books, was one of the worst disasters of European history. That battle fought in the heart of Armenia had as a consequence, within ten years, the conquest of three fourths of Asia Minor by the Turks. It is true that the progress of the Turks was aided by the unbelievable absence of "Christian patriotism" among the Byzantine generals who were disputing the throne. It was one of these pretenders who in 1078 . . . himself called the Turks as allies and installed them in Nicaea near the Sea of Marmora and facing Constantinople. Three years later a younger member of the Seljuk family drove out the Byzantines and founded an independent Turkish kingdom of Asia Minor with Nicaea as its capital; this was the nucleus of our historic Turkey. During this same time other Turkish chiefs in Syria took

The Middle Ages

Jerusalem from the Arabs of Egypt (1071) and Antioch from the Byzantines (1085). Under the third Seljuk sultan, Malik-Shah (1072–1092) the Turkish Empire was extended from Bukhara to Antioch. Malik-Shah, the grandson of nomads who had come out of the depths of central Asia, was able in 1087—in a gesture curiously symbolical—to wet his sword in the waters of the Mediterranean.

These events, the last of which unfolded under the pontificate of Urban II (1088–1099), would have profound reverberation in the West. The collapse of the Byzantine Empire after Manzikert, the absence of any reaction in the face of the occupation of Asia Minor by the Turkish race and by Islam, imposed on the West the conviction that in the face of such failure and in order to save Europe, now directly menaced, the nations of the West would have to intervene. Our ancient chroniclers were not mistaken here. William of Tyre[1] would see in the disaster of Manzikert the definite elimination of the Greeks as protagonists for Christendom, the historical justification for the entry into the scene of the Franks to replace these partners now out of the game. In fact, it was time to think about the situation. From Nicaea, where Islam had a foothold, Constantinople could be surprised at any instant. The catastrophe of 1453 could have occurred in the last years of the eleventh century. . . . This was one of the motives which would cause Urban II, fourteen years after the taking of Nicaea, to undertake the preaching of the First Crusade. There is no need to imagine a direct appeal from the Byzantine emperor Alexius Comnenus in order to explain such a resolution. The feeling which Urban had of his duties as guide and defender of Christendom suffice to clarify his policy. It was a policy with a large vision if there ever was one, a policy which, from the height of the pontifical throne erected at Clermont-Ferrand, embraced not only Jerusalem where the wars between the Egyptians and the Seljuks had resulted in new massacres of the Christians, but also the question of the straits, "the arm of St. George," as one said then, always under the menace of a Turkish surprise attack.

On 27 November 1095, the tenth day of the Council of Clermont, Urban II called all of Christendom to arms. This was an appeal of the pontiff for the defense of the faith menaced by a new Muslim invasion, the call of the true heir of the Roman emperors for the defense of the West, of the highest European authority for the safeguarding of Europe against Asiatic conquerors who were the successors of Attila and the precursors of Mohammed II.[2] The cry "God wills it!" was the answer from all sides to his proclamation; it was taken up by Urban himself, who made it the cry of a general rallying and demanded that the future soldiers of Christ mark themselves with the sign of the cross. The "crusade" was born, an idea . . . which launched princes and commoners to the extremity of the East. The crusading idea of the Council of Clermont can only be compared in that respect with the Panhellenic idea of the congress of Corinth in 336 B.C., which launched Alexander the Great and all of Greece on the conquest of Asia.

CLAUDE CAHEN

The content [of Cahen's longer article in *Past and Present,* referred to above] can be summarized as follows. The crusaders departed for the East with the conviction that they were going to the aid of eastern Christendom, which had been overpowered by the Turkish conquest, and that they were fighting for the maintenance of pilgrimages which that conquest had also imperilled. The real situation was quite different. The Turkish conquest had only been disastrous for the *Greek Christians of Asia Minor;* it was not disastrous either for the other Christians in Asia Minor or for the Christians in the rest of the Muslim world and in particular for those in Palestine, all of whom had preserved their traditional situation in Muslim lands. As for the pilgrims, if they were prevented from being able to reach the Holy Land by way of Asia Minor, those who came directly to Palestine by sea were not bothered any more than before. Contrary interpretations rest on misunderstandings and tendentious confusions. Certainly there were always small matters for complaint, but there was no more of that at the end of the eleventh century in Palestine than before, and it was the West which had the greater sensitivity on this matter. At the outset the crusaders conducted an expedition into Palestine which was justified only in

[1] An important historian of the crusading movement and of the Latin Kingdom of Jerusalem. [Editor's note].

[2] Attila was the ferocious leader of the Huns in the fifth century; Mohammed II was the leader of the Ottoman Turks who captured Constantinople in 1453. [Editor's note].

From C. Cahen, "L'Islam et la Croisade," *Relazioni del X Congresso Internazionale di Scienze Storiche,* Vol. III: *Storia del Medioevo* (Florence, 1955), pp. 625-28. Used by permission of G. C. Sanzoni, Editore. Translated by the editor.

terms of assistance to Byzantium. It is that partial substitution of purpose which it is necessary to explain.

Included among the questions which the second part of my article in English briefly poses is naturally that concerning how it came to pass in the West that a project was conceived which, if I am not wrong, did not exactly correspond to the demands of the situation in the East. Naturally, there was a whole set of general conditions favorable to the project in the West. Furthermore, I think that it is necessary to exclude the idea of the influence of the Italian maritime cities; although they profited from the Crusade, they seem to me to have been engaged in it with extreme prudence and to have been very little disposed toward crusading in the beginning. The Crusade was the work of people for whom economic conditions could certainly play a part, but not commercial motives. Whatever the case may be in this respect, the whole set of general conditions does not entirely explain the conception of the Crusade. It is difficult not to give a notable role to the papacy. From my point of view as an orientalist, how can one view the conception of the papacy? There are two questions to consider: the attitude of the papacy toward the Muslims in general, and its attitude toward the eastern Christians.

Towards the Muslims, the Papacy adopted a policy of giving encouragement to Christian reconquest in the West before doing so in the East, and there is no doubt that the western experience influenced the ultimate eastern decision. What is remarkable is that, whereas in the East the Crusade would appear as a reply to the Turkish offensive (although that offensive did not unloose all the consequences that are ordinarily imagined), in the West the Christian reconquest first began as a result of the general weakening of Islam and . . . presents itself in the immediate setting as an initiative that was in no way provoked. This is absolutely clear in Sicily and in Spain. Quite the reverse, in the latter case it was the Christian offensive which would provoke a stiffening of Islam, the appeal to the Almoravides, and the establishment in Spain of a harsh Muslim regime which followed upon a period of remarkable tolerance. That Christian offensive was not the doing of the papacy alone; perhaps the initial idea even owed nothing to the papacy. But the papacy actively interested itself in this matter—in Sicily after its alliance with the Normans, and in Spain from the pontificate of Alexander II. The idea which would later

be transferred to the Orient with certain new characteristics would certainly find circumstances favorable there as a result of the Turkish offensive, but it was anterior to the Turkish invasion and it was born independently of that offensive.

However, the bringing together of a certain number of well known facts concerning the papal policy in the western Mediterranean basin suggests that the struggle against Islam did not always interest the papacy and that papal policy had at the same time another end which the struggle against Islam might assist in attaining—so much that papal policy ceased to be interested in this struggle when it no longer served that end. This policy involved as close as possible an attachment to the papacy—within the framework of the Gregorian reform—of those Christian societies which by virtue of circumstances had too much autonomy vis-à-vis the papacy: the Greeks in Sicily and the Spaniards. It was known that in Spain this policy did not proceed without difficulty. On the contrary, Gregory VII enjoyed perfectly cordial relationships with a Muslim prince of North Africa. . . . And later when the Normans would make peace with the Muslim prince of Tunisia, the ancient Suzerain of the Sicilians who had given up claim to the island, the papacy seemed to have been as reserved as the Normans in the expedition of the Pisans and Genoese against Madhia in Tunisia. Therefore, there was no policy of systematic aggressiveness against the Muslims except where aggressiveness might result in the organization of a new Christendom more closely bound to the Holy See. In North Africa there were too few Christians.

It seems to me that in the East the problem for the papacy was exactly of the same order. There existed in the East a Christendom which, without being properly speaking heretical, was directed by leaders whom Rome could not support: Byzantine Christianity. There was—aside from the heretical Christians of the East of which little was known —the Christianity of the Greek rite but of the Arabic language and of much more hesitant behavior than that of Byzantium, namely, the Christianity of the patriarchates of Antioch and Jerusalem, perhaps also the Armenians, who had shown a certain desire for contacts with Rome and thought very little of Byzantium. Conditions were excellent to organize . . . a Roman Christianity in Syria-Palestine which would help to neutralize Byzantine influence in the East and to bring about a change of heart in the patriarch of Constantinople, just as the papacy had obtained a change of heart of the almost autonomous prelates of Spain. I have certainly ventured far from my territory as an orientalist here, but the consideration in their entirety of all the Mediterranean aspects of the problem appears to me to render that line of explication as an hypothesis which, if not demonstrable, is at least unavoidable. . . .

MARSHALL W. BALDWIN

THE BYZANTINE PROBLEM

Urban II's motives for summoning the First Crusade may have been more complex than Grousset suggests; perhaps, as Cahen hints, the Muslim threat to the West was not as great as has been assumed, and perhaps Urban II was tempted to think that a war against the Muslims in the East would bring the Christians of Syria, Palestine, and Armenia closer to Rome. But there was another "eastern" problem that may have had a bearing on Urban's decision and plans. This was the question of the relationship between Byzantium and the papacy. Is it possible that this issue was foremost in the Pope's mind as the idea of a crusade was formulated in the period just before the Council of Clermont? Many historians are inclined to believe that the Byzantine problem was crucial in Urban's thoughts and that the crusading movement was undertaken to try to resolve that problem advantageously.

The Byzantine policy of the papacy and the state of relationships between Rome and Constantinople in the eleventh century are so complex that it is almost impossible to treat them briefly. The following selection, attempting to summarize major recent positions on the policy of the papacy with respect to Byzantium, will do no more than introduce the student to the basic issues. It does make perfectly clear that the papacy had a major stake in Byzantine affairs and that these matters were related to the crusading movement. Marshall W. Baldwin of New York University is one of the leading American specialists in crusading history.

The motives behind the launching of the First Crusade have always been at once a source of interest and a problem to modern historians. The importance of understanding so significant a development at its very inception is obvious, but truthworthy contemporary evidence is difficult to find. Bishop Adhemar of Puy, whom Urban II had appointed as legate and chief of the expedition, and who presumably was aware of the pope's intentions, died in August, 1098, before the goal had been reached. Urban himself died on July 29, 1099, just two weeks after the capture of Jerusalem by the crusaders, and left as indication of his plans only his celebrated speech at Clermont (1095) and a few letters. Since Pascal II, as is well known, lacked the enterprising statesmanship of his illustrious predecessor, the initiative passed into the hands of ecclesiastics and laymen in the east. It is incorrect, therefore, to assume that all the actions of these local rulers and churchmen conformed to papal plans. A number of the early chronicles of the crusade were written by men who had been in the Levant and, as a consequence, the Levantine point of view colored the writings of contemporary historians in Europe. Even

From Marshall W. Baldwin, "Some Recent Interpretations of Pope Urban's Eastern Policy," *The Catholic Historical Review*, XXV (1939–40), pp. 459–66. Reprinted by permission of *The Catholic Historical Review*.

the accounts of Urban's speech at Clermont were compiled probably some years after the event and were doubtless affected by what had subsequently taken place. As a consequence of this absence of adequate contemporary evidence, Urban's motives have too often been judged by modern historians in the light of what resulted from the First Crusade, and a bewildering variety of conclusions has been drawn from later events. This is especially noticeable in the natural tendency to consider the crusade in relation to significant contemporary developments in Europe. Since there is as yet no general agreement among scholars as to the proper interpretation of Urban's policy in the First Crusade, no categorical statements can safely be made. Several recent studies, however, have thrown some new light on the problem. A brief summary of these may serve to state the case as it now stands and perhaps contribute to a better understanding of Urban's original intentions.

One problem which has concerned a number of scholars is the connection between the First Crusade and papal Byzantine policy. By 1095 the latter had two aspects. First, the desire to end the Greek schism of 1054 involved dealings with Byzantine ecclesiastics. Second, the advances of the Seljuk Turks had forced eastern emperors to seek aid in the West. Michael VII, for example, had approached Gregory VII. In this manner, important negotiations between the popes and the Byzantine emperors were opened and there appeared to Gregory VII the possibility of achieving the long sought for religious reconciliation through the offering of military assistance. Gregory, of course, could not carry out his project. But a similar opportunity confronted Urban II, and historians have debated the question whether Urban also considered military aid to the Byzantine emperor as a means of reconciling the Byzantine church.

It is no longer doubted that Emperor Alexius actually requested Urban's assistance at the Council of Piacenza in March, 1095, and that the pope seriously considered the appeal. What is not clear is whether, in preaching the crusade six months later at Clermont, Urban viewed the projected expedition as a means of effecting reunion. An affirmative answer to this question has been given by the Reverend Bernard Leib, S.J.[1] In a comprehensive survey of papal policy, in which even relations with Russia were

included, Father Leib maintained that, despite the schism of 1054, relations between Greek and Latin Christians were such as to warrant the hope of reunion. Negotiations which Urban II opened in 1089 came to naught largely owing to the opposition of his enemies, in particular the anti-pope, Guibert. Thus, in Leib's view, the crusade opened a new opportunity for healing the schism. Unfortunately, the new political considerations which the crusade presented, the lack of discipline among the crusaders and especially their misunderstandings with the Greeks ruined the pope's plan and served only to stiffen the dogmatic opposition of the Byzantine clergy.

Leib's work was severely criticized, especially by Erich Caspar and Walther Holtzmann, both prominent German students of papal history.[2] The latter published about the same time an important article on papal Levantine policies in the second half of the eleventh century, in which he discussed in detail the various reunion negotiations and the plans for military action against the Turks and concluded that the First Crusade had no immediate connection with Urban's efforts to achieve a religious reconciliation.[3] Although reunion was close to the pope's heart, as is shown by his negotiations in 1089 and by his renewed efforts in 1098–9, the crusade grew out of entirely different factors, such as the Turkish situation and the Cluny reform movement. Therefore, although at Piacenza in March, 1095, Urban had simply considered sending aid to Alexius, by the time he had reached Clermont in November of the same year, he had decided on Jerusalem as the goal. This change, Holtzmann thought, perhaps resulted from the pope's journey through southern France and may well have been brought about by the persuasion of such men as Adhemar of Puy and Raymond of Saint-Gilles, who later played prominent rôles on the expedition to Jerusalem. Thus, in addition to clarifying Urban's Byzantine policies before 1095, Holtzmann also called attention to the marked change in the pope's plans between the Council of

[1] B. Leib, *Rome, Kiew et Byzance à la Fin du XIe Siècle* (Paris, 1924), especially 179 ff. and 319 ff.

[2] E. Caspar in *Byzantinische Zeitschrift*, XXVI (1926), 102; W. Holtzmann in *Historische Zeitschrift*, CXXXIV (1926), 98–100. But see also the less unfavorable notice of L. Halphen in *Bibliothèque de lÉcole des Chartes*, LXXXV (1924), 376–9.

[3] "Studien zur Orientpolitik des Reformpapsttums und zur Entstehung des ersten Kreuzzuges," *Historische Vierteljahrschrift*, XXII (1924–5), 167–99. There is a brief summary in *Historische Zeitschrift*, CXXXII (1925), 359 by A. Hofmeister. Holtzmann's conclusions regarding the negotiations of 1089 were further substantiated by his discovery and publication of two Greek documents ("Der Unionsverhandlungen zwischen Alexios I und Urban II im Jahre 1089," *Byzantinische Zeitschrift*, XXVII (1928), 38 ff.).

Piacenza in March, 1095, where the appeal of Alexius was heard and the Council of Clermont in November, 1095, where the First Crusade (something vastly different from a mere expedition to help Constantinople) was launched.

In an article on Urban's crusade plans, Augustin Fliche, the noted French historian of the eleventh century papacy, helped to explain this significant change by discussing in detail the pope's journey from Piacenza to Clermont through southern France.[4] Urban stopped at various places. But the visits most significant for the crusade were: Le Puy where he met Adhemar, recently returned from a pilgrimage to the Holy Land; Cluny, the heart of the reform movement and in close touch with the Spanish situation; and Saint-Gilles. The visit to Raymond of Saint-Gilles, which took the pope considerably out of his way, Fliche especially emphasized. Raymond IV, count of Toulouse, friend of the church and already known for his exploits in Spain, may well have been as influential as Adhemar of Puy in broadening Urban's plans. Certainly at Piacenza Urban apparently only considered sending a small force to aid Alexius, whereas at Clermont the idea of an expedition to recover the Holy Land had fully matured in his mind. According to Fliche, however, the pope had in mind only one army under the direction of Adhemar with Raymond as his lieutenant, and must have been thoroughly surprised to find three other armies and hordes of peasants taking the road to Jerusalem.

Other historians, especially those engaged in surveying European conditions in general, have been less interested in the problem of Constantinople and its place in Urban's policy than with the relation of the First Crusade to contemporary European developments, in particular the investiture controversy. It has been frequently asserted, for example, that Urban's purpose in the crusade was the reestablishment of his leadership over Christendom, seriously threatened as a result of the struggle with the Holy Roman Empire. Others have denied this. Some have held that the pope sought to relieve the pressure of

the Muslims in Spain by an attack in the east. Students of the crusaders' states in the Levant have attributed to the papacy plans for a church state in Jerusalem or possibly a papal fief bound to the Holy See by ties similar to those which the popes maintained with some of the smaller European kingdoms.

It is in consideration of such manifestly divergent interpretations of competent scholars that a recent book by Carl Erdmann takes on considerable significance.[5] The author has made an exhaustive and penetrating analysis of the origin and development of the crusade idea, the holy war. He concludes that, far from being an outgrowth of eleventh century conditions, the crusade idea has its roots deep in the Christian past; that it represents a gradual transformation of the early idea of the spiritual "soldier of Christ" to the temporal defender of the church and the pope of later days. Thus, the First Crusade, in fact all crusades, are simply examples of the holy war. Erdmann's book has been reviewed at length by several distinguished scholars and it would be superfluous to repeat here what others have said. There has been universal agreement as to the significance of the book and the competence of the author. The book has even been called "a complete repertory of all the facts and all the doctrines which throw light on the attitude of the church toward the feudal world during the tenth and eleventh centuries." The principal criticism has been directed against the author's too strict adherence to his main thesis and his consequent insistence on fitting all crusades into the same pattern. What particularly concerns the present discussion is Erdmann's treatment of Urban II. In his final chapter and in an appendix of some length, he has given one of the most comprehensive and thorough studies of Urban's eastern policy which has so far appeared.

This eastern policy, the author maintains, was less an original conception than the natural consequence of the efforts of his predecessors, especially Gregory VII. Urban's innovations were in method rather than in principle. Nevertheless, in pushing the war against the infidel, the pope showed a remarkable grasp of all the elements in the situation. He associated the papacy with the mid-Mediterranean expansion of the Pisans and the Normans. He coordinated the holy war in Spain with that in the Orient without, however, failing to realize that, from the

---

[4] "Urbain II et la Croisade," *Revue d'Histoire de l'Église de France*, XII (1927), 289–306. In a more recent article ("Les Origines de l'Action de la Papauté en vue de la Croisade," *Revue d'Histoire ecclésiastique*, XXXIV (1938), 765–75), Fliche discusses the significant fact that by the eleventh century the papacy, not the empire (as formerly), was already recognized as the leader in promoting the defense against Islam. Moreover, in view of the fact that the emperor was under the ban of the church at the time, it was natural for Urban to turn elsewhere for assistance.

[5] *Die Entstehung des Kreuzzugsgedankens (Forschungen zur Kirchen- und Geistesgeschichte*, ed. E. Seeberg, E. Caspar, W. Weber, VI, Stuttgart, 1935).

The Byzantine Problem

military and geographic standpoint, the two developments were distinct. Urban was not so naïve as to think that events in Asia necessarily affected the Iberian peninsula. Moreover, he placed the Spanish war on a par with the crusade to the Holy Land by offering the same indulgence for both. In 1099 when the archbishop of Toledo appeared in Rome hoping to join the crusaders in the Levant, the pope sent him back to Spain.

As far as the east itself was concerned, Urban's policy involved two factors at first: ecclesiastical reunion with the Byzantine church, and military aid to the eastern empire. Undoubtedly he hoped that the offering of military assistance might enhance the prospects for reunion and in the years 1089–91 both were considered. Whether ecclesiastical reunion entered into the plans for the crusade in 1095–6 it is unfortunately impossible to say and "conjectures are fruitless." It is only certain that the crusade did not mean the abandonment of hopes for reunion, as Urban's efforts in 1098–99 indicate. But Erdmann insists (and here he differs markedly from other interpretations) that the military plan of Clermont was not the radical departure from the ideas of Piacenza that was once supposed. Even at Piacenza it was not merely a question of protecting Constantinople. Military action to push back the frontiers of Islam, possibly even to Syria and Palestine, may very well have been intended. Further, the traditional explanation of Clermont is not entirely satisfactory. Since the accounts of the pope's speech were written some years after the event, they were probably influenced by the anti-Byzantinism current in Europe after 1100. Thus, the actual goal of the expedition, Jerusalem, seems to have been read back with exaggerated emphasis into the reports of the speech and eventually to have influenced the interpretation of modern historians. Relying upon such evidence as can be found prior to 1099 and discounting the reports of pilgrims returning from Palestine, the author maintains that even at Clermont, the freeing of the "Oriental Church," a defensive war of a united Christendom against the infidel in the east as in Spain, was Urban's purpose. Already the participants in the Spanish war had been offered the same indulgence given pilgrims to Jerusalem. But pilgrims were not supposed to be armed. Therefore, Urban's great innovation at Clermont was to extend the customary Jerusalem pilgrimage indulgence to all who went to Jerusalem "for the freeing of God's church," and thus officially to proclaim for the first time the idea of the armed pilgrimage. Con-

stantinople and Jerusalem, then, were not two conflicting objectives, were not an "either-or," but an "as well-as." Jerusalem was a necessary "Marschziel" not the "Kriegziel," and the First Crusade was merely the culmination of the long development of the holy war idea.

Finally, Erdmann holds that while it is true Urban won great moral authority as a result of the crusade, it is a question whether such was his design. Apparently, at least as far as can be learned from his own statements, the pope had no intention of binding the crusaders to a papal over-lordship or of founding a church state in the Levant. Such notions originated later in the east. Urban's statesmanship differed from Gregory VII's in what Erdmann describes as his capacity for limitation. He was content to "place himself at the head of a popular movement without obtaining direct advantage therefrom" (p. 325).

It is clear that this interpretation of the origins of the First Crusade differs in many respects from any hitherto held and is, of course, open to the same criticism which has been made of the main body of the book. Urban is made to fit into a plan; and although the pope is credited with statesmanlike qualities of a high order, his great initiative and originality are denied. In a sense he becomes a follower rather than a leader. The impression is given that the author has sought somewhat too ingeniously to minimize the difference between Clermont and Piacenza in order that the crusade may appear "as a simple continuation of the previous Orient policy of the popes" (p. 303). On the other hand, in approaching the important subject of the crusade from the standpoint of papal policy, Erdmann has performed a signal service in questioning a number of broad generalizations and in calling attention to the danger of confusing actual results with original intentions. He has demonstrated Urban's grasp of the European situation as a whole, political and religious, in the east and in Europe. Not all the questions which have puzzled scholars have been satisfactorily answered, but here is an interpretation of the pope's eastern policy based on painstaking and thorough analysis which, if it is not accepted, will have to be reckoned with in the future.

In spite of the difficulties and disagreements evident in this brief discussion, certain lines of thought have been clarified by the recent studies of Urban II's policies and the relatively certain can more easily be distinguished from the uncertain. The connection between Spain and the Orient has been placed in its proper light. The relation between the crusade and the reunion of the churches remains uncertain, although important contributions have been made to a better understanding of papal Byzantine policy. Equally uncertain is Urban's attitude toward the prospective crusaders' states in the Levant. In view of previous theories Erdmann's opinion that the pope planned neither a church state nor a papal fief in Jerusalem is significant. His statements also lend support to those who are not inclined to view the First Crusade as a papal counteroffensive in the investiture struggle. Finally, while there has never been any doubt as to Urban's abilities, the breadth of his statesmanship, his understanding of the manifold interrelations of European and Mediterranean politics and his capacity for coördinating separate undertakings are now more clear than ever before. This remains true whether the First Crusade is regarded as merely the culmination of a long development or as a spectacular and original achievement.

HILMAR C. KRUEGER

MATERIAL CONCERNS

Piety and politics loomed large as factors causing the Crusades. But even Urban II was aware of men's material urges and ambitions, and he was not reluctant to suggest that valuable rewards awaited the successful crusaders, as his speech at Clermont reveals. It is therefore impossible to overlook the economic factors at play in the crusading enterprise. Professor Hilmar C. Krueger of the University of Cincinnati, a leading American expert on the economic history of medieval Italy and especially Genoa, analyzes these factors in the following selection. His remarks make it obvious that many who participated in the Crusades stood to benefit from holy war. To what extent was that their prime motive? It remains for the student to place this aspect of the Crusades in relation to other forces that have been identified as causes for the assault on the East. The final answer may lie in one's view of human nature.

The Crusades were part of a pan-European expansionist movement that pushed into all directions, partially under the impetus or guise of Christianity. The conquest of England by Duke William of Normandy, the foundation of another Norman Kingdom in the Two Sicilies, the Spanish campaigns of the Christian knights of Spain and France, and the Saxon Crusade across the Elbe, the expeditions of the Scandinavian sailors into the northern seas and the Christian settlements in Iceland and Greenland, the acceptance of Roman Christianity by St. Stephen and his Hungarian subjects were all parts of the same expansionist movement, some antecedent, others contemporary, to the more phenomenal overseas expansion. To a great degree this general development made the Crusades possible and acceptable. In all areas the developments continued beyond the end of the twelfth century.

The economic aspects of the Crusades were as varied as the participants. There is little need and no method to weigh and evaluate the varied causes for this overseas expansion. Admittedly, religious, political, and social forces existed in addition to the more material economic factors. Pope Urban II appealed successfully to all interests and by no means did he overlook the economic and material aspects. That these economic interests influenced consider-

From Hilmar C. Krueger, "Economic Aspects of Expanding Europe," in *Twelfth-Century Europe and the Foundations of Modern Society*, ed. Marshall Claggett, Gaines Post and Robert Reynolds (Madison, Wisconsin: University of Wisconsin Press, 1961), pp. 69–72. Reprinted with permission of the copyright owners, the Regents of the University of Wisconsin.

ably the activities of some of the crusading elements may be gathered from the denunciations of them when some of the crusades failed to reach the expectations of the more spiritually minded.

In a measure the Crusades were evidence that the Peace of God and the Truce of God had failed. The varied accounts of Pope Urban's speeches refer to bloody strife, plundering and pilfering, homicide and sacrilege, hatreds and dissensions. These actions were economic liabilities for western Europe and any diminution of them was of economic profit to the communities and groups among whom they existed. Urban's references to the actions were couched in terms of religion, humanity, and social conscience, but the economic losses from war and plunder cannot be denied and the gains from their absence cannot be overlooked.

To the feudal barons, "aforetime robbers" who were to become soldiers of Christ, the pope gave promise of material gains. He promised to the overseas crusaders what the bishops and princes of the north had offered to the Saxon colonists and settlers. "The possessions of the enemy will be yours, too, since you will make spoil of his treasures. . . ." "Wrest that land from the wicked race, and subject it to yourselves, that land which, as the scripture says, 'floweth with milk and honey.'" He obviously hoped to gain the support of the landless or land-poor barony, who possessed little property because of the rules of inheritance or the ill fortune of the feudal wars. He knew, too, the inevitable result of increasing population whose land "is too narrow . . . nor does it abound in wealth; and it furnishes scarcely enough food for its cultivators."

The economic gains that were promised to the feudal barons were also obtained by them. The great princes at the head of their feudal levies carved out the largest estates, but lesser barons established themselves as well. As the crusading armies marched southward from Asia Minor into Syria and Palestine, individual leaders conquered and claimed their personal principalities. In that fashion Tancred established himself in Cilicia, Baldwin in the County of Edessa, and Raymond of Toulouse in the County of Tripoli. They often quarreled with one another in complete disregard of the common cause and the Kingdom of Jerusalem and certainly not in the interests of the Holy Sepulcher and the papal see. With them their own personal ambitions ranked first, and they demanded before anything else the

establishment of their own political authority along feudal lines which gave them the customary economic returns in fees, services, fines and products. The lesser barons generally became vassals and enjoyed similar gains, but on a smaller scale. Many of the barons, who had nothing to return to in western Europe, established residence in the Levant and their descendants became part of the Frankish aristocracy of the East. Fulcher of Chartres exclaimed: "He who in Europe owned not so much as a village is lord of a whole city out here. He who was worth no more than a few pence now disposes of a fortune. Why should we return to the West when we have all we desire here?"

While the feudal barons formed the majority of the fighting men in the crusading campaigns, the Italian townsmen and merchants were so essential to the whole movement that it would have collapsed without their support. After the First Crusade all western armies travelled eastward, by sea, and even in the First Crusade the naval and military support of Genoa and Pisa was considerable. Pope Urban II recognized the importance of the towns and merchants for the movement and accordingly sent itinerant propagandists into the cities to preach the crusades or had local preachers perform the job.

Since the Italian towns had been fighting the Moslems for several centuries, the papal preachers had no difficulty persuading the Italian merchants to coöperate. The Italians had fought the Arabs for three hundred years before 1095, at first defensively, then offensively. All the great Italian cities, Naples, Rome, Pisa, and Genoa in the west, Bari, Ancona, and Venice on the Adriatic, had been attacked and plundered by the Arabs. In the early tenth century the south Italian cities had wiped out the last Arab base in Italy, and in the early eleventh century Genoa and Pisa had driven the Arabs from the Tyrrhenian Sea. In 1087 a combined force of Italian cities, under the leadership of a papal legate, attacked Mehdia in North Africa, plundered a merchant suburb, gained compensation for damages done to their ships by Arab pirates, and obtained free access to the area for their merchants. The victory cleared the western Mediterranean of Arab pirates and competitors. To the Italian cities the call of Pope Urban II sounded like an invitation to help clear the eastern Mediterranean as well and to obtain similar commercial privileges.

To the Italian merchants the Crusades always appeared to be extraordinary economic opportunities. From the very start the Italians gained financial rewards. Their ships carried the crusaders and their equipment, even their horses, to the Holy Land, and then supplied the Crusaders with food, drink, and, on occasion, with timber, manpower, and siege machinery. Genoa and Pisa commandeered all possible ships in their domains for transport purposes and ordered the construction of more and larger vessels. The transport services were a source of immediate income for the communes, merchants, and shipowners. The Fourth Crusade is good evidence that financial return loomed large in the aims of the shipowners and merchants. The Crusades gave to the Italian cities much of the liquid capital that was needed in the capitalistic developments that were just beginning. Furthermore, this capital came from sources unrelated to the Italian towns, from western feudal barons and kings. It was money which the Italians could not have obtained otherwise.

In addition to these immediate monetary returns Genoa, Pisa, and Venice received promises of quarters in the coastal towns of Syria and Palestine.

These promises were generally made in private agreements between the Italian cities and the baronial leaders, the kings of France and England, and the kings of Jerusalem. Often they were made under pressure of the moment and then forgotten when the pressure was lifted. However, the Italians, especially the Genoese, established themselves well enough to enjoy long-term rewards and profits. In at least a dozen coastal towns of the Levant the Italians possessed throughout most of the twelfth century residential and commercial quarters, from which they gained an income from rentals, leases, harbor dues, and court fines. In these centers the Italian merchants carried on their trade with the European colonists and feudal residents, with Arab traders, and with their associates and agents who worked in the area. The Italian quarters of the Levant became the centers of exchange for Oriental and European goods and markets for the western imports that increased as the century wore on. The Oriental trade was highly profitable and another source of capital in the new money economy of the period. The Crusades were the strongest influence on the development of medieval trade and industry.

5

MEDIEVAL CULTURE: ITS PLACE IN
THE HISTORY OF CULTURE

Economic revival and the Crusades were only two manifestations of the vitality surging through European society in the eleventh, twelfth, and thirteenth centuries. To complete the picture of the "first" Europe equal attention ought to be given to other aspects of society. For these centuries witnessed the creation of vigorous systems of monarchical government, the development of cities and city life, the perfection of papal government, the establishment of new monastic orders, and an extensive reformation of religious life, to mention but a few of the most outstanding signs of resurgence. These interlocking movements provided European society with bone and muscle; society as a whole became orderly, secure, and affluent to a degree unknown during the several previous centuries. These accomplishments compel the serious student of history to abandon any notion that he might have had about the High Middle Ages as a "dark age."

Should there still be a lingering doubt about the constructive, positive character of this age, perhaps the case can be clinched by introducing the skeptics to the cultural accomplishments of the era stretching from mid-eleventh to early fourteenth century. Here in the realm of the intellect and the spirit, in the creations of the poet, the storyteller, the architect, the sculptor, the painter, the philosopher, and the scholar is the crowning glory of the "first" Europe. In our final problem concerning the Middle Ages we shall concentrate our attention on this aspect of medieval history.

It is not easy to find an intelligible approach to medieval cultural life. Anyone who has studied deeply a golden age in cultural history—for example, fifth-century Athens or the Italian Renaissance—is tempted to illustrate the glory of his beloved era by parading the accomplishments of the age before his audience, as if to say that the sheer magnitude of achievement is proof of vitality and excellence. There is not room here to undertake this kind of display of medieval culture. Nor perhaps would such an exercise in cataloging be very profitable in terms of conveying a true appreciation of medieval cultural life.

There is only one sure way to grasp the full meaning of medieval cultural life—or that of any other age. That is to immerse oneself in the works of the thinkers, writers, and artists of the age. No one can comprehend medieval thought, appreciate medieval tastes, or share medieval feelings unless he has experienced at first hand the humanism of John of Salisbury, the logical acuity of Abelard, the vast learning of Albertus Magnus, the capability of systematic thought of Thomas Aquinas, the power of symbolization of the authors of the *Romance of the Rose,* the range of imagination of Chrétien of Troyes, the emotional power of the Latin hymnists and the troubadour poets, the sense of space and form of the architect who conceived the cathedral at Amiens, the love of humanity of the sculptor whose statues adorn the cathedral at Chartres, or the cosmic vision of Dante. It would take no less than a lifetime to capture the full genius reflected in even these few figures, let alone all the rest of the cultural figures who graced the age.

Perhaps there is another angle of approach to medieval cultural life that will serve a useful purpose at this stage of our study of Western civilization. Students who have just begun to acquire some knowledge about medieval cultural achievements will undoubtedly be prompted to ask a series of related questions. Where does medieval culture fit into the total stream of cultural history? What difference did it make in the history of mankind that Thomas Aquinas, Dante, and all the other medieval cultural leaders lived and created? Was the cultural achievement of the High Middle Ages unique in the larger story of man's intellectual and artistic striving? Or do medieval cultural monuments represent a link in a continuum that extends backward and forward, a link that joins an earlier chapter in cultural history with a later? Was medieval cultural activity a baneful chapter in cultural history that had to be undone before a more sophisticated and meaningful intellectual and artistic life could evolve? Or did it represent a golden age whose main features must be reincarnated?

The following selections provide some representative responses to these questions.

In so doing they will introduce the student to the broad area of cultural history, an aspect of history which is exciting and stimulating to many scholars. For to place medieval culture in the total stream of history, the cultural historian is forced to generalize about such things as "the medieval mind," "the spirit of the Middle Ages," and "the world view of medieval man." He is compelled to involve himself in comparative history, since he must place one culture in some relationship to others. He is driven to tracing elusive influences in thought and style across extensive periods. Finally, he is forced to place a value on the achievements of one age in relation to others. These kinds of issues have evoked immensely provocative responses from historians. And they have produced considerable amounts of historical hokum. We shall let each student decide what he thinks of cultural history after he has sampled the following attempts to deal with medieval culture.

VOLTAIRE

MEDIEVAL CULTURE: A BARREN FIELD

Our first effort to locate medieval culture in the stream of history comes from the pen of Voltaire, the eighteenth-century French genius whose name is almost synonymous with the cult of reason that characterized the Enlightenment. A prodigiously active writer whose works were read all over Europe, Voltaire made his mark chiefly as a caustic critic of what he felt were the evils of his age: prejudice, despotic government, privilege, superstition, ignorance. In many respects the Roman Catholic Church symbolized all these abuses and was therefore the prime target for his barbs. This view made him little sympathetic with that chapter of history during which the Church's influence had been paramount.

The passage below is taken from Voltaire's *Essay on Manners,* a long discourse on universal history which sought to show that the course of history comprised a struggle of the forces of reason and enlightenment against superstition, faith, and obscurantism. His reflections on medieval culture are set down after he has colorfully narrated medieval history down to 1450 in terms of wars, feudal anarchy, and assorted other miseries. This long narrative account makes no reference to medieval culture; all Voltaire's thoughts on the subject are contained in the following passage—the brevity of which may be the best index to Voltaire's views concerning the place of medieval culture in the total history of civilization.

Willing to turn from the repetition of so many miseries and mutual quarrels, the dismal objects of history and the commonplaces of human wickedness; I shall now examine mankind as members of society, inquire into their private lives, and in what manner the arts were cultivated among them.

From *The Works of Voltaire*, William F. Fleming (Paris, London, New York, Chicago: E. R. Dumont, c. 1901),Vol. XXVI, pp. 42, 46, 54, 56–57, 58, 59–60.

Toward the close of the thirteenth century, and in the beginning of the fourteenth, it appears to me, that they began in Italy, notwithstanding the dissensions which prevailed everywhere, to emerge from that brutality which had in a manner overwhelmed Europe, after the decline of the Roman Empire. . . . [Voltaire discusses certain advances in the practical arts, but paints a general picture of misery and discomfort as part of the European scene in the Middle Ages]. But it was not thus in the beautiful and trading cities of Italy. There the people lived in affluence and ease. With them alone the sweets of life seemed to have taken up their residence, and riches and liberty inspired their genius, and elevated their courage. . . . [Voltaire now discusses Dante, Petrarch, Boccaccio, Cimabue, Giotto, and Brunelleschi, all of whom are represented as creative artists who elevate Italy above barbarism.]

But although this light seems to have shone only in Italy, yet there were not wanting some persons of talents in other countries. St. Bernard and Abelard, who lived in France in the twelfth century, may be considered as men of great genius, but their language was a barbarous jargon, and their Latin was a tribute which they paid to the bad taste of the times. The Latin hymns in rhyme, which were composed in the twelfth and thirteenth centuries, are the very quintessence of barbarism. It was not thus that Horace sung the secular games. The scholastic divinity of those times, which was the bastard offspring of the Aristotelian philosophy, badly translated, and as ill understood, did more injury to understanding and the polite studies than ever the Huns and Vandals had done. . . .

[Voltaire speaks briefly of the state of the arts in the East—in the Arab world, arguing that there were signs of good taste and intelligence there.] What did they know in Germany, France, England, Spain, and the northern parts of Lombardy? Nothing but barbarous and feudal customs equally tumultuous and uncertain, duels, tournaments, scholastic divinity,

and magic. They still celebrated in several churches the festival of the ass, and that of the innocents and fools. An ass was brought before the altar, and the people sang the whole anthem to him: "Amen, Amen, Asine; eh, eh, eh, Mr. Ass! eh, eh, eh, Mr. Ass." A company of fools marched at the head of every procession in plaited gowns, hung round with bells and baubles, and this fashion is still kept up in some towns of the Low Countries, and in Germany. As to our northern nations, all their literature consisted in certain farces, written and exhibited in the vulgar tongue, with the titles of "The Foolish Mother," "The Prince of Fools," etc. Nothing was to be heard but stories of revelation, people possessed by evil spirits and fascinations. . . .

Immediately preceding these times of the fourteenth century, our Europe was . . . depopulated and impoverished by the Crusades. If we go back from these Crusades to the times which followed after the death of Charlemagne we shall find them not less unhappy, and still more ignorant. The comparison of those ages with our own should fill us with a due sense of the happiness we now enjoy, notwithstanding the almost invincible propensity we have to admire and praise the past at the expense of the present. . . .

As some few monarchs and pontiffs worthy of better times could not stop the general torrent of disorder, so neither could a few fine geniuses, born in the darkness of the northern nations, allure to those climates the arts and sciences. Charles V, king of France, who made a collection of over nine hundred volumes, at least a century before the Vatican library was founded by Nicholas V, in vain endeavored to encourage learning in his kingdom. The soil was not yet prepared for bearing those exotic fruits. There has been a collection of some of the wretched productions of those times: this is like collecting a heap of flints from the rubbish of an old house, when we are surrounded by beautiful palaces. . . . Learning was unknown, and taste yet more so. . . .

J. J. WALSH

MEDIEVAL CULTURE: *NE PLUS ULTRA*

From the hostile Voltaire we pass to the opposite extreme in the form of an evaluation of medieval culture by James J. Walsh, a physician with a strong and deeply felt interest in medieval history. Dr. Walsh first began to express his views on medieval culture in the form of lectures, delivered first in Roman Catholic circles in New York and then all over the United States. Eventually in 1907 he published his mature concepts in a book, *The Thirteenth, Greatest of Centuries,* which has since enjoyed a wide audience. As an amateur historian, Dr. Walsh felt free to move on a grand scale across medieval cultural life and to cast his judgments in heroic terms; this quality of his work is shared by other famous "amateurs" who have exercised a considerable influence in shaping favorable attitudes toward the Middle Ages by their perceptive treatments of medieval culture; one thinks especially of Henry Adams' *Mont St. Michel and Chartres* and Henry Osborn Taylor's *The Medieval Mind.*

In reading the following selection the student should seek out the criteria Walsh uses to judge the cultural achievements of the Middle Ages. Do his criteria for cultural excellence have validity or do his standards of judgment so weigh the balance that his conclusions are meaningless? A student ought also to inquire whether Walsh presents any solid evidence to support his case. Then he might be able to say whether Voltaire or Walsh is closer to a valid evaluation of medieval culture in the perspective of world history.

It cannot but seem a paradox to say that the Thirteenth was the greatest of centuries. To most people the idea will appear at once so preposterous that they may not even care to consider it. A certain number, of course, will have their curiosity piqued by the thought that anyone should evolve so curious a notion. Either of these attitudes of mind will yield at once to a more properly receptive mood if it is recalled that the Thirteenth is the century of the Gothic cathedrals, of the foundation of the university, of the signing of Magna Charta, and of the origin of representative government with something like constitutional guarantees throughout the west of Europe. The cathedrals represent a development in the arts that has probably never been equaled either before or since. The university was a definite creation of these generations that has lived and maintained its usefulness practically in the same form in which it was then cast for the seven centuries ever since. The foundation stones of modern liberties are to be found in the documents which for the first time declared the rights of man during this precious period.

A little consideration of the men who, at this period, lived lives of undying influence on mankind, will still further attract the attention of those who have not usually grouped these great characters together. Just before the century opened, three great rulers died at the height of their influence. They are still and will always be the subject of men's thoughts and of literature. They were Frederick Barbarossa, Saladin, and Richard Coeur De Lion. They formed but a suggestive prelude of what was to come in the following century, when such great monarchs as St. Louis of France, St. Ferdinand of Spain, Alfonso the Wise of Castile, Frederick II of Germany, Edward

From James J. Walsh, *The Thirteenth, Greatest of Centuries,* 12th ed. (New York: Fordham University Press, 1952), pp. 1–17. Reprinted by permission.

I, the English Justinian, Rudolph of Hapsburg, whose descendants still rule in Austria, and Robert Bruce, occupied the thrones of Europe. Was it by chance or Providence that the same century saw the rise of and the beginning of the fall of that great Eastern monarchy which had been created by the genius for conquest of Jenghiz Khan, the Tatar warrior, who ruled over all the Eastern world from beyond what are now the western confines of Russia, Poland, and Hungary, into and including what we now call China.

But the thrones of Europe and of Asia did not monopolize the great men of the time. The Thirteenth Century claims such wonderful churchmen as St. Francis and St. Dominic, and while it has only the influence of St. Hugh of Lincoln, who died just as it began, it can be proud of St. Edmund of Canterbury, Stephen Langton, and Robert Grosseteste, all men whose place in history is due to what they did for their people, and such magnificent women as Queen Blanche of Castile, St. Clare of Assisi, and St. Elizabeth of Hungary. The century opened with one of the greatest of the Popes on the throne, Innocent III, and it closed with the most misunderstood of Popes, who is in spite of this one of the worthiest successors of Peter, Boniface VIII. During the century there had been such men as Honorius IV, the Patron of Learning, Gregory IX, to whom Canon Law owes so much, and John XXI, who had been famous as a scientist before becoming Pope. There are such scholars as St. Thomas of Aquin, Albertus Magnus, Roger Bacon, St. Bonaventure, Duns Scotus, Raymond Lully, Vincent of Beauvais, and Alexander of Hales, and such patrons of learning as Robert of Sorbonne, and the founders of nearly twenty universities. There were such artists as Gaddi, Cimabue, and above all Giotto, and such literary men as the authors of the Arthur Legends and the Nibelungen, the Meistersingers, the Minnesingers, the Troubadours, and Trouvères, and above all Dante, who is universally considered now to be one of the greatest literary men of all times, but who was not, as is so often thought and said, a solitary phenomenon in the period, but only the culmination of a great literary movement that had to have some such supreme expression of itself as this in order to properly round out the cycle of its existence.

If in addition it be said that this century saw the birth of the democratic spirit in many different ways in the various countries of Europe, but always in such form that it was never quite to die out again,

the reasons for talking of it as possibly the greatest of centuries will be readily appreciated even by those whose reading has not given them any preliminary basis of information with regard to this period, which has unfortunately been shrouded from the eyes of most people by the fact that its place in the midst of the Middle Ages would seem to preclude all possibility of the idea that it could represent a great phase of the development of the human intellect and its esthetic possibilities.

There would seem to be one more or less insuperable objection to the consideration of the Thirteenth as the greatest of centuries, and that arises from the fact that the idea of evolution has consciously and unconsciously tinged the thoughts of our generation to such a degree, that it seems almost impossible to think of a period so far in the distant past as having produced results comparable with those that naturally flow from the heightened development of a long subsequent epoch. Whatever of truth there may be in the great theory of evolution, however, it must not be forgotten that no added evidence for its acceptance can be obtained from the intellectual history of the human race. We may be "the heirs of all the ages in the foremost files of time," but one thing is certain, that we can scarcely hope to equal, and do not at all think of surpassing, some of the great literary achievements of long past ages.

In the things of the spirit apparently there is very little, if any, evolution. Homer wrote nearly three thousand years ago as supreme an expression of human life in absolute literary values as the world has ever known, or, with all reverence for the future be it said, is ever likely to know. The great dramatic poem Job emanated from a Hebrew poet in those earlier times, and yet, if judged from the standpoint of mere literature, is as surpassing an expression of human intelligence in the presence of the mystery of evil as has ever come from the mind of man. We are no nearer the solution of the problem of evil in life, though thousands of years have passed and man has been much occupied with the thoughts that disturbed the mind of the ruler of Moab. The Code of Hammurabi, recently discovered, has shown very definitely that men could make laws nearly five thousand years ago as well calculated to correct human abuses as those our legislators spend so much time over at present, and the olden time laws were probably quite as effective as ours can hope to be, for all our well intentioned purpose and praiseworthy efforts at reform. . . .

. . . Perhaps, then, the prejudice with regard to evolution and its supposed effectiveness in making the men of more recent times superior to those of the past, may be considered to have very little weight as an *a priori* objection to the consideration of the Thirteenth Century as representing the highest stage in human accomplishment. . . .

To most people the greater portion of surprise with regard to the assertion of the Thirteenth as the greatest of centuries will be the fact that the period thus picked out is almost in the heart of the Middle Ages. It would be not so amazing if the fifth century before Christ, which produced such marvelous accomplishments in letters and art and philosophy among the Greeks, was chosen as the greatest of human epochs. There might not even be so much of unpreparedness of mind if that supreme century of Roman History, from fifty years before Christ to fifty years after, were picked out for such signal notice. We have grown accustomed, however, to think of the Middle Ages as hopelessly backward in the opportunities they afforded men for the expression of their intellectual and artistic faculties, and above all for any development of that human liberty which means so much for the happiness of the race and must constitute the basis of any real advance worth while talking about in human affairs. It is this that would make the Thirteenth Century seem out of place in any comparative study for the purpose of determining proportionate epochal greatness. The spirit breathes where it will, however, and there was a mighty wind of the spirit of human progress abroad in that Thirteenth Century, whose effects usually miss proper recognition in history, because people fail to group together in their minds all the influences in our modern life that come to us from that precious period. . . .

In taking up the thesis, The Thirteenth the Greatest of Centuries, it seems absolutely necessary to define just what is meant by the term great, in its application to a period. An historical epoch, most people would concede at once, is really great just in proportion to the happiness which it provides for the largest possible number of humanity. That period is greatest that has done most to make men happy. Happiness consists in the opportunity to express whatever is best in us, and above all to find utterance for whatever is individual. An essential element in it is the

opportunity to develop and apply the intellectual faculties, whether this be of purely artistic or of thoroughly practical character. For such happiness the opportunity to rise above one's original station is one of the necessary requisites. Out of these opportunities there comes such contentment as is possible to man in the imperfect existence that is his under present conditions.

Almost as important a quality in any epoch that is to be considered supremely great, is the difference between the condition of men at the beginning of it and at its conclusion. The period that represents most progress, even though at the end uplift should not have reached a degree equal to subsequent periods, must be considered as having best accomplished its duty to the race. For purposes of comparison it is the amount of ground actually covered in a definite time, rather than the comparative position at the end of it, that deserves to be taken into account. This would seem to be a sort of hedging, as if the terms of the comparison of the Thirteenth with other centuries were to be made more favorable by the establishment of different standards. There is, however, no need of any such makeshift in order to establish the actual supremacy of the Thirteenth Century, since it can well afford to be estimated on its own merits alone, and without any allowances because of the stage of cultural development at which it occurred.

John Ruskin once said that a proper estimation of the accomplishments of a period in human history can only be obtained by careful study of three books—The Book of the Deeds, The Book of the Arts, and the Book of the Words, of the given epoch. The Thirteenth Century may be promptly ready for this judgment of what it accomplished for men, of what it wrote for subsequent generations, and of the artistic qualities to be found in its art remains. In the Book of the Deeds of the century what is especially important is what was accomplished for men, that is, what the period did for the education of the people, not alone the classes but the masses, and what a precious heritage of liberty and of social coordination it left behind. To most people it will appear at once that if the most important chapter of Thirteenth Century accomplishment is to be found in the Book of its Deeds and the deeds are to be judged according to the standard just given of education and liberty, then there will be no need to seek further, since these are words for which it is supposed that there is no actual equivalent in human life and history for at least several centuries after the close of the Thirteenth.

As a matter of fact, however, it is in this very chapter that the Thirteenth Century will be found strongest in its claim to true greatness. The Thirteenth Century saw the foundation of the universities and their gradual development into the institutions of learning which we have at the present time. Those scholars of the Thirteenth Century recognized that, for its own development and for practical purposes, the human intellect can best be trained along certain lines. For its preliminary training, it seemed to them to need what has since come to be called the liberal arts, that is, a knowledge of certain languages and of logic, as well as a thorough consideration of the great problems of the relation of man to his Creator, to his fellowmen, and to the universe around him. Grammar, a much wider subject than we now include under the term, and philosophy constituted the undergraduate studies of the universities of the Thirteenth Century. For the practical purposes of life, a division of post-graduate study had to be made so as to suit the life design of each individual, and accordingly the faculties of theology, for the training of divines; of medicine, for the training of physicians; and of law, for the training of advocates, came into existence. . . .

It is, however, much more for what it accomplished for the education of the masses than for the institutions it succeeded in developing for the training of the classes, that the Thirteenth Century merits a place in the roll of fame. This declaration will doubtless seem utterly paradoxical to the ordinary reader of history. We are very prone to consider that it is only in our time that anything like popular education has come into existence. As a matter of fact, however, the education afforded to the people in the little towns of the Middle Ages, represents an ideal of educational uplift for the masses such as has never been even distantly approached in succeeding centuries. The Thirteenth Century developed the greatest set of technical schools that the world has ever known. The technical school is supposed to be a creation of the last half century at the outside. These medieval towns, however, during the course of the building of their cathedrals, of their public buildings and various magnificent edifices of royalty and for the nobility, succeeded in accomplishing such artistic results that the world has ever since held them in admiration, and that this admiration has increased rather than diminished with the development of taste in very recent years.

Nearly every one of the most important towns of England during the Thirteenth Century was erecting a cathedral. Altogether some twenty cathedrals remain as the subject of loving veneration and of frequent visitation for the modern generation. There was intense rivalry between these various towns. Each tried to surpass the other in the grandeur of its cathedral and auxiliary buildings. Instead of lending workmen to one another there was a civic pride in accomplishing for one's native town whatever was best. Each of these towns, then, none of which had more than twenty thousand inhabitants except London, and even that scarcely more, had to develop its own artist-artisans for itself. That they succeeded in doing so demonstrates a great educational influence at work in arts and crafts in each of these towns. We scarcely succeed in obtaining such trained workmen in proportionately much fewer numbers even with the aid of our technical schools, and while these Thirteenth Century people did not think of such a term, it is evident that they had the reality and that they were able to develop artistic handicraftsmen—the best the world has ever known.

With all this of education abroad in the lands, it is not surprising that great results should have flowed from human efforts and that these should prove enduring even down to our own time. Accomplishments of the highest significance were necessarily bound up with opportunities for self-expression, so tempting and so complete, as those provided for the generations of the Thirteenth Century. The books of the Words as well as of the Arts of the Thirteenth Century will be found eminently interesting, and no period has ever furnished so many examples of wondrous initiative, followed almost immediately by just as marvelous progress and eventual approach to as near perfection as it is perhaps possible to come in things human. Ordinarily literary origins are not known with sufficient certainty as to dates for any but the professional scholar to realize the scope of the century's literature. Only a very little consideration, however, is needed to demonstrate how thoroughly representative of what is most enduring in literary expression in modern times, are the works in every country that had origin in this century.

There was not a single country in civilized Europe which did not contribute its quota and that of great significance to the literary movement of the time. In Spain there came the Cid and certain accompanying products of ballad poetry which form the basis of the national literature and are still read not only by scholars and amateurs, but even by the people generally, because of the supreme human interest in them. In England, the beginning of the Thirteenth Century saw the putting into shape of the Arthur Legends in the form in which they were to appeal most nearly to subsequent generations. Walter Map's work in these was, as we shall see, one of the great literary accomplishments of all time. Subsequent treatments of the same subject are only slight modifications of the theme which he elaborated, and Mallory's and Spenser's and even our own Tennyson's work derive their interest from the humanly sympathetic story, written so close to the heart of nature in the Thirteenth Century that it will always prove attractive.

In Germany, just at the same time, the Nibelungen-Lied was receiving the form in which it was to live as the great National epic. The Meistersingers also were accomplishing their supreme work of Christianizing and modernizing the old German and Christian legends which were to prove such a precious heritage of interest for posterity. In the South of Germany the Minnesingers sang their tuneful strains and showed how possible it was to take the cruder language of the North, and pour forth as melodious hymns of praise to nature and to their beloved ones as in the more fluent Southern tongues. Most of this was done in the old Suabian high German dialect, and the basis of the modern German language was thus laid. The low German was to prove the vehicle for the original form of the animal epic or stories with regard to Reynard, the Fox, which were to prove so popular throughout all of Europe for all time thereafter.

In North France the Trouvères were accomplishing a similar work to that of the Minnesingers in South Germany, but doing it with an original genius, a refinement of style characteristic of their nation, and a finish of form that was to impress itself upon French literature for all subsequent time. Here also Jean de Meun and Guillaume de Lorris wrote the Romance of the Rose, which was to remain the most popular book in Europe down to the age of printing and for some time thereafter. At the South of France the work of the Troubadours, similar to that of the Trouvères and yet with a spirit and character all its own, was creating a type of love songs that the world recurs to with pleasure whenever the lyrical aspect of poetry becomes fashionable. The influence of the Troubadours was to be felt in Italy, and before the end of the Thirteenth Century there were many writers of short poems that deserve a place in what is best in literature. Men like Sordello, Guido Cavalcanti, Cino da Pistoia, and Dante da Maiano, deserve mention in any historical review of literature, quite apart from the influence which they had on their great successor, the Prince of Italian poets and one of the immortal trio of the world's supreme creative singers—Dante Alighieri. With what must have seemed the limit of conceit he placed himself among the six greatest poets, but posterity breathes his name only with those of Homer and Shakespeare.

Dante, in spite of his giant personality and sublime poetic genius, is not an exception nor a solitary phenomenon in the course of the century, but only a worthy culmination of the literary movement which, beginning in the distant West in Spain and England, gradually worked eastward quite contrary to the usual trend of human development and inspired its greatest work in the musical Tuscan dialect after having helped in the foundation of all the other modern languages. Dante is the supreme type of the Thirteenth Century, the child of his age, but the great master whom medieval influences have made all that he is. That he belongs to the century there can be no doubt, and of himself alone he would be quite sufficient to lift any period out of obscurity and place it among the favorite epochs, in which the human mind found one of those opportune moments for the expression of what is sublimest in human thought.

It is, however, the book of the Arts of the Thirteenth Century that deserves most to be thumbed by the modern reader intent on learning something of this marvelous period of human existence. There is not a single branch of art in which the men of this generation did not accomplish excelling things that have been favorite subjects for study and loving imitation ever since. Perhaps the most marvelous quality of the grand old Gothic cathedrals, erected during the Thirteenth Century, is not their impressiveness as a whole so much as their wonderful finish in detail. It matters not what element of construction or decoration be taken into consideration, always there is an approach to perfection in accomplishment in some one of the cathedrals that shows with what thoroughness the men of the time comprehended what was best in art, and how finally their strivings after perfection were rewarded as bountifully as perhaps it has ever been given to men to realize.

Of the major arts—architecture itself, sculpture and painting—only a word will be said here since they will be treated more fully in subsequent chapters. No more perfect effort at worthy worship of the Most High has ever been accomplished than is to be seen in the Gothic cathedrals in every country in Europe as they exist to the present day. While the movement began in North France, and gradually spread to other countries, there was never any question of mere slavish imitation, but on the contrary in each country Gothic architecture took on a national character and developed into a charming expression of the special characteristics of the people for whom and by whom it was made. English Gothic is, of course, quite different to that of France; Spanish Gothic has a character all its own; the German Gothic cathedrals partake of the heavier characteristics of the Northern people, while Italian Gothic adds certain airy decorative qualities to the French model that give renewed interest and inevitably indicate the origin of the structures.

In painting, Cimabue's work, so wonderfully appreciated by the people of Florence that spontaneously they flocked in procession to do honor to his great picture, was the beginning of modern art. How much was accomplished before the end of the century will be best appreciated when the name of Giotto is mentioned as the culmination of the art movement of the century. As we shall see, the work done by him, especially at Assisi, has been a source of inspiration for artists down even to our own time, and there are certain qualities of his art, especially his faculty for producing the feeling of solidity in his paintings, in which very probably he has never been surpassed. Gothic cathedrals in other countries did not lend themselves so well as subjects of inspiration for decorative art, but in every country the sacred books in use in the cathedral were adorned, at the command of the artistic impulse of the period, in a way that has made the illuminated missals and office books of the Thirteenth Century perhaps the most precious that there are in the history of book-making.

It might be thought that in sculpture, at least, these Thirteenth-Century generations would prove to be below the level of that perfection and artistic expression which came so assuredly in other lines. It is true that most of the sculptures of the period have defects that make them unworthy of imitation, though it is in the matter of technique that they fail rather than in honest effort to express feelings appropriately within the domain of chiseled work. On the other hand there are some supreme examples of what is best in sculpture to be found among the adornments of the cathedrals of the period. No more simply dignified rendition of the God Man has ever been made in stone than the statue of Christ, which with such charming appropriateness the people of Amiens have called *le Beau Dieu*, their beautiful God, and that visitors to their great cathedral can never admire sufficiently, admirably set off, as it is, in its beautiful situation above the main door of the great cathedral. Other examples are not lacking, as for instance some of the Thirteenth-Century effigies of the French kings and queens at St. Denis, and some of the wonderful sculptures at Rheims. In its place as a subsidiary art to architecture for decorative purposes, sculpture was even more eminently successful. The best example of this is the famous Angel Chair of Lincoln, one of the most beautiful things that ever came from the hand of man and whose designation indicates the belief of the centuries that only the angels could have made it.

In the handicrafts most nearly allied to the arts, the Thirteenth Century reigns supreme with a splendor unapproached by what has been accomplished in any other century. The iron work of their gates and railings, even of their hinges and latches and locks, has been admired and imitated by many generations since. When a piece of it is no longer of use, or loosens from the crumbling woodwork to which it was attached, it is straightway transported to some museum, there to be displayed not alone for its antiquarian interest, but also as a model and a suggestion to the modern designer. This same thing is true of the precious metal work of the times also, at least as regards the utensils and ornaments employed in the sacred services. The chalices and other sacred vessels were made on severely simple lines and according to models which have since become the types of such sacred utensils for all times.

The vestments used in the sacred ceremonials partook of this same character of eminently appropriate handiwork united to the chastest of designs, executed with supreme taste. . . . It is said by those who are authorities in the matter that Thirteenth-Century needlework represents what is best in this line. It is not the most elaborate, nor the most showy, but it is in accordance with the best taste, supremely suitable to the objects of which it formed a part. It is, after all, only an almost inevitable appendix to the beautiful work done in the illumination of the sacred books, that the sacred vestments should have been quite as supremely artistic and just as much triumphs of art.

As a matter of fact, every minutest detail of cathedral construction and ornamentation shared in this artistic triumph. Even the inscriptions, done in brass upon the gravestones that formed part of the cathedral pavements, are models of their kind, and rubbings from them are frequently taken because of their marvelous effectiveness as designs in Gothic tracery.

Their bells were made with such care and such perfection that, down to the present time, nothing better has been accomplished in this handicraft, and their marvelous retention of tone shows how thorough was the work of these early bellmakers.

The triumph of artistic decoration in the cathedrals, however, and the most marvelous page in the book of the Arts of the century, remains to be spoken of in their magnificent stained-glass windows. Where they learned their secret of glassmaking we know not. Artists of the modern time, who have spent years in trying to perfect their own work in this line, would give anything to have some of the secrets of the glassmakers of the Thirteenth Century. Such windows as the Five Sisters at York, or the wonderful Jesse window of Chartres with some of its companions, are the despair of the modern artists in stained glass. The fact that their glass-making was not done at one, or even a few, common centers, but was apparently executed in each of these small medieval towns that were the site of a cathedral, only adds to the marvel of how the workmen of the time succeeded so well in accomplishing their purpose of solving the difficult problems of stained glasswork.

If, to crown all that has been said about the Thirteenth Century, we now add a brief account of what was accomplished for men in the matter of liberty and the establishment of legal rights, we shall have a reasonably adequate introduction to this great subject. Liberty is thought to be a word whose true significance is of much more recent origin than the end of the Middle Ages. The rights of men are usually supposed to have received serious acknowledgment only in comparatively recent centuries. The recalling of a few facts, however, will dispel this illusion and show how these men of the later middle age laid the foundation of most of the rights and privileges that we are so proud to consider our birthright in this modern time. The first great fact in the history of modern liberty is the signing of Magna Charta which took place only a little after the middle of the first quarter of the Thirteenth Century. The movement that led up to it had arisen amongst the guildsmen as well as the churchmen and the nobles of the preceding century. When the document was signed, however, these men did not consider that their work was finished. They kept themselves ready to take further advantage of the necessities of their rulers and it was not long before they had secured political as well as legal rights.

Shortly after the middle of the Thirteenth Century the first English parliament met, and in the latter part of that half century it became a formal institution with regularly appointed times of meeting and definite duties and privileges. Then began the era of law in its modern sense for the English people. The English common law took form and its great principles were enunciated practically in the terms in which they are stated down to the present day. Bracton made his famous digest of the English common law for the use of judges and lawyers and it became a standard work of reference. Such it has remained down to our own time. At the end of the century, during the reign of Edward I, the English Justinian, the laws of the land were formulated, lacunae in legislation filled up, rights and privileges fully determined, real-estate laws put on a modern basis, and the most important portions of English law became realities that were to be modified but not essentially changed in all the after time.

This history of liberty and of law-making, so familiar with regard to England, must be repeated almost literally with regard to the continental nations. In France, the foundation of the laws of the kingdom were laid during the reign of Louis IX, and French authorities in the history of law, point with pride, to how deeply and broadly the foundations of French jurisprudence were laid. Under Louis's cousin, Ferdinand III of Castile, who, like the French monarch, has received the title of Saint, because of the uprightness of his character and all that he did for his people, forgetful of himself, the foundations of Spanish law were laid, and it is to that time that Spanish jurists trace the origin of nearly all the rights and privileges of their people. In Germany there is a corresponding story. In Saxony there was the issue of a famous book of laws, which represented all the grants of the sovereigns, and all the claims of subjects that had been admitted by monarchs up to that time. In a word, everywhere there was a codification of laws and a laying of foundations in jurisprudence, upon which the modern superstructure of law was to rise.

This is probably the most surprising part of the Thirteenth Century. When it began men below the rank of nobles were practically slaves. Whatever rights they had were uncertain, liable to frequent violation because of their indefinite character, and any generation might, under the tyranny of some consciousless monarch, have lost even the few privileges they had enjoyed before. At the close of the Thirteenth Century this was no longer possible. The laws had been written down and monarchs were bound by them as well as their subjects. Individual caprice might no longer deprive them arbitrarily of their rights and hard won privileges, though tyranny might still assert itself and a submissive generation might, for a time, allow themselves to be governed by measures beyond the domain of legal justification. Any subsequent generation might, however, begin anew its assertion of its rights from the oldtime laws, rather than from the position to which their forbears had been reduced by a tyrant's whim.

Is it any wonder, then, that we should call the generations that gave us the cathedrals, the universities, the great technical schools that were organized by the trades guilds, the great national literatures that lie at the basis of all our modern literature, the beginnings of sculpture and of art carried to such heights that artistic principles were revealed for all time, and, finally, the great men and women of this century—for more than any other it glories in names that were born not to die—is it at all surprising that we should claim for the period which, in addition to all this, saw the foundation of modern law and liberty, the right to be hailed—the greatest of human history?

JOHN HERMAN RANDALL, JR.

MEDIEVAL CULTURE:

AN INDISPENSABLE LINK IN A CHAIN

Perhaps Walsh has gone too far in judging the thirteenth century as the greatest of centuries and in arguing by implication that the culture of the Middle Ages represents the most splendid of all human achievements. If one is unwilling to give to the Middle Ages the summit position in the world's cultural biography, can we still find for it some significant position? Many scholars have done so by viewing medieval cultural history primarily as an indispensable chapter which produced certain crucial developments that served as a prelude for later growth.

An example of this interpretation is supplied by John Herman Randall, Jr., a professor of philosophy at Columbia University. Randall's basic concerns are with the configuration of modern thought, especially in its scientic aspects. In his well-known *The Making of the Modern Mind* he felt it necessary to begin his account of modern intellectual history with the Middle Ages where he discerned the formulation of certain basic concepts without which the modern mind would be incomprehensible. The following essay, read at a conference on the humanities held at the University of Pennsylvania in 1941, seeks to identify the crucial medieval contributions that undergird modern thought. The student should try to isolate those elements of medieval cultural history which Randall holds to be significant in the larger picture of European thought. Perhaps he will be tempted to ask whether Randall is being too selective and thus guilty of overlooking vital aspects of medieval culture. Can a historian fully comprehend the genius of an age by fitting it into a larger historical continuum? This issue eternally arises to plague the historian who tries to make his knowledge of the past fit into a larger picture.

To dwell today on the continuity of a European culture once more in the midst of profound transformation is both irony and wisdom. It is irony, for there are many to tell us that the continuity has at last ended: it is an autopsy we have come to perform. It is wisdom, for there are others, with longer perspectives if no less touched by the tragedies of men, who recall how often civilization has died in Europe in the past, and wonder if this can truly be the end. For the history of Europe is the tale of one crisis and radical transformation after another. In contrast to the stability of other great civilizations, Europe has never crystallized, but has remained flexible in the face of the new problems its energies have created. It has been the very essence of its culture to be revolutionary. That is at once its tragic destiny and its chief glory. . . .

Men are aware of the changes, not the continuities in the present; for it is not continuities that demand the decision in which living consists. It is only in the past that they emerge, in the backward look of the historian. He can take the most revolutionary idea, that came to its discoverer with the insistent compulsion of novelty, and lay bare its long history, the gradual stages by which men slowly worked it out. In their revolt against the tyranny of intellectual authority, the pioneers of seventeenth-century science were conscious as few others of making a sharp break with the past, of wiping the slate clean and starting afresh with reason alone. Yet every one of them, we now know, was influenced in a thousand ways by the intellectual traditions on which he drew. And the very conceptions of reason they severally trusted for liberation came to them scarred with the battles and worn with the uses of their long histories. Descartes, of them all, had the utmost contempt for the past. Today he has won his fitting reward. For the foremost historian of medieval thought has calmly awarded him the post of the greatest of those

who stand in the long tradition that stems from St. Augustine. Especially is this continuity exhibited in the ideas that are so widely shared as to be a social possession. Though human nature be infinitely plastic, and the new-born babe can take on with ease any of the myriad forms of culture man has devised for himself, those institutionalized habits are themselves extraordinarily tough, and even when pressure has grown intolerable change but slowly. This toughness and vitality of intellectual traditions ardent revolutionaries learn to their sorrow, and nostalgic conservatives might well recall to their joy.

So the tale of the birth of modern European culture is a tale of continuity in change. The Middle Ages were invented by intellectual revolutionaries; they have now been destroyed by the historians and scholars of our generation, who have refused at last to take those boasts at their face value. To their leaders the Renaissance and the Reformation were desperate leaps back over the immediate past to the purity of an earlier and a wiser time. But the historian, soberly examining their claims to novelty—or to a novel antiquity—has pushed each of the distinctive ideas for which they stood further and further back into those very Middle Ages from which they were trying to escape. After all, we find, there were so many rebirths of ancient learning, so many reformations of the Church to its original holiness! The modernity of the Middle Ages has now been made a familiar story; and so has the medieval character of modern times. The scholars have pushed continuity ahead as well as backward. Modern ideas, we discover, did not really make their appearance till the Age of Enlightenment; what men earlier so bravely felt and thought was mere compromise and transition. And now the wise tell us that the heavenly city the eighteenth-century philosophers worshipped, and even their adored reason itself, link them, too, far

From John Herman Randall, Jr., "Unifying Factors in the Development of Modern Ideas," *Studies in Civilization*, University of Pennsylvania Bicentennial Conference (Philadelphia, 1941), pp. 105–18. Reprinted by permission of the University of Pennsylvania Press.

more closely to the great classic tradition of ages past than to the manifold irrationalisms of the present and the earthly purgatory to which we soberly look forward. St. Francis, we discover, was fundamentally modern, St. Marx medieval; and though not the whole truth, what we discover is true. There has been plenty of change, revolutionary change; but these revelations of our scholars may serve to illustrate the underlying continuity that permeates the development of European ideas from the very beginnings of Western civilization. There has been continuity in each of the major senses in which we find it exhibited in human histories. There has been the gradual and continuous change that, slowly accumulating, finally reaches spectacular achievement, or wins general acceptance. There has been the sheer persistence of intellectual materials, of assumptions, methods, and attitudes. And there has been the preservation of old ideas bent to new uses in the face of the novel experience.

In every field of European culture we find a continuous development in all these senses, with no sharp break, from the eleventh century on. . . . Intellectually, there is . . . the eager appropriation of more and more of the materials of the ancient world to meet the needs of new experience and the demands for a more potent method. All the problems of medieval and modern thought have arisen from the conflict of new knowledge and experience with traditional thought and values. The first clash came with the impact of Aristotelian science on the Augustinian wisdom in the twelfth century. The problems it generated, and the solutions with which men met them, have ever since remained the central and organizing problems of modern thought. The story of natural science, chief glory of modern times, once began in 1543 with Copernicus. It has been pushed back through the Paduan school of the fifteenth century, through the Masters of Paris in the fourteenth, to the Oxford group of the thirteenth and the School of Chartres in the twelfth. And modern philosophy, which every schoolboy knew sprang full-grown from the brow of Descartes, has revealed the potent traditions of later medieval times, which controlled the assumptions and dictated the methods of the seventeenth-century system-builders. Today the first modern philosopher is no longer Descartes, it is St. Thomas—unless indeed it be St. Augustine! Without a knowledge of those two intricate and subtle bodies of ideas, the subsequent course of the most modern European thinking grows quite unintelligible. . . .

. . . Whatever strand one singles out of the intellectual life of Western civilization, it proves to run back to what we still name the Middle Ages. No longer do we find a great gulf between the thirteenth century and what we used to call *the* Renaissance. The Middle Ages form the essential prelude to the development of modern ideas. They have become for us the first stage in modern times. . . .

. . . There is one continuity that asks for special emphasis. We have heard much of the unity of medieval civilization. That heritage too was not lost: European culture remained a unity. . . .

The unity of modern culture has not been such a unity of belief, of creed and dogma—though the Great Tradition, coming down through the Middle Ages from Greek thought, has given it a direction and a backbone in the midst of all the criticisms and extensions that moderns have made. It has not been a unity of faith—though there has been a persisting core of common and shared ideals and values, whatever the devices to which men have turned to give them social embodiment. The unity of modern culture has been a unity of problems confronted, of novel experience to be assimilated and understood, of novel beliefs to be worked somehow into the accepted pattern of living. European thinkers may have wandered into far lands: but again and again they have been called back to meet the same insistent difficulties. And those common problems have repeatedly forced divergent ideas and intellectual methods to face the compulsions of a common world and a common life. Starting with the same heritage of ideas, men developed them in diverse ways as their experience differed. Characteristic traditions, so widely shared as to be almost national, took form as early as the fourteenth century, when the philosophies the later world was to use as its tools and methods first received clear-cut expression. Their subtle but inescapable differences in attitude and approach reappear in the efforts of the intellectual pioneers of the seventeenth century to meet their new problems; they have persisted to this day, coloring political, religious, scientific, and philosophic thought.

Yet time and again these differing intellectual traditions have confronted the same fundamental problems of European social experience; and confronting them, have been led, each by its own route, to converge once more. There have been the problems of economic life, with different incidence, to be sure, in different lands, but still with a common pattern — the growth of commerce, the rise of business, the new ideals they generated, the new demands for an altered political control. There have been the common problems of industrial and technological civilization, which have forced all lands, each in its own way, to resort to the same devices, and to wage the same bitter quarrels over the same alternative methods. The same expanding commerce broke down the medieval social synthesis, and rendered both its institutions and its ideals inadequate; it provoked the same individualistic reaction, the same demand for the cardinal freedom to build up the modern world. All medieval and modern thought has been colored by the necessity of vindicating an ever growing individualism against the earlier medieval collectivism. The great intellectual movements — the Thomistic protest against Platonic realism, the rebellion of nominalism against Thomism, the Renaissance, the Reformation, the scientific thought of the seventeenth century, the Enlightenment, the Romantic rebellion, the liberalism of the nineteenth century — all have been successive waves of individualism in conduct, religion, and thought. Now that machine technology has built up a new social structure within the ruins of the old, quite irrelevant to the whole ideology of freedom and individuality, Europeans have had to reverse the whole current of their intellectual tradition to get back somehow to a collectivism adequate for a common industrial age. This helps to explain why the task is so hard, why it often seems easier to try to wipe out the past completely, instead of remolding it to meet new needs. Terrific pressure has called for heroic remedies.

And always there has been, for every tradition, the steady advance of science, with its new knowledge to be somehow reconciled with older beliefs, and its new methods to be assimilated and employed. Of all the factors unifying modern ideas, the inescapable fact of science has been the most influential. Just so in the thirteenth century it was likewise science, in the body of Aristotelian thought, that made possible the medieval synthesis. In its continuous if wayward advance, ever injecting new concepts and new methods into some painfully won adjustment, science has been the chief begetter of common intellectual problems, and the chief source of common intellectual methods. And even today it forms the main body of ideas that still remain a common possession of a divided Europe, the principal legacy of the rich achievements of the modern

era to those in the future who have the wit to wield it.

Both the continuity and the unity of European thought I wish to illustrate in terms of what has persisted during the entire medieval and modern period as the central unifying problem of all. It arose as the major issue in the thirteenth century: the differing positions taken determined the main outlines of the distinctive philosophies left as a heritage to modern times. It is still the basic intellectual issue in the European conflict today, lifting it above a mere struggle for power to genuine conflict of method — or, if we prefer, of ideals. It touches on and involves in the end every one of those major ideas that have formed the core of European intellectual life.

The thirteenth century knew it as the problem of the relation of reason to faith, of science to wisdom. In our sophistication, we are apt to phrase it differently. We call it the problem of the relation of science to human values, of our knowledge of the means and mechanisms by which we wield power over nature and over ourselves to the ends of action, the social ideals to which that power is directed. It is the question of the relation of Truth to Good. In what way is truth a means to the social good? What is the good which knowledge must serve, whose good is it in the end, and by what means is it to be determined?

This is the basic problem of a dynamic culture, one whose knowledge and therefore whose power is increasing and expanding. What it can do is forever coming into conflict with what it thinks it ought to do, with its accustomed pattern of behavior. Its faith — its inherited ideals and goals — is forever being upset by new knowledge, bringing the power to do new things. That new power carries with it the opportunity to realize old goals that had formerly seemed unattainable: it liberates from the bondage of ignorance and weakness. But it has its own compulsions: much that men had done with impunity it now makes impossible. To act in the familiar way with magnified power is become far too dangerous; or it is excluded by the other things men must do to fulfill the promise of their new resources. For the knowledge that is power is no mere instrument for effecting accustomed ends: it brings with it new goals of its own, and imposes its own conditions and responsibilities. It raises inescapably the question of the uses to which it can be put. Science, far from being irrelevant to values, impinges upon them at every turn. A society that lives by science is bound by the conditions and responsibilites of its power. . . .

Now the Middle Ages inherited from Greek thought two major traditions, two basic ways of dealing with this central problem. There is the way we may broadly call humanism, which makes of truth a means to achieving the good of man. It subordinates science to values, and takes knowledge as an instrument of power. And there is the way we may call naturalism, the way of scientific understanding. It finds truth no mere means, but an essential part of human good. For it, science is itself a supreme value, and there is no greater power than understanding itself. It is the glory of the medieval synthesis that it succeeded in uniting these two ways, in bringing together humanism and naturalism, in identifying science with wisdom and truth with good. It is the tragedy of Europe that since then the two ways, save for a brief coöperation again in the eighteenth century, have parted company. Wisdom has been divorced from science, truth from good, to their mutual confusion. The central problem of European culture has been to create a scientific humanism that would bring them together once more, as they were united in the thirteenth century.

Humanism the Middle Ages found in the philosophy of St. Augustine — the Platonic Augustine of the medieval thinkers, not the Manichaean of the Reformation. Science and naturalism it found in Aristotle — a science which made the problem easier than it has been in modern times, for it did not exclude man from its scope, and it saw human life not as something divorced from nature, but rather as the illustration of the fullest development of nature's processes. In the solution of St. Thomas, Aristotelian naturalism was nicely inserted within the framework of the Augustinian humanism, subtly transforming it at every turn, and creating the pattern of a scientific humanism as the central core of the European tradition.

Augustine set wisdom above science, as its source and criterion. He made truth depend on good, and subordinated knowledge to the control of values. Science in the end is of worth only in the measure that it contributes to the beatitude that is salvation. And that good which is the object of wisdom is also the object of faith; in the last analysis it is faith which supplies the goals which knowledge must serve. In contrast, St. Thomas made the vision of truth itself the highest good, that truth which is the source of all other truths. In understanding he found man's true well-being, and in knowledge the supreme excellence. The goals of human living are not

furnished by a faith imposed upon knowledge from above; they are found rather through the scientific analysis of the proper function of a rational animal.

Both Augustine and Thomas shared the common methods of reason and experience; but they meant quite different things by them. For Augustine, experience was something inner, private, and immediate; it was found by turning away from the world to the soul. And reason likewise was to be reached by analyzing the soul to discover the Master within. It was an object of intellectual intuition, of faith and loyalty. For Thomas, experience was open and public, the operation of man's powers in coöperation with the powers of this world. The starting-point of analysis was not the inward vision of the soul, but rather common observation and the obvious facts. And reason likewise was common to all; it was found in that most public of all human functions, language and communication. It was man's expression of the structure of his common world. The Augustinian philosophy of experience is the ancestor of all the idealisms of modern times; and, in its Ockhamite versions, which embraced a positivistic vision of science, of all the empiricisms. And all, in the end, fall back on faith to determine the goals of living. The Thomistic philosophy of being is the ancestor of all science, of all appeal to observation and testing, and to the rational principles by which facts are rendered intelligible.

In the seventeenth century the content of science changed: it now brought an understanding of nature rather than of human life, in terms that left life unintelligible. And the salvation men sought was no longer beatitude in eternity, but frankly the power and the glory of this world. The power to which the way of humanism made science an instrument became dominion over nature's forces; the end of knowledge was now to extend the bounds of human empire over nature. No longer was science the servant of wisdom, of human good. It was the handmaiden of a power aimed indifferently at good or ill — to the effecting of all things possible. Francis Bacon is the prophet and the consummate spokesman of what the humanist way made out of the new science. That science must indeed aim at "truth in speculation," but it must be a truth that will bring "freedom in operation" — the sheer power to do. And the understanding which the way of naturalism made the supreme value likewise ceased to be the understanding of human good. It became the sheer knowledge of what is, and of man as a part of the great Scheme of things. . . . To the humanist modern science brought the freedom of power, to the naturalist the freedom of understanding; but both it robbed of the treasure they had enjoyed during the Middle Ages, the freedom that is the service of the Good.

Yet the great and insistent problem all men were forced to face was the problem of Freedom, of finding liberation from the institutions of the medieval world, religious, economic, political. And since the goal of emancipation was so clear, the absence of wisdom did not at first prove serious. Men knew what they wanted, and proceeded to secure it. The good was given; the major question was how to secure it. By the eighteenth century the individualistic values were so widely accepted that a new synthesis proved possible. They were firmly established by both reason and experience. Because no sober man of common sense would presume to doubt them, it was not realized that only the intense need of liberation supported the generous and humane ideals of that Enlightenment synthesis. Men forgot that Reason supplies no premises of its own, but depends for the principles it so nicely elaborates on some accepted values: it binds men together only when they already share a common faith. And they forgot also that experience can unite men only when it is common, when it is the shared tradition of a group.

So long as Europe overwhelmingly demanded emancipation from the past, the fact that its intellectual methods of reason and experience were impotent of themselves to unite men in a common wisdom was of little practical moment. But the difficulties broke out so soon as men passed from mere emancipation to the harder tasks of constructing new institutions. Even before the coming of industrialism, the major problem of European thought had begun to shift from Freedom to Organization. At first, it was the need to integrate the national cultures of the post-Napoleonic world. Then, with ever increasing pressure, came the problem of organizing economic life to realize the promise of technology, and to enable it to continue functioning. Freedom was no longer enough; there was need of wisdom once more. Where could men find the necessary wisdom? By what ideas could they be reunited? In a culture drenched with generations of struggle to achieve individualism, how could they enlist the coöperative support of men to effect the necessary social control and directions of technology?

The common need of unification turned men again to their two inherited methods of achieving wisdom. Following the way of humanism, they again sought a wisdom that would control and direct science and its terrifying power over nature. Science was irrelevant to human good, the moderns had taught; it was disruptive and chaotic. It must be brought to order by a unifying social faith in some other superior good. In that good was to be the true embodiment of reason and experience.

In its desperate search for social organization, Europe has tried a number of different unifying ideas: . . . it appealed to the Church . . .; the mighty and potent idea of the Nation; the idea of the Working-Class, of the Toiling and Oppressed Masses. . . .

These are all potent ideas, rooted in the very core of European culture; their power for good or ill seems still inexhaustible. They form the several unifying faiths to which Europe has fled in its bitter struggle to escape centuries of individualism. They are the social goods set up to control all knowledge, the wisdom that is to overcome the anarchy of science. That truth is not true which does not derive from them and their strength; that knowledge is false which does not lead men to their Truth. They repeat, in our day and generation, the pattern of the old Augustinian solution, the ministry of all science to the power that can bring salvation.

Over against them is set the other method, the method that founds wisdom, not on some social faith external to science, but on science itself. For it, the good that will unite men in its service is not to be imposed on knowledge from without. It must be itself determined by knowledge, and it must embrace science, not dominate it. The understanding and power of science, it holds, are essential to wisdom: truth is the source of good. The values that will bind men together are not to be found in a superior Reason that can be reached only by faith, or in an Experience that is an appeal to a limited and divisive tradition. They are discoverable only in a common and public reason and experience indissolubly married in the critical methods of scientific inquiry and verification. This way, the way of a scientific humanism, repeats today the wisdom of St. Thomas.

These two ways of relating science and wisdom, truth and good, were struggling in the Middle Ages; they are still in conflict today. They are the legacy of centuries of European thought upon its most profound problem. They are the two ideas between which men can choose in their common need. The goal is set: we must learn how to organize our society so that we may live with technology, and with those peoples who have already taken its demands seriously. The issue that still remains open, the great question at stake in the present tragic conflict, concerns the method of achieving that organization. We too can resort to a unifying faith that will raise some social good above truth, the good of the nation, or the good of a class. . . . We too can turn to the wisdom of Augustine. Or we can adopt the fuller wisdom of Thomas. We can learn from the great Augustinian tradition, the great tradition of humanism, that science must be bent to the service of the Good: in disinterested science, in a science that disdainfully refuses to take account of values, in a science that deliberately eschews wisdom, there is no salvation. But the Good to which science ministers must be a good itself determined by scientific methods, a good of which science is an essential part.

CRANE BRINTON

MEDIEVAL CULTURE:
AN ENTITY SUI GENERIS

Many historians would protest what Voltaire, Walsh, and Randall have tried to do in the preceding selections. They would insist that medieval culture can best be comprehended if it is examined in its own right and judged as an entity with its own characteristics. Crane Brinton, a Harvard scholar who is one of America's most eminent historians, provides a case for this view. Brinton's major scholarly works have been devoted to the era of the French Revolution. However, his is the kind of mind that expands from specialized research to a wider vision of human achievement. In *Ideas and Men* he tried to synthesize the total history of Western culture. This task required placing the Middle Ages in some meaningful relationship to a larger picture. After examining various aspects of medieval thought and expression, Brinton wrote the following passage which he entitled "An Evaluation of Medieval Culture."

Brinton asks the reader to identify the over-arching concepts which characterize medieval culture and to appreciate their uniqueness. The student must judge whether medieval culture makes more sense when approached from this perspective than when treated in the way the previous commentators have done. The issue raised here is basic to all historical studies: the problem of the unique, nonrepetitive character of each moment in man's existence. For if medieval history and culture are to be judged *sui generis*, then must we not judge our own culture without reference to past models? Does this make the study of the past essentially meaningless? Or can we draw a deeper meaning by grasping what is unique in each episode of the past?

The historian who attempts to make generalizations about the rise, maturing, and fall of cultures (or societies, or civilizations) confronts in the Middle Ages a serious problem. The more common classification adopted by such historians—or philosophers of history—in recent times is to set up a Graeco-Latin culture lasting roughly from the Greeks of Homer to the Romans of the fifth century A.D. and a modern Western culture beginning in the Dark Ages and going on to the present (which present many of them regard as the decadent last days of our culture). . . . Now in such a view, the Dark Ages appears as the infancy, the Middle Ages as the youth, of our modern culture. The Middle Ages, in other words, is not in itself a culture. On the other hand, many of those who have most deeply studied the Middle Ages, including most of the modern lovers of the period, regard it as, so to speak, a culture-in-itself, not merely a prelude to our own. They think of the Middle Ages as rising to a peak in the thirteenth century and then falling off in the next two centuries. Those of them who most dislike the modern world think of the decline as continuous to the present. . . .

With these warnings, we may return to the problem with which we set out. It is possible, though the formula is oversimple, to reconcile the view of the Middle Ages as a beginning, a youth, of modern Western society with the view of the Middle Ages as in itself a peak, a flourishing, a kind of maturity. If you focus on the political and economic integration of the territorial subgroups in Western society (nations), then there are two clear sequences in our history—one from the diversity of independent, economically primitive city-states, tribes, and nations of roughly 1000 B.C. to the unified, wealthy, complex One World of the Roman Empire, and another from the extreme feudal disintegration and economic primitiveness of the Dark Ages to the present, when there are but seventy-odd independent political units in the whole world, when economic development has reached heights unknown before, and when this process of integration seems to many well on its way toward a universal state. If you focus on smaller and more detailed problems, such as that of the development of representative parliamentary institutions, or that of the growth of banking, or of scientific thought, you find a low point which is almost a break (not quite) in the Dark Ages, and you find unmistakable beginnings in the Middle Ages, from which development has been in some sense continuous to the present. In such lights, the Middle Ages appear clearly as a beginning of things modern.

If, however, you focus as well as you can on medieval culture *as a whole*, on what we have somewhat weakly called a "way of life," on medieval notions of right and beauty and man's place in the scheme of things, you can hardly help accepting something of the thesis that the Middle Ages deserves to be ranked as an achievement in living different from, though clearly related to, our own. You cannot read Dante, or Aquinas, or Chaucer, or look at the cathedral of Chartres, or even study a detailed map of a medieval self-sustaining manor, without feeling that you are in another world. Indeed that world will probably seem to a twentieth-century American who will take the trouble to live himself into both, a world more different from his own than that of fifth-century Athens.

We can here do no more than indicate certain broad generalizations about this medieval world, certain notes of medieval culture, certain signs of its taste or flavor.

First of all, there is the immediacy, the common-sense acceptance, of the supernatural, which we have of course already encountered. There are millions of men and women in the twentieth century who as good Christians believe in Christianity. Many of them would be gravely offended were we to suggest that their belief is one whit less strong than that of their medieval ancestors. But even for believers today the boundaries of the supernatural have been pushed back, and whole regions of their conscious life made subject to the regularities we think of as natural. They may pray for rain; but they also read the weather reports drawn up by meteorologists who, whatever their religion, do not believe that God interferes directly with cold fronts. Moreover, there are today millions of men and women —no one knows quite how many—who do not believe in the immortality of the human soul, and for whom, therefore, the notion of heaven and hell is meaningless, or actually offensive. There are a great many more for whom heaven and hell have become very vague concepts indeed; they believe in immortality, heaven, and hell, but as rather remote

From Crane Brinton, *Ideas and Men, The Story of Western Thought*, 2nd ed., pp. 190–201. © 1963. Reprinted by permission of Prentice-Hall, Inc., Englewood Cliffs, N. J.

things, closer acquaintance with which can be indefinitely postponed. Hell, particularly, has for many moderns lost its bite; it has become for them a place for distinguished sinners only, much like the Greek hell.

Not so for the men of the Middle Ages. God, as we have pointed out, was as real, as present for them, as the weather is for us, heaven or hell for each man as certain as sunshine or rain. Medieval intellectuals for the most part held that God made things happen on this earth in accordance with certain regularities basically directed for man's good—that is, that the universe was basically moral and therefore that much was known and predictable. Their God was a reliable God, in something of the same sense that modern scientists think nature reliable. Some of this sense of regularity, if only in the form of what we like to call common sense, undoubtedly was shared by the masses, or they could hardly have gone about their daily living. None the less, there is widespread among the medieval masses, and even among the intellectuals, a feeling of the irrationality, the uncertainty, the *unexpectedness* of life on this earth. At one most obvious level, this comes out in the prevalence of what we now call superstition in the Middle Ages. The slightest dip into medieval writing brings up an example—that eggs laid on Good Friday are good to put out fires, that elves sour milk, that the king's touch can cure scrofula, and many, many more. True, many of these superstitions are still alive, and we have added some of our own. But the range and depth of medieval superstition puts ours in the shade. . . .

The immediacy of the supernatural (of which superstition is merely the trivial and undignified part) is clear in a work that must at least be sampled by anyone attempting to understand the Middle Ages. The hell, purgatory, and heaven of Dante's *Divine Comedy* were as real to him as London was to Dickens. His hell, as has often been remarked, is the most concrete of the three. Dante was a very great poet, but he was also an embittered and exiled politician who saw his Florence and his Italy take a course that outraged his moral sense. He put his enemies in hell—in his book—as part of a polemic process as natural to him as the much more abstract fulminations that have to satisfy a modern Trotskyite. The quality of fantasy, which a modern attempting to deal with the supernatural can hardly avoid, is simply not in Dante's *Inferno*. He takes his reader to a hell so convincing that any

attempt of an illustrator to paint it takes the edge off, makes it less true. This applies notably to the work of the best-known of Dante's illustrators, the French nineteenth-century artist Gustave Doré, who only succeeds in making Dante's hell what we call "romantic"—which it is not.

Nevertheless, the romantic writers of the nineteenth century—Walter Scott will come to mind at once—found something they were looking for in the Middle Ages, which they brought back into good cultural repute. That something they distorted by overemphasis, but it is there, and is the second note of medieval culture we must try to bring out. It is another phase of the medieval acceptance of the supernatural as natural. Truth, we like to say, is stranger than fiction. But we moderns do not really mean by that saying that we believe our daily life is filled with wonders. We mean, for example, that out of hundreds of real murder cases that come up in our courts *one* shows a degree of human depravity and ingenuity that goes beyond the imaginings of the wildest of detective fiction. The overwhelming majority of actual murders we know to be by no means up to fictional standards in interest. They are, in fact, routine affairs, as crime goes. Put in more general terms, we accept a sort of commonsense statistical view, in which instances are strung along a classical distribution curve; 100 per cent is as rare as 0 per cent, and there is a great bulge around 50 per cent.

The men of the Middle Ages were not statistically minded. We should overdo paradox if we asserted that for the medieval mind the rare instance was as common as the usual instance; but we should not greatly overdo paradox if we asserted that for the medieval mind the rare instance is, humanly speaking, quite as *typical*, quite as good as, or even better than, the usual instance as a sign to man of what the universe is like. The medieval man was not put off by the extreme; he expected it, looked for it, put it concretely into his art. The world of his imagination (he would not have admitted it *was* a world of mere imagination) was filled with horrors and marvels, perfect heroes and perfect villains, monsters and saints. And somehow, for most of us today, the monsters stay in the mind better than the saints. We find Dante's Inferno more convincing than his Paradise. Were those of us who have been exposed at all to medieval cultural history to call up at random some sort of concrete image of the Middle Ages, the most frequent would probably be

The Middle Ages

that brooding gargoyle of Notre Dame in Paris which has been reproduced on thousands of post cards.

This medieval push toward the extreme, toward the grotesque or toward the sublime, is often described as a striving toward the infinite, the endless, a refusal to accept the apparent limits of the material world of sense experience. A favorite practice among philosophical historians of culture—Spengler again will do as a concrete instance—is to contrast the Greek temple and the Gothic cathedral. The Greek temple stands foursquare on solid ground, accepting man's own commonplace dimensions, its basic shape no more heroic and heavenstorming than a box; the Gothic cathedral soars, transcends by daring inventions like the pointed arch and the flying buttress the vertical limitations of earlier building, seeks to translate into stone the longing of the medieval soul for the infinite. The Greek temple is geometry; the Gothic cathedral, algebra. The Greek temple accepts; the Gothic cathedral aspires. The Greek temple looks as if man made it; the Gothic cathedral looks as if the forest grew it.

Now these contrasts are fundamentally sound. A Greek temple and a Gothic cathedral are very different things, and the differences are in part expressions of different human attitudes toward the beautiful and the good. You can argue that there are material or technical reasons why the medieval architects built one way, the Greeks another—differing religious ceremonies needing to be housed, differing engineering techniques that set differing problems. But the fact remains that the men of the Middle Ages wanted something the Greeks had not wanted. They wanted height; the architects of the cathedral at Beauvais in France wanted it so much that they built the seemingly impossible apse that exists today and tried to construct an even more impossible tower, which unfortunately but quite naturally fell.

Nor is the famous simile of the Gothic forest without suggestiveness. We go from suggestiveness to the fanciful if we say that because their Germanic and Celtic ancestors had grown up in the primeval forest of a northern climate they built their church aisles to look like forest aisles, while the Greeks had no such pattern in their Mediterranean environment. But certainly the finished Gothic church, not only in its structural lines but in its ornamental details —the leafy foliage of its capitals, the tracery of its vaults, its statues, which seem to grow out of the whole building, the thousand details of ornamentation flowering from it—looks less planned, more spontaneous, than a Greek building, or one of our own.

The impression is helped by the fact that very few Gothic cathedrals were built all of a piece. They were strung out over several generations, as the money came in, and the builders of each part built in the variant of the Gothic style fashionable in their day. (Remember that the practice of picking from the grab bag of history a particular style, Doric, Gothic, Colonial, Mission, and the like is strictly limited to modern times; until these times men have always built in their own contemporary style, just as, for example, they always dressed their actors in the style of their own day.) So the favorite Gothic church of the connoisseur, the cathedral of Chartres in France, still has in its crypt the round arches of the pre-Gothic romanesque style; it has on its west front a south tower in the simple, relatively unornamented style of early Gothic, a north tower richly ornamented in a later style, and elsewhere statues, porches, rose windows made by many different hands over several centuries. Yet the building is a magnificent whole, and no hodgepodge; neither, of course, is a forest.

This second note of medieval culture—call it spontaneity, imaginative exuberance, the search for the extraordinary, the striking, the romantic, the striving for the infinite, no phrase quite spans the reality—this note can be heard in everything medieval. We have chosen to find it in architecture, but it could be found equally well in the rich tangle of medieval literature. Dante's was—for a man of the Middle Ages—a disciplined mind, and his style has none of the looseness, quaintness, exuberance of the knightly romances; but the effect of his epic as a whole, when contrasted with that of his master Vergil, is quite like that of a Gothic cathedral contrasted with a Greek temple. Even his great political work, the Latin *De Monarchia*, is a welter of argument and fancy compared with the logical neatness of Aristotle's political writing.

A third note of medieval culture, less pleasing to its modern admirers, is the frequence of violence. Murder and sudden death were not as unusual to medieval man as to modern man. We must be careful here, as always with big generalizations. The lover of the Middle Ages may well reply that modern warfare kills far more effectively than did the medieval, that nothing in medieval annals is any worse than what went on in the concentration camps of the last war. He is right, of course, but he must be reminded of our modern successes in medicine and in provisioning large populations. For all our terrible wars, we have up to the moment maintained a larger population in the West than ever before. But the real point is the absence in the Middle Ages, in spite of the Christian tradition, of a feeling for the relative permanence of human life. Men simply did not expect life to be without hazard. Indeed, they saw the hand of God in the decision of violence. One of the best known of medieval institutions is that of trial by combat, a procedure limited to conflicts among the knightly class. As a last resort, a dispute could be settled by combat between the disputants or between their champions, and the decision was seen as the direct intervention of God who gave victory to the right. Gradually through the Middle Ages this procedure was supplanted by legal processes that became the foundation of our own.

We need not labor the point. The upper classes, heirs of the rough fighter of the Dark Ages, carried on well into the more advanced culture of the Middle Ages the tradition of violence in which their fathers had been bred. We have seen how this tradition was gradually formalized into the mock violence of late chivalry. The Church and the growing territorial states both had a part in the gradual substitution of orderly processes of law for this appeal to force. Growing trade brought with it growing protection of industry and commerce, until the robber baron was tamed. Even so, the grave social conflicts of the later Middle Ages brought renewed violence of another kind, and terrible plagues, like the Black Death of the fourteenth century, added their toll. Later medieval literature and art . . . came to be obsessed with death.

If we put all this together, we have a whole that does not altogether fit with some of the things we have said earlier about the Middle Ages. Our notes sum up as a pervading sense of the uncertainties and irregularities of life, indeed as the *cultivation* of these qualities. We have a culture that hardly distinguishes between the supernatural and the natural, a culture of credulity and superstition, a culture of unearthly mysticism and of very earthly crudity and violence, a culture of extremes and contradictions, a culture forever oscillating between a

search for the Holy Grail and a search for the next meal. What has become of the moderation, the "whiggishness" of Aquinas? Where is that quality of maturity that made us rank the thirteenth century in some respects with the fifth century B.C.? It looks as if this medieval culture really were a sort of childhood or at best obstreperous youth, for which the gargoyle is a fitting symbol.

We shall have to let many of our contradictions about the Middle Ages stand. Indeed, they can stand the more serenely because, though all human cultures contain contradictory, logically mutually inconsistent elements, the Middle Ages is conspicuous in Western history as an age of strongly marked contrasts. One of the firmest notes of medieval culture is that of contrast and contradiction, at its clearest perhaps in the contradiction between the high Christian ideals of its formal culture, of Scholasticism and chivalry, and the "spotted actuality." Just because the Middle Ages at their best took the Christian way of life so seriously, indeed so literally, does the coarseness, the violence, the eccentricity, and also the *routine* and dullness, of much of their daily life force itself on our attention.

But if our notes of other-worldliness, belief in the supernatural, striving after the infinite, violence, and contrast between Christian ideals and a not very Christian performance must stand, we must none the less make several qualifications in them. First, though much of medieval culture seems like the culture of an age of immaturity—credulity, love of extremes, more pleasing traits like the freshness of imagination, the unbuttoned joy, the simplicity that so captivated the later romantics—the notion that medieval culture did attain a real maturity is by no means false. This maturity comes out clearly in almost any form of medieval art. We have in our account perhaps focused overmuch on an analytical approach that has neglected the chronological development of medieval culture. The Middle Ages are by no means all of one piece. They have their own youth, their own primitive stage, which we call the Dark Ages. They flower in the thirteenth, to modern Neo-Scholastics the "greatest of centuries." They have their own falling off in the fourteenth and fifteenth centuries.

Let us take a few examples. The world of the *Chanson de Roland*, the ninth-century world as it was preserved in epic tradition, has the qualities of the youthful, the primitive. It is a simple, dignified world of strong men with clear-cut loyalties. It is a simple world economically and socially, as far as we can discern these matters. But no sensible man would call the world reflected in Dante's *Divine Comedy* a simple, youthful world. Dante, like Aquinas, is a mature man living in a most complex civilization. . . . .

This cycle from youth to age appears perhaps at its clearest in medieval church architecture. Here the beginnings lie in the rather heavy, round-arched romanesque of the early Middle Ages. With the invention of the pointed arch true Gothic begins. In its early period—which some today think its best—Gothic architecture is relatively simple. It is content with vaulting lighter and higher than romanesque, a vaulting that does not, however, seem to strain for height. Its carving is natural, graceful, and subordinated to the lines of the building. Its statues are also skillfully adapted to the architect's purpose. The best of them—for example, those of the west front at Chartres—have the quality historians of art have labeled "primitive," a quality also found in Athenian sculpture just before the great age of Phidias. The window tracery—perhaps the easiest sign of a particular Gothic period for the layman—is still simple. Gradually the style gets more complicated, more ornamented. There is a mature middle period in which daring use of the flying buttress and other devices enables the architects to give an impression of great height, and to flood their churches with light from many windows. Sculpture attains a perfection that is not the realism of the Greeks, but another high realism with no trace of the primitive distortion of anatomy. Such, for instance, are the statues of the cathedrals at Amiens and Rheims. Window tracery is freer, more flowing, more decorated.

Then in the later medieval centuries comes the overripeness which is a sign that the style is growing old. Notably in France there is a striving for impossible height which brings on disaster like the fall of the central tower at Beauvais. Ornamentation, both inside and outside the building, gets out of hand, so that one finds western fronts like that at Rouen which are adorned like a wedding cake. The Virgin no longer smiles naturally—she smiles ineffably. The natural is again distorted, but melodramatically, not simply as with the primitives; or the distortion is "realistic," and the Virgin looks like an attractive peasant girl. The window tracery, carrying out in great complexity the suggestion of the flame, sets the tone for what in France especially is called the *flamboyant* (flaming) period of late Gothic. The word "flamboyant" itself has come in this way to suggest overelaboration and ostentation. In England, later Gothic did not follow French models into striving for great height. Characteristically, those who believe the English are congenitally moderate like to say, English architects never did attempt the soaring naves and towers of the French. Yet English Gothic, too, shows the excesses of an exhausted style. The tracery of its later period, instead of following the theme of a flame, adopts that of vertical lines, and is called the "perpendicular." English perpendicular is thus in its ornamentation almost obsessed with the theme of height, and carries this out in tracery and vaulting.

So too in many other phases of cultural life one can trace in the later Middle Ages a falling off from an earlier balance and maturity. Even in formal philosophical thought, Scholasticism, after the great peak of the thirteenth century, begins to abandon the moderation of Aquinas and to spin out its arguments into the hair-splitting logic that gave its humanist opponents of the Renaissance good grounds for attack. We have already noted how in its decay chivalry became a series of formal acts divorced from the new life around it.

Our remaining difficulty is less serious than it may appear at first sight to be. We have maintained that especially in its great period the Middle Ages was a society of status in which the individual had a relatively secure place, a society in which the individual had known duties and rights, had *roots*. In contrast to our still very competitive modern society, we have argued that the medieval man had a peace of mind most of us moderns do not have. And yet the notes of medieval culture as we have tried to sum them up suggest anything but balance, moderation, security. Striving for the infinite, the ineffable, expecting the miraculous as we expect the statistically established, living in an age of violence and sudden death, never free from the menace of famine and disease, imperfectly protected by little more than custom and religious feeling from abuse of power by feudal authorities, the medieval man seems on the surface to have been intolerably insecure.

Three considerations should soften this contradiction. First, the balance we have found in medieval life is at its best only briefly, at the height of medieval culture in the twelfth, thirteenth, and early fourteenth centuries. Even then there was violence and uncertainty enough, but not the widespread violence and change we find in the fifteenth century, which was unmistakably a time of troubles for Western man.

Second, the phrase we have used above, "little more than custom and religious feeling," gives things a misleading modern twist. Again, in the high Middle Ages, custom and religious feeling were of incalculably more strength than we moderns can easily realize. Consider the relation of feudal lord and serf. If the lord were to beat the serf, seduce his daughter, take away his holding of land, there was in most of the medieval West no court, no police power, no civil organization to which the serf could apply for redress. There was no "constitution," no "bill of rights" in our modern sense. Even the English Magna Charta of 1215 was not, in fact, a legal document for the protection of the common man. But most lords did not commonly beat serfs, seduce their daughters, take away their livelihood. One simple set of facts shows this, and is a refutation of the widespread view that the Middle Ages was a chaos of poverty and oppression from which the West was somewhat inexplicably freed by the Renaissance and Reformation. From the eleventh century on, in spite of private wars, pestilence, famine, imperfect protection of commerce, the lot of the western European peasant steadily improved, at least until the breakup of the relatively self-sufficient manorial economy began to produce the modern uncertainty associated with production for sale in money. Serfs in France as well as in England gradually attained the status of freemen, not by any statute of wholesale emancipation as in nineteenth-century Russia, but by the slow working of economic and legal processes which, basically, enabled western European serfs to *earn* their freedom. They could not have done this in a chaotic society without the steady force of law and custom, nor, of course, in an absolutely fixed society of caste.

Finally, and most important, if hardest for us to understand, the security of medieval life was a very different thing from what we in the mid-twentieth century understand by security. The medieval man did not count on the kind of life on earth we accept as something given. He did not expect our physical comforts and luxuries, did not expect to avoid smallpox by vaccination, did not expect good roads, did not, in short, expect a thousand things we take for

granted. He was used to a hard life (in our terms), used to violence and uncertainty. Nothing in his philosophy—and we use the word philosophy advisedly, even of the common man—led him to expect that his life on earth could actually be very different from what it had always been. Such beliefs do not mean that the medieval man expected nothing, that he was never discontented. A shrewish wife, for instance, was as unpleasant to live with in the thirteenth as in the twentieth century.

But—and we are getting toward the heart of the matter—in no class of society would the thirteenth-century husband dream of trying to divorce his wife for "mental cruelty," or indeed for any other reason. Marriage was for him made in heaven, even if it were not well made. God had made marriage indissoluble. So too with many other aspects of human life, which we tend to regard as arrangements a man can make or unmake on his own initiative, and on his own responsibility. For the medieval man, much of his life was out of his own hands, in the hands of God working through society. We come back to the inescapable fact of the penetration of medieval life by the Christian attitude—not the Christian attitude at its perfection of spiritual striving, though the Middle Ages made a more natural place for this than our own—but the Christian attitude in its acceptance of the world as a place of probation, of toil and sorrow for the human soul. It is no accident that one of the best-known passages of Dante is

E'en la sua volontate è nostra pace;
Ella è quel mare al qual tutto si move
Ciò ch' ella crea, e che natura face.

"And in his will is our peace: that will is the ocean to which moves everything that it creates or that nature makes."

The Christian promise of salvation in an afterlife for the man or woman who lives on earth according to the precepts of the Church no doubt helps explain the Christian hold over the medieval mind. But the notion of religion as an opiate is a product of the modern mind, which thinks—or hopes—that suffering is not in the order of things. Christianity for the medieval man not merely gave promise of a better life in the next world; it gave to this uncertain life of violence, striving, imperfection, and want on earth meaning, limits, and purpose that came near to closing, for most men, the gap between what they had and what they wanted. Medieval man was more nearly than we *resigned* to a world he could not greatly change. He felt secure in the midst of what we should regard as insecurity—violence, physical want, hardship, even fears bred of ignorance of what we regard as natural phenomena. He felt this security precisely because he was keenly aware of his own weakness. He was neither ashamed of nor disturbed by this weakness; it was not his fault, nor was it, humanly speaking, anyone's fault—certainly one could not be impious enough to attribute the fault to God. The medieval man *felt* as truth what in a later philosopher, Leibnitz, was no more than a rather insincere intellectual formula—that this is the best of all possible worlds. Not a happy, not a contented world, for in such a world men would usurp the place of God. It was, quite simply, God's world.

PITIRIM A. SOROKIN

MEDIEVAL CULTURE:
A SPECIMEN OF A UNIVERSAL TYPE

As one grasps the substance of Brinton's description of medieval culture, he might wonder whether the values, ideas, and modes of expression it reflects are really so unique to this one era. Is it not possible that medieval culture is but one example of a universal approach to human existence? Have there not been comparable or even duplicate cultural patterns developed in other settings and in other ages? Many significant historians, exemplified best in our century by Oswald Spengler and Arnold J. Toynbee, have so argued. The final selection in this treatment of medieval culture offers a sample of this approach. Unfortunately, the sample must be abbreviated, for historians who take this approach to cultural history compose immense works to make their case. Their basic undertaking involves a comparative study of cultures and thus they are compelled to encompass all human experience. Such endeavors always end in multivolume productions of extreme complexity from which it is nearly impossible to extract a brief summation of the historians' ideas that makes sense.

Our spokesman for such an approach will be Pitirim Sorokin, a Russian-born sociologist who, after a stormy career in revolutionary Russia, came to the United States to take up a teaching and scholarly career at the University of Minnesota and Harvard. His major work is a massive, four-volume study entitled *Social and Cultural Dynamics*. This work begins with a generalized theory of culture too complex to summarize adequately. In essence, Sorokin reduces all varieties of cultural expression across all history to three basic types: ideational, sensate, and idealistic. Each of these types represents a distinctive mentality and a unique view toward life that permeates all modes of expression and activity. An "ideational" culture is one which sees reality primarily in terms of non-material being, which rejects the world revealed by the senses and which emphasizes the spiritual aspects of existence. It is a culture that is predominately *religious*. A "sensate" culture finds reality in the world of the senses; it rejects the spiritual, supersensory side of existence, and emphasizes physical well-being and control of the material world for the sake of human comfort and happiness. It is a culture that is fundamentally *scientific*. An "idealistic" culture is one that harmonizes and synthesizes the spiritual and material dimensions of life, usually with the intention of understanding and utilizing the material world in order to enhance the spiritual powers of man. In any particular society and age, one of these types dominates. By a dynamic process it gives way in time to another which in turn is replaced by still another or by the first.

After expounding his generalized theory of culture, Sorokin then surveys vast stretches of cultural history in an effort to relate the diverse particulars of cultural history to his generalized types. In his investigations of the art, music, literature, and philosophy of the twelfth, thirteenth, and early fourteenth centuries he finds a series of characteristics which fit together in such a way as to convince him that medieval culture is a prime example of one of his universal types. Moreover, he finds in the culture of that period a striking resemblance to cultures of other ages, especially that of fifth century B.C. Greece. Thus medieval culture emerges as a recurring type. Again the length of Sorokin's discussion calls for abbreviation. We will present only his treatment of medieval art, trusting that this material will illustrate his approach. In fact, he finds in medieval art features that are repeated in every other aspect of medieval culture; thus art becomes for him the chief index to the nature of medieval culture, to medieval literature, music, architecture, philosophy, science, theology, and political theory.

For the period from about the sixth to the thirteenth century the Christian art was the only major, logically integrated art. The division of high art into the religious and the secular was practically nonexistent at that period. The course of this Western Christian art was in essentials similar to that of the Byzantine art. Throughout this period it remained essentially Ideational with an Idealistic treatment of the empirical-visual phenomena. It is true that from about the ninth century (the Carlovingian Renaissance) the elements of Visualism began to filter into that art. Nevertheless, up to the end of the twelfth century Ideationalism was the dominant characteristic of that art. . . .

Being almost entirely religious, it is concerned mainly with religious, transcendental, and conceptual symbols, and when it deals with "worldly" scenes, animals, and persons, it represents them in an Ideational Idealistic form. Its method is the same whether it treats the figures of music, geometry, philosophy; or scenes of the Annunciation, of the

Last Judgment, of the Visitation, of the Crucifixion; or plants and symbolic animals like Tritons, centaurs, griffons; not to mention the figures of Christ and the saints and the virtues. If after the eleventh century the figures of the Vices and devils are not particularly attractive, the reason is that the negative values had of necessity to be negatively idealized, that is, exaggerated in their negative traits. But the tide of Sensate Visualism was rising.

Later on I shall present detailed data as to the manifestation of this rise of Visualism. For the present it is enough to mention a few of its symptoms. Representation of animal and plant lore becomes more pronounced in the art of the twelfth century, as compared with that of the preceding period. Half-moral historical scenes and figures of a secular character, like the images of Alexander the Great, of Roland, of the Arthurian cycle and the Knights of the Round Table, of the minstrels and troubadours, and so on, occur more and more often. The images of women more often appear now. And the technique begins

From Pitirim A. Sorokin, *Social and Cultural Dynamics*, 4 vols. (New York, 1937), Vol. 1, pp. 319–26. Copyright 1937, The Bedminster Press. Reprinted by permission.

to change, though slightly and almost imperceptibly, nevertheless definitely in the direction of Visualism.

This rising tide of Visualism and ebb of Ideationalism resulted, in the thirteenth and partly in the fourteenth century, in one of those rare, but recurrent sublime blends of both styles in the form of the supreme idealistic art of these centuries, an art in all its essential traits similar to the great Idealistic art of Greece of the fifth and, in part, of the fourth centuries B.C. It should be noted here that such an Idealistic art appeared again when the dominant Ideational style was declining and the moderate Visualism was rising. But not when Visualism was falling and Ideationalism rising. . . .

Only the Ideational man and the Ideational culture which begin to pay more and more attention to the empirico-sensory world but which by one half, at least, are still in the supersensate world of Ideationalism, seem to be able to produce the great Idealistic art, as a blend of both styles. Such exactly was the situation in the thirteenth century in Western culture generally, and especially in its art. As in Greece of the fifth century B.C., here again we are in an age of faith, all-embracing, understanding, and justifying all, including this world. It still does not see the central value in this world and in the earthly life. It sees this in the supersensory world; but the divine plan of this supersensory world somehow now includes also this earthly world and gives to it its meaning, blessing, and justification. Hence the art of the thirteenth century included (like the *Speculum majus* of Vincent of Beauvais): (I) the mirror of nature (humblest animals and plants), (2) the mirror of science (seven Muses of the *trivium* and the *quadrivium,* plus the eighth of philosophy), (3) the mirror of the virtues and of religion. This was the chief division. For the main place in art was given naturally (naturally in an Idealistic culture) to the representation of the providentially controlled march of humanity, in which "it sees only Christ and looks only for Christ in it." . . .

Since the dead and death itself were idealized in that art, it goes without saying that all the other phenomena were presented in the same spirit of idealized serenity, calm, and charm, as the results of the unshakable faith and inner certitude of the believing soul. If previously the Virtues were represented as fighting the Vices, now "by a much more profound comprehension of the essence of Virtue the Artists represent them in a state of repose; they

show us that their presence in the soul gives to it imperturbable stillness and peace."

All the other earmarks of the Idealistic art are clearly shown by the art of the thirteenth century, this apex of the Christian European art. Here are a few of its characteristics — already familar to us.

(I) It was not an art for art's sake, but the "Bible in the stone." Art was a means for the expression of the sublime religious conscience of the people. . . .

(2) We have already seen that its figures were idealized, even the dead. Most of its statues are remarkable from this standpoint. Their postures, gestures, expressions, appearance, all are lighted by the sublime serenity of the religious and moral ideal.

(3) The art of the thirteenth and of the preceding centuries, like that of the fifth B.C. and before, was an expression of a collective ideal, and thus it was a collective work. All in some way participated in it, especially in the building of the cathedrals. . . .

(4) Again like the art of the fifth century B.C., the art of the thirteenth century "tends to convince but not to disturb emotionally."

(5) Since it was a collective work and a realization of the ideal of the collectivity, the leading artists played only the role of the *primus inter pares.* They themselves neither regarded it as their own achievement only, nor were anxious to stamp their names and to take copyrights for it. Nor did they do it for the art's sake only. They did it as their service to God, *ad gloriam Dei,* for the realization of the ideal and not at all for the sake of a sensuous beauty or for a sensate enjoyment. Though the names of some of the leaders, like Villard de Honnecourt, are known, most of the artists remained anonymous, and their mood was very different from the Visual-individualistic artist who, at least, wants to immortalize himself through his creation. . . .

(6) The technique of art of the period was already so greatly developed that not without reason most of the investigators compare it and its creations with the technique of Phidias and of other great Greek masters of the fifth century. How such a miraculous development of the technique itself was possible does not concern us here. But the fact of such a miraculous ripening in a relatively short time is beyond doubt. This perfect Visual technique given into

the hands of faithful and imperturbably idealistic souls permitted the miracle of the art of the thirteenth century, just as was the case previously with the Greek art of the fifth century. . . .

(7) As in the Greek classical art, there is calm and quiet and a lack of dynamism (the Platonic ideas do not change); there is no "show" and nothing *malerisch;* there is no patheticism, no sentimentality, no emotionalism; and there is no disorder. From the expressions of the visages to the chevelure or to the plaits of the drapery, everything is harmonious and perfect but free from the sweet and sentimental orderliness or "perfection" of a perfumed doll. Likewise the art of the preceding centuries, as well as of the thirteenth century, had a "contemptuous attitude towards [Sensate] virtuosity, was free from dilettantism, and disdainful of art for the sake of art."

Such was this golden age of the idealistic art of Christian Europe.

The Middle Ages

III

The Eve of the Modern World

1250-1648

INTRODUCTION

Modern historians have largely abandoned the old and familiar notion that history is a series of well-defined periods such as "classical antiquity" or "the Middle Ages," connected by transitional epochs. While retaining the conventional labels, they have replaced the static, orderly, and artificial idea of structure with the idea of continuum—what we might call the continuity of change. It is a Heraclitean view which sees every age as an age of transition and great historical changes as the products of accumulation of forces rather than dramatic, cataclysmic happenings.

Yet, even within the concept of the historical continuum there are some ages in which the tempo of change is so marked and the product of change so significant that they can only be properly described as transitional ages. Such a one is the period with which the following problems are concerned—Western Europe in the four crowded centuries between 1250 and 1648. There was not a major facet of the life of Western Europe that did not, in this period, experience change so fundamental that the Europe of the seventeenth century was more like the Europe of every age that followed than it was like any time that had gone before.

The church which, in the thirteenth century, had been a formative force in European politics had, by 1648, been virtually excluded from the councils of political decision. Religion was still a political force to be contended with but it was no longer the unitary religion of medieval Catholicism. The Reformation had brought an end to that and, while the evangelical sects still multiplied and wrangled among themselves, by 1648 a broad belt had been drawn across the European continent to divide Catholic Europe from Protestant Europe. And the division it represented was irrevocable. The last great effort of the Catholic Hapsburg monarchy to turn back the clock of religion and politics had failed and religious division was to remain a permanent part of the European cultural and political scene.

The political frontiers which had marked the Europe of the thirteenth century were gone. For the diplomats who redrew the map of Europe at the Peace of Westphalia (1648) and at the Peace of the Pyrenees (1659) had created the essential shape of modern Europe. A handful of the major powers with which Innocent III had dealt remained but under the rule of constitutional forms and royal dynasties unknown to the thirteenth century. On the periphery of the medieval Europe the barbaric kingdoms of Scandinavia had taken form and intruded into the affairs of the older powers. Gustavus Adolphus, the king of Sweden and "Lion of the North," had played as major a role in the conflicts of central Europe in the seventeenth century as had the German emperor. On the open eastern frontier a major new power had shouldered its way into the family of European nations: the Duchy of Muscovy had become Russia. The menace of the Turks which had threatened and frightened the Europe of the Middle Ages and generated that series of quixotic adventures we call the Crusades was fading into insignificance; the Ottoman Empire was becoming the "sick man of Europe," the object no longer of the fear of the European powers and shortly to be an object of their cupidity. Beyond Europe itself a new world had opened to the enterprise of Europeans. To those remote places of which thirteenth-century men had only been able to speculate, the men of the seventeenth century sailed their ships, planted colonies, founded charter companies, began to carve out overseas empires, and undertook the translation of the ethos of Western Europe to the wider world.

Much of the motivation which had driven men to open that wider world was economic. Indeed, the economic forces which had flourished in the thirteenth century had come to the maturity of their medieval form and had evolved into their modern counterparts. The European money market had long since shifted to the north Atlantic seaboard. The Flemish towns had enjoyed their late medieval prosperity and decayed. The great chartered mercantile companies of Holland and England had appeared with such capital assets and annual volume of trade and profits as to shame the wealth of even the greatest medieval monarchies. Their syndics wielded a power greater than the great Khan and the long arm of their naval policy reached to the other side of the world.

The social structure of medieval Europe had been similarly transformed. The concept of privilege was still dominant and few men even theorized yet about the broad-based democracy that we know in our time. In many parts of Europe the social forms of medieval feudalism still persisted. But, by the mid-seventeenth century, those forms were rapidly becoming moribund under the pressure of two formative forces of the modern world, the nation state and the middle class. Both these forces had existed in embryo in the High Middle Ages and had come to maturity in the four centuries with which we are here concerned. The stubborn barons who could still defy the kings of the thirteenth century had become the self-seeking *frondeurs* or captive courtiers of the seventeenth. The middle class, which had come into precarious existence in the medieval towns, had by the seventeenth century become the most important social class of Western Europe. The men of this class had re-built the European economic machinery. They had in some nations redrawn the charts of government and even in those nations where royal absolutism prevailed they were the men and the class closest the throne. The parliaments and assemblies and political parties which these men dominate in Western Europe today were already forming in the seventeenth century.

The intellectual preoccupation of the thirteenth century was scholasticism. It was the century of Albertus Magnus, St. Thomas Aquinas, and Duns Scotus. But by 1648 even the frame of reference within which scholasticism had meaning was fundamentally changed. Men were still concerned with the state of their souls, whether Catholic or Protestant. The vocabulary of religion was still familiar to the man in the street after more than a century of Reformation and Counterreformation. But Europe was weary of religious wars and of the causes that spawned them. The vision of eternity was being replaced by the vision of the here and now. Not only was there a physical world to be explored and exploited but a new world of the mind was opening, the world of science, that most modern characteristic of the modern world. By 1648 Leibnitz and Newton were already born; Robert Boyle was about to start his revolutionary experiments in chemistry; and Blaise Pascal had already published one of the landmark works in spatial mathematics.

In nearly every sense the four centuries from the mid-thirteenth to the mid-seventeenth were the seed time of our world. The "new Europe" which the Middle Ages had created was rapidly becoming modern Europe.

It is to be expected that an age of such significance as this should have attracted the curious attention of historians for they are perennially concerned to search for cause and to probe for the origins of things. It is equally to be expected that their attention should have led to controversy. This is in the nature of the historiographic process no matter what the period under consideration. But when the period is significant, as this one is, and complex, as it is also, major (and often acrimonious) differences of interpretation are nearly inevitable. They abound in the critical literature of this transitional age between medieval and modern history.

It is the purpose of the five problems that follow to illuminate some of the most important of these controversies. Some of the problems represent flat differences of opinion. Others represent shades of opinion within a broad area of general agreement. Some represent the evolution of a critical position through two or three generations of historical revision. But altogether they give to the interested student some insight into both the multiplicity and subtlety of historical forces and the continually vital process of restudying the past. The student must realize that there is really no such thing as "the dead past"; that no moment of past time is ever completely known; and that no historical controversy is ever conclusively solved.

1

THE DECLINE AND FALL OF THE MEDIEVAL PAPACY

The century and a half before the great jubilee year 1300 had been a time of accelerating growth and accomplishment in the history of Western Europe. Towns had sprung up and prospered; a flourishing network of trade had knit these together and quickened material life; the formless chaos of feudalism seemed to be giving way before the wealth and power and order of the national monarchies. The century and a half after 1300 presents almost exactly the opposite picture. It was a time of general war and devastation, of revolutions and upheaval, of famine and pestilence, and a pervasive attitude of despair and resignation. And it was a time of such crisis in the history of the papacy that this "greatest of medieval institutions" was fundamentally altered.

The striking success of the popes in asserting their primacy in the church in the course of the twelfth and thirteenth centuries had made the history of the papacy almost synonymous with the history of the church. Thus the series of shocks, both external and internal, which battered the papacy in the centuries between the High Middle Ages and the eve of the Reformation was of basic importance in the history of the church and of Western Europe. For the troubles of the papacy must be set within a generally troubled time. The changes that overtook that institution were not so alien to nor so distinct from the changes, equally drastic and painful, to which other institutions were being subjected.

For reasons that are still not entirely clear, the curve of European economic prosperity which had climbed steadily upward for some two centuries dropped sharply downward in the early fourteenth century and general economic recovery did not begin until well after the middle of the fifteenth century. War and pestilence complicated the economic troubles and contributed to them. Agricultural productivity declined and land which had been reclaimed and settled in the thirteenth century expansion reverted to forest and waste. Settled agricultural villages disappeared and Europe seemed to be retreating. In the mid-fourteenth century came the Black Death, the most devastating of medieval plagues. But even before the Black Death there is evidence of a sharp decline in population which was accelerated by the pestilence. Labor shortages resulted and, of course, aggravated the problem of agricultural production. The towns and cities as well as the countryside were declining in population. The effects of the plague were especially bad in the crowded and unsanitary cities. But trade and exchange, the life blood of the cities, was declining also. The volume of trade in northern Europe in 1400 may actually have been less than it was a century before.

Such conditions as these spread alarm in every direction and triggered savage social revolts and equally savage reprisals. At the same time that economic conditions had their effects in other spheres, military, political, and social events contributed heavily to the pattern of economic troubles. Germany and the Empire were in chronic disorder. Kings and antikings fought for a title which had become almost meaningless and, on a lesser scale, the sovereign territorial lords of Germany fought bitterly with each other. Before the middle of the fourteenth century the Hundred Years' War had broken out between England and France, and within a generation had come to involve most of the powers of Western Europe. It was a particularly destructive war, not only because of the tactic of wholesale devastation which was widely employed, but because of the long periods of nominal peace between major engagements which set loose upon the helpless countryside of western France rapacious bands of soldiers to live off the land. Thus the Hundred Years' War, like the chronic military disorder of Germany, was really a series of small and destructive local wars. Moreover, for long periods of time, the government of France —which had been the most stable and centralized power in Europe—was in collapse, and the institutions which had so painfully built over the centuries seemed to be dissolving.

In these desperate times men could see no rhyme nor reason to their problems. They could not fathom the changes that were destroying their lives and fortunes. They rebelled savagely and senselessly. The records of the age are filled with the accounts of peasant revolts and, in the cities, uprisings among the working people. Men were angry, frustrated, and in despair. And they turned, in their desperation, to the most extreme and neurotic expressions of religious fervor. Had the church been able to seize and direct this blind and desperate religious fervor the history of this period might have been very different. But the church as an institution was too deeply involved in the very forces from which men turned. It was too much of the world to take leadership of an otherworldly reaction. And it is against this general background of what Wallace K. Ferguson has called "a changing world" that we must consider the changes that affected the papacy and contributed to its precipitate decline.

The chain of events was triggered by the pontificate of Boniface VIII (1294–1303).

The Decline and Fall of the Medieval Papacy   **227**

This ambitious and intemperate pope chose to test his exalted notions of papal sovereignty against the power of the French monarchy and that shrewd and able monarch Philip IV: and he lost. But he lost more than a skirmish, for he had failed to realize that the concept of an international spiritual and temporal kingdom of the church, under the rule of the monarchical papacy, was no longer compatible with the rising spirit of the national monarchy. He had set himself and the papacy against the wave of the future.

The victory of the French king overshadowed the selection of Boniface's successor, and the cardinals, fearful of French reprisal, elected a French cleric as Clement V. Shortly Clement took up residence, not at Rome, but at the French city of Avignon obviously within the reach of the French king and apparently subservient to him. For more than seventy years—until 1378—and through seven popes, the papacy remained in exile at Avignon, the so-called Babylonian Captivity of the Church. French popes preferred French clerics to important church positions, and the interests of France seemed to predominate in papal policy. Criticism mounted from every quarter, criticism not only of the scandalous partisanship of the popes, but of their even more scandalous worldliness. And they had no defense. It is probable that this period was the most crucial in the decline of papal prestige in the later Middle Ages.

In 1378 the papacy was restored to Rome but was immediately divided by a disputed election. The result was the Great Schism. An Italian pope reigned in Rome; a French pope returned to Avignon. And their successors perpetuated the condition for forty years. The nations of Europe, already divided on a dozen secular issues, were now divided in religious obedience. The abuses which had been the scandal of the "Babylonian" papacy became even more flagrant, and the criticism and popular hostility to the church more strident.

In their desperation to heal the schism, well intentioned men in both papal camps sought a solution in the summoning of general councils. The first of these was called at Pisa in 1409 to begin the Conciliar Movement. It lasted through the fifteenth century and it must be counted a failure. The schism was finally healed, but the need for reform which was an issue of more pressing importance was not met. The popes chose to fight the councils rather than the problems the councils raised. The monarchical sovereignty of the popes was chosen as the prize to be preserved. And the popes preserved it; but at the cost of their prestige, their spiritual authority and the general condition of the church. On the eve of the Reformation, the traditional church was as ill-prepared as it had ever been to face a major challenge.

In the selections that follow, a number of scholars look at different aspects of this history of the papacy in the fourteenth and fifteenth centuries. The general account of events is not in dispute among them any more than whether the Reformation or the French Revolution actually happened. Nor is the overall significance of the events in dispute. Their significance, indeed, is what makes them well worth repeated study. The scholars whose work is represented here are in disagreement but on matters of emphasis, balance, proportion, causes, and the relative weight of evidence. These differences are in the best tradition of historical revision to which this whole work is directed.

LUDWIG PASTOR

THE CONVENTIONAL VIEW

Ludwig Pastor (1854–1928) devoted most of his long life to the writing of his massive, documentary *The History of the Popes, from the Close of the Middle Ages.* The first volume appeared in 1886. The sixteenth was published posthumously in 1933. He is the greatest representative in modern scholarship of what may be called the "conventional view" of the causes and consequences of the decline of the medieval papacy, the view from which later revisionist scholars must dissent. While there is no one place in the first few books of his history where Pastor "capsulizes" a thesis, the excerpts which make up the following selection clearly reflect his view.

As the earlier historian Edward Gibbon had surveyed the melancholy course of the decline of Rome from the perspective of the high empire, so Pastor—who resembles Gibbon in many ways—surveyed what was to him the equally melancholy decline of the medieval papacy from the perspective of the thirteenth century and the eminence to which Innocent III had raised the papacy above both church and state. But there is a basic difference between Gibbon and Pastor. Gibbon was a harsh and unrelenting judge of his subject: Pastor was a sympathetic witness for his. He was a devoted Catholic, a pupil and disciple of the Catholic apologist-historian Johannes Janssen, a professor of history in the traditionally Catholic University of Innsbruck, and a scholar loaded with the honors of his church in recognition of his scholarship. Yet, despite his religious commitment, Pastor should not be regarded as a narrow, sectarian advocate. He based his work solidly upon documents and relentlessly followed wherever those documents led his argument. Indeed, he was more severe in his judgments than many of his less orthodox predecessors had been for the simple reason that he cared more and thus he responded more heatedly when he discovered evidence of misconduct, gross errors of policy, and personal venality which detracted from the exalted theory of the papacy to which he subscribed.

As the student studies this selection, he should look for the major tenets of Pastor's interpretation and seek to answer such questions as: What were the consequences of the papacy's removal to Avignon? What was the reason for the Great Schism?

What were its consequences? Did the papacy have any realistic alternative to the actions and policies it actually pursued during this period? Perhaps even more important, the student should compare this selection closely with those that follow in this section with an eye to the question: To what extent, despite his careful scholarship, did Pastor's Catholic orthodoxy distort his narrative?

The disastrous struggle between the highest powers of Christendom, which began in the eleventh century and reached its climax in the thirteenth, was decided, apparently to the advantage of the Papacy, by the tragical downfall of the house of Hohenstaufen. But the overthrow of the Empire also shook the temporal position of the Popes, who were now more and more compelled to ally themselves closely with France. In the warfare with the Emperors, the Papacy had already sought protection and had found refuge in that kingdom in critical times. The sojourn of the Popes in France had, however, been only transitory. The most sacred traditions, and a history going back for more than a thousand years, seemed to have bound the highest ecclesiastical dignity so closely to Italy and to Rome that, in the eleventh, twelfth, and thirteenth centuries, the idea that a Pope could be crowned anywhere but in the Eternal City, or could fix his residence for the whole duration of his Pontificate out of Italy, would have been looked upon as an impossibility.

A change came over this state of things in the time of Clement V. (1305–1314), a native of Gascony. Fearing for the independence of the Ecclesiastical power amid the party struggles by which Italy was torn, and yielding to the influence of Philip the Fair, the strong-handed oppressor of Boniface VIII., he remained in France and never set foot in Rome. His successor, John XXII., also a Gascon, was elected, after prolonged and stormy discussions, in 1316, when the Holy See had been for two years vacant. He took up his permanent abode at Avignon, where he was only separated by the Rhone from the territory of the French King. Clement V. had lived as a guest in the Dominican Monastery at Avignon, but John XXII. set up a magnificent establishment there. The essential character of that new epoch in the history of the Papacy, which begins with Clement V. and John XXII., consists in the lasting separation from the traditional home of the Holy See and from the Italian soil, which brought the Popes into such pernicious dependence on France and seriously endangered the universal nature of their position.

O good beginning!
To what a vile conclusion must Thou stoop.[1]

The words of the great Italian poet are not exaggerated, for the Avignon Popes, without exception, were all more or less dependent on France. Frenchmen themselves, and surrounded by a College of Cardinals in which the French element predominated, they gave a French character to the government of the Church. This character was at variance with the principle of universality inherent in it and in the Papacy. The Church had always been the representative of this principle in contradistinction to that of isolated nationalities, and it was the high office of the Pope, as her Supreme Head, to be the common Father of all nations. This universality was in a great degree the secret of the power and influence of the Mediaeval Popes.

The migration to France, the creation of a preponderance of French Cardinals, and the consequent election of seven French Popes in succession, necessarily compromised the position of the Papacy in the eyes of the world, creating a suspicion that the highest spiritual power had become the tool of France. This suspicion, though in many cases unfounded, weakened the general confidence in the Head of the Church, and awakened in the other nations a feeling of antagonism to the ecclesiastical authority which had become French. The bonds which united the States of the Church to the Apostolic See were gradually loosened, and the arbitrary proceedings of the Court at Avignon, which was too often swayed by personal and family interests, accelerated the process of dissolution. The worst apprehensions for the future were entertained.

The dark points of the Avignon period have certainly been greatly exaggerated. The assertion that the

[1] Dante, *Parad.*, xxvii, 59, 60.

From Ludwig Pastor, *The History of the Popes, from the Close of the Middle Ages*, ed., tr. F. I. Antrobus, 6th ed. (London: Kegan Paul, Trench, Trubner & Co. Ltd., 1938), Vol. I, pp. 57–174 with deletions. The elaborate documentation is not reproduced here; the reader is referred to the edition cited. Reprinted by permission of Routledge & Kegan Paul Ltd.

The Eve of the Modern World

Government of the Avignon Popes was wholly ruled by the "will and pleasure of the Kings of France," is, in this general sense, unjust. The Popes of those days were not all so weak as Clement V., who submitted the draft of the Bull, by which he called on the Princes of Europe to imprison the Templars,[2] to the French King. Moreover, even this Pope, the least independent of the fourteenth century Pontiffs, for many years offered a passive resistance to the wishes of France, and a writer, who has thoroughly studied the period, emphatically asserts that only for a few years of the Pontificate of Clement V. was the idea so long associated with the "Babylonian Captivity" of the Popes fully realized. The extension of this epithet to the whole of the Avignon sojourn is an unfair exaggeration. The eager censors of the dependence into which the Avignon Popes sank, draw attention to the political action of the Holy See during this period so exclusively, that hardly any place is left for its labours in the cause of religion. A very partial picture is thus drawn, wherein the noble efforts of these much-abused Pontiffs for the conversion of heathen nations become almost imperceptible in the dim background. . . .

With the most ample recognition of the worldwide activity of the French Popes, it cannot be denied that the effects of the transfer of the Holy See from its natural and historical home were disastrous. Torn from its proper abode, the Papacy, notwithstanding the individual greatness of some of the Avignon Pontiffs, could not maintain its former dignity. The freedom and independence of the highest tribunal in Christendom, which, according to Innocent III., was bound to protect all rights, was endangered, now that the supreme direction of the Church was so much under the influence of a nation so deeply imbued with its own spirit, and possessing so little of the universal. That France should obtain exclusive possession of the highest spiritual authority was a thing contrary both to the office of the Papacy and the very being of the Church.

This dependence on the power of a Prince, who in former times had often been rebuked by Rome, was in strange contradiction with the supremacy claimed by the Popes. By this subjection and by its worldliness, the Avignon Papacy aroused an opposition which, though it might for a moment be overborne

while it leant on the crumbling power of the Empire, yet moved men's minds so deeply that its effects were not effaced for several centuries. Its downfall is most closely connected with this opposition, which was manifested, not only in the bitter accusations of its political and clerical enemies, but even also in the letters of its devoted friend St. Catherine, which are full of entreaties, complaints, and denunciations. The Papal Government, founded as it was on the principle of authority, built up in independence of the Empire, and gaining strength in proportion to the decay of that power, was unable to offer any adequate resistance to this twofold stream of political and religious antagonism. The catastrophe of the great Schism was the immediate consequence of the false position now occupied by the Papacy. . . .

The disastrous effects produced by the residence of the Popes at Avignon were at first chiefly felt in Italy. Hardly ever has a country fallen into such anarchy as did the Italian peninsula, when bereft of her principle of unity by the unfortunate decision of Clement V. to fix his abode in France. Torn to pieces by irreconcilable parties, the land, which had been fitly termed the garden of Europe, was now a scene of desolation. It will easily be understood that all Italian hearts were filled with bitter longings, a regret which found voice in continual protests against the Gallicized Papacy. . . .

The unmitigated condemnation of the Avignon Popes must have been based in great measure on Petrarch's unjust representations, to which, in later times and without examination, an undue historical importance has been attached. He is often supposed to be a determined adversary of the Papacy; but this is a complete mistake. He never for a moment questioned its divine institution. We have already said that he was outwardly on the best terms with almost all the Popes of his time, and received from them many favours. They took his frequent and earnest exhortations to leave Avignon and return to desolate Rome as mere poetical rhapsodies, and in fact they were nothing more. If Petrarch himself, though a Roman citizen, kept aloof from Rome; if, though nominally an Italian patriot, he fixed his abode for many years, from motives of convenience, or in quest of preferment, in that very Avignon which he had bitterly reproached the Popes for choosing, and which he had called the most loathsome place in the world, must not the Babylonish poison have eaten deeply into his heart? How much easier it would have been for Petrarch to have re-

---

[2] The reference here is to the pope's assistance in Philip IV's attack on the Order of Knights Templar.

turned to Rome than it was for the Popes, fettered as they were by so many political considerations!

But however much we may question Petrarch's right to find fault with the moral delinquencies of the Court at Avignon; however much we may, in many respects, modify the picture he paints of it, no impartial inquirer can deny that it was pervaded by a deplorable worldliness. For this melancholy fact we have testimony more trustworthy than the rhetorical descriptions of the Italian poet. Yet it must in justice be borne in mind that the influx of thousands of strangers into the little French provincial town, so suddenly raised to the position of capital of the world, had produced all the evils which appertain to densely populated places. Moreover, even if we are to believe all the angry assertions of contemporaries as to the corruption prevailing in Avignon, evidence is not wanting, on the other hand, of ardent yearnings for a life conformable to the precepts of the Gospel. . . .

[*The pontificate of John XXII, in almost every sense the apogee of the Avignonese papacy, was followed by those of Benedict XII (1334–1342), Clement VI (1342–1352), Innocent VI (1352–1362), Urban V (1362–1370), and Gregory XI (1370–1378). All these popes were French prelates and all—except Gregory XI—continued their residence at Avignon. But they were not unaware of the bitter criticism their continued exile generated nor certainly of the many political and financial, as well as spiritual, disadvantages they suffered. There was mounting pressure for them to return to Rome. Some halting gestures were made in that direction: Urban V visited Rome briefly. Then Gregory XI did return and in 1378, died in Rome. Editor's note.*]

After an interval of seventy-five years a Conclave again met in Rome, and on its decision depended the question whether or not the injurious predominance of France in the management of the affairs of the Church should continue. Severe struggles were to be expected, for no slight disunion existed in the Sacred College.

Of the sixteen Cardinals then present in Rome, four only were of Italian nationality. Francesco Tibaldeschi and Giacomo Orsini were Romans, Simone da Borsano and Pietro Corsini, natives respectively of Milan and Florence. These Princes of the Church were naturally desirous that an Italian should occupy the Chair of St. Peter. The twelve foreign or "Ultra-montane" Cardinals, of whom one was a Spaniard and the others French, were sub-divided into two parties. The Limousin Cardinals strove for the elevation of a native of their province, the birthplace of the last four Popes. Of the six remaining members of the Sacred College, two were undecided, and the four others, of whom the Cardinal of Geneva was the leader, formed what was called the Gallican faction.

No party accordingly had the preponderance, and a protracted Conclave was to be anticipated. External circumstances, however, led to a different result. Before the Cardinals entered on their deliberations, the Municipal authorities of Rome had besought them to elect a Roman, or at any rate an Italian, and while the Conclave was proceeding, the governors of the districts appeared, and presented the same petition. The populace gathered round the Vatican in the greatest excitement, demanding, with shouts and uproar, the election of a Roman. The Cardinals were compelled to make haste, and as no one of the three parties was sufficiently powerful to carry the day, all united in favour of Bartolomeo Prignano, Archbishop of Bari, a candidate who belonged to no party and seemed in many respects the individual best fitted to rule the Church in this period of peculiar difficulty. He was the worthiest and most capable among the Italian prelates. As a native of Naples, he was the subject of Queen Joanna, whose protection at this crisis was of the greatest importance. A long residence in Avignon had given him the opportunity of acquiring French manners, and ties of equal strength bound him to Italy and to France. On the 8th April, 1378, he was elevated to the supreme dignity, taking the name of Urban VI.

Great confusion was occasioned by a misunderstanding which occurred after the election. The crowd forcibly broke into the Conclave to see the new Pope, and the Cardinals, dreading to inform them of the election of Prignano, who was not a Roman, persuaded the aged Cardinal Tibaldeschi to put on the Papal Insignia and allow the populace to greet him. Hardly had this been done, when, apprehensive of what might happen when the deception was discovered, most of the Cardinals sought safety in flight. Finally, confidence was restored by the assurance of the City authorities that Prignano's election would find favour with the people. It is plain then that the election itself was not the result of compulsion on the part of the Roman populace. If, however, the least suspicion of constraint could be attached to it, the subsequent bearing of the Cardinals was sufficient to completely counteract it. As soon as tranquillity was restored Prignano's election was announced to the people and was followed by his Coronation. All the Cardinals then present in Rome took part in the ceremony, and thereby publicly acknowledged Urban VI. as the rightful Pope. They assisted him in his ecclesiastical functions and asked him for spiritual favours. They announced his election and Coronation to the Emperor and to Christendom in general by letters signed with their own hands, and homage was universally rendered to the new Head of the Church. No member of the Sacred College thought of calling the election in question; on the contrary, in official documents, as well as in private conversations, they all maintained its undoubted validity. . . .

The new Pope was adorned by great and rare qualities; almost all his contemporaries are unanimous in praise of his purity of life, his simplicity and temperance. He was also esteemed for his learning, and yet more for the conscientious zeal with which he discharged his ecclesiastical duties. . . .

But Urban VI. had one great fault, a fault fraught with evil consequences to himself, and yet more to the Church; he lacked Christian gentleness and charity. He was naturally arbitrary and extremely violent and imprudent, and when he came to deal with the burning ecclesiastical question of the day, that of reform, the consequences were disastrous.

The melancholy condition of the affairs of the Church at this period is clear from the letters of St. Catherine of Siena. The suggestions of reform which she had made repeatedly and with unexampled courage had unfortunately not been carried out. Gregory XI. was far too irresolute to adopt energetic measures, and he also attached undue weight to the opinions of his relations, and of the French Cardinals, by whom he was surrounded; moreover, he was fully occupied by the war with Florence, and this was perhaps the chief cause of his inaction. Whether, if longer life had been granted to him, he would really have undertaken the amendment of the clergy, it is impossible to say. One thing is certain, that at the date of the new Pope's accession the work had still to be done. . . .

The plans of reform entertained by Urban VI. filled the French King, Charles V., with wrath. The free and independent position, which the new Pope had from the first assumed was a thorn in the side of the King, who wished to bring back the Avignon days. Were Urban now to succeed in creating an Italian majority in the Sacred College, the return of the Holy See to its dependence on France would be greatly deferred, if not indeed altogether prevented. Charles V therefore secretly encouraged the Cardinals, promising them armed assistance, even at the cost of a cessation of hostilities with England, if they would take the final step, before which they still hesitated. Confident in his powerful support, the thirteen Cardinals assembled at Anagni, on the 9th August, 1378, published a manifesto, declaring Urban's election to have been invalid, as resulting from the constraint exercised by the Roman populace, who had risen in insurrection, and proclaiming as a consequence the vacancy of the Holy See.

On the 20th September they informed the astonished world that the true Pope had been chosen in the person of Robert of Geneva, now Clement VII. The great Papal Schism (1378–1417), the most terrible of all imaginable calamities, thus burst upon Christendom, and the very centre of its unity became the occasion of the division of the Church. . . .

Christendom had never yet witnessed such a Schism; all timid souls were cast into a sea of doubt, and even courageous men like Abbot Ludolf of Sagan, its historian, bewailed it day and night.

Anti-popes, indeed, had already arisen on several occasions, but in most cases they had very soon passed away, for, owing their elevation to the secular power, it bore more or less clearly on its very face the stamp of violence and injustice. But in the present instance all was different; unlike the Schisms caused by the Hohenstaufens or Louis of Bavaria, that of 1378 was the work of the Cardinals, the highest of the clergy. And, moreover, the election of Urban VI. had taken place under circumstances so peculiar that it was easy to call it in question. It was impossible for those not on the spot to investigate it in all its details, and the fact, that all who had taken part in it subsequently renounced their allegiance, was well calculated to inspire doubt and perplexity. It is extremely difficult for those who study the question in the present day with countless documents before them, and the power of contemplating the further development of the Schism, to estimate the difficulties of contemporaries who sought to know which of the two Popes had a right to their obedience. The extreme confusion is evidenced by the fact that canonized Saints are found amongst the adherents of each of the rivals. St. Catherine of Siena, and her namesake of Sweden, stand opposed to St. Vincent Ferrer and the Blessed Peter of Luxemburg, who acknowledged the French Pope. All the writings of the period give more or less evidence of the conflicting opinions which prevailed; and upright men afterwards confessed, that they had been unable to find out which was the true Pope.

To add to the complications, the obedience of Germany to Urban VI. and that of France to Clement VII. was far from complete, for individuals in both countries attached themselves to the Pope, from whom they expected to gain most. The allegiance of the Holy Roman Empire to Urban was evidently of an unstable character, since ecclesiastics in Augsburg fearlessly, and without hindrance, accepted charges and benefices from the hands of the Antipope and his partisans, and itinerant preachers publicly asserted the validity of his claim. Peter Suchenwirt, in a poem written at this period, describes the distress, which the growing anarchy within the Church was causing in men's minds, and earnestly beseeches God to end it. "There are two Popes," he says; "which is the right one? . . ."

It has been well observed that we can scarcely form an idea of the deplorable condition to which Europe was reduced by the schism. Uncertainty as to the title of its ruler is ruinous to a nation; this schism affected the whole of Christendom, and called the very existence of the Church in question. The discord touching its Head necessarily permeated the whole body of the Church; in many Dioceses two Bishops were in arms for the possession of the Episcopal throne, two Abbots in conflict for an abbey. The consequent confusion was indescribable. We cannot wonder that the Christian religion became the derision of Jews and Mahometans.

The amount of evil wrought by the schism of 1378, the longest known in the history of the Papacy, can only be estimated, when we reflect that it occurred at a moment, when thorough reform in ecclesiastical affairs was a most urgent need. This was now utterly out of the question, and, indeed, all evils which had crept into ecclesiastical life were infinitely increased. Respect for the Holy See was also greatly impaired, and the Popes became more than ever dependent on the temporal power, for the schism allowed each Prince to choose which Pope he would acknowledge. In the eyes of the people, the

simple fact of a double Papacy must have shaken the authority of the Holy See to its very foundations. It may truly be said that these fifty years of schism prepared the way for the great Apostacy of the sixteenth century.

It is not within the scope of the present work to recount all the vicissitudes of the warfare between the claimants of the Papal throne—for Urban VI. received immediately a successor. Neither side would yield, and the confusion of Christendom daily increased and pervaded all classes of society. The Cardinals of the rival Popes were at open variance, and in many dioceses there were two Bishops. This was the case in Breslau, Mayence, Liege, Basle, Metz Constance, Coire, Lubeck, Dorpat, and other places, and even the Religious and Military Orders were drawn into the schism.

The conflict was carried on with unexampled violence. While the adherents of the Roman Pope reprobated the Mass offered by the "Clementines," the "Clementines" in their turn looked on that of the "Urbanists" as a blasphemy; in many cases public worship was altogether discontinued. "The depths of calamity," as St. Catherine of Siena said, "overwhelmed the Church." "Mutual hatred," writes a biographer of the Saint, "lust of power, the worst intrigues flourished amidst clergy and laity alike, and who could suppress these crimes? God alone could help, and He led the Church through great and long-continued tribulation back to unity, and made it plain to all that men may indeed in their wickedness wound her, but they cannot destroy her, for she bears within a divine principle of life." Therefore, even amid the direst storm of discord, St. Catherine could write, "I saw how the Bride of Christ was giving forth life, for she contains such living power that no one can kill her; I saw that she was dispensing strength and light, and that no one can take them from her, and I saw that her fruit never diminishes, but always increases." . . .

The literature of this period, a field as yet but little explored, testifies to the general distress caused by the Schism. Touching lamentations in both prose and verse portray the desolation and confusion of the time, and this was aggravated by epidemics. "Whose heart," cries Heinrich von Langenstein, "is so hardened as not to be moved by the unspeakable sufferings of his Mother, the Church?" . . .

From these complaints it is evident how keenly

the need of a Supreme Judge, Guardian, and Guide in ecclesiastical affairs was felt.

Naturally, men did not stop at mere expressions of sorrow, but went on to inquire into the origin of the evil which was bringing such dishonour on the Church. The most clear-sighted contemporary writers point to the corruption of the clergy, to their inordinate desire for money and possessions—in short, to their selfishness—as the root of all the misery. This is the key note of Nicolas de Clémangis' celebrated book, "On the Ruin of the Church" (written in 1401); and in a sermon delivered before the Council of Constance, the preacher insisted that "money was the origin of the Schism, and the root of all the confusion."

It cannot, however, be too often repeated that the ecclesiastical corruption was in great measure a consequence of the Avignon period, and of the influence which State politics had acquired in matters of Church government. The rupture, produced by the recreant French Cardinals, was, in reality, nothing but the conflict of two nations for the possession of the Papacy; the Italians wished to recover it, and the French would not let it be wrested from them.

Those who raised their voices to complain of the corruption and confusion of Christendom were not always men of real piety or moral worth. In many cases they might with advantage have begun by reforming their own lives. Some of them went so far as to charge all the evils of the day upon the ecclesiastical authorities, and stirred up laity and clergy against each other; such persons only destroyed that which was still standing. Others, again, clamoured for reform, while themselves doing nothing to promote it. But at this time, as at all periods in the history of the Church, men were found who, without making much noise or lamentation, laboured in the right way—that is, within the limits laid down by the Church—for the thorough amendment of all that was amiss. . . .

The crisis which the Church passed through at this juncture, is the most grievous recorded in her history. Just when the desperate struggle between the rival Popes had thrown everything into utter confusion, when ecclesiastical revenues and favours served almost exclusively as the reward of partisans, and when worldliness had reached its climax, heretical movements arose in England, France, Italy, Germany, and, above all, in Bohemia, and threatened the very constitution of the Church. This was most natural; the smaller the chance of reform being effected by the Church, the more popular and active became the reform movement not directed by her; the higher the region that needed, but resisted reform, the more popular did this movement become. . . .

The appearance of John Wyclif in England was a matter of far greater moment than heresies of this kind, which were forcibly repressed by the Inquisition. The errors of the Apocalyptics and the Waldenses, of Marsiglio, Occam, and others, were all concentrated in his sect, which prepared the transition to a new heretical system of a universal character, namely, Protestantism. His teaching is gross pantheistic realism, involving a Predestinarianism which annihilates moral freedom. Everything is God. An absolute necessity governs all, even the action of God Himself. Evil happens by necessity; God constrains every creature that acts, to the performance of each action. Some are predestined to glory, others to damnation. The prayer of the reprobate is of no avail, and the predestined are none the worse for the sins which God compels them to commit. Wyclif builds his church on this theory of predestination. It is, in his view, the society of the elect. As an external institution, accordingly, it disappears, to become merely an inward association of souls, and no one can know who does or does not belong to it. The only thing certain is that it always exists on earth, although it may be sometimes only composed of a few poor laymen, scattered in different countries. Wyclif began by a conditional recognition of the Pope, but afterwards came to regard him, not as the Vicar of Christ, but as Anti-Christ. He taught that honour paid to the Pope was idolatry, of a character all the more hideous and blasphemous, inasmuch as divine honour was given to a member of Lucifer, an idol, worse than a painted log of wood, because of the great wickedness he contains. Wyclif further teaches that the Church ought to be without property, and to return to the simplicity of Apostolic times. The Bible alone, without tradition, is the sole source of faith. No temporal or ecclesiastical superior has authority, when he is in a state of mortal sin. Indulgences, confession, extreme unction and orders, are all rejected by Wyclif, who even attacks the very centre of all Christian worship, the Most Holy Sacrament of the Altar.

These doctrines, which involved a revolution, not only in the Church, but also in politics and society, made their way rapidly in England. Countless disciples,—poor clergy whom Wyclif sent forth in opposition to the "rich Church which had fallen away to the devil,"—propagated them through the length and breadth of the land. These itinerant preachers, in a comparatively short time, aroused a most formidable movement against the property of the Church, the Pope, and the Bishops. But a change suddenly took place. King Richard the Second's marriage with Anne, the daughter of the King of Bohemia, was a great blow to the cause of Wyclif in England. The Courts of Westminster and of Prague were of one mind in regard to the affairs of the Church and other important political questions, and would have done anything rather than show favour to Wyclif and his companions, or to France and her anti-Pope, Clement VII.

On the other hand, as this marriage led to an increase of intercourse between England and Bohemia, Wyclif's ideas found entrance into the latter country. English students frequented the University of Prague, and Bohemians that of Oxford; and Wyclif's treatises were widely spread in Bohemia. John Huss, the leader of the Bohemian movement, was not merely much influenced, but absolutely dominated by these ideas. Recent investigations have furnished incontestable evidence that, in the matter of doctrine, Huss owed everything to Wyclif, whose works he often plagiarized with astonishing simplicity.

The opinions of the Bohemian leader, like those of Wyclif, must necessarily have led in practice to a social revolution, and one of which the end could not be foreseen, since the right to possess property was made dependent on religious opinion. Only "Believers," that is to say, the followers of Huss, could hold it, and this right lasted as long as their convictions accorded with those that prevailed in the country. Argument is needless to show that such a theory destroys all private rights, and the attempt to make these principles—so plausibly deduced from the doctrines of the Christian religion—serve as the rule for the foundation of a new social order, must lead to the most terrible consequences. The subsequent wars of the Hussites evidently owed their peculiarly sanguinary character in great part to these views. If Huss declared war against social order, he also called in question all civil authority, when he espoused Wyclif's principle, that no man who had committed a mortal sin could be a temporal ruler, a bishop, or a prelate, "because his temporal or spiritual authority, his office and his dignity would not be approved by God."

Whether Huss realized the consequences of such doctrines, or merely followed his master, may remain an open question; one thing, however, the most enthusiastic admirer of the Czech reformer cannot dispute—namely, that doctrines which must have rendered anarchy permanent in Church and State imperatively required to be met by some action on the part of the civil and ecclesiastical authorities. The results of the opinions promulgated by Huss soon became apparent in the Bohemian Revolution in which the idea of a democratic Republic and of a social system based on communistic principles took practical form. . . .

During the earlier years of the Schism, efforts had been made to establish the legality of the one, and the illegality of the other Pope, by means of arguments founded on history and on Canon Law, but in consequence of French intrigues the question had only become more and more obscured. As time went on, conscientious men, who anxiously strove to understand the rights of the case, were unable to decide between claims which seemed to be so equally balanced, while in other cases passion took no account of proofs, and power trampled them under foot. Despair took possession of many upright minds. The Schism seemed an evil from which there was no escape, a labyrinth from which no outlet could be found. The path of investigation which, by the lapse of time and in consequence of the prevailing excitement, had necessarily become more and more difficult, seemed to lead no further. The University of Paris, which suffered much from the discord of Christendom, now sought to assume the leadership of the great movement towards unity. In 1394 her members were invited to send in written opinions as to the means of putting an end to the Schism. In order that all might express their opinions with perfect freedom it was decided that the documents should be placed in a locked chest in the Church of St. Mathurin. The general feeling on the subject is manifested by their number, which amounted to ten thousand. Their examination was to be the work of a Commission formed of members from all the Faculties of the University. Three propositions emerged from this mass of documents. The first was the voluntary retirement of the two Popes (Cessio). The second the decision of the point of law by a commission selected by the two Popes (Compromissio). The third, an appeal to a General

The Eve of the Modern World

Council. The University recommended the voluntary retirement of both Popes as the simplest and safest course, and as rendering a fresh election of one whom both parties would acknowledge, possible. The endeavours to restore unity by this means were carried to their further point under Gregory XII., after the failure of the French scheme of forcibly imposing peace on the Church by the common action of all the western powers. They seemed at first in Gregory's case to promise success, but all hopes of the kind soon proved delusive.

[*And there was left open to the church only the appeal to a General Council. It was this impasse which produced the Conciliar Movement and extended it on through most of the fifteenth century with further damage to the universal authority and prestige of the papacy. The way was thus prepared for the coming of the Reformation, in Pastor's phrase, "the great Apostacy of the sixteenth century." Editor's note.*]

GUILLAUME MOLLAT

A MAJOR REVISIONIST VIEW

Guillaume Mollat, the French cleric and church historian, was one of the major figures of the first generation of modern scholars to undertake a revision of views of this period in the history of the papacy. The first edition of his *The Popes at Avignon* appeared in 1912, while Pastor's magisterial volumes were still issuing from the press. The ninth French edition, published in 1950, was much enlarged and substantially revised in light of recent scholarship, much of it Mollat's own. He had worked the archives as assiduously as Pastor, devoting his attention almost exclusively to the Avignonese popes and to the papal "system" which emerged under their hands. He had written on papal fiscal measures in Brittany, on the civil and canon law, and starting in 1950 he published a series of studies, based on his long archival research, dealing with the letters patent and the private and public papers of the Avignonese popes Benedict XII, Urban V, Gregory XI, and Clement V. But his major interpretive work was *The Popes at Avignon*, from which the following selection is taken.

Mollat deals in this book with only a portion of the problem with which we saw Pastor concerned in the previous selection, but it is a crucial portion of the general problem if the student will recall the position that Pastor took on the Avignonese popes and their "pernicious dependence on France," the beginning, as he saw it, of a string of causation leading to the undoing of the medieval papacy.

In *The Popes at Avignon*, Mollat undertakes to reassess the "general opinion" to which, he claims, Pastor had yielded with regard to the Babylonian Captivity. From this reassessment emerges a very different estimation of the popes' motives in not returning to Rome, a very different view of the papacy's relations with the French kings, and a very different explanation of the papal fiscal policies, usually explained in terms of moral lapse, weakness, or avarice. The student should observe carefully the "case" Mollat makes in each instance. He should determine whether the almost clinical refusal of the author to take a moral position—in spite of his being a member of the Catholic clergy—works to distort his narrative in the same way that the advocacy of Pastor might have distorted his. He should consider that Mollat, while a churchman, was also a Frenchman and what effect this might have had upon his point of view. And finally, he should reflect a bit on the basic critical problem of historical revision: not so much the patient study and restudy of the documents as the patient "rethinking of the past."

Between 1305 and 1378 seven popes succeeded one another on the throne of St Peter and lived, more or less continuously, in Avignon, on the banks of the Rhône.

Was it an unheard-of occurrence and in fact a "scandal" in the annals of the Church for them to reside outside Rome? The majority of non-French writers . . . seem to suggest it. Yet, for all they were bishops of Rome, a large number of the popes were elected and crowned elsewhere than at Rome and governed the world from some place other than Rome. During the latter half of the thirteenth century their subjects' unrest made it impossible for the popes to reside in the Eternal City and they were obliged to emigrate, to such an extent that it became exceptional for them to live in Rome.

Nothing is more enlightening in this respect than the itinerary followed by the popes throughout the half-century preceding their installation at Avignon. After a stay of five months and a few days in Rome, where he suffered the greatest restriction of his liberty and had his authority impeded by the noble families, Benedict XI (1303–04) left for Perugia where he died. According to Ferreto Ferreti of Vicenza, he was thinking of making an indefinite stay in Lombardy. His predecessor, Boniface VIII (1294–1303), was much less frequently to be found at the Lateran palace than at Anagni, Orvieto or Velletri. Celestine V (1294), the holy hermit, never saw Rome; elected at Perugia and crowned at Aquila, he proceeded to Sulmona, Capua and Naples, where he renounced his title. Nicholas IV (1288–92) was elected at Rome and sometimes resided at Santa Maria Maggiore; but he lived as a rule at Rieti and Orvieto. Honorius IV (1285–7), after his election at Perugia, liked to live at Santa

Sabina; only in the extreme heat of summer did he retreat to Tivoli or Palombara. Martin IV (1281–5), a Frenchman, elected at Viterbo, *ubi tunc residebat Romana Curia*,[1] never went outside Tuscany and Umbria. Also elected at Viterbo, Nicholas III (1277–80) was unusual in being crowned at Rome; he divided his time between that city, Sutri, Vetralla and Viterbo. John XXI (1276–7) never left Viterbo, where he had been elected and where he died and was buried beneath the walls of his own palace. Innocent V and Adrian V occupied the pontifical throne for brief periods only, during the first six months of the year 1276. After two months' stay in Rome, Gregory X (1271–6) went to Orvieto and then to France, where he summoned the fourteenth oecumenical council at Lyons. His return journey to Italy was made in short stages, with many halts in "the sweet land of Provence." He went to Orange, Beaucaire and Valence and back to Vienne, in order to return to Italy by way of Switzerland and he died at Arezzo. The French Pope Clement IV (1265–8) did not issue a single document from Rome. He went to Perugia, Assisi, Orvieto, Montefiascone and Viterbo. Urban IV (1261–4), another Frenchman, had only three residences, Viterbo, Montefiascone and Orvieto; he died in his litter on the way from Orvieto to Perugia. Alexander IV (1254–61) was elected and crowned at Naples, and had a liking for Anagni and Viterbo; at the beginning and end of his pontificate, he spent a few months at the Lateran Palace, and died at Viterbo. Innocent IV (1243–54), who was elected and consecrated at Anagni, spent only a very short time at Rome; he was obliged to flee from Frederick II and to take refuge at Lyons from 1244 until 1251. When he returned to Italy, he settled in the peaceful

[1] "Where the Roman Curia resided at that time. [Editor's note].

From G. Mollat, *The Popes at Avignon, 1305–1378*, tr. Janet Love from the 9th French edition (New York and London, 1963), pp. xiii–xxii, 343–44. Reprinted by permission of Thomas Nelson & Sons Ltd., London; a paperback edition is published by Harper & Row, Inc., New York.

country of Umbria and then went to Naples, where he died. . . .

The establishment of the papacy outside Rome in the fourteenth century, then, does not constitute an unheard-of revolution in history; it was brought about and prepared by a long series of circumstances and events. The really extraordinary and unprecedented circumstance is the prolonged residence of the popes outside Italy. Moreover the Italians, once they were deprived of the considerable advantages provided by the presence of the papacy, did not fail to follow Petrarch and St Catherine of Siena in copious expressions of blame and complaint. Ughelli — to quote only one of the best known — goes so far as to assert that the transference of the Holy See to Avignon was a greater disaster for his country than the barbarian invasions. German scholarship has echoed these sentiments. Gregorovius declares that the Avignon popes were the "slaves" of the kings of France; Hase refers to them as "bishops of the French court"; Martens maintains that they would not have dared to exercise any sovereign authority without the approval of the French kings. Pastor yields to the general opinion: he reproaches the papacy with having caused the Church to lose its universality by becoming French and thus arousing popular suspicion and feelings of hostility; he alleges that this move precipitated the decline of religious feeling. Other writers, both in France and elsewhere, have bitterly denounced the excessive concern of the court at Avignon with finance, the looseness of its morals, its extravagant tastes, its nepotism and absolutism. In a word, according to the majority of historians, the Avignon papacy was the source of the greatest evils for the Church and, in the last analysis, the chief cause of the great schism of the West. Whatever may have been claimed in its defence, the judgment of history remains unfavourable towards it. Is this judgment confirmed or invalidated by the publication of the Papal Registers and the studies that have appeared since the opening of the Vatican Archives? A statement of the facts will make a reply possible.

We shall endeavour, in the following pages, to study in detail and with reference to the texts of the Archives, the pontificates of Clement V, John XXII, Benedict XII, Clement VI, Innocent VI, Urban V and Gregory XI. These have usually been the victims of prejudice caused by a chauvinism which is not, on this occasion, French. We are not writing a defence, but an historical account, sketching biographies, clarifying policy and describing institutions without any preconceived notion save that of stating what the texts imply.

THE ESTABLISHMENT OF THE HOLY SEE AT AVIGNON

The chronicler Ptolemy of Lucca reports that as soon as Bertrand de Got was elected pope, "he determined to fix his residence in the Comtat-Venaissin and never to cross the Alps." This is a misstatement. It is true that the cardinals' letters, giving notice of the election, were expressed in such a way as to deter Clement V from going to Italy. They depicted that country as given over to anarchy and the Papal States as devastated by war. Nevertheless, the pope announced his intention of going to Italy as soon as peace was made between the kings of England and France, and the crusade organised. He chose the place for his coronation on imperial soil, at Vienne in Dauphiné, a town on the main road to Italy. He invited only a limited number of cardinals to his coronation: two bishops, two priests and two deacons.

Although Clement V subsequently changed his plans, he still had every intention of leaving France, where circumstances had detained him. In 1306 the ambassador of Aragon wrote to James II: "The pope signified [to the cardinals] that it was his intention to stay here until the coming month of March. For then he will give leave to the court to cross the Alps and will meet with the king of France at Poitiers, that he may persuade him to receive the cross and ratify the peace between himself and the king of England. And from that time forward, without tarrying in any other place, my said lord the pope will go to Italy." According to the same ambassador, during the meeting at Poitiers in 1308, the supreme pontiff expressed his joy at encountering Philip the Fair, for it was his intention to go to Rome but to entertain the king before his departure. On 11 April 1308, Clement was considering the restoration of the ciborium to the high altar of St John Lateran and said: "By the grace of God we propose to put back with our own hands the most famous wooden altar in the place where it formerly was." Moreover, in the next year he was promising that within the space of two years he would himself crown the Emperor Henry VII at Rome. Why did Clement V not carry out these intentions that he had so often expressed?

The pope's object in choosing to hold his coronation at Vienne and not on Italian soil was to attract the kings of France and England to the ceremony and to take advantage of their presence to work for the conclusion of a lasting peace between them. In this he was carrying out a cherished plan of the late Boniface VIII, who had dreamt of going to France to settle the Anglo-French differences. Like his predecessor, Clement V considered that the crusade would be impossible without the effective co-operation of France and England. Such co-operation could not properly be sought until the day when the two countries had signed the peace. Clement V worked untiringly to reconcile them. He arranged the marriage of Isabella of France with the future Edward II. Despite his efforts, final reconciliation was not achieved until 1312.

On 28 November 1306, however, Clement V declared that peace negotiations, which by that date were well advanced, could have been completed by the intervention of nuncios alone. But other causes hindered his departure for Rome. Chief among these was the pressure exercised by the French court. As early as July and August 1305, French ambassadors sought Clement V and reminded him that the action brought against the deceased Boniface VIII was not yet finished. The pope, anxious to avoid a renewal of this action, made a concession that was to have considerable consequences: he decreed that his coronation should now take place not at Vienne but at Lyons. On 14 November 1305 this ceremony was performed in that city in the presence of Philip the Fair. It was followed by very important negotiations. The king of France was insistent that the trial of Boniface VIII should be renewed. It was agreed that this should be discussed at a future meeting; with the result that Clement V was obliged to put off until a more favourable time his departure for Italy.

The pope made his way from Lyons to Mâcon and Cluny and then reached Languedoc by way of Nevers, Bourges, Limoges and Périgueux. An illness which almost proved fatal helped to keep him for nearly a year in the Bordeaux area (May 1306 – March 1307) and prevented the proposed meeting with Philip the Fair from taking place at Michaelmas 1306. After a partial recovery, Clement V once more set out on his journeyings and reached Poitiers in April 1307. Here he could come to no understanding with the king of France, who refused to agree to all the proposed compromises to end the lawsuit against Boniface VIII, which was still hanging fire. They parted without coming to any decision. On 13 October 1307 a sensational event took place: the mass arrest of the Templars. A further interview with Philip the Fair became necessary. This, too, took place at Poitiers (May–July 1308). The king's demands on this occasion were such that Clement V resolved not to proceed with his enterprise. He could not contemplate going to Rome. It would have been madness to leave Philip the Fair master of the situation on the eve of the opening of the Council of Vienne, where decisions would be taken gravely affecting the interests of the Church, and where in particular the scandalous trial of the Templars would be debated. In complete agreement with the cardinals, Clement V decided to transfer the court to Avignon (August 1308).

This city possessed valuable assets. Rapid and frequent communication with Italy was ensured by both land and water routes. It was near France but not dependent upon her. There was nothing to fear from the suzerains of Avignon, the Angevin princes of Naples; their energies were largely absorbed in defending the integrity of their kingdom of the Two Sicilies against the encroachments of the ambitious house of Aragon, and in the promotion of Guelph interests in the rest of the peninsula; moreover, were they not vassals of the Church? Lastly, the city of Avignon formed an enclave in the Comtat-Venaissin, a possession of the Holy See. No town could provide the papacy with a more peaceful refuge and more powerful guarantees of independence and security.

Once he had taken this decision, Clement V made his way by short stages across the south of France. In March 1309 he entered Avignon and so inaugurated the papacy's long exile which was to last for more than seventy years and which, through ill-justified comparison with the sojourn of the Chosen People in a strange land, has come to be known as "the Babylonian captivity."

The pope's establishment at Avignon still remained provisional in character. Clement V lived unpretentiously in the convent of the Dominicans. He caused only the registers of letters of his two predecessors to be brought from Italy, and left the greater part of the pontifical treasure at the church of St Francis of Assisi. He stayed for only a very short time in Avignon itself, preferring the towns and castles of the Comtat-Venaissin.

The Eve of the Modern World

The lawsuit brought against Boniface VIII caused the supreme pontiff the gravest anxiety between 1309 and 1311. Clement V was skilful enough to succeed in delaying the proceedings as much as possible and ultimately in silencing the worst accusers of the dead pope. As for the trial of the Templars, this was settled at the Council of Vienne (16 October 1311–6 May 1312). At the very moment when Clement might have gone to Italy, his health, never very robust, took a turn for the worse. According to the chronicler Ptolemy of Lucca, who had his information from the lips of the pope's confessor, it declined rapidly after the promulgation, at the Council of Vienne, of the Constitution *Exivi de Paradiso*. The pope, feeling that his end was near, dictated his will on 9 June 1312. His sickness grew worse in the course of the years 1313 and 1314 and finally overcame him on 20 April 1314.

Even if Clement V had enjoyed better health, he could not have crossed the Alps in 1312 or 1313. Henry VII's entry into Italy had set the whole country in revolt. From 7 May 1312, Rome served only as a battlefield where Guelphs and Ghibellines attacked each other brutally. Henry VII lost no time in treating the papacy as an enemy and in defying the threat of excommunication against anyone attacking the king of Naples. In such circumstances who can blame Clement V for staying in the Comtat-Venaissin? Where else could he have found so safe a refuge?

Under the successors of Clement V, Rome and Italy, despite their peoples' protestations and repeated appeals, remained inhospitable to the papacy. "Ah! Italy, abode of sorrow," wrote Dante, "vessel without a helmsman amidst a dreadful storm, no longer art thou mistress of thy peoples, but a place of prostitution. Now, those who live in thy dominions wage implacable war amongst themselves; those protected by the same wall and the same ramparts rend each other. Search, unhappy country, around thy shores and see if in thy bosom a single one of thy provinces enjoys peace." Italy was indeed incessantly laid waste by war in the reign of John XXII. In 1332 the pope contemplated crossing the Alps, after Bertrand du Poujet's victories over the Ghibellines. He conceived the plan of pacifying Lombardy and Tuscany, and then proceeding to Rome. Bologna, which had yielded to the Church, was provisionally chosen as a place of residence. Preparations for the pope's reception were made: a citadel was built at the Galliera gate; an order even reached Rome itself for the pontifical dwellings to be restored and the gardens cultivated afresh. The rebellion of Bologna and the completion of arrangements for the crusade put a speedy end to the pope's plans. In 1333 the king of France was appointed captain-general of the Christian army. That year and the next negotiations were more active than ever between the courts of Paris and Avignon. The departure of the Holy See for Italy would have displeased Philip VI—who had been much angered by the intentions of John XXII—and would have hindered the preparations for the expedition which seemed definitely arranged; undoubtedly it would have gravely compromised the ultimate success of the crusade.

At the beginning of his pontificate, Benedict XII listened to the grievances of the ambassadors sent him by the Romans. In a Consistory held in July 1335, he decided, with the unanimous consent of his cardinals, that the court would leave Avignon about the first of the following October and transfer provisionally to Bologna. The cardinals changed their minds in a second Consistory. They considered it best to postpone the departure for Italy, for, in addition to the many difficulties of the journey itself, they thought that a move on the part of the Holy See would interfere with the plans for the crusade and the settling of urgent business. Moreover, an investigation made on the spot gave ample evidence that sedition at Bologna was still causing too much unrest to justify the transfer of the Holy See within its walls. The cardinals' foresight was justified. Bologna speedily revolted once more against the Church; elsewhere, in Romagna and in the Marches, the nobles were planning to become independent; while at Rome revolution reigned from 1347 until 1354.

Under Clement VI war became inevitable. It was to devastate Italy until the day when the fierce sword of Albornoz conquered the various tyrants, great and small, who were disturbing the peace. Urban V thought this a favourable moment to re-establish the papacy in Rome. As is well known, the hostility of his own subjects forced him to return to Avignon. The pope's fears were not illusory. Under Gregory XI the Roman factions were once more aroused. They plotted to massacre the foreigners who made up the papal court and the non-Italian cardinals, so as to compel the pope to settle forever in the Eternal City. What is worse, a Roman cardinal, in order to seize the triple crown for himself, is alleged to have had the dire thought of making an attempt on the life of Gregory XI. According to other contemporaries, if Gregory XI had left Italy again, as he had shown that he intended to do, the Romans would have created an antipope in opposition to him. In any event, the precautions taken by the supreme pontiff on 19 March 1378 show clearly how much he feared serious trouble after his death.

To sum up, the fact that for many years the popes did not live in Italy is explained by that country's persistent hostility. The popes of the fourteenth century were bound to have fresh in their minds the memory of the attempt on the life of Boniface VIII perpetrated at Anagni; this attack had only been made possible by the connivance of the Romans.

The continued residence of the popes on the banks of the Rhône is thus adequately explained and even justified by the need to put an end to the suit brought against Boniface VIII and to wind up the trial of the Templars, by the imminence of the crusade, by the attempts at conciliation between France and England, and above all by the unsettled state of Italy. To these primary causes must be added some secondary ones: the preponderance of French cardinals in the Sacred College and their marked distaste for Italian soil; the construction by Benedict XII of the Palace of the Popes, at once an admirable work of art and a fortress which for long guaranteed the most complete security; the purchase of Avignon from Joanna I, queen of Naples, in 1348; Clement VI's devotion to his country; the age and infirmity of Innocent VI; the manoeuvres and intrigues of the kings of France, who wished to keep the papal court within their sphere of influence; and the popes' anxiety to preserve friendly relations with the only genuine allies on whom they could count in the bitter conflict with Louis of Bavaria.

CONCLUSION

It was for long customary to judge the Avignon popes only in the light of the malevolent accounts of contemporary chroniclers, and the tendentious writings of Petrarch, St Catherine of Siena and St Bridget of Sweden. All these used to be accepted quite uncritically and without question.

Since, however, documents from the archives were published, though only in an abridged form some seventy or eighty years ago, it has become possible to modify the judgment of history which had hitherto remained uniformly unfavourable to the Avignon papacy.

In the first place, the Avignon popes have frequently been criticised for being too humble in their attitude towards France, and too willing to modify their general policy to suit the particular convenience of the French royal house. In certain instances, such as the trial of the Templars, and in the case of certain popes, such as Clement V and Benedict XII, this criticism still seems justified. But to take a more general view, the diplomatic activities of the Avignon popes were carried on with a real independence both in the East and in the West, and in their foreign policy they unremittingly pursued a threefold aim: to bring peace to Europe, to conquer the Holy Land and to recapture the Papal States.

It must be admitted that the Avignon popes failed to realise their plans for a Crusade. It is difficult to decide how Utopian such plans were, in view of the political situation in fourteenth-century Europe. The popes may well have thought that their influence over the princes of Christendom was still sufficient to justify a hope of success in the noble enterprise. Indeed, throughout the century, their arbitration and intervention were constantly requested, or at least accepted, except in the case of the imperial election, which was now beyond the Roman pontiff's sphere of influence.

The most commonly held grievance against the Avignon popes is that they continued to stay on the bank of the Rhône, far from the Eternal City, which seemed abandoned "without hope of return." On this particular point, the results of our historical investigations are quite unambiguous. Italy was plunged into political anarchy and could not guarantee safe shelter to the papacy. Throughout the fourteenth century the popes tried, with varying success, to restore peace in the peninsula and to take their place once more among the small states that were in process of formation. The victories of Cardinal Albornoz and his skilful policy, which was carried on by Gregory XI, eventually made Rome once more a fitting habitation for the pope.

The Italian policy of the Avignon popes provides at least an explanation and to a certain extent an excuse for their financial system, which was in many ways a new one, and which was eventually to cause serious harm to Christian countries. This discontent was to come into the full light of day at the time of the Great Schism of the West.

The financial policy of the Avignon popes was

closely linked with the increasing tendency to centralise the administration of the Roman Church. This tendency received a lively impetus from, and was very similar to, the corresponding centralisation which was going on in the various European states during the fourteenth and fifteenth centuries as a result of the constitution of national monarchies. It was to give rise to the dangerous forces of reaction which almost carried the day at the Council of Basle.

In conclusion, the religious activities of the Avignon popes stand out in the zeal with which they put down heresy, reformed the religious orders and brought the knowledge of the Gospel to distant lands.

PETER PARTNER

ANOTHER VIEW OF PAPAL FISCALITY

In the following selection, the British scholar Peter Partner limits the focus of our larger problem still further to the question of "Papal Finance and the Papal States." But again, as in the case of the selection from Mollat, this is an extremely important aspect of the problem. Most of the charges that the "general opinion" has leveled against the popes of the later Middle Ages and early modern times go back ultimately to the "secularization of the papacy" and its concern for temporalities at the expense of its ancient spiritual functions. The most often cited evidence of papal temporality is, moreover, the concern of the popes with finance: the historical record reveals a tissue of complaints and charges against the financial policies of the papacy going back from modern scholarship through the Reformation to the strident critics of the fourteenth and fifteenth centuries. It is to these two causally related issues—the secularization of the papacy and papal finance—that Partner addresses himself in this article.

The base of Partner's argument is the well-accepted fact that from the eighth century the papacy played a double role as an international spiritual power on the one hand and as an Italian secular state on the other. He goes on to argue that the maintenance and successful operation of the papal state in Italy was essential to the success of the papacy in its international dimension. But the very bureaucratic practices which were necessary to the successful operation of the papal state were precisely those that brought down upon the papacy the storm of criticism for its secularism. He traces the course of the popes' recovery of the papal state and the increasingly successful administration of it through the opening years of the Reformation and observes the paradox that when the Reformation did break, it was at the moment when the popes were less guilty of the "money-grabbing" with which they were charged than they had been for centuries.

The student should "test" this paradox the author presents. He should note the modern pragmatic defense Partner presents for the papal bureaucracy and for the widely criticized practices of nepotism and the sale of church offices. And he should note the role of the various secular powers in forcing upon the papacy those very secular practices which they then took occasion to criticize.

Machiavelli never missed a chance to bait the Church, and the Papal State does not escape his irony. He taunts the Popes as old and ailing men, unfit for war and dogged by approaching death. The inefficiency of their rule was proverbial; few of them could stand up to the fearful physical and mental gymnastics required of a Renaissance prince. Of all rulers, only they "possess states and do not defend them, have subjects and do not govern them."

This is savage and penetrating, but it is far from being the whole truth. Machiavelli, who considered persons rather than bureaucracies, forgot that the Papal State was managed by the Roman curia, which was probably the most efficient, tenacious and conservative bureaucracy in Europe. Most officers of the Papal court were lawyers, and the claims of the Papacy, which was itself the fount of Canon Law in the West, were pressed by them inexorably from one pontificate to another. They were ambitious and competent men, whose integrity tended to be that of the good civil servant rather than that of the good priest, and to their legal minds the enforcement of the financial rights of the Papacy was of the first importance. And when it is considered how often temporal princes had seized, corrupted and misused the Papacy in its moments of political impotence, their view seems neither nonsensical nor necessarily self-interested.

Papal revenues arose from both "spiritual" and "temporal" sources—that is, in part from a great variety of taxes concerned with the conferment of benefices and the spiritual primacy of the Papacy, in part from the money tribute paid by certain kingdoms, and in part from the government of the lands that the Papacy directly controlled. It was this last, the "Patrimony of St. Peter" of the Middle Ages, the "temporal power" of modern times, that aroused Machiavelli's scorn.

The Pope had since the early Middle Ages been a political ruler as well as a landlord; his worldly rule was based on the so-called "donations" of the Frankish kings in the eighth century. After many vicissitudes, he found himself in the thirteenth century in control of a loosely-knit state, which in the west included Rome and its district, the ancient Latium as far south as Terracina and Ceprano, and as far north as the river Pescia, running inland along the Sienese border into Umbria, to Città della Pieve, Perugia and Città di Castello. On the Adriatic it extended from Ravenna and Bologna in the north (with suzerainty over Ferrara and some neighbouring areas), south down the coast to Ascoli Piceno, and eastwards into the mountainous interior to the Duchy of Spoleto. The two richest areas of this territory were the great town of Bologna, and the southeastern area known as the March of Ancona, which had a flourishing sea trade, and an agriculture of the open countryside, which did not, as elsewhere in central Italy, cling round the walls of the cities. But in the earlier Middle Ages the Papal hand lay lightly on the March, where the communes were as independent as they were prosperous, and lighter still on Romagna, the area in all Italy most prolific of tyrants, of semi-autonomous *signori* whose profession was arms and who, whenever not rigorously coerced, denied all but the nominal suzerainty of the Pope. The country south of Rome was sterile, dominated by the Roman baronage, disorderly, and usually administered at a loss. To the north of Rome, in that part of northern Latium and Umbria known as the Patrimony of St. Peter in Tuscia, Papal rule was strongest. The whole State was one of the five great powers of Italy, an equal to Milan, Venice and the Kingdom of Naples, had it not been worked on by such powerful centrifugal forces, and governed by such short-lived rulers. But the Papal lands tended to be thought a mere source of income rather than a State to be governed. They were ruled through the same bureau, the Apostolic Chamber, that collected the spiritual taxes, and the Pope sometimes appeared in his dominions to be more a tax-collector than a prince.

When the reform of the Church was discussed in the fifteenth century it was recognized by all but the extreme radicals that the Pope and Cardinals should have a substantial income, to pay for the central administration of the Church and for that expensive pageantry which the Middle Ages associated with princely power. Reformers at the great Council of Constance in 1414–1418 tended to say that the

From Peter Partner, "Papal Finance and the Papal State," *History Today*, VII (1957), pp. 766–74. Reprinted by permission of Peter Partner.

Papacy should maintain itself from its worldly revenues, and cut the spiritual ones, whose collection fostered corruption and worldliness, to a minimum. But here they ignored the most tragic part of the problem facing the later medieval Papacy. The Popes might indeed have sacrificed a large part of their spiritual revenues, had they been certain of their power to collect the temporal ones. But the disorders of Italy, rebellion within the Papal State and aggression without, constantly forced them to impose heavy spiritual taxes in order to deal with political rebellions, or even to prevent the Papal State from crumbling away altogether. The abolition of spiritual taxes, and the democratic constitution which the extreme "conciliar" party wanted to force on the Papacy, would have meant the destruction of the Papal State.

These problems changed little in essence for centuries, and, if the situation is viewed from the point of view of the Papal curia, the "periods" in which Papal history has been marked out by modern historians appear rather artificial. We are accustomed to think of the Renaissance as the epoch when the Papacy was an Italian principate, with the Borgia in the forefront of the scene. But although it was exercised only with difficulty, the effective rule of the Popes over their temporal state dates at the latest from the second half of the thirteenth century. This is rather more than a century after the consolidation of the powers of the kings of England and France, but Papal rule lacked a score of the advantages enjoyed by the developing national state. From the thirteenth century, however, the Papal State possessed a complex system of government, a network of provincial rectors, a system of law, a developed central administration. But the role of the temporal power was much complicated by its Janus face—the spiritual primacy of St. Peter; from the time of the Carolingian donations of the eighth century one face of the Papacy was turned inward to Italy and the other outward to Europe, with important consequences for the history of Italy and of the Church. The two aspects of policy are interlocked: the "universal" policy of the Papacy led to a bitter struggle with the Emperors, which led in turn to the seizure by the Empire of whole provinces of the State of the Church. On the other hand, the European prestige of the Papacy afforded many political advantages to the temporal power, and from the spiritual power the Popes drew the money that made possible the decisive conquest of their own patrimony.

This conquest was not easy, and its methods were complex. When Boniface VIII died miserably in 1303, after his bitter humiliation at Anagni at the hands of the agents of Philip the Fair of France and of the Roman family of Colonna, one of the oldest techniques for furthering the temporal power seemed to have ended in defeat and discredit. We have the habit of judging those Popes who enriched their own families at the expense of the Church rather hardly, and of automatically calling a "nepotistic" Pope a bad one. But this is a somewhat prim and anachronistic view of a practice that to contemporaries was not essentially immoral; and it also underrates the practical effectiveness of a realistic policy. The Pope had few troops at his command; and in central Italy the disruptive forces of communes, tyrants and barons were too self-seeking and too sophisticated to be coerced into political obedience by purely spiritual fulminations. If a Pope were to reduce the temporal power to order, he would be best elected from one of the great Roman baronial families—a Conti, a Savelli, an Orsini—so that he might use the military and political force of his family in the service of the Roman Church. This policy was adopted throughout the thirteenth century, and the rise of the temporal authority from impotence to power is convincing proof of its effectiveness; but it had its dangers. The Church paid a heavy price in grants of money and land, and in a certain decline of moral stability. Quarrels and civil war often followed the death of a Pope, when the jealous and perhaps despoiled nobles of one family would fall upon another, which under the rule of their dead kinsman had been enjoying the fruits of office. A further peril was the Pope who pressed the claims of his family with such indiscretion as to attack the whole basis of temporal government. Such a Pope was Boniface VIII, such another was Alexander Borgia, a pair disparate in their moral outlook, but similar in having plans for their families of such grandiosity as to threaten to secularize the whole temporal power. Boniface gave the Caetani family an enormous quantity of money and land, and—encouraged, it is true, by motives unconnected with family—mercilessly expropriated their Colonna enemies. He thus drew down a vengeance that caused disorder and ruin in the Papal State for a good many years, and was a contributory cause of the transfer of the Holy See to Avignon in 1309, where for almost seventy years the Popes remained in the so-called "Babylonian Exile."

It has long been usual to reprove the Avignonese

Popes for their rapacity and for a certain degree of moral turpitude, and to allege the entire decadence of the authority of the Holy See in Italy to be a result of their refusal to desert the pleasant wines of Provence for the bitter beverage of rebellion and danger that would be forced on them in Rome. It is doubtful if the first branch of this charge can be proved; and the second is certainly unjust. The fourteenth century was the epoch of the universal financial domination of the Papacy, which, using its Italian bankers as a European credit system, enforced its taxes and its system of distributing clerical office in every corner of the Church, and enjoyed thereby an immense revenue. But the Papacy at Avignon was not, for this reason, a different entity from the Papacy at Rome. Its system was a development of the already highly articulated organization in use at Rome: the methods of Boniface VIII were not in this respect very different from those of his Avignonese successors, nor was his income so very much less than theirs. And, similarly, the Avignonese Popes were far from forgetting their responsibilities to the temporal power; not only were they anxious for peace so that they might return to Italy, but they wanted to rule with a firmer hand in the Papal State, to suppress tyrants and rebellious barons, to limit the independence of the towns. To this end legates and commissioners were sent from Avignon to Italy charged with commissions of reform, to combat the corruption of the rectors and the intrusion of local interests into Papal government. It was a hard struggle; and, as is common in medieval government, each wave of war and unrest seems to present a picture of irreparable chaos, only to recede and to leave the central authority in a slightly stronger position than before. The times demanded a combination of subtlety and brutal strength. The old hegemony of the free cities, which had been glad to accept Papal protection on limited terms, was ending, and everywhere was being succeeded by the rule of the tyrant, the *signore*. The Papacy did its best to play off one *signore* against another, and, where it could, to assert the *signoria* of the Church against any city which gave it the opportunity. Thus the city of Rome, which in the thirteenth century had much increased its independence vis-à-vis the Popes, in the succeeding century lost ground; in 1347 the dictatorship of Cola di Rienzo, that exotic propagandist of a united Italy under a reborn classical Rome, marks one of the last effective stands of the commune of Rome against Papal authority.

The great agent of the Avignonese Popes in their reconquest of the temporal power was the Spanish Cardinal Gil Albornoz, who between 1353 and 1367 re-established the authority of the Church in every part of the State, and enacted a legal code that was to remain in force in the Papal State until 1817. What other legates had attempted piecemeal, Albornoz achieved in gross. Without finally crushing the tyrants of Romagna, he forced them at least to pay tribute; he built or repaired a network of fortresses, and enjoyed an immense personal prestige from which Papal government as a whole benefited. It proved beyond his power to break the influence of the Visconti, the tyrants of Milan, and the mediocre support he received in this enterprise from the curia assured its failure. Thirty years before John XXII had conducted a comparable war against the Visconti, designed perhaps to impose the influence of the Church over the whole of North Italy, and this policy also had failed. The Papacy at its strongest was able to arbitrate but not to dominate in Italy—a fact repugnant to Machiavelli and to those Italian patriots who disliked the balance of power, and wished one of the Italian states to become strong enough to unite the peninsula.

The military effort to re-establish the temporal power needed money; and most of this was supplied from the "spiritual" revenues of the Church. The Avignonese Popes did not spend all their revenues on clothes and on the construction of their admirable palace; John XXII spent over three-fifths of his income on the Italian wars, and some of his successors spent a similar amount. The temporal princes, many of whom were far on the way toward the creation of the national state, blackmailed the Popes into giving them a substantial share of the clerical taxes nominally due to the Papacy. But the Church groaned under the weight of taxes, the more so because, as time advanced, the princely middlemen took a larger percentage, forcing an increase to be made in gross taxes to maintain the same net income. This state of affairs, which involved a cure of souls being treated principally as the object of legal rights, aroused increasing protest from the truly pious, who saw spiritual things being treated as earthly chattels, from the impoverished clergy and, ironically enough, from many of the princes, who used the pietistic outcry as a lever to get themselves better terms from the Papacy. Denunciations of these Papal exactions was to become a Protestant commonplace, although the part played by the princes was discreetly omitted and has been dragged back to the light only by the labours of modern scholarship.

The Papacy finally returned to Rome in 1377. It was at once afflicted in the following year by the longest and most pernicious schism of the Middle Ages. Until 1417, the Church was without a certain head, and the allegiance of Europe was divided between two and sometimes three claimants to the tiara. The consequences were in every way disastrous. Christendom almost lost its nerve; clerical taxes were collected with more and more difficulty; the power of temporal rulers in Church affairs and their share in clerical taxation both increased sharply. But in one respect the influence of the Schism on Papal power was less deadly than is often thought. Losing many of their spiritual taxes, the Popes were thrown back upon the temporalities. The Cardinals, who had had the right to enjoy half the temporal income, could no longer enforce their claim. The turbulence of the times favoured the Popes, in that the communes could no longer easily maintain themselves outside the larger political units, and the decay of their political and financial privileges was accelerated. Boniface IX, by the time of his death in 1404, was as complete a master of the Papal State as any Pope before him; and, although in the latter part of the Schism the temporal power drifted into utter ruin, the effects of his work were not entirely lost.

The Schism was the great crisis of Papal finance, a crisis more severe and decisive than the Reformation. Early in 1417, the income of the Holy See (then vacant) was nil. It was no longer practical for the Popes to impose arbitrary taxes, or even to collect ordinary ones, without making terms with the temporal rulers, who did not thereby neglect their own interests. The "tenth," the direct tax for the extraordinary needs of the Papacy, became extremely difficult to impose outside Italy. Some taxes were entirely abolished at the Council of Constance. The income of Martin V, the Pope elected at Constance in 1417, was at first between a quarter and a third of that of the Avignonese Popes. Ways out were found; but the decay of the whole tax-collecting system meant that a steep moral price had to be paid in order to maintain even this modest income. The chancery taxes, imposed on anyone who had to seek an official document from the Papal court, were very much increased. Dispensations and compositions of various kinds were charged at a high rate; the indulgence became financially important. No one of these measures brought in a huge sum,

but together they kept the curia from bankruptcy. The newly discovered alum mines at Tolfa were a windfall for the Popes. The sale of offices, an institution more respectable in the Middle Ages than now, but even then rather shocking in a clerical context, had begun seriously in the Papal court during the Schism. At the start providing a real additional income, this practice had the effect of multiplying the number of offices held; and when, late in the fifteenth century, whole colleges of new offices were created at a stroke, it turned into a system of State life-annuities. The salaries of the venal offices were on the average about eleven per cent of the purchase price; percentage charges were made when an office was sold by one holder to another. The capital invested grew by 1520 to between two and a half and three million ducats, and the annual interest absorbed a huge sum. Thus there grew up a kind of privileged stock exchange, to which entry was reserved for the officials of the Roman curia — a fact that had disastrous results for the many attempts made by the Popes to reform the curia.

These expedients were insufficient to cure the basic malaise of Papal finances, which were saved from disaster only by a large increase of the income from the temporal power. From being negligible at the beginning of the Avignonese period, this grew steadily with the spread of effective Papal suzerainty, so that by the third quarter of the fifteenth century Papal budgets estimate that over half Papal income was derived from the Papal State. Perhaps the revenues actually due were not increased a great deal; what was decisive was the regularity of their collection, a factor depending entirely on firmness of government. This was achieved in the same intermittent, wasteful but effective fashion as before. Martin V (Pope from 1417–1431) proved to be the refounder of the temporal power in Italy. A Colonna, he used the system of nepotism with great success, and, having found central Italy in chaos and the lands of the Church in the hands of tyrants, at his death he left the Papal State swollen in wealth and extent, and governed with a firm hand. The power of the Pope in the more distant provinces, Romagna and the March of Ancona, increased steadily as the tyrants there were brought to order. The most effective repression in these provinces since Albornoz' time was conducted by Cesare Borgia, who had his father lived would have tried to turn the whole of central Italy into a duchy or a kingdom of his own. But Julius II turned Borgia's work to the service of the Church — the observation is Machiavelli's. By the time of that fierce pontiff's death in 1513, the Papal State had little more to fear from internal enemies; and, although it led to the sack of Rome in 1527, the Spanish domination in Italy protected the Popes from external foes. The last serious communal rebellion was that of Perugia in 1539; and from this period until the French Revolution the Papal State led a relatively tranquil existence.

The effect of this seems to have been that, from the pontificate of Julius II, Papal revenues rose steeply, and for the first time regained the level they had in their heyday in the fourteenth century—but with the difference that, instead of being drawn from the clerical estate all over Europe, they were provided mainly by the inhabitants of the Papal State. In the medieval phrase, the Pope was "living of his own." The Reformation period, in which criticism of Papal "bloodsucking" reached its peak, was thus a period in which the "spiritual" taxes in fact sank to a low proportion—perhaps a quarter—of Papal revenue. Taxation for the benefit of the Church was still not lacking in Europe; but the naïve criticism of the reformers overlooked the long line of middlemen who stood between the tax-payer and Rome.

Once the Papal budget had been balanced, it was,

in theory, at last possible to plan a drastic reform of the Roman court, which would iron out its complex and irritating bureaucratic anomalies, and disperse the tribe of clerical hangers-on. But for a long time no such reform was attempted, partly because of the spendthrift dilettantism of Popes like Leo X (Pope from 1513–1521), partly because of political crises, but perhaps most of all because a hoary and conservative bureaucracy would not permit its leader to encroach on ancient privilege. Papal income continued to rise. But not until the Council of Trent was a root-and-branch reform of the Roman curia attempted. By that time Papal finances were predominantly the finances of the Papal State; the losses occasioned by the Tridentine reforms were met by increases in the salt tax.

From a financial point of view the Reformation is therefore a paradox; the final outburst against Papal money-grabbing came at the moment when the Popes were less guilty under this charge than they had been for many centuries. If the reformers had turned their attention to the growing share of Church revenues which was enjoyed by the temporal princes, they might have had a more realistic view of the situation.

WALLACE K. FERGUSON

A MODERN SYNTHESIS

The following selection is taken from an article, "The Church in a Changing World: A Contribution to the Interpretation of the Renaissance," by the eminent American historian of the Renaissance, Wallace K. Ferguson. In it he presents a new interpretation of this period in the history of the church which he states more elaborately in his recently published book, *Europe in Transition 1300–1520*. Despite its small compass, this article takes a broader view even than the selection from the much more comprehensive work of Pastor. The result is to present this segment of the history of the church and the papacy as a distinct period in church history, a major period of transition between the high Middle Ages and modern times. It is part of the author's general argument in favor of the Renaissance as a distinct historical period.

In this article Ferguson's argument is that the church and the papacy were able to dominate the Christian world in the age of Innocent III because that world was still predominantly feudal; that, with the crisis of Boniface VIII, the church and papacy began to lose ground as feudalism gave way before the rising national monarchies and the general changes in society marking the passing of feudalism; that the changes for which the late medieval popes have been criticized were actually awkward and ill-contrived accommodations to these changed material conditions of institutional life; and that, after the upheaval of the Reformation, the church regained its strength and the papacy its integrity not by counterreformation but by a return to fundamental spirituality.

The student should compare the treatment of the Avignonese papacy in this selection with its treatment in the preceding ones. He should note Ferguson's argument that the popes of the fifteenth century turned to the consolidation of their secular power in Italy and behaved like other contemporary Italian princes; and he should note the difference between this argument and the one advanced by Partner in the previous selection. He should note how Ferguson explains the Conciliar Movement in terms not of the reform of abuses but in terms of a fundamental conflict of constitutional theory. And finally, the student should attempt to follow the systematic development of the author's "thesis."

The historical interpretation of that phase in the development of European civilization represented by the fourteenth, fifteenth, and sixteenth centuries poses a problem that has aroused much interest and no little controversy among scholars in the ninety-odd years since Burckhardt first treated these centuries as a period in the history of Italian civilization and labeled it the Renaissance. Since then, scholars who did not share Burckhardt's preconceptions, or who were interested primarily in other countries or in some particular aspect of culture, have presented widely divergent views of the spirit, content, and chronological limits of the Renaissance,[1] with the result that the value of the concept for purposes of periodization has been greatly vitiated. Much of the confusion concerning the Renaissance arises, I think, from the fact that it has been used indiscriminately as a style concept or to denote an intellectual movement, and that, when considered as a historical period, it has commonly been regarded from the point of view of one country or one particular cultural or religious interest, so that its interpretation has been constructed upon too narrow a foundation. It seems to me that, if we consider the economic, social, and political, as well as the intellectual, aesthetic, and religious life of the centuries from 1300 to 1600, we shall find a certain unity of development in all the countries of western Europe. It seems to me, too, that, if the various aspects of their civilization are related to one another in a reasonably well co-ordinated synthesis, these three centuries may be treated as a period in the history of western European civilization as a whole, and that such a periodic concept may have sufficient validity to serve as a useful, if not indispensable, instrument of historical thought. For this period the term Renaissance may not be well chosen, but it is still the only commonly accepted term we have for a crucially important historical period, and one that cannot be treated satisfactorily by the simple device of attaching it to either the medieval or the modern age, or by dividing it between them.

It is, indeed, the distinguishing characteristic of these centuries that they are neither medieval nor modern, but represent a transitional stage which has a character of its own. In a paper read at the meeting of the Modern Language Association in December, 1950,[2] I defined the Renaissance as a period characterized by the gradual shift from one fairly

[1] For review of the major trends in the interpretation of the Renaissance, see W. K. Ferguson, *The Renaissance in Historical Thought* (Boston, 1948).

[2] W. K. Ferguson, "The Interpretation of the Renaissance: Suggestions for a Synthesis," *Journal of the History of Ideas*, XII (1951), 483–95.

From Wallace K. Ferguson, "The Church in a Changing World: A Contribution to the Interpretation of the Renaissance," *American Historical Review*, LIX (1953), pp. 1–18. Reprinted by permission of the American Historical Association and the author.

well co-ordinated and clearly defined type of civilization to another, yet at the same time possessing in its own right certain distinctive traits and a high degree of cultural vitality. As a more precise hypothesis I suggested that it was a transition from a civilization that was predominantly feudal and ecclesiastical in its social, political, and cultural manifestations and agrarian in its economic foundations, to one that was predominantly national, urban, secular, and laic, in which the economic center of gravity had shifted from agriculture to commerce and industry and in which a simple money economy had evolved into capitalism. What I want to consider here is the problem of the Church and the papacy in this synthesis. To what extent do they fit? And to what extent does this approach to the interpretation of the Renaissance serve to illuminate a crucial segment in the history of the Church?

The conception of this period as peculiarly an age of transition makes it necessary to establish first of all a fairly definite idea of the nature of the civilizations that preceded and followed it. But, since historical thought tends naturally toward a genetic treatment and, indeed, cannot avoid the problem of causation, the interpretation of a transitional age is necessarily bound up more closely with the age out of which it grew than with that into which it later developed. By far the greater part of the controversy over the character of the Renaissance has concentrated attention upon its relation to the Middle Ages. This is the essential problem of the Renaissance scholar. The question of the relation of the Renaissance to the following period belongs rather to scholars whose field of interest is the early modern period. That is their genetic headache; let us leave it to them. This may seem an irresponsible attitude, and I may be following too closely the example of that little bird, the prototype of all historians, who always liked to fly backwards, because he didn't care where he was going but liked to see where he had been. I think, however, that in so far as our interest is concentrated upon the transitional age itself, we must consider of first importance the question of what were the causes, nature, and extent of change. And that leads us back inevitably to the Middle Ages. As Carl Becker once remarked, a historian can describe anything only by first describing what it successively was before it became that which it will presently cease to be.

The origins of the Church, of course, carry us back to a period before the Middle Ages. From that early period it inherited not only its basic doctrine but also the concept of universality and the hierarchical organization that have remained constant throughout its history. In considering what was peculiarly medieval in the Church, however, and therefore likely to change with the passing of medieval civilization, we need go no further back than the centuries in which feudalism was taking shape, that is, roughly the eighth, ninth, and tenth centuries. In these centuries, if we accept Pirenne's thesis, western Europe had been reduced to an almost purely agricultural economy. And I think we might describe feudalism as fundamentally the adaptation of social and political organization to an economy in which land was almost the only form of wealth. Under these circumstances, central governments lacked the financial resources to govern effectively, so that legal jurisdiction and governmental authority were parceled out among the great landholders. Under these circumstances, too, the clergy, as one of the two classes that did not work the land yet had a very important function to perform, became a landholding class. Even earlier, in the Merovingian period, bishops had become administrative officers with secular rule over their cities. Now, as feudal lords, the bishops and abbots became the rulers of fiefs, barons ecclesiastical with sovereign rights in their baronies. From this period on, the Church was committed to the exercise of temporal authority and to great possessions. But, by the nature of feudal tenure, a lord was also a vassal. And the barons ecclesiastical were at the same time vassals of secular lords: kings or emperors. From this arose much interference by laymen in the election of church officials, and the ill-omened figure of Simon Magus cast its shadow across the Church. This was the period in which the Church was most completely feudalized. In their dual capacity as feudal vassals and church officers, prelates were forced to divide their services, often somewhat unequally, between God and Mammon, but they also exercised a great deal of independent authority. The utter inadequacy of fiscal income made effective central government almost impossible for either the papacy or the monarchies, so that the conflict of secular and spiritual interests operated on the level of diocese and fief rather than of Church and state in the broader sense.

The eleventh century marked the beginning of a tremendous revival in every branch of medieval civilization. Regular commercial relations were re-established between Italy and the Levant. From the seacoasts trade spread inland until the whole of western Europe was covered with a network of trade routes along which traveled not only merchants but also pilgrims, crusaders, students, and churchmen on official business. At intervals along these trade routes old cities revived or new ones sprang up. They became centers of local trade and skilled industry and, at the same time, furnished a market for surplus agricultural products. The twelfth and thirteenth centuries were characterized by a steadily growing prosperity in both country and city. The population of western Europe probably doubled during this period. Money economy, reintroduced through commerce and industry in the cities, spread to the countryside and made possible the partial conversion of landed wealth into fluid wealth that could be mobilized and concentrated. But, though this economic revival received its initial impetus from trade and depended for its continuing growth on the growth of cities, European society still retained in main outlines the structure which had been given it by the feudal system and the Church. The vigorous culture which made the twelfth and thirteenth centuries the classic period of medieval civilization was preeminently the culture of the feudal nobility and the clergy.

Feudalism, indeed, lasted long after the passing of that condition of almost exclusive agricultural economy in which it had been formed and which had justified its existence. The rights and privileges of the dominant feudal classes were protected by their monopoly of military force, by long-established jurisdictional authority, and by custom so ingrained that no other form of social and political organization could be imagined. As Joseph Calmette has observed, feudalism had become a kind of Kantian category, in terms of which the medieval mind perceived the social world.[3] Nevertheless, the growth of a money economy made possible, even in this period, the gradual recovery by central governments of some of the powers that had been lost in practice, if not in theory, during the early feudal era. In the early stages of this development, however, the government of the Church was in a position to take advantage of the new situation to better effect than were the feudal monarchies. Though partially feudalized in practice, the Church had never been as feudalized in theory as were the secular states. Its hierarchical principle was deeply rooted in both tradition and dogma. The feudal system, it is true, was also in theory hierarchical; but the feudal hier-

archy consisted of a fortuitous network of personal relations which changed its form with each generation and which the accidents of marriage and inheritance rendered increasingly chaotic. The hierarchy of the Church, on the other hand, was a rationally organized administrative system, modeled upon that of the Roman Empire. Whereas the secular monarchies could establish effective state government only by destroying the feudal hierarchy as a political reality, the ecclesiastical monarchy had only to tighten its control of the hierarchy to make it an effective instrument of central government.

Even so, this was no easy task, for the officers of the Church were also vassals of emperors or kings. Bishops resisted the extension of papal authority not only because it infringed upon their independent diocesan jurisdiction but also because, in many cases, they felt a prior loyalty to the king or emperor who had nominated and enfeoffed them. This was the most serious obstacle to the growth of a strong centralized government in the Church. The vigorous assertion of the papal monarchy by Gregory VII led inevitably to the Investiture Controversy with the emperors and to less overt conflicts with other kings and princes. It also led to an unprecedented expansion of the claims of papal supremacy from the ecclesiastical into the temporal sphere. For, so long as the officers of the Church were also temporal lords, whose support was essential to secular rulers, the government of the Church could not be disassociated from that of the state. An effective papal monarchy within the Church could, therefore, be achieved only by establishing papal supremacy over the secular states. In this the popes were never entirely successful, but in the age of Innocent III they came very close to the fulfillment of their ambition. In their contest with the powers of this world the popes could count on the immense spiritual authority conferred upon them by unchallenged faith in the saving power of the Church. Their spiritual weapons were not yet blunted by overuse. They enjoyed the prestige of leading the military might of Christendom against the infidel; and they were actively supported by all the reforming elements in the monastic orders, by the doctors of the new scholastic learning, and by the development of canon law in the new universities. It must not be forgotten that the assertion of papal supremacy began as a reform movement at a time when reform of the Church was sadly needed. There is something, too, in Heinrich von Eicken's theory that the supremacy of the Church over temporal governments was the logical

[3]Joseph Calmette, *Le Monde féodal* (Paris, 1946), p. 169.

extension into practice of the ascetic conviction of the worthlessness of all things worldly.[4] At any rate, the concern with temporal affairs, which threatened eventually to secularize the Church, had in the twelfth century the full support of St. Bernard and all the most ascetic elements in both the secular and regular clergy.

Despite all these advantages, it is doubtful whether the papacy or the Church as an institution could have achieved the dominant position they held in the age of Innocent III if political and social life had not still been cast in the feudal mold—and that not only because secular governments were still too much weakened by feudal particularism to resist the encroachments of the spiritual authority upon the temporal sphere. The privileged legal status of the clergy fitted naturally into a society in which all legal status depended upon social status. The immunity of the clergy from secular jurisdiction was only one of many immunities, akin to that of the burghers or any other corporate body. The ecclesiastical courts and the canon law competed not with state courts and state law but with a bewildering variety of feudal and urban courts and laws. Everywhere the Church had the advantage that its institutions were universal, while those of the secular world were local and particular. The universality of the Church, indeed, found its perfect complement in the particularism and localism of feudal society. There could be little real conflict between a knight's loyalty to his immediate lord and the Christian's loyalty to the head of the *Respublica Christiana*. Seldom did these centruies witness any type of warfare between the extremes of the localized feudal brawl and the crusade against the infidel. Finally, it was largely due to the conditions of life in a feudal society that the clergy were able to maintain a practical monopoly of education. As the only class in society which had a felt need for these things, the clergy became the principal protagonists of learning, music, and art. They were thus able to give them a direction consonant with their own interests, and to place upon them the stamp of a universal uniformity that did much to impede the growth of national sentiment or national cultures. The feudal nobilty had their vernacular literatures—troubadour lyric, chanson, romance, or Minnesang—but serious thought served the Church. The best brains of Europe functioned below a tonsure. And what medieval men had of visual beauty or the concourse of sweet sounds they owed to the universal Church.

The conditions so uniquely favorable to papal supremacy and to the dominant position of the Church in European society lasted until about the end of the thirteenth century. Even before that time, however, there were signs, though the cloud was no larger than a man's hand, that the halcyon days were passing. The conflict between the thirteenth-century popes and the viper brood of the Hohenstaufen ended in the practical destruction of the Empire. But, in the process, the papacy lost something of the moral prestige that had been its greatest asset in the days of the Investiture Controversy. A moral conflict had degenerated into a squabble over territorial sovereignty in Italy. The spiritual weapons of the Apostolic See had been used too freely in defense of the material patrimony of St. Peter, and popes had too often cried crusade when there was no crusade. So far as any contemporary could observe, however, the papacy was stronger than ever. The Empire was shattered, and, during the greater part of the thirteenth century, France was ruled by a saint and England by a pious fool, neither of whom would offer effective resistance to the spiritual ruler of Christendom. When in 1300 Boniface VIII proclaimed the first Jubilee Year, it seemed as though all Europe had come to Rome to pour its varied coinage into the papal coffers. Two years later, in the bull *Unam Sanctam*, Boniface proclaimed in uncompromising terms the subjection of the temporal to the spiritual authority and concluded by declaring that, for all human creatures, obedience to the Roman pontiff is altogether necessary to salvation. The storm that broke immediately thereafter indicated the extent to which conditions had changed. Philip the Fair was no saint, and Edward I no pious fool. Nor were these sovereigns content to act as mere feudal suzerains within their kingdoms. The reigns of these two kings mark the first decisive stage in the transition from feudal to national monarchy, and a national monarch, determined to be master in his own state, could scarcely tolerate either the papal claims to supremacy or the immunity of the clergy from royal jurisdiction and royal taxation. In the rising national monarchies the papacy met for the first time a secular power too strong for it. The arrest of the aged pope at Anagni marked the end of a period which had opened with an emperor standing barefoot in the snow before the gates of Canossa.

[4] Heinrich von Eicken, *Geschichte und System der mittelalterlichen Weltanschauung* (Stuttgart, 1923), pp. 325 ff.

The crisis precipitated by the conflict between Boniface VIII and Philip the Fair led to a series of events which seriously undermined the authority and prestige of the papacy; the long exile at Avignon under the shadow of the French monarchy, the scandal of the Great Schism, the conciliar movement, and the anarchy in the Papal States. All of these events aggravated the difficulties inherent in the position of the Church in a changing world. Yet their significance may easily be exaggerated. The anarchy in the Papal States which made Rome unsafe was not new. There had been schisms before the Great Schism, and antipopes before Clement VII. As Guillaume Mollat has recently pointed out, the absence of the popes from Rome was not unprecedented nor necessarily disastrous.[5] It has been calculated, indeed, that "between the years 1100 and 1304, that is, two hundred and four years, the popes lived one hundred and twenty-two outside Rome and eighty-two in Rome: a difference of forty years in favor of absence."[6]

What seems to me more significant than these external events in the history of the papacy is the profound though gradual change which took place in the whole civilization of western Europe in the three centuries following 1300. It was a change caused by the interaction of political and social factors, complicated by shifts in the social balance and by the imponderable element of a changing *Weltanschauung*. But one factor at least was, I think, of basic importance: the expansion within feudal society of a money economy during the preceding two or three hundred years. By the end of the thirteenth century it had begun to disintegrate a system never intended for it. Even before that time, the manorial system, with its exchange of labor and produce for the use of land and its closely integrated relation of landholders to dependent workers, had begun to be replaced by a system of cash payments—of rents, leases, and wages. The result was a fundamental change in the economic and social foundations of feudalism. The disrupting effect of this change was aggravated by widespread famines in the early years of the fourteenth century, by the depopulation of Europe resulting from the Black Death and the succession of only relatively less fatal epidemics that followed, by the devastation of France during the Hundred Years' War, by the cessation of coloniza-

[5] Guillaume Mollat, *Les Papes d'Avignon* (Paris, 1949), pp. 9 ff.

[6] Louis Gayet, *Le Grand Schisme d'Occident* (Florence, 1889), p. 3.

tion and of the assarting of waste land, in short by a series of economic crises and depressions which bred intense social unrest and seriously undermined the economic stability of the feudal classes, including the landholding clergy, and loosened their hold upon the land and its people.

At the same time that the economic and social foundations of feudalism were crumbling, the political and jurisdictional powers of the feudal nobles were being absorbed by the central governments in the great national states and in the smaller principalities of Germany and the Netherlands, as they had been already in the city-states of Italy. The money economy which undermined the independence of the feudal classes served to increase the powers of central government. Money furnished the sinews of administration as of war, and though the total wealth of the European states may not have increased materially during the period of economic crisis from 1300 to about 1450, governments everywhere were learning to utilize the available wealth to better effect by levying new taxes, by imposing import, export, and excise duties, by borrowing from the great Italian banking houses, and, in general, by evolving a more efficient fiscal system. The change in military technique from the feudal array to the royal armies and mercenary companies of the Hundred Years' War is but one symptom of a process which, by the end of the fifteenth century, had subordinated feudal particularism to royal absolutism and had transformed the feudal vassal of the Middle Ages into the courtier of the early modern period.

Meanwhile, in the urban centers of commerce and industry an equally fundamental change was taking place. Even before 1300, in Italy and the Netherlands, a simple money economy had begun to develop into an embryonic capitalist system. That development continued steadily during the following centuries and spread to all parts of western Europe. The first hundred and fifty years or so of this period, it is true, lacked the steadily expanding prosperity of the preceding centuries. There were periods of acute depression and social unrest in all the great commercial and industrial cities during the fourteenth century. Some cities declined, while others grew. It is difficult to estimate how much the wealth of the cities actually increased during this period. There is, however, ample evidence of an increasing concentration of wealth and of a revolutionary development in the techniques of capitalist business enterprise.

One result, the cultural and religious implications of which I shall return to later, was the spread of lay education in the cities; another, the growth of an urban patriciate composed of laymen who had the wealth, leisure, and cultivated taste to fit them for active participation in any form of intellectual or aesthetic culture. Still another result, the implications of which are more germane to my present argument, was the evolution by merchants, bankers, and financiers of new and more efficient methods of book-keeping and accounting, as well as of more efficient techniques for the mobilization and transportation of money in large quantities. The development of state fiscal systems, the more rational accounting introduced into state chanceries, the hard-headed calculation behind the pious façade of royal policies, even the national bankruptcies that mark this period, are all evidence of the application to public finance of techniques and attitudes first worked out in the domain of private capitalist enterprise.

All of these changes operated, directly or indirectly, to alter the character of medieval society; and, inasmuch as the Church had adapted itself with remarkable success to medieval conditions, any change was almost certain to be prejudicial to it. And, in fact, it did become increasingly difficult for the Church to maintain its dominant position in society and for the papacy to maintain the temporal supremacy it had won in the feudal era. At the same time, the papacy could not conceivably abandon without a struggle powers and privileges which the Church had possessed for centuries and had exercised for the good of the Christian community and for the salvation of souls. Not only would the abandonment of its traditional policy have involved encroachment upon too many vested interests; it would also have involved a grave dereliction of duty, the abdication of a responsibility for the moral government of Christendom that had been asserted by saints and popes and rationalized by centuries of canon law and scholastic argument. But to maintain its position under the new conditions, the government of the Church would have to fight with new weapons. It would have to meet the growing centralization of state administration with an increased centralization in the administration of the Church; and, as money became more and more the essential source of power, it would have to rival the fiscal system of state governments by establishing a more efficient fiscal system of its own. Or so it must have seemed to anyone likely to achieve high office in

the Church. There were mystics, like the spiritual Franciscans, who felt differently, and reformers, like John Wycliffe, whose conviction that wealth and power were a hindrance rather than a help to the Church drove them into heresy. But mystics are seldom successful politicians, even ecclesiastical politicians, and spiritually-minded reformers who advocated a return to apostolic poverty or the abandonment to Caesar of the things that were Caesar's were not likely to rise to positions of great authority in an institution committed to great possessions and to the exercise of temporal power. Yet the fiscal system and the concentration of administrative authority in the papal curia, both of which were developed with such skill by the fourteenth- and fifteenth-century popes, should not be considered simply the result of official will to power or avarice in high places. To the hierarchical mind there must have seemed no alternative. The changing policy of the Church as it strove to meet changing conditions must have seemed merely the continuation through new methods of the traditional policy of the preceding centuries. No Biblical injunction warned of the danger of putting old wine into new bottles.

Nevertheless, the development within the Church of a highly organized and centralized fiscal system implied more than the mere adaptation to old ends of a new means. Hitherto, the papal supremacy had been founded largely upon moral authority. The wealth of the Church had remained, even after the reintroduction of money economy, to a great extent decentralized. It was wealth drawn largely from land and held by the officers of the local church organization. By the end of the thirteenth century, however, the increased circulation of money, together with the growth of new techniques of bookkeeping, banking, and exchange, had made possible an effective system of taxation in both Church and state. Thereafter, the centralization of governmental authority and the elaboration of a fiscal system went hand in hand. In this the papacy was simply keeping pace with the secular governments. But the results were different, for the Church was not a secular institution devoted solely to secular ends, though its officers may occasionally have lost sight of this fact in their preoccupation with *Realpolitik*. The possession of wealth had always carried with it the threat of a materialism that might sap the spiritual vigor of the Church. Since the days of Peter Damiani preachers had complained that men were inspired to seek office in the Church by avarice and ambition. So long as the wealth of the Church remained decentralized, however, its central government had remained relatively uncontaminated. Under the new conditions not only the wealth but the materialism that went with it, seemed to be concentrated in an unprecedented degree in the papal curia. Contemporary wits noticed that the word Roma furnished an acrostic base for the apothegm *radix omnium malorum avaritia*.

Nor did the danger end there, for the blight of fiscality spread throughout the Church. The increasing demands of the papal curia forced preoccupation with finance upon all the officers of the Church down to the parish level. And the effort of the papal chancery to introduce a fiscal system into an institution 'hat had never been designed for it led inevitably to the systematization of simony and to traffic in spiritual goods. The fourteenth-century popes, it is true, were very largely successful in gaining that control of the nomination of prelates for which the medieval popes had labored in vain. But, as Dean Inge once remarked, in matters of religion nothing fails like success. The reservation to the papal curia of the right of nomination to vacant benefices throughout Christendom did not achieve a reform of the Church. On the contrary, fiscal pressures, diplomatic negotiations with secular princes, and nepotism in the curia made papal provisions the source of new abuses: absenteeism, duplication of offices, traffic in expectancies, the outright sale of benefices, and close calculation of the financial value of every office. Through the imposition of annates and *servitia* the system also imposed a crushing tax upon benefices, so that many of the charitable and other services expected of the local clergy were left undone. I need not describe here the fiscal expedients to which that financial genius, John XXII, and the other popes of this period resorted. Nor need I emphasize their deleterious effects upon clerical morality. These things are well enough known. Conditions were doubtless never as bad as the reforming preachers would have us believe. One cannot, however, entirely ignore the evidence of a cloud of witnesses to the effect that secular and material interests had done much to corrupt the spiritual character of the clergy, high and low. The pamphlet literature of the conciliar movement furnishes ample evidence of a widespread demand for reform of the Church in head and members, and of a growing conviction that reform could be achieved only by depriving the papal monarchy of some of its sovereign powers.

The conciliar movement, however, was by its very nature doomed to failure. Its constitutional theory ran counter to the trend of growing absolutism in the state as well as in the Church. The position of the bishops had been weakened by many of the same political and economic factors as had undermined the independence of the feudal nobles. The principle of free canonical election, for which the councils strove, had for centuries been no more than partially realized, and it was now a lost cause. It served the interest of the kings no more than of the popes. Finally, the whole conception of the ecumenical council as an international body governing a universal Church had become partially anachronistic. In practice, at any rate, it was vitiated by the intrusion of national governments, national interests, and national sentiments, which divided the councils and frustrated the attempt to impose a permanent control upon the papal executive.

The popes were thus able to weather the storm of the conciliar movement, and they emerged with their theoretical sovereignty intact and with a stronger hold than ever upon the administration of the Church. If so much was won, however, much also was lost. During the crisis years of the Captivity and the Schism the popes had gradually abandoned in practice their claims to supremacy over secular rulers. The fifteenth-century popes made their peace with kings and princes through a series of tacit agreements or formal concordats, by which they shared the nomination of church officers and the taxation of the clergy with the secular rulers. In England, the Statute of Provisors, which the fourteenth-century parliaments had used as an instrument to check papal provisions to English benefices, was allowed to become a dead letter. The English kings were content to leave to the popes the right of provision, and incidentally the annates or *servitia* paid by those who received their benefices by papal collation, on the tacit understanding that a certain number of royal ministers or favorites would be nominated. A similar tacit agreement to share some of the fruits of the papal right of provision in Germany with the emperor and the electors underlay the formal Concordat of Vienna of 1448, by means of which Nicholas V won the emperor Frederick III away from the Council of Basel. The French monarchy, long accustomed to special consideration by the Avignonese popes, proved more difficult to deal with. The Pragmatic Sanction of Bourges in 1438 was a unilateral assertion of the liberties of the Gallican Church, and for more than half a century it remained a threat to the principle of papal sovereignty. The theory of papal authority was finally saved by the Concordat of Bologna in 1516, but only at the cost of surrendering to Francis I the most profitable fruits of control of the national church.

In the system of concordats the papacy made its first adjustment to a world of strong secular states. The popes made such practical concessions as were necessary, without apparent impairment of their own *plenitudo potestatis*. For an estimate of the results we can scarcely do better than quote Professor McIlwain's masterly summary:

They were concessions only. But they were concessions guaranteed by a bilateral document in the nature of a treaty, which implies two treaty-making powers. The concordats were in fact the price the Papacy paid for its victory over the councils and it was a price heavier than appeared at the time. They were a tacit acknowledgment of the sovereignty of national states and they mark the virtual end of the medieval theory that Christendom in its secular aspect is one great state as in its spiritual it is a single Church. From such an admission the logical inference must come sooner or later that the Church is *in* every nation instead of embracing all nations, and this can ultimately mean only that its functions are primarily spiritual and that its participation in secular matters is never justifiable except for a spiritual end — *ad finem spiritualem*.[7]

That was undoubtedly the ultimate result; but it was not the moral immediately drawn from the situation by the popes in the century between the Council of Basel and the Council of Trent. Having failed to maintain the universal sovereignty that had been possible in the feudal age, they concentrated their attention upon restoring their temporal sovereignty in their own states. In this transitional stage, the popes became Italian princes. They suppressed the independent despotisms in the Papal States by force; they employed armies of mercenaries, waged wars, made and broke alliances, and in general took their place as one of the powers in the state system of Europe. In this period political expediency dominated papal policy, though fiscal considerations were not neglected. The College of Cardinals now included members of the ruling families of Italy and the chief ministers of the great European states. Never before had the papacy seemed so securely established as a temporal power, but never before had its power seemed so purely temporal as it did in the age of Alexander VI and Julius II. This was its period of greatest peril. On the one hand the pope, as

temporal ruler of the states of the Church, was no more than a third-rate power, on the level more or less of Milan or Florence. In the game of power politics he was no match for France or Spain. In 1527 the papacy that had chosen to live by the sword came very close to perishing by the sword, and thereafter the popes, as temporal rulers, were drawn into the Spanish sphere of influence, becoming satellites whose foreign policy was dominated by Spanish kings. On the other hand, the preoccupation of the papal curia with temporal politics during these crisis years made it peculiarly unfitted to combat the spiritual revolution that broke out in Germany and that, within two generations, separated half of northern Europe permanently from the Church of Rome. The papacy survived this crisis too, with its sovereignty over what remained of the Church strengthened rather than weakened; but it did so only by ceasing to compete with secular states upon their own terms, by withdrawing into the spiritual sphere in which its authority was unchallenged, by restating the doctrines of the Church in the spirit of the great scholastic age, by employing the militia of the Society of Jesus rather than hired mercenaries, and by leaving coercive jurisdiction to the secular arm of state governments. Not that the temporal power of the papacy, the privileged status of the clergy, and the great possessions of the Church were completely abandoned in the Counter-Reformation. Much remained that would be whittled away only very gradually in the following centuries. But, by the end of the sixteenth century, the main lines which were to be followed in the Church's adjustment to the modern world were already clearly indicated. The transition from medieval to modern forms was nearly complete.

So far I have concentrated attention primarily upon the papacy and the Church in their relation to the secular states. That, however, is only a part of the problem of assessing the position of the Church in the changing civilization of the Renaissance. The relation of the Church to contemporary changes in culture, religious sentiment, and general *Weltanschauung* is of equal if not greater importance, but it is less easy to summarize in a brief paper. Here I can do no more than make a few general observations.

One factor of primary importance for the whole cultural evolution of the Renaissance period, it seems to me, was the growth of lay education. This was not an entirely unknown phenomenon in the Middle Ages. As James Westfall Thompson and oth-

[7]C. H. McIlwain, *The Growth of Political Thought in the West* (New York, 1932), p. 352.

ers have demonstrated, there was more literacy, at least, among medieval laymen then historians used to suppose, though that is not saying very much.[8] Nevertheless, the magnificent intellectual and aesthetic achievements of the twelfth and thirteenth centuries, if we exclude the vernacular literature of chivalry, was almost entirely the work of clerics and was patronized, organized, and directed by the Church *ad majorem Dei gloriam*. Under feudal conditions the nobles had little use for learning and less for art, while the burghers had not yet acquired the wealth, social security, or independent cultural tradition that would enable them to compete with the clergy in this sphere. In Italy, however, before the end of the thirteenth century, and in other countries of western Europe somewhat later, the social and economic development of the cities had reached a point where literacy was a necessity, and higher education a possibility, for the middle and upper classes of the urban population. To this end the growth of communal governments staffed by lay administrators, increasing prosperity, and the gradual evolution of a more self-confident burgher tradition all contributed. But on a purely material level the major factor, I think, was the expansion of business enterprise which accompanied the transition from itinerant to sedentary commerce, and the growth of capitalist forms of business organization. This involved, on the one hand, bookkeeping, written instruments of credit and exchange, accurate calculation of profit and loss, complicated negotiations with distant agents or partners, and a much more precise definition of civil law, all of which made literacy indispensable for everyone connected with business in any managerial capacity and also called into being a numerous learned class of lay lawyers, scribes, and notaries. On the other hand, it resulted in the concentration of wealth and the accumulation of surplus capital which furnished the means for lay patronage of literature, learning, and the arts. It also created a new class of leisured *rentiers,* who lived on inherited wealth and were free to devote themselves to intellectual or aesthetic interests. The concentration of both wealth and political power in royal or princely courts served the same purpose in slightly different ways. Such courts became centers for the patronage and dissemination of lay culture, and so exposed the courtly nobility to a wider range of cultural interests than had been available in the isolated baronial castles of the feu-

dal era. After 1450 the invention of printing vastly increased the lay reading public and tipped the scale decisively in favor of lay participation in all forms of literary culture; but that epoch-making invention was itself the answer to a demand already large enough to ensure its being a profitable venture.

The spread of lay education and lay patronage and the growth of a distinct class of lay men of letters greatly expanded the secular content of Renaissance culture. This does not imply any necessary decline in religious sentiment. On the contrary, it was accompanied in many places by a pronounced growth in lay piety. Nevertheless, it was detrimental in many ways to the dominant position which the Church had acquired in medieval society. It deprived the Church of its exclusive control of higher education and the clergy of their monopoly of learning and serious thought. And it created a rival, if not an antagonist, to the ecclesiastical culture of the preceding centuries. Evidence of this may be found everywhere in Renaissance music and art, as well as in literature and learning. The revival of antiquity is but one aspect, if the most prominent, of this general trend. Humanism grew up largely as a lay interest, the offspring of lay education, though many humanists were technically clerics. It was, at any rate, not controlled and directed by the Church as scholasticism had been, and it may even be said to have imposed itself upon the Church in the person of such popes as Nicholas V and Pius II and the scores of humanists highly placed in the ecclesiastical hierarchy. In the long run, humanism of the Erasmian variety inspired the most telling attacks upon the temporal power, wealth, and materialism of the Church in the period just preceding the Protestant Reformation.

The reforming Christian humanism of the Erasmian circle represents another aspect of the danger to the medieval Church inherent in the spread of lay education. As I noted in passing, this was accompanied in many places by a distinct revival of lay piety. But the lay piety inspired by mystical preachers like Eckhart and Tauler, and represented by such movements as that of the Friends of God in the Rhineland or the *Devotio Moderna* in the Netherlands, was in large part a reaction against the sacerdotalism of the Church, its mechanization of the means of salvation and the materialism of the contemporary clergy. It is clear that in these years of crisis the Church was not satisfying the spiritual needs of many thoughtful and pious laymen. Left to find their own way toward a

[8]J. W. Thompson, *The Literacy of the Laity in the Middle Ages* (Berkeley, 1939).

sense of personal communion with Christ, they read the New Testament and devotional works which, while entirely orthodox, still had the effect of shifting the emphasis in religious thought from the services of the Church to the inner life of faith and a loving devotion to the person of Christ. It was this peculiarly lay piety that Erasmus, who had been taught in his early years by the Brethren of the Common Life, introduced to a wide circle of educated readers in the *Enchiridion Militis Christiani* and a score of other works less ostensibly devotional.

It may be, too, that the growing bourgeois ethic, if I know what I mean, was in these centuries drifting away from the moral teaching and ascetic ideals of the medieval Church. The pious burgher, sober and hard-working, may well have resented the attitude of the doctors of the Church who barely tolerated commercial activity; and he may also have been tempted to regard the monks, especially such monks as he saw about him, as men who had not so much fled the pleasures and temptations of the world as escaped from its responsibilities. Finally, the intellectual independence which education gave to laymen, together with the individualism fostered by a complex and changing society, might well have made men less ready to accept without question the absolute authority of the Church in matters of doctrine or the claim of the clergy to be the indispensable purveyors of the means of salvation. There has, I think, been a good deal of confused thinking concerning the relationship of capitalism to Protestantism. Nevertheless, I think there can be little doubt that the economic and social conditions which made possible a widespread lay literacy and stimulated a growing sense of self-confident individualism did, at the same time, create an intellectual and moral atmosphere favorable to the reception of Luther's doctrine of the freedom of a Christian man and the priesthood of all believers.

Consideration of the Protestant Reformation, however, except as it affected the Catholic Church, lies beyond the scope of the present discussion. The Church survived this crisis also, with its membership sadly diminished but with its divinely inspired authority strongly reaffirmed. Though papal infallibility was not yet a dogma, the popes after Trent enjoyed an absolute authority in matters of faith and morals greater than that of even their most authoritative medieval predecessors. In the cultural and religious, as well as in the political and administrative fields, the Counter-Reformation completed the Church's

adjustment to the modern world. Since then it has changed but relatively little. Yet, if I have assessed aright the predominant characteristics of modern civilization, it was no more than a partial adjustment, and was in some respects a reaction. It was certainly no surrender to the new elements that had grown up within Western civilization since the High Middle Ages. It was rather an orderly retreat to a previously prepared position. The withdrawal of the Church into the spiritual sphere in which its authority could still be exercised in absolute fashion involved not only the abdication of temporal supremacy but also the partial rejection of the secular philosophies, the natural sciences, and large areas of the autonomous lay culture that grew out of the Renaissance. While making concessions where concessions were unavoidable, and abandoning such claims to authority in secular matters as changing conditions had made untenable, the Church returned after the Counter-Reformation, though in a more purely spiritual sense, to the conception of its nature and function that had been formulated in the twelfth and thirteenth centuries. What it could not dominate it rejected, and so maintained, in an ever-shrinking sphere, the authoritative direction of human activity that, in the Middle Ages, had approached a universal domination of the temporal as well as the spiritual life of the Christian community.

But if the Church thus finally succeeded in adapting the medieval ideal to the realities of the modern world, it did so only after a series of well-nigh disastrous crises, which lend to its history during the transitional period a special character. If we consider the events and the changes in ecclesiastical polity that fill the years between the death of Boniface VIII and the period of reconstruction after the Council of Trent, and if we take as the common factor in all of them the efforts, often misguided or self-defeating, of the Church and the papacy to maintain the position they had achieved during the Middle Ages in the midst of a social complex that was being radically altered by new economic, political, and cultural forces, we may, I think, safely conclude that the three centuries of the Renaissance constitute a distinct period in Church history, and that to treat them as such will serve to clarify much that might otherwise remain obscure. The Renaissance Church and the Renaissance papacy were neither medieval nor modern; rather they were caught in a state of uneasy maladjustment between two worlds. It is the distinguishing mark of a genuinely transitional period that the unresolved conflict between traditional institutions and ways of thinking on the one hand, and, on the other, changing economic, political, and social conditions creates a state of acute crisis. The Renaissance was such a period, and the effects of the conflict, as well as the fundamental causes, are, I believe, nowhere more clearly evident than in the history of the Church.

2

RENAISSANCE HUMANISM: CHRISTIAN OR PAGAN?

The men, events, and movements we study today under the term, "The Renaissance" have been studied since their own times and their importance has been continuously recognized. The Renaissance popes, the wealth of Venice or Florence, the speculations of Machiavelli, the poetry of Petrarch, the scholarship of Erasmus, the saintliness of Thomas More were not discovered "only yesterday." But the containing concept of the Renaissance as an historical period with its own distinctive characteristics, its own form, and its own limits is a comparatively new concept in historical scholarship, scarcely more than a century old. And it has been a strife-torn century. For there is almost no aspect of the concept of the Renaissance that has not been called into question, including the concept itself. Medievalists have contended that the vaunted newness of the Renaissance was not new at all and that the whole movement was an inseparable extension of the Middle Ages. They have claimed that the salient characteristic of individualism was by no means unique with the Renaissance and that medieval scholars, politicians, and entrepreneurs were fully as individualistic as Petrarch, Ludovico Sforza, or Cosimo de' Medici. Critics have probed and questioned every major figure and work identified with the Renaissance. They have disputed the primacy of Italy within the Renaissance framework and recently they have raised the question of whether the florescence of the Renaissance was related to the traditional economic factor of surplus or was a response to severe economic depression. But virtually all critics of the Renaissance except the most unregenerate, have recognized that humanism was the most characteristic movement of the age. Indeed, if the Renaissance culture is to be set off at all from that of the preceding age, it is because it was a humanistic culture.

Much has been written on "The Age of Humanism" and "The World of Humanism." The term has been defined so narrowly that it becomes little more than the enthusiastic study of Latin and Greek and so broadly that it becomes a universal philosophy. Yet the basic character of the movement, fundamental and important as it is to the whole concept of the Renaissance, remains obscure. Scholars can agree that this writer was a humanist and that one was not. There is even reasonable agreement as to what constitutes humanistic influence in the plastic arts, in the music, the drama, and the literature of the period. But fundamental agreement on the definition of humanism itself remains to be found. Part of the problem is a confusion of terms and definitions, as the student will see in the selections that follow. Part of it is the divergence of points of view among the critics themselves.

Part of it is simply the scope and complexity of the movement. But since humanism is so crucial to the concept of the Renaissance the questions about the nature of humanism are correspondingly crucial. Among them one of the most important is the extent to which humanism was a pagan revival.

This problem has been implicit from the beginning of the systematic study of the Renaissance, as we see in the first selection that follows from Jacob Burckhardt. This is natural enough because of the close identification of humanism with classical antiquity—which is to say pagan antiquity—and the enthusiasm with which the humanists embraced all things classical possibly, it has been suggested, even classical paganism. The problem was complicated and judgment prejudiced by the behavior of many of the humanists themselves, on the one hand, in their open adulation of everything ancient and, on the other, in their flaunting of the commonly accepted canons of Christian behavior. In a few dramatic instances they rejected those canons; some even did so on the philosophic grounds of preferring the ancient systems. Thus the double charges of paganism and libertinism have each lent credence to the other and the result has been a kind of stereotype of corrupt "pagan-tinged" Italian humanism.

Another stereotype has contributed to this tradition by contrast, the stereotype of Christian humanism. This stereotype describes the humanism that flourished in those "more Christian" lands north of the Alps as sharply opposed to the pagan or pagan-tinged humanism of Italy. Men had no trouble identifying Erasmus or Thomas More, John Colet or LeFevre d'Etaples as Christians. Their writings were persistently concerned with the Christian tradition, the texts of the Church fathers, and with scripture. And the libertine element, which was so damaging to the reputation of Italian humanism, was largely lacking in their personal lives. While this stereotype is as dangerous and limiting as any other stereotype, the concept of Christian humanism as such still occurs, even in the respected modern critical literature of the Renaissance, as the student will see in the selection from Harbison.

But, nonetheless, this double tradition has made a basis for the pagan thesis in interpreting Renaissance humanism. Scholars have begun, however, to reexamine the roots of the charge. They have begun to restudy the individual humanists themselves, their specific works, and their contemporary reputations. They have begun to frame new definitions. And, in all, this revisionist movement has begun to raise some of the questions which are dealt with in the selections to follow from Walser and Kristeller.

JAKOB BURCKHARDT

THE PAGAN THESIS

With the publication in 1860 of Jacob Burckhardt's *The Civilization of the Renaissance in Italy* the modern study of the Renaissance as an historical period began. This pioneering work was a brief essay rather than an exhaustive, multivolume treatise but in it Burckhardt raised most of the fundamental questions of Renaissance scholarship. Much of subsequent scholarship has been devoted to proving or disproving the Burckhardtian position on one or another of these questions; to filling in the skeletal outlines of his work with more detailed enquiry; and to following out the implications of his thought.

Burckhardt identified the humanists as those who had fashioned the new intellectual framework of the Renaissance and pointed out that the source of their inspiration was the revival of antiquity. As they sought to identify with their beloved antiquity they turned their backs upon the Christian tradition that was their medieval heritage with the result that Burckhardt bluntly declared, "This humanism was in fact pagan." Thus the problem with which the following selection from *The Civilization of the Renaissance in Italy* deals is close to the center of the complex "Burckhardt Thesis."

Some of the leading elements of this thesis are the protean individualism that Burckhardt ascribed to Renaissance men, the essential worldliness he saw in their outlook, and the importance of classicism and the revival of antiquity in promoting that worldliness. All these parts of the larger general argument are to be found in the present selection. The student should observe how they are related to Burckhardt's position on the question of Renaissance paganism. But, most basically, the student should be aware that Burckhardt's position in this regard is actually a point of view and that many of the same "facts" which he uses to prove Renaissance humanism pagan, later writers will use to rescue it from precisely that indictment.

These modern men, the representatives of the culture of Italy, were born with the same religious instincts as other mediaeval Europeans. But their powerful individuality made them in religion, as in other matters, altogether subjective, and the intense charm which the discovery of the inner and outer universe exercised upon them rendered them markedly worldly. In the rest of Europe religion remained, till a much later period, something given from without, and in practical life egotism and sensuality alternated with devotion and repentance. The latter had no spiritual competitors, as in Italy, or only to a far smaller extent.

Further, the close and frequent relations of Italy with Byzantium and the Mohammedan peoples had produced a dispassionate tolerance which weakened the ethnographical conception of a privileged

From Jakob Burckhardt, *The Civilisation of the Period of the Renaissance in Italy*, tr. S. G. C. Middlemore, 2 vols. (London: C. Kegan Paul & Co., 1878), Vol. II, pp. 297–320 with deletions.

Christendom. And when classical antiquity with its men and institutions became an ideal of life, as well as the greatest of historical memories, ancient speculation and scepticism obtained in many cases a complete mastery over the minds of Italians.

Since, again, the Italians were the first modern people of Europe who gave themselves boldly to speculations on freedom and necessity, and since they did so under violent and lawless political circumstances, in which evil seemed often to win a splendid and lasting victory, their belief in God began to waver, and their view of the government of the world became fatalistic. And when their passionate natures refused to rest in the sense of uncertainty, they made a shift to help themselves out with ancient, oriental, or mediaeval superstition. They took to astrology and magic.

Finally, these intellectual giants, these representatives of the Renaissance, show, in respect to religion, a quality which is common in youthful natures. Distinguishing keenly between good and evil, they yet are conscious of no sin. Every disturbance of their inward harmony they feel themselves able to make good out of the plastic resources of their own nature, and therefore they feel no repentance. The need of salvation thus becomes felt more and more dimly, while the ambitions and the intellectual activity of the present either shut out altogether every thought of a world to come, or else caused it to assume a poetic instead of a dogmatic form.

When we look on all this as pervaded and often perverted by the all-powerful Italian imagination, we obtain a picture of that time which is certainly more in accordance with truth than are vague declamations against modern paganism. And closer investigation often reveals to us that underneath this outward shell much genuine religion could still survive.

The fuller discussion of these points must be limited to a few of the most essential explanations.

That religion should again become an affair of the individual and of his own personal feeling was inevitable when the Church became corrupt in doctrine and tyrannous in practice, and is a proof that the European mind was still alive. It is true that this showed itself in many different ways. While the mystical and ascetical sects of the North lost no time in creating new outward forms for their new modes of thought and feeling, each individual in Italy went

his own way, and thousands wandered on the sea of life without any religious guidance whatever. All the more must we admire those who attained and held fast to a personal religion. They were not to blame for being unable to have any part or lot in the old Church, as she then was; nor would it be reasonable to expect that they should all of them go through that mighty spiritual labour which was appointed to the German reformers. The form and aim of this personal faith, as it showed itself in the better minds, will be set forth at the close of our work.

The worldliness, through which the Renaissance seems to offer so striking a contrast to the Middle Ages, owed its first origin to the flood of new thoughts, purposes, and views, which transformed the mediaeval conception of nature and man. The spirit is not in itself more hostile to religion than that "culture" which now holds its place, but which can give us only a feeble notion of the universal ferment which the discovery of a new world of greatness then called forth. This worldliness was not frivolous, but earnest, and was ennobled by art and poetry. It is a lofty necessity of the modern spirit that this attitude, once gained, can never again be lost, that an irresistible impulse forces us to the investigation of men and things, and that we must hold this inquiry to be our proper end and work. How soon and by what paths this search will lead us back to God, and in what ways the religious temper of the individual will be affected by it, are questions which cannot be met by any general answer. The Middle Ages, which spared themselves the trouble of induction and free inquiry, can have no right to impose upon us their dogmatical verdict in a matter of such vast importance. . . .

In the course of the fifteenth century the works of antiquity were discovered and diffused with extraordinary rapidity. All the writings of the Greek philosophers which we ourselves possess were now, at least in the form of Latin translations, in everybody's hands. It is a curious fact that some of the most zealous apostles of this new culture were men of the strictest piety, or even ascetics. Fra Ambrogio Camaldolese, as a spiritual dignitary chiefly occupied with ecclesiastical affairs, and as a literary man with the translation of the Greek Fathers of the Church, could not repress the humanistic impulse, and at the request of Cosimo de' Medici, undertook to translate Diogenes Laertius into Latin. His contemporaries, Niccolò Niccoli, Giannozzo Manetti, Donato Acciaiuoli, and Pope Nicholas V, united to a

The Eve of the Modern World

many-sided humanism profound biblical scholarship and deep piety. In Vittorino da Feltre the same temper has been already noticed. The same Maffeo Vegio, who added a thirteenth book to the "Æneid," had an enthusiasm for the memory of St. Augustine and his mother Monica which cannot have been without a deeper influence upon him. The result of all these tendencies was that the Platonic Academy at Florence deliberately chose for its object the reconciliation of the spirit of antiquity with that of Christianity. It was a remarkable oasis in the humanism of the period.

This humanism was in fact pagan, and became more and more so as its sphere widened in the fifteenth century. Its representatives, whom we have already described as the advanced guard of an unbridled individualism, display as a rule such a character that even their religion, which is sometimes professed very definitely, becomes a matter of indifference to us. They easily got the name of atheists, if they showed themselves indifferent to religion, and spoke freely against the Church; but not one of them ever professed, or dared to profess, a formal, philosophical atheism. If they sought for any leading principle, it must have been a kind of superficial rationalism—a careless inference from the many and contradictory opinions of antiquity with which they busied themselves, and from the discredit into which the Church and her doctrines had fallen. This was the sort of reasoning which was near bringing Galeotto Martio to the stake, had not his former pupil, Pope Sixtus IV, perhaps at the request of Lorenzo de' Medici, saved him from the hands of the Inquisition. Galeotto had ventured to write that the man who lived uprightly, and acted according to the natural law born within him, would go to heaven, whatever nation he belonged to.

Let us take, by way of example, the religious attitude of one of the smaller men in the great army. Codrus Urceus was first the tutor of the last Ordelaffo, Prince of Forlì, and afterwards for many years professor at Bologna. Against the Church and the monks his language is as abusive as that of the rest. His tone in general is reckless to the last degree, and he constantly introduces himself in all his local history and gossip. But he knows how to speak to the edification of the true God-Man, Jesus Christ, and to commend himself by letter to the prayers of a saintly priest. On one occasion, after enumerating the follies of the pagan religions, he thus goes on: "Our theologians, too, quarrel about 'the guinea-pig's

tail,' about the Immaculate Conception, Antichrist, Sacraments, Predestination, and other things, which were better let alone than talked of publicly." Once, when he was not at home, his room and manuscripts were burnt. When he heard the news he stood opposite a figure of the Madonna in the street, and cried to it: "Listen to what I tell you; I am not mad, I am saying what I mean. If I ever call upon you in the hour of my death, you need not hear me or take me among your own, for I will go and spend eternity with the devil." After which speech he found it desirable to spend six months in retirement at the home of a wood-cutter. With all this, he was so superstitious that prodigies and omens gave him incessant frights, leaving him no belief to spare for the immortality of the soul. When his hearers questioned him on the matter, he answered that no one knew what became of a man, of his soul or his body, after death, and the talk about another life was only fit to frighten old women. But when he came to die, he commended in his will his soul or his spirit to Almighty God, exhorted his weeping pupils to fear the Lord, and especially to believe in immortality and future retribution, and received the Sacrament with much fervour. We have no guarantee that more famous men in the same calling, however significant their opinions may be, were in practical life any more consistent. It is probable that most of them wavered inwardly between incredulity and a remnant of the faith in which they were brought up, and outwardly held for prudential reasons to the Church.

Through the connexion of rationalism with the newly born science of historical investigation, some timid attempts at biblical criticism may here and there have been made. A saying of Pius II has been recorded, which seems intended to prepare the way for such criticism: "Even if Christianity were not confirmed by miracles, it ought still to be accepted on account of its morality." The legends of the Church, in so far as they contained arbitrary versions of the biblical miracles, were freely ridiculed, and this reacted on the religious sense of the people. Where Judaizing heretics are mentioned, we must understand chiefly those who denied the Divinity of Christ, which was probably the offence for which Giorgio da Novara was burnt at Bologna about the year 1500. But again at Bologna in the year 1497 the Dominican Inquisitor was forced to let the physician Gabriele da Salò, who had powerful patrons, escape with a simple expression of penitence, although he was in the habit of maintaining that Jesus was not God, but son of Joseph and Mary, and conceived in the usual way; that by his cunning he had deceived the world to its ruin; that he may have died on the cross on account of crimes which he had committed; that his religion would soon come to an end; that his body was not really contained in the sacrament, and that he performed his miracles, not through any divine power, but through the influence of the heavenly bodies. This latter statement is most characteristic of the time; Faith is gone, but magic still holds its ground.

With respect to the moral government of the world, the humanists seldom get beyond a cold and resigned consideration of the prevalent violence and misrule. In this mood the many works "On Fate," or whatever name they bear, are written. They tell of the turning of the wheel of Fortune, and of the instability of earthly, especially political, things. Providence is only brought in because the writers would still be ashamed of undisguised fatalism, of the avowal of their ignorance, or of useless complaints. . . .

We cannot on the other hand, read without a kind of awe how men sometimes boasted of their fortune in public inscriptions. Giovanni II Bentivoglio, ruler of Bologna, ventured to carve in stone on the newly built tower by his palace, that his merit and his fortune had given him richly of all that could be desired—and this a few years before his expulsion. The ancients, when they spoke in this tone, had nevertheless a sense of the envy of the gods. In Italy it was probably the Condottieri who first ventured to boast so loudly of their fortune.

But the way in which resuscitated antiquity affected religion most powerfully, was not through any doctrines or philosophical system, but through a general tendency which it fostered. The men, and in some respects the institutions of antiquity were preferred to those of the Middle Ages, and in the eager attempt to imitate and reproduce them, religion was left to take care of itself. All was absorbed in the admiration for historical greatness. To this the philologians added many special follies of their own, by which they became the mark for general attention. How far Paul II was justified in calling his Abbreviators and their friends to account for their paganism, is certainly a matter of great doubt, as his biographer and chief victim, Platina, has shown a masterly skill in explaining his vindictiveness on other grounds, and especially in making him play a ludicrous figure. The charges of infidelity, paganism, denial of immortality, and so forth, were not made against the accused till the charge of high treason had broken down. Paul, indeed, if we are correctly informed about him, was by no means the man to judge of intellectual things. It was he who exhorted the Romans to teach their children nothing beyond reading and writing. His priestly narrowness of views reminds us of Savonarola, with the difference that Paul might fairly have been told that he and his like were in great part to blame if culture made men hostile to religion. It cannot, nevertheless, be doubted that he felt a real anxiety about the pagan tendencies which surrounded him. And what, in truth, may not the humanists have allowed themselves at the court of the profligate pagan, Sigismondo Malatesta? How far these men, destitute for the most part of fixed principle, ventured to go, depended assuredly on the sort of influences they were exposed to. Nor could they treat of Christianity without paganizing it. It is curious, for instance, to notice how far Gioviano Pontano carried this confusion. He speaks of a saint not only as "divus," but as "deus";[1] the angels he holds to be identical with the genii of antiquity; and his notion of immortality reminds us of the old kingdom of the shades. This spirit occasionally appears in the most extravagant shapes. In 1526, when Siena was attacked by the exiled party, the worthy canon Tizio, who tells us the story himself, rose from his bed on the 22nd July, called to mind what is written in the third book of Macrobius, celebrated Mass, and then pronounced against the enemy the curse with which his author had supplied him, only altering "Telus mater teque Juppiter obtestor" into "Tellus teque Christe Deus obtestor."[2] After he had done this for three days, the enemy retreated. On the one side, these things strike us as an affair of mere style and fashion; on the other, as a symptom of religious decadence.

[1] "Divus" and "deus" were both classical Latin words for God. Apparently Pontano preferred these to the more medieval flavored "sanctus," the usual word for saint. [Editor's note.]

[2] "Mother Earth and thou Jupiter I beseech." "Earth and thou Christ God I beseech." [Editor's note.]

The Eve of the Modern World

ERNST WALSER

PAGAN FORM: CHRISTIAN SUBSTANCE

Although Ernst Walser was a student of Burckhardt at Basel, his mature scholarship marks a decisive shift away from the position taken by his master on almost every fundamental point. He disputed the most basic of Burckhardt's assumptions, asserting that the Renaissance was not a distinct, integral period. He based his assertion upon the detailed study of the works of the most significant Renaissance humanists from which he concluded that these key figures in the conception of the Renaissance actually represented no more than a continuation of typically medieval modes of thought. The key point in Walser's thesis is his denial that Renaissance humanism was basically pagan and his contrary assertion that the humanists remained fundamentally Christian and orthodox, as their medieval predecessors had been. The following excerpt from Walser's most important book concentrates on this point.

He argues first that most of the instances of alleged humanistic paganism are actually no more than the Renaissance enthusiasm for the "style" of antiquity or evidence merely of the critical philological skepticism and anticlericalism of the age; and that such attitudes did not destroy fundamental Christian belief. He contends that even the most damaging evidence of apparent pagan revival is not to be accepted. He argues that the Florentine Neoplatonists, customarily regarded as the clearest and most consistent example of the revival of a classical philosophic system, "were of the deepest Christian piety" and not essentially different from the earlier medieval Christian thinkers who borrowed bits and pieces of classical thought. He argues that the famous carnival songs and practices associated with Lorenzo de' Medici, and again usually regarded as pagan revivals, are not so much revivals as survivals of the ancient and durable nature magic common to Europe and, in Italy, merely disguised in classical dress, thus becoming another evidence of the "purely external, formal and fashionable" manifestation of Renaissance paganism.

We are confronted by the accusation that the study of antiquity was responsible for the destruction of Christian belief in the Quattrocento or that it was at least certain proof of the irreligiosity of the age. The charge against the humanists for their disbelief is based on their aesthetic paganism, on their critical skepticism, and on their anti-clericalism. Therefore, paganism, criticism, and anti-curialism will be dealt with before we finally take a stand regarding the positive religious elements.

At the outset we are confronted with the accusation of heathenism or paganism. Are we not to consider as completely valid the . . . charge of Erasmus[1] when it is supported by the eloquent lament of preachers like Savonarola or by such an impeccable witness as Machiavelli?

Let us attempt to get hold of the problem at a more

[1] A reference to Erasmus' impatience with rhetorical archaisms in his dialogue *Ciceronianus*. [Editor's note.]

From Ernst Walser, *Studien zur Weltanschauung der Renaissance* in *Gesammelte Studien zur Geistesgeschichte der Renaissance* (Basel, 1932), pp. 102–17. Used by permission of Benno Schwabe & Co. Translated by the editor.

fundamental level: on what basis does that which is new in the Renaissance admiration of antiquity actually rest? The remembrance of the power and splendor of the Roman Empire, after its fall, had never been extinguished in the hearts of mankind; above all not in Italy. In this instance the spectacle of antiquity's continuing survival would be tantamount to a history of its whole cultural development: and Germanic, Greek, and Arabic influences appear as negligible factors in the face of the on-flowing continuum of Roman antiquity. Many an administrative institution of antiquity survived through the Middle Ages in Italy; here Roman law continued in effect; Latin continued to be regarded here as a national language so that the newly formed vernacular began to be written only at a time when other peoples of the post-classical world already possessed a real literature in their vernaculars. In Italy ancient heathen religious concepts, barely disguised under a robe of Christianity, continued in constant procession through the dark centuries as well as through those illuminated by art and knowledge. Timorous legends of Nero, Vergil, and Augustus grew up like ivy around the powerful ruins of a lost world.

Thus in Italy Roman antiquity was considered, throughout the Middle Ages, not as a period of foreign domination—as was the case in other countries—but rather as a thoroughly national past. And every attempt at Italian unification, from the Middle Ages down to the present, has had strength, driving force, and the prospect of continuing success only if undertaken in the holy name of ancient Rome. Moreover, antiquity continued to be perpetuated by the schools. In the study of the ancient authors there came to life and exhausted itself the concept of each and every field of knowledge from the fall of Rome until into the twelfth century.

This preoccupation with antiquity, however, did not pass through the centuries as a constantly diminishing force: it was rather as if antiquity were borne to the barren shore of mankind like a powerful, recurring wave. The Irish monks of Charlemagne, the Benedictine abbeys under the Ottonians pored over the classical authors, transcribed their works, and carried on textual criticism which was as good as—or even better than—that of the earlier Renaissance humanists. It was the period of high scholasticism that first made a distinction between ancient and Christian knowledge by accomplishing the co-

lossal task of creating a new and harmoniously constructed Christian world view from a mixture of classical and Christian elements. It was first in high scholasticism that all the branches of knowledge became a solidly joined structure which ascended from the Seven Liberal Arts to philosophy and then to its completely overshadowing discipline, theology. This, however, did not prevent rational and mystic thinkers—even in the Middle Ages—from surrendering themselves to rather bold speculations which remained unmolested by the church as long as they did not give offense to revealed religion. Thus we see a group of individual religious thinkers in whose works all the classical philosophic systems are repeated no less often than will be the case with the humanists.

Thus while the actual Renaissance begins with Petrarch, there is in its involvement with pagan antiquity, the collecting of ancient authors, and the sifting of their texts, nothing essentially different from what was already being done in the purely medieval Carolingian and Ottonian pre-Renaissances. Even the medieval princes had accepted the *Roman de Titus Livius* and the *Prouesses du bon chevalier Jules César* into their curiosity cabinets. But by the mid-fourteenth century we sense that a new era and a new attitude toward antiquity are beginning.

The new decisive factor which Petrarch and his followers add and which rises over mankind like a dawn of understanding is the profoundly sensitive perception not of the content of the classics but rather of their formal beauty. The deepest roots of humanism and the great common bond that ties all humanists together is neither individualism nor politics, philosophy nor common religious ideas (in all these things their opinions were widely different): the great common bond is simply artistic sensitivity. Moreover, there is in it—especially as literature is concerned—a conscious reaction against the overly dry, rational work of scholasticism. Nor can it be said that humanism emanated by any means from one particular caste: neither from the scholars nor the priests nor the laity. Rather its ideas appealed to widely dispersed men of the most varied occupations and positions—school masters, priests, bishops, merchants, lawyers. Generally speaking, at first it was a case of a few isolated individuals who were caught up in the new enthusiasm while the great mass of their professional and social compeers continued to persist in the traditional. It is therefore

The Eve of the Modern World

incorrect when Philippe Monnier,[2] for example, speaks of a fundamental opposition between the Italian humanists and the monks since capable men in orders like Marsilio, Traversari, and Aliotti were among the most enthusiastic partisans of humanism. On the other hand, thoroughgoing humanists like Salutati, Niccoli, and others were friendly in the extreme toward the monks. No, the opposition to the humanists was assembled from all possible class levels and camps, just as was the community of humanists itself. The opponents were in part defenders of the scholastic method: in part, to be sure, they were monks, but only those mystic and ignorant ascetics of the stamp of Jacopone da Todi, who had of old also been deadly enemies of scholasticism along with every other variety of learning.

The new-found aestheticism developed like a pervasive cloud and expressed itself especially well in literature. Its herald was Francesco Petrarca although he was not its inventor, for such deep flowing movements go beyond the energy of a single man.

His poetry found receptive hearts and kindled in them the flame of poetry. The poet of Laura writes in annoyance of the flocks of would-be poets who disturbed him daily in his quiet cell at Vaucluse with the ill-bred children of their muse: it was especially painful to convince poetizing cardinals of the hopelessness of their efforts. Lawyers and physicians, craftsmen of every description flocked to him; and he views with horror the time when not only fishermen, hunters, and peasants will make rhymes but even the oxen before the plow will ruminate verses. Even a dry and matter of fact nature like Salutati began with Latin verses of dubious beauty: fortunately he later tended to restrict himself to the epistle and the treatise. However, this poetical fire was soon extinguished once more and into its place moved that element which became typical of the entire Renaissance: eloquence. Petrarch, even as a boy, upon reading the speeches of Cicero and before he completely understood the meaning of the words, felt himself deeply moved by their soft ring and the quiet, flooding harmony of their rhythm. . . .

Thus the forms of antiquity developed into the outward means of expression—whether the rhetoric was false or genuine—for the whole cultural life of Italy. And from this time on, certain purely medieval heirlooms of knighthood and chivalry wrapped

[2] *Le Quattrocento* (New Edition, 1908), I, 124 ff.

themselves in the stylish little mantle of antiquity, masquerading as "feeling for nature" and Neoplatonism (just as neo-humanist concepts and ideals did). Thus we find a complete ladder of purely outward paganism.

The lowest rung of humanistic study was, beyond a doubt, the passion for citing authorities. Already in the Middle Ages writers were wont to parade their erudition by deploying in rank and file everything (and on every occasion) that might serve as an authority. This was all the more justified since in that time more wrangling went on by citing authorities than by real proofs. A frightening example of this is to be had in the otherwise rather vigorous tracts of the Swiss Felix Hemmerli. The humanists also—especially those of the early period—freely imitated this wretched practice except that from now on are cited not only the great scholastics but classical authors in great profusion. In these classical citations then we see simply the expression of scholarly vanity, ever self-renewing and blooming from a truly eternal rootstock: but there is no unbelief here. Under the same heading are to be placed the classical expletives *Per Jovem, Dii boni, Edepol,* etc. behind which it is foolish to suspect a decrease in Christian belief and thought (although especially zealous and ignorant monks occasionally did so). Thus countless examples of contemporary matters—in both church and state—represented in classical dress present a low level understanding of antiquity and truly deplorable taste. This is the typical form of paganism. And it is precisely on this point that the most exacting examination of the facts is necessary in order to decide whether this is simply a literary fashion (which is the case in the overwhelming majority of cases) or whether there is here a spirit in opposition to Christianity. In the carry-over of classical form and usage to contemporary things the humanist school master was the preeminent performer: as in the case when the rhetorician Porcellius traveled self-importantly between the battle lines of the brawling mercenary captains Piccinino and Sforza in order to sing their deeds in heroic style after the model of the battles of Scipio and Hannibal. Also belonging to purely formal paganism are many expressions which cannot be allowed to deceive us even when they concern matters of Christian religion. The Middle Ages had arrived at similar results from the opposite direction in that the circle of Old Testament prototypes and prophecies (Adam as a symbol of Christ, the Tree of Knowledge as a symbol of the cross, etc.) had also been extended to heathen mythology (Leda as a symbol of the Immaculate Conception). Even though Dante, in purely formal pagan terms, calls the Redeemer *Giove crocifisso,* he was not aware of committing any greater sacrilege than contemporary medieval theologians who had explained Vergil's *Fourth Eclogue* or Aeneas (after the example of Fulgentius) in Christian symbolic terms. In like fashion, in his *Africa,* Petrarch has both the goddesses Rome and Carthage appear before Jupiter at Olympus begging for help before the battle of Zama: the father of the gods explains to them that he himself will descend to earth after ten years of Saturn's rule and will redeem mankind by his own ignominious death. Boccaccio in *Filocolo, Fiammetta,* and *Ameto* presents veritable masterpieces of disguising contemporary things in classical dress.

Similar examples run through the entire Italian Quattrocento and Cinquecento and are found no less often in France. The devout Guillaume Budé calls Christ a two-headed Janus (to explain the unity of divine and human nature), a Mercury (interpreter of heavenly and earthly wisdom), Prometheus (who brought mankind the true fire from heaven), Hercules Alexicacus (destroyer of the monster), and Achilles. Job, on the other hand, is one of the philosophers persecuted by Fortune. Ronsard, in his *Hymne de l'Hercule chrétien,* described the life of Christ by illustrating every phase of the Redeemer's life with a deed of Hercules. I also class with these superficial paganisms the cult of Mercury which the overwrought Ciriaco d'Ancona promoted: his language and personality are here strikingly reminiscent of Rabelais' Limousin pupil! The pious epics of the time of Leo X and Clement VII are also rich in such illustrations. Take, for example, the unspeakable work of Sannazzaro, *De partu virginis:* God the Father after he has instructed the heavenly legions in the mysteries of the redemption—in a meeting at Olympus—inspires them with sympathy for sinful mankind. A delegation of *genii* (Laetitia, Concordia, Right-Love, etc.) tie on their wings and escort scantily clad Horae in their flight down to the shepherds of the field. At this the constellations are enraptured and the moon (with unwitting humor) contemplates the dance of joy already going on among the stars. Then we pass into the depths where the river god Jordan is sitting by the Crystal Urn with his daughter rivers and is relating a prophecy of Proteus which the latter had heard from Apollo and in which the nereids are pictured swimming toward Christ as he walks on the ocean and a trembling Neptune kisses

his foot. Among the small and stupid humanists paganism assumed the ridiculous form of hollow, pedantic Ciceronianism which Erasmus rightly ridiculed. In 1529 a professor at Bologna, Romolo Amaseo, announced in the solemn welcoming address for the Emperor Charles V and Pope Clement VII, that he would rather be the dead servant of Cicero than to have to live in such a grim and miserable present. But in the same manner as the leading humanists of the foregoing century had made fun of such silliness, on this occasion Bembo made no less a fool of the valiant Amaseo.

We note then: the newly awakened aestheticism, with reference to the forms of classical antiquity, expresses itself in a long gradation which runs from the most sensitive taste to the worst fashion fad. However, it would be altogether incorrect to infer a diminished Christianity from these tricks of speech contrived on the model of classical rhetoric. Precisely those examples cited from Erasmus' *Dialogus Ciceronianus* should, one and all, be set under the rubric of the completely harmless and purely external paganisms.

The same comments concerning purely superficial and formal paganism in literature must certainly also be made in art. Classical fruit garlands, putti, and the like become henceforth a part of ornamental accessory just as do the undraped figures in the background of Michelangelo's Holy Family in the Uffizi. And these certainly do not prove the decline of orthodoxy any more than does the fact that Lippi's Madonna in the Annunciation is sitting in a splendidly decorated Renaissance room. And when the classical fashion (or fad) occasions the closest association of pagan mythology and Christian ideas in the pious epics of a Sannazzaro why then should not the same happen in art? When Filarete admits Aesopian fables, classical emperors, virtues and scenes like Ganymede and Leda into the ornamentation of the doors of St. Peter's one no more takes offense at this ornamental paganism than one does at Proteus and Apollo who, in Sannazzaro, prophesy the birth of Christ. These bronze reliefs prove nothing either about the faith of the artist or that of the patron. This latter was none other than Eugenius IV, a foe of liberal humanistic study, who would certainly have been man enough to send the doors and the artist *a casa il diavolo* if the depiction had offended him. People felt all the less injured by this ornamental paganism since church sculpture of the Middle Ages was accustomed to represent much

The Eve of the Modern World

worse things: unedifying *novella* subjects (not just the ribald adventure of the harnessed Aristotle but also the lewd revenge of Virgil the magician on the Roman women); animal and human grotesques; indeed downright phallic images. . . . Moreover, people viewed all things connected with procreation with a beautiful simplicity which is still characteristic of the south European today and of which admirable preachers like St. Bernardino da Siena spoke. The medieval (and earlier south European) concept of the sacred was constituted quite differently from ours: what crude hocus-pocus our clergy performed with the "Fools' Mass" and the "Asses' Mass" not only at carnival but even at the ecclesiastical primitial celebrations! Probably for this reason the church dances of the sixteenth century were held in a holy place in order to insure the recovery of those stricken with the "dancing sickness" through the magical influence of the Lord's house. Therefore, when Savonarola, revered for the ardor of his convictions and for his martyr's death, damns all colorful pomp and thundering music, out of his own gloomy asceticism, as the heathenizing work of the devil and longs for the times (and when were they really?) when the sacramental cup was of wood and the priests of gold, we certainly will not believe every word. It is equally unjustified though to damn his opponent, Fra Mariano da Genazzano, as a hypocrite and aesthetic heathen (as did the romantically naive description of Villari) simply because he spoke out for a reasonable and nonascetic exercise of religion and declined to indulge in hysterical and apocalyptic prophecies in order to teach fear and horror to his listeners!

Much more difficult to judge than the paganism of external form is the paganism of content. It is true that Stoic, Neoplatonic, and Epicurean precepts frequently appear in the writings of the humanists: and in their ultimate consequences all these systems are anti-Christian. But are these mementos of classicism not already to be found in scholasticism? The medieval thinkers borrowed from all these theories just as much as they could use for their own speculations but anything beyond this they completely rejected. Does not the basically scholastic nominalism lead to crass materialism in the final analysis; and, on the other hand, does not its adversary, medieval realism, lead to pantheism of the purest sort? And we see the same thing with the humanists. To be precise, the stoicism of Petrarch and Salutati is tied into a fundamental sympathy with the most severe monastic asceticism.

As early as the first years of the fifteenth century Cardinal Francesco Zabarella (d.1417) departed from the crude medieval popular concept of *porcus Epicuri* (probably stemming from a Horatian source) and condemned the hedonism of Epicurus only where the philosopher considered his goal to be coarse and sensual rather than purely spiritual joy. This latter point of view was represented by Niccoli in the treatise of Lorenzo Valla, *De voluptate*. To be precise, the Neoplatonists such as Marsilio Ficino, Pico della Mirandola and their numerous followers in Italy and France were of the deepest Christian piety. To be sure, there were individual thinkers in the fifteenth and sixteenth centuries who were no longer Christians and who found their comfort in life as in death in the train of thought of heathen philosophers. Their number, however, is no greater than it was in the preceding centuries and the proof of their paganism has a claim to accuracy only when it is verified by numerous unequivocal signs and is not merely reasoned from a few Stoic or Epicurean sentences.

The criticism of the *Canti carnascialeschi* also seems to me rather intricate. It is known that A. F. Grazzini, who lived a generation after Lorenzo de' Medici, ascribed to the Magnifico the innovation in the carnival songs "di variare non solamente il canto ma le invenzioni e il modo di comporre le parole."[3] Pasquale Villari explains this as if Lorenzo had accustomed his fellow citizens to this sort of spectacle in the devilish intention of choking off their sentiments of liberty by such corruption. Popular amusement with parades and songs at carnival time, as at the beginning of May, were an invention neither of the Medici nor the Renaissance. As for the *Calendimaggio* festivals, they go back at least to the battle of Campaldino in 1265. The fifteenth century added to this the greator splendor and mythological ornamentation of *trionfi* such as that of *Bacco ed Arianna*. The greater splendor resulted from the greater prosperity and improved standard of living which is clearly demonstrated by the development of Florentine household furnishings. The classical costumes resulted from the joy in the newly discovered "forms" of antiquity. Not very much can be inferred from such external trappings. For example, even the brave Gessner in the eighteenth century styled his hair in "antique" fashion and, with his upright old Zurich comrades, held idyllic "lamb-pious" fests

[3]Not only of modifying the song but the improvisations and the manner of composing the words. [Editor's note.]

—without consequently becoming a pagan! And furthermore, many earlier Italian dance songs, in word and rhythm, directly recall Lorenzo de' Medici. The old French and old Provençal May and dance tunes admonish young women, as do the *canti*, to enjoy life and to exchange the *jaloux* (the poor stupid husband) for a youthful lover. We need not take this any more literally for the Middle Ages than for the Renaissance. The fact that Florentine women did not actually carry out such foolish advice was assured less by the barbaric laws against adultery than by husbands themselves who always carried their daggers loose in their scabbards. Finally, it would be well to remember the stream of bluntly realistic and erotic love songs which came down, together with the idealistic ones, from the time of the Sicilians—and also the unbelievable mass of crudity that both lords and ladies of the Renaissance faithfully took over from the Middle Ages. All these mitigating factors are still not sufficient to explain the strange fact that the sole object of all the *Canti carnascialeschi* we know (with only negligible exceptions) was the repugnantly graphic description of the crudest love pleasures with a forwardness which makes it barely conceivable how such literal depictions would sound in the streets in the ears of an entire population. Unfortunately nothing is preserved of the women's dance songs prior to the twelfth century: this includes the *obscina et turpea cantica cum choris foemineis*[4] from seventh century France as well as the *cantiunculae* and *naeniae, quarum aliae*

maleficiorum aliae stupri causa[5] of the tenth century which Italian women performed on the calends of January and March and on St. John's Day. But does not this call to *copula* together with the circumstances of the procession open the question whether we might not suspect an ancient custom in these *canti* which, in the final analysis, rests upon a fertility ritual. In all Europe similar symbols were widespread at such carnivals and spring festivals. Even the May King—who was also to be found in Florence and who still appears in the dance songs of Lorenzo de' Medici—belongs to the spring magic for which Mannhardt has assembled a persuasive mass of evidence. This explains by itself the licentious content. Thus Lorenzo il Magnifico is not to be credited with the invention of the whole carnival "carryings-on" but rather with only its more sumptuous setting and classical trappings.

The paganism of the Renaissance, with all its thousandfold forms in literature, art, folk festivals, etc. is a purely external, formal and fashionable element. In the case of very isolated individuals, it can be used as decisive proof of unbelief. But it would be thoroughly wrong to use it in its totality as evidence of a decline in orthodoxy, of the growth of indifference, of the decline of public morality, etc. The few Renaissance men who were actually convinced anti-Christians did not hold this view out of either indifference or paganism but rather out of a religious disposition or even out of a deep need for other forms of belief.

[4] Filthy and obscene songs with female choruses. [Editor's note.]

[5] Songs and incantations some of which were associated with witchcraft, others with lust. [Editor's note.]

PAUL OSKAR KRISTELLER

A NEW VIEW OF THE PROBLEM

Like Ernst Walser, Paul Oskar Kristeller has spent most of his life dealing in detail with the actual works of individual humanists, studying their writings and editing their texts, especially those of the major humanistic philosophers such as Marsilio Ficino. From the study of these sources he brings, again like Walser, a new point of view to bear upon the question of the alleged paganism of the Renaissance.

He agrees with Walser, calling "the Renaissance a fundamentally Christian age."

The Eve of the Modern World

He agrees to an extent with one of Walser's principal points, that much of the striking newness an older generation of scholars saw in the Renaissance was actually a continuation of medieval patterns of thought and action. He stresses the vigorous continuity of medieval religious forms and practices right through the Renaissance, as well as the "persistence of church doctrine, institutions, and worship."

But much of the case Kristeller makes for "Christian humanism" is derived from his well known theory about the nature of humanism itself, that it was essentially "neither religious nor antireligious, but a literary and scholarly orientation that could be and, in many cases, was pursued without any explicit discourse on religious topics by individuals who otherwise might be fervent or nominal members of one of the Christian churches." Moreover, he asserts that, within the frame of this concept, the humanists returned to the classical texts of Christianity as they had earlier returned to the texts of pagan antiquity and applied their scholars' tools not in the restoration of paganism but in the salutary work of "sacred philology."

Thus to the extent that he recognizes a traditional conflict at all, Kristeller sees the humanists not as neopagans in conflict with Christianity but as professional scholars, practitioners of the "new learning," in conflict with the professional methodology of scholasticism.

In reading this selection the student should observe whether Kristeller changes the ground or the terms of the traditional argument. And, if he does so, does he produce a more sensible case, does he "define the problem away," or does he make the problem conform to his definition?

Many historians of the last century tended to associate the Italian Renaissance and Italian humanism with some kind of irreligion, and to interpret the Protestant and Catholic Reformations as expressions of a religious revival which challenged and finally defeated the un-Christian culture of the preceding period. The moral ideas and literary allegories in the writings of the humanists were taken to be expressions, real or potential, overt or concealed, of a new paganism incompatible with Christianity. The neat separation between reason and faith advocated by the Aristotelian philosophers was considered as a hypocritical device to cover up a secret atheism, whereas the emphasis on a natural religion common to all men, found in the work of the Platonists and Stoics, was characterized as pantheism. This picture of the supposed paganism of the Renaissance which was drawn by historians with much horror or enthusiasm, depending on the strength of their religious or irreligious convictions, can partly be dismissed as the result of later legends and preconceptions. In part, it may be traced to charges made against the humanists and philosophers by hostile or narrow-minded contemporaries, which should not be accepted at their face value. Most recent historians have taken quite a different view of the matter. There was, to be sure, a good deal of talk about the pagan gods and heroes in the literature of the Renaissance, and it was justified by the familiar device of allegory, and strengthened by the belief in astrology, but there were few, if any, thinkers who seriously thought of reviving ancient pagan cults. The word pantheism had not yet been invented, and although the word atheism was generously used in polemics during the later sixteenth century, there were probably no real atheists and barely a few pantheists during the Renaissance. The best or worst we may say is that there were some thinkers who might be considered, or actually were considered, as forerunners of eighteenth-century free thought. There was then, of course, as there was before and afterwards, a certain amount of religious indifference and of merely nominal adherence to the doctrines of the Church. There were many cases of conduct in private and public life that were not in accordance with the moral commands of Christianity, and there were plenty of abuses in ecclesiastic practice itself, but I am not inclined to consider this as distinctive of the Renaissance period.

The real core of the tradition concerning Renaissance paganism is something quite different: it is the steady and irresistible growth of nonreligious intellectual interests which were not so much opposed to the content of religious doctrine, as rather competing with it for individual and public attention. This was nothing fundamentally new, but rather a matter of degree and of emphasis. The Middle Ages was certainly a religious epoch, but it would be wrong to assume that men's entire attention was occupied by religious, let alone by theological, preoccupations. Medieval architects built castles and palaces, not only cathedrals and monasteries. Even when the clerics held the monopoly of learning, they cultivated grammar and the other liberal arts besides theology, and during the High Middle Ages, when specialization began to arise, nonreligious literature also expanded. The thirteenth century produced not Thomas Aquinas alone, as some people seem to believe, or other scholastic theologians, but also a vast literature on Roman law, medicine, Aristotelian logic and physics, mathematics and astronomy, letter-writing and rhetoric, and even on classical Latin poetry, not to mention the chronicles and histories, the lyric and epic poetry in Latin and in the vernacular languages. This development made further progress during the Renaissance period, as a glance at the inventory of a manuscript collection or at a bibliography of printed books will easily reveal, and it continued unchecked during and after the Reformation, whatever the theologians of that time or later times may have felt about it. If an age where the nonreligious concerns that had been growing for centuries attained a kind of equilibrium with religious and theological thought, or even began to surpass it in vitality and appeal, must be called pagan, the Renaissance was pagan, at least in certain places and phases. Yet since the religious convictions of Christianity were either retained or transformed but never really challenged, it seems more appropriate to call the Renaissance a fundamentally Christian age.

To prove this point, it would be pertinent in the first place to state that the medieval traditions of religious thought and literature continued without interruption until and after the Reformation, and that Italy was no exception to this rule. The study of theology and canon law, and the literary production resulting from it, tended to increase rather than to decline, a fact that is often overlooked because historians of these subjects have paid less attention to that period than to the earlier ones, except for the material directly connected with the Reformation controversies. German mysticism was succeeded during the very period with which we are concerned by the more practical and less speculative *Devotio Moderna* in the Low Countries, a movement that produced such an important document as the *Imitation of Christ,* contributed to a reform of secondary education all over Northern Europe, and had a formative influence on such thinkers as Cusanus and Erasmus. Effective preachers made a deep impression on the learned and unlearned alike all over fifteenth-century Italy, and sometimes led to revivalist movements and political repercussions, of which Savonarola is the most famous but by no means an isolated instance. In Italy no less than in the rest of Europe, the religious guilds directed the activities of the laity and exercised a tremendous influence upon the visual arts, music, and literature. Partly in connection with these guilds, an extensive religious literature of a popular character was circulated, which was composed either by clerics or by laymen, but always addressed to the latter and usually in the vernacular languages. These facts, along with the persistence of church doctrine, institutions, and worship, would go a long way to prove the religious preoccupations of the Renaissance period.

Yet we are not so much concerned with the undoubted survival of medieval Christianity in the Renaissance as with the changes and transformations which affected religious thought during that period. As a distinguished historian has put it, Christianity is not only medieval, but also ancient and modern, and thus it was possible for Christian thought during the Renaissance to cease being medieval in many respects, and yet to remain Christian. This novelty is apparent in the new doctrines and institutions created by the Protestant and Catholic Reformations, a topic on which I shall not attempt to elaborate. I shall merely show that the humanist movement, as we have tried to describe it in our first lecture, had its share in bringing about those changes in religious thought.

The view that the humanist movement was essentially pagan or anti-Christian cannot be sustained. It was successfully refuted by the humanists themselves when they defended their work and program against the charges of unfriendly theologians of their own time. The opposite view, which has had influential defenders in recent years, namely that Renaissance humanism was in its origin a religious movement, or even a religious reaction against certain antireligious tendencies in the Middle Ages, seems to me equally wrong or exaggerated. I am convinced that humanism was in its core neither religious nor antireligious, but a literary and scholarly orientation that could be and, in many cases, was pursued without any explicit discourse on religious topics by individuals who otherwise might be fervent or nominal members of one of the Christian churches. On the other hand, there were many scholars and thinkers with a humanist training who had a genuine concern for religious and theological problems, and it is my contention that the way they brought their humanist training to bear upon the source material and subject matter of Christian theology was one of the factors responsible for the changes which Christianity underwent during that period. The most important elements in the humanist approach to religion and theology were the attack upon the scholastic method and the emphasis upon the return to the classics, which in this case meant the Christian classics, that is, the Bible and the Church Fathers.

In order to understand the significance of these attitudes, we must once more go back to antiquity and the Middle Ages. Christianity originated in a Jewish Palestine which had become politically a part of the Roman Empire, and culturally a part of the Hellenistic world. At the time when the new religion began to spread through the Mediterranean area, its sacred writings which were to form the canon of the New Testament were composed in Greek, that is, in a language which showed the marks of a long literary and philosophical tradition, and in part by authors such as Paul, Luke, and John, who had enjoyed a literary and perhaps a philosophical education. In the following centuries, the early Apologists, the Greek Fathers, and the great Councils were engaged in the task of defining and developing Christian doctrine, and of making it acceptable to the entire Greek-speaking world. Thus the reading and study of the Greek poets and prose writers was finally approved, with some reservations, whereas the teachings of the Greek philosophical schools were subjected to careful examination, rejecting everything that seemed incompatible with Christian doctrine, but using whatever appeared compatible to bolster and to supplement Christian theology. After the precedent of Philo the Jew, Clement of Alexandria and the other Greek Fathers went a long way in adding Greek philosophical methods and notions, especially Stoic and Platonist, to the doctrinal, historical and institutional teachings contained in the Bible, and in creating out of these diverse elements a novel and coherent Christian view of God, the universe, and man. At the same time, a similar synthesis of ancient and Christian elements was achieved by the Latin Fathers of the Western Church. Writers like Arnobius, Cyprian, Lactantius, and Ambrose embody in their writings the best grammatical and rhetorical training, based on the Roman poets and orators, that was available in their time. Jerome added to his consummate Latin literary education that Greek and Hebrew scholarship which enabled him to translate the entire Bible from the original languages into Latin. Augustine, the most important and complex of them all, was not only an excellent and cultured rhetorician according to the standards of his time, but also made use of the allegorical method to justify the study of the ancient Roman poets and prose writers. Furthermore, Augustine was a learned and productive philosophical and theological thinker, who left to posterity a substantial body of writings in which traditional religious doctrine was enriched with novel theological ideas like the City of God, original sin, and predestination, and also with philosophical conceptions of Greek and especially Neoplatonic origin, like the eternal forms in the divine mind, the incorporeality and immortality of the soul, conceptions which appear more prominently in his earlier, philosophical writings, but which he did not completely abandon even in his later years when he was engaged in Church administration and in theological controversies with the heretics of his time. Thus Christianity, during the first six centuries of its existence, which still belong to the period of classical antiquity, absorbed a large amount of Greek philosophical ideas and of Greek and Latin literary traditions, so that some historians have been able to speak, with a certain amount of justification, of the humanism of the Church Fathers. In recent years, it has become customary among theologians and historians to ignore or to minimize the indebtedness of Philo, Augustine, and the other early Christian writers to Greek philosophy. I must leave it to the judgment of present-day theologians and their followers whether they are really serving their cause by trying to eliminate from Christian theology all notions originally derived from Greek philosophy. Certainly those historians who follow a similar tendency and deny the significance of Greek philosophy for early Christian thought can be corrected through an objective study of the sources.

During the early Middle Ages, the Latin West had very limited philosophical and scientific interests, as we have seen, but it continued as best it could the grammatical and theological studies sanctioned by Augustine and the other Latin Fathers; and a number of Spanish, Irish, Anglo-Saxon and Carolingian scholars achieved distinction in this way. In the history of theology, a marked change from the pattern of the patristic period occurred with the rise of scholasticism after the eleventh century. What was involved was not merely the influx of additional philosophical sources and ideas, both Platonist and Aristotelian, of which we have spoken in the preceding lectures. Much more important was the novel tendency to transform the subject matter of Christian theology into a topically arranged and logically coherent system. There was no precedent for this either in the Bible or in Latin patristic literature, although certain Greek writers like Origen and John of Damascus had paved the way. The desire for a topical arrangement found its expression in the collections of sentences and church canons which culminated in the twelfth century in the *Libri Sententiarum* of Peter Lombard and the *Decretum* of Gratian which for many centuries were to serve as the standard textbooks of theology and of canon law. At the same time, the rising interest in Aristotelian logic led to the endeavor, first cultivated in the schools of Bec, Laon, and Paris, to apply the newly refined methods of dialectical argument to the subject matter of theology, which thus became by the standards of the time a real science. It is this method of Anselm, Abelard, and Peter Lombard which dominates the theological tradition of the high and later Middle Ages, including Bonaventura, Aquinas, Duns Scotus, and Ockham, not the older method of Peter Damiani or St. Bernard, who tried in vain to stem the rising tide of scholasticism and whose influence was hence confined to the more popular and practical, less scientific areas of later religious literature.

If we remember these facts concerning the history of theology in the West, we can understand what it meant for a Renaissance humanist with religious convictions to attack scholastic theology and to advocate a return to the Biblical and patristic sources of Christianity. It meant that these sources, which after all were themselves the product of antiquity, were considered as the Christian classics which shared the prestige and authority of classical antiquity and to which the same methods of historical and philological scholarship could be applied. Thus Petrarch shuns the medieval theologians except St. Bernard and quotes only early Christian writers in his religious and theological remarks. Valla laments the harmful influence of logic and philosophy upon theology and advocates an alliance between faith and eloquence. And Erasmus repeatedly attacks the scholastic theologians and emphasizes that the early Christian writers were grammarians, but no dialecticians. In his rejection of scholastic theology and his emphasis on the authority of Scripture and the Fathers, even Luther no less than John Colet is in agreement with the humanists, whereas the attempt to combine the study of theology with an elegant Latin style and a thorough knowledge of the Greek and Latin classics characterizes not only many Italian humanists and Erasmus, but also Melanchthon, Calvin, and the early Jesuits.

If we try to assess the positive contributions of humanist scholarship to Renaissance theology, we must emphasize above all their achievements in what we might call sacred philology. Valla led the way with his notes on the New Testament, in which he criticized several passages of Jerome's Vulgate on the basis of the Greek text. He was followed by Manetti, who made a new translation of the New Testament from Greek into Latin and of the Psalms from Hebrew into Latin, a work which has not yet been sufficiently studied. Erasmus' edition of the Greek New Testament is well known. It is this humanist tradition of biblical philology which provides the background and method for Luther's German version of the entire Bible from the Hebrew and Greek, as well as for the official revision of the Vulgate accomplished by Catholic scholars during the second half of the sixteenth century, and for the official English version completed under King James I. The theological exegesis of the Bible and of its various parts had always been an important branch of Christian literature ever since patristic times. It was temporarily overshadowed, though by no means eliminated, by the predominance of Peter Lombard's *Sentences* in the theological curriculum of the later Middle Ages, but it derived new force in the sixteenth century from the emphasis of Protestant theology upon the original source of Christian doctrine. To what extent the exegesis of that period was affected by the new methods and standards of humanist philology, seems to be a question which has not yet been sufficiently investigated.

An even wider field was offered to humanist scholarship by the large body of Greek Christian literature of the patristic and Byzantine period. Some of this material had been translated into Latin towards the end of antiquity and again during the twelfth century. Yet it is an established fact not sufficiently known or appreciated that a large proportion of Greek patristic literature was for the first time translated into Latin by the humanists and humanistically trained theologians of the fifteenth and sixteenth centuries. This applies to many important writings of Eusebius, Basil, and John Chrysostom, of Gregory of Nazianzus and of Nyssa, not to mention many later or lesser authors, or the writings which had been known before and were now reissued in presumably better Latin versions. Early in the fifteenth century, Leonardo Bruni translated Basil's letter which defended the reading of the pagan poets on the part of Christian students, and this welcome support of the humanist program by a distinguished Church author attained such a wide circulation that we may assume that it was used in the classroom. About the same time, Ambrogio Traversari, a monk with a classical training, dedicated a considerable amount of his energy to the translating of Greek Christian writers, thus setting an example to many later scholars, clerics, and laymen alike. These Latin versions attained great popularity as the numerous manuscript copies and printed editions may prove. They were often followed by vernacular translations, and in the sixteenth century, by editions of the original Greek texts. Thus we must conclude that the Renaissance possessed a much better and more complete knowledge of Greek Christian literature and theology than the preceding age, and it would be an interesting question, which to my knowledge has not yet been explored, whether or to what extent the newly diffused ideas of these Greek authors exercised an influence on the theological discussions and controversies of the Reformation period.

Whereas a considerable proportion of Greek Christian literature was thus made available to the West through the labors of the humanists, the writings of the Latin Church Fathers had been continuously known through the Middle Ages, and never ceased

to exercise a strong influence on all theologians and other writers. Yet in this area also humanist scholarship brought about significant changes. The humanists were fully aware of the fact that authors like Ambrose and Lactantius, and especially Jerome and Augustine, belong to the good period of ancient Latin literature, and hence must be considered as "Christian classics." Consequently, some of their works were included in the curriculum of the humanistic school, as in that of Guarino, and regularly listed as recommended readings by humanist educators like Bruni, Valla, Erasmus, and Vives. Thus the Latin Fathers were read in the humanistic period no less than before, but they were grouped with the classical Latin writers rather than with the medieval theologians, and this fact could not fail to bring about a change in the way in which they were read and understood.

Moreover, the new philological methods of editing and commenting which the humanists had developed in their studies of the ancient authors were also applied to the Latin Church Fathers. We know in the case of Augustine that many manuscript copies and printed editions of the fifteenth century were due to the efforts of humanist scholars, and that Vives composed a philological commentary on the City of God, with which he was said in true humanist fashion to have restored St. Augustine to his ancient integrity. The application of humanist scholarship to Latin patristic literature culminated in the work of Erasmus, who prepared for a number of the most important writers critical editions of their collected works. His example was followed by Protestant and Catholic scholars alike, and later in the sixteenth century, the pope appointed a special committee of scholars for the purpose of publishing the writings of the Fathers in new critical editions.

Another field in which humanist scholarship was applied to the problems which concerned the churches and theologians was the study of ecclesiastic history. The critical methods developed by the humanists for the writing of ancient and medieval history on the basis of authentic contemporary documents and evidence were first applied to church history by Valla in his famous attack on the Donation of Constantine. In the sixteenth century, the Magdeburg Centuriatores used this method to rewrite the whole history of the church from the Protestant point of view, and later in the century, Cardinal Baronius and his assistants undertook the same task for the Catholic side.

The humanist interest in early Christian literature was not limited to philological and historical preoccupations, but also had its doctrinal consequences in philosophy and theology. Just as the philological study of the pagan philosophers led the way towards a revival of Platonism and of other ancient philosophies, and more specifically to a new kind of Aristotelianism, so the humanistic study of the Bible and of the Church Fathers led to new interpretations of early Christian thought, that are characteristic of the Renaissance and Reformation period. Thus the attempt to interpret the Epistles of Paul without the context and superstructure of scholastic theology was made by scholars like Ficino, Colet, and Erasmus before it had such powerful and decisive results in the work of Luther. Even more significant and more widespread was the influence exercised during the Renaissance by St. Augustine. . . .

I think we are now at last prepared to offer a meaningful interpretation of the term "Christian humanism" that is so often applied to the Renaissance or to earlier periods. Confining the term humanism, according to the Renaissance meaning of the words humanist and humanities, to the rhetorical, classical, and moral concerns of the Renaissance humanists, regardless of the particular philosophical or theological opinions held by individual humanists, and of the theological, philosophical, scientific, or juristic training which individual scholars may have combined with their humanist education, we might choose to call Christian humanists all those scholars who accepted the teachings of Christianity and were members of one of the churches, without necessarily discussing religious or theological topics in their literary or scholarly writings. By this standard, practically all Renaissance humanists,

before and after the Reformation, were Christian humanists, since the alleged cases of openly pagan or atheistic convictions are rare and dubious. But it is probably preferable to use the term Christian humanism in a more specific sense, and to limit it to those scholars with a humanist classical and rhetorical training who explicitly discussed religious or theological problems in all or some of their writings. In this sense, neither Aquinas nor Luther were Christian humanists, for the simple reason that they were theologians, but not humanists as that term was then understood, although Luther presupposes certain scholarly achievements of humanism. On the other hand, we must list among the Christian humanists not only Erasmus, Vives, Budé, and More, but also Calvin, the elegant Latin writer and commentator of Seneca; Melanchthon, the defender of rhetoric against philosophy, who had more influence on many aspects of Lutheran Germany than Luther himself and who was responsible for the humanistic tradition of the German Protestant schools down to the nineteenth century; and finally the Jesuit Fathers, many of whom were excellent classical scholars and Latin writers, and who owed part of their success to the good instruction offered in their schools and colleges in the then fashionable humanistic disciplines. For the tradition of humanist learning by no means came to an end with the Protestant or Catholic Reformations, as might appear if we look only for the headlines of the historical development. It survived as vigorously as did the tradition of Aristotelian scholasticism, cutting across all religious and national divisions, flourishing at Leiden and Oxford no less than at Padua and Salamanca, and exercising as formative an influence upon the minds of the philosophers and scientists trained in the schools and universities of the seventeenth and eighteenth centuries.

E. HARRIS HARBISON

NEW THESIS OR OLD?

The following selection is from a series of essays by the late E. Harris Harbison entitled *The Christian Scholar in the Age of the Reformation*. The very title of the work betrays the author's underlying assumption with reference to the neopaganism of the humanistic movement, which is that the humanist was essentially Christian and remained so in spite of "the impact of the Revival of Learning upon the Christian scholar and his sense of calling." On this point Harbison is apparently in agreement with Walser and Kristeller. But his interpretation is quite different from either of theirs. His central thesis is that, while the Renaissance humanists remained Christian scholars as their predecessors had been, the Revival of Learning provided for them a new frame of reference of classical paganism which they were never quite able to square with that of traditional Christianity: and that ultimately the Christian scholar had to choose between his Christian and his scholarly calling.

The selection takes the form of a survey of selected humanists from Petrarch through Valla and Pico to the English scholar John Colet whose life and work reached to the eve of the Reformation. The author uses these figures to illustrate the various ways in which these men adjusted to the contradictions between classicism and Christianity; and he obviously prefers Colet as "the first to be able to absorb a good deal of the philological and historical interests and attitudes of the New Learning and to direct them to a purpose fully Christian." This preference awakens echoes of an earlier generation of scholars which made a clear distinction between the pagan humanists of the Italian Renaissance and the Christian scholars of the Northern Renaissance.

The student should attempt to "test" the thesis that Harbison presents against the case presented by Walser and Kristeller. How, for example, does Harbison's view square with the importance Kristeller attaches to "sacred philology"? He should consider the consistency between Harbison's underlying assumption and his main thesis. And he should ask whether Harbison has put himself closer to the revisionists or the traditionalists.

The implications of all this [i.e. the humanists' developing sense of historical time and distance] for the scholar who took his commitment to the Christian religion seriously were confused and unclear at first. It had not been easy to domesticate Greek philosophy in medieval Christianity, but Aquinas and others had done it. Abelard had found Christian uses for dialectic but was suspicious of grammar and rhetoric: "What has Horace to do with the Psalter, Virgil with the Gospel, Cicero with the Apostle?" he asked, echoing Jerome. The line of least resistance for the Christian Humanist was to castigate dialectic (and Scholasticism in general) as unchristian, to ask with Erasmus what has Aristotle to do with Christ, and to sing the praises of grammar and rhetoric as potential allies of Christian belief. This the Humanists did, from Petrarch on, but it was not so easy to persuade either themselves or others as it might have seemed. And it is this that gives the study of the Christian scholar and his calling during the Reformation its interest. For one thing, to reject Abelard and Aquinas was to be driven back to the equally fundamental questions raised by Jerome and Augustine as scholars and Christians. And to think more and more as historians and less and less as philosophers was to raise a disturbingly new question for Christian thinkers: What if there had been a breach of historical continuity within Christianity itself, a breach between a primitive apostolic Church close to its Founder's spirit and a corrupted institution of a later and darker age which had unwittingly broken the tie that bound it to Christ? What if the new history, archaeology, and philology should appear to shake to its foundations the structure of Christianity as a set of timeless beliefs? There was work enough for Christian scholars to do as a result of the Revival of Learning.

New Thesis or Old?

To suggest some of the facets of the problem we must select and concentrate as we did in the preceding chapter. The most important figures to understand if one would know something of the impact of the Revival of Learning upon the Christian scholar and his sense of calling are Petrarch, Lorenzo Valla, Pico della Mirandola, and John Colet. With these four we shall be concerned in this chapter.

Francesco Petrarca, or Petrarch (1304–1374), was the first to feel deeply the personal implications of the new scholarly interests and perspectives which we have discussed—or at least the first to be articulate about his doubts and worries. More clearly than anyone of his generation, Petrarch was able to conceive Roman antiquity historically, as it had been, a pagan society of infinite attractiveness. He knew this society was dead, but he found by experience that he could revive its greatest figures and their thoughts in his imagination and live in spiritual friendship with them. This gave peculiar poignancy to his sense of the gulf between the *Respublica Romana* and the *Respublica Christiana,* between civic and monastic ideals, between Cicero and Christ. He knew that the Voice might reproach him for being a Ciceronian rather than a Christian as it had reproached Jerome. But characteristically, it was an imaginative literary dialogue, not a vision, in which the conflict within him took place between his love for pagan antiquity and his devotion to Christianity. This was his *Secret,* the famous dialogue between St. Augustine and himself which he wrote in 1342 at the age of thirty-eight and always kept by his bedside to remind him of his soul-searchings at the height of his intellectual powers. The problem is Jerome's primarily, but the Father who Petrarch feels will best understand his own passions and problems is not Jerome but the author of the *Confessions.* The Augustine of the dialogue is a curious mixture, part Augustine as he was, part Petrarch's prudish medieval conscience. He is always right in his argument with Petrarch's more human half, but he is not always understanding enough of human failings. He wins the argument but loses Petrarch's soul.

Petrarch's *Secret* is an extraordinarily subtle piece of self-analysis. Augustine lays bare Petrarch's spiritual anatomy with the relentless touch of a skilled soul-surgeon: his infatuation for Laura, which Augustine insists was never so high-minded or ennobling an affair as Petrarch maintains it was; his ambition for literary fame, which the saint says

is more soaring and limitless than Petrarch is aware of; and his *accidia,* his inner melancholy and malaise, the result of a hopelessly divided mind and will. When Petrarch blames all these failings on external circumstances and agencies, Augustine brings him relentlessly back to their internal roots. The trouble is "your overcrowded mind," he says; you have "no considered plan"; you "can never put your whole strength to anything" because of the "worrying torment of a mind angry with itself [which] loathes its own defilements, yet cleanses them not away." Read Seneca or Cicero, he says, or for that matter read your own book on *Tranquillity of Soul;* you are "a past-master in the whole field," but like too many other writers of your generation, you do not practice what you preach.[1]

The root of the trouble, it develops, is a deep dichotomy between occupation and conscience. No man of his generation was ever more engrossed and seduced by the pleasures of scholarship and writing than Petrarch. All his life he sought some satisfying moral justification of the work he loved—in vain. He quoted Cicero's definition of glory to Augustine—"the illustrious and world-wide renown of good services rendered to one's fellow-citizens, to one's country, or to all mankind"—with the implication that this was what *he* was doing. But Augustine was not taken in: "Why and wherefore, I ask, this perpetual toil, these ceaseless vigils, and this intense application to study? You will answer, perhaps, that you seek to find out what is profitable for life. But you have long since learned what is needful for life and for death. What was now required of you was to try and put in practice what you know, instead of plunging deeper and deeper into laborious inquiries, where new problems are always meeting you, and insoluble mysteries, in which you never reach the end. . . . You write books on others, but yourself you quite forget."[2] Does this mean, asks Petrarch, that I must drop my work entirely? Yes, says Augustine, Rome has been celebrated before; think only on your approaching death. Petrarch says he wishes Augustine had told him all this earlier. "I will pull myself together and collect my scattered wits, and make a great endeavor to possess my soul in patience," he concludes,

[1] *Petrarch's Secret. . . .* trans. Wm. H. Draper, London, Chatto and Windus, 1911, pp. 45–46, 99, 138. The quotations that follow are used by permission.

[2] *Ibid.,* pp. 166–170.

"but I have not strength to resist that old bent for study altogether." The "true order" is "that mortal men should first care for mortal things, and that to things transitory, things eternal should succeed." Meanwhile he prays that God will lead him "safe and whole out of so many crooked ways."[3]

In the course of the dialogue, Petrarch raised anew the question which had haunted both Augustine and Abelard, the question of the relation between learning and goodness, or more precisely, the problem of scholarship and sex: can a sinner be a good scholar? "Remember," says Augustine to Petrarch on the subject of Laura, "remember how ill your profession accords with a life like this; think how this woman has injured your soul, your body, your fortune."[4]

The whole question of learning and goodness came up again twenty-five years later in an amusing way. In 1366 four Venetian noblemen amused themselves after a good dinner by debating and declaring a formal legal sentence to the effect that Petrarch was certainly a good man but a poor scholar, "a good man without learning." This cut Petrarch to the quick. He waited a year, then wrote an elaborate answer in the classical form of an invective entitled *On my own ignorance and that of many others*. His line of defence—ignoring for the moment the various layers of irony—is that he may not know much but neither does anybody, and he is at least a devoted Christian, which is more than his enemies can say. At the same time he is careful to display his erudition by saturating the essay with classical quotations. Furthermore, he sketches the reply *he* would make if he were to be accused of Ciceronianism as Jerome was: "My incorruptible treasure and the superior part of my soul is with Christ; but because of the frailties and burdens of mortal life, which are not only difficult to bear but difficult merely to enumerate, I cannot, I confess, lift up, however ardently I should wish, the inferior parts of my soul, in which the irascible and concupiscible appetites are located." Cicero has done him no harm and much good, he insists. Augustine and Jerome both had the same experience. "I even feel sure that Cicero himself would have been a Christian if he had been able to see Christ and to comprehend his doctrine," he adds, as Augustine had thought of Plato.[5] Yet in all this there is no real justification of the scholarly or literary calling. In fact there is a deep undercurrent

of anti-intellectualism which seems more than merely ironical: "It is safer to strive for a good and pious will than for a capable and clear intellect. . . . It is better to will the good than to know the truth. . . . In this life it is impossible to know God in his fulness; piously and ardently to love Him is possible. . . ."[6] "It will be enough if I succeed in being wise within the limits of sobriety; and this can be achieved without much learning, even without any, as is clearly shown by the long line of illiterate saints of both sexes."[7] And yet Petrarch spent years of his life working over a scholarly book *On Illustrious Men* of classical antiquity and had really very little love for "illiterate saints."

It is too easy to make fun of Petrarch. A badly integrated personality, we would say today—and send him to the psychoanalyst's couch. But Petrarch's emotional tensions were the warning of a new era in the history of Christian scholarship. The particular kind of reconciliation between classicism and Christianity which was represented by Aquinas in philosophy, Dante in poetry, and the Gothic Cathedral in art could not last forever because it was based on hazy and inaccurate notions of the past, both classical and Christian. The rise of history, archaeology, and philology as scholarly disciplines was bound to sharpen the differences between Athens and Jerusalem and reveal the shaky historical foundations of the so-called medieval synthesis of Greek reason and Christian faith. As the philological and historical attitudes spread, they would reveal that the gulf between the classical point of view and the Christian was far wider than either Aquinas or Dante suspected. What Petrarch did was to dramatize and popularize these new scholarly attitudes. Elaboration of the disciplines themselves he left to others, but he did demonstrate vividly the psychological tensions that might result if the disciplines were taken seriously. Try as he might, Petrarch could never quite bring his scholarly activity and his Christian faith into any organic relationship with each other. He could never gain a sense of calling as a Christian and a scholar. His failure was an omen of how difficult the task was to be in the next

[5] *The Renaissance Philosophy of Man*, ed. Ernst Cassirer, P. O. Kristeller, and J. H. Randall, Chicago, University of Chicago Press, 1948, pp. 113–115. Copyright 1948 by the University of Chicago. The quotations that follow from Petrarch and Pico are used by permission.

[6] *Ibid.*, p. 105.

[7] *Ibid.*, p. 127.

[3] *Ibid.*, pp. 176, 184–192.

[4] *Ibid.*, p. 163.

New Thesis or Old?

two centuries of growing secularism and deepening religious strife.

The destructive possibilities, both for good and ill, of the new attitudes which accompanied the Revival of Learning became abundantly evident a century after Petrarch in the career of Lorenzo Valla (1405 – 1457), Valla exemplified better than anyone else of his generation and the triumph of grammar and rhetoric over dialectic, of the historical over the philosophical attitude. He had probably the keenest critical intelligence of any of the Italian Humanists. Like Jerome he was primarily a philologist—and like Jerome he was always getting into violent literary quarrels. Like Abelard he seems to have been primarily concerned to make his generation think, question, ponder its unexamined beliefs and assumptions.

His book On the Elegancies of the Latin Language (published 1444) was for its day a model of the best critical method in linguistic study and served as the foundation of good Latin style and sound method for later Humanists, notably Erasmus. Unlike Jerome, Valla's restless intellect applied the methods learned in philology to the criticism of doctrines and institutions. At twenty-six years of age he wrote a dialogue On Pleasure which attacked Petrarch's naive reconciliation of Stoicism with Christian ethics, questioned the validity of good works as a conscious moral goal and suggested ironically that a life lived according to Epicurean principles was a better introduction than Stoicism to the eternal bliss reserved for Christians. Soon he was applying his criticism to Scholasticism and monasticism. The Schoolmen, he said, really did not know their Aristotle, and they wrote very bad and obscure Latin; they should have paid more attention to rhetoric than to dialectic, which was after all a barren method. The monks, he said, had falsely usurped the name of "religious" and were trying to dodge the secular duties demanded of all Christians; there was only one moral perfection, he insisted, open to layman and cleric alike; the monks were rather a sect than a religion. His most famous work was his conclusive proof, on historical and philological grounds, that the Donation of Constantine, upon which so much of the papal claim to temporal power was based, was an arrant forgery. Typical of his method were his remarks about the "satraps" which the author of the document incautiously mentioned. "What have satraps got to do with the case?" asks the outraged historian and philologist. "Numskull, blockhead! Do Caesars speak thus? Are Roman decrees usually drafted thus? Whoever heard of satraps being mentioned in the councils of the Romans?"[8]

If the new criticism could be applied to the Donation of Constantine, why could it not be applied equally well to other documents of the Christian tradition? Valla's originality lay in his insight that if collation of manuscripts, analysis of language, and examination of historical context got one closer to the mind of Cicero or of Aristotle, the same techniques would presumably get one closer to the mind of the Fathers, or of St. Paul, or perhaps of Moses. No document was so sacred as to be exempt from philological analysis, providing that fundamental doctrines were not questioned. Valla demonstrated that a letter from King Abgar of Edessa to Jesus was apocryphal. He proved that the mystical writings attributed to Dionysius the Areopagite could not possibly have been written by a contemporary of St. Paul's, as generations of medieval students had believed. He argued that the Apostles' Creed was the work not of the Apostles but of the Council of Nicaea. But most important of all, he took in hand three Latin and three Greek codices of the New Testament and demonstrated that the Latin Vulgate was full of grammatical misunderstandings and unhappy translations. Paul had written extremely well in Greek, he pointed out; it was a shame that his meaning was so often twisted or obscured by the translator. He could not believe that the New Testament Vulgate was Jerome's work. Jerome was too good a scholar and stylist for that. The New Testament verses scattered through his works are always better translated than they are in the Vulgate. Either Jerome had nothing to do with it, or the copyists had ruined his work. . . .

He had the instincts of a true critic, writes his biographer: "to compare, to judge, to illuminate, to correct, to show literature the way to become a supremely effective force in ameliorating society."[9] But how much of this could be called Christian motivation we shall never know and it is useless to inquire. To assess the precise extent to which an individual mind or a whole society has become what we call "secularized" is the most difficult problem the historian of this period has to face. Valla never protested his Christian motives in the

[8] The Treatise of Lorenzo Valla on the Donation of Constantine, trans. C. B. Coleman, New Haven, Yale University Press, pp. 84 – 85.

[9] Girolamo Mancini, Vita di Lorenzo Valla, Florence, 1891, p. 331.

way Abelard and Petrarch felt called upon to do; nor did he ever proclaim his contempt for Christianity. His work exemplifies nicely how faint and fluctuating is the line that separates the religious from the secular in the motivation of critical scholarship at the close of the Middle Ages. What Valla did as a scholar was indispensable to Erasmus, Luther, and Calvin—and they all spoke well of him. He demonstrated what historical and philological criticism could accomplish. But we will never be able to fathom the combination of worldly motives, disinterested love of truth, and Christian aims, that inspired his work.

The ideal scholar, if there were one, would be composed of equal parts of critical ability and appreciative capacity. The two are not often united in the same man. Valla was long on critical acumen but short on appreciative insight (into Scholasticism, for instance). The most spectacular scholar of the next generation, Giovanni Pico della Mirandola (1463–1494), was long on the power of appreciation and short on critical penetration. Valla was a philologist who had little patience with philosophy; Pico, a philosopher who had no great interest in philology. If Valla illustrated the benefits and potential dangers of criticism, Pico demonstrated the strengths and weaknesses of a sort of indiscriminate appreciation as the foundation of scholarly work.

It is hard to describe Pico and make him believable. The attempt somehow reminds one of that remark of Montaigne's about stories of the same witch appearing one day in one place and the next a thousand miles away: "To tell the truth I would not believe my own eyes in such a case."[10] Apparently Pico had everything: brains, good looks, noble birth, money, ambition, and enormous energy. Above all, he had an insatiable thirst for learning, which he attempted to slake at Bologna, Padua, Florence, Rome, and Paris. In 1486 at the tender age of twenty-four—"full of pride and desirous of glory," his nephew-biographer tells us—he went to Rome and published nine hundred Theses or propositions drawn from the lore of all ages and places, Eastern and Western. To the startled scholarly world he proposed to defend these propositions before all comers and offered to pay the traveling expenses of any debaters who should come from a distance. The Pope was unimpressed. "This young man wants someone to burn him some day," he remarked. A

[10] *Essays,* III, II.

papal commission censured thirteen of the propositions—such as that Christ did not really and truly descend into Hell but only *quoad effectum,* and that no one's beliefs are simply the product of his will alone. Pico wrote a hasty *Apology* but this got him into more trouble. He fled to Paris where he was imprisoned for a short time, then escaped to Florence where he remained under the protection of Lorenzo de' Medici during most of his few remaining years. This conflict with ecclesiastical authority shook him deeply. Looking back on it, he told his nephew he thought it was by God's special providence that he had thus been falsely accused of heresy so that he would come to his senses, give up "the voluptuous use of women," to which he had been addicted, and correct his evil ways. Just what the character of his "conversion" was, it is hard to say. He sold his hereditary lands, burned some youthful love poetry, and talked of going out barefoot to preach Christ—after he finished writing "certain books" he had in hand. He came increasingly under the influence of Savonarola, who insisted in a sermon preached after his death that Pico had determined to become a Dominican friar. But he remained a layman, and except that he concentrated somewhat more on purely religious problems, the change in his life apparently did not affect his whole conception of learning, as it had Augustine's. In 1494 at the early age of thirty-one he died of a fever in three days of illness. . . .

One thing is evident. Pico was no more able than Petrarch or Valla to attain any clear sense of calling as a Christian scholar. Petrarch never found any final reconciliation between the Ciceronian and Christian halves of his split personality. Valla never made explicit the Christian roots (if there were any) of his philological crusade. Pico's personal devotion to Christ, the only-begotten Son, never found any adequate place in his vast and indiscriminate syncretism. All three considered themselves scholars and Christians, but none of the three had any consciousness, so far as I have been able to discover, of organic relationship between personal piety and scholarly endeavor.

Here, it would seem, is the importance of John Colet (1467?–1519). Colet was the first to be able to absorb a good deal of the philological and historical interests and attitudes of the New Learning and to direct them to a purpose fully Christian. In him personal piety and professional purpose interpenetrated each other so thoroughly that when his friends wrote about him, the scholar always recalled the Christian and the Christian the scholar. "In London there is John Colet, Dean of St. Paul's, who has combined great learning with a marvellous piety," Erasmus wrote to a friend. Later he said that he had never seen "a more highly-gifted intellect," adding immediately that Colet liked to bend this intellect to what would fit him for immortality. At table, Erasmus reported, his conversation was "all either about literature or about Christ." "A book was ever his companion on the road, and his talk was always of Christ." Thomas More said of him after his death: "None more learned or more holy has lived among us for many ages past."[11]

The thing that strikes the historian most about Colet at this distance is the extraordinary balance and harmony in him between conflicting impulses and aims which tore other men of his generation to pieces—or made hypocrites of them. In a little devotional tract that he wrote, an admonition to the reader is repeated like a refrain: order your life "by reason and grace." And its last words are: "Use well temporal things. Desire eternal things. Finis."[12] The balance between this world and the next in his mind gave him an inner assurance that made those who knew him best rely on him for judgment and courage. He had the power, as Lupton notes, "of uniting and attaching others to himself, or rather of drawing them through himself to a higher object."[13] He did not come by this emotional stability easily. "It was but a very small portion of this religious spirit that he owed to nature," Erasmus thought. By nature he was irascible, covetous, and inclined to sensuous pleasures. He had to discipline these three weaknesses all his life, "by philosophy and sacred studies, watching, fasting, and prayer"—that is, by both mind and will. His anger sometimes blazed out in righteous indignation. He founded St. Paul's School with the money he inherited from his wealthy merchant father, partly because he knew his tendency to covetousness. He never married (he was ordained priest in 1498) and his dinners were notoriously frugal, "yet," says Erasmus, "if an occasion ever presented itself, either of conversing with ladies, or being a guest at sumptuous repasts, you might have seen some traces of the old nature in him." Erasmus concluded the warm pen-portrait which is the chief source of our knowledge of Colet's life by remarking that although he never noted any sign of human weakness in his saintly friend Vitrier, "In Colet were some traits which showed him to be but man." . . .

Colet was no Humanist in the ordinary sense of the word. He seems never to have felt any guilty love for pagan literature like Jerome or Petrarch. He saw no value in reading the ancient poets and philosophers. In his Oxford lectures he specifically condemned the idea that a man had to study the classics in order to understand Scripture. Truth is understood by grace, grace is procured by prayers, and prayers are heard through devotion and self-denial.[14] Man's natural reason has no autonomous power of arriving at the truth without God's aid. Theology is not a "science" to be attained by reason—this was Aquinas' error, he thought—it is a "wisdom" revealed to faith by the divine illumination.[15] Colet steeped himself in Paul's radical pessimism about the natural man and emerged an Augustinian—almost a "Lutheran," in fact—on the helplessness of the unaided intellect. In his lectures on the Dionysian writings, he showed how much he had absorbed of the Neo-Platonic doctrine that mere learning will never save a man. "Not knowledge, but love, leads to eternal life. . . . Ignorant love has a thousand times more power than cold wisdom." He condemned "indiscriminate erudition," saying that it dulled Christian innocence and simplicity.[16] Probably he was referring to the Schoolmen, but it is not impossible that he was thinking of Pico.

Yet when all is said on the side of Colet's narrow intellectual interests and almost puritanical Christianity (he had absorbed Paul's view of marriage as a mere concession to human infirmity), the fact remains that he was able to direct a penetrating mind and a devout heart into a brief scholarly career of considerable significance. Within the Christian tradition itself, his tastes were not narrow or dogmatic. He read heretical books with attention, says Erasmus, and got more out of them than he did out of

[11] Erasmus to Servatius Roger, 8 July 1514, Allen, *Opus Epistolarum*, I, Ep. 296; Erasmus, *Vitrier and Colet*, pp. 31–32, 26; Thomas More to a Monk, 1519–20, *The Correspondence of Sir Thomas More*, ed. Elizabeth F. Rogers, Princeton, 1947, p. 192.

[12] "A ryght fruitfull monicion concernynge the order of a good christen mannes lyfe," in Lupton, *Life*, pp. 305–310.

[13] Lupton, *Life*, p. 265.

[14] Colet, *I Corinthians*, p. 110.

[15] Rice, "John Colet and the Annihilation of the Natural," *loc. cit.*, pp. 152–161.

[16] Colet, *Two Treatises on the Hierarchies of Dionysius*, ed. J. H. Lupton, London, 1869, p. 219; Erasmus, *Vitrier and Colet*, p. 37.

The Eve of the Modern World

orthodox scholastic hair-splitters.[17] His scholarly ideal, even when he failed to live up to it in his own writing, was directness and simplicity. He once read a copy of Reuchlin's *Cabalistica* and wrote Erasmus that he was not really qualified to discuss it, but that as he read, it seemed to him at times that "the wonders were more verbal than real."[18] What came to his mind in commenting on Romans 1:17 was quite characteristic. He chose to remark on how simple was the Apostles' method of citation when quoting from the Old Testament (in this case, Paul was quoting "The just shall live by faith" from Habakkuk). In contrast, he said, modern theologians and lawyers are so afraid no one will believe them that they pile citation upon citation to show off their erudition.[19]

Christian scholarship to Colet begins in prayer and divine illumination; it concerns itself with the whole of a scriptural writer's thought and his historical surroundings; it moves on from historical analysis to ethical and religious understanding; and it ends in social reform and the deepening of personal piety. Unlike any of the moving spirits of the Revival of Learning in Italy whom we have considered, Colet was able to adapt the historical and philological approach to the reverent study of Scripture and to bring his own Christian piety into fruitful relationship with humanistic scholarship. His example was to have important effects upon the greatest scholar of the age, Erasmus of Rotterdam.

[17] Erasmus, *Vitrier and Colet*, p. 38.

[18] Lupton, *Colet*, pp. 225–226.

[19] Colet, *Romans*, p. 209.

3

THE REFORMATION: THE PROBLEM OF CAUSE

There was in the medieval church a long prior history of religious dissent stretching back for centuries before the Protestant Reformation. Time after time dissent had taken the shape of monastic reform movements—the Cluniac reform of the tenth and eleventh centuries, the Cistertian Order of the twelfth century, and the mendicant orders of the thirteenth. And these movements had succeded, in their times, in reforming and reinvigorating the church. There had been individual critics who had railed against the church; others who quietly lamented its perennial corruption; and mystics who had turned from it to look for God within themselves. Dissent had expressed itself in the form of violent heretical movements which increased in frequency and virulence through the High Middle Ages in spite of the best efforts of the Church, first to ignore them, then to correct them, and finally to destroy them.

In a hundred ways the church had somehow dealt with its dissenters and contained them. But with the increasing internal troubles of the church in the fourteenth and fifteenth centuries and the increasing pressure of conflicts with the emerging national monarchies, the vigor which in earlier ages had been summoned to deal with religious dissent had begun to fail. At the same time the abuses which had long lent credence to the charges of critics of the church were on the increase. The church of the High Middle Ages had committed itself to continued concern for temporalities: the church of the later Middle Ages now bore the onus of that commitment. The need for reform was so patent that it became the major program of the whole string of church councils that stretched across the fifteenth century. The cry for reform of the church in head and members was raised again and again. Many highly placed churchmen were concerned for church reform, even most of the fifteenth century popes were for it. But they refused to accept even a program of reform with which they were in fundamental agreement from the hands of the hated councils, and the energies which might have been effectively employed in reform were dissipated in constitutional strife. The Conciliar Movement was a massive failure and with it faded the hope for either systematic constitutional change or reform of the church. Heretical critics multiplied and men of good will turned in despair to lay religious movements, to fanatic revivalists, and to their own dark thoughts. There seemed no alternative but the violence of religious revolution: and this came at last with the Protestant Reformation. In this context the Reformation becomes part of the pattern of dissent running back through the history of the church. But is this pattern a fundamental cause of the Reformation or is it merely its historical setting and background? Two of the selections that follow take opposing views on this question.

Much of the modern speculation about the causes of the Reformation focuses on the square and stalwart figure of Martin Luther, who seems to embody so much of its strength and purpose in himself. His importance is certainly fundamental in any discussion of the Reformation. But many scholars see the basic cause of the Reformation—either to praise or to condemn it—in the troubled soul of Luther and in the truculence and success with which he maintained his convictions. They reject the notion that the background to the Reformation was its cause. They point out that the condition of the church was no worse in the early sixteenth century than it had been for centuries: indeed, there were some signs of recovery. They point out that there was astonishingly little that was either original or new in Luther's position, that much of what he said had been said before by Hus, Occam, Wyclif and others. Thus, they say, why should Luther have succeeded in making a religious revolution when earlier reformers had failed, except for some special magic in the man himself? The scholars who take this position subscribe to some variety of what has been called the "hero thesis" in history, which sees the moving force of things in great men rather than in the ebb and flow of large, impersonal forces. Three of the following selections set forth the view that Luther was the cause of the Reformation—but they see Luther in very different ways.

The student should be aware that the two points of view represented in the selections of this problem, while important, are not the only points of view. For example, if it is true that much of what Luther said Hus had said before, why was it that the spark of Luther's words caught fire in so many other men of his time? Was it only the man Luther himself? If the abuses of the church were on their way to being cured, why were so many men ready to follow Luther to the destruction of the church? Is it not possible to see the cause of the Reformation in the coincidence of the man and his time? Is there not a middle ground on which the critic may stand?

HENRY CHARLES LEA

THE EXTERNAL VIEW

One of the oldest and most durable explanations for the Reformation is that it was a reaction against the abuses of the medieval church and a movement to correct those abuses. The very term Reformation reflects this contention. Among the most passionate advocates of this view was Henry Charles Lea (1825–1909) from whose chapter-essay, "The Eve of the Reformation" in the *Renaissance* volume of the old *Cambridge Modern History,* the following selection is taken.

Lea argues that it is an error to regard the Reformation as primarily a religious movement; that "the motives, both remote and proximate, which led to the Lutheran revolt were largely secular rather than spiritual"; and that "the existing ecclesiastical system was the practical evolution of dogma, and the overthrow of dogma was the only way to obtain permanent relief from the intolerable abuses of that system." He goes on to detail the familiar story of church abuse—the corrupt and cynical financial practices of the papacy and its agents, the intrusion of the church into the proper affairs of the emerging secular states, the conflict of lay and ecclesiastical courts for jurisdiction. He concludes that, on the one hand, the church forfeited the respect and confidence of the secular world by its very secularism and, on the other, destroyed true spirituality by its dependence on the empty forms of religious observance.

The student should note, in light of our previous problem, Lea's gratuitous charge that Renaissance humanism was both paganistic and a contributing factor to the coming of the Reformation. He should weigh the reasons Lea gives for the Reformation's having occurred in Germany. But most of all the student should observe that Lea's concept of the cause of the Reformation is basically external. This view is predictable enough given the fact that the bulk of Lea's writings—including the massive *A History of the Inquisition of the Middle Ages* and *History of Sacerdotal Celibacy in the Christian Church*—was devoted to the examination of the institutions of the medieval church, and that his verdict on those institutions was fundamentally negative. In the final analysis, then, the student should ponder whether the external view of cause can really be entertained for so fundamental a religious revolution as the Reformation.

As the sixteenth century opened, Europe was standing unconscious on the brink of a crater destined to change profoundly by its eruption the course of modern civilisation. The Church had acquired so complete a control over the souls of men, its venerable antiquity and its majestic organisation so filled the imagination, the services it had rendered seemed to call for such reverential gratitude, and its ac-

From Henry Charles Lea, "The Eve of the Reformation," Chapter XIX of *The Cambridge Modern History,* Vol. I: *The Renaissance* (New York, 1907), pp. 653–57, 660, 665–68, 673–80, 686–87, 690–91. Reprinted by permission of the Cambridge University Press.

knowledged claim to interpret the will of God to man rendered obedience so plain a duty, that the continuance of its power appeared to be an unchanging law of the universe, destined to operate throughout the limitless future. To understand the combination of forces which rent the domination of the Church into fragments, we must investigate in detail its relations with society on the eve of the disruption, and consider how it was regarded by the men of that day, with their diverse grievances, more or less justifying revolt. We must here omit from consideration the benefits which the Church had conferred, and confine our attention to the antagonisms which it provoked and to the evils for which it was held responsible. The interests and the motives at work were numerous and complex, some of them dating back for centuries, others comparatively recent, but all of them growing in intensity with the development of political institutions and popular intelligence. There has been a natural tendency to regard the Reformation as solely a religious movement; but this is an error. In the curious theocracy which dominated the Middle Ages, secular and spiritual interests became so inextricably intermingled that it is impossible wholly to disentangle them; but the motives, both remote and proximate, which led to the Lutheran revolt were largely secular rather than spiritual. So far, indeed, as concerns our present purpose we may dismiss the religious changes incident to the Reformation with the remark that they were not the object sought but the means for attaining that object. The existing ecclesiastical system was the practical evolution of dogma, and the overthrow of dogma was the only way to obtain permanent relief from the intolerable abuses of that system. . . .

This sovereignty was temporal as well as spiritual. The power of the Pope, as the earthly representative of God, was illimitable. The official theory, as expressed in the *De Principum Regimine,* which passes under the name of St Thomas Aquinas, declared the temporal jurisdiction of kings to be simply derived from the authority intrusted by Christ to St Peter and his successors; whence it followed that the exercise of the royal authority was subject to papal control. . . .

While it is true that the extreme exercise of papal authority in making and unmaking Kings was exceptional, still the unlimited jurisdiction claimed by the Holy See was irksome in many ways to the sovereigns of Europe and, as time wore on and the secular authority became consolidated, it was endured with more and more impatience. There could be no hard and fast line of delimitation between the spiritual and the temporal, for the two were mutually interdependent, and the convenient phrase, *temporalia ad spiritualia ordinata,* was devised to define those temporal matters, over which, as requisite to the due enjoyment of the spiritual, the Church claimed exclusive control. Moreover it assumed the right to determine in doubtful matters the definition of this elastic term and the secular ruler constantly found himself inconveniently limited in the exercise of his authority. The tension thence arising was increased by the happy device of legates and nuncios, by which the Holy See established in every country a representative whose business it was to exercise supreme spiritual jurisdiction and to maintain the claims of the Church, resulting in a divided sovereignty, at times exceedingly galling and even incompatible with a well-ordered State. Rulers so orthodox as Ferdinand and Isabel asked the great national Council of Seville, in 1478, how they could best prevent the residence of legates and nuncios who not only carried much gold out of the kingdom but interfered seriously with the royal pre-eminence. In this they only expressed the desires of the people; for the Estates of Castile, in 1480, asked the sovereigns to make some provision with respect to the nuncios who were of no benefit and only a source of evil.

Another fruitful source of complaint, on the part not only of the rulers but of the national Churches, was the gradual extension of the claim of the Holy See to control all patronage. Innocent III has the credit of first systematically asserting this claim and exploiting it for the benefit of his Cardinals and other officials. The practice increased, and Villani tells us that, in 1319, John XXII assumed to himself the control of all prebends in every collegiate church, from the sale of which he gathered immense sums. Finally the assertion was made that the Holy See owned all benefices and in the rules of the papal Chanceries appear the prices to be charged for them, whether with or without cure of souls, showing that the traffic had become an established source of revenue. Even the rights of lay patrons and founders were disregarded and in the provisions granted by the popes there was a special clause derogating their claims. Partly this patronage was used for direct profit, partly it was employed for the benefit of the Cardinals and their retainers, on whom pluralities were heaped with unstinted hand,

and the further refinement was introduced of granting to them pensions imposed on benefices and monastic foundations. Abbeys, also, were bestowed *in commendam* on titular abbots who collected the revenues through stewards, with little heed to the maintenance of the inmates or the performance of the offices. In the eager desire to anticipate these profits of simony, vacancies were not awaited, and rights of succession, under the name of expectatives, were given or sold in advance. The deplorable results of this spiritual commerce were early apparent and formed the subject of bitter lamentation and complaint, but to no purpose. . . .

Another ecclesiastical abuse severely felt by all sovereigns who were jealous of their jurisdiction and earnest in enforcing justice was the exemption enjoyed by all ranks of the clergy from the authority of the secular tribunals. They were justiciable only by the spiritual Courts, which could pronounce no judgments of blood, and whose leniency towards clerical offenders virtually assured to them immunity from punishment—an immunity long maintained in English jurisprudence under the well-known name of Benefit of Clergy. So complete was the freedom of the priesthood from all responsibility to secular authority that the ingenuity of the doctors was taxed to find excuses for the banishment of Abiathar by Solomon. The evil of this consisted not only in the temptation to crime which it offered to those regularly bred to the Church and performing its functions, but it attracted to the lower orders of the clergy, which were not bound to celibacy or debarred from worldly pursuits, numberless criminals and vagabonds, who were thus enabled to set the officers of justice at defiance. The first defence of a thief or assassin when arrested was to claim that he belonged to the Church and to display his tonsure, and the episcopal officials were vigilant in the defence of these wretches, thus stimulating crime and grievously impeding the administration of justice. Frequent efforts were made by the secular authorities to remedy these evils; but the Church resolutely maintained its prerogatives, provoking quarrels which led to increased antagonism between the laity and the clergy. The *Gravamina* of the German Nation, adopted by the Diet of Nürnberg, in 1522, stated no more than the truth in asserting that this clerical immunity was responsible for countless cases of adultery, robbery, coining, arson, homicide, and false-witness committed by ecclesiastics; and there was peculiar significance in the declaration that, unless the clergy were subjected to the secular

Courts, there was reason to fear an uprising of the people, for no justice was to be had against a clerical offender in the spiritual tribunals. . . .

Under the circumstances the Holy See could inspire neither respect nor confidence. Universal distrust was the rule between the States, and the papacy was merely a State whose pretensions to care for the general welfare of Christendom were recognised as diplomatic hypocrisy. When, in 1462, Pius II took the desperate step of resolving to lead in person the proposed crusade, he explained that this was the only way to convince Europe of his sincerity. When he levied a tithe, he said, for the war with the infidel, appeal was made to a future Council; when he issued indulgences he was accused of greed; whatever was done was attributed to the desire to raise money, and no one trusted the papal word; like a bankrupt trader, he was without credit. This distrust of the papacy with regard to its financial devices for the prosecution of the war with the Turk was universally entertained, and it lent a sharper edge to the dissatisfaction of those called upon to contribute. . . .

In every way the revenues thus enjoyed and squandered by the Curia were scandalous and oppressive. To begin with, the cost of their collection was enormous. The accounts of the papal agent for first-fruits in Hungary, for the year 1320, show that of 1913 florins collected only 732 reached the papal treasury. With a more thorough organisation in later periods the returns were better; but when the device was adopted of employing bankers to collect the proceeds of annates and indulgences, the share allotted to those who conducted the business and made advances, was ruinously large. In the contract for the fateful St Peter's indulgence with the Fuggers of Augsburg, their portion of the receipts was to be fifty *per cent*. Even worse was it when these revenues were farmed out, for the banker who depended for his profits on the extent of his sales or collections was not likely to be overnice in his methods, nor to exercise much restraint over his agents. Europe was overrun with pardon-sellers who had purchased letters empowering them to sell indulgences, whether of a general character or for some church or hospital; and for centuries their lies, their frauds, their exactions, and their filthy living were the cause of the bitterest and most indignant complaints.

Even more demoralising were the revenues derived

from the sale of countless dispensations for marriage within the prohibited degrees, for the holding of pluralities, for the numerous kinds of "irregularities" and other breaches of the canon law; so that its prescriptions might almost seem to have been framed for the purpose of enabling the Holy See to profit by their violation. Not less destructive to morals were the absolutions, which amounted to a sale of pardons for sin of every description, as though the Decalogue had been enacted for this very purpose. There was also a thriving business done in the composition for unjust gains, whereby fraudulent traders, usurers, robbers, and other male-factors, on paying to the Church a portion of their illegal acquisitions, were released from the obligation of making restitution. In every way the power of the keys and the treasure of the merits of Christ were exploited, without any regard for moral consequences. . . .

In fact, one of the most urgent symptoms of the necessity of a new order of things was the complete divorce between religion and morality. There was abundant zeal in debating minute points of faith, but little in evoking from it an exemplary standard of life—as Pius II said of the Conventual Franciscans: they were generally excellent theologians but gave themselves little trouble about virtue. The sacerdotal system, developed by the dialectics of the School-men, had constructed a routine of external observances through which salvation was to be gained not so much by abstinence from sin as by its pardon through the intervention of the priest, whose super-natural powers were in no way impaired by the scandals of his daily life. Except within the pale of the pagan Renaissance, never was there a livelier dread of future punishment, but this punishment was to be escaped, not by amendment but by confession, absolution, and indulgences. This frame of mind is exemplified by the condottiere Vitelozzo Vitelli who, when after a life steeped in crime, he was suddenly strangled by Cesare Borgia, in 1502, felt no more poignant regret than that he could not obtain absolution from the Pope—and that Pope was Alexander VI. Society was thoroughly cor-rupt—perhaps less so in the lower than in the higher classes—but no one can read the Lenten sermons of the preachers of the time, even with full allowance for rhetorical exaggeration, without recognising that the world has rarely seen a more debased standard of morality than that which prevailed in Italy in the closing years of the Middle Ages. Yet at the same time never were there greater outward manifesta-

tions of devotional zeal. A man like San Giovanni Capistrano could scarce walk the streets of a city without an armed guard to preserve his life from the surging crowds eager to secure a rag of his gar-ments as a relic or to carry away some odour of his holiness by touching him with a stick. Venice, which cared little for an interdict, offered in vain ten thousand ducats, in 1455, for a seamless coat of Christ. Siena and Perugia went to war over the wedding-ring of the Virgin. At no period was there greater faith in the thaumaturgic virtue of images and saintly relics; never were religious solemnities so gorgeously celebrated; never were processions so magnificent or so numerously attended; never were fashionable shrines so largely thronged by pilgrims. In his *Encheiridion Militis Christiani,* written in 1502 and approved by Adrian VI, then head of the Uni-versity of Louvain, Erasmus had the boldness to pro-test against this new kind of Judaism which placed its reliance on observances, like magic rites, which drew men away from Christ; and again, in 1519, in a letter to Cardinal Albrecht of Mainz, he declared that religion was degenerating into a more than Ju-daic formalism of ceremonies, and that there must be a change.

A priesthood trained in this formalism, which had practically replaced the ethical values of Christian-ity, secure that its supernatural attributes were unaffected by the most flagitious life, and selected by such methods as were practised by the Curia and imitated by the prelates, could not be expected to rise above the standards of the community. Rather, indeed, were the influences, to which the clergy were exposed, adapted to depress them below the average. They were clothed with virtually irrespon-sible power over their subjects, they were free from the restraints of secular law, and they were con-demned to celibacy in times when no man was ex-pected to be continent. For three hundred years it had been the constant complaint that the people were contaminated by their pastors and the com-plaint continued. . . .

The popular literature of the period similarly reflects this mingled contempt and hatred for the priesthood. The Franciscan Thomas Murner, who subsequently was one of the most savage opponents of Luther, in the curious rhymed sermons which, in 1512, he preached in Frankfort-on-the-Main, and which, un-der the names of the *Schelmenzunft* and the *Nar-renbeschweerung,* had a wide popularity, is never tired of dwelling on the scandals of all classes of the

The Eve of the Modern World

clergy, from bishops to monks and nuns. All are worldly, rapacious, and sensual. When the lay lord has shorn the sheep, the priest comes and fairly disembowels it, the begging friar follows and gets what he can and then the pardoner. If a bishop is in want of money he sends around his fiscal among the parish priests to extort payment for the privilege of keeping their concubines. In the nunneries the sister who has the most children is made the abbess. If Christ were on earth to-day He would be betrayed, and Judas would be reckoned an honest man. The devil is really the ruler of the Church, whose prelates perform his works; they are too ignorant to discharge their duties and require coadjutors — it would be well for them could they likewise have substitutes in hell. The wolf preached and sang mass so as to gather the geese around him, and then seized and ate them; so it is with prelate and priest who promise all things and pretend to care for souls until they get their benefices, when they devour their flocks. The immense applause with which these attacks on the abuses of the Church were everywhere received, and others of a similar character in Eulenspiegel, Sebastian Brant's *Narrenschiff*, Johann Faber's *Tractatus de Ruine Ecclesie Planctu*, and the *Encomium Moriae* of Erasmus, their translation into many languages and wide circulation throughout Europe, show how thoroughly they responded to the popular feeling, how dangerously the Church had forfeited the respect of the masses, and how deeply rooted was the aversion which it had inspired. The priests hated Rome for her ceaseless exactions and the people hated the priests with perhaps even better reason. So bitter was this dislike that, in 1502, Erasmus tells us that among laymen to call a man a cleric or a priest or a monk was an unpardonable insult. . . .

While thus the primary cause of the Reformation is to be sought in the all-pervading corruption of the Church and its oppressive exercise of its supernatural prerogatives, there were other factors conducing to the explosion. Sufficient provocation had long existed, and since the failure at Basel no reasonable man could continue to anticipate relief from conciliar action. The shackles which for centuries had bound the human intellect had to be loosened, before there could be a popular movement of volume sufficient to break with the traditions of the past and boldly tempt the dangers of a new and untried career for humanity. The old reverence for authority had to be weakened, the sense of intellectual independence had to be awakened and the spirit of enquiry and of more or less scientific investigation had to be created, before pious and devout men could reach the root of the abuses which caused so much indignation, and could deny the authenticity of the apostolical deposit on which had been erected the venerable and imposing structure of scholastic theology and papal autocracy.

It was the New Learning and the humanistic movement which supplied the impulse necessary for this, and they found conditions singularly favourable for their work. The Church had triumphed so completely over her enemies that the engines of repression had been neglected and had grown rusty, while the Popes were so engrossed in their secular schemes and ambition that they had little thought to waste on the possible tendencies of the fashionable learning which they patronised. Thus there came an atmosphere of free thought, strangely at variance with the rigid dogmatism of the theologians, and even in theology there was a certain latitude of discussion permissible, for the Tridentine decrees had not yet formulated into articles of faith the results of the debates of the Schoolmen since the twelfth century. It is a remarkable proof of the prevailing laxity that Nicholas V commissioned Gianozzo Manetti to make a new translation of the Bible from the original Hebrew and Greek, thus showing that the Vulgate was regarded as insufficient and that it enjoyed no such authority as that attributed to it at Trent. In view of this laxity it is not surprising that in Italy the New Learning assumed various fantastic shapes of belief — the cult of the Genius of Rome by Pomponio Leto and his Academy, the Platonism of Marsiglio Ficino, the practical denial of immortality by Pomponazzi, and the modified Averrhoism of Agostino Nifo. So long as the profits of the Curia or the authority of the Pope remained undisputed there was little disposition to trouble the dreamers and speculators. Savonarola declares, with some rhetorical exaggeration, that culture had supplanted religion in the minds of those to whom the destinies of Christianity were confided, until they lost belief in God, celebrated feasts of the devil, and made a jest of the sacred mysteries. In the polite Court circles of Leo X, we are told, a man was scarce accounted as cultured and well-bred unless he cherished a certain amount of heretical opinion; and after Luther's doctrines had become rigidly defined Melanchthon is said to have looked back with a sigh to the days before the Reformation as to a time when there was freedom of thought. It is true that there was occasional spasmodic repression. Pico della Mirandola, because of thirteen heretical propositions among the nine hundred which he offered to defend in 1487, was obliged to fly to Spain and to make his peace by submission; but, as a rule, the humanists were allowed to air their fancies in peace. When the disputations of the schools on the question of the future life became overbold and created scandal, the Lateran Council, in 1513, forbade the teaching of Averrhoism and of the mortality of the soul; but it did so in terms which placed little restraint on philosophers who shielded themselves behind a perfunctory declaration of submission to the judgment of the Church. . . .

The combination of all these factors rendered an explosion inevitable, and Germany was predestined to be its scene. The ground was better prepared for it there then elsewhere, by the deeper moral and religious earnestness of the people and by the tendencies of the academies and associations with which society was honeycombed. In obedience to these influences the humanistic movement had not been pagan and aesthetic as in Italy, but had addressed itself to the higher emotions and had sought to train the conscience of the individual to recognise his direct responsibility to God and to his fellows. But more potent than all this were the forces arising from the political system of Germany and its relations with the Holy See. The Teutonic spirit of independence had early found expression in the *Sachsenspiegel* and *Sächsische Weichbild*—the laws and customs of Northern Germany—which were resolutely maintained in spite of repeated papal condemnation. Thus not only did the Church inspire there less awe than elsewhere in Europe, but throughout the Middle Ages there had been special causes of antagonism actively at work.

If Italy had suffered bitterly from the *Tedeschi,* Germany had no less reason to hate the papacy. The fatal curse of the so-called Holy Roman Empire hung over both lands. It gave the Emperor a valid right to the suzerainty of the peninsula; it gave the papacy a traditional claim to confirm at its discretion the election of an Emperor. Conflicting and incompatible pretensions rendered impossible a permanent truce between the representatives of Charlemagne and St Peter. Since the age of Gregory VII the consistent policy of Rome had been to cripple the Empire by fomenting internal dissension and rendering impossible the evolution of a strong and centralised government, such as elsewhere in Europe was gradually overcoming the centrifugal

forces of feudalism. This policy had been successful and Germany had become a mere geographical expression—a congeries of sovereign princes, petty and great, owning allegiance to an Emperor whose dignity was scarce more than a primacy of honour and whose actual power was to be measured by that of his ancestral territories. The result of this was that Germany lay exposed defenceless to the rapacity and oppression of the Roman Curia. Its multitudinous sovereigns had vindicated their independence at the cost of depriving themselves of the strength to be derived from centralised union. Germany was the ordinary resource of a Pope in financial straits, through the exaction of a tithe, the raising of the annates, or the issue in unstinted volume of the treasure of the merits of Christ in the form of an unremitting stream of indulgences which sucked up as with a sponge the savings of the people. Nor could any steady opposition be offered to the absorption of the ecclesiastical patronage by the Curia, through which benefices were sold or bestowed on the cardinals or their creatures, and no limits could be set on appeals to the Holy See which enlarged its jurisdiction and impoverished pleaders by involving them in interminable and ruinous litigation in the venal Roman Courts. . . .

If Germany was thus the predestined scene of the outbreak, it was also the land in which the chances of success were the greatest. The very political condition which baffled all attempts at self-protection likewise barred the way to the suppression of the movement. A single prince, like the Elector Frederick of Saxony, could protect it in its infancy. As the revolt made progress other princes could join it, whether moved by religious considerations, or by way of maintaining the allegiance of their subjects, or in order to seize the temporalities and pious foundations, or, like Albrecht of Brandenburg, to found a principality and a dynasty. We need not here enquire too closely into the motives of which the League of Schmalkalden was the outcome, and may content ourselves with pointing to the fact that even Charles V was, in spite of the victory of Mühlberg, powerless to restore the imperial supremacy or to impose his will on the Protestant States.

The progress of the Reformation, and still more so that of the Counter-Reformation, lie outside the limits of the present chapter; but it may be concluded by a few words suggesting why the abuses which, in the sixteenth century, could only be cured by rending the Church in twain, have to so large an extent disappeared since the Reformation, leading many enthusiasts to feel regret that the venerable ecclesiastical structure was not purified from within—that reform was not adopted in place of schism. The abuses under which Christendom groaned were too inveterate, too firmly entrenched, and too profitable to be removed by any but the sternest and sharpest remedies.

PRESERVED SMITH

ANOTHER VIEW FROM THE OUTSIDE

The following passage is from the introductory chapter of *The Age of the Reformation* by Preserved Smith (1880–1941), who may be taken as a fair representative of the reaction of his generation of Reformation scholars against the generation of Henry Charles Lea. Like Lea, Smith deals in this selection with the financial abuses of the old church, with its secularism, with the immorality of the clergy, and the consequent evil reputation of the clergy in the eyes of laymen on the eve of the Reformation. He even cites the same passage from Pius II which Lea had used. He points out, like Lea, the barrenness of the religious formalism that the sixteenth century had inherited from the medieval church and the inability of that formalism to cope with the vigorous new spirit beginning to stir in the generation of Martin Luther.

But there are fundamental differences between Lea and Smith, beginning with their basic assumptions. Smith denies that the "principal cause" of the Reformation "was the corruption of the church," an assumption diametrically opposed to that of Lea. Thus, Smith's recitation of many of the same charges and arguments that Lea had used stemmed from a very different motive: "though the corruptions of the church were not a main cause of the Protestant secession, they furnished good excuses for attack." What Lea presented as basic causes, Smith regards as pretexts.

Another difference the student should note is the difference in tone between the two selections. Where Lea exhibits outraged moral conscience, Smith adopts a tone almost of mocking superiority. For he belonged to a generation of rationalistic historians who thought they were beginning at last to understand the past in terms of larger social and economic patterns which had not been understood either by their predecessors or by their subjects, the blind wretches who had struggled vainly against those patterns in ages past. Thus, while Smith disagrees with the external view taken by Lea, his own view of the causes of the Reformation is itself external. As he says in the concluding chapter of this same book, "The Reformation, like the Renaissance and the sixteenth-century Social Revolution, was but the consequence of the operation of antecedent changes in environment and habit, intellectual and economic."

In the eyes of the early Protestants the Reformation was a return to primitive Christianity and its principal cause was the corruption of the church. That there was great depravity in the church as elsewhere cannot be doubted, but there are several reasons for thinking that it could not have been an important cause for the loss of so many of her sons. In the first place there is no good ground for believing that the moral condition of the priesthood was worse in 1500 than it had been for a long time; indeed, there is good evidence to the contrary, that things were tending to improve, if not at Rome yet in many parts of Christendom. If objectionable practices of the priests had been a sufficient cause for the secession of whole nations, the Reformation would have come long before it actually did. Again, there is good reason to doubt that the mere abuse of an institution has ever led to its complete otherthrow; as long as the institution is regarded as necessary, it is rather mended than ended. Thirdly, many of the acts that seem corrupt to us, gave little offence to contemporaries, for they were universal. If the church sold offices and justice, so did the civil governments. If the clergy lived impure lives, so did the laity. Probably the standard of the church (save in special circumstances) was no worse than that of civil life, and in some respects it was rather more decent. Finally, there is some reason to suspect of exaggeration the charges preferred by the innovators. Like all reformers they made the most of their enemy's faults. Invective like theirs is common to every generation and to all spheres of life. It is true that the denunciation of the priesthood comes not only from Protestants and satirists, but from popes and councils and canonized saints, and that it bulks large in medieval literature. Nevertheless, it is both a *priori* probable and to some extent historically verifiable that the evil was more noisy, not more potent, than the good. But though the corruptions of the church were not a main cause of the Protestant secession, they furnished good excuses for attack; the Reformers were scandalized by the divergence of the practice and the pretensions of the official representatives of Christianity, and their attack was envenomed and the break made easier thereby. It is therefore necessary to say a few words about those abuses at which public opinion then took most offence.

Many of these were connected with money. The common man's conscience was wounded by the smart in his purse. The wealth of the church was enormous, though exaggerated by those contemporaries who estimated it at one-third of the total real estate of Western Europe. In addition to revenues from her own land the church collected tithes and taxes, including "Peter's pence" in England, Scandinavia and Poland. The clergy paid dues to the curia, among them the *servitia* charged on the bishops and the annates levied on the income of the first year for each appointee to high ecclesiastical office, and the price for the archbishop's pall. The priests recouped themselves by charging high fees for their ministrations. At a time when the Christian ideal was one of "apostolic poverty" the riches of the clergy were often felt as a scandal to the pious.

Though the normal method of appointment to civil office was sale, it was felt as a special abuse in the church and was branded by the name of simony. Leo X made no less than 500,000 ducats annually from the sale of more than 2000 offices, most of which, being sinecures, eventually came to be regarded as annuities, with a salary amounting to about 10 per cent. of the purchase price.

Justice was also venal, in the church no less than in the state. Pardon was obtainable for all crimes for, as a papal vice-chamberlain phrased it, "The Lord wishes not the death of a sinner but that he should pay and live." Dispensations from the laws against marriage within the prohibited degrees were sold. Thus an ordinary man had to pay 16 grossi for dispensation to marry a woman who stood in "spiritual relationship" to him; a noble had to pay 20 grossi for the same privilege, and a prince or duke 30 grossi. First cousins might marry for the payment of 27 grossi; an uncle and niece for from three to four ducats, though this was later raised to as much as sixty ducats, at least for nobles. Marriage within the first degree of affinity (a deceased wife's mother or daughter by another husband) was at one time sold for about ten ducats; marriage within the second degree was permitted for from 300 to 600 grossi. Hardly necessary to add, as was done: "Note well, that dispensations or graces of this sort are not given to poor people." Dispensations from vows and from the requirements of ecclesiastical law, as for example those relating to fasting, were also to be obtained at a price.

From *The Age of the Reformation* by Preserved Smith, pp. 20–29, copyright 1920, 1948. Used by permission of the publishers, Holt, Rinehart and Winston, Inc.

The Eve of the Modern World

One of the richest sources of ecclesiastical revenue was the sale of indulgences, or the remission by the pope of the temporal penalties of sin, both penance in this life and the pains of purgatory. The practice of giving these pardons first arose as a means of assuring heaven to those warriors who fell fighting the infidel. In 1300 Boniface VIII granted a plenary indulgence to all who made the pilgrimage to the jubilee at Rome, and the golden harvest reaped on this occasion induced his successors to take the same means of imparting spiritual graces to the faithful at frequent intervals. In the fourteenth century the pardons were extended to all who contributed a sum of money to a pious purpose, whether they came to Rome or not, and, as the agents who were sent out to distribute these pardons were also given power to confess and absolve, the papal letters were naturally regarded as no less than tickets of admission to heaven. In the thirteenth century the theologians had discovered that there was at the disposal of the church and her head an abundant "treasury of the merits of Christ and the saints," which might be applied vicariously to anyone by the pope. In the fifteenth century the claimed power to free living men from purgatory was extended to the dead, and this soon became one of the most profitable branches of the "holy trade."

The means of obtaining indulgences varied. Sometimes they were granted to those who made a pilgrimage or who would read a pious book. Sometimes they were used to raise money for some public work, a hospital or a bridge. But more and more they became an ordinary means for raising revenue for the curia. How thoroughly commercialized the business of selling grace and remission of the penalties of sin had become is shown by the fact that the agents of the pope were often bankers who organized the sales on purely business lines in return for a percentage of the net receipts plus the indirect profits accruing to those who handle large sums. Of the net receipts the financiers usually got about ten per cent.; an equal amount was given to the emperor or other civil ruler for permitting the pardoners to enter his territory, commissions were also paid to the local bishop and clergy, and of course the pedlars of the pardons received a proportion of the profits in order to stimulate their zeal. On the average from thirty to forty-five per cent. of the gross receipts were turned into the Roman treasury.

It is natural that public opinion should have come to regard indulgences with aversion. Their bad moral effect was too obvious to be disregarded, the compounding with sin for a payment destined to satisfy the greed of unscrupulous prelates. Their economic effects were also noticed, the draining of the country of money with which further to enrich a corrupt Italian city. Many rulers forbade their sale in their territories, because, as Duke George of Saxony, a good Catholic, expressed it, before Luther was heard of, "they cheated the simple layman of his soul." Hutten mocked at Pope Julius II for selling to others the heaven he could not win himself. Pius II was obliged to confess: "If we send ambassadors to ask aid of the princes, they are mocked; if we impose a tithe on the clergy, appeal is made to a future council; if we publish an indulgence and invite contributions in return for spiritual favors, we are charged with greed. People think all is done merely for the sake of extorting money. No one trusts us. We have no more credit than a bankrupt merchant."

Much is said in the literature of the latter Middle Ages about the immorality of the clergy. This class has always been severely judged because of its high pretensions. Moreover the vow of celibacy was too hard to keep for most men and for some women; that many priests, monks and nuns broke it cannot be doubted. And yet there was a sprinkling of saintly parsons like him of whom Chaucer said

Who Christes lore and his apostles twelve
He taught, but first he folwed it himselve,

and there were many others who kept up at least the appearance of decency. But here, as always, the bad attracted more attention than the good.

The most reliable data on the subject are found in the records of church visitations, both those undertaken by the Reformers and those occasionally attempted by the Catholic prelates of the earlier period. Everywhere it was proved that a large proportion of the clergy were both wofully ignorant and morally unworthy. Besides the priests who had concubines, there were many given to drink and some who kept taverns, gaming rooms and worse places. Plunged in gross ignorance and superstition, those blind leaders of the blind, who won great reputations as exorcists or as wizards, were unable to understand the Latin service, and sometimes to repeat even the Lord's prayer or creed in any language.

The Reformation, like most other revolutions, came

not at the lowest ebb of abuse, but at a time when the tide had already begun to run, and to run strongly, in the direction of improvement. One can hardly find a sweeter, more spiritual religion anywhere than that set forth in Erasmus's *Enchiridion,* or in More's *Utopia,* or than that lived by Vitrier and Colet. Many men, who had not attained to this conception of the true beauty of the gospel, were yet thoroughly disgusted with things as they were and quite ready to substitute a new and purer conception and practice for the old, mechanical one.

Evidence for this is the popularity of the Bible and other devotional books. Before 1500 there were nearly a hundred editions of the Latin Vulgate, and a number of translations into German and French. There were also nearly a hundred editions, in Latin and various vernaculars, of *The Imitation of Christ.* There was so flourishing a crop of devotional handbooks that no others could compete with them in popularity. For those who could not read there were the *Biblia Pauperum,* picture-books with a minimum of text, and there were sermons by popular preachers. If some of these tracts and homilies were crude and superstitious, others were filled with a spirit of love and honesty. Whereas the passion for pilgrimages and relics seemed to increase, there were men of clear vision to denounce the attendant evils. A new feature was the foundation of lay brotherhoods, like that of the Common Life, with the purpose of cultivating a good character in the world, and of rendering social service. The number of these brotherhoods was great and their popularity general.

Had the forces already at work within the church been allowed to operate, probably much of the moral reform desired by the best Catholics would have been accomplished quietly without the violent rending of Christian unity that actually took place. But the fact is, that such reforms never would or could have satisfied the spirit of the age. Men were not only shocked by the abuses in the church, but they had outgrown some of her ideals. Not all of her teaching, nor most of it, had become repugnant to them, for it has often been pointed out that the Reformers kept more of the doctrines of Catholicism than they threw away, but in certain respects they repudiated, not the abuse but the very principle on which the church acted. In four respects, particularly, the ideals of the new age were incompatible with those of the Roman communion.

The first of these was the sacramental theory of sal-vation and its corollary, the sacerdotal power. According to Catholic doctrine grace is imparted to the believer by means of certain rites: baptism, confirmation, the eucharist, penance, extreme unction, holy orders, and matrimony. Baptism is the necessary prerequisite to the enjoyment of the others, for without it the unwashed soul, whether heathen or child of Christian parents, would go to eternal fire; but the "most excellent of the sacraments" is the eucharist, in which Christ is mysteriously sacrificed by the priest to the Father and his body and blood eaten and drunk by the worshippers. Without these rites there was no salvation, and they acted automatically *(ex opere operato)* on the soul of the faithful who put no active hindrance in their way. Save baptism, they could be administered only by priests, a special caste with "an indelible character" marking them off from the laity. Needless to remark the immense power that this doctrine gave the clergy in a believing age. They were made the arbiters of each man's eternal destiny, and their moral character had no more to do with their binding and loosing sentence than does the moral character of a secular officer affect his official acts. Add to this that the priests were unbound by ties of family, that by confession they entered into everyone's private life, that they were not amenable to civil justice—and their position as a privileged order was secure. The growing self-assurance and enlightenment of a nascent individualism found this distinction intolerable.

Another element of medieval Catholicism to clash with the developing powers of the new age was its pessimistic and ascetic other-worldliness. The ideal of the church was monastic; all the pleasures of this world, all its pomps and learning and art were but snares to seduce men from salvation. Reason was called a barren tree but faith was held to blossom like the rose. Wealth was shunned as dangerous, marriage deprecated as a necessary evil. Fasting, scourging, celibacy, solitude, were cultivated as the surest roads to heaven. If a good layman might barely shoulder his way through the strait and narrow gate, the highest graces and heavenly rewards were vouchsafed to the faithful monk. All this grated harshly on the minds of the generations that began to find life glorious and happy, not evil but good.

Third, the worship of the saints, which had once been a stepping-stone to higher things, was now widely regarded as a stumbling-block. Though far from a scientific conception of natural law, many men had become sufficiently monistic in their philosophy to see in the current hagiolatry a sort of polytheism. Erasmus freely drew the parallel between the saints and the heathen deities, and he and others scourged the grossly materialistic form which this worship often took. If we may believe him, fugitive nuns prayed for help in hiding their sin; merchants for a rich haul; gamblers for luck; and prostitutes for generous patrons. Margaret of Navarre tells as an actual fact of a man who prayed for help in seducing his neighbor's wife, and similar instances of perverted piety are not wanting. The passion for the relics of the saints led to an enormous traffic in spurious articles. There appeared to be enough of the wood of the true cross, said Erasmus, to make a ship; there were exhibited five shin-bones of the ass on which Christ rode, whole bottles of the Virgin's milk, and several complete bits of skin saved from the circumcision of Jesus.

Finally, patriots were no longer inclined to tolerate the claims of the popes to temporal power. The church had become, in fact, an international state, with its monarch, its representative legislative assemblies, its laws and its code. It was not a voluntary society, for if citizens were not born into it they were baptized into it before they could exercise any choice. It kept prisons and passed sentence (virtually if not nominally) of death; it treated with other governments as one power with another; it took principalities and kingdoms in fief. It was supported by involuntary contributions.

The expanding world had burst the bands of the old church. It needed a new spiritual frame, and this frame was largely supplied by the Reformation. Prior to that revolution there had been several distinct efforts to transcend or to revolt from the limitations imposed by the Catholic faith; this was done by the mystics, by the pre-reformers, by the patriots and by the humanists.

ROLAND H. BAINTON

A SYMPATHETIC VIEW FROM THE INSIDE

The following passage from the best-selling biography, *Here I Stand: A Life of Martin Luther,* by Roland H. Bainton represents the nearly complete departure of contemporary scholars from the "environmental" or "external" analysis of the causes of the Reformation such as we have seen in the excerpt from Henry Charles Lea and, to a degree, in that from Preserved Smith. Bainton's view may in contrast be called an essentially interior view. The Reformation was to him neither primarily a social revolution nor the result of the movement of massive, impersonal economic forces. It was primarily a religious revolt and it was generated in the religious disquiet of a single man—Martin Luther. As Bainton says, ". . . Luther was above all else a man of religion. The great outward crises of his life which bedazzle the eyes of dramatic biographers were to Luther himself trivial in comparison with the inner upheavals of his questing after God." By the same token, such things as the corruption of the church, the peculiar socio-political configuration of the Holy Roman Empire, the emergence of capitalism, and the intellectual revolution of Renaissance humanism, while perhaps not trivial, must be relegated by such a view to the status of contributing background factors rather than primary causes of the Reformation.

In this selection Bainton deals in some detail with the series of inner crises in

Luther's young manhood which led him to that "revelation" which may be called the starting point of the Reformation. The first of these crises was the terror-stricken vow to become a monk, made in the midst of a thunderstorm. The second was the "terror of the holy" that overtook him at the celebration of his first mass. The third was his realization of a "way out" for him from the hopelessness of man's sin and the awfulness of God's majesty through a new understanding of scripture, in particular of the famous passage from Romans which "became to me a gate to heaven" and the origin of the cardinal Lutheran doctrine of justification by faith.

On a sultry day in July of the year 1505 a lonely traveler was trudging over a parched road on the outskirts of the Saxon village of Stotternheim. He was a young man, short but sturdy, and wore the dress of a university student. As he approached the village, the sky became overcast. Suddenly there was a shower, then a crashing storm. A bolt of lightning rived the gloom and knocked the man to the ground. Struggling to rise, he cried in terror, "St. Anne help me! I will become a monk."

The man who thus called upon a saint was later to repudiate the cult of the saints. He who vowed to become a monk was later to renounce monasticism. A loyal son of the Catholic Church, he was later to shatter the structure of medieval Catholicism. A devoted servant of the pope, he was later to identify the popes with Antichrist. For this young man was Martin Luther.

His demolition was the more devastating because it reinforced disintegrations already in progress. Nationalism was in process of breaking the political unities when the Reformation destroyed the religious. Yet this paradoxical figure revived the Christian consciousness of Europe. In his day, as Catholic historians all agree, the popes of the Renaissance were secularized, flippant, frivolous, sensual, magnificent, and unscrupulous. The intelligentsia did not revolt against the Church because the Church was so much of their mind and mood as scarcely to warrant a revolt. Politics were emancipated from any concern for the faith to such a degree that the Most Christian King of France and His Holiness the Pope did not disdain a military alliance with the Sultan against the Holy Roman Empire. Luther changed all this. Religion became again a dominant factor even in politics for another century and a half. Men cared enough for the faith to die for it and to kill for it. If there is any sense remaining of Christian

civilization in the West, this man Luther in no small measure deserves the credit.

Very naturally he is a controversial figure. The multitudinous portrayals fall into certain broad types already delineated in his own generation. His followers hailed him as the prophet of the Lord and the deliverer of Germany. His opponents on the Catholic side called him the son of perdition and the demolisher of Christendom. The agrarian agitators branded him as the sycophant of the princes, and the radical sectaries compared him to Moses, who led the children of Israel out of Egypt and left them to perish in the wilderness. But such judgments belong to an epilogue rather than a prologue. The first endeavor must be to understand the man.

One will not move far in this direction unless one recognizes at the outset that Luther was above all else a man of religion. The great outward crises of his life which bedazzle the eyes of dramatic biographers were to Luther himself trivial in comparison with the inner upheavals of his questing after God. For that reason this study may appropriately begin with his first acute religious crisis in 1505 rather than with his birth in 1483. . . .

The Church taught that no sensible person would wait until his deathbed to make an act of contrition and plead for grace. From beginning to end the only secure course was to lay hold of every help the Church had to offer: sacraments, pilgrimages, indulgences, the intercession of the saints. Yet foolish was the man who relied solely on the good offices of the heavenly intercessors if he had done nothing to insure their favor!

And what better could he do than take the cowl? . . .

The Eve of the Modern World

These were the ideas on which Luther had been nurtured. There was nothing peculiar in his beliefs or his responses save their intensity. His depression over the prospect of death was acute but by no means singular. The man who was later to revolt against monasticism became a monk for exactly the same reason as thousands of others, namely, in order to save his soul. The immediate occasion of his resolve to enter the cloister was the unexpected encounter with death on that sultry July day in 1505. He was then twenty-one and a student at the University of Erfurt. As he returned to school after a visit with his parents, sudden lightning struck him to earth. In that single flash he saw the denouement of the drama of existence. There was God the all-terrible, Christ the inexorable, and all the leering fiends springing from their lurking places in pond and wood that with sardonic cachinnations they might seize his shock of curly hair and bolt him into hell. It was no wonder that he cried out to his father's saint, patroness of miners, "St. Anne help me! I will become a monk." . . .

Luther in later life remarked that during the first year in the monastery the Devil is very quiet. We have every reason to believe that his own inner tempest subsided and that during his novitiate he was relatively placid. This may be inferred from the mere fact that at the end of the year he was permitted to make his profession. The probationary period was intended to give the candidate an opportunity to test himself and to be tested. He was instructed to search his heart and declare any misgivings as to his fitness for the monastic calling. If his companions and superiors believed him to have no vocation, they would reject him. Since Luther was accepted, we may safely assume that neither he nor his brethren saw any reason to suppose that he was not adapted to the monastic life. . . .

Thus he might have continued had he not been overtaken by another thunderstorm, this time of the spirit. The occasion was the saying of his first mass. He had been selected for the priesthood by his superior and commenced his functions with this initial celebration.

The occasion was always an ordeal because the mass is the focal point of the Church's means of grace. Here on the altar bread and wine become the flesh and blood of God, and the sacrifice of Calvary is re-enacted. The priest who performs the miracle of transforming the elements enjoys a power and

privilege denied even to angels. The whole difference between the clergy and the laity rests on this. The superiority of the Church over the state likewise is rooted here, for what king or emperor ever conferred upon mankind a boon comparable to that bestowed by the humblest minister at the altar?

Well might the young priest tremble to perform a rite by which God would appear in human form. But many had done it, and the experience of the centuries enabled the manuals to foresee all possible tremors and prescribe the safeguards. The celebrant must be concerned, though not unduly, about the forms. . . .

The day began with the chiming of the cloister bells and the chanting of the psalm, "O sing unto the Lord a new song." Luther took his place before the altar and began to recite the introductory portion of the mass until he came to the words, "We offer unto thee, the living, the true, the eternal God." He related afterward:

At these words I was utterly stupefied and terror-stricken. I thought to myself, "With what tongue shall I address such Majesty, seeing that all men ought to tremble in the presence of even an earthly prince? Who am I, that I should lift up mine eyes or raise my hands to the divine Majesty? The angels surround him. At his nod the earth trembles. And shall I, a miserable little pygmy, say 'I want this, I ask for that'? For I am dust and ashes and full of sin and I am speaking to the living, eternal and the true God."

The terror of the Holy, the horrors of Infinitude, smote him like a new lightning bolt, and only through a fearful restraint could he hold himself at the altar to the end.

The man of our secularized generation may have difficulty in understanding the tremors of his medieval forebear. There are indeed elements in the religion of Luther of a very primitive character, which hark back to the childhood of the race. He suffered from the savage's fear of a malevolent deity, the enemy of men, capricious, easily and unwittingly offended if sacred places be violated or magical formulas mispronounced. His was the fear of ancient Israel before the ark of the Lord's presence. Luther felt similarly toward the sacred host of the Savior's body; and when it was carried in procession, panic took hold of him. His God was the God who inhabited the storm clouds brooding on the brow of Sinai, into whose presence Moses could not enter with unveiled face and live. Luther's experience, however, far exceeds the primitive and should not be so unintelligible to the modern man who, gazing upon the uncharted nebulae through instruments of his own devising, recoils with a sense of abject littleness.

Luther's tremor was augmented by the recognition of unworthiness. "I am dust and ashes and full of sin." Creatureliness and imperfection alike oppressed him. Toward God he was at once attracted and repelled. Only in harmony with the Ultimate could he find peace. But how could a pigmy stand before divine Majesty; how could a transgressor confront divine Holiness? Before God the high and God the holy Luther was stupefied. For such an experience he had a word which has as much right to be carried over into English as *Blitzkrieg*. The word he used was *Anfechtung*, for which there is no English equivalent. It may be a trial sent by God to test man, or an assault by the Devil to destroy man. It is all the doubt, turmoil, pang, tremor, panic, despair, desolation, and desperation which invade the spirit of man.

Utterly limp, he came from the altar to the table where his father and the guests would make merry with the brothers. After shuddering at the unapproachableness of the heavenly Father he now craved some word of assurance from the earthly father. How his heart would be warmed to hear from the lips of old Hans that his resentment had entirely passed, and that he was now cordially in accord with his son's decision! They sat down to meat together, and Martin, as if he were still a little child, turned and said, "Dear father, why were you so contrary to my becoming a monk? And perhaps you are not quite satisfied even now. The life is so quiet and godly."

This was too much for old Hans, who had been doing his best to smother his rebellion. He flared up before all the doctors and the masters and the guests, "You learned scholar, have you never read in the Bible that you should honor your father and your mother? And here you have left me and your dear mother to look after ourselves in our old age." . . .

This second upheaval of the spirit set up in Luther an inner turmoil which was to end in the abandonment of the cowl, but not until after a long interval. In fact he continued to wear the monastic habit for three years after his excommunication. Altogether he was garbed as a monk for nineteen years. His development was gradual, and we are not to imagine him in perpetual torment and never able to say mass without terror. He pulled himself together and went on with the appointed round and with whatever new duties were assigned. The prior, for example, informed him that he should resume his university studies in order to qualify for the post of lector in the Augustinian order. He took all such assignments in stride.

But the problem of the alienation of man from God had been renewed in altered form.

Luther set himself to learn and expound the Scriptures. On August 1, 1513, he commenced his lectures on the book of Psalms. In the fall of 1515 he was lecturing on St. Paul's Epistle to the Romans. The Epistle to the Galatians was treated throughout 1516–17. These studies proved to be for Luther the Damascus road. The third great religious crisis which resolved his turmoil was as the still small voice compared to the earthquake of the first upheaval in the thunderstorm at Stotternheim and the fire of the second tremor which consumed him at the saying of his first mass. No *coup de foudre*, no heavenly apparition, no religious ceremony, precipitated the third crisis. The place was no lonely road in a blinding storm, nor even the holy altar, but simply the study in the tower of the Augustinian monastery. The solution to Luther's problems came in the midst of the performance of the daily task.

His first lectures were on the book of Psalms. We must bear in mind his method of reading the Psalms and the Old Testament as a whole. For him, as for his time, it was a Christian book foreshadowing the death of the Redeemer.

The reference to Christ was unmistakable when he came to the twenty-second psalm, the first verse of which was recited by Christ as he expired upon the cross. "My God, my God, why hast thou forsaken me?" What could be the meaning of this? Christ evidently felt himself to be forsaken, abandoned by God, deserted. Christ too had *Anfechtungen*. The utter desolation which Luther said he could not endure for more than a tenth of an hour and live had been experienced by Christ himself as he died. Rejected of men, he was rejected also of God. How much worse this must have been than the scourging, the thorns, the nails! In the garden he sweat blood as he did not upon the cross. Christ's descent into hell was nothing other than this sense of alienation from God. Christ had suffered what Luther suffered, or rather Luther was finding himself in what Christ had suffered, even as Albrecht Dürer painted himself as the Man of Sorrows.

Why should Christ have known such desperation? Luther knew perfectly well why he himself had had them: he was weak in the presence of the Mighty; he was impure in the presence of the Holy; he had blasphemed the Divine Majesty. But Christ was not weak; Christ was not impure; Christ was not impious. Why then should he have been so overwhelmed with desolation? The only answer must be that Christ took to himself the iniquity of us all. He who was without sin for our sakes became sin and so identified himself with us as to participate in our alienation. He who was truly man so sensed his solidarity with humanity as to feel himself along with mankind estranged from the All Holy. What a new picture this is of Christ! Where, then, is the judge, sitting upon the rainbow to condemn sinners? He is still the judge. He must judge, as truth judges error and light darkness; but in judging he suffers with those whom he must condemn and feels himself with them subject to condemnation. The judge upon the rainbow has become the derelict upon the cross.

A new view also of God is here. The All Terrible is the All Merciful too. Wrath and love fuse upon the cross. The hideousness of sin cannot be denied or forgotten; but God, who desires not that a sinner should die but that he should turn and live, has found the reconciliation in the pangs of bitter death. It is not that the Son by his sacrifice has placated the irate Father; it is not primarily that the Master by his self-abandoning goodness has made up for our deficiency. It is that in some inexplicable way, in the utter desolation of the forsaken Christ, God was able to reconcile the world to himself. This does not mean that all the mystery is clear. God is still shrouded at times in thick darkness. There are almost two Gods, the inscrutable God whose ways are past finding out and the God made known to us in Christ. He is still a consuming fire, but he burns that he may purge and chasten and heal. He is not a God of idle whim, because the cross is not the last word. He who gave his Son unto death also raised him up and will raise us with him, if with him we die to sin that we may rise to newness of life.

Who can understand this? Philosophy is unequal to it. Only faith can grasp so high a mystery. This is the foolishness of the cross which is hid from the wise and prudent. Reason must retire. She cannot understand that "God hides his power in weakness, his wisdom in folly, his goodness in severity, his justice in sins, his mercy in anger."

How amazing that God in Christ should do all this; that the Most High, the Most Holy should be the All Loving too; that the ineffable Majesty should stoop to take upon himself our flesh, subject to hunger and cold, death and desperation. We see him lying in the feedbox of a donkey, laboring in a carpenter's shop, dying a derelict under the sins of the world. The gospel is not so much a miracle as a marvel, and every line is suffused with wonder.

What God first worked in Christ, that he must work also in us. If he who had done no wrong was forsaken on the cross, we who are truly alienated from God must suffer a deep hurt. We are not for that reason to upbraid, since the hurt is for our healing.

Repentance which is occupied with thoughts of peace is hypocrisy. There must be a great earnestness about it and a deep hurt if the old man is to be put off. When lightning strikes a tree or a man, it does two things at once—it rends the tree and swiftly slays the man. But it also turns the face of the dead man and the broken branches of the tree itself toward heaven. . . . We seek to be saved, and God in order that he may save rather damns. . . . They are damned who flee damnation, for Christ was of all the saints the most damned and forsaken.

The contemplation of the cross had convinced Luther that God is neither malicious nor capricious. If, like the Samaritan, God must first pour into our wounds the wine that smarts, it is that he may thereafter use the oil that soothes. But there still remains the problem of the justice of God. Wrath can melt into mercy, and God will be all the more the Christian God; but if justice be dissolved in leniency, how can he be the just God whom Scripture describes? The study of the apostle Paul proved at this point of inestimable value to Luther and at the same time confronted him with the final stumbling block because Paul unequivocally speaks of the justice of God. At the very expression Luther trembled. Yet he persisted in grappling with Paul, who plainly had agonized over precisely his problem and had found a solution. Light broke at last through the examination of exact shades of meaning in the Greek language. One understands why Luther could never join those who discarded the humanist tools of scholarship. In the

Greek of the Pauline epistle the word "justice" has a double sense, rendered in English by "justice" and "justification." The former is a strict enforcement of the law, as when a judge pronounces the appropriate sentence. Justification is a process of the sort which sometimes takes place if the judge suspends the sentence, places the prisoner on parole, expresses confidence and personal interest in him, and thereby instills such resolve that the man is reclaimed and justice itself ultimately better conserved than by the exaction of a pound of flesh. Similarly the moral improvement issuing from the Christian experience of regeneration, even though it falls far short of perfection, yet can be regarded as a vindication of the justice of God.

But from here on any human analogy breaks down. God does not condition his forgiveness upon the expectation of future fulfillment. And man is not put right with God by any achievement, whether present or foreseen. On man's side the one requisite is faith, which means belief that God was in Christ seeking to save; trust that God will keep his promises; and commitment to his will and way. Faith is not an achievement. It is a gift. Yet it comes only through the hearing and study of the Word. In this respect Luther's own experience was made normative. For the whole process of being made new Luther took over from Paul the terminology of "justification by faith."

These are Luther's own words:

I greatly longed to understand Paul's Epistle to the Romans and nothing stood in the way but that one expression, "the justice of God," because I took it to mean that justice whereby God is just and deals justly in punishing the unjust. My situation was that, although an impeccable monk, I stood before God as a sinner troubled in conscience, and I had no confidence that my merit would assuage him. Therefore I did not love a just and angry God, but rather hated and murmured against him. Yet I clung to the dear Paul and had a great yearning to know what he meant.

Night and day I pondered until I saw the connection between the justice of God and the statement that "the just shall live by his faith." Then I grasped that the justice of God is that righteousness by which through grace and sheer mercy God justifies us through faith. Thereupon I felt myself to be reborn and to have gone through open doors into paradise. The whole of Scripture took on a new meaning, and whereas before the "justice of God" had filled me with hate, now it became to me inexpressibly sweet in greater love. This passage of Paul became to me a gate to heaven. . . .

If you have a true faith that Christ is your Saviour, then at once you have a gracious God, for faith leads you in and opens up God's heart and will, that you should see pure grace and overflowing love. This it is to behold God in faith that you should look upon his fatherly, friendly heart, in which there is no anger nor ungraciousness. He who sees God as angry does not see him rightly but looks only on a curtain, as if a dark cloud had been drawn across his face.

Luther had come into a new view of Christ and a new view of God. He had come to love the suffering Redeemer and the God unveiled on Calvary. But were they after all powerful enough to deliver him from all the hosts of hell? The cross had resolved the conflict between the wrath and the mercy of God, and Paul had reconciled for him the inconsistency of the justice and the forgiveness of God, but what of the conflict between God and the Devil? Is God lord of all, or is he himself impeded by demonic hordes? Such questions a few years ago would have seemed to modern man but relics of medievalism, and fear of demons was dispelled simply by denying their existence. Today so much of the sinister has engulfed us that we are prone to wonder whether perhaps there may not be malignant forces in the heavenly places. All those who have known the torments of mental disorder well understand the imagery of satanic hands clutching to pull them to their doom. Luther's answer was not scientific but religious. He did not dissipate the demons by turning on an electric light, because for him they had long ago been routed when the veil of the temple was rent and the earth quaked and darkness descended upon the face of the land. Christ in his utter anguish had fused the wrath and the mercy of God, and put to flight all the legions of Satan.

The Eve of the Modern World

HARTMANN GRISAR

A HOSTILE VIEW FROM THE INSIDE

In the following passage another scholar, the Jesuit Hartmann Grisar (1845–1932) sees the basic cause or, in this case, the basic blame for the Reformation in the same critical period of Luther's life and in much the same series of events as does Bainton. The passage is taken from his *Martin Luther, His Life and Work,* a somewhat abbreviated and sharpened work based upon Grisar's larger and more famous *Luther,* Eng. tr. E. M. Lamond, 6 vols. (London: Herder, 1913–17). Grisar is probably the most important modern Catholic scholar of Lutheranism but he is still very much in the mainstream of a hostile tradition going back to the age of the Reformation itself. While some of the partisan reactions of the traditional Catholic biography no longer enjoy a place in Grisar's pages, his "home base" in interpreting Luther and the Reformation is always Catholic orthodoxy, understandably enough, and from this base his view of Luther is often hostile. This is true in spite of his considerable and perceptive insight into the psychology of religion, in spite of his candid admission that "the existing discontent" with the condition of the church "accelerated the revolution," and in spite even of his formidable knowledge of his subject. Largely then as a result of Grisar's point of view there emerges from his account of the same events quite a different picture of Martin Luther. Instead of the frightened and solitary religious striving against "the terror of the holy" and finally finding illumination in his understanding of St. Paul, we find a rebel, wilfully distorting the rules of his own order and arrogantly preferring his own interpretation of scripture and Christian tradition to that of the church. Grisar finds Luther selfish, overbearing, and neglectful of his proper religious duties. He finds him misled by his attraction to mysticism and excessive in his ascetic exercise. In short, what Grisar builds is a case of Luther's suffering from "a serious aberration." What other interpretation is open to him?

LUTHER'S FIRST BIBLICAL LECTURES— HIS MYSTICISM

The first lectures of the new professor of Biblical science were delivered in the years 1513 to 1515 and dealt with the Psalms. Those of his pupils who were monks and had to recite the Divine Office in choir, were particularly interested in the Psalms. The interpretation offered them by Luther has been preserved in his works. It is, however, not an explanation made in accordance with our modern ideas, but rather a collection of allegorical and moral sentences based upon the text, as was the custom in those days. Luther justly abandoned this allegorical manner of interpretation in later life. Non-Catholics have endeavored, without justification, to discover in these lectures the germs of his later teaching. His manner of expression is often indefinite and elastic and generally more rhetorical than theologically correct. His teaching on justification, grace, and free will, is, like his other doctrines, still fundamentally Catholic, or at least can be so interpreted if the dog-

From Hartmann Grisar, S. J., *Martin Luther, His Life and Work,* adapted from the 2nd German edition by F. J. Eble, ed. A. Preuss (Westminster, Md., 1950), pp. 58–70. Reprinted by permission of The Newman Press.

matic teaching of the Church is properly understood. Still there are a few indications of the coming change. Take, for instance, his emphatic assertion that Christ died for all men and his exaggerated opposition to the doctrine of justification by means of good works. In general these lectures reveal talent, religious zeal, and fertile imagination—qualities which must have charmed his auditors to an unusual degree.

Luther was very amiable and communicative towards his pupils. His entire personality, the very gleam of his eye, exerted a certain fascination over those who associated with him.

The young professor of Sacred Scripture displayed a pronounced inclination towards mysticism. Mysticism had always been cultivated to a certain extent in the religious orders of the Catholic Church. The reading of Bonaventure had pointed Luther, even as a young monk, to the pious union with God at which Mysticism aims. Toward the close of his lectures on the Psalms, he became acquainted with certain works on Mysticism which he imbibed with great avidity. They were the sermons of Tauler and the tract "Theologia deutsch." They dominate his thoughts in 1515. Although these works were not designed to do so, they helped to develop his unecclesiastical ideas. His lively experience of the weakness of the human will induced him to hearken readily to the mystical voices which spoke of the complete relinquishment of man to God, even though he did not understand them perfectly. His opposition to good works opened his mind to a fallacious conception of the doctrines of those books of the mystical life. It appeared to him that, by following such leaders, his internal fears could be dispelled by a calm immersion in the Godhead.

John Tauler, an ornament of the Dominican Order (died in 1361), was a famous preacher in the pulpits of Strasburg. His writings and sermons are filled with profound thoughts and have a strong popular appeal. They abound in attractive imagery and are replete with devotion. Tauler stands four-square on the basis of Catholic teaching and the best scholastic theology. Two points in his mystical admonitions found a special echo in Luther's soul, namely, the interior calmness with which God's operations are to be received, and the darkness which fills the souls of pious persons, of whom he speaks consolingly. Luther, however, introduced his own erroneous ideas into the teaching of Tauler. His demand that

the soul be calmly absorbed in God, Luther interpreted as complete passivity, yea, self-annihilation. And what Tauler says concerning trials arising from the withdrawal of all religious joy, of all emotions of grace in the dark night of the soul, he referred directly to his own morbid attacks of fear, to which he endeavored to oppose a misconceived quietism, a certain repose generated by despair. In brief, he tried to transform all theology into what he called a theology of the Cross. Misconstruing Tauler's doctrine of perfection he would recognize only the highest motives, namely, reasons of the greatest perfection for himself as well as for others. Fear of divine punishment and hope of divine reward were to be excluded.

These were extravagances which could not aid him, but, on the contrary, involved great danger to his orthodoxy; in fact, constituted a serious aberration. But he trusted his new lights with the utmost self-confidence. Writing of Tauler to his friend Lang at Erfurt, who was also fascinated by the works of that mystic, Luther compares him with contemporary and older theologians and says that while Tauler was unknown to the Schoolmen, he offered more real theology than the combined theological professors of all the universities.

The other mystical writer who interested him, was discovered by Luther in a manuscript. He lived in the fourteenth century and was the author of the "Theologia deutsch." His name is unknown to us. He was a priest at Frankfort on the Main. His work, which is a didactic treatise on perfection, is Catholic, although not exempt from obscurities. Luther esteemed it as a book of gold, particularly in view of its praise of the sole domination of God in the soul that suffers for Him. He edited this book, at first incompletely, in 1516, then in its entirety, in 1518. It is remarkable that a book on Mysticism was his first publication. Soon he occupied himself with the mystical writings of the so-called Dionysius the Areopagite, the father of Mysticism, and with those of Gerard Groote, a more modern author.

His style in those days, as also later on, reveals how profoundly he was animated by the devout tone of these mystics. Thus, in writing to George Leiffer, a fellow-monk at Erfurt, who was afflicted by persecutions and interior sufferings, he says (1516): "Do not cast away thy little fragment of the Cross of Christ, but deposit it as a sacrosanct relic in a golden shrine, namely, in a heart filled with gentle charity.

For even the hateful things which we experience, are priceless relics. True, they are not, like the wood of the Cross, hallowed by contact with the body of the Lord, yet, in as far as we embrace them out of love for His most loving heart and His divine will, they are kissed and blessed beyond measure." In discussing the idea of self-annihilation under the guidance of God, which was his favorite thought in these days, he shows that he has gone astray. He says that man should not choose among good works, but abandon himself to God's inspiration, as the steed is governed by the reins. In an address delivered in 1516 he declares: "The man of God goeth, whithersoever God directs him as a rider. He never knows whither he is headed; he is passive rather than active. He journeys ever onward, no matter what the condition of the road, through water, mud, rain, snow, wind, etc. Thus are the men of God who are led by the divine spirit." Such are the doctrines which he opposed to those who became distasteful to him on account of their insistence on good works and what he called their Pharisaical observance of external practices.

On May 1, 1515, a chapter of the Augustinian congregation was held at Gotha under the presidency of Staupitz. Luther preached the sermon at the opening assembly. The theme which he selected treated of the contrasts which must have developed in the monasteries of the congregation, namely, the "little saints" and their calumnies against the monastic brethren who disagreed with them in matters of discipline. With extreme acerbity, and employing the crudest and most repulsive figures of speech, he scourged their criticism of others as inspired by love of scandal and malevolent detraction. Apparently the majority of the brethren of his Order sided with him, for they elected him to the office of rural vicar, i.e., special superior of a number of monasteries as the representative of Staupitz.

At stated times he visited the monasteries thus entrusted to him. There were eleven of them, including Erfurt and Wittenberg. After the middle of April, 1516, he made a visitation of the congregations of the Order at Dresden, Neustadt on the Orla, Erfurt, Gotha, Langensalza, and Nordhausen. The letters written by him during his term of office as rural vicar, which normally lasted three years, contain practical directions and admonitions concerning monastic discipline and are, in part, quite edifying. Some of his visitations, however, were conducted with such astonishing rapidity that no fruitful results

could be expected of them. Thus the visitation of the monastery at Gotha occupied but one hour, that at Langensalza two hours. "In these places," he wrote to Lang, "the Lord will work without us and direct the spiritual and temporal affairs in spite of the devil." At Neustadt he deposed the prior, Michael Dressel, without a hearing, because the brethren could not get along with him. "I did this," he informed Lang in confidence, "because I hoped to rule there myself for the half-year."

In a letter to the same friend he writes as follows about the engagements with which he was overwhelmed at that time: "I really ought to have two secretaries or chancellors. I do hardly anything all day but write letters. . . . I am at the same time preacher to the monastery, have to preach in the refectory, and am even expected to preach daily in the parish church. I am regent of the studium [i.e., of the younger monks] and vicar, that is to say prior eleven times over; I have to provide for the delivery of the fish from the Leitzkau pond and to manage the litigation of the Herzberg fellows [monks] at Torgau; I am lecturing on Paul, compiling an exposition of the Psalter, and, as I said before, writing letters most of the time. . . . It is seldom that I have time for the recitation of the Divine Office or to celebrate Mass, and then, too, I have my peculiar temptations from the flesh, the world, and the devil."

INTERIOR STATE

The last sentence quoted above contains a remarkable declaration about his spiritual condition and his compliance with his monastic duties at that time. He seldom found time to recite the Divine Office and to say Mass. It was his duty so to arrange his affairs as to be able to comply with these obligations. The canonical hours were strictly prescribed. Saying Mass is the central obligation of every priest, especially if he is a member of a religious order. If Luther did not know how to observe due moderation in his labors; if he was derelict in the principal duties of the spiritual life; it was to be feared that he would gradually drift away from the religious state, particularly in view of the fact that he had adopted a false Mysticism which favored the relaxation of the rule. As rural vicar, it is probable that he did not sustain among the brethren the good old spirit which the zealous Proles had introduced into the society. Of the "temptations of the flesh" which he mentions we learn nothing definite. He was not yet in conflict with his vows. His wrestlings with the devil may signify the fears and terrors to which he was subject.

He continued to be on good terms with his friend Staupitz, who was interested in the young monk's manifold activities. Staupitz also posed as a mystic, and favored the spiritual tendency which Luther followed. This talented and sociable man was very popular as a useful adviser in the homes of the rich and as an entertainer at table. Whilst Luther could not accompany him on such errands, he enjoyed his company on monastic visitations. In July, 1515, he accompanied Staupitz to Eisleben, when the latter opened the new Augustinian monastery at that place. As he walked in his sacerdotal vestments in the procession through the city of his birth at the side of his vicar, who carried the Blessed Sacrament, Luther was suddenly seized with unspeakable fright at the thought of the proximity of Christ. On mentioning the incident to his superior afterwards, the latter comforted him by saying: "Your thought is not Christ," and assuring him that Christ did not desire this fear. At times, in consequence either of a disordered affection of the heart or of overwork, he was so distressed that he could not eat or drink for a long time. One day he was found seemingly dead in his cell, so completely was he exhausted as a result of agitation and lack of food. His friend Ratzeberger, a physician, mentions this incident, without, however, indicating the exact time of its occurrence. Luther was relieved of this pitiable condition by recourse to music, which always stimulated him. After he had regained his strength, he was able once more to prosecute his labors. As a result of his suffering and worry he became very much emaciated.

Did Luther subject himself to extraordinary deeds of penance at any period of his monastic life, as he frequently affirmed in his subsequent conflict with the papacy and monasticism, when he was impelled by polemical reasons to describe himself as the type of a holy and mortified monk, one who could not find peace of mind during his whole monastic career? Holding then that peace of mind was simply impossible in the Catholic Church, he arbitrarily misreprepresents monasticism, in order to exhibit in a most glaring manner the alleged inherent impossibility of "papistic" ethics to produce the assurance of God's mercy. "I tormented my body by fasting, vigils, and cold. . . . In the observance of these matters I was so precise and superstitious, that I imposed more burdens upon my body than it could bear without danger to health." "If ever a monk got to heaven by monkery, then I should have got there." "I almost died a-fasting, for often I took neither a drop of water nor a morsel of food for three days."

Such exaggerated penitential exercises were prohibited by the statutes of the congregation, which were distinguished for great discretion, and insisted upon proper moderation as a matter of strict duty.

The above picture of singular holiness is produced not by early witnesses, but by assertions which Luther made little by little at a later period of life. The established facts contradict the legend. Perhaps his description is based partly on reminiscences of his distracted days in the monastery, or on eccentric efforts to overcome his sombre moods by means of a false piety. His greatest error, and the one which most betrays him, is that he ascribes his fictitious asceticism to all serious-minded members of his monastery, yea, of all monasteries. He would have it that all monks consumed themselves in wailing and grief, wrestling for the peace of God, until he supplied the remedy. It is a rule of the most elementary criticism finally to cut loose from the distorted presentation of the matter which has maintained itself so tenaciously in Protestant biographies of Luther.

It may be admitted that, on the whole, Luther was a dutiful monk for the greatest part of his monastic life. "When I was in the monastery," he stated on one occasion, in 1535, "I was not like the rest of men, the robbers, the unjust, the adulterous; but I observed chastity, obedience, and poverty."

Yet, after his transfer to Wittenberg, and in consequence of the applause which was accorded to him there, the unpleasant traits of his character, especially his positive insistence on always being in the right, began to manifest themselves more and more disagreeably. In his opinion, the Scholastic theologians, even the greatest among them, were sophists. They were a herd of "swine theologians," while he was the enlightened pupil of St. Paul and St. Augustine. The finer achievements of Scholasticism, especially those of its intellectual giant, Thomas of Aquin, were scarcely known to him. Could his confused mysticism perhaps supplement his deficient knowledge of Scholasticism? No, it only made him more self-conscious and arbitrary in the sphere of theology. He gave free vent to his criticism of highly respected ascetical writers. An example of his egotistical excess in this respect is furnished by his glosses for the year 1515, which he indited on the Psalter of Mary, a work of Mark of Weida. In addition to these characteristics, there was his peculiar irritability, which is strikingly exhibited in his correspondence during 1514. The theologians of Erfurt, led by Nathin, had reproved him for taking the doctorate at Erfurt instead of at Wittenberg, since the Erfurt school had claims on him as one of its own pupils. It is possible that some harsh words were exchanged in regard to this matter. The young professor in a letter addressed to the monastery at Erfurt says that he had well nigh resolved to "pour out the entire vial of his wrath and indignation upon Nathin and the whole monastery" on account of their lies and mockery. They had received two shocking letters (litterae stupidae) from him, for which he now wants to excuse himself, though his indignation "was only too well founded," especially since he now heard even worse things about Nathin and his complaints against his (Luther's) person. In the meantime, God had willed his separation from the Erfurt monastery, etc.

The ill-feeling between Nathin and his Erfurt colleagues, on the one hand, and Luther and his monastic partisans on the other, arose from the controvery concerning the stricter observance of the rule within the Order.

OPPOSITION TO SELF-RIGHTEOUSNESS AND RELIGIOUS OBSERVANCE

Contradictory conceptions of monastic life continued to be harbored in the Augustinian congregation even after the settlement of the contention with regard to Staupitz's plans of union.

Those brethren who treasured the ancient monastic discipline, protected by papal privileges and exemptions, were accused of self-righteous Pharisaism and of disobedience towards the General of the order by Luther and his party. They were the "Little Saints" against whom he had inveighed in his impetuous address at Gotha. In his lectures and sermons he reproached, though often only in allusions, their "observantine" practices, their adherence to the doctrine of good works, and their want of charity. His invectives, however, were

launched with a bitterness which those concerned assuredly did not merit, even though there might have been reasons for complaint. It may be said that the ancient and the modern wings opposed each other in the Wittenberg monastery. Probably there was friction also in the monastery at Erfurt, where Luther's friend Lang was prior, as well as in other monasteries of the congregation. Luther's monastery, however, was the center of the contention. The young students of the Order brought with them their divergent views out of the cloisters whence they came and they carried the new atmosphere of Wittenberg along with them when they left. Luther's partisans at Wittenberg boasted that they were more closely attached to the General of the Order at Rome than their opponents. The General, they contended, was not in favor of the singularities of the Observantines.

At the commencement of his first series of lectures on the Psalms, Luther delivered a sarcastic address on the obedience due to religious superiors. "How many do we not find," he says, "who believe they are very religious, and yet they are, if I may so express it, only men of an extremely sanguine temperament (sanguinicissimi) and true Idumaeans [i.e., paganminded]. There are people who so revere and praise their monastic state, their order, their Saints, and their institutions, that they cast a shadow upon all others, not wishing to grant them their proper place. In a very unspiritual manner they are humble followers (observantes) of their fathers and boast of them. Oh, the frenzy that prevails in this day! It has almost come to this that every monastery repudiates the customs of all others and is imbued with such pride as to preclude taking over or learning anything at all from another. That is the pride of Jews and heretics, with which we, unfortunate ones, are also encompassed," etc. In the addresses which he delivered in the monastery church he frequently alludes to the obstinate pride of the Jews and heretics, in condemnation of those members of his order or of other orders who adhered to the strict observance. These "Observantines, exempted and privileged characters"—thus he fulminates in another lecture, are devoid of obedience, which is the very soul of good works. It will be seen—he continues—how detrimental to the Church they are; in the interests of the rule, they were determined to insist upon exceptions; "but that is a light that comes from the devil."

This was the contest which led the fiery monk to enter upon doubtful ways. His opposition to the so-called doctrine of self-righteousness caused him to form a false conception of righteousness; instead of attacking an heretical error, he combated the true worth of good works and the perfections of the monastic life.

Voluntary poverty, as practiced by the mendicants, was one of the foundations of his Order. The inmates of monastic houses were to live on alms according to the practice introduced by the great Saint Francis of Assisi and for the benefactions received were to devote themselves gratis to the spiritual needs of their fellowmen. Many abuses, it is true, had attached themselves to the mendicant system; self-interest, avarice, and worldly-mindedness infected the itinerant mendicants. But in his explanation of the Psalms Luther attacks the life of poverty *per se:* "O mendicants! O mendicants! O mendicants!" he pathetically exclaims, "who can excuse you? . . . Look to it yourselves," etc. He places the practice of poverty in an unfavorable light. In his criticism of the "self-righteousness of his irksome enemies, he confronts them with the righteousness of the spirit that cometh from Christ. These people, whom he believed it his duty to expose, were guilty, in his opinion, of a Pharisaical denial of the true righteousness of Christ. His righteousness, and not our good works, effect our salvation; works generate a fleshly sense and boastfulness. These thought-processes evince how false mysticism, unclear theological notions, a darkening of the monastic spirit, and passionate obstinacy conspired in Luther's mind.

In the years 1515 and 1516, the phalanx of the self-righteous, the *justitiarii,* as he styles them, again constitute the object of his attacks. There is Christ, the hen with its protecting wings, which he must defend against the vultures that pounce upon us in their self-righteousness. These enemies of the sweet righteousness imputed to us by God are "a pestilence in the Church; intractable, nay, rebellious against their superiors, they decry others and clothe themselves with the lamb-skins of their good works."

An Augustinian friend of his, George Spenlein, having become weary of certain persecutions, had had himself transferred from Wittenberg to the monastery at Memmingen. Luther sent him a peculiar letter of condolence on April 8, 1516. According to this missive, it would seem that the self-righteous Spenlein had been for a long time "in opposition to the self-righteousness of God, which had been bestowed most lavishly and gratuitously upon him by Christ"; whereas he (Spenlein) desired to stand before God with his own works and merits, which, of course, is impossible. He (Luther), too, had harbored this notion, and says he still wrestles with this error. "Learn, therefore, my sweet brother," thus he addresses Spenlein in the vocabulary of mysticism, "learn to sing to the Lord Jesus and, distrusting yourself, say to Him: Thou, O Lord Jesus, art my righteousness, but I am Thy sin. Thou hast accepted what was mine and hast given to me what was Thine. Oh, that thou wouldst boldly appear thyself as a sinner, yea, be a sinner in reality; for Christ abides only in sinners." "But, if you are a lily and a rose of Christ, then learn to bear persecution with patience, lest your secret pride convert you into a thorn."

The germ of Luther's reformatory doctrine is plainly contained in this species of Mysticism. Step by step he had arrived at his new dogma in the above described manner. The system which attacked the basic truths of the Catholic Church, was complete in outline. Before giving a fuller exposition of it, we must consider the individual factors which cooperated in its development in Luther's mind.

Confession and penance were a source of torturing offense to the young monk. Can one obtain peace with God by the performance of penitential works? He discussed this question with Staupitz on an occasion when he sought consolation. Staupitz pointed out to him that all penance must begin and end with love; that all treasures are hidden in Christ, in whom we must trust and whom we must love. These words contain nothing new; but the exhortation to combine love with penance entered the inflammable soul of Luther as a voice from heaven. According to his own expression, it "clung to his soul as the sharp arrows of the mighty" (Ps. CXIX, 4); henceforward, he says, he would execrate the hypocrisy by means of which he had formerly sought to express a "fabricated and forced" penitential spirit during the tortures of confession. Now that the merits of Christ covered everything, penance appeared easy and sweet to him. He expresses himself on this point in a grateful letter to Staupitz, written in 1518.

On the occasion referred to, it is probable that Staupitz, as was his custom, expressed himself in a vague and sentimental manner, rather than in clear theological terms. His writings are susceptible of improvement in many respects. The influence which he exerted on Luther was not a wholesome one. He was too fond of him to penetrate his character. He perceived in him a rising star of his congregation, a very promising ornament of his Order. Even in the most critical period anterior to Luther's apostasy, he eulogized his courage and said: Christ speaks out of your mouth, — so well it pleased him that Luther, in the matter of righteousness and good works, ascribed everything to Christ, to whom alone glory should be given. Certain of a favorable response on the part of his superior, Luther wrote thus in the above letter to him: "My sweet Saviour and Pardoner, to whom I shall sing as long as I live (Ps. CIII, 33), is sufficient for me. If there be anyone who will not sing with me, what is that to me? Let him howl if it please him." The short-sighted Staupitz sided with Luther even after he had been condemned by the Church.

Nor was Staupitz the man who could thoroughly free Luther from his doubts about predestination, although Luther says he helped him. His general references to the wounds of Christ could not permanently set the troubled monk aright. He should have placed definitely before him the Catholic dogma, based on Sacred Scripture, that God sincerely desires the salvation of all men, and should have made clear to the doubter that voluntary sin is the sole cause of damnation. But he himself seems not to have grasped these truths, for in certain critical passages of his writings he allows them to retreat before a certain mysterious predestination. Luther's fear of predestination constituted the obscure substratum of his evolving new religious system. Recalling Staupitz's exhortations, he says, in 1532: We must stop at the wounds of Christ, and may not ponder over the awful mystery. The only remedy consists in dismissing from our minds the possibility of a verdict of damnation. "When I attend to these ideas, I forget what Christ and God are, and sometimes arrive at the conclusion that God is a scoundrel. . . . The idea of predestination causes us to forget God, and the *Laudate* ceases and the *Blasphemate* begins." The part which these struggles had in the origin of

his new doctrine, is to be sought in Luther's violent efforts to attain to a certain repose in the face of his presumptive predestination.

It is also remarkable that the last-quoted utterance is followed by one concerning his "great spiritual temptations." In contrast with the struggles of despair which he underwent, he is not deeply impressed by ordinary temptations. "No one," he writes, "can really write or say anything about grace, unless he has been disciplined by spiritual temptations." His opponents, he says elsewhere, not having had such experiences, it behooved them to observe silence. When his doctrine encountered opposition in Rome, he wrote to Staupitz that Roman citations and other matters made no impression on him. "My sufferings, as you know, are incomparably greater, and these force me to regard such temporal flashes as extremely trivial." He meant "doubtlessly, personal, inward sufferings and attacks which were connected with bodily ailments . . . , whereby, as formerly, he was always seized with fear for his personal salvation when he pondered on the hidden depths of the divine will."

In his interpretation of the Epistle of St. Paul to the Romans, given during the years 1515 and 1516, Luther completely unfolded his new doctrine.

NORMAN O. BROWN

A VISCERAL VIEW FROM THE INSIDE

We have identified in the last two selections what Protestant scholarship has come to call Luther's "Thurmerlebnis" or "experience in the tower," that is, the sudden understanding of the famous passage from St. Paul, that "gate to heaven" which eventually led Luther to the fundamental premise of his theology and made a religious revolution. Bainton noted with some delicacy that "the solution to Luther's problem came in the midst of the performance of the daily task." Grisar (in a passage not included in the previous selection) was considerably more direct. In the present selection Norman O. Brown is more direct still and, with the same candor as Luther himself exhibited, states that this central experience of divine illumination came to Luther "on the privy in the tower." What is more to the point, he asserts that this is not simply an unfortunate or embarrassing incident that history and Luther might well have left unrecorded. On the contrary, he insists that what, in another frame of reference, is an uncomfortable triviality, in his view reveals "a hidden connection between higher spiritual activity and lower organs of the body."

We have already observed that contemporary scholarship has tended to abandon the "external" concept of the causes of the Reformation and to seek its more basic cause in the history of the man Luther. Brown's thesis is an example of another approach to this search, the psychoanalytic approach. Without exception, the books and articles which have attempted to demonstrate this approach have been attacked—and in many instances they have deserved attack. Psychoanalytic interpreters have been faulted for their historical inaccuracy, their ignorance of theology, and the presuppositions of their methodology. It has been charged, for example, that even in the case of Luther about whom we have more day-to-day, ordinary information than about any other man of his time, we still cannot know enough that is pertinent to psychoanalysis to make a trustworthy judgment. It has even been charged that the basic assumption of psychoanalysis—that man is always and in every age motivated by self-interest—fails as an assumption when dealing with an essentially religious man.

This selection from Brown's *Life Against Death, The Psychoanalytical Meaning of History*, while certainly still controversial, is one of the most solid representatives of its type and the student must attempt to assess not only the work but the method.

Luther describes the circumstances under which he received the illumination which became the fundamental axiom of the Protestant Reformation—the doctrine of justification by faith—in the following words:

These words "just" and "justice of God" were a thunderbolt in my conscience. They soon struck terror in me who heard them. He is just, therefore He punishes. But once when in this tower I was meditating on those words, "the just lives by faith," "justice of God," I soon had the thought whether we ought to live justified by faith, and God's justice ought to be the salvation of every believer, and soon my soul was revived. Therefore it is God's justice which justifies us and saves us. And these words became a sweeter message for me. This knowledge the Holy Spirit gave me on the privy in the tower.

Luther with his freedom from hypocrisy, his all-embracing vitality, and his all-embracing faith, records the scene of his crucial religious experience with untroubled candor. It was in a tower of the Wittenberg monastery, where the privy was located. Grisar explains, "In olden times it was very usual to establish this adjunct on the city wall and its towers, the sewage having egress outside the town boundaries."

Luther's candor has been too much for the Lutherans. Recognizing the crucial importance of the "experience in the tower," the *Thurmerlebnis,* as it is called in Lutheran hagiography, Lutheran scholars have either monkeyed with the texts in an attempt to separate the tower from the privy, or else interpreted the tower not as a geographical location but as an allegory of spiritual captivity. It was thus left to the Jesuit Father Grisar (1911) to recover the facts, only to be received by outcries, from Harnack and a pack of lesser Lutherans, that he was hitting below the belt, indulging in "vulgar Catholic polemics."

When the smoke of controversy died away, the location of the *Thurmerlebnis* was established, but both the Jesuit and his Lutheran critics were agreed that the location was of no significance. Grisar agreed with Harnack that "the locality in which Luther first glimpsed this thought is of small importance"; he agreed with the Lutheran Scheel that Roman Catholics, like all Christians, believe that God is present everywhere.

Psychoanalysis, alas! cannot agree that it is of no significance that the religious experience which in-

From Norman O. Brown, *Life Against Death, The Psychoanalytical Meaning of History* (Middletown, Conn., 1959), pp. 202–3, 206–210, 211–17. Reprinted by permission of Wesleyan University Press and Routledge & Kegan Paul Ltd.

augurated Protestant theology took place in the privy. The psychoanalytical theory of infantile sexuality and its sublimation insists that there is a hidden connection between higher spiritual activity and lower organs of the body. Ever since Freud's essay on "Character and Anal Erotism" (1908), psycho-analysis has accepted as a demonstrated theorem that a definite type of ethical character, exhibiting a combination of three traits—orderliness, parsimony, and obstinacy—is constructed by the sublimation of a special concentration of libido in the anal zone, and it is therefore labeled the anal character. . . .

At the abstract theoretical level, psychoanalytical paradox and historical common sense are so far apart that one can only despair of ever unifying them. It therefore seems inevitable that progress will be made, if at all, by concrete empirical investigation. And since in general psychoanalytical considerations grope so far beneath the surface that they can easily be dismissed as arbitrary constructions not based on facts, such concrete empirical investigations must take as their point of departure, not psychoanalytical imputations as to what may (or may not) be going on in the Unconscious, but historical fact.

Such a solid point of departure is provided by the historical fact that the Protestant illumination came to Luther while seated on the privy. Such historical facts are hard to come by (few of the world's great men had Luther's honesty), and historical science should make the most of them. The hypothesis to be investigated is that there is some mysterious intrinsic connection between the Protestant illumination and the privy. The issue is: What exactly does the privy mean to Luther? But since the theory of sublimation is at stake in such an investigation, we cannot use the theory of sublimation to impute to Luther's unconscious meanings for the privy. Rather we must rely on the historical evidence of his writings for documented fact as to what the privy meant to Luther (in psychoanalytical terms, his "associations" to the idea of the privy). Such an empirical investigation of Luther's writings reveals the existence of a middle term, unexplored by both the psychoanalysts and the historians, connecting the privy with Protestantism on the one hand and capitalism on the other. This middle term is the Devil.

Psychoanalytical studies of the Devil, following Freud himself, have emphasized the Oedipal aspect of the Devil, his status as a father-substitute, the ambivalent combination of emulation of and hostility against the father in the Devil, and the identity of God and the Devil (as father-substitutes) underlying their opposition. The persistently anal character of the Devil has not been emphasized enough. The color pre-eminently associated with the Devil and the Black Mass is black—not because of his place of abode (a circular explanation) but because of the association of black and filth. "The painters paint the Devil black and filthy," says Luther. Equally persistent is the association of the Devil with a sulphurous or other evil smell, the origin of which is plainly revealed in the article "De crepitu Diaboli" in an eighteenth-century compendium of folklore. The climax of the ritual of the Witches' Sabbath was to kiss the Devil's posteriors or a facial mask attached to the Devil's posteriors. In the central ceremony of the Black Mass, as the Queen of the Sabbath lay prone, "The sacred host was prepared by kneading on her buttocks a mixture of the most repulsive material, faeces, menstrual blood, urine, and offal of various kinds." Hence Dante makes the still point of the turning world, round which he passes upward to Purgatory, Satan's anus; hence Bosch, in the panel depicting this world as Hell, enthrones Satan on a privy, from which the souls that have passed out of his anus drop into the black pit.

Luther's idea of the Devil is a compound of current folklore, personal experience, and theological speculation; but of these ingredients the element of personal experience is decisive. It is an error to think of Luther's diabolism, or the general diabolism of the period, as a reverberation of a medieval theme. The age which gave birth to Protestantism experienced the Devil with a peculiar immediacy, power, and pervasiveness, and Luther, who personally experienced the Devil with more immediacy, power, and pervasiveness than any other leader of the age, is in this respect only the most representative man of the age. Personal experience was the touchstone by which Luther tested current folklore of the Devil; and personal experience was, of course, the touchstone for his theological speculations.

In Luther's personal encounters with the Devil—remember we are dealing with materialized apparitions—the anal character of the Devil is sensuously perceived and sensuously recorded by Luther (in his Table-Talk) with a gross concreteness that latter-day Protestantism cannot imagine and would not tolerate. An encounter with the Devil is for Luther an encounter with something black and "filthy." Latter-day Lutheranism has encouraged the circulation of the stories of how the Devil threw ink at Luther, and Luther threw ink at the Devil; here the anality has a thin but sufficient disguise. But there is no disguise in Melancthon's additional details: "Having been worsted by this saying the Demon departed indignant and murmuring to himself, after having emitted a crepitation of no small size, which left a train of foul odour in the chamber for several days afterwards." Personal experience therefore authorized Luther to give credibility to the story of a Lutheran pastor to whom the Devil appeared in the confessional, blasphemed Christ, and "departed leaving a horrible stench." The materialized anality which is the Devil consists not only of anal smells but also anal sights; twice at least Luther was assaulted by an apparition of the Devil "showing him his posterior." And, as passages too numerous to cite show, Luther's most general word for the assaults of the Devil is the homely German verb *bescheissen*.

As striking as the anality of the Devil's attacks is the anality of Luther's counterattacks. When Luther pours verbal abuse at the Devil or throws the ink at him, the anality of his weapons is perhaps disguised. But there is no disguise when Luther records that in one encounter, when Lutheran doctrines had not sufficed to rout the Devil, he had routed him *"mit einem Furz"*—the same weapon the Devil used against Luther in Melancthon's story. Personal experience therefore authorized Luther to tell with approval the story of the lady who had routed the Devil with the same device. Other anal weapons employed by Luther in his fight with the Devil—my language is here more refined than Luther's—are injunctions to "lick (or kiss) my posteriors" or to "defecate in his pants and hang them round his neck," and threats to "defecate in his face" or to "throw him into my anus, where he belongs."

The last quotation exhibits the psychic logic and psychoanalytical understanding underlying Luther's warfare with the Devil. The Devil is virtually recognized as a displaced materialization of Luther's own anality, which is to be conquered by being replaced where it came from. The same pattern of anal attack and counterattack is exhibited in Luther's notions of witchcraft. Luther says that "people who eat butter that has been bewitched, eat nothing but mud"; and as a counterattack on the witchcraft that is spoiling the butter-churning, he recommends "Dr. Pommer's plan" as the best—"Dr. Pommer came to the res-

cue, scoffed at the Devil, and emptied his bowels into the churn."

Given the importance of the Devil in Lutheran theology—a subject to which we shall come in a moment—it is Luther's grossly concrete image of the anal character of the Devil that made the privy the appropriate scene for his critical religious experience. And the appropriate comment is not that milk-and-water piety, proposed by nineteenth-century Lutherans and assented to by the Jesuit Grisar, that "God is everywhere." We are reminded of Luther's acid test of a Christian teacher: "Does he know of death and the Devil? Or is all sweetness and light?" Protestantism was born in the temple of the Devil, and it found God again in extremest alienation from God. The dark ambivalence of the situation is expressed in Luther's story of the proper answer to the Devil given by a monk sitting on the privy:

Monachus super latrinam
Non debet orare primam?
Deo quod supra,
Tibi quod cadit infra.

The situation is apparently proverbial. Sir John Harrington wrote the same answer to the Devil on an emblem hung in the privy of his house: "To God my pray'r I ment, to thee the durt." Whether or not there was a materialized apparition of the Devil in Luther's experience in the tower, the Devil was present in some sense of psychic reality. Again we must remember the intimate and everyday familiarity of Luther's experience with the Devil. The Wartburg castle was full of devils, who never left him at peace but "behave in such a way that he is never alone even when he seems to be so." In his old age Luther's steps were dogged by two particular devils, who walked with him whenever he went in the dormitory (*auf dem Schlafhause*). And the Wittenberg cloister, where the *Thurmerlebnis* took place, was no less full of devils.

We have established the relation between the Devil and anality. We have now to establish the relation between the Devil and Protestantism. Everybody knows that Luther and Luther's Protestantism are haunted by a sense of the Devil; every time we sing *"Ein feste Burg"* and celebrate the victory over our "ancient foe" it stares us in the face. But rationalists nursed on eighteenth-century Enlightenment, and optimists nursed on nineteenth-century Liberalism,

The Eve of the Modern World

who themselves cannot take the Devil seriously, could not take Luther's Devil seriously. We are reminded of Baudelaire's epigram—"The neatest trick of the Devil is to persuade you he does not exist." Luther's diabolism was regarded as either an individual psychological aberration or as a hang-over from medieval superstition. In this spirit Troeltsch, Weber, Tawney and their countless followers (including Fromm) have defined Protestantism simply as a new relation to God. Thus Troeltsch: "The whole change of view in Protestantism is summed up and expressed in its Idea of God"; the essence of Protestantism is "the reduction of the whole of religion . . . to that idea of God."

But Protestantism and its social and psychological implications must be understood as a new relation to the Devil, a relation which explains the new relation to God. If we want to understand Luther, we may, if we like, take neither his God nor his Devil seriously, and substitute psychological explanations for both. What we may not do is to take one seriously and explain away the other. . . .

"Far from decreasing the power of the Devil in the world, the Reformation brought him strong reinforcements"; so speaks the Devil's most authoritative historian. The psychological premise of Protestantism is conviction of sin. Protestantism, as a new relation to God, is a response to a new experience of evil. The novelty consists first in the scope and intensity of the evil experienced, and second in the sense of absolute powerlessness in the face of it. This new experience of evil reaches back into the waning period of the Middle Ages; Protestantism and Protestant diabolism are the offspring of a long gestation. Huizinga writes of the fifteenth century:

Is it surprising that the people could see their fate and that of the world only as an endless succession of evils? Bad governments, exactions, the cupidity and violence of the great, wars and brigandage, scarcity, misery and pestilence—to this is contemporary history nearly reduced in the eyes of the people. The feeling of general insecurity which was caused by the chronic form wars were apt to take, by the constant menace of the dangerous classes, by the mistrust of justice, was further aggravated by the obsession of the coming end of the world, and by the fear of hell, of sorcerers and of devils. The background of all life in the world seems black. Satan covers a gloomy earth with his sombre wings.

In Luther this experience of omnipresent and uncontrollable evil generates the theological novelty that this world, in all its outward manifestations, is ruled not by God but by the Devil. "It is an article of faith," says Luther, "that the Devil is *Princeps mundi, Deus huius seculi*." It is an article of faith, based on experience: "The Devil is the lord of the world. Let him who does not know this, try it. I have had some experience of it: but no one will believe me until he experiences it too." "The world and all that belongs to it must have the Devil as its master." "We are servants in a hostelry, where Satan is the householder, the world his wife, and our affections his children." "The whole world is possessed by Satan." "The whole world is enslaved to his machinations." "The world is the Devil and the Devil is the world." "Everything is full of devils, in the courts of princes, in houses, in fields, in streets, in water, in wood, in fire."

Luther finds the autonomous demonic power of evil not only in the macrocosm of society but also in the microcosm of the individual. It is his experience of the dominion of Satan over the individual that generates another theological innovation, the denial of free will; Melancthon (in 1559) and other critics correctly apprehend the trend of Luther's thought when they call his predestinarianism Manichaean. Luther's predestinarianism is partly based on a sense of the power of temptation—"No man could face the devil with his free will"—but at a deeper level it is based on the sense that temptation and sin are the work of an autonomous force outside of the individual. The result is to eliminate the traditional notion of vices, faults for which the individual is responsible, and substitute the Devil. "The German reformer and his disciples thus filled Germany with devils by diabolizing all vices." A Lutheran compilation, the *Theatrum Diabolorum* (1569), lists the new discoveries, the devil of blasphemy, the dance-devil, the laziness-devil, the pride-devil, etc.

Not content with diabolizing the vices, Luther diabolizes the virtues also. Man is justified not by works but by faith alone; and faith is not a virtue in our power but a gift of God. The whole domain of traditional virtue, pejoratively re-evaluated as mere "works," is handed over to the Devil. "For seeing that, outside of Christ, death and sin are our masters and the devil our God and sovereign, there can be no power or might, no wit or understanding whereby we could make ourselves fit for, or could even strive after, righteousness and life, but on the contrary we must remain blind and captive, slaves of sin and the devil." Therefore, "in the man who does not believe in Christ not only are all sins mortal, but even his good works are sins." Hence piety in the Romish style is the devil's work: "The Devil lets his own do many good works, pray, fast, build churches, establish Masses and holy days, and behave as if he were quite holy and pious." "Men of holy works (die Werkheiligen) are Satan's captive servants, no matter how much they appear outwardly to surpass others in good works and in strictness and holiness of life." Thus the Devil as "lord of the world," so that "men must think, speak and do what the Devil wills," is the guiding spirit behind the traditional religious virtue of pious works. . . .

True, Luther cannot permit his experience of dualism to submerge Christianity's traditional faith in the monarchy of God; to reconcile the two he has such formulations as that God *permits* the Devil to rage or that God *withdraws* to leave space for the Devil. But the net effect is still to recognize the Devil's power as a positive antidivine structure in its own right. Hence when Luther is arguing for man's lack of free will, he does not simply argue from the omnipotence of God, but also from the power and rights of the Devil and from original sin, which established and perpetuates Satan's domination over mankind. "In the Protestant Church, the Devil must have his pay, and the Devil's pay is the soul of the sinner. Thus ever since the days of the Reformation, Satan's power in this world has considerably increased." According to the more merciful Catholic tradition, even those who had made pacts with the Devil might, even in the eleventh hour, be saved by some outward act of penitence (the "works" that Luther despised) or by the intercession of the saints (another concept that fell victim to Protestant fundamentalism). The new Lutheran notion of inescapable damnation takes over the Faust legend and makes it a profound symbol of modern man.

Nor does Christian faith withdraw the Christian from the domination of Satan. Here the central doctrine is the impossibility of overcoming sin, a Lutheran innovation which, as Troeltsch says, is all the more remarkable for being a divergence from Pauline Christianity. The doctrine of the impossibility of overcoming sin can be deduced from the doctrine of the vanity of good works, and it results in the Lutheran dualism between the inner world of grace and the outer world of works, the world of the spirit and the world of the flesh. Following Troeltsch's explication of the Lutheran position, we may say

that an active fulfillment of the Christian ideal is impossible upon earth and realizable only in the future life. Hence the Lutheran conception of grace and of the impossibility of overcoming sin leaves no outwardly visible distinction between Christian and non-Christian. Christianity consists in the inner possession of grace, not in any outward achievement. Although to some extent faith should issue in good works, such good works affect neither the quality of Christian piety nor the fact of personal salvation. This is tantamount to saying—and Luther says it—that the Christian remains under the dominion of the Devil, and nevertheless is lord over the Devil and the Devil has no power over him. This paradox means that the Christian is split into two dimensions, spirit that belongs to Christ and flesh that belongs to the Devil. Again we see the tremendous extension of the Devil's empire in Protestantism. The whole realm of visible reality, the world and the flesh, belong to the Devil; God has retired into invisibility—*Deus absconditus*. . . .

It would be hard to find a clearer illustration of the actuality and effective power of that death instinct which Freud postulated and which the non-Freudian world has ridiculed. For hell, Luther said, is not a place, but is the experience of death, and Luther's devil is ultimately personified death. Luther's new *theologia crucis* rejects the traditional Aristotelian-Thomistic goal of actualizing the potentialities of life as *amor concupiscentiae*, and calls us to experience hell on earth, to experience life on earth as ruled by the death instinct, and to die to such a death-in-life, in the hope of a more joyful resurrection. . . .

It is the hope of a more joyful resurrection that alone saves Luther from the dominion of death. Satan is the lord of this life, but there is another life where Christ is King, and to have faith in the existence of that other life is to conquer this death-in-life while in it. To make psychological sense of Luther's central paradox we had to invoke Freud's two immortal antagonists, the life instinct and the death instinct. Under Luther's symbols, we perceive that Luther sees this life as being under the domination of the death instinct. Those who take Freud's *Civilization and Its Discontents* seriously can only agree, and must recognize Luther's insight as a decisive advance in the task, as old as human history, of reclaiming id territory for the human ego. This recognition of life as death-in-life reflects and crystallizes an immense withdrawal of libido from life. In other words, whereas in previous ages life had been a

The Eve of the Modern World

mixture of Eros and Thanatos, in the Protestant era life becomes a pure culture of the death instinct. Luther's faith and grace—the hope of a more joyful resurrection—form an enclave in the dominion of death which will not bow the knee and call death life, but on the other hand they form no real exception to the fact that death has dominion over life. Luther cannot affirm life, but can only die to this death-in-life. Therefore for him, too, holy living is holy dying. "God . . . makes alive by slaying."

Thus the insight of Protestantism is its insight into the dominion of death in life, and its service to life and to love is its hope in another life which would be true life. The positive features in Luther are his diabolism and his eschatology. Actually the diabolism and the eschatology are two sides of the same coin. It would be psychically impossible for Luther to recognize the Devil's dominion over this world (Luther is not yet de Sade) without the faith that the Devil's dominion is doomed, and that the history of man on earth will end in the kingdom of God, when grace will be made visible. Hence it is an integral part of Luther's position to believe, as the earliest Christians had, that he is living in the last age of time. In fact, in Luther's eyes the new power of the Devil points to the end of time: our devils are far worse than those known in previous ages; compared to ours, medieval devils are child's play; the whole age is Satanic; the world cannot last much longer, and "from so Satanic a world" Luther would fain be "quickly snatched."

4

CALVINISM AND REVOLUTION

Important as Luther was as the first major reformer—whether or not the "cause" of the Reformation—his younger contemporary, the French reformer Jean Calvin was probably more important. For Lutheranism and, for that matter, most of the Protestant groups and sects which developed prior to the Calvinist movement were closely related to ethnic, national, regional, or class interests. It was only with Calvinism that the Reformation gained an internationalism and universality to set against the ancient, ecumenical claims of Catholicism.

The center of the Calvinist universe was Geneva, the "Protestant Rome." It was to this Swiss city that the young Calvin fled from persecution in his native France in 1536. It was at this very time that his religious ideas were beginning to crystalize. With the exception of one brief exile, Calvin spent the rest of his life in Geneva, intent upon making that city the Protestant "City of God." To an astonishing extent he succeeded.

Calvinism, like most of the evangelical sects, was a militant and concerned faith and from Calvin's Geneva a steady stream of preachers and missionaries and agents went out to preach the reformed doctrine, to enter into the religious and political strife of the time, and to seize upon local movements and protests and convert their disparate energies to Calvinism. All across Europe the division between Catholic and reformed had hardened into implacable hostility and this religious hostility had embittered older economic or political or sectional differences. The wars of religion had already begun and Calvinism was rapidly becoming a dominant factor in them. As the fortunes of religious war and persecution swayed back and forth, religious refugees came to Geneva—from the England of Mary Tudor, from the Huguenot south of France, from the Low Countries, and the Rhine valley. And in time they returned to their countries strengthened in faith and determination by the iron doctrines of Calvinism. By the later sixteenth century Calvinism had, in one way or another, set its stamp upon the Huguenot movement in France, the Reformed Church of the Low Countries and Germany, English Puritanism, and Scots Presbyterianism. Wherever Calvinism went, and in whatever form, it was followed by political upheaval and revolution. The formation of the Huguenot church in France was followed by the formation of the Huguenot party and the outbreak of the Wars of Religion. With the appearance of organized Calvinism in the Low Countries the long smouldering hostility to Spain became a war for independence from which eventually emerged the Protestant-Calvinist Dutch Republic. The civil war which broke out at last in England in the 1640's is customarily called the Puritan — that is to say, Calvinist — Revolution.

This seductive sequence of religious and political events, repeated time and again, has naturally enough suggested that Calvinism *caused* the religious wars and revolutions. Indeed, the suggestion has become a thesis. And it is that thesis which is the subject of the selections which follow in this problem. The selections represent widely divergent views with reference to this traditional framework of interpretation but, in one sense or another, they all test the thesis. And the student, as he ponders the readings, should do the same. He might ask himself, is what seems the logical conclusion really a logical conclusion at all or a form of the logical fallacy expressed in the dictum *post hoc ergo propter hoc?* Do the facts, as marshalled by the authorities quoted here, bear out the thesis? Is it generally supportable enough to be a thesis or do we impose upon very different and very complex sets of events the dangerous oversimplification of "the single cause"?

RUPERT E. DAVIES

THE THEOLOGICAL BASIS

The central problem of this section is posed by the question, to what extent was Calvinism a principal cause for the rash of social and political revolutions that broke out among the European states of the later sixteenth and seventeenth centuries? In the last three selections we shall look at specific cases in France, the Low Countries, and England. But in this first selection we must be concerned with a necessary item of background. Calvinism was primarily a theological system and, no matter how important its socio-political implications may have been, they were nonetheless implications. Thus we must see if there is a "Doctrine of Revolution" inherent in Calvin's theology. For this purpose we turn to an important critical book by Rupert E. Davies, *The Problem of Authority in the Continental Reformers,* and specifically to that portion of the book devoted to Calvin who, in this frame of reference, Davies regards as the most important of the major reformers.

The basis of Calvin's concept of authority is starkly simple: "Religious truth is to be found in the Word of God, and elsewhere only in so far as it is derived from the Word of God; there is no appeal from the Word of God, and no man, nor any body of men, is competent to set aside, add to, or disagree with, the Word of God." Thus the Bible becomes the source of supreme authority for individual men. It is also the source of authority for the church because the "visible Church" is composed of those who model their lives upon the Word of God and model the form of their ecclesiastical organization upon the principles and precedents to be found in the Word of God.

If the Word of God is the supreme authority in man's private life and in his religious life, is it not also the supreme authority in his relations with the exterior world—the state? And if the state fails to conform to the Word of God, what is the Christian citizen to do? This is the burden of the following selection. The student should note carefully the arguments that are developed with a view to applying them to the "cases" he will encounter later in this section.

What, on Calvin's view, is the relation of the Word of God to the State, in the sense of the legally constituted government? Does the Bible exercise authority over it? We must first discover the nature of the State in Calvin's idea of it. All power and authority belong ultimately and essentially to God. In view of the corruption of mankind God has delegated some of His power to men by directly setting up governments and magistrates, which will be necessary as long as man remains in his imperfect state—that is, as long as he remains on earth; they are "the vicars of God," "the ministers of the divine justice," their tribunals are "the throne of the living God," their mouths "the organ of the divine truth." Their God-given functions are "to cherish and protect the outward worship of God, to defend the sound doctrine of piety and the position of the Church, to adjust our lives to the society of men, to conform our characters to civil justice, to reconcile us to one another, to nourish common peace and tranquillity." This divine institution and these divine functions give magistrates a divine vocation, one that is not only "holy and legitimate in the sight of God, but also most sacred, and one that is by far the most honourable of all vocations in the whole life of mortals." In the performance of its functions the State has the right and duty to shed the blood of its citizens in punishment, since it is carrying out the judgements of God, and it also has the right and duty to declare and prosecute war against other States for

the protection of its citizens, although it will do everything in its power to preserve peace.

It is very clear that Calvin thus ascribes complete independence to the State in virtue of its direct divine institution. And this independence includes independence of the Church; or rather, it implies complete distinctness of province. The Church is concerned with the "soul, or the inner man," the State "with the setting up of civil and external justice of morals." Thus a man lives under two "regiments." The State may not interfere with the Church, though it is charged with the task of facilitating and protecting its operations, but the Church must not interfere with the State either.

Here, perhaps, it is necessary to pause. It is well known that in Calvin's Geneva the Church took a much greater part in politics than it has been allowed to do in any ancient or modern State, and as large a part as it took in any medieval State. It appears difficult to reconcile this fact with Calvin's conception of the functions of Church and State. No respectable reconciliation is in fact possible. Calvin's theory was what we have stated it to be. In conformity with it, Calvin himself never sought or obtained any magistracy at Geneva (although he sat on the constitutional commission of 1543); he was not even a citizen until 1559; and he exerted no influence in politics, as far as he knew, except as a

From Rupert E. Davies, *The Problem of Authority in the Continental Reformers, A Study in Luther, Zwingli, and Calvin* (London, 1946), pp. 130–38. Reprinted by permission of the Epworth Press.

The Theological Basis

private man and not as representative of the Church. He was probably unaware that any breach of his theory had occurred during his lifetime in Geneva. But here he did not see things as they really were. There were factors in the actual situation with which his theory had not reckoned. In the first place, he was himself constantly consulted on all matters which affected the city's welfare and always gave his advice on religious grounds; it was frequently taken, and his influence on politics came more and more to be virtually the interference of the Church through its leading minister. Secondly, his great love for the city of Geneva made him extremely zealous that it should be the model of a Christian city, and so he was the more urgent in his advice when it was asked for, and this intensified the impression of ecclesiastical interference. But the third factor was by far the most important: in Calvin's view, private morals were part of man's inner life and therefore within the scope of the Church; to deal with them and punish breaches of the moral law, he set up the Consistory, which was a Church court imposing spiritual penalties, including excommunication. But everyone in Geneva was a Church member, and the city was virtually identical with the congregation, so that excommunication was tantamount to banishment; and it is impossible to seclude the sphere of morals in such a way that the civil law is not related to them, so that the Consistory necessarily invaded the province of the State on numerous occasions. Thus the Church did not in practice allow the State the independence which Calvin's theory ascribed to it. A struggle naturally ensued, from which the Church emerged victorious over the State, although Calvin thought that it had merely vindicated its own rights, whereas in fact it had virtually disfranchised the State. Thus Reformed Geneva out-medievalized the Middle Ages, and the Church securely held the two swords. But Calvin's theory is not in the least affected, and to it we now return.

It is clear that it is a Biblical theory, based on the thirteenth chapter of the Epistle to the Romans, and supported by various passages in the Old and New Testaments. And Calvin quotes Scripture to prove his case at every point, according to his usual custom. Especially does he use the Biblical arguments to confute the anarchists and pacifists, who both denied in effect that government was necessary for Christians. But he nowhere says of the State what he has emphasized in respect of the Church, that it is created and formed by the Word of God, but only that it is set up by God. It seems, then, that Calvin

thought of the State as having a function and authority, within its proper limits, which was derivative not from the Word, but only from God Himself. This function and authority are described and confirmed by the Word, but not created by it.

Calvin does not shift from this position when he treats of two other major aspects of politics — the right form of constitution and the nature and authority of law. On the former question, he says that it is useless for private men to speak and argue. For a great deal depends on circumstances, and even if one looks at the matter abstractly it is by no means easy to determine the best constitution. For himself, Calvin says, he has a preference for aristocracy — an interesting preference, in view of the democratic strain in his ideas of Church government, but one which he indulged when sitting on the Constitutional Commission of 1543 in Geneva, if the result of that commission's work may be used as evidence — and gives several reasons for this. But it has been "brought about by the divine providence that different regions" of the earth's surface "should be administered under different constitutions."

It is evident from this that Calvin regarded each constitution as having been determined and established by the will and direct act of God — he says in so many words in the course of the passage just quoted that God "set up an aristocracy among the Jews . . . until such time as He produced in David the archetype of Christ." Moreover, he nowhere says that we are to learn the true form of polity from the Bible, for although he uses the aristocracy, which he imagined the pre-Davidic Jews as having, as an argument in favour of his personal preference for that form of government, he does not regard the argument as in any way decisive; in fact, the implication of the passage is that we are not to go to the Bible for instructions in the matter, but rather to accept the already existing divine arrangements. It might be thought that he came to this conclusion because the Bible in various places approves of various types of polity and therefore consultation of it on this point would not be particularly fruitful, but in view of his general position in this regard it is legitimate to treat the conclusion as genuinely arrived at from Calvin's true premises.

In his treatment of law, Calvin first of all denies at some length the contention that the Mosaic law should be taken as the model of all subsequent legislation; having divided it into the moral law, the

The Eve of the Modern World

ceremonial law, and the judicial law, he says that only the first is universally applicable and that the third gives a juridical system suited to the Jews and intended for them only. Each State has to make its own laws according to the circumstances of its time and place and characters of its people, and it is entitled to make special laws, often of particular severity, in times of emergency; these laws are to be founded on one principle of the moral law—which is written, not only in the books of Moses, but on the consciences of all humanity and is rightly called Natural Law—and that principle is equity ((aequitas); but otherwise they are to be as different as circumstances demand. He goes on from this point to show that it is quite legitimate for Christians to go to law, so long as they are free from the spirit of litigiousness, despite the apparent prohibition of St. Paul in I Corinthians vi. I ("Dare any of you, having a matter against his neighbour, go to law before the unrighteous?").

We see that the position here is much the same as it is with forms of constitution; in fact, Calvin himself explicitly equates the two matters, and adds to what he has previously said about constitutions the remark that they must aim at equity. Law must differ from place to place and age to age and country to country as circumstances demand. The Bible does not prescribe the character and content of such laws; in fact, the actual legislation which it does contain is to be disregarded as being of a purely temporary nature. But there is one difference which is worthy of note. Constitutions are of direct divine appointment; laws are made by the government which results from the constitution, and their authority, like that of the taxes which a government may impose, is divine only at the first remove. But this fact does not affect the relation of the law to the Word of God, which is not invoked in the matter at all.

It may be objected that as laws (and, according to Calvin's afterthought, constitutions) are to be expressions of the principle of equity, and as the principle of equity is derived from the Word of God, they are after all subordinate to the Bible. But this objection takes no account of the sharp distinction between morals and law in the mind of Calvin, morals being within the province of the Bible and the Church, law within the province of the State. It is quite true that this distinction cannot really be maintained and that the attempt to maintain it had unpleasant results in practice in Geneva; it is also true that Calvin's de-

mand that laws should be based on the moral principle of equity is a virtual, though unconscious, admission that the distinction is untenable. But Calvin did make and maintain the distinction, and we must therefore deny that Calvin subordinated law to the Word of God.

The last aspect of politics with which Calvin deals in the Institutes is the question of the subject's obedience to his rulers. This was, of course, a matter of supreme importance to those of the Reformed faith, in view of widespread persecution, actual or imminent, at the time at which Calvin was writing. He discussed it therefore with care and at length. What he has to say follows logically from what he has said about the nature and functions of governments, constitutions, and laws. The authority of rulers is from God; therefore they are to be obeyed; to resist one's ruler is to resist God. It is quite true, he points out, that it is difficult to see in many rulers the representatives of God, but God is using them for His purposes none the less. The ruler has, of course, duties towards us, but they are not our business. We must do our duty, and, if need be, suffer as a consequence. If we feel disposed to rebel because of the sin or incapacity of our rulers, we must resist the temptation; their punishment will be carried out in due course by God Himself, and it is no concern of ours.

So far Calvin seems almost to have overstated the conclusion which follows from the delegation of divine power to human rulers—no doubt in his eagerness to prevent civil strife in as many countries as possible and to clear the Protestants of the charge of stirring up rebellion and internal dissension. But he has two modifications to make. Firstly, he says: "I am speaking all the time about private persons. For if there are now any magistrates of the people set up to restrain the licence of kings (as, for instance, the ephors who were opposed to the Spartan kings, or the tribunes of the people who were opposed to the Roman consuls, or the officers of the demos who were opposed to the Athenian Senate; and whatever power in present circumstances the three orders have in individual kingdoms when they hold their primary assemblies), so far am I from forbidding their opposition in accordance with their office to the mad licence of kings that, if they connive at the unrestrained aggressions of kings and their outrages against the humble common people, I assert that their deceit amounts to criminal treachery; for they are fraudulently betraying the liberty of the people which God has ordained them to protect." We are entitled to suppose that the "opposition" here virtually enjoined on "magistrates of the people" may take violent forms, and we have therefore here a concession to those who assert the right to rebel which is capable of having important practical consequences. Yet it must be observed that the right of the "magistrates of the people" to oppose the ruler is derived from their own position as rulers, and therefore set up by God; there is nothing here to limit the duty of subjects to obey.

In the last section of all he makes the second, and larger, modification. "But in the obedience which we have decided to be due to the commands of our rulers, we must always make this exception—or rather, this must be our primary consideration—that it may not lead us away from our obedience to Him, to whose will the wishes of all kings must be subject, to whose decrees their commands must give way, to whose majesty the emblems of their majesty must submit." We are to disobey the commands of our rulers when they are against God; and this he interprets by saying that we must "endure anything rather than turn away from piety." In other words, as his examples from the Old Testament show, we are to disobey when we are commanded to follow a false religion—and only then. There is no sign, however, that we, as private citizens, are to go farther than passive disobedience; violent action is not open to us.

This whole account of the duties of subjects is, of course, amply established and confirmed throughout by the evidence of Holy Writ, and in a certain sense it is true to say that the subject is to obey his rulers and rebel against his rulers because he is commanded to do so by the Bible. He is thus subject in his political relations to the authority of Scripture. But the principal reason why he is so to obey is the fact that the rulers' power comes to them straight from God, whom it is his prime duty in the whole of life to obey, and the principal reason why he is on certain occasions to rebel is the fact that the rulers on these occasions have ceased to be the instruments of God and have set themselves against Him, and consequently obedience to God involves disobedience to the rulers. And there is certainly nothing in the whole account to suggest that the rulers have their power from any source but God, or that they are subordinate to the Word of God. Thus Calvin here, it appears, is strictly consistent with his general view of government.

A charge of inconsistency might, however, be brought against him on one count. A subject is to disobey his rulers when they command anything against God; now only the Bible reveals what is against God. Therefore it seems that the subject disobeys his rulers whenever they issue a command which is contrary to the Bible; and this means that the rulers, despite Calvin's professions to the contrary, are to legislate after all in accordance with the Bible. But the inconsistency dissolves if we remember once again Calvin's distinction between the provinces of Church and State. The State, if it truly conceives its function, cannot possibly issue commands which are against God; if it does issue such commands, it must be that the State has gone beyond its province and intruded on that of the Church and Bible. And the permission on certain occasions to disobey means in fact permission to disobey when the State has exceeded its functions.

Here, perhaps, it is worth while comparing Calvin's view of politics with that of Luther. Both Reformers held that God set up the State directly, and that the State therefore derives its authority from God, and not from the Word. But whereas Luther asserts that the State once set up must govern and make its laws according to the prescriptions of the Word, Calvin says that it does so in its own derived right. Thus Calvin takes a step, wholly alien to the thought of Luther, in the direction of autonomizing the State. He is, of course, nowhere near to saying that the State is autonomous in the sense of being independent of divine law altogether; but he does free it from any subordination to Church or Bible. It is ironical, therefore, that while Luther's Church became subservient to the State, Calvin's Church aimed at and often achieved domination of the State.

We may now sum up as follows the scope and nature of the Bible's authority according to Calvin: for the individual in religious matters, the Bible is completely authoritative; in political matters he is under its authority to the extent of being commanded authoritatively by it to obey his rulers, but much more he is under the authority of God as mediated to him by his rulers. The Church derives all its authority from the Bible, and the Bible is for it completely authoritative. The State derives its authority immediately from God, and the Bible has no authority over it.

It is clear that we cannot ascribe to Calvin the Biblical totalitarianism which we found in the case of

Luther; and the former's partial recognition of the autonomy of the State and of the individual in his political relations puts him beyond the Middle Ages. We have, too, in Calvin the beginnings of the distinction between religious and other kinds of truth, implied by the right of the State to publish its own valid ordinances. Of course, the distinction in Calvin is merely inchoate, since the State's edicts are to him derived from God, but the door has been pushed slightly ajar for the State to enter later with a claim of absolute right to speak in its own sphere, and then for science, art, and the rest to do the same.

J. E. NEALE

THE WARS OF RELIGION: A SPECIAL CASE?

The clearest and most often cited example of Calvinist revolution are the so-called Wars of Religion in France. Even this conventional label betrays the thesis. And it is thoroughly understandable: Calvin was French himself; he felt most deeply the religious disabilities under which "true religion" suffered in France; he directed his most passionate efforts to the conversion of his fellow Frenchmen; and he was successful to the extent that the earliest major organization of Calvinism outside the city of Geneva itself was the Huguenot organization in France. It is to that organization that we turn in the following selection excerpted from Sir John Neale's *The Age of Catherine de Medici*. There are several chapter-essays in the book dealing with various aspects of the Wars of Religion, but we are concerned with his chapter on the religious background and the formation of the Huguenot church organization which Neale regards as "the most striking feature in the history of the French Calvinist . . . movement." In this assessment he is in basic agreement with Davies, the author of the preceding selection, who said in an earlier passage of his book, "It is in the matter of church government that [Calvin's] influence has been, and remains, most profound and far reaching." The shape of the Huguenot church became the shape of the Huguenot rebel state that supported the Wars of Religion.

While Neale's account is not cluttered with special pleading or religious partisanship he, nonetheless, is in substantial agreement with the conventional thesis that the religious wars were caused by the special character of Calvinism. He contends, for example, that the French reform movement "was bound to assume the shape of rebellion." The student should keep this idea in mind as he deals with the last two selections in this section for he must decide if the thesis which explains so well the Wars of Religion in France can be equally well applied to the Dutch Revolt or the English Civil War; or whether the case of the Wars of Religion is a special case.

Our story begins in March 1559 with the Peace of Cateau-Cambrésis. It was primarily a peace between Spain and France, though England too was a party, for Mary Tudor had entered the war in the train of

From J. E. Neale, *The Age of Catherine de Medici* (New York, 1959), pp. 9–11, 13–22, 24–32. Reprinted by permission of Barnes & Noble, Inc., and Jonathan Cape Ltd.

her husband, Philip II, and had lost Calais. This peace marks the close of an epoch in European as well as French history.

The most obvious change in the European scene was its new rulers. Only three to four years before, Philip II had taken over Spain and the Spanish Netherlands from his father, the Emperor Charles V; in England Elizabeth had become Queen the previous November; and in France celebrations connected with the Peace were to result in the death of Henry II and thus lead to the gradual emergence of the Queen-Mother, Catherine de Medici, as the director of French policy. By a striking coincidence all three of these rulers were long-lived. Catherine de Medici died at the turn of the year 1588-89: she was sixty-nine. Philip II died in 1598: he was seventy-one. Elizabeth died in 1603: she was sixty-nine. The second half of the sixteenth century was dominated by these three personalities, and, according to one's national standpoint, is the Age of Philip II, of Elizabeth, or of Catherine de Medici.

The Peace of Cateau-Cambrésis closed the period of the Italian Wars, which had gone on intermittently for over sixty years and ended, from the French point of view, in complete humiliation. France finally gave up the challenge to Spanish hegemony in Italy, and Italy was left to itself and Spain. The Italian states could no longer disturb the peace by playing off one great power against another; they passed out of the main current of international affairs.

The Italian Wars were ended. So also was the second great theme of that period of history—the German Reformation. After years of disorder and civil war, in which the Emperor had tried and failed to accomplish the miracle of uniting rival theologies in a compromise, exhaustion and realism had propounded their own solution—the solution which is described by the Latin tag, *cuius regio eius religio*: the prince determines the faith of his kingdom. The sixteenth century was totalitarian in its political creed: its motto was "One King, One Faith." Germany preserved this creed in its Reformation settlement, but paid a heavy price. It shattered itself. The Prince, not the Emperor, was the beneficiary of the German Reformation; and a country which in law was a federal state became in consequence a confederation of states. German unity had to wait until the nineteenth century—or perhaps one should say, until the twentieth. The Reformation settlement was

embodied in the Peace of Augsburg in 1555; and thereafter Germany, like Italy, receded from the main current of European affairs and did not re-emerge until the eve of the Thirty Years War, half a century or so later. In that half-century it is western Europe that occupies the stage of history.

Modern research, with its emphasis on economic factors, has a very up-to-date reason for the making of the Peace of Cateau-Cambrésis: money, or rather, the lack of it. Of that I must say a word in a later chapter. But in the mind of the King of France, Henry II, who wanted peace so desperately that he was prepared to surrender almost anything, money was not the only reason. He had an overwhelming desire to tackle a domestic problem, the urgency of which had been growing in recent years. That problem was heresy; and it is the theme of this chapter.

We have all heard, maybe to the point of staleness, about the causes of the Reformation; about the state of the Catholic Church in the early sixteenth century, about worldly and non-resident bishops, ignorant and unspiritual clergy, and the monasteries. The story is the same in France, only perhaps more so, for there, in addition to the general slackness of the age, there was a peculiar reason for the deplorable condition of the Church. It was the Concordat of 1516; an agreement made between the French monarchy and the Papacy, which can only be described as a deal in the spoils of the Gallican Church. It gave the King the nomination to bishoprics, abbeys, and conventual priories in France; and its effect can be put quite briefly. Not a single French bishop obtained his post because of religious zeal or spiritual worthiness. Fifty per cent of benefices were given for Court services, the rest to please influential local magnates; and benefices were actually given to two Italian princes to further French diplomacy in Italy. These appointments were regarded, not as ecclesiastical preferment, but as grants of revenue, a conception that was blatant enough when the grants consisted of all future vacant benefices until their combined revenue should reach a certain sum. . . .

In its early phases the French Reform movement was moderate and respectable. It was the spiritual facet of Humanism, a blending of Erasmian and Lutheran impulses, and had the King's sister for patron. Though admirable in many ways, it lacked the qualities to shape a great rebel cause. Indeed, neither Lutheranism nor Humanism possessed the

The Eve of the Modern World

practical genius required for sustained and successful rebellion. This may seem a strange remark when one thinks of the explosive force of the Lutheran Reformation in Germany: it had been dynamic enough to rouse a whole nation and had accomplished a revolution. But the practical success of the movement had been due to the support of the secular princes. It was they and not Luther who had supplied the Lutheran Church with its organization. Luther was a mystic, not an administrator. To him the Church was not an organized, earthly society, but an invisible body, the mystic communion of saints; and it needed the mundane mind of the Prince to fetch the Church down from the heavens, where Luther had left it suspended, and clothe it in the necessary garments to move about the earth. There were no essential Lutheran doctrines about the form of church organization, and everywhere the Prince supplied that form. Consequently we find the Lutheran Church episcopal in one state and non-episcopal in another. . . .

If French Protestantism had remained Lutheran it would indeed have been a weak plant.

It would have been weak because in the nature of things the Reformation in France could not count on the support of the King. However much on occasions the French monarchy might seem to wobble, there can be little doubt that it was fated to remain Catholic. What had it to gain from going Reformist? In the all-important business of appointing to bishoprics and wealthy abbeys, the King of France, under the Concordat of 1516, was as much the Head of the Church as Henry VIII of England. A government that was desperately and permanently bankrupt, as France was for the next half-century, that relied on its ecclesiastical patronage to pay officials and courtiers, and that in dire need was able to tax the Church without mercy, could not afford to discard a system which served it so well.

True, the French King might have broken with Rome and, like Henry VIII, become the titular as well as the practical Head of the Church. There was an old and strong tradition of Gallicanism in the French Church, a tradition of national independence which might seem to have suggested a move of this sort; and in the first year or two of our period there actually was an occasional hint to the Papacy that if it did not mind its p's and q's France might follow the example of England. But even if such a change had been practical policy, it would not have satisfied the

Reformers. On doctrinal questions a breach with Rome would no doubt have brought some concessions to Protestants, but the last thing the Reformers wanted was the perpetuation of that scandalous laxity and irreligion associated with royal control of the Church. No. The French monarchy was fated to remain Catholic. Its vested interests in the *ancien régime* were too great, and so also were those of powerful elements in the country. Moreover, though Protestant communities developed in Paris and were troublesome, this city was always staunchly, nay fanatically Catholic. It was not an accident that England ultimately took the religious complexion of its capital: London was worth a sermon. Nor was it an accident that France ultimately took the religious complexion of its capital: Paris was worth a Mass.

Thus the French Reform movement, being opposed to the interests of the monarchy, was bound to assume the shape of rebellion. Now, there are certain essentials for prolonged and successful rebellion; and the chief is organization. Here lies the significance of Calvinism. If I am inclined to stress organization over against doctrine or anything else, the reason is my profound conviction of its vital importance. Much of English history, Scottish history, and Dutch history in the second half of the sixteenth century might be written round the organization of Calvinism; and I am often tempted to speak of this period as the Age of Calvin, although in fact Calvin died in 1564. . . .

The theological or doctrinal aspect of Calvinism need not detain us. On this subject it is sufficient to note that at a moment when the inherent individualism of the German Reformation was producing confusion in Protestant theology, Calvin, with his legal training and the clarity and rigour of the French genius, rethought Protestant theology into an ordered and logical system. The Gallic qualities of his mind naturally fitted his teaching to become the Protestant gospel of the French people. There was one doctrine of Calvinism—that of predestination, to which Calvin was driven by the relentless logic of his thought—which deserves mention because of its value to a fighting faith. In time of hazard and persecution it was no small fortification to the spirit to know that one was among the elect, predestined by God to salvation.

But it is not the theology, it is the organization of this Church that is the most striking feature in the history of the French Calvinist, or, as it was called,

Huguenot movement. Unlike Luther, Calvin did not regard the organization of the Church as a negligible consideration and let the State have its own way. It was an integral part of his teaching. After all, the secret of the power wielded throughout the centuries by the Catholic Church lay in its organization and discipline as well as its dogma. And, as one eminent French historian has put it, Calvin's unique achievement, the sign of his originality, was to construct a new Catholicism outside the old and opposed to it.

This organization, which is better known to most of us by the name Presbyterian, must be examined in some detail. The officers of Calvin's Church were divided into three categories: ministers, elders, and deacons. The elders joined with the ministers in the government and discipline of the Church, while the deacons had charge of the sick and poor. In appearance the scheme had a democratic basis since each minister—and the same was true of elders and deacons—had ultimately to be elected by the particular congregation that he was to serve. But in fact Calvin's Church was oligarchic and conservative. The real choice of candidates for the ministry was in the hands of the body of ministers, who put them through a preliminary and searching examination of their doctrinal views and knowledge of scripture, their preaching ability, and their moral fitness. In Geneva Calvin gave the title of the Venerable Company to his ministers, and he meant them to live up to the title. Discipline was the very essence of his Church, among both officers and rank and file.

Each individual church, in the scheme of ecclesiastical government for countries like France, was governed by its minister and elders, the laity in the persons of the elders joining with the ministry here as throughout the whole organization. Minister and elders together formed a disciplinary committee known as the Consistory, which, by domiciliary visits or otherwise, maintained a constant supervision over the mode of life of every member of the church; an activity which Queen Elizabeth, to whom the Genevan system was anathema, described as an intolerable inquisition to pry into people's lives. This committee might even, and in France did, exercise a minor police power.

Above the Consistory, or ruling body of the single church, was another committee known in France as the Colloquy. It consisted of the ministers and elders of a number of neighbouring churches, grouped into a district, over which they exercised a general supervision, dealing with business brought to them by the individual churches. Above the Colloquy was the Synod, also a governing body of ministers and elders. In a large country like France there would be Provincial Synods, and, capping the whole ecclesiastical organization, a National Synod.

Think what this organization meant; think, especially, how well it was adapted to the cause of rebellion. Isolation, which breeds fear, doubt, and surrender in all but the most courageous, was impossible. No sooner was a community formed than it was organized; no sooner were there several communities than they were linked together by the Colloquy; and on top of this came the Provincial Synod and finally the National Synod to weld all the churches into a single unit.

Throughout every grade of this organization ran the remarkable Calvinist discipline, which maintained unity of belief and a high code of personal conduct. . . .

So much for the organization and discipline of the Calvinist Church. We must next see how Calvin meant his Church to fit into the State. Once more he was precise and logical. State and Church were separate powers, but they were fused, first by the assumption that every citizen would be a member of the Church, and secondly by the unique position accorded to the Bible. Calvin regarded the Bible as the word of God, in the full and literal sense. Consequently, in a godly society it should be the fundamental law both of the State and the Church. Now the Bible is full of moral injunctions, and the Old Testament in particular, with its Mosaic laws, embodies a whole penal code. These injunctions and this code, being the word of God, should therefore be part of the law of the State: for example, death is the punishment for adultery in the Old Testament, and it should be the same in the Calvinist State. From our point of view the conception reveals a monstrous confusion of morality and law; the sort of confusion which, in a minor degree perhaps, the contemporary totalitarian State has made. But it is not my object to condemn or praise; and I hasten to make a final point about Calvin's State. It is this: since the Bible was to be the fundamental law of the State, and since the professional expositors of the Bible were the ministers, it followed that the ministers would in fact dominate State as well as Church. In other words, Calvin's State would be a theocracy; a

The Eve of the Modern World

natural conclusion, for he drew his inspiration from the Old Testament and the Israelitish theocracy.

This in brief was Calvin's theory of Church and State — his vision of Utopia. In the course of the centuries many authors have written Utopias; few indeed have had the opportunity and the ideal conditions for putting them to the actual experiment. This perfect and rarest of Fortune's gifts was Calvin's. Geneva became his theocracy. . . .

It was from Geneva that the French Huguenot movement was organized. From here and neighbouring Protestant cities, Protestant literature was carried secretly through France by colporteurs and distributed surreptitiously by booksellers. It is significant that between 1549 and 1557 no less than fifty-six printers and booksellers sought refuge in Geneva. From here also missionaries went forth. As Huguenot congregations were formed it was to Geneva that they applied for ministers, and it was there that they sent their young men to be trained for the ministry. On questions of government and policy they were continually writing to Calvin. Once more I think that a contemporary parallel may be helpful. Calvin's Geneva was in many ways like Moscow during those years after the war of 1914–1918 when the Soviet State dreamed of a world communist revolution: it was as much a thorn in the side of the French government as Moscow in the side of capitalist Germany before 1933.

Though this account of Calvin and Geneva has not, I hope, exceeded the length that their place in French history warrants, it is time that we examined the growth of the Calvinist movement in France itself.

First, let us look at the classes of people who responded to Reformist propaganda. We can best begin with the one class that it scarcely touched — the peasantry. With certain exceptions they were hostile. They were completely illiterate and thus could not be affected by the clandestine literature that played so large a part in Huguenot propaganda; and as was inevitable with people rooted to the soil, they were profoundly conservative. They were attached to the worship of saints and the cult of the dead; and it was only when Reformist ideas began to grip the nobility and gentry that any of them were won over to the cause, and then by tenant-loyalty rather than religious conversion.

As might be expected, it was among the educated,

at the universities, that the new doctrine spread first. Many university teachers and also tutors in noble households were converted, and in due course influenced the minds of their pupils. Medical men, lawyers, and notaries, and other professional men figured prominently in Huguenot ranks. The lawyer class in France was very large and, in comparison with the less bureaucratic government of England, was used in great numbers in the administration of the country. They formed almost an estate in themselves, and their traditions were anti-clerical. It was generally from the rank and file of the profession that Huguenot converts were obtained. They played an important part in the movement, for they were able secretly to shelter heretics from the operation of the laws against them.

These professional men were mostly the sons of merchants, whose trade connections with other countries brought them into touch with new-fangled ideas, and who, by their independent spirit and quality of mind, as a class were everywhere inclined to anticlericalism and heresy. In France they had additional cause for discontent in the grave financial drain caused by the Italian Wars. Their professional sons had no small part in converting them to Calvinism; and the organization of the Huguenot Church, by providing through the offices of elders and deacons for bourgeois laity in church government, appealed to their *amour-propre*. The spirit of Calvinism was, as I have said, essentially oligarchic and bourgeois.

Among the clergy, the bishops kept more or less clear of the infection. Only four went over to Geneva; five more were restless. Otherwise, in contrast with the English Reformation, the episcopacy was the great obstacle to heresy. It was the lower clergy and especially the Friars who became Huguenots. For three centuries the Friars had been the militia of the Church. They thronged the universities, and by their preaching, their mysticism, and their contacts with the people, were the true leaders of the crowd. They were a great asset and a great nuisance: speculators in doctrine and rebels against discipline, their tradition was one of independence and turbulence. They proved readily accessible to Genevan ideas, and were invaluable in the early stages of the Reform movement as peripatetic preachers of heresy, profiting by the non-residence of bishops and the immunities of their orders to overrun the country. They provided the new Church in France with its first ministers. But their indiscipline and their democratic spirit, both of which Calvin loathed, detracted from their service. One of Calvin's correspondents described them as "these horrible beasts"; and Calvin himself was far from enamoured of such turbulent pioneers.

The nobility—a class which included what we in England would term the country gentry—was the last class to be won over in large numbers. Very few were Calvinists in 1547, but twelve years later the situation had changed remarkably. Education and the influence of their women-folk were important factors in their conversion. With the women it was religious feeling—a revulsion against the moral and religious laxity of Francis I's reign; but with their men-folk the motive was often revolt against a social and political regime of which they were the victims. Moreover, they had lost a good deal by the Concordat of 1516, before which they had been able to secure high ecclesiastical positions for their sons. They tended to be anticlerical and anticipated spoils for themselves in the form of Church lands if the Reform movement triumphed.

The recruiting of the lesser nobility—the country gentry—was of great practical service. They might be described as the Storm-Troopers of the Huguenot movement. As a class they were entitled and accustomed to carry swords, and they therefore constituted a natural protection for meetings of heretic congregations. There was need for this. At first Huguenot congregations met in secret and often at night, in cellars or in the countryside outside the towns. Their meetings were illegal and liable to be broken up by the authorities. A more frequent danger was attack by hostile bands of Catholics, for, as the movement spread, it inflamed passions, as the growth of the Nazi movement did in Germany; and just as there were incessant clashes and fights between Communists and Nazis in the days before Hitler succeeded to power, so there were clashes and fights between Catholics and Huguenots. The gentry were needed to protect the Huguenot ministers and their flocks from assault, and congregations often met with a body of armed protectors forming a circle of defence round them. The churches came to place themselves, each under some nobleman as their protector.

As the number of converts increased, the situation deteriorated, breeding further aggression on both sides, for there were few ministers available in the earlier stages of the movement and congregations were therefore apt to grow so large that they were forced to meet in public. Secrecy was no longer possible. An extract from the minutes of the Consistory of Mans, dated August 6th, 1561, illustrates this transition to public meetings: "It has been decided that M. Merlin shall commence to preach publicly under the town hall of this town on Sunday next at 7.0 a.m. Superintendents will make haste to warn faithful noblemen (gentilshommes) so that all the faithful of this town shall be at the meeting." After this beginning, the minister at Mans preached in public four times a week.

Naturally, when secret meetings gave place to public, ministers were no longer able to exercise adequate control over the recruiting of their audiences, and rowdy elements appeared, only too ready to start image-breaking. Moreover, there was an impulse, which the ministers could not well restrain, to seize buildings, especially churches, for Huguenot services. This was often done in a hot-headed and riotous way. In Languedoc and Guienne bands of fanatics drove priests and worshippers out of churches and attacked convents. Similar happenings took place in other parts of the country, though occasionally, where Catholics were lukewarm, amicable arrangements were made with them and churches were shared between the new and the old faiths.

The change from secret to open worship—a significant stage in the Huguenot story—took place during the years 1560 and 1561. Disorder spread through France. Where Catholics were in a majority they turned on the Huguenots and engaged in bloody strife; where the Huguenots were strong, extremists often got out of hand and terrorized the Catholics.

Speaking in general terms—for it would be wearisome, and not very illuminating, to discuss the question in detail, province by province—the Huguenot movement tended to be strong in centres of international trade; for example, at Lyons, the great entrepôt near to the Genevan and German centres of Protestantism, and in the east in Brittany where trade connections with England and the Netherlands encouraged its growth. Normandy too was badly infected with heresy, though here the chief inducement was social and political discontent among the gentry of a province where the evils of French government were exceptionally rife. The movement also flourished in the south, from the Rhône and Provence through Languedoc to the King of Navarre's territory in the south-west. Paris had heretics, but remained predominantly and fervently Catholic: the Huguenot stronghold over against Catholic Paris was Orleans, where some idea of the numbers may be gathered from the fact that in May 1561 five to six thousand persons attended Communion and more than ten thousand followed Protestant funerals. In May 1561 there were said to be two thousand one hundred and fifty separate Huguenot churches in France.

The important years for the organization of the Church were 1555 to 1559. Since 1555 the separate churches had been organizing themselves, largely under the influence and direction of Calvin, who wanted to put a stop to disorder and establish a responsible ministry and proper discipline. Then in May 1559 the first National Synod was held in Paris. The meeting was in a lodging house, so that the coming and going would not attract attention; and the number present may have reached fifty. They were obscure men, for as yet the nobility had not imposed itself upon the leadership of the Church; and all of them risked death by their presence. They drew up a confession of faith and articles of discipline, including a constitution or organization for the whole Church. . . .

Such an organization—the organization of a rebel movement within the State—would be remarkable at any time in any State. It is nothing short of astounding to find it within the sixteenth-century State.

That is not all. I have already noted how the nobility, when they joined the movement, naturally took over the protection of congregations. During the turbulent years 1560 and 1561 most of the individual churches placed themselves under a noble protector. Consistories and Synods encouraged this, and the nobility took their place, by right of birth, on the governing bodies of the churches they protected.

The dangerous possibilities of this development were soon evident. The French nobility still retained the old feudal traditions which grouped the lesser nobles under the leadership of greater noblemen, and these in turn under still greater, until the few greatest noblemen in the land were reached—a feudal pyramid. Obviously, this grouping of the nobility fitted perfectly into the pyramid organization of the Huguenot Church, with its district, provincial, and national bodies. And so the Church was able and indeed tempted to create a military organization coinciding with its ecclesiastical organization. The individual church had its captain, the Colloquy its colonel, and the Province its general (chef-général). This was the military organization devised in November 1561 for the provinces of Bordeaux and Toulouse.

At this point I can, for the moment, leave my story, for I am verging on the political problem of the age—the subject of my next chapter. I would merely ask you to consider the amazing character and terrifying possibilities of this organized heretical party; consider also the passions that its growth had aroused in France. And I know no better way to secure an imaginative grasp of the situation than to reflect on the turbulent history of the ideological movements in our own days—the history of the Fascist movement in Italy, and better still of the Nazi movement in Germany. Governments have collapsed before them.

PIETER GEYL

THE DUTCH REVOLT: A REVISIONIST VIEW

The following selection from the writings of the eminent Dutch historian Pieter Geyl represents a radical departure from the general thesis we have been examining in this section. He reviews the conventional interpretation, i.e. that it was the Calvinist temper of the Dutch that led them to rebel against Spain, strengthened them in their heroic resistance, and finally led them to the formation of their independent and staunchly Protestant state. And then he examines the facts: there was a long tradition of Dutch language and culture, predating by centuries the formation of a Dutch state; there was, moreover, a long tradition of self-government which was offended by "the relentless policy of centralization and autocracy pursued by the royal government"; in the early and crucial years of the rebellion the Protestants were a minority everywhere, not only in the Catholic south but in the allegedly Protestant north; and finally, the most significant fact was the course of military action in the war itself and the military advantage represented by the natural defensive lines of the great rivers. The result is that "the true explanation, then, of the division of the Netherlands into a Protestant north and a Catholic south is the exact opposite of the current one. . . ." Thus cause and effect are reversed and rather than Calvinism causing the revolt, the triumph of Calvinism is the result of a revolt which was successful on other than religious grounds.

Of course Geyl is dealing with only a part of the general thesis — its application to the Dutch revolt — and he claims nothing more. He does indicate that the whole thesis "would bear discussion of a more general theoretical character." The student should attempt such a discussion for himself. He should note the revisionist methodology, so well demonstrated by Geyl, of testing a plausible theory against hard fact and see if he can apply this methodology to the other parts of our theory and to those other regions of Europe where Calvinism is said to have been the prime cause in making revolution.

The problem I shall here discuss — the problem of the modern State and my own Netherlands history — is one that posed itself before me very early in my career. It is a problem that would bear discussion of a more general theoretical character than I shall venture upon. I shall write as a practicing historian — which is what I am — who has come up against a problem that required some thinking out, some grappling with theory.

The Dutch State resulted from revolution and war in the closing decades of the sixteenth century; but there had been a long history in the Low Countries before it came into existence — a long history when the Dutch language was spoken and Dutch literature flourished, when people felt and thought about religion in ways which still have a meaning today, when churches were built which still dominate our towns and villages, and pictures painted in which we can still recognize ourselves.

If there was no Dutch State, there had been, ever since the migrations and settlement of the Franks in

the sixth century after Christ, a Dutch linguistic area. The extent of this linguistic area has remained extraordinarily constant throughout the centuries. The linguistic boundary separating Dutch from French still runs where it ran when the Frankish colonization was completed some thirteen centuries ago. Expressed in present-day political terms it runs right through Belgium, so that the Dutch linguistic area now embraces Holland (or the Kingdom of the Netherlands, to use the official description) and the northern half of Belgium, commonly called Flanders. (Let me say in passing that this name *Flanders,* historically speaking, belongs only to the western part, the ancient County of Flanders. Flanders in the modern sense of the Dutch-speaking region of Belgium, extends also over the ancient Duchy of Brabant and other districts still further East. Similarly *Holland* is originally no more than the northwestern part of the Kingdom which is now commonly so called. The ancient county was later on only one of the seven provinces constituting the Dutch Republic.)

Now the point that needs stressing is that this ancient

The Eve of the Modern World

(and still modern) Dutch linguistic area is not co-terminous with the Dutch State as it suddenly sprang into existence in the course of the sixteenth-century revolt against Philip II of Spain. It is much larger. The Dutch State comprises not quite two thirds of the Dutch-speaking people in the Low Countries and the region which remained outside at the critical moment in the last quarter of the sixteenth century was the region in which the Middle Ages—with towns like Ghent and Bruges, Antwerp and Brussels—Dutch literature and civilization had had their earliest and most significant development.

It is a fact deserving careful attention that the linguistic area had never been the basis of any political formation. In the late Carolingian times part of it owed allegiance to the French Kingdom, another part to the German Kingdom; but, as time went on, in both cases this allegiance came to mean less and less. The reality were the feudal principalities—duchies, counties, bishoprics; and these gradually became completely independent. At last, in the fifteenth and early sixteenth centuries, a union was brought about by an outside power, the French Dukes of Burgundy, and their successors the Hapsburg rulers. But in this union the French-speaking provinces—as the old principalities now came to be called—Hainaut, Namur, Artois, and the rest—were combined with the Dutch-speaking provinces, Holland, Gelderland, Groningen, Brabant, Flanders and the rest; and the whole of the Netherlands came, moreover, to be connected with the extensive Hapsburg Empire, and in the end more especially with Spain. The Burgundian-Hapsburg rulers had meanwhile brought the beginnings of a central administration to the Low Countries; the governor and his councils resided at Brussels.

Within the framework thus created it was a natural development for a national sentiment, a sentiment of belonging together, to grow up. But the Burgundian-Hapsburg rule had at the same time introduced subjection to a foreign system, and it was in opposition to this domination, in opposition particularly to the purely Spanish tendencies of the rule of Philip II, that the national sentiment became more keenly aware of itself. It was fully awakened in the revolt in which all the seventeen provinces, with the single exception of Luxemburg, participated from 1576 on, under a States General meeting in a revolutionary fashion at Brussels.

Everybody knows that this union was broken up in the course of the resulting war and that only a group of Northern provinces achieved independence, becoming the Protestant Republic of the Seven United Provinces, while the Southern provinces were reduced to obedience and became, under the sovereignty of Spain, an advanced post of the great Counter-Reformation movement. Today the Dutch Kingdom is still preponderantly Protestant, or at least non-Catholic, and the Kingdom of Belgium homogeneously Catholic. The great question is: how did this separation, and how did this divergence in religion, come about?

There is one answer to this question which I am afraid is the one which will occur spontaneously to most of you. It is that it must have been because Protestantism steeled the Northern rebels—the Dutch—to a successful resistance, while the Southern rebels—the Belgians—being Catholics, did not have the heart to persevere in the struggle. It is the answer that is still to be found in innumerable English and American textbooks and that indeed until fairly recently used to be given, in various disguises, or to a greater or lesser extent attenuated or qualified, by both Dutch and Belgian historians. But it never agreed with the facts.

You should note, first of all, that at the outset, before opposition had developed into revolt and war had altered the face of things, the Protestants were not more numerous in the North than they were in the South (and everywhere they constituted no more than a small minority). When in 1576 all the provinces united against the King of Spain—by the so-called Pacification of Ghent—it was not long before in all of them, in the provinces of Flanders and Brabant no less than in the Northern provinces, the Protestant minority managed to get hold of the positions of power and actually were in command of the rebellion. How was this possible? For one thing, because the only armed force which was from the start at the disposal of the Prince of Orange, the Sea Beggars, had helped the Protestants into the saddle four years earlier in the Northwestern provinces of Holland and Zeeland. If they managed in 1572 to revolutionize those two provinces alone it was not because their inhabitants were so much readier to welcome them, but because their geographical position invited attack from oversea and their soil offered special advantages for defence against Spanish attempts at reconquest. These partisan bands were composed of the exiles of the abortive rebellious movement of 1566–7; they were drawn from all the provinces; and they were Protestants to a man. The rebellious spirit in the country, however, was by no means exclusively caused by the new religion. It was primarily due to the irritation of a people wedded to their medieval tradition of self-government at the relentless policy of centralization and autocracy pursued by the royal government. But the Protestant minority, placed in a position of power by the armed invaders in 1572, were the most determined, in fact irreconcilable, enemies of the King, and that was in itself another reason why they came to occupy the leading positions everywhere. Revolutions are always led by minorities, and so it was here. It had been so in Holland and Zeeland from 1572 on, and soon after 1576 in Brabant and Flanders as well the Protestants came to the top.

But now the Spanish Government had got another army ready, which under the Duke of Parma, from 1578 onward, set about conquering the rebellious Netherlands. This army started from the outlying province of Luxemburg and in the course of not very many years managed to reduce to obedience a considerable part of the country. The fall of Antwerp (the great commercial metropolis of the Netherlands at that time) in 1585 completed the conquest of Flanders and Brabant. But Parma also took the whole East, up to the extreme North; Groningen made its submission as early as 1580. In 1590 Parma's advance was definitely halted, and the rebels, reduced now to a small group of Northwestern provinces clustered round Holland, set in a counteroffensive, by which they recovered part of the ground lost.

The religious convictions of the populations had little to do with these movements of conquest and reconquest. One glance at the map will show you that Parma's farthest advance, about 1590, was bounded by the strong strategic barrier of the rivers traversing the Netherlands from East to West (the Rhine and the Maas) and by the river Ysel. How strong this barrier is we learned to our cost in September 1944, when Montgomery was held up at Arnhem and the liberation of exactly the same portion of the Netherlands—all the country north of the great rivers and west of the Ysel—was delayed by a terrible eight months. If Parma was never able to cross that barrier, if the rebels on the contrary were able to take the offensive and push him back, it was because he was ordered by Philip to intervene in the French civil war and had to divide his forces. The counteroffensive, led by Maurice of Orange, Wil-

liam the Silent's son, was again conditioned by the geographic factor. It was easy to recover the country east of the river Ysel, but not because the population there were in sympathy with their "deliverers." On the contrary they were overwhelmingly Catholic—much more so than Flanders and Brabant had been, although today that region, Groningen for instance, is solidly Protestant. But in those years the Groningers clung to the Spaniards as their protectors from the heretics. If they were "delivered," and then Protestantized, it was because the region was too far removed from the base of Spanish power in the South. To push on south of the great rivers, on the contrary, was a task beyond the power of Maurice. It would have meant a head-on attack on the main strength of the Spanish position.

Meanwhile, these military events were deciding the fates of the two religions contending for mastery. As soon as Parma and his Spaniards had recovered their hold on a district, Protestantism was strictly suppressed; most of the Protestants in fact emigrated—the majority settling in the provinces which were still holding out, in the North, that is, where they strengthened the Protestant element. The rebels, on their part, were all the time carrying on a reverse process of Protestantization, in which all means of pressure were used. This was a process, however, for which time was needed, and only where the rebellion survived for a generation or longer could the majority of the population be brought over to the new church.

The true explanation, then, of the division of the Netherlands into a Protestant North and a Catholic South is the exact opposite of the current one. It is not because the South was Catholic and the North Protestant that the rebellion failed here and succeeded there: it is because the rivers enabled the rebellion to entrench itself in the North, while Spain recovered the provinces situated on the wrong side of the strategic barrier, that in course of time there sprang into existence this dual system of the Protestant Northern Republic and the Catholic Southern Netherlands, of Protestant Holland and Catholic Belgium.

I have now given you, reduced to its simplest form, and somewhat dogmatically, an argument which I adumbrated for the first time more than thirty years ago and which I have since set out on many occasions, elaborating certain aspects of it or indicating its implications in connection with a variety of top-

The Eve of the Modern World

ics. Here I shall discuss something of the historiographical background to the conflicting views on this matter. I never discovered any new facts. The relevant facts were not unknown nor are they in dispute. Is it not remarkable, then, that historians both in Holland and Belgium either completely overlooked them, or at least gave them little attention, failed to draw the obvious conclusion, and commonly wrote as if the separation had been a perfectly natural event and the emergence of a Holland and a Belgium, the one Protestant and the other Catholic, was the consummation of divergent tendencies inherent in the history and character or civilization of the populations?

Seeley, in his little book on *The Growth of English Policy,* refers to "that curious sort of optimistic fatalism to which historians are liable" and which in England caused them to argue (as he puts it) "that the loss of our American colonies was not only inevitable, but was even a fortunate thing for us." It is in that spirit exactly that Simon Stijl, about 1770, in a popular one-volume *History of the United Netherlands,* wrote that "one of the principal causes to which our Republic owes its durability resides in its *correct size.* Had it been smaller, its neighbours would have despised it. Had it been larger, it would have become unmanageable." Remember that this "correct size" of the Republic of the Seven Provinces was less than one third of that of the single state of Pennsylvania. Remember also that this paean to its durability was written twenty-five years before it was overthrown for good and all by the armies of the French Revolutionary Republic. And in fact this was not the first occasion, nor was it to be the last, on which the break-up of the old seventeen Netherlands into two unrelated small states left both helpless in the face of foreign invasion.

Here is another example of the way in which historians dealt with the problem. In 1860 Fruin wrote: "It was no passing misunderstanding that brought about the separation; it was a profound difference between the northern and the southern provinces, in origin, in national character, . . . in religion. . . ."

Now, Fruin is a historian of a very different stamp from Stijl. He is the acknowledged master of the modern, methodical school in Holland, and his work is still very highly regarded. There is no glamour about Fruin. He is pre-eminently critical. He does not paint, he tries to explain. When he was a rising scholar, the reading public in Holland as well as in the rest of the world was captivated by the moving and colorful work of Motley. Fruin devoted to Motley's *The Rise of the Dutch Republic,* and later on to its sequel, two very long essays, small books really, very deferential in tone; but the effect of the story as told anew by the critic is to make the reader realize that Motley had sacrificed everything to his sense of the dramatic and that he had no real understanding of the problems of Dutch history. Today nobody—among Dutch or Belgian historians at least—will take Motley's views and explanations seriously any longer, but everybody will study Fruin's magisterial essays. It is all the more amazing, then, that a scholar of this calibre could go so utterly wrong in discussing the causes of the Netherlands split.

He says that it was due to *difference in origin.* Apparently he was thinking of the difference between the Dutch-speaking section and the Walloons. But the line of political separation did not follow the linguistic boundary. The fact that requires explanation on the contrary is the splitting-up of the Dutch-speaking population.

He says that it was due to *difference in religion.* But, as he knew very well, Protestantism was no less strong in the South than it was in the North. The homogeneous Catholicism of present-day Belgium and the preponderance of Protestantism in present-day Holland cannot have caused a sixteenth-century event.

He says that the separation was due to *difference in national character.* No more is needed to answer this than to quote another English historian, Maitland, who once described national character as "a wonder-working spirit, at the beck and call of every embarrassed historian, a sort of *deus ex machina,* which is invoked to settle any problem which cannot readily be solved by ordinary methods of rational investigation."

In the present case "rational investigation" will yield the solution readily enough, if only it is resorted to. But the most surprising thing of all is that Fruin never once mentions the Spaniards when enumerating the causes of the split. Antwerp held out for a year when Parma laid siege to it in 1584, and yet we find Fruin and a host of writers, both Dutch and Belgian, speaking as if the separation were due to mutual misunderstanding or incompatibility. . . .

The revolt and the separation in the late sixteenth

century form critical points in the debate outlined; and if time permitted it could be shown from Belgian writers as well as Dutch how other details came to be misrepresented under the influence of contemporary preoccupations. But it is obvious that the whole course of Netherlands history *before* the separation must present difficulties to anyone placing himself on the modern State point of view.

Yet this was generally done, and the first author to do it systematically and with really brilliant synthetic power, was Henri Pirenne, the first volume of whose *Histoire de Belgique* appeared in 1900. Here the past was uncompromisingly subjected to a conception inspired by the modern State. In his preface Pirenne announces quite plainly that it is his aim to bring out ''the character of unity presented by the older history of Belgium.'' Of Belgium? He means, of course, of the regions which were at one time, many centuries later, to constitute Belgium. For in the days of Caesar or of Charlemagne, or even of Philip the Good or Charles V, Belgium really was still far to seek. But Pirenne sees it coming all the time. He does not for a moment conceal the fact that we are in the presence here of an unusual phenomenon: the exchange of influence between, the gradual growing together into one nation of, Germanic and Romance populations, Flemings and Walloons. But he is all the time out to show how criss-cross connections, economic, political, social and cultural, led to a similarity of conditions and bound together the regions on either side of the linguistic boundary.

It is clear to me that there is a large element of artificiality in this conception of Pirenne's. Given the unmistakable present-day political inspiration, one would on general grounds expect this to be the case; but the imposing work actually abounds in passages, as well as in omissions, where the constructive intention can be seen to have done violence to the unruly multiplicity of historic reality. . . .

The most striking expression of these views is to be found in a little book, *Nederland en België*, published in 1905 by a young historian, Colenbrander, who was to be one of the leading men of his gener-

ation. It was inspired entirely by Pirenne. The Flemings, by Pirenne's theory, had been skillfully and unostentatiously detached from the Dutch, and had been safely, and to all outward seeming honorably, incorporated in a mystic Belgian unity stretching back into the remotest ages. It now remained for Dutch historiography to show that a similar unity had from ancient times embraced the regions which in the late sixteenth century came to constitute the Protestant Republic, forerunner of the contemporary Kingdom. What the argument required particularly was a demonstration of the original and innate difference that had caused Dutch and Flemings to diverge. Colenbrander found evidence in religious movements, in schools of painting, in architecture. The method has been applied many times since, by writers on art, on literature and on religion, and also by the political historians, to prove that a Dutch nation existed in the midst of the feudal confusion, or in a corner of the Burgundian-Hapsburg State, before ever a Dutch State had been born—a nation already complete with all the virtues which present-day Dutchmen love to regard as being their own: soberness and simplicity, a strong spiritual awareness under a reserved exterior, a nation, in short, of regular little Calvinists before ever Calvinism had been thought of.

How easy a game it is! The civilization of the medieval Netherlands was a rich one and richly diversified; features to suit a particular argument can always be discovered and, if isolated and arranged in a certain way, can be used to produce the desired impression. How easy a game, but how unprofitable! These ingenious speculations might have some interest if the separation of the sixteenth century had indeed been a voluntary one. The assumption that this is so underlies the whole argument of Colenbrander, just as it did that amazing passage of Fruin. Like Fruin, Colenbrander seems to forget about Parma and his Spanish army; and although I have always been ready to meet the speculators on their own ground, the recollection of the way in which things actually came to pass in the sixteenth-century war of liberation and reconquest is enough to brush their fallacies aside as so many cobwebs.

CHRISTOPHER HILL

THE "PURITAN REVOLUTION":
A SUMMARY OF REVISION

The politico-religious doctrines of Calvinism came to the British Isles largely through the agency of John Knox who brought Presbyterianism to Scotland by way of Geneva and the Marian exiles, those English Protestants who had fled their country during the brief Catholic revival of Mary Tudor's reign, who had been deeply affected by Calvinist influences during the exile, and who returned to England under Elizabeth as the Puritans, the most familiar label for the English Calvinists. Their strength and their explosive religious doctrines grew through the long reign of Elizabeth to become the major force in the civil war which came under her Stuart successors, which took the life of a king, which for a generation established a Protestant "Rule of Saints," and which ended in the Stuart restoration.

The above is a sketch of the conventional thesis that the English civil war was a "Puritan Revolution." Its greatest exponent was the nineteenth century English historian Samuel R. Gardiner whose many books—including a ten-volume *History of England from the Accession of James I to the Outbreak of the Civil War*—and whose awesome archival research gave to his position a seemingly unassailable orthodoxy. But the forces of historical revision are irreverent and twentieth-century scholars have assailed the unassailable. Of all the facets of the general problem we have dealt with, none has been more besieged by revision than that of the English Puritan Revolution. And in no area has the revision been more subtle and sophisticated. In view of the complexity of the interpretations the following selection has been chosen, the chapter entitled "Recent Interpretations of the Civil War," from *Puritanism and Revolution* by Christopher Hill. It is precisely what its title claims, a summary statement of recent scholarship on the problem written by one of the most eminent authorities on the subject.

The student should not only follow these arguments with reference to their specific subject but should attempt to apply them, where they are applicable, to the parallel problems of continental Calvinism and revolution.

In 1913 R. G. Usher wrote: "The English Revolution of 1640 is as much an enigma today as it was to Charles. It is a riddle which has to be solved. No one has tried to solve it because all assumed it was solved by repeating the Grand Remonstrance. Every Englishman born since 1800 has . . . been born into a view of English history."[1]

Anyone who has studied the pages of the *Economic History Review* recently will agree that the English Revolution is still an enigma, though not now be-

[1] R. G. Usher, *The Historical Method of S. R. Gardiner*, p. 156.

cause historians repeat the Grand Remonstrance. One school of thought appears to believe (roughly) that the revolution was caused by the rise of the gentry during the century before 1640. Another school believes (roughly) that it was caused by that section of the gentry which was declining during the same period. The subscriber pays his guinea and takes his choice. The object of this essay is to take stock of the present state of the controversy over the causes of the civil war.

We have to start with Gardiner. His eighteen volumes on the history of England between 1603 and 1656, supplemented by Firth's *Last Years of the Protectorate*, established fifty years ago an interpretation of the civil war as "the Puritan Revolution," a struggle for religious and constitutional liberty. Gardiner's immense learning and mastery of the then available sources, his narrative gifts and his knack of hitting on the telling quotation—all this has made his authority very difficult to overthrow.

Yet Usher long ago pointed out Gardiner's bewildering eclecticism of method; and the case against Gardiner has been reinforced by much detailed research published since he wrote, especially in the field of economic history. A. P. Newton's *Colonizing Activities of the Early Puritans* showed that Pym and many of the Long Parliament's leaders had important trading connections. J. U. Nef's *Rise of the British Coal Industry*, and other works by Nef himself, Wadsworth and Mann, Ramsay, Dobb, Court and others have established the existence of something like an industrial revolution in the century before 1640. Professor Tawney's *The Agrarian Problem of the Sixteenth Century*, Professor Arkhangelsky's two volumes on *The Agrarian Legislation of the English Revolution* (in Russian) and Mrs. Thirsk's articles[2] have revealed agrarian problems whose depth Gardiner does not seem to have suspected. All these works—and many more could be cited—suggest that far more importance should be given to economic developments in preparing for civil war than Gardiner allowed. Moreover, Professor Tawney's *Religion and the Rise of Capitalism*, popularizing a great deal of German work on that sub-

ject, stated a connection between Puritanism and the rise of capitalism which most historians would now accept, even if they differed about which was cause and which effect. It is difficult to go on speaking about "the Puritan Revolution" *tout court*.

Finally, since the publication of Professor Namier's great works on eighteenth-century politics, historians have got into the habit of asking new questions. They have become more interested in the "connections," whether of patronage or economic interest, of historical characters, than in their proclaimed political principles. The "Namier method" has already been extended forward to analyse nineteenth-century parliaments and back to the fifteenth century. The witenagemot still awaits Namierization: not so the Long Parliament.

Today, then, the "Puritan Revolution" is in eclipse, though many of its assumptions still haunt our thinking. The view which explains the civil war as a struggle for liberty is little more acceptable to historians trained to ask "liberty for whom to do what?" It is a question to which many answers can be given. Liberty for witch-hunters to burn witches, and liberty for wicked capitalists to grind the faces of the poor, have been two of the simpler and least convincing, which I shall not be discussing.

In many ways the reaction against Gardiner has been healthy. "The Puritan Revolution" was a nineteenth-century invention: there is virtue in going back to explanations current in the seventeenth and eighteenth centuries. Men so diverse in their political outlook as Winstanley, Harrington, Hobbes, Baxter, Clarendon, all explained the civil war in terms of social forces which we are today less likely to dismiss than Gardiner was.[3] We hardly need to be reminded, in this ideological age, that there were more reasons than religious conviction for supporting a "protestant" foreign policy which expressed itself in war to open up the Spanish empire to English trade; that a greedy citizen of London might object to paying tithes no less than a pious Quaker; we observe remarks like that of the servant giving notice: "I would have the liberty of my conscience, not to be catechized in the principles of religion,"[4] because we now realize that the liberating effects of

[2] Mrs. Thirsk has shown that large numbers of royalists regained their confiscated estates even before 1660 ("The Sales of Royalist Land during the Interregnum," *Economic History Review*, Second Series, V, pp. 188–207; "The Restoration Land Settlement," *Journal of Modern History*, XXVI, pp. 315–28). Space has not permitted a discussion of this very important contribution, which must modify our view of the Restoration.

[3] But Gardiner had his moments of insight. Cf. his excellent analysis of the social function of Scottish Presbyterianism in his *History of the Great Civil War* (1901), I, pp. 226–8.

[4] T. Edwards, *Gangraena* (1646), p. 138.

toleration extended beyond the purely religious sphere.

But many of the reactions against Gardiner have so far been rather negative. To be told that many of those whom we call "Presbyterians" opposed the establishment of a Presbyterian church in England, and that many of those whom we call "Independents" were Presbyterian elders,[5] is helpful in so far as it stops us thinking of the two great parties as primarily religious groupings. But that is only half our problem. Gardiner's interpretation of the English Revolution will no longer do: yet no alternative interpretation has yet acquired general acceptance, and none has been put forward, in this country, which can compare with Gardiner's in scope and solidity.[6] It is noteworthy that in the *Oxford* and the *Penguin Histories of England* the volumes dealing with this period are among the least satisfactory in the series. They have not escaped from Gardiner, though they supply the evidence for showing that his (and their) interpretation is no longer convincing.

II

Professor Tawney came nearest to establishing a new orthodoxy, especially in his still unpublished Ford Lectures of 1936, and in "The Rise of the Gentry" (*Economic History Review*, XI, No. 1) and *Harrington's Interpretation of his Age* (*Raleigh Lecture*, 1941). Professor Tawney's views are familiar and easily accessible, so I shall not attempt to summarize them: they amount to an adaptation of Harrington's theory that the civil war was fought to redress the balance of property which had been upset by the redistribution of land in the century before 1640. This position seemed to be strengthened by an article by Mr. Stone, "An Anatomy of the Elizabethan Aristocracy," which suggested that a majority of the peerage was heavily indebted by the end of Elizabeth's reign, and was saved only by subsidies from her successor. Mr. Stone's figures, however, were criticized by Professor Trevor-Roper, and Mr. Stone himself modified some of his original statements, though he did not abandon his general argument.[7]

In 1953 Professor Trevor-Roper produced his own rival interpretation. Criticizing Professor Tawney's use of the concept "gentry," he argued that the civil war was caused not by the rise but by the decline of a section of the gentry. The really big profits in the century before 1640 were made not by farming but by holding court office, by the practice of the law, or by taking part in industry or trade. The "mere gentry," those who enjoyed none of these alternative sources of income, inevitably got into financial difficulties.[8] They struggled to get positions at court. Essex's revolt in 1601, and Gunpowder Plot in 1605, are to be seen as desperate attempts by the "outs" to get "in."[9] So apparently is the civil war. Professor Trevor-Roper explains that as a gentleman became impoverished, he retired to his estates and set about economic reorganization. For this he needed "an ideology of economy, of retrenchment." Such an ideology he found either in Roman Catholicism or in extreme Puritanism. His adherence to either of these beliefs would complete his isolation from the Court and strengthen the bonds between himself and others of his like who had been through similar experiences. Independency and Roman Catholicism are both creeds of the declining gentry.[10]

A summary so bald cannot do justice to the vigour and cogency with which Professor Trevor-Roper argues his case. He has certainly established the need for more, and more reliable, statistics before we can safely generalize about "the gentry" in this period. He has performed a useful service in emphasizing the importance of court office as a source of windfall profits for the fortunate few. Nevertheless, on balance, I do not myself feel happy about the thesis as a whole. . . .

Even if we could accept the equation of Independents with declining gentlemen, it would not help us to explain the civil war. For when the war began the men in control at Westminster were not those whom we call Independents, and certainly not declining gentlemen; they were great peers like Warwick, Essex, Manchester (the last named a *court* peer who had bought out the declining *Royalist* Cromwell); Hampden, the richest commoner in England; Pym,

---

[5] J. H. Hexter, "The Problem of the Presbyterian Independents," *American Historical Review*, XLIV, pp. 29–49.

[6] The only one known to me is a two-volume collective work published in the U.S.S.R. in 1954 entitled *The English Bourgeois Revolution of the 17th century*, whose 800 large pages interpret the revolution in Marxist terms as "one of the most important turning-points in English, European, and world history."

[7] *Econ. H. R.*, XVIII, Nos. 1 and 2; *Second Series*, III, No. 3; IV, No. 3.

[8] H. R. Trevor-Roper, *The Gentry, 1540–1640* (*Econ. H. R. Supplement*), pp. 24–31.

[9] *Ibid.*, pp. 32, 38–42.

[10] *Ibid.*, p. 31.

government employee and treasurer of a City company; Holles, son of a gentleman rich enough to buy an earldom. When the Five Members escaped from the King's attempt to arrest them in January 1642, they did not flee to the backwoods: they retired to the City of London, where they were warmly welcomed. The civil war might not have been won without the Independents, but they did not start it. Professor Trevor-Roper speaks always of Presbyterians and Royalists as though they were "on the same side,"[11] which is absurd in the years before 1647.

But the point at which Professor Trevor-Roper's analysis seems to me least satisfactory of all is his attitude to religion. For him the economic needs of a declining gentleman might be expressed either by Roman Catholicism or by Independency, and it seems to have been of no significance which of the two he happened to take up. For the declining gentry were behind all the political upheavals of the early seventeenth century—Essex's revolt, Gunpowder Plot, 1642. Even if this thesis fitted the English facts (which it does not), it would still be intolerably provincial. For over a century before 1640 men all over Europe had been suffering, dying, and killing for what they held to be high ideals; from the sixteen-twenties a great war was being waged on the Continent over ideological issues which aroused the intensest excitement in England and created a profound cleavage of opinon about questions of foreign policy. Professor Trevor-Roper asks us to see in all this only a reflection of the financial difficulties of a section of the English gentry. The spiritual wrestlings of a Milton, a Vane, a Roger Williams are nothing but the epiphenomena of economic decline. The idea is difficult to discuss seriously. Only three brief points may be made. First, if we are to look for causal connections between recusancy and economic decline, it is surely less likely that a gentleman turned Catholic because of poverty than that his poverty was caused by recusancy fines. Secondly, radical Puritanism is specifically associated by contemporaries with the towns, as indeed similar creeds had been all over Europe since Calvin's day. Thirdly, one of the few generalizations we can make about the civil war is that Catholics and Independents were on opposite sides. So if they were both declining gentlemen fighting to get back to the spoils of office, both "outs" trying to become "ins," on which side were the "ins"? Perhaps they were the Clubmen, the only neutralist party?

[11] Op. cit., pp. 33–4, 42–3, 53.

III

Professor Trevor-Roper has had second thoughts on the Independents, published in a brilliantly argued essay on "Oliver Cromwell and his Parliaments."[12] In this "the Independents" are divided into two sharply contrasted categories. The first is "the Whigs" —men like Hesilrige, Scot, Bradshaw, Slingsby Bethel. These are in fact those whom most of us regard as the main parliamentary leaders of the Independents, though for Professor Trevor-Roper they have now become "the republican usurpers." The second category comprises "those ordinary Independent gentry whom Cromwell represented," the back-benchers and the officers.[13] This distinction has validity: but what remains now of the thesis that it was the Independents, the declining gentry, "who made the revolution"? To define the Independents proper in such a way as to exclude the majority in the Rump, and simultaneously to attribute the making of the revolution to them, is like saying that the French Revolution was "made" by those Jacobins who were to support Napoleon after 1802. How many of those now claimed as the real Independents even sat in Parliament before 1645? It surprises Professor Trevor-Roper, but need surprise no one else, that those who sought to create "an Independent political caucus" for Cromwell in the Parliaments after the expulsion of the Rump "were not real Independents but, all of them, ex-royalists"—Ashley-Cooper, Wolseley, Broghill.[14] A "real" Independent is clearly a rare bird. It seems to me that in refining and improving his definition to suit his argument Professor Trevor-Roper has destroyed his own thesis about the causes of the civil war. . . .

IV

Another recent work which discusses the line-up in the civil war is that of Messrs. Brunton and Pennington, *Members of the Long Parliament*. This book has been rightly praised by many reviewers, and it contains a wealth of valuable information. If I dwell on what seem to me its less satisfactory aspects it is, first, because I believe some reviewers have claimed

[12] In *Essays Presented to Sir Lewis Namier* (ed. R. Pares and A. J. P. Taylor), pp. 1–48. On p. 28 Professor Trevor-Roper is mistaken in saying that the Instrument of Government preserved the old property qualifications.

[13] *Ibid.*, pp. 16, 20, 45–6; cf. Professor Trevor-Roper in *Annales* (1956), p. 493.

[14] *Ibid.*, pp. 18, 46–7. Wolseley was born in 1630.

too much for it (indeed, more than its authors would); secondly, because I believe harm may be done if it is too easily assumed that its negative conclusions are irrefutable; and thirdly because I believe methodological considerations of some importance for future work on the subject are involved.[15]

The authors analysed the personnel of the Long Parliament, and asked themselves whether this analysis threw light on the causes of the civil war. Their conclusions were entirely negative. Gentlemen, lawyers, and merchants were found among M.P.s on either side. The only significant difference was that the average age of Royalist M.P.s was thirty-six, that of their opponents forty-seven. Therefore, the authors concluded, attempts to explain the civil war in terms of class divisions are unfounded.

This conclusion may be criticized on two grounds. First, I believe the facts have in certain important respects been incorrectly interpreted; secondly, even if the interpretation were correct, the conclusion would not follow.

(I) Even on Messrs. Brunton and Pennington's own analysis, significant differences between the two groups of M.P.s can be seen. Though there were merchants on either side, they were not equally divided. Of the London merchants elected to the House of Commons, the twelve monopolists were expelled; in the civil war they naturally supported the court through which their profits had come. Of the remaining nineteen London merchants, eighteen were Parliamentarians. The one exception, George Lowe, held estates in Wiltshire and was connected by marriage with Edward Hyde.[16] Provincial merchants were more equally divided. But in the Eastern Association merchants were solidly Parliamentarian, and even in the Royalist-occupied areas a small majority among the merchant M.P.s had the courage to declare for Parliament.[17] The authors did not ask how many of the Royalist merchants were royal officials like the customs farmer and Duchy of Lancaster official who were returned for the borough of Lancaster, presumably thanks to Duchy pressure. Nor did they ask how many were members of urban governing oligarchies maintained in their privileged

position by the royal charters which the Levellers and Diggers wanted to abolish. The Royalist M.P.s Hooke and Long "represented actually the merchant oligarchy of Bristol,"[18] a city in which, Sir Samuel Luke was told in 1643, "they are all Roundheads . . . except the major and 2 or 3 aldermen."[19]

Similarly, to say that the numbers of gentlemen on either side were roughly equal does not get us very far. The authors warn against the dangers of dividing the landed from the mercantile interest, especially in the clothing counties.[20] But should we not attempt to divide *within* the landed interest? The economic life of most gentlemen in Cumberland or Wales was very different from that of gentlemen in Norfolk or Surrey. Messrs. Brunton and Pennington brush aside altogether too lightly the distinction between the economically-advanced south and east of the country, which was Parliamentarian, and the economically-backward north and west, which was Royalist. Mr. Pennington admits that "a study of how the estates of landed members were managed might reveal an economic line of cleavage corresponding to the political one."[21] Until this question has been investigated it is premature to tell us what the answer to it is.

The authors also note that

among county families it is easier to find Parliamentarian than Royalist members who were exploiting local assets and opportunities. More characteristic of the Royalists are the supplementary sources of income that could be picked up through connections at the court and in the capital.[22]

This contrast between local economic activity (whether in industry or agriculture) and the economic parasitism of the Court would be a profitable field of research for those looking for divisions between M.P.s (and among the gentry as a whole). And were such activities only local? Mrs. Keeler notes some 60 M.P.s known to have been members of trading companies, and there were no doubt many more:

---

[15] See a review of *Members of the Long Parliament* by B. Manning in *Past and Present*, No. 5 (1954) and a discussion between Messrs. Manning and Pennington in *ibid.*, No. 6.

[16] Keeler, *op. cit.*, pp. 257–8.

[17] Brunton and Pennington, *op. cit.*, p. 62.

[18] Keeler, *op. cit.*, pp. 47, 53.

[19] Ed. I. G. Philip, *Journal of Sir Samuel Luke* (Oxfordshire Record Society), p. 218; cf. the similar remarks in John Corbet's *Historical Relation of the Military Government of Gloucester* (1645), in *Bibliotheca Gloucestrensis* (1823), I, p. 14.

[20] Brunton and Pennington, *op. cit.*, p. 73.

[21] *Past and Present*, No. 6, p. 88. This most important reservation was mentioned in the last dozen lines of *Members of the Long Parliament*.

[22] Brunton and Pennington, *op. cit.*, pp. 166–7.

The "Puritan Revolution": A Summary of Revision   335

most of them seem to have been Parliamentarians.[23] A thorough exploration of all these business activities, central and local, might even help us towards answering Messrs. Brunton and Pennington's rhetorical question: "What is it that makes one great grandson of a Tudor copyholder or a Tudor judge a progressive bourgeois and another a feudal aristocrat?"[24] We are at least more likely to find the answer here than in even the most exhaustive examination of members' pedigrees. Independency, the authors note, was strong among M.P.s from the clothing counties: it was weakest in the north and west.[25]

Further, to divide members of the House of Commons into two parties, labelled "Royalist" and "Parliamentarian," and then to treat all members of the two groups as statistically equivalent, is misleading. Side by side with men prepared to sacrifice property to principle, like Henry Marten or Sir Bevil Grenville, our authors perforce list the marginal turncoat on either side who had no principles at all. They were aware of the dangers here, and they may be right in arguing that no other division was possible. But statistics so compiled are of highly dubious value. Mr. Pennington recognizes that "the crucial problem" is the M.P.s who were firm opponents of Strafford (and, we might add, continued to oppose the Court throughout 1641) and yet fought for the King.[26] Mrs. Keeler's book shows the very large number of M.P.s who no doubt owed their place in the Commons to their opposition to the government and yet ultimately changed sides. Nineteen Cornish M.P.s swung over to the King between the summer of 1642 and the end of 1643.[27]

There might be many reasons for this: fear of the consequences of treason;[28] fear for the safety of one's estates; alarm at social disorder (anti-enclosure riots, refusal of rents, pressure of London citizens on M.P.s, "mechanick preachers"). . . .

Another reason for changing sides might be the possession of estates in areas occupied by the royal forces. Something approaching 100 M.P.s who transferred their support to the King after 1642 came from areas controlled by Royalist armies in the early stages of the war. . . .

As in dealing with Professor Trevor-Roper's views about management of the Commons, so here we are faced with the larger question of the applicability of "the Namier method" to periods of acute political crisis. The method was originally devised to illuminate English politics at the accession of George III. It would be difficult to find a period in the whole of English history when the political nation was more "at one in all fundamental matters." It was therefore legitimate to apply a technique of analysis which ignored political principles, or treated them as rationalizations of economic or other interests. But if we go even a few years forward—to the Wilkes question—or a few years back—to the Jacobites, to 1688—principles begin to rear their inconvenient heads.[29] Here the Namier method is of more limited value, as its author specifically warned. Messrs. Brunton and Pennington analyse their M.P.s into family groupings, local groupings, economic groupings, patronage groupings, age groupings. (It may reasonably be argued that family and regional groupings were also economic groupings more often than Messrs. Brunton and Pennington recognize.[30]) But none of their groups are united by ideas. Yet there was in the House of Commons a group of republicans; perhaps some M.P.s even took their religion seriously enough to work together with men of like convictions?[31]

About the relation of M.P.s to the electorate questions must also be asked which would have been less relevant in 1760. Politics then was what went on at Westminster. But a civil war by definition transcends the limits of the old governmental institutions. The war was maintained not so much by the 500 M.P.s as by the citizens of London, Hull, Gloucester, Plymouth; by the freeholders of Buckinghamshire riding up to London to defend John Hampden; by the russet-coated captains of Cromwell's Ironsides; by the members of the sectarian congregations. Even if Messrs. Brunton and Pennington had established (as they have not) that there

[23] Keeler, op. cit., pp. 25, 30; Brunton and Pennington, op. cit., pp. 162–4.

[24] Ibid., p. 178

[25] Ibid., pp. 43–4.

[26] Past and Present, No. 6, p. 87.

[27] R. N. Worth, Buller Papers, p. viii.

[28] See a discussion of this point between the Oxinden cousins in The Oxinden Letters, 1607–43 (ed. D. Gardiner), pp. 308–9.

[29] I owe this point, as so much more, to discussions with Professor Richard Pares.

[30] Keeler, op. cit., p. 30; Manning, Past and Present, No. 5, p. 72.

[31] "Mr. Pennington finds it difficult to understand the division into the parties in the Commons because he ignores the ideas that underlie it" (Manning, Past and Present, No. 6, p. 90.)

were no significant economic divisions between M.P.s on the two sides, they would have proved very little about the division in the country. The House of Commons was elected on the same franchise as had prevailed since 1430: naturally men of the same social types as in previous Parliaments were returned. Parliament contained a cross-section of the ruling class. The two houses were divided because the ruling class was divided. What needs analysis, if we are to understand the civil war, is the exact nature of this division; and, secondly, its relation to division in the country at large and in the electorate.

How did any particular M.P. get into Parliament? The contestants at Great Marlow were all gentlemen, but they represented such different interests that we need different categories to place them in. Whitelocke and Hoby "stood for the liberty of the commons in the election," with the support of shopkeepers and labourers as well as of the burgesses and "the ordinary sort of townsmen"; their opponent John Borlace, son-in-law of Attorney-General Bankes, was a great local landowner. Men feared that "if they left Mr. Borlace out . . . he would not let them buy any wood of him, but do them many ill turns." Bankes had to give Borlace the seat for his borough of Corfe Castle, vacated by the expulsion of Windebanke from the Commons.[32] In Essex "it was said amongst the people that if Nevill [the royalist candidate] had the day they would tear the gentlemen to pieces." The victorious candidates were of course also gentlemen: but gentlemen clearly with a difference. The defeated candidate thought that the 40s. freehold qualifications should be raised to £20. "Then gentlemen would be looked up to."[33] The only Royalist returned from Northamptonshire was M.P. for Higham Ferrers, a borough in the Queen's jointure.[34] In general it was a Royalist commonplace that corporations were "nurseries of schism and rebellion." Messrs. Brunton and Pennington give away a larger point than they appear to realize when they admit that, at the time of Pride's Purge, "in the country generally there were undoubtedly the beginnings of a resistance by the small men, the propertyless and the oppressed," but "little sign of a class division" in Parliament.[35] This means either that Pride's Purge bore no relation to events in the country, or that Messrs. Brunton and Pennington are looking for the wrong sort of connections.

V

Fortunately Mr. Pennington too has had second thoughts, or rather has pressed his investigations beyond Westminster into the depths of the country. The simultaneous publication in 1957 of excellent studies of the county committees of Staffordshire and Kent has very sensibly added to our understanding of social divisions in the provinces.[36] In each county two parties appeared in the course of the civil war. The compromise-peace party drew its main strength from the old ruling families, concerned primarily with the preservation of their property and dominant influence. The win-the-war party, in each county, was led by members of leading families who were directly engaged in military operations, but in general its members were of markedly lower social origin. Inevitably it looked to London for a national lead and a national military organization. Religious radicals gravitated towards this group, but the conflict within county committees, which corresponds to the national rivalry between Presbyterians and Independents, was not primarily religious. Originally a dispute about military tactics, it soon revealed itself as also a social quarrel. The old ruling families were ousted from control of both counties in the middle sixteen-forties. . . .

The civil war, then, cannot be explained merely by looking at M.P.s. Men did not die and kill one another for four years over issues which can be satisfactorily analysed by a method evolved for a period in which there were no serious political disagreements. The civil war was fought about issues of principle which roused large numbers of men to heroic activity and sacrifice. To say that account should be taken of these issues need not lead us back to Gardiner's conception of "the Puritan Revolution."

The methods, the techniques of analysis employed by Messrs. Brunton and Pennington, and by Mr.

[32] M. R. Frear, "The Election at Great Marlow in 1640," *Journal of Modern History*, XIV, No. 4, pp. 437–45; Brunton and Pennington, *op. cit.*, p. 167.

[33] *C.S.P. Dom.*, 1639–40, pp. 608–9. The writer added that raising the franchise "would save the ministers a great deal of pains in preaching [away] from their own churches"—an interesting side-light on the political role of the pulpit.

[34] Keeler, *op. cit.*, p. 57; cf. p. 64.

[35] Brunton and Pennington, *op. cit.*, p. 182.

[36] Ed. D. H. Pennington and I. A. Roots, *The Committee at Stafford, 1643–5*; A. M. Everitt, *The County Committee of Kent in the Civil War*.

Stone and Professor Trevor-Roper, seem to me in danger of giving a false emphasis which, unless very great care is taken to guard against it, would render their interpretations as lop-sided as Gardiner's, though on the opposite side. By their exclusive concentration on interests, whether economic, geographical, or those of patronage, the impression is given that all politics is a dirty game, struggles for the spoils of office, the "ins" versus the "outs," that principles are merely rationalizations. I do not believe that material conflicts are the only ones deserving serious analysis. This approach indeed brings its own refutation. The civil war did, after all, take place, but Messrs. Brunton and Pennington supply no adequate explanation of that fact. Professor Trevor-Roper has to dismiss as "futile" the deliberate waging of war for trade, colonies and markets by the Commonwealth and Protectorate.[37] Yet these policies were to be followed by successive governments for the next 175 years. The men of undeniable political principle, whose theories of democracy inspired the American revolutionaries, the Radicals and Chartists, and are still alive today, he dismisses as "the lunatic fringe," who were able to become vocal only because of the degeneration of politics after 1643. This is not dealing very seriously with history.

VI

An earnest evangelical once expostulated with Baring-Gould about the chorus of "Onward Christian Soldiers." Dangerous concessions to ritualism, he thought, were made in the words

With the cross of Jesus/Going on before.

Baring-Gould accepted the criticism with due solemnity, and suggested that the low church gentleman might prefer to sing

With the cross of Jesus/Left behind the door.

"The Puritan Revolution" is dead and buried, and I do not want to resurrect it; but need Puritanism be left altogether behind the door? The importance of economic issues has been established; but we still have to find a synthesis which will take cognizance of this and yet give some explanation of why in 1640 not only M.P.s but a large number of other people thought bishops the main enemy; why there were so many conflicts before 1640 over the

appointment of lecturers in town corporations; why, when the troops got drunk of a Saturday night in 1640, their animal spirits were worked off in the destruction of altar rails; why Cromwell's Army marched into battle singing psalms.

The following points, I would suggest, will have to be included in our ultimate synthesis:

(i) A much more serious study needs to be made of the political effects of the "industrial revolution" of the century before 1640. Professor Nef's valuable suggestions in his *Rise of the British Coal Industry* have not been properly followed up. The struggle over monopolies was not only of financial and constitutional importance; it was also of the greatest consequence for the future of capitalism in industry that there should be freedom of economic development. Further knowledge here might help us to a clearer understanding of the support which towns (except sometimes their ruling oligarches) and the rural industrial areas gave to the parliamentary cause.

(ii) When Dr. Valerie Pearl's eagerly awaited thesis on the City of London is published, we shall have a clearer picture of politics there in the crucial years 1640–3. We shall know more about the links between the ruling oligarchy of aldermen and the Court, which made the City government Royalist, and isolated it from the majority of the Common Council and of City voters, who were radical Parliamentarians: and about the fierce conflicts which led to the violent overthrow of the royalist clique in the winter of 1641, just in time to make the City a safe refuge for the Five Members. But more work is still needed on London politics after 1643, and on political struggles in other towns.

(iii) We should also, I believe, look more closely at colonial and imperial policies. Since Newton's book we all recognize the crucial importance of the Providence Island Company, but this was after all one of the smaller companies. The full political effect of disputes over colonial questions on the origin and progress of the revolution has never been fully worked out.[38] But when we find the Witney blanket-makers asking the House of Lords in 1641 to protect the rights and privileges of the Royal

---

[37] Trevor-Roper, *The Gentry*, p. 43.

[38] Cf. Manning, *Past and Present*, No. 5, p. 71. There are some valuable chapters on this subject in the Russian work quoted on p. 6, n. 2 above.

Africa Company, we can image how many people's lives were already affected by freedom of export.[39]

(iv) Professor Campbell and Dr. Hoskins have directed our attention to the rising yeoman;[40] but there has been no full analysis of his economic problems in relation to government policy, nor of those of the small clothiers and artisans generally. Yet traditionally these classes are believed to have formed the backbone of the New Model Army, and most contemporaries agree in putting them solidly on the parliamentary side, at least in the south and east. There is a danger that in riveting our attention on the gentry we may underestimate social groups which were at least of equal importance once the old stable social structure began to crumble, and whose grievances helped to make it crumble.

(v) This brings us to a subject one mentions with diffidence — the people of England. Gardiner and the Whigs often assumed too lightly that Parliament represented "the people," that it is easy to know what "the people" wanted. But the modern tendency is again to throw the baby out with the bath water, and to leave out of account those who actually fought the civil war. Tenants no doubt often turned out to fight as their landlords told them, London demonstrations could be organized, the rank and file of the New Model Army were not all as politically sophisticated as the Agitators. Granting this, the evidence still suggests that in 1640 there was a real popular hostility to the old régime whose depth and intensity needs analysis and explanation, and whose influence on the course of events after 1640 we almost certainly tend to underestimate. The consumers and craftsmen who suffered from the high prices caused by monopolies, the peasants whom Laud's good intentions failed to protect,[41] and who thought the time had come to throw down enclosures in 1640–1; the ordinary citizens who resisted the Laudian attempt to increase tithe pay-

ments; the small men for whom the parson of the established church (*any* established church) was "Public Enemy No. 1"; the members of the sectarian congregations of the sixteen-forties and -fifties whose naïve but daring speculations have still to be properly studied in their social setting[42] — it was these men, not M.P.s or "the gentry," rising or declining, who bore the brunt of the civil war. It would also be interesting to have studies of those who fought for the King. But I suspect that in the Royalist areas the traditional "feudal" machinery still worked, landlords brought out their tenants, the militia was officered by the gentry of the county. The New Model was an army of a new type.

(vi) On the gentry, let us admit that we still do not know enough. I personally believe that the contemporary analyses of Winstanley, Harrington, Hobbes, Baxter, and Clarendon are still the safest guides, and that Professor Tawney is more right than Professor Trevor-Roper. But we should stop generalizing about "the gentry." Professor Trevor-Roper himself points out the regional differences which made a gentleman with £150 a year in Devon comparable with one who had far more in the home counties.[43] We also need to know more about different types of estate management and leasing policies, about investments in trade and industry, before we can begin to see the way in which the rise of capitalism was dividing the gentry into different economic classes. We need more studies of individual families like Dr. M. Finch's admirable *The Wealth of Five Northamptonshire Families, 1540–1640;*[44] more documents like those of the Herbert and Percy families edited respectively by Dr. Kerridge and Mr. James.[45] We also need more regional inquiries like those of Professor Dodd and Messrs. Everitt and Pennington and Roots, and local documents like the minutebook of Bedford Corporation. Such local studies will divert us from exclusive attention to the small group of men at Westminster, and help us to see the deeper social currents on which the politicians were floating.

---

[39] *Victoria County History of Oxfordshire*, II, pp. 247–8. Viscount Wenman, whose family had risen to a peerage through the Witney wool trade, represented Oxfordshire in the Long Parliament.

[40] M. Campbell, *The English Yeoman*; W. G. Hoskins, *Essays in Leicestershire History*.

[41] It is significant that when the Levellers, the party of the small men, were using every stick to beat the Parliamentarian leaders, even going so far as to say that England used to be merrier before the Reformation, they never, to the best of my knowledge, argued that things had been better under Laud and Charles I. If the prosperity and "social justice" of the sixteen-thirties had had any reality for the small men, it is very unlikely that they would not have used this argument.

[42] But cf. P. Zagorin, *A History of Political Thought in the English Revolution*.

[43] *The Gentry*, p. 52.

[44] Publications of the Northhamptonshire Record Society, Vol. XIX (1956).

[45] Ed. E. Kerridge, *Surveys of the Manors of Philip, First Earl of Pembroke and Montgomery, 1631–2* (Wilts. Archaeological and Natural History Society, Records Branch, Vol. IX, 1953); ed. M. E. James, *Estate Accounts of the Earls of Northumberland, 1562–1637* (Surtees Society, Vol. CLXIII, 1955).

(vii) Professor Trevor-Roper has done a great service in drawing our attention to the significance of control of the state. But this was not important merely as a source of spoils, of windfall wealth for individuals. The state was an instrument of economic power, maintaining monopolists and customs farmers, fining enclosers, endangering property by arbitrary taxation; in different hands the same instrument was used to confiscate and sell land, to pass the Navigation Act which challenged the Dutch to fight for the trade of the world, to conquer Ireland and grab Spanish colonies. Yet the relation of individuals and groups to the state power still needs fuller investigation.

(viii) We also need far more understanding of ideas, especially at the point where they interact with economics. Over twenty years ago Mr. Wagner wrote a fascinating article on "Coke and the Rise of Economic Liberalism."[46] This line of thought needs fuller working out; it may prove as important as that summarized in Professor Tawney's *Religion and the Rise of Capitalism*. Contemporaries were influenced by legal theories little less than by religion: Lilburne held the Bible in one hand, Coke in the other. It is therefore important to take legal history out of the hands of the lawyers, as religious history has been taken away from the theologians, and to relate both to social development. Law deals with property relations, and liberty and property were the two things most strongly and consistently emphasized in the Long Parliament in 1640–1. The fact that after 1640 (and after 1660) Sir Edward Coke was regarded as *the* legal authority, whereas before 1640 his writings were suppressed by the government, shows the importance of clarity about the exact relation of his legal doctrine to the social and economic changes of the seventeenth century.

(ix) Finally, questions of religion and church govern-

ment should not be "left behind the door." We must have a better explanation of their importance for contemporaries than the theory that Puritanism helps landowners to balance their income and expenditure, or encourages the bourgeoisie to grind the faces of the poor. Professor Haller has shown us how the Puritan ministers acted as organizers of something approaching a political party;[47] and the ministers were more interested in religion than economics. Puritanism means Vane and Milton and Bunyan as well as Alderman Fowke, who was "not much noted for religion, but a countenancer of good ministers" and who was "deeply engaged in Bishops' lands."[48] We are in no danger today of forgetting those who fought well because they thought they were fighting God's battles. We must remember too the vision of Bacon and George Hakewill and John Preston, of a freer humanity glorifying God by abolishing evil through profounder knowledge of the world in which men live. Bacon's influence in inspiring revolt against the past became widespread only after the political revolution of the sixteen-forties:[49] modern science entered Oxford behind the New Model Army. The connections of religion, science, politics, and economics are infinite and infinitely subtle. Religion was the idiom in which the men of the seventeenth century thought. One does not need to accept the idiom, or to take it at its face value, to see that it cannot be ignored or rejected as a simple reflex of economic needs. Any adequate interpretation of the English Revolution must give full place to questions of religion and church government, must help us to grasp the political and social implications of theological heresy. . . .

[47] W. Haller, *The Rise of Puritanism, passim.*

[48] Quoted in J. Stoughton, *History of Religion in England,* III, p. 148.

[49] Cf. R. F. Jones, *Ancients and Moderns,* pp. 48–69, 122. For Preston, see pp. 239–74 below.

[46] *Economic History Review,* VI, No. 1.

5

THE THIRTY YEARS' WAR

It has been claimed that not one year of the seventeenth century was free of major war somewhere in Western Europe. The claim is almost true. Thus the century that has come to mark the birth of the modern world saw to it that that world should be born in conflict.

Because general wars were so typical of the century and because the results of these wars were of such importance to the shaping of modern Europe, the Thirty Years' War was chosen as the topic of this problem. This struggle was certainly the most important war of that century. It was also chosen for another reason: as we shall see in the first selection following, there is not a single major assertion of the traditional interpretation of the Thirty Years' War which has not come under attack in recent critical scholarship. Indeed the revision has been so complete that even the concept of the Thirty Years' War as a special, separable topic is virtually lost. In approaching the subject, on the one extreme scholars have gone back along the chain of causation well beyond the events which are traditionally alleged as the immediate causes of the war — the disputed succession to the throne of Bohemia and the Bohemian insurrection of 1618. At the other extreme they have tended to see the Peace of Westphalia, the general settlement which traditionally marks the end of the war, as the conclusion of only a limited portion of the war and to make the Peace of the Pyrenees (1659) the breaking point of the century. They have lengthened the focus of their interpretations to take in not simply Germany and central Europe, but a sphere of interconnected conflicts reaching from Poland and the Baltic to the Spanish New World and the Dutch East Indies; and in temporal terms reaching back to the so-called Wars of Religion in the previous century.

There is substantial disagreement as to the relationship between the cycle of religious wars in the sixteenth century and the greater wars of the seventeenth. Some scholars still insist that the Thirty Years' War was essentially a war of religion and, while their construction is more sophisticated than that of many writers of earlier generations, the earlier assertion remains. There are more scholars who tend to reduce the element of religious causation not only in the Thirty Years' War but even in the earlier religious wars. They see a sequence of two or three rounds of war beginning with the Habsburg-Valois conflict of the early sixteenth century, then expanding to the wars in France, the Low Countries, and off the channel coast in the later sixteenth century — but still tied fundamentally to the same string of cause, the European menace of Habsburg hegemony. They tend to view the Thirty Years' War and the Franco-Spanish conflict of the seventeenth century as a major expansion and extension of this same causal theme. And, to project the subject a bit beyond the limits of this problem, they then show that the ascendancy of France in the second half of the century and the wars that flowed from the policies of Louis XIV represented only a shift in the center of power from Spain to France and the emergence of a new threat of French hegemony.

As the student studies the revisionist selections that deal with this problem, he should keep in mind this larger politico-military context. And he should ask himself the question whether with such wholesale revision of a traditional subject we may see emerging not so much a new orthodoxy as a new controversy. But regardless of the specific interpretations of the Thirty Years' War and whether one accepts or rejects one or another of them, we can see in the early seventeenth century the

The Thirty Years' War   341

thread of the major theme which runs through western history from the "first Europe" of the High Middle Ages to the mid-seventeenth century, the rise of the modern state.

S. H. STEINBERG

THE THIRTY YEARS' WAR: A GENERAL REVISION

The following selection, while perhaps not entirely "A New Interpretation," as the author claims, may still be taken as one of the best examples of this generation's almost total revision of the traditional picture of the Thirty Years' War. That traditional picture may be sketched in the following terms. The war began with the Bohemian uprising of 1618; the Bohemian phase was followed in 1625 by the phase of Danish intervention; in 1630 began the Swedish phase; and the last was the French phase which ended in 1648 with the general peace settlement of Westphalia which conclusively redrew the map of Europe. Each of these standard periods of the war was dominated by its identifying personalities—Ferdinand II, Frederick V, Christian IV, Wallenstein, Gustavus Adolphus, and Richelieu. The causes of the war were seen as German constitutional and religious issues held over from the later Middle Ages and the Reformation and which were gradually broadened as non-German powers entered the war and complicated it with dynastic politics until the war which had begun as "the last war of religion" ended in being the first war of modern political issues. Finally, the Thirty Years' War has been traditionally viewed as one of the most brutal and destructive of conflicts and writers have dwelt in horrified fascination upon this theme.

There is not a single element of the foregoing picture that Steinberg and other revisionist scholars have not challenged. Steinberg, in this selection, points out that the war did not arise from German causes—either constitutional or religious—but was from the beginning part of the larger dynastic conflict of Bourbon and Habsburg and that "seen against this European background, German affairs are of minor importance." Moreover, he claims, "the conception of the Thirty Years' War as a 'war of religion' has been abandoned to a large extent," or has at least been demoted from cause to pretext. Even the time-honored theme of the brutal destructiveness of the war has been questioned.

The author of the most recent book on the "Thirty Years' War" sums up its causes and results as follows.[1] "The larger issue was that between the

[1] C. V. Wedgewood, *The Thirty Years War* (1938), p. 31, 65, 526.

dynasties of Hapsburg and Bourbon. . . . But . . . the geography and politics of Germany alone give the key to the problem. The signal for war was given . . . in May, 1618, by revolt in Bohemia. There was no compulsion towards a conflict.

. . . The war solved no problem. Its effects, both immediate and indirect, were either negative or disastrous. Morally subversive, economically destructive, socially degrading, confused in its causes, devious in its course, futile in its result, it is the outstanding example in European history of meaningless conflict."

Apart from the first dozen words quoted here almost every word of this statement is debatable. However, Miss Wedgwood only voices what may be called the *consensus gentium;* and it will take time and patience to uproot the prejudices and misconceptions of historians which have been strongly backed by playwrights, novelists and poets.[2] To Miss Wedgwood's version the following may be opposed. The various European wars fought between 1609 and 1660 decided the issue between the dynasties of Hapsburg and Bourbon. France's need to break her encirclement gives the key to the problem. Open warfare ensued over the Hapsburg effort to strengthen their grip on France to the north and north-east (truce with the Netherlands and attempted seizure of Jülich-Cleve, April, 1609). The only alternative to armed conflict was tame submission to Hapsburg domination. The series of wars ending with the peace of the Pyrenees (1659) solved the outstanding problem of Europe: the final overthrow of the Hapsburg hegemony established the principle of the balance of power, which henceforth would militate against every attempt to set up a single-state rule over Europe. The immediate effects of most of the wars were negligible; cumulatively and indirectly, they were momentous. Morally, the age of rationalism affirmed the equality of the Christian denominations and, implicitly, the freedom of worship and thought; economically, the age of mercantilism rid Europe from the curse of the American gold which had wrecked the economics of the sixteenth century; socially, the age of absolutism dissolved the feudal structure of society. It is the outstanding example in European history of an intrinsically successful settlement.

The traditional concept of the Thirty Years' War is

based on two main groups of sources: deliberate official propaganda and unwittingly one-sided private records. The first reflect the opinions of the victorious powers—France, Sweden, the Netherlands, Brandenburg; the second, those of the educated middle class which was hit hardest by the economic upheaval of the time. That these distortions should have gained credence may perhaps be ascribed to two failings of the nineteenth-century schools of German historians: they consciously or unconsciously made the political interests of the Prussian monarchy the criterion by which they judged the course of German history; and they preferred narrative sources and dispositive documents to administrative and business records.

Now of the two German powers which gained most by the peace of Westphalia—Brandenburg and Bavaria—the latter lapsed into a state of indolence and complacency after the death of Maximilian I (1651), whereas in the former, Frederick William I, the Great Elector, pursued a vigorous policy of aggrandizement. He was a master of political propaganda, the first to put over the identification of Hohenzollern and German interests; and he laid the foundations of the Prussian monarchy in the ideological sphere as well as in that of power politics. In Samuel von Pufendorf (1632–94) he secured as court historiographer a scholar and pamphleteer of European reputation who had already served the Dutch, Swedish and Palatine governments. Pufendorf's interpretation of the Thirty Years' War was taken up by Frederick the Great in his *Mémoires pour servir à l'histoire de la maison de Brandebourg,* and has become part and parcel of the national-liberal historiography of the nineteenth century.

The original "atrocity" propaganda emanating from Berlin had a double aim: for home consumption it was meant to accentuate the magnitude of the political, economic and cultural successes, real or alleged, of the Great Elector by painting the background as black as possible; while at the same time the darker aspects of his policy—the abandonment of the peasantry to the tender mercies of the Junkers, the oppressive taxation of the poorer classes in general and of the townspeople in particular, the tax exemption of the Junkers, and the inordinate expenses for the standing army—could, to the more

---

[2] There can be no doubt that Schiller's *Geschichte des Dreissigjährigen Krieges,* first published in 1792, and his dramatic trilogy *Wallenstein* (1799) have crystallized and popularized the main features of the traditional concept.

From S. H. Steinberg, "The Thirty Years' War: A New Interpretation," *History,* XXXII (1947), 89–102. Reprinted by permission of the editor of *History.*

The Thirty Years' War: A General Revision

gullible, be justified as unavoidable consequences of the war. As an instrument of foreign policy, the Brandenburg version of the Thirty Years' War— Brandenburg as the defender of the protestant religion and of the "German liberties" against Hapsburg interference and foreign aggression in general—was meant to serve the shifts and vagaries of the Great Elector's policy: one aspect or another of this picture could always be turned against his *pro tempore* enemy—the emperor, Sweden, Poland, France, Denmark—and incidentally win for him the moral support of the German and Dutch Protestants or of the anti-Hapsburg German Catholic princes, or the latent German patriotism of the liberal professions.

This picture of the Thirty Years' War, born of the needs of the Brandenburg propaganda of 1650–90, more or less coincided with the historical preconceptions of nineteenth-century national liberalism. The current version of the Thirty Years' War therefore largely reflects the Prusso-German attitude of Bismarck's fight against the German middle states, Austria and France, the *Kulturkampf* against the Roman Church, and the cultural and economic expansionism of the Hohenzollern Empire.

While the official records reflect the light in which the victorious party wished the nexus and causality of events to be seen, the private sources—chronicles, annals, diaries, letters—chiefly show the results of the war as experienced by those who lost most. These documents have been used to fill in the lurid details of famine and starvation, epidemics and cannibalism, ruin of town and country, decline of civilization, extinction of large sections of the population and complete pauperization of the remainder. It is not the purpose of the present paper to glorify the Thirty Years' War; and much misery, brutality, cruelty and suffering no doubt added to the terror and slaughter of purely military actions. But nothing is gained by putting the Thirty Years' War in a class by itself: its destructive aspects are common to every war—and were in any case smaller than those of "total war" in the twentieth century—and an impartial assessment of the facts will lead to the conclusion that some of the features most commonly attributed to it are unconnected with the war itself, while others have been generalized and exaggerated. The generalization of isolated events, the exaggeration of facts and, above all, figures, the special pleading for a particular cause, lay the contemporary chroniclers and diarists less open to crit-

icism than modern historians who have failed to recognise the distorted perspective from which these accounts have been written: for the compilers of town chronicles, parish registers, family albums and personal diaries, all belonged to the same class of educated, professional men—clerks, priests, officials, lawyers—who were hit by every vicissitude of the times, and always hit hardest. Whenever circumstances forced upon the treasury a cut in expenditure, it was the educational and cultural departments which were the first victims.[3]

The very term "Thirty Years' War" is fraught with misunderstanding. Seventeenth-century authors speak of the military events of the first half of the century as "wars," "*bella*" in the plural and clearly distinguish between the "*bellum Bohemicum,*" "*bellum Suecicum*" and so forth. The figure "thirty" and the singular "war" seems to occur for the first time in Pufendorf's *De statu imperii Germanici* (1667). One of the liveliest and still most readable pamphlets of seventeenth-century political science, its success was immediate and far-reaching: German, French, English and Dutch translations, popular adaptations and polemical treatises secured the rapid spread of its arguments throughout Europe. Here we have already all the well-known theses of later historians: the Bohemian revolt of 1618 as the beginning, the peace of Wesphalia as the end of the war; its character as a religious conflict; its extension over the whole of Germany; the omission of its European setting; the economic ruin and exhaustion; and the insinuation that Austria is a foreign power like France and Turkey.

From the political point of view the Thirty Years' War offers two aspects: the general European, and the particular German one. Both issues can be traced to the foreign and home policies of the emperors Maximilian I and Charles V. In the European field, Maximilian started the antagonism between the houses of Hapsburg and Valois by claiming the inheritance of Charles the Bold of Burgundy, and made it permanent by marrying his only son to the daughter and heiress of the Spanish world-monarchy. He thereby welded a ring of Hapsburg possessions round France which every French statesman was bound to try his utmost to break.

[3]To give an illustration: as a result of a general change in financial policy, the imperial city of Goslar, from 1625 to 1630, reduced its expenditure from 221,744 guilders to 54,342 guilders; expenditure on defence dropped from 590 to 460 guilders, on schools from 102 to 4 guilders.

In Germany, Maximilian deliberately wrecked the last prospect of equitable settlement of the constitutional dispute between centralism and federalism. As at the same time the imperial crown became hereditary in the house of Hapsburg, in all but legal prescription, he made this dynasty the permanent champion of that centralism which had become unattainable and was therefore by force of circumstances reactionary; so that any combination of forces, which for different reasons might be opposed to the Hapsburgs or the empire or centralisation, might appear as fighting for progress.

Charles V, Maximilian's grandson, intensified this development. He completed the total encirclement of France by acquiring the duchy of Milan, subduing the papacy, and drawing Portugal, England, Denmark and Poland into the Hapsburg orbit. The very greatness of his successes made a reaction inevitable. The exploits of Elizabethan England, the secession of the Spanish Netherlands, the alliance between France and the German Protestants (1552), the pacification of France by the edict of Nantes (1598) — are all signs of the growing restiveness against Hapsburg universalism. In fact, during the fifty years following the death of Charles V (1558) all European powers were jockeying for position.

France was obviously the rallying point of every opponent of Hapsburg domination throughout the whole of western Europe and the New World. The aggressive and expansionist policies of Louis XIV and Napoleon I have obliterated the fact that up to the death of Mazarin (1661) it was France which was the protagonist of the European balance of power against the domination of the continent by a single power.

The political struggle was accompanied by an ideological struggle. The antagonism between the old and the new faith made itself felt in the early stages of the conflict, and religious catchwords and propaganda were meant as sincerely or insincerely as were in more recent times the slogans of democracy and totalitarianism. The Hapsburgs, it is true, represented all the life-forces and the spirit of the reformed church of Rome; and the defeat of the Hapsburgs undoubtedly benefited the Protestant powers of Sweden, the Netherlands, England and Brandenburg. But the victory was chiefly a victory of Catholic France, which during the war was successively led by two cardinals of the Roman church; and the papacy itself had from 1523 to 1644 consistently opposed the Hapsburgs and even lent its support to the Protestant hero, Gustavus Adolphus of Sweden.

France could become the ideological leader of Europe as well as its political protagonist as she herself had solved the fight between Protestantism and Catholicism in a *tertium quid* which transcended both these sixteenth-century points of argument. Because the French leaders — the Protestants Henry IV and Sully and the Catholics Richelieu and Mazarin alike — recognized that the absolute claims inherent in every religious system were irreconcilable, they replaced religious standards, by the criterion of the *raison d'état*. This enabled France to destroy Protestantism within her own frontiers and to save Protestantism in Germany, Sweden and the Low Countries, to secure religious unity at home, and to perpetuate the split of western Christendom abroad. Catholic apologists tried in vain to counter this onslaught of secularism by elaborating a *ragione della chiesa*; it has never been a serious challenge to the *raison d'état*.

Seen against this European background, German affairs are of minor importance. Germany, as such, i.e. the "German section of the Holy Roman Empire," was not at all involved in any of the European wars of the period. The individual German states entered and left one war or another as partisans of the European antagonists; only the emperor was engaged in every conflict, not, however, as German king, but as the head of the Austrian branch of the house of Hapsburg. The German wars started in 1609 with the war of the Jülich-Cleve succession and ended in 1648 with the treaties of Münster and Osnabrück. They decided the political future of the empire, in that the last attempt to set up a centralistic government was defeated in favour of a loose confederation of virtually independent states. The concerted action by which the electors forced the emperor to dismiss his generalissimo Wallenstein in 1630 was their last achievement as a corporate body. They, too, who for centuries had represented the federal principle of the German constitution, henceforth showed an ever diminishing concern with the affairs of the empire and were content to look after their own interests. However, the constitution agreed upon in 1648 proved its soundness in that it lasted for more than 200 years, until 1866, with the short interval of the Napoleonic settlement. The wars also decided the dynastic rivalries within the leading German houses — curiously, every time in favour of the younger branch: the Palatine Wittelsbachs, the Thuringian Wettiners and the Wolfenbüttel Guelphs had to give way to their cousins of Bavaria, Saxony and Hanover, who henceforth formed the leading group of German powers. The most far-reaching result, however, was the rise of the electorate of Brandenburg, before 1609 the least important of the bigger principalities; it came to equal Bavaria and Saxony and was to outstrip them in the following century.

The conception of the Thirty Years' War as a "war of religion" has been abandoned to a large extent since it has been recognized that religious divisions coincided largely with political, constitutional and economic ones. It will always remain a matter of dispute which of these motives was decisive at a given moment. It does, however, seem that rational considerations of political and economic gains determined the policies of the cabinets to the same extent to which religious emotions held a strong sway over the masses, sufficient to whip up their passions in battle and to make them endure with fortitude their plight in adversity. The Swedes, under Gustavus, fought for the pure gospel, caring little for the *"dominium maris Baltici"* and knowing nothing of the French subsidies on which they subsisted; while Tilly's men were fired by an equal zeal for the Holy Virgin, with no stake in the power politics of the Wittelsbachs and ignorant of the pope's support of the heretic Swede.

Political and dynastic, religious and personal motives are inextricably mixed in the actions of the champions of the Protestant and Catholic causes. Both Gustavus Adolphus of Sweden and Maximilian of Bavaria were fervent devotees of their creeds. At the same time, the Lutheran establishment was also Gustavus's strongest bulwark against the claims to the Swedish throne, made by his Catholic cousin, Sigismund of Poland; and as the Palatine Wittelsbachs had assumed the leadership of the Protestant estates of the empire, the head of the Bavarian branch found safety and prospect of gain in rallying the Catholic princes under his standard. The struggle for the *"dominium maris Baltici"* set Gustavus in opposition to Protestant Denmark, Catholic Poland and Orthodox Russia. The occupation of the Hartz mines by the imperial forces (1624) endangered the Swedish copper market; Wallenstein's appointment as "General of the Atlantic and Baltic Seas" (1628) threatened Sweden's maritime position: her vital interests demanded armed intervention against the Catholic Hapsburgs and alliance with Catholic France, and the edict of restitution (1629) only added religious zeal to the dictates of power politics. Likewise, political considerations brought Maximilian into conflict with the Lutheran imperial cities of Swabia and Franconia, Catholic Austria and Spain, and the Calvinistic Netherlands and Palatinate; but after he had overawed the cities and, in alliance with Austria and Spain, crushed the elector Palatine, his interests as a prince of the empire and member of the college of electors made him turn against the Hapsburgs as his chief opponents. The reduction of the dominant position of the emperor and the removal of the Spaniards from the empire were from 1627 onward his overriding aims which, in co-operation with the pope, Catholic France and Lutheran Saxony, were brought to a successful consummation.

The ruinous effect of the war years on German economic and cultural life has been very much exaggerated. War is by its very nature destructive, and the wars of the seventeenth century are no exceptions. But all the campaigns of the period 1609–1648 were of short duration and the armies themselves of a very small size.[4] It was only the districts of primary strategic importance which had to bear the brunt of successive invasions in the seventeenth century, as they have been the focal points of every fight in central Europe, from Caesar's to Eisenhower's campaigns: the Rhine crossings of Breisach and Wesel, the Leipzig plain, the passes across the Black Forest and the roads to Regensburg and the Danube Valley. Other tracts of Germany were hardly affected at all, some only for a few weeks; the majority of towns never saw an enemy inside their walls.

From the middle of the thirteenth century the towns were the undisputed masters of German economics. Even agriculture, if not brought under direct control of city financiers, was at least completely dependent upon the town markets for home consumption as well as exportation (with the notable exception of

[4] The Catholic League had an effective strength of about 15,000 men; Gustavus Adolphus landed in Germany with 15,000 men; the imperial army under Wallenstein may have exceeded 20,000 men; Bernhard of Weimar received French subsidies for 18,000 men — Richelieu had originally only bargained for 14,000; Condé's army in 1645, the strongest French contingent to be employed in Germany, numbered 12,000 men. The numbers of "regiments," "squadrons," "standards" etc. are meaningless in themselves: for instance, in the battle of Breitenfeld, the 15,000 troops of the League were organized in 10 regiments, the 15,000 imperialists in 28 regiments.

the Teutonic Order in Prussia, whose totalitarian economy comprised production as well as commerce and excluded the citizen middlemen). This whole system of German economics was breaking down in a series of disastrous events from the middle of the sixteenth century: the south German cities were ruined by the repeated bankruptcies of the Spanish crown (1557, 1575, 1596, 1607), in which they lost every financial gain accumulated in the preceding century. The Hanse towns of North Germany were equally hit by the sack of Antwerp (1585) and the closing of the London Steelyard (1598) which deprived them of the two western pillars of their trading system; and even more by the separation of the Netherlands from Spain. The new republic vigorously asserted its independence in the economic sphere, intruding into the Baltic trade, hitherto the jealously-guarded monopoly of the Hanse.

About 1620 the German towns still presented an outward picture of opulence and solidity—very much emphasized to the casual observer by the splendour of their architectural achievements, as shown in Mathias Merian's topographical engravings published from 1640. Yet the foundations of their prosperity had gone, and the big inflation of the years 1619–23 only set the seal upon the utter ruin of German economics which had started some fifty years earlier. . . .

The part of the economic structure which was hit hardest by the immediate effects of the war was agriculture, especially for medium-sized and small farmers. To big land-owners, on the other hand, the war itself, the maintenance of troops over wide distances and the new methods of logistics and commissariat as introduced by Wallenstein and Gustavus Adolphus, offered fresh possibilities of enrichment. In fact, the seventeenth century is the period of the growth of the big *latifundia* of the Junkers at the smallholders' expense. The eviction of peasants, and the sequestration of peasant land by the lord of the manor had started at the end of the sixteenth century, caused by the steady rise of corn prices which made large-scale farming and bulk selling more profitable. The depopulation of the countryside and the disappearance of whole villages were in full swing before the first shot of the "Thirty Years' War" was fired, and went on long after the conclusion of the peace of Westphalia.

On the other hand, the improved organization of the

commissariat resulted in increasing the apparent burdens of occupied countries. Indiscriminate pillaging by a band of marauders may have done greater damage, but it appeared as a natural phenomenon, whereas the methodical requisitioning by quartermasters was felt the more irksome as it was planned and therefore rigid, thorough and therefore inescapable, fixed in writing and therefore long remembered and resented.

Ignorance of scientific demography and inability to visualize large figures account for the legend of the enormous loss of population, which is variously given as ranging from a third to half or more of the total. All these figures are purely imaginary. Such statistical surveys as were occasionally made were always designed to support some special pleading: to obtain a grant in aid, a reduction of payments, or an alleviation of services.[5] The main sources, however, are contemporary reports and, rarely, records of deaths, to the virtual exclusion of registers of births. In view of the huge birthrate this neglect amounts to thirty to fifty per cent[6]; in other words, exactly that third or half by which the population is said to have been reduced. It is, of course, indisputable that the irregular movements of troops, especially of ill-disciplined mercenaries, and the migration of refugees greatly contributed to the spreading of epidemics, such as the various kinds of typhoid (the greatest terror of the seventeenth century) or, to a lesser degree, of the plague and syphilis. On the other hand, the mortality of the urban population shows a surprising likeness in a place which was far remote from the European battlefields, and one which was right in their midst: it has been computed at seventy *per mille* for London in 1620–43, and at sixty-eight *per mille* for Frankfurt in 1600–50.

What actually happened was an extensive inner migration chiefly from the agrarian countryside into the industrial town, and from the economically retrograde town to the prosperous one. As with the ownership of movable and immovable property, so with regard to the population it is more appropriate to speak of redistribution than of destruction.

[5] For example, the district of Militsch in Silesia in 1619 furnished the government in Breslau with a list of 976 men available for military service; whereas at the actual census, 1,527 men had been recorded in this category.

[6] These percentages are based on eighteenth-century statistics (when the birthrate was already beginning to decline) for Prussia and Saxony where the surplus of births over deaths was 30 per cent. and 50 per cent. respectively.

The net result is that of an all-round, though very limited increase. This almost imperceptible rise, and over long periods, virtual stagnation, is characteristic of every community of a predominantly agricultural type. Keeping in mind the vagueness of the term "Germany," it seems safe to assume a population of fifteen to seventeen million in 1600. A loss of five to eight million by 1650 could not possibly have been made good by 1700, for which year a population of seventeen to twenty million is fairly well documented. . . .

The Thirty Years' War, put in its proper perspective, was therefore not such a catastrophe as popular historians have made out. Perhaps the one irreparable damage Germany sustained in the first half of the seventeenth century was that German civilization and German politics parted company. This separation may be the greatest misfortune of German history.

H. R. TREVOR-ROPER

THE LARGER PATTERN OF CAUSE

In the following selection the eminent British historian of the seventeenth century, H. R. Trevor-Roper, is concerned to argue by analogy from the instance of the Thirty Years' War to the general question, "Why do Great Wars Begin?" But in the process he adopts a point of view with reference to the causes of the Thirty Years' War which is at considerable variance with the traditional picture of those causes and in agreement with one of the several recent reinterpretations. To Trevor-Roper the causes of the war are no longer to be seen in terms of Germany or the empire but rather in terms of the complexity of European international relations. He treats the Bohemian revolt of 1618 — the immediate cause of the war in the traditional view — as only one in a string of incidents (and not an especially important one at that) any of which might have set off general war. But, in the larger argument, Trevor-Roper holds that it is never incidents that cause great wars but rather the policy decisions of great powers. And, in the instance of the Thirty Years' War, he argues that the great power whose deliberate policy decision caused the war was Spain. He argues that the Thirty Years' War did not really break out in 1618 in Bohemia but in 1621 with the Spanish declaration of war. He argues that it was not the issues of religion or the imperial constitution that caused its outbreak but the decision of Habsburg Spain to take the offensive once more in her two-centuries-old attempt to gain the hegemony of Europe. And we may extend his argument to presume that he would mark the end of the war not with the Peace of Westphalia in 1648 but the Peace of the Pyrenees in 1659. In this analysis we lose even the concept of the Thirty Years' War: it becomes part of a larger whole rather than an entity in itself. We turn now to the question of why it began.

Why, indeed? Several times in history the pattern has recurred, we see a general peace, apparently welcome to all powers, but beneath this peace we see fear and suspicion constantly threatening it. No

From H. R. Trevor-Roper, "Why Do Great Wars Begin?," *Horizon*, V (Nov. 1962), pp. 32–41. Reprinted by permission of American Heritage Publishing Co., Inc.

power wants war, but each fears that some incident will create war. The atmosphere is combustible and therefore a spark may set the world ablaze. Consequently when a spark does fly, there is a rush to isolate or stifle it. Even those who might profit by a fire in that quarter are too frightened to exploit it; for it might spread. And so the peace is kept; the various danger spots are guarded; even their dangers are preserved, not eliminated, for to eliminate them is to touch them and to touch them is to set them off. And then, suddenly a spark flies which is not isolated; the complex system of insurance suddenly fails; the wind blows, and all the danger spots are simultaneously alight: it is general war. . . .

On such occasions it is customary to say that the incidents lead to the war: they generate a fear whose pressure is irresistible, and cause men to build up armaments which must be used. In other words, the war is inevitable: it is only a question of time. This may be so, but since the question is open, perhaps it is worthwhile to look back at the outbreak of the greatest, most destructive war in preindustrial Europe: the Thirty Years' War, which is customarily dated from the last of a series of such incidents, the Bohemian Revolt of 1618. . . .

Obviously there were opportunities for incidents everywhere. But if we wish to find a pattern in these incidents, we must always look to Spain. After all, it was Spain that had made the peace of the great powers: in 1598, in 1604, in 1609 the Spanish monarchy, bankrupt but still powerful, had wound up the wars of Philip II with France, England, and Holland. It was Spain that kept the peace; and it was Spain that, in the end, broke it. The Thirty Years' War is generally thought of as a German war; but it was the Spanish Hapsburgs who dominated their cousins in Vienna and Prague, and it was the Spanish declaration of war in 1621 that made the local German war into a European war. . . .

The Spanish empire in Europe consisted of Flanders and Italy. Since its chief problem was the revolt of the Netherlands, its most essential communications were between Spain and Flanders, across or around the huge intervening body of France. In the old days the regular route had been by sea, from Laredo or Coruna to Flushing. But now the Dutch held Flushing and with the English commanded the sea lanes, so that Spanish forces—men, munitions, money—all had to reach Flanders by land. They sailed from Barcelona or Naples to Genoa (nominally free but in fact a Spanish protectorate) and assembled in Milan. Then they marched north, over the Alps, along the Rhine to the Low Countries. On this route there was one solid Spanish steppingstone: Franche-Comté, on the borders of France and Switzerland. There were also imperial fiefs, like Alsace, held by the Austrian Hapsburgs. Then there were theoretically independent states that, in fact, were safely Spaniolized, like the prince-bishoprics of Cologne or Liège: no trouble came from them. And there were allied states like the Catholic cantons of Switzerland which, by treaty, allowed free passage to Spanish (but only Spanish) troops. As long as Spanish power was firm, all these could be managed.

But there were other spots which were more difficult. There was Savoy: its duke had a mountainous terrain and an army and could be very troublesome, especially if supported by France. Then there was the Palatinate on the middle Rhine. The Elector Palatine was a dangerous enemy: he was a Calvinist, the titular leader of the activists among the German Protestants, and he had a vote in the making of emperors. It was most inconvenient that his castle of Heidelberg should overlook a sector of the Spanish route. And finally there were other petty German principalities which the chance of election or heredity might place in the wrong hands.

Moreover there was another vital area. To the Spanish Hapsburgs it was essential that their Austrian cousins rule the Holy Roman Empire: the emperor was overlord of the German princes on the Rhine; he ruled over Alsace; he also held legal rights over a number of princes in Italy. But the Austrian Hapsburgs in 1609 were inconveniently weak; they were also childless and there was no agreed heir. For those reasons it was necessary to Spain to have means of communicating with Austria and means of influencing imperial elections. These necessities raised two other areas to the status of danger spots. To communicate with Austria, Spain needed to control the land route from Milan to the Tirol; to influence elections it needed to control the otherwise irrelevant kingdom of Bohemia.

The land route from Milan to the Tirol ran through the Valtelline passes to the south of Switzerland. The inhabitants of the Valtelline were Catholics, but they were subject to the Swiss Grisons, who were Protestants. This made matters difficult. To secure the pass, the Spanish governor of Milan had built a fort near Lake Como. This provoked the Grisons, who looked round for sympathy. They found it in France. They also found it in Venice, the last of the independent republics of Italy, conscious of its historic greatness. Venice also felt itself strangled by the Hapsburgs. By land, the Austrian Hapsburgs overhung it from north and east, the Spanish Hapsburgs from the west. By sea, the Austrians encouraged the Bosnian pirates, its enemies in the Adriatic, and the Spaniards dominated the outlet of the Adriatic at Apulia. The Venetians had no desire to see the Valtelline closed and the two enemies joining hands to encircle them.

As for the kingdom of Bohemia, its claim to be a danger spot was purely political, not strategic. The king of Bohemia was an elector to the Empire, and in the present balance of power he might even control the deciding vote. It was therefore essential to Spain that the Bohemian Diet should elect the Spanish candidate to the Bohemian crown. This candidate was the Archduke Ferdinand of Styria, who would then, according to the Spanish plan, help to elect himself emperor. In 1609 this plan was not yet complete, least of all in Madrid, but the Spanish ambassador had built up a solid party in Prague by lavish distribution of favors, honors, promises, and pensions, and was prepared for the future.

Thus all the danger spots name themselves: the Rhineland, the Palatinate, Savoy, Venice, the Valtelline, Bohemia. Incidents that occurred elsewhere could be settled locally, but incidents in these places invariably endangered the peace.

The first trouble came in the Rhineland. Scarcely had the truce between Spain and Holland been signed, and the last great war wound up, when a disputed succession in Jülich-Cleves, on the lower Rhine, lauched a general crisis. The Duke of Cleves who' had died had been a Catholic, but two rivals now claimed the throne, both Protestants. A Protestant prince on the lower Rhine! To Spain such a thought was impossible, and one of the claimants, to ensure Spanish support, promptly turned papist. But the dispute remained and soon engaged all Europe. Henri IV of France allied himself with the German Protestants and with the Duke of Savoy. There was general mobilization. Savoy prepared to pounce on Milan. Henri IV had his queen crowned as his regent in his stead and set out to the Rhineland front. Then, quite suddenly, all was over: in the streets of Paris an assassin sprang into the royal coach, stabbed and killed Henri IV. With that sudden coup

the course of history was stayed. The anti-Spanish alliance collapsed.

But other crises soon followed. In 1613 there was another disputed succession. This time it was in Montferrat, an exposed enclave lying between Milan and Savoy. The Duke of Savoy claimed control over it, refused mediation, occupied it, defied Spain, expelled the Spanish ambassador, sent back his Spanish decorations. Successive Spanish governors of Milan made war against him. He was defeated in the field, forced to submit, but bobbed up again with foreign support, unofficial but valuable.

While Savoy was fighting against Spain by land, Venice was engaged in a fierce struggle by sea against the Bosnian pirates who enjoyed the protection of the Archduke Ferdinand. Before long Venice found itself at war with the Archduke himself on land, and a Dutch fleet brought Dutch soldiers through the Straits of Gibraltar to fight for Venice. And then another force entered the ever-widening fight. The Spanish viceroy of Naples, the Duke of Osuna, was a man of wild visions and ruthless methods. He sent troops by land through a protesting Italy to assist Milan against Savoy, and he sent a fleet—his own fleet, flying his own personal flag—into the Adriatic to destroy the ships of Venice, with which Spain was not even at war. He had an ally in Venice in the Spanish ambassador there, the Marquis of Bedmar, who was equally self-willed and independent. There can be no doubt that Osuna and Bedmar were determined to destroy Venice.

And yet in fact the Italian crisis came to nothing just as the Rhineland crisis had done. The great powers were never engaged. The governor of Dauphiné might make war, but the government of France was still. The Archduke Ferdinand might be at war, but the Emperor, his sovereign, did not stir. The governors of Milan and Naples might act, but Madrid remained uncommitted. Dutch soldiers fought in Italy, but the Dutch government remained at peace. It seemed as if the great powers would only fight through agents. The second crisis had passed.

Immediately it was followed by a third, a fourth, a fifth: 1618 was a year of crises. On May 18 there was one in Venice. On that morning the inhabitants of the city awoke to see two corpses hanging upside down from the public gibbet. Their legs were broken, a sign that they were guilty of treason. Five days later a third corpse joined them, mutilated by torture. No explanation was given: the Venetian Inquisitors of State never explained; they acted, and left the public to guess. But all agreed that there had been a deep plot against the independence of the city. Osuna and Bedmar had planned a sudden coup: Bedmar had organized the fifth column within, Osuna had his fleet ready to strike without. But Venice had struck first. Osuna and Bedmar of course protested their innocence; but whereas the cautious Bedmar continued his diplomatic career and was made a cardinal of the Church, the impetuous Osuna was afterward recalled, accused of seeking to make himself king of Naples, and died in prison. On all sides the matter was dropped.

In Bohemia, meanwhile, the Spaniards had won a great victory. The old Emperor, who was also the king of Bohemia, persuaded the Bohemian Diet to pre-elect the Spanish candidate, the Archduke Ferdinand, as next king when the Emperor should die. That guaranteed the crown of Bohemia. Indirectly, it ensured that the imperial election should go as the Spaniards wished. And further, by a secret treaty signed with the Archduke, the Spaniards agreed that he should be the next emperor. The King of Spain himself had claims, but by this treaty he renounced them. He renounced them in exchange for solid assets: for Alsace, an essential stage on the route to Flanders; for the Tirol, which linked Italy with Germany; and for the imperial fiefs in Italy. Thus at one blow Spain had secured Bohemia and the Empire for the most dependable of its allies and fastened its own hold over its European communications. At least it had been done so on paper.

In fact it had not. In fact, on May 23, 1618, three days after the ruin of the Spanish conspiracy in Venice, the Spanish conspiracy was ruined in Prague also. On that day the Protestant nobility of Bohemia revolted, threw the Hispanophile Catholic ministers out of the window of the Hradčany Castle, and set up a revolutionary government. The first act of this government was to expel those constant allies of Spain, the Jesuits. The second was to look round for a Protestant heir to replace the pre-elected Archduke. Only a radical prince would accept such a revolutionary throne, and therefore their eyes lit on the most radical of German princes: the Calvinist Elector Palatine, whose own capital of Heidelberg was such a nuisance on the Spanish Rhineland route.

The revolution in Prague, coinciding with the delivery of Venice, sent a thrill of excitement through all Protestant Europe. All the enemies of Spain were roused. Two months later the Protestant party in the Valtelline murdered their Catholic enemies, whom they accused of "Hispanismus," seized control of the pass, and so cut Milan off from the Tirol. At the same time Savoy and Venice made a formal alliance against future aggression. The following year Venice and Holland made a defensive alliance against Spain, and on the death of the Emperor the members of the Bohemian Diet formally elected the Elector Palatine as their king.

From this point on, historians say, general war was certain. Of course it is easy to say this because in fact war did break out: the Thirty Years' War is conventionally dated from the Bohemian revolt. But let us look a little more closely at the course of events after that revolt. We may find that the easy answer is not necessarily the true or only answer. The causes of war are so important that we ought to take nothing for granted.

The first fact to notice is that the Bohemian revolt was far less fatal than might appear. It did not in fact lead to the loss of the Empire. In 1619, while the Bohemian Diet was electing its new Protestant king in Prague, the Archduke, as legal king of Bohemia, was in Frankfort helping to elect himself emperor. Therefore the major part of Spanish policy was undamaged. The Empire was safe. All that was lost was Bohemia. Moreover, it seemed that Bohemia could be isolated. The Archduke had been legally elected, and his election could not be superseded. The election of the new king was illegal; even his own father-in-law, the king of England, refused to support him, and a French envoy succeeded in persuading the two German leagues—the Catholic League and the Evangelical Union—to remain neutral. The Bohemian rebels had overplayed their hand. They had even given a moral advantage to Spain.

It was an advantage which Spain was quick to seize. In 1620 a Spanish army under Spinola marched from the Netherlands and occupied the Palatinate. The Elector could hardly complain: he had deserted his own country to usurp a crown elsewhere and, in the general view, deserved what he got. In the same year the Spanish governor of Milan carried out a successful coup in the Valtelline. Under his patronage the Catholics in the valley suddenly rose and in the "Holy Butchery" massacred their Protestant rulers and placed the vital corridor under Spanish protection. A few months later a Bavarian army acting for the Hapsburgs totally defeated the usurping king of Bohemia and drove him headlong from Prague. By the spring of 1621 all, it seemed, was over; the *status quo* had been restored; the danger of general war was past.

Thus when we look closely at the facts we see that the last of the "incidents" did not, of itself, precipitate a general war. The revolt in Prague no more created the war than the conspiracy in Venice had done, or the war in the Adriatic, or the war over Montferrat, or the affair of Jülich-Cleves, or the Palatinate, or the Valtelline. And yet, later, in 1621, real war broke out, bringing devastation and revolution to Europe for the next three decades. How then did this happen? To seek an answer to this question we must turn away from the facile assumption that war rises spontaneously out of "incidents" and look instead at the men who create incidents and are the real makers of history.

The European war that broke out in 1621 was caused not by accumulated accidents but by human decisions. Those decisions were taken in Madrid. The questions we must ask are: Who were the men who made those decisions and why did they make them? I believe that it is perfectly possible to answer these questions. The men were a party of Spanish officials who came to power in Madrid in 1621, and they made war deliberately because, unlike their predecessors, they believed that war would be more profitable to Spain than peace. . . .

And who were these men? Essentially they were two. First there was Baltasar de Zúñiga, the advocate of a forward policy throughout Europe. He had been ambassador to the Archduke Albert and then to the Emperor, and had always opposed the truce in the North and argued action in Bohemia. He was now the most powerful figure in Madrid. Secondly there was the new King's young tutor, Gaspar de Guzmán, Zúñiga's nephew, who would dominate Spain for the next twenty-two years as the Count-Duke of Olivares. Behind them stood the whole party: the party of the pushing, powerful, uncontrolled governors and ambassadors throughout the Empire who had long been openly impatient of the restraining peace which all the great powers were conspiring to keep. For years these men had fretted at the weakness of politicians in Madrid. They had longed to throw into action the armies they commanded and maintained, the fifth columns they had created and

nursed. With the change of government, they found politicians who shared their views.

But why should anyone want war in 1621? . . .

The answer is not difficult to find. It is to be found in their own statements. These men believed that, in spite of appearances, Spain was losing the peace. This loss was not a loss of territory (Spanish territory had been constantly increasing), nor even merely a loss of trade (Spanish trade had never been much). It was something far greater than this. Beneath the surface of spectacular peaceful triumphs the whole Spanish "way of life" was being undermined by a more successful rival ideology that had its headquarters in Amsterdam, the capital of those insubordinate, invincible, unpardonable heretics and rebels, the Dutch.

For the Spanish peace had, in some respects, represented the victory and spread of a way of life. It was the triumph of princely bureaucracy, of an official class in a monarchical society, living to a large extent on taxes which grew as it grew. This official class had by now an official ideology, an ideology of the court: an ideology shared even by the great merchants, who farmed the taxes and felt themselves half courtiers; and consecrated by the Church, which was a court-Church, and particularly by the religious orders—most of all by the courtliest of all orders, the Jesuits, who at this time were the invariable allies of Spain. Such a system had its outward charm, of course. The bureaucracy patronized official art and architecture; it advertised itself and its solidity through magnificent buildings, which we admire today, and magnificent shows and pageants, which dissolved overnight. But it also had its weakness. Though it created a form of state-capitalism, it discouraged private trade and industry. Everywhere we see the same spectacle: industry and commerce crushed under bureaucracy; merchants shifting their capital into the purchase of land, titles, or offices; peasants oppressed by taxes; craftsmen fleeing to other lands.

This "Spanish" way of life was not confined to the Spanish empire, or even to Catholic countries. Wherever Spanish influence was felt, it was encouraged. We see it in France, the France of Marie de Médicis; we see it in England, the England of James I and the Duke of Buckingham. But over against it there was another way of life, the ideology of the country opposed to the court: of country

The Eve of the Modern World

landlords opposed to court magnates, of lesser merchants opposed to the great monopolists of the court, of taxpayers opposed to taxeaters. This ideology was conservative: it was nationalistic, for it opposed an international system; it was anti-Spanish, and anticlerical, for that system was operated by Spain and Rome; and against the ostentatious consumption of the court, it was "puritan." This ideology had been suppressed—indeed could hardly exist—in Spain and Spanish Italy; it seethed below the surface in England and France; but in Venice and Holland, in different forms, it ruled. Against Venice and Holland, therefore, all the hatred of Spanish officialdom was directed.

Of course, if the Spanish peace had really been consolidating Spanish power in Europe, there would have been no need for action: Spain could have waited till the dwindling "puritan" generation had died out. But the Spanish officials were convinced that time was not on Spain's side. They believed that the purpose of peace was to recover from the bankruptcy of war, to renew military strength, to create new resources for final victory. And that, it was only too clear, had not been done. Behind the façade of its wealth and strength, Spain had sunk deeper into bankruptcy, deeper into feebleness. Meanwhile its old enemies were using the peace to grow in power and prosperity. The courtly clerical, aristocratic system of Spain might be magnificent, but it did not work. The ideology of the Dutch might be heretical, rebellious, vulgar, but it worked. Time therefore was on their side. Fortunately, said the Spanish officials, the balance of power was still on the side of Spain, provided Spain struck, and struck now. . . .

In Madrid [these] arguments were driven home by Baltasar de Zúñiga himself. It seemed to him as if the Spaniards had shed their blood only to fill the veins of subject nations: "We have left our own country deserted and sterile in order to people and fertilize the lands we have conquered." Therefore, the Carthage on the Zuider Zee must be destroyed: the treasure of Spain that had been secretly drained away to the north must be brought back by force. Was it not for this day that Zúñiga himself and his fellow imperialists had worked so hard, throughout the Spanish Peace, to secure the vital corridors—the Valtelline, Alsace, the Palatinate? Now they had secured them all. Were they then not to strike?

When these arguments were first advanced in Madrid, there was resistance. How, men asked, could Spain face the cost of war? With his dying voice, the Archduke in Brussels urged that the truce be prolonged. "We must suppose," he protested, "that even if all Europe is destined to be subject to one monarch, that time is not yet." But as the old rulers died off, the new prevailed; and besides, they had other allies. The Councils of Portugal and the Indies, representing the East and West India trades, agreed with Zúñiga and Coloma. Those men had long suffered from the Dutch. In the years of the war the Dutch had seized half the East Indies from Portugal; in the years of peace they had stolen the trade of the West Indies. It was vain to hope of defeating them at sea, but a well-aimed blow by land would solve the problem. Struck in the heart, the octopus would loosen its distant tentacles. Thanks to this argument, and this support, the party of war prevailed. The truce was denounced. The half-settled troubles of Germany were swept up into a general war.

Thus we can answer our question. The Thirty Years' War, as a general war, was not created by the Bohemian and German incidents which officially began it. These could have been settled, or at least localized, as so many other such incidents had been. Perhaps no general war ever arises out of mere incidents. General wars arise because the governments of great powers, or the men behind such governments, want war and exploit incidents. . . .

The Larger Pattern of Cause

CARL J. FRIEDRICH

"THIS GREATEST OF THE RELIGIOUS WARS"

One of the traditional assumptions about the Thirty Years' War was that it was a war of religion. Now, as we have seen, most modern revisionist scholars tend either to reject this assumption or move it to a much lower priority position in the list of causes. Yet is it possible to separate religion from politics—or from anything else—in the early seventeenth century? This is essentially the question that Carl J. Friedrich poses in his treatment of the Thirty Years' War in his influential book, *The Age of the Baroque,* from which the following selection is taken. He flatly calls it "this greatest of the religious wars," and states that "without a full appreciation of the close links between secular and religious issues, it becomes impossible to comprehend the Thirty Years' War."

Such a position is itself a form of revision in that it is a sophisticated restatement of an older thesis but within a new framework. Friedrich is as well aware of the play of dynastic power politics in this age as is Steinberg or Trevor-Roper. Indeed he holds that the war was a transition between the age of religious war and the age of political war and that the reason why the forces of the counterreformation won most of the battles and yet lost the war was "that the forces of the modern state were predominantly on the other side." He feels that the new framework within which we must understand this play of religious and secular forces is the concept of the baroque in which religion and politics, faith and power are mixed, in spite of contradiction; and that contradiction itself is an essential part of the baroque that modern men easily misunderstand.

It has been the fashion to minimize the religious aspect of the great wars which raged in the heart of Europe, over the territory of the Holy Roman Empire of the German Nation. Not only the calculating statecraft of Richelieu and Mazarin, but even Pope Urban VIII's own insistence lent support to such a view in a later age which had come to look upon religion and politics as fairly well separated fields of thought and action. Liberal historians found it difficult to perceive that for baroque man religion and politics were cut from the same cloth, indeed that the most intensely political issues were precisely the religious ones. Gone was the neopaganism of the renaissance, with its preoccupation with self-fulfillment here and now. Once again, and for the last time, life was seen as meaningful in religious, even theological, terms, and the greater insight into power which the renaissance had brought served merely to deepen the political passion brought to the struggle over religious faiths.

Without a full appreciation of the close links between secular and religious issues, it becomes impossible to comprehend the Thirty Years' War. Frederick, the unlucky Palatine, as well as Ferdinand, Tilly and Gustavus Adolphus, Maximilian of Bavaria and John George of Saxony, they all must be considered fools unless their religious motivation is understood as the quintessential core of their politics. Time and again, they appear to have done the "wrong thing," if their actions are viewed in a strictly secular perspective. To be sure, men became increasingly sophisticated as the war dragged on; but even after peace was finally concluded in 1648, the religious controversies continued. Ever since the Diet of Augsburg (1555) had adopted the callous position that a man must confess the religion of those who had authority over the territory he lived in—a view which came to be known under the slogan of "*cujus regio, ejus religio*"—the intimate tie of religion and government had been the basis of the Holy Empire's tenuous peace. Born of the spirit of its time—Lutheran otherworldliness combining with Humanistic indifferentism—this doctrine was no more than an unstable compromise between Catholics and Lutherans, the Calvinists being entirely outside its protective sphere. But in the seventeenth century not only the Calvinists, who by 1618 had become the fighting protagonists of Protestantism, but likewise the more ardent Catholics, inspired by the Council of Trent, by the Jesuits and Capuchins, backed by the power of Spain and filled with the ardor of the Counter Reformation, had come to look upon this doctrine as wicked and contrary to their deepest convictions.

When Ferdinand, after claiming the crown of Bohemia by heredity, proceeded to push the work of counter reformation, his strongest motivation was religious; so was the resistance offered by the Bohemian people, as well as Frederick's acceptance of the crown of Bohemia on the basis of an election. Dynastic and national sentiments played their part, surely, but they reinforced the basic religious urge. The same concurrence of religious with dynastic, political, even economic motives persisted throughout the protracted struggle, but the religious did not cease to be the all-pervasive feeling; baroque man, far from being bothered by the contradictions, experienced these polarities as inescapable.

If religion played a vital role in persuading Ferdinand II to dismiss his victorious general, it was even more decisive in inspiring Gustavus Adolphus to enter the war against both the emperor and the League. The nineteenth century, incapable of feeling the religious passions which stirred baroque humanity and much impressed with the solidified national states which the seventeenth century bequeathed to posterity, was prone to magnify the dynastic and often Machiavellian policies adopted by rulers who professed to be deeply religious, and the twentieth century has largely followed suit in denying the religious character of these wars. But it is precisely this capacity to regard the statesman as the champion of religion, to live and act the drama of man's dual dependence upon faith and power that constituted the quintessence of the baroque. The Jesuits, sponsors of the baroque style in architecture all over central and southern Europe, advised Catholic rulers, but more especially Ferdinand II, concerning their dual duties. The somber and passionate driving force behind so much unscrupulousness was religious pathos in all its depth. What the Catholics did, elicited a corresponding pattern of thought and action in the Protestant world: Maurice of Nassau and James I, Gustavus Adolphus and Cromwell, as well as many minor figures of the European theater, conceived of themselves as guardians of the "secrets of rule," the *arcana imperii,* to be employed for the greater glory of God and the Christian religion. . . .

The five battles of the White Mountain, Lutter am Barenberge, Breitenfeld, Lützen and Nördlingen, were the decisive ones of the great war; after Nördlingen many a bloody engagement was fought, but none turned the scale as these battles had done. It is a startling testimony to the inner weakness of the cause of the Counter Reformation that in spite of losing only one of these great encounters, it could not win the war in the end. The deeper reason was that the forces of the modern state were predominantly on the other side.

In any case, the battle of Nördlingen had sufficiently reduced the power of Sweden and with it the prospects of a sweeping Protestant predominance, to strengthen negotiations begun earlier in 1634 for an all-round compromise. In contrast to the French cardinal, who protested a desire for a general peace while fanning the flames of war, the German emperor and his estates proceeded to treat of peace among themselves and eventually arrived at a settlement which acknowledged the existing state of affairs. The peace of Prague (1635), the third of the peace treaties by which the great war was punctuated, might have brought the conflict to an end thirteen years earlier than the peace of Westphalia, had it not been for Swedish and French determination to reduce the Hapsburg power further and to secure extensive compensations for their sanguinary and financial efforts up to that time. The peace of Prague expressly challenged such pretensions by providing that any lands lost to either the emperor or one of the states, like Lorraine and Mecklenburg, should be restored to them, if necessary by force of arms. An army for the entire Empire was provided, and the liberation of German territories from foreign armies was made the express purpose of this army. As for the problem of religious peace, the doctrine of "cujus regio, ejus religio" was by implication reaffirmed, and the Edict of Restitution by similar implication set aside. Instead, it was provided that the ecclesiastical domains, foundations, monasteries and the like should be divided on the basis of actual possession at the time of the peace of Passau and, for those acquired after Passau, the date of November 12, 1627 should serve, but for a forty-year period only. There was a certain number of exceptions, and since Ferdinand was unwilling to grant religious toleration in his crownlands, especially Bohemia, in spite of strong Saxon representations, it was agreed that this matter might be further negotiated.

As a whole, the peace of Prague constituted an attempt to rally all German estates behind the ancient constitution and unite them against the foreign invaders, especially Sweden and France. . . . Obviously this settlement was bound to look to France and Sweden more like a defensive alliance than like a peace treaty. Estates threatened by either French or Swedish forces could not but look upon the document in a similar light, since adherence to its terms entailed joining forces with the emperor and hence might bring about conquest by his enemies. As a result, its conclusion did not bring peace, but an intensification of the war.

The historian may well be pardoned for not reviewing the sorry tale of this long-drawn-out disaster. Largely it was the story of a Swedish-French-Spanish struggle. In 1637, Emperor Ferdinand passed away, unsuccessful and a victim of his bigotry and his delusions. Recurrently responsible for the continuation of the great war which he had himself allowed to get under way, he could look upon his crown lands, as well as upon the larger Empire, for which he was in his own conception of rulership the God-appointed shepherd, as not only devastated and exhausted, but also as no more Christian in the Catholic way than when he ascended his throne.

In 1635 Richelieu had finally *declared* war upon the Austrian Hapsburgs—France would never admit it meant the Empire—after having *participated* in it certainly since the entrance of Gustavus Adolphus. This step was in a sense the result of the battle of Nördlingen, in which the Spanish Hapsburgs had combined with their Austrian kinsmen to defeat the

Protestants and Swedes. French intervention was also intended to counteract the peace of Prague. Since this peace had all but reunited the Empire, Richelieu was determined to split it again. He believed that the time had come to launch the final assault upon Hapsburg power, and if not utterly to destroy it, in any case to reduce it to the point where it could no longer threaten the imperial ambitions of France. If in the course of this, France secured Alsace and reached the Rhine, so much the better; but such was not a primary or initial goal of French policy. More important by far was the prospect of wresting control of Franche-Comté and the Spanish Netherlands from the Hapsburgs, since these territories constituted the eastern prong of the vise in which the Hapsburgs had held France for generations. If it meant the continuation of the war in Germany for another thirteen years, this was a regrettable incident to the more important goal of securing France against Hapsburg power.

The French aggression, though seemingly well supported by Sweden, the Netherlands, and the German Protestants, did not at first work out well. The Spanish, invading from the Netherlands, all but captured Paris; elsewhere, too, the French met defeat, due to incompetent commanders and lack of logistic support for badly organized armies. But in the face of these reverses, Richelieu showed his accustomed fortitude and perseverance, as told in another chapter. In due course, the internal weakness of Spain, highlighted by the successful revolt of Portugal in 1640, was revealed in the crushing defeat at Rocroy (1643), which ended the legend of the invincibility of the Spanish infantry. The emperor thereupon authorized peace negotiations. Spain lost almost fifteen thousand men and never recovered from the disaster. . . .

After Rocroy, the Bavarian army had once again become the mainstay of the imperial position. It had successfully defended Württemberg against Turenne and Condé. But its dominance was due in part to General Piccolomini's being needed in the Netherlands, while General Gallas, through incompetence, wrecked the imperial forces in a vain attempt to check a Swedish attack upon Denmark (1644). Fortunately Queen Christina, now eighteen, mounted the throne of Gustavus Adolphus in that year. Determined to help secure peace, she insisted that the Swedish plenipotentiaries actively promote the negotiations. Furthermore, the Dutch, after Rocroy, had finally decided that France had become a greater danger than Spain, and were therefore quite willing to help further the peace which they more than others had ever been prepared to welcome. Finally, Pope Urban VIII, often the champion of the French cause, while at the same time keenly concerned over his own power, had died. In his place, the weaker and unaggressive Innocent X had mounted St. Peter's throne; by merely failing to support Mazarin and the French position with the energy of his predecessor, Innocent enhanced the chances of peace.

Actually, beginning about 1641, the preliminaries of a peace had for a number of years been under negotiation. They took definite shape after Rocroy when the emperor decided to go ahead. Crosscurrents of policy had previously caused the negotiations to be divided into halves. At Münster the treaty between the Austrian Hapsburgs, their allies and France was being negotiated, while at Osnabrück, some miles away, the Swedes negotiated with the Empire and its estates. There were endless wrangles over etiquette and protocol, but these disputes were often baroque designs, hiding deeper policy conflicts. Thus the refusal of the French ambassador to meet the Spaniard presumably served Mazarin's desire to avoid a peace settlement with Spain; seemingly senseless insistence upon forms for the furtherance of concrete policy was frequent.

The real difficulties arose from the complexity of the situation. France and Sweden both insisted that they were at war with the Hapsburgs, rather than the Empire, since part of the estates were on their side. The estates on their part insisted upon participation, not only to protect their territorial rights, but also to settle the constitutional and other internal issues from which the war had originated; for under the constitution of the Empire these were issues of immediate concern to them. . . .

Unfortunately, two other factors besides the resulting clumsy procedure contributed to the extreme slowness of the negotiations. One was the fact that a number of other powers were brought into the negotiations. Richelieu's aspiration to make France the arbiter of Christianity favored this extension, but so did a variety of other ambitions, including the Holy See's similar desire. Thus Spain and the United Provinces, Portugal and Venice, Denmark, Poland and a number of others appeared on the scene. And while no peace was agreed upon between France and Spain, such a peace was worked out between Spain and the United Provinces.

The other, and perhaps the more serious difficulty, resulted from the failure to arrange for a cessation of hostilities, while the congress met. For not only was the course of negotiations continually being affected by the shifting fortunes of the battlefield, but some of the negotiating powers, notably Sweden and France, were thereby induced to intensify their war activities, in order to force a decision or effect an alliance. A striking illustration was the frightful devastation of Bavaria by French troops, undertaken in order to force the elector to abandon his connection with the emperor, May to October, 1648. At that point, fortunately, the peace was concluded, and the outrages came to an end. There can be little doubt that this would have happened much sooner if there had been a cease-fire agreement at the start, but the parties were too far apart at the outset to make this kind of agreement possible. So for five years they wrangled, maneuvered and shifted at Münster and Osnabrück, living in plenty while the surrounding countryside starved, and while terrible destruction was wrought upon the helpless mass of the people, not only in Germany, but in Italy, eastern France and elsewhere.

The main political and territorial provisions of the treaty, now generally known as the Treaty of Westphalia of 1648, were as follows: (I) Each German principality was declared a sovereign member of the body known as the Empire, and hence could declare war and make peace at its own discretion. (2) Alsace, with the exception of the free imperial city of Strassburg, was ceded to France, and the forcible acquisition of the bishoprics of Metz, Toul and Verdun by France was confirmed. (3) Sweden acquired the western parts of Pomerania (including Stettin) and the bishoprics of Bremen and Verden, thereby securing control of the mouths of three great German rivers: the Weser, the Elbe and the Oder. (4) Brandenburg, starting on its career of expansion, added most of eastern Pomerania to its possessions, along with the contested lands of the former bishoprics of Magdeburg, Halberstadt and Minden. (5) Saxony was confirmed in the possession of Lusatia. (6) Both France and Sweden, through their territorial acquisitions, were placed in a position to interfere in the affairs of the Empire at any time; since the treaties reaffirmed the constitution (Articles 8 of Osnabrück, 62–66 of Münster), any breach of the constitution was made a concern of France and

Sweden; besides, Sweden was given the status of an estate of the Empire for Bremen, etc. (Article 10 of Osnabrück). France's full sovereignty over Alsace[10] precluded this status. (7) The vexatious question of the electorate and Palatinate, which had been so largely involved in the continuation of the war after 1622, was resolved by creating a new electoral office, so that both the duke of Bavaria and the son of Frederick could become electors; at the same time the Lower Palatinate along the Rhine was given back to the Elector Palatine, while the Upper Palatinate remained with Bavaria. (8) Status of full sovereignty was formally accorded to the United Provinces and Switzerland, which had hitherto been bound to the Empire by a shadowy dependence. (9) Calvinists, at the insistence of Brandenburg, were given equal status with Lutherans, and the year 1624 was chosen for determining ecclesiastical control, while the terms of the religious peace of Augsburg were relaxed and greater toleration enjoined upon rulers. (10) On the imperial courts, the number of Catholic and Protestant judges was to be equal thereafter. The terms of treaty precluded objections by the church; consequently, Pope Innocent X forthwith condemned the treaty as unacceptable. While this ban was never lifted, the treaty remained as a symbol of the emergence of the modern state and of the system of many such states, facing each other as strictly secular sovereigns. The Counter Reformation's long-drawn-out struggle to recapture the unity of Christendom by force of arms had ended in failure.

The negotiations for the Treaty of Westphalia initiated what became a standing operating procedure of the new diplomacy; congresses of ambassadors at the end of a war to try to negotiate a peace settlement on the basis of the sovereign equality of victor and vanquished. This method with all its faults seems in retrospect superior to the more recent practice of dictating peace terms: its often elaborate compromises resulted in a greater degree of genuine pacification. But not always. The vague and in important respects contradictory provisions of the Treaty of Westphalia concerning Alsace served as a welcome pretext for Louis XIV when he decided to challenge them in the next generation. It is interesting that French opposition opinion—rather paradoxically, considering the substantial French gains under the settlement—attacked the treaty savagely and delayed its signing by France until 1651. Indignation was leveled at Mazarin because he had failed to establish peace with Spain at the same time. The anger of the public over this was an important in-

gredient of the commotion which led to the Fronde.

But throughout Germany the announcement of the conclusion of peace was greeted with such joy as the utterly exhausted populace could still muster. There were celebrations upon celebrations, and all the baroque poets burst into heavily ornate song to welcome the dove of peace. . . .

In spite of the tendency of historical scholarship to tone down the doleful tales which are traditionally associated with the Thirty Years' War, there can be little doubt that its effects were not only disastrous in terms of the immediate future, but that the aftereffects of this war thwarted German life for a hundred years. It was only in the period of Goethe and Schiller that the German people seemed to shake off the pallor that had hung over the nation's cultural life. To be sure, there were noble exceptions, such as Leibniz and Bach, but on the whole the loss in human creative talent as well as the material devastation in town and country could not be overcome until after a long convalescence. Even worse, in the long run, was the institutional confusion which the war brought about. The perpetuation of a vast array of principalities large and small could only serve to prevent the growth of a healthy national spirit related to a suitable government and constitution. For a system of social order and government which had served well enough within the context of the medieval unity of church and empire could in the age of the sovereign state and nation lead only to endless frustrations and eventual violence in the search for a solution. It may be a bit far-fetched to trace an explanation of the violence of Fascist nationalism in Germany back to the Thirty Years' War. But that the "monstrosity" which the young Pufendorf saw in the German constitution had something to do with the rise of Prussia few will deny. In any case, the Thirty Years' War marked the effective end of the medieval dream of universal empire, until the revolutionary first Napoleon revived it on a novel basis. . . .

All in all, the toll in human suffering resulting from this greatest of the religious wars was staggering, the results in terms of the religious objectives practically nil. The high hopes of Ferdinand II and his Counter Reformation associates were finished, as were the Calvinists' projects for a predominantly Protestant Empire. The activities on both sides had merely succeeded in demonstrating that rather than surrendering their religious convictions, Germans would di-

The Eve of the Modern World

vide permanently into many principalities, each governed according to the formula of the religious peace of Augsburg: *"Cujus regio, ejus religio."* A vicious doctrine on the face of it, it nonetheless provided a tolerable compromise for the Germans as a people; a man could remove from one "sovereignty" to another, if compelled by religious scruples. Thus religion triumphed, in a negative sense, over the political requirements of building a modern national state. The outcome of the Thirty Years' War in this sense permanently shaped the course of German history, in contrast with England and France, where the religious wars led, eventually, to a consolidation of religious views, favoring Protestant predominance in one, Catholic in the other. To modify the "forcing of conscience" inherent in such unity, religious toleration—the willingness to let the individual decide for himself—served as the pathmaker for a later more pronounced individualism. In Germany, each "state" patriarchally protected the individual's conscience, while the nation remained a cultural community without firm political framework. Protestant Prussia and Saxony, Catholic Austria and Bavaria, not to mention the dozens of lesser princes, nobles and "free" cities, could proceed to develop a political absolutism, untempered by cultural aspirations. The fatal split in German thought and action between the realm of the spirit and the realm of material power had been started. The modern state emerged from the Treaty of Westphalia in all the kingdoms, duchies and principalities, but it was a crippled, barebones "state," a mere apparatus—a bureaucracy serving princely aspirations for power and aggrandizement. The nation remained outside.

ROBERT ERGANG

THE ALL-DESTRUCTIVE WAR?

One of the commonplaces of the traditional view of the Thirty Years' War is that it was the very exemplification of brutality, devastation, and suffering. It is as if historians, looking back through the horror of modern general war, had taken the Thirty Years' War not only as the first such conflict in its scope and duration but as the terrible forecast of the cost of modern war in misery, loss of life, and destruction of property. And yet, modern scholars have begun to call even this venerable tradition of the Thirty Years' War into question. Steinberg, in the first selection of this section, speaks of the "atrocity propaganda" to which he attributes so much of the tradition. Carl J. Friedrich, in the selection just past, speaks of "the tendency of historical scholarship to tone down the doleful tales which are traditionally associated with the Thirty Years' War"—even though he disagrees with the tendency. One of the modern scholars who subscribes to this revisionist view is Robert Ergang from whose monograph, *The Myth of the All-destructive Fury of the Thirty Years' War,* the following selection is taken.

The student should note in particular the author's use of what might be called historical perspective as a basic tool. With reference, for example, to the destruction of villages, he points not to the immediate effects of the war but to long-term economic changes which can be traced back to the Middle Ages. With reference to the reputed loss of population, he points to the fairly uniform incidence of epidemic disease before, after, and during the war and to the fact that the loss of population was more apparent than real owing to the large number of displaced persons.

> The student should also test Ergang's answers (and those of Steinberg) to the question, why did contemporary records present so unrelieved a picture of disaster? Are their answers persuasive?

In their eagerness to disprove the myth of the all-destructive fury of the Thirty Years' War certain revisionist historians have gone too far in the other direction. Thus some have contended that affairs in Germany took a turn for the better as early as 1617 as a result of the adoption of a more vigorous policy by the Habsburgs. The wide differences of opinion must be ascribed not only to the personal prejudices of the historians but also to the nature of the "evidence" upon which the opinions rest. Before we can arrive at a definitive answer regarding the destructive effects of the war the documents, chronicles, reports, and parish records must be critically re-examined and many monographs must be written. Even then certain lacunae will remain because so many essential materials were destroyed during and since the Thirty Years' War. Many special studies by German scholars have already appeared. The best we can do at the present time is to consider briefly the conclusions revisionist scholars have reached, so that from them we may derive a more authentic view of the general effects of the war.

The revisionist trumpet was sounded soon after the middle of the nineteenth century. As early as 1857 G. Brückner requested a thorough-going critical re-examination of the primary sources for the purpose of ascertaining if the destruction of the war had been exaggerated. "Historical truth no less than national feeling demand it," he stated. The call seems to have fallen on deaf ears. Other historians also advocated a re-examination of the evidence with no better results. Indeed, during the succeeding years the trend was rather in the direction of greater exaggeration. In the decade of the nineties, however, a number of historians sharply questioned the myth. Thus R. Wuttke stated:

It is an exaggeration if the decline of Germany, the loss of its trade position is ascribed to the effects of the war. Contemporary reports take pleasure in dwelling on the special horrors, and in summarily making the war responsible for the lack of moral backbone and spirit of enterprise which characterized the seventeenth century.

The real impetus, however, for a re-examination of the question came from B. Erdmannsdörffer's *Deutsche Geschichte vom westfälischen Frieden bis zum Regierungsantritt Friedrichs des Grossen*, in which he discussed the problem at some length. Soon a number of German scholars turned their attention to some phase or other of the problem.

After a careful re-examination of the evidence revisionist historians have concluded that practically all the reports of cannibalism have no foundation in fact. O. Meinardus took it upon himself to trace to its sources the story which has Melchior der Schütz and his band of men kill and devour 500 human beings. "After careful and thorough-going research in the printed literature of Silesian history as well as in the Silesian archives," he found no mention whatever of cannibalism or the hunt for human beings. He did, however, find mention of Melchior der Schütz. In the Royal Archives at Breslau he found the record of a criminal case which was tried in the winter of 1653–1654 with Melchior Hedloff, also known as "Schütze Melchior," as the defendant. Melchior was accused of having murdered 251 people while committing robberies over a period of eleven years. The court record states that he buried his victims in various places. The only reference to cannibalism is in the accusation that on one occasion he had killed a pregnant woman and eaten the heart of her unborn child. His purpose in doing this, the record states, was "to make him more fierce, so he could rage with greater fury and be more respected." Thus, in so far as cannibalism was involved, it was based on superstition and not motivated by hunger. As the author states in the title of his study, the story of Melchior's cannibalism is "an historical fable."

A broader study of reports of cannibalism was made by F. Julian who reminds us that such stories are not peculiar to the Thirty Years' War, but are "typical of longer periods of war and famine." He takes eight stories of cannibalism and shows how they were borrowed from past history as far back as ancient times. Some of the other stories, he says, are the products "of unbounded exaggeration of individual occurrences for purposes of propaganda." Hearsay also played an important part in the creation and

From Robert Ergang, *The Myth of the All-destructive Fury of the Thirty Years' War* (Pocono Pines, Pa.: Craftsmen Press, 1956), pp. 16–22, 24–27. Reprinted by permission of the author; available through Richard S. Barnes, Bookseller, 1628 North Welles St., Chicago 14, Ill.

The Eve of the Modern World

circulation of such stories. "Many a clergyman," he states, "wrote down in his parish records what he heard as a proof of the gravity of the times." A number of these stories, he believes, were "typical inventions which were put into circulation only after the Thirty Years' War." Julian further shows how rumors of cannibalism in the vicinity of Zweibrücken were started by the writer of a *Kollektenbrief*[1] who, in an effort to excite sympathy, stated, "The dearth of food is so great that the dead are no longer safe in their graves." When this device proved successful others adopted it and before long a goodly number of cannibalist stories were in circulation. "There is," Julian writes in summing up his studies, "no credible confirmation of these extreme incidents in the source materials that have been examined up to this time." The only exception he is ready to make is in regard to reports of cannibalism during the siege of Breisach (1638). "In the besieged Breisach," he writes, "an exceptional case of cannibalism turned up which probably can be accepted as an actual happening."

Revisionist historians have also presented evidence to show that barbarities were the exception rather than the rule. Historians of the old school give the impression that plundering and burning, rape of children and old women, cannibalism, and perversions of all kinds were ordinary every-day occurrences. In most of the stories the soldiers are the perpetrators of the horrible deeds. Armies are depicted as "great bands of robbers, held together solely by their lust for murder and their inordinate desire for plunder." The soldiers, almost without exception, are painted in the darkest colors. Thus one historian wrote, "The soldiers were nothing but highway robbers, who maimed and tortured the country people to make them give up their last remaining property." Another stated, "Nowhere in the armies, as regards both officers and common soldiers, was there order and discipline." Undoubtedly some of the troops did at times commit terrible cruelties and were guilty of senseless slaughter, rapine, arson, destruction, and plundering. It was, in a sense, an age of inhumanity in the rest of Europe as well as in Germany. Many of the reports must, however, be ascribed to exaggeration and atrocity propaganda. The latter is, of course, not limited to the Thirty Years' War. . . .

Actually most of the soldiers who participated in the Thirty Years' War were not permitted to disobey military regulations with impunity. Both Tilly and Gustavus Adolphus enforced a rather strict discipline. In Wallenstein's armies the discipline was less strict, but only because he permitted it. Even Wallenstein had no intention of destroying villages and towns and devastating districts, for he preferred to collect "contributions" from them. His correspondence frequently expresses concern for the civilian population. The distinguished German historian Leopold von Ranke wrote that when Wallenstein's armies marched into a district "there was no lack of violence, as is recorded with a righteous indignation in the local chronicles and in correspondence. At the same time it is clear that a certain order was preserved." Another historian writes that in the records of Wismar there are many reports of thefts and burglaries supposedly committed by Wallenstein's soldiers stationed in and about that city. One report states the conditions were so bad that "shrouds were being stolen out of coffins in broad daylight," a characteristic exaggeration of the period. The historian adds, however, "The most drastic punishments were meted out as a means of maintaining discipline among these troops. According to the records gallows were erected during the night of September 9, 1628, and at dawn, by the personal order of Wallenstein, fourteen men were hanged for refusing to obey orders." According to the regulations of all armies the soldiers were to pay for the food they consumed. The districts in which they were quartered were to furnish them only lodging, salt and vinegar, light and wood, and hay and straw for their horses. E. von Frauenholz states that the average pay for cavalrymen was fifteen gulden per month and for foot soldiers from six to ten. This, he feels, was adequate for the purchase of food and necessaries, if the stipend was paid. Vast sums were sent into Germany for this purpose from Sweden, France, Holland, Spain and England. On occasion cities reported a considerable increase in business from armies that passed their way. Oxenstierna, the Swedish general, succeeded in getting a raise in pay for the Swedish soldiers on the plea that German merchants and artisans had raised their prices so high that the pay of the soldiers no longer sufficed to purchase the necessaries of life.

Not until the middle period of the war did the discipline become less strict with the result that plundering and barbarism increased. Even then the authorities did not cease their efforts to enforce

---

[1] A letter asking religious brethren living in other parts of Germany or in Holland, England, France and Switzerland, to relieve the need of those in the war area by taking up collections.

order and discipline. A general order, issued from imperial headquarters on August 1, 1641, reads in part:

Swearing will be punished the first time according to the discretion of the authorities; thereafter it is punishable with death. Stealing a cow or horse, secretly or by force, will without judgment and investigation, and without mercy, be punished by hanging. If one is in possession of a stolen horse and cannot show from whom it was purchased, he will be punished as if he were the thief. Whoever mistreats or tortures a civilian or attacks anyone on the highway will pay with his life.

Although the prohibitions were clear, they were at times openly flouted, particularly when the troops did not receive the stipend they had been promised. The fact that they were not paid gave the troops an excuse for demanding food from peasants and towns-people. Such a search for food and fodder often resulted in other things being taken. At no time did the high command condone plundering of friendly districts, but at such times as the military authorities failed to pay their troops they could hardly enforce their prohibitions. Strict enforcement would have caused troops to desert to the enemy. Nevertheless, on occasion, to curb the worst excesses, the authorities summarily hanged those apprehended in the act of plundering or maltreating civilians. The perpetrators of most of the misdeeds, it appears, were small marauding bands, the members of which were often deserters from the large armies. If the marauding force was not too large the peasants often defended their property vigorously, and at times successfully. When reports about such bands reached the larger army camps detachments of troops were usually sent out to capture the marauders and hang them on the nearest trees. At times, of course, enemy forces deliberately devasted certain areas to weaken the opposition. But this was not a common occurrence.

Pillage and theft did not necessarily mean complete disappearance of wealth, as some historians have contended. Most of the salable articles were quickly sold and the money was put into circulation. F. Kaphahn states that the soldiers "spent their money with subtler-women, tavern keepers, merchants and tradesmen." Thus many of the valuables which the marauders took from the peasants and townspeople were not lost to the country.

But there is a brighter side to the picture. In the contemporary records there are laudatory as well as critical comments. Many chronicles of the decade of the thirties and forties report that such veteran troops as those of the French general Turenne were well-behaved. Ranke approvingly quoted Count Khevenhueller (1588–1650) who in the *Annales Ferdinandei* praises the conduct of the soldiers, stating that the country was not devastated and burned, that the people were not driven from home and manor, that everything was well-cultivated and harvested, and that soldier and peasant got along well together.

Revisionist historians have also shown that such statements as "thousands of villages disappeared completely from the map" are not based on fact. This is not to gainsay that many villages were completely destroyed and for a time deserted by their inhabitants. Most of them, however, were soon rebuilt. W. Zahn writes regarding Brandenburg, "A large percentage of the villages were burned during the course of the war, but they were all rebuilt; hence the assumption is unfounded that the numerous deserted villages are attributable to the Thirty Years' War." J. Gebauer states emphatically, "Let one thing be finally and clearly established: In Brandenburg's narrower or wider precincts not one single village was permanently destroyed by the great war; the devastated and deserted villages of the countryside were one and all laid waste in the last centuries of the Middle Ages." O. Kius asserts that in Thuringia "no village was permitted to lie in ruins." Regarding Saxony R. Wuttke writes, "In Saxony there can be no question of the destruction of entire villages, as has been reported from other parts of Germany." W. Arnold states that in Hesse individual farms were deserted, but that there is no evidence to show that a single village disappeared. G. Mehring states that in Württemberg no large villages disappeared completely "only individual estates and smaller hamlets." "There is no doubt," another historian writes regarding Württemberg, "that parts of our country suffered terribly . . . but only in very rare instances was the devastation permanent. Even during the war years many who had sought refuge in the cities dared to return to their villages and to rebuild them if they had been destroyed." In Austria, A. Grund states, no villages were abandoned during the period from 1500 to 1683. On the contrary, fourteen villages were repeopled during this period.

This does not mean, however, that there were no deserted villages or ruins of villages in Germany after the war. W. Beschorner shows that many of the villages which were supposed to have disappeared during the Thirty Years' War actually disappeared long before that time. "In numerous instances," he wrote, "it has been proved by the records, often right down to the day and year, that villages which, according to folk tradition were burned or deserted by their inhabitants during the Thirty Years' War, had vanished from the earth much earlier, some as early as the thirteenth, fourteenth, and fifteenth centuries." Finally, F. Kaphahn states, "As it has been proved ever more clearly, the war had no part, or no considerable part, in causing the permanent desertion of villages. This took place almost exclusively in the thirteenth and fourteenth centuries." The reason for leaving the villages was that the soil was too poor for intensive cultivation.

In general, devastation in the agricultural districts was not as widespread and as permanent as historians of the old school have pictured it. The war undoubtedly interfered with the cultivation of the land in many places and in some the tilling of the soil was suspended entirely for some years. But the war did not ruin the fertility of the soil; on the contrary, the fact that the soil was uncultivated for a time may have helped to restore its fertility. Cultivation was resumed at the earliest possible time where the soil was fertile. E. Gothein asserts that "dwellings rose on the land surprisingly quickly and the arable land was soon put under the plow." In 1649 the Cistercian Mauritz Vogt wrote regarding Bohemia and Moravia: "In this year the subjects who had previously lived in the woods again became good cultivators, and cities, castles, markets and villages shook the sad ashes from their ruins and all will within a short time be resplendent with new roofs. In 1657 Cardinal Harrach wrote, "There is no doubt that Bohemia suffered tremendous damage and devastation during the war . . . but now everything hereabouts has been rebuilt." The French Field Marshal Grammont who had been in Westphalia in 1646 said when he visited it again in 1658 that all traces of the war had disappeared. K. Schmidt in his *Geschichte des dreissigjährigen Krieges* (1848) describes the destruction and devastation in superlatives, but then adds:

As a result of the newly awakened activity cultivation of the soil was restored so quickly that it would be difficult to find a better example of German industry. Soon the fields were blooming and better towns and villages were arising from the ashes. Trade and commerce revived on the highroads and in the markets, and science and art rose to higher levels than ever before.

Ilse Hoffman made a careful study of the diaries and reports of English travelers who visited Germany during the two decades after the Peace of Westphalia. She found that what they saw in most parts of Germany was not devastation, but thriving villages, well-cultivated fields, and plentiful crops. "Where one expected," she wrote, "to find descriptions of neglected acres, uncultivated vineyards or deserted stretches . . . one hears only a few years after the Peace of Westphalia the old song of the rich fertility of the German countryside." Schiller described a parallel situation in his *Jungfrau von Orleans* when he has Thibaut say:

Unworried can we view the desolation,
For steadfast stand the acres which we till.
The flames consume our villages, our corn
Is trampled 'neath the tread of warrior steeds;
With the new spring new harvests reappear,
And our light huts are quickly reared again.

Livestock was not replaced so quickly, but in this respect, too, the loss has been greatly exaggerated. The heavy losses in certain districts cannot be used as a norm for Germany as a whole. If at all possible the peasants would hide their cattle in woods, swamps, and caves at the approach of armies and marauding bands. E. Brückner shows that in some parts of Germany the number of sheep, pigs, and cattle increased during the war. On the other hand, the number of horses declined sharply, causing more and more peasants to use oxen to cultivate their fields. One reason for the decline of the number of horses was that so many were "used up" by the cavalry regiments of the time. We find that even near the end of the war many districts were able to furnish large numbers of sheep, pigs, and cattle. Thus in 1646 the Duchy of Laubach sent 600 cattle into the imperial camp in Bavaria and in the fall of 1647 General Montecucculi was able to obtain 1000 sheep, 150 steers and 160 pigs on a raid in the vicinity of Cassel. F. Beyhoff writes regarding the city of Giessen, "Despite the chaos of the war there were still many cattle in Giessen in 1648: 76 horses, 12 yoke oxen, 600 young and old steers, and 2900 sheep." . . .

Most controversial is the question of the loss of population. Since no general census was taken in Germany there are no reliable figures either for 1618 or for 1648 on which to base an estimate. Members of the old school gave such varying estimates for the decline of the population as from thirty to twelve million, from thirty to eighteen million, from twenty-one to thirteen million, from sixteen to six million, from sixteen to four million. In no instance are we told how the losses were computed. Neither are we informed whether the decline takes into account the population of the territories formally separated from the Holy Roman Empire by the peace, i.e., Switzerland and the Dutch Netherlands. In one respect there is almost unanimity. Most historians agree with the statistician who in the second half of the seventeenth century estimated the number of those killed in battle at 325,000. The number of civilians killed by soldiers was, according to the parish records, very small. Furthermore, there is little evidence to show that famine was a great destroyer. The greatest loss of life resulted from epidemics, epidemics of dystentery, typhus, and bubonic plague. The fact is often overlooked that there were epidemics before and after the war. From the fourteenth to the eighteenth centuries they were recurring phenomena. On the eve of the Thirty Years' War a series of epidemics claimed many lives in different parts of Germany and in neighboring countries. After the war epidemics caused loss of life on a large scale in the Rhine region (1665–1670), Austria (1678–1681), and Silesia and Saxony (1681). During the war they raged first in one, then in another part of Germany at various times. Cities far removed from the fighting suffered equally with those near the battlefields. Hence the war must not be held primarily responsible for the epidemics, although the dearth of the necessities of life in certain districts, caused by the devastations of the war, probably weakened the resistance of the inhabitants to disease. Even if epidemics did claim many times as many lives as warfare the decline of the population would still have been small.

In endeavoring to arrive at an estimate of the loss of life one must take into account the fact that there was a large floating population in Germany during the period of the Thirty Years' War. Consequently what was often regarded as destruction of the population was only dislocation of the population. Smaller or larger groups, composed of servants, the families of soldiers, dispossessed peasants, and rabble, usually moved along in the wake of the armies. There is little agreement among historians as to the size of these groups. While some believe the numbers were large, others argue that they were not. Furthermore, it was not uncommon for the entire population of a village to leave at the approach of an army. Often the local parson or priest would then note in the parish records that the village was depopulated. Later, after the army or armies had passed,

some peasants would return, while others remained in the fortified cities. "The cities," one historian wrote, "which were surrounded with earthworks and walls with substantial gates and whose citizens were well trained in defense were certainly able to defend themselves, particularly during the first years of the war." Many cities were able to obtain *Schutzbriefe* (letters of protection) from the commanding generals through payment of large sums of money.

To such cities the inhabitants of neighboring villages often fled in considerable numbers. In Weimar, for example, the number of "strangers" was fifty per cent larger than that of native citizens. During the period from 1634 to 1648 some 2000 peasants from neighboring villages lived in the city of Heilbronn where crude shelters were put up for them in every available space. "It is well known," another historian writes, "that the city of Lübeck was spared by the war. It was neither besieged nor surrounded and was therefore a safe refuge for many fugitives, especially for the Holstein nobility." Even W. Menzel whose writings helped to give the myth a wider circulation stated that the principal reason for the rapid growth of the population in Württemberg, one of the hardest hit sections of Germany, immediately after the war was "the return of a large part of the many who had left the fatherland after the battle of Nördlingen in 1634 to take refuge in Switzerland." G. Brückner states that in Germany generally the gradual return after the war of scattered peasants to the villages in which they had originally lived "explains in part the fact that the population appeared to increase so rapidly from 1649 to 1659." F. Beyhoff sums up the situation in the words:

It is an altogether erroneous procedure to attempt to assess the decline of the population by trying to ascertain the size of the population immediately after the war. At this time the population was still in a fluctuating movement started by the war and had not returned to a quiet state. Certainly during the war a great shift of population had taken place from territory to territory. Many thousands had fled from their homes to seek safety at a distance. Only gradually did they return.

To be sure, certain parts of Germany did suffer heavy population losses, but the sharp decline in some districts was offset at least in part by gains in others. The population of Saxony, for example, increased from 25,965 in 1608 to 46,317 in 1659. The population of many cities, including Würzburg, Strassburg, Hamburg and Bremen, increased during the war. Moreover, such figures as are available in specialized studies show that in many cities the population decline was not as drastic as had been stated. In contrast to the statement that at the end of the war "the city of Berlin contained but 300 citizens," F. Faden has shown that the population of Berlin numbered about 7,500 in 1643 and was even larger in 1648. F. Riegler, after reexamining the parish records, asserts that the population of the free city of Schwäbisch-Hall was 1279 in 1618, 1326 in 1631 and 1106 in 1650. "One would think," he comments, "that the misery of the last war years would have resulted in an even greater depopulation of the city, in a sharp decline in the number of inhabitants. This was not the case." K. Weiss takes issue with Schiller for stating that "Nuremberg buried more than ten thousand of its inhabitants." "The figures given by Schiller," he says, "are too high."

Revisionists have also shown that the so-called Franconian decree is spurious. Among the earlier historians who cited it was M. Menzel, and since that time it has been cited again and again as proof of the calamitous decline of the population. The "decree," supposedly issued "with the assent of the spiritual princes" by the diet of Franconia meeting at Nuremberg on February 15, 1650, forbids all males under sixty to become monks during the succeeding ten years, gives the Catholic clergy the right to marry, and permits each layman to take two wives. F. Julian, after careful investigation, calls it "the bigamy swindle," asserting that no meeting of the Franconian diet was held on the date cited. He further states that the story first made its appearance early in the eighteenth century and is patently the work of a practical joker. G. Wolf, too, labels it "an invention."

As to actual figures for the whole of Germany revisionists differ widely among themselves. R. Hoeniger states, "According to my estimate the total population of Germany at the end of the war was only two or three million less than it had been in 1618. In the decade of the forties the population resumed its growth, so that at the end of the war the loss may have been as low as one or two million." This estimate has been vigorously denounced as being too low. Hoeniger undoubtedly went too far in his reaction, but his statements did stimulate a wide interest in the subject. Special studies which appeared during the succeeding two decades presented revised figures for the losses in specific localities. But the figures for other localities and districts still stand in need of critical reexamination. Although many historians disagreed with Hoeniger regarding the total losses, some joined him to form "the left wing" of the revisionist group. W. Windelband, who remained conservative in other respects, writes, "The assertion that the total losses were as high as a third of the population is to be regarded with a healthy skepticism. In some places, however, a decline of as much as a fifth can be established with considerable certainty."

The right wing of the revisionist group is far more conservative. Günther Franz, for example, estimates the population decline for Germany as a whole at one third. In doing so he still accepts the old figures which set the population loss in some districts as high as 60 to 70 per cent. More cautious are the conclusions of G. Oestreich who finds it impossible to arrive at "an accurate estimate" until historians have marshalled more facts. "The figures quoted in the reports and records of the time," he writes, "are exaggerated beyond all bounds."

The present writer agrees that it will be impossible to arrive at a reliable figure until more records have been critically reexamined and correlated. The estimates of the conservative revisionists are largely based on figures collected by members of the old school who were trying to paint the picture as black as possible. Even though the decline of the population was as large for certain localities as stated, emigration and dislocation have not been adequately considered as factors in the decline. It is the opinion of this writer that when more local figures are carefully reexamined they will show that the total decline of the population in the Holy Roman Empire from 1618 to 1648 was considerably less than the one-third estimated by the conservative revisionists. Johann Peter Süssmilch (1707–1767), whom the German economist Wilhelm Roscher regards as the outstanding population expert of the eighteenth century, asserted long before the myth of the all-destructive fury of the Thirty Years' War was created that by the early eighteenth century "the population losses had not only been recovered, but many sections of Germany were so thickly populated that they could send, nay were almost forced to send, colonists to America and other parts of the world." More than a century later Karl Biedermann, before he was influenced by Freytag's *Bilder aus der deutschen Vergangenheit,* denounced those who stated that it required more than a century to restore the population of Germany to the size it had been in

1618. He was willing to agree that the population of certain districts, as, for example, parts of Franconia and Thuringia, had suffered a sharp decline, but "for the whole of Germany, and even for larger sections of Germany, this has been denied by the most scrupulous statisticians of the last century."

234567890